MANUAL DE GRAMÁTICA

SIXTH EDITION

MANUAL DE GRAMÁTICA

Grammar Reference for Students of Spanish

SIXTH EDITION

ELEANOR DOZIER
CORNELL UNIVERSITY

ZULMA IGUINA
CORNELL UNIVERSITY

Australia • Brazil • Canada • Mexico • Singapore • United Kingdom • United States

CENGAGE

Manual de gramática: Grammar Reference for Students of Spanish,
Sixth Edition
Eleanor Dozier and Zulma Iguina

Product Director: Beth Kramer

Senior Product Manager: Martine Edwards

Product Development Manager: Katie Wade

Managing Content Developer: Harriet C. Dishman

Associate Content Developer: Daniel Cruse

Marketing Director: Michelle Williams

Senior Content Project Manager: Esther Marshall

Art Director: Brenda Carmichael

Manufacturing Planner: Betsy Donaghey

IP Analyst: Jessica Elias/Christina Ciaramella

IP Project Manager: Farah Fard

Production Service: Lumina Datamatics, Inc.

Compositor: Lumina Datamatics, Inc.

Cover and Text Designer: Brenda Carmichael

Cover Image: catwalker/Shutterstock

© 2017, 2013, 2008 Cengage Learning, Inc.

ALL RIGHTS RESERVED. No part of this work covered by the copyright herein may be reproduced or distributed in any form or by any means, except as permitted by U.S. copyright law, without the prior written permission of the copyright owner.

> For product information and technology assistance, contact us at
> **Cengage Customer & Sales Support, 1-800-354-9706**
> **or support.cengage.com.**
>
> For permission to use material from this text or product, submit all requests online at **www.cengage.com/permissions.**

Library of Congress Control Number: 2015947848

Student Edition:
ISBN: 978-1-305-65822-6

Loose-leaf Edition:
ISBN: 978-1-337-10072-4

Cengage
200 Pier 4 Boulevard
Boston, MA 02210
USA

Cengage is a leading provider of customized learning solutions with employees residing in nearly 40 different countries and sales in more than 125 countries around the world. Find your local representative at: **www.cengage.com.**

To learn more about Cengage platforms and services, register or access your online learning solution, or purchase materials for your course, visit **www.cengage.com.**

Printed in the United States of America
Print Number: 04   Print Year: 2021

CONTENTS

To the Student   xxiii

Chapter 1 Overview   1

- **A** Sentence Components   2
- **B** Verb Structure   5
- **C** Sentence Structure   6
  - 1 Independent Clauses   6
  - 2 Main or Principal Clauses   7
  - 3 Dependent or Subordinate Clauses   7
- **D** Subject–Verb Agreement   13

Chapter 2 Nouns and Noun Determiners   19

- **A** Nouns and Their Equivalents   20
  - 1 Introduction   20
    - a. Definition   20
    - b. Noun equivalents   20
    - c. Noun companions   22
  - 2 Nouns: Gender and Number   23
    - a. Gender **(Género)**   23
    - b. Number **(Número)**   25
  - 3 Personal **a**   26

v

B Noun Determiners 28

1 Articles 28
a. Definite articles 28
   (1) Subjects 29
   (2) Titles 30
   (3) Languages 30
   (4) Possessives vs. Articles 31
b. Indefinite articles 32

2 Adjectives 34
a. Demonstrative adjectives 34
b. Possessive adjectives 35
c. Forms of descriptive adjectives 36
   (1) Common adjective endings 36
   (2) Adjectives with short and long forms 37
d. Position of descriptive adjectives 38
e. Comparisons 43
   (1) Comparisons of inequality 43
      (a) With adverbs, adjectives, and nouns 43
      (b) With a numerical expression, use **de** instead of **que** 43
      (c) With a verb or clause as second part of comparison 44
   (2) Comparisons of equality 46
      (a) **Tanto(-a, -os, -as)... como** 46
      (b) **Tanto como** 46
      (c) **Tan... como** 46
f. Superlatives 46

Chapter 3 Pronouns 49

A Personal Pronouns 50

1 Grammatical Functions of Personal Pronouns 50
a. Subject 50
b. Direct object complement 50

      c. Indirect object complement with direct object   51

      d. Indirect object complement without direct object   51

      e. Transitivity   52

2 Subject Pronouns   53

    Subject pronoun usage   53

    Usage of **usted, tú, vosotros,** and **vos**   56

3 Direct Object Pronouns   57

      a. Formation and usage   57

      b. Stressed and unstressed object pronouns (direct or indirect object)   59

      c. **Lo:** The neuter (invariable) pronoun   60

4 Indirect Object Pronouns   60

5 Required Repetitive Object Pronouns   62

      a. Direct object pronouns   62

      b. Indirect object pronouns   63

6 Order of Object Pronouns when Combined   63

7 Position of Object Pronouns   64

8 Prepositional Object Pronouns   66

B Se   68

1 Introduction   68

2 Reflexive Pronouns   69

      a. Reflexives   69

      b. Reciprocals   70

3 **Se me** Construction: Accidental **se**   71

- **4** Impersonal **se** 74
  - a. Introduction 74
  - b. The passive voice and the impersonal **se** 75
    - (1) Agent present (subject of the action: stated) 75
    - (2) No agent: not impersonal (subject of the action: absent but implied) 75
    - (3) No agent: impersonal (subject of the action: absent and irrelevant) 75
  - c. Impersonal **se** with inanimate objects 76
  - d. Impersonal **se** with persons 76
  - e. Impersonal **se** with both human and inanimate objects 77
  - f. Impersonal reflexive construction: **uno** 78

C Demonstrative and Possessive Pronouns 78

- **1** Demonstrative Pronouns 78
- **2** Possessive Pronouns 79

D Interrogatives 81

- **1** **¿Qué?** 81
- **2** **¿Cuál(es)?** 81
- **3** **¿Qué?** vs. **¿Cuál?** with **ser** 81
- **4** *How?* 83
  - a. *How?* + *verb* = **¿Cómo?** 83
  - b. *How?* + *adj.* or *adv.* ≠ **¿Cómo?** 84
  - c. *How much / many?* = **¿Cuánto(a)(s)...?** 85
- **5** Word order 85

E Exclamatives 85

- **1** **¡Qué!** + *noun* 86
- **2** **¡Qué!** + *modified noun* 86
- **3** **¡Qué!** + *adj.* 86
- **4** **¡Qué!** + *adv.* 87

- **5** ¡Cómo! + *verb* 87
- **6** ¡Cuánto! + *verb* 87
- **7** ¡Cuánto(a)! + *noun* 87
- **8** ¡Cuántos(as)! + *noun* 88
- **9** ¡Quién(es)! + *verb* 88

F Indefinites and Negatives 88

G Relative Pronouns 92

- **1** Formation and Usage 92
- **2** Relative Pronouns with no Preposition 94
- **3** Relative Pronouns with a Preposition 94
    - a. **El cual/el que** 94
    - b. **Que** after **a/de/en/con** 94
- **4** Additional Uses 95
    - a. **Lo que/lo cual** (Invariable) 95
    - b. **El que** 95
    - c. **Lo que** 96
    - d. **Cuyo** 96
    - e. **Donde** 96
    - f. *Who* 97
        - (1) Interrogative pronoun: **¿Quién?** 97
        - (2) Relative pronoun: **Que** 97
        - (3) **El cual/el que** 97
    - g. *What* 97

Chapter 4 Prepositions, Adverbs, Conjunctions, and Transitions 99

A Prepositions 100

- **1** Function of Prepositions 100

2 Verbs Used without Prepositions 102

3 Individual Prepositions 103
- a. **A** 103
  - (1) Usage 103
  - (2) Personal **a** 103
  - (3) Expressions with **a** 104
  - (4) Verbs with **a** 105
- b. **Con** 107
  - (1) Usage 107
  - (2) Expressions with **con** 107
  - (3) Verbs with **con** 107
- c. **De** 108
  - (1) Usage 108
  - (2) Expressions with **de** 109
  - (3) Verbs with **de** 109
- d. **En** 111
  - (1) Usage 111
  - (2) Expressions with **en** 112
  - (3) Verbs with **en** 112
- e. **Para** 114
  - (1) Usage 114
  - (2) Expressions with **para** 114
- f. **Por** 115
  - (1) Usage 115
  - (2) Expressions with **por** 116
  - (3) Verbs with **por** 117

4 List of Expressions with Prepositions (English–Spanish) 118

5 Review of Expressions with Prepositions 119

B Adverbs 121

1 Definition 121

2 Adverbs Ending in **-mente** 121

3 Word Order 122

4 Multiple-Function Words 122

- 5 Adverbs of Time   124
- 6 Adverbs of Manner   126
- 7 Adverbs of Quantity   128
- 8 Adverbs of Confirmation, Doubt, or Negation   129
- 9 Adverbial Phrases   132
- 10 Adverbs of Place   133
- 11 Related Adverbs and Prepositions   136

C Conjunctions   138

- 1 Usage   138
- 2 Conjunctions of Coordination   138
- 3 Conjunctions of Subordination   139

D Transitions   140

Chapter 5 Verbs: Formation   147

A Indicative Mood   148

- 1 Present Indicative   148
  - a. Regular verbs   148
  - b. Stem-changing verbs   148
  - c. Spelling-changing verbs   150
  - d. Classified irregular verbs   152
  - e. Other irregular verbs   153
- 2 Aspects of the Past Indicative   154
  - a. Imperfect indicative   154
  - b. Preterite   155
  - c. Present perfect indicative   158
  - d. Pluperfect indicative   158

3 Future 159
   a. Simple future 159
   b. Future perfect 160

B Conditional Mood 160

1 Present Conditional 160

2 Conditional Perfect 161

C Subjunctive Mood 162

1 Present Subjunctive 162
   a. Regular verbs 162
   b. Stem-changing verbs 162
   c. Irregular verbs 163

2 Imperfect Subjunctive 165

3 Present Perfect Subjunctive 166

4 Pluperfect Subjunctive 167

D Imperative Mood 167

1 Direct Commands 167
   a. **Tú** 167
   b. **Usted/ustedes** 169
   c. **Vosotros** 170
   d. **Nosotros** 171

2 Indirect Commands 172

E Infinitive 173

1 Present Infinitive 173

2 Perfect Infinitive 173

F Participle 173

    1 Present Participle or Gerund 173

    2 Past Participle 174

Chapter 6 Verbs: Usage 177

Preliminary Definitions 178

A Present Indicative 178

B Aspects of the Past Indicative Tense: Preterite vs. Imperfect and Pluperfect 179

    1 Past Conditions, Beliefs—Imperfect 180

    2 Changed Conditions, Reactions—Preterite 181

    3 Actions, Single or Consecutive—Preterite 182

    4 Habitual Actions or Events—Imperfect 182

    5 Finite Habitual and Repeated Actions—Preterite 182

    6 Actions—Beginning, Middle, End 182

        a. Preterite: Beginning and/or end 183

        b. Imperfect: Middle, in progress, interrupted 183

    7 Imperfect as Parallel to the Present 184

    8 Projected Actions/Indirect Discourse—Imperfect 184

    9 *Would*—Contexts and Translations 185

    10 **Saber** and **conocer** 185

    11 Modal Auxiliaries in the Past 186

        a. **Acabar de** + *infinitive* 186

        b. **Deber** + *infinitive* 186

        c. **Ir a** + *infinitive* 187

        d. **Poder** + *infinitive* 187

        e. **Querer** + *infinitive* 187

        f. **Tener que** + *infinitive* 188

12. **Ser** in Sentences with Relative Clauses 188
13. The Preterite and the Present Perfect 189
14. The Pluperfect 189

C Compound Tenses 191

1. Introduction 191
2. Perfect Tenses 192
   a. Present perfect indicative 192
   b. Future perfect 192
   c. Past perfect (pluperfect) indicative 192
   d. Conditional perfect 193
   e. Present perfect subjunctive 193
   f. Pluperfect subjunctive 193
3. Simple Progressive Tenses 194
   a. Introduction 194
   b. Present progressive 194
   c. Future progressive 195
   d. Past progressive 195
   e. Conditional present progressive 195
   f. Subjunctive present progressive 196
   g. Subjunctive imperfect progressive 196
4. Perfect Progressive Tenses 196
   a. Introduction 196
   b. Indicative present perfect progressive 196
   c. Indicative future perfect progressive 197
   d. Indicative pluperfect progressive 197
   e. Conditional perfect progressive 197
   f. Subjunctive present perfect progressive 197
   g. Subjunctive pluperfect progressive 198
5. Modal Auxiliaries 198

D Ways of Expressing the Future   199

E Conditional   200

  1. Introduction   200
  2. Courtesy with Conditional of Modal Auxiliaries   200
  3. Hypothetical Situations Implied or Stated   200
  4. Future of the Past   201
  5. Probability in the Past   201

F Probability   201

G Subjunctive   203

  1. Introduction   203
  2. Nominal Clauses   203
     a. Definition and usage   203
     b. Subjunctive after expressions of emotion   205
     c. Subjunctive after expressions of volition and Influence   206
     d. Subjunctive after expressions of doubt and negation of reality   209
     e. Subjunctive after impersonal expressions with **ser**   211
  3. Adjectival Clauses   213
     a. Definition   213
     b. Usage   213
  4. Adverbial Clauses   215
     a. Definition   215
     b. Usage   215
  5. Sequence of Tenses   219
     a. Introduction   219
     b. Chronological relativity   219
     c. Aspect relativity   225

    d. Tense relativity from indicative to subjunctive 226
     (1) Main clause in the present set 226
     (2) Main clause in the past set 227

 6 *If* (**si**) Clauses 228
   a. Sequence of tenses 228
   b. **Como si** *(As if)* 230

 7 **Ojalá** 230

 8 Expressions of Leave-Taking 231

H Infinitives and Present Participles 234

 1 Infinitives 234
   a. Present infinitive 234
   b. Perfect infinitive 237

 2 Present Participles 237

I Verbs Like **gustar** 239

 1 Formation 239
 2 Word Order 240
 3 Verbs Similar to **gustar** 241
 4 Articles 243
 5 Changes in Meaning 244

J Reflexive Verbs 245

K Indirect Discourse 252

 1 Introduction 252
 2 Verb-Tense Changes 253
 3 No Verb-Tense Changes 254
 4 Person Changes 255
 5 Time Changes 255

- **6** Other Changes 257
  - a. Connectives 257
  - b. *This, that,* and the other 257
  - c. Verbs of communication 257
  - d. A note about word order with indirect interrogatives 258

Chapter 7 Ser, estar, haber, hacer, and tener 259

A Overview 260

B Ser vs. estar 262

- **1** With Equal Elements: **ser** 262
- **2** With Adjectives 262
  - a. Predicate Adjectives 262
    - (1) **Aburrido** (*boring* vs. *bored*) 264
    - (2) **Bueno** (*good* vs. *in good health, tasty*) 264
    - (3) **Callado** (*quiet by nature* vs. *silent now*) 265
    - (4) **Ciego** (*blind* vs. *blinded figuratively or momentarily*) 265
    - (5) **Cómodo** (*comfortable object* vs. *comfortable person*) 265
    - (6) **Frío** (*cold as norm or not, used with objects*) 265
    - (7) **Listo** (*clever [person or animal]* vs. *ready*) 265
    - (8) **Maduro** (*mature* vs. *ripe*) 266
    - (9) **Rico** (*wealthy* vs. *delicious*) 266
    - (10) **Verde** (*green* vs. *unripe*) 266
    - (11) **Vivo** (*smart, bright person* vs. *alive*) 266
  - b. Expressions with *to be* 266
  - c. Impersonal expressions 268
- **3** With Prepositions and Adverbs 268
  - a. **De** 268
  - b. Time and place 269
- **4** With Past and Present Participles 270

      a. With present participles   270
      b. With past participles: Passive voice and resultant condition   270
        (1) Formation of the passive voice   270
        (2) A note about the passive voice   271

C **Estar** vs. **haber**   273

D Expressions with **estar** and **tener**   274

   1 Expressions with **estar**   274
   2 Expressions with **tener**   274

E Time Expressions   275

   1 Introduction   275
      a. Counting forward   275
      b. Counting backward   275
   2 Duration   276
      a. Counting back from the present   276
      b. Counting back from a moment in the past   277
   3 *Ago*   278

Chapter 8 Lexical Variations   279

A Introduction   280

B Terms and Expressions   280

   1 **Acabar**   280
   2 *Apply*   281
   3 *Ask*   282
   4 *At*   283

5	*Attend* 284
6	*Because* 285
7	*Become* or *get* 285
8	*But* 287
9	*Come* and *go* 288
10	**Despedir** 289
11	*Exit* and *success* 289
12	*Go* and *leave* 290
13	*Guide* 292
14	*Know* 292
15	*Learn* 293
16	*Meet* 294
17	*Order* 295
18	*Pensar* 295
19	People vs. Machines 296
20	*Play* 298
21	*Put* 299
22	*Realize* 300
23	*Serve* 300
24	*Spend* 301
25	*Take* 301
26	*Time* 303
27	*What* 304

C False Cognates and False Friends   305

Chapter 9 Orthography 313

A General Information 314

1. The Alphabet 314
2. Representation of Letters by Sound 316

B Consonants: Spelling Issues 318

1. **B, V** 319
2. **K, C, Qu, S** 321
    a. The sound /k/ 321
    b. The sounds /s/ and /z/; **seseo** 322
       (1) The letter s 322
       (2) The letter c + e, i 322
       (3) Stem changes for verbs ending in **-cer** or **-cir**: c → z 323
    c. Words ending in **-ción, -sión, -tión, -xión** 323
3. **G, Gu, Gü, J** 324
    a. The sound /g/; silent u; ü 324
    b. The sound /j/ 325
    c. Verb spelling changes to maintain the /j/ or /g/ sound of the stem 327
       (1) Verbs ending in **-ger** /jer/ or **-gir** /jir/: g → j 327
       (2) Verbs ending in **-guir** /gir/, **-gar** /gar/, **-guar** /guar/: **gu → g; gu → gü** 327
4. **H** 329
    a. Pronunciation of the letter **h** 329
    b. Spelling with the letter **h** 329
    c. Homophones 330
5. **X** 333
    a. The letter **x** pronounced /s/ 333
    b. The letter **x** pronounced /ks/ 333
    c. The letter **x** pronounced /j/ 334
    d. Spelling with the letter **x** 335

6 Ll, Y, Í 335
  a. The sound /y/   335
  b. Spellings for the Sound /y/   336
  c. Lists of common words ending in **-ia, -illa,** and **-ía**   336

7 R, RR 340
  a. The sound /r/   340
  b. The sound /rr/   340
  c. Spelling with **r** and **rr**   341
  d. Soft **d, r**   341

8 *Ch, Ph, Th* → C/Qu, F, T 342
  a. *Ch* → **C/Qu**   342
  b. *Ph* → **F**   342
  c. *Th* → **T**   343

9 Double Consonants 343

C Vowels and Accents   344

1 Syllabification   344
  a. Consonants: Their role in syllables   344
  b. Multiple vowels   345

2 Stress   347
  a. Categorization of words by stress   347
  b. Rules for written accents   348
  c. Special cases   348
    (1) Adverbs ending in -**mente**   348
    (2) Monosyllables   349
    (3) Non-monosyllabic homonyms   350
      (a) **Aun** vs. **Aún**   350
      (b) **Solo**   350
      (c) Demonstrative pronouns   351
      (d) Exclamative and interrogative adjectives, pronouns, and adverbs   351

D Linking between Words: Synalepha   354

1 Same Letter   355

2 Vowel + Vowel   355

3 Consonant + Vowel   356

E Capitalization 357

F Numbers 360
    1 Cardinal Numbers 360
    2 Ordinal Numbers 366
    3 Fractions 369

G Punctuation 371
    1 Terminology 371
    2 Differences between English and Spanish Punctuation 372
        a. Questions and exclamations 372
        b. Dialogue 372
        c. Quotations 373
        d. End of line word division 373

H Dialectal Variation, Norm, Register 374
    1 Dialectal Variation 375
        a. Pronunciation 375
        b. Vocabulary 376
        c. Grammar 377
    2 Norm 377
    3 Register 377
    4 Useful Websites 378

I Summary of 2010 *Ortografía* Changes 378

Ejercicios 381

Verb Tables A-1
    A Lista de modelos de conjugación A-2
    B Modelos de conjugación (Verb Tables) A-3
    C Mini-índice de verbos A-26

Index I-1

TO THE STUDENT

This grammar program is designed not only as a reference tool, but also as a study tool. We hope that it will serve you when you need to understand or review a certain grammar point, but more significantly, that you will learn to make effective use of it as a resource to help you attain a higher level of accuracy in your own oral and written expression, and to better comprehend what you read and hear.

AS A STUDY TOOL

When you approach the study of grammar, we recommend that you apply a few basic principles:

- **Timing** Study what your instructor assigns in grammar at a time of day when your mind is alert, and as soon as possible. If you leave it for the last minute, you are not going to absorb as much as you might if you start promptly.
- **Dosage** To maintain your attention at its highest level of receptivity, it is best to practice in frequent small doses, rather than spend a lot of time all at once. A steady daily routine will always serve you best.
- **Practice** As you study the rules, test your understanding frequently by practicing with the self-correcting exercises in MindTap or the print text. This will help the information take better hold in your memory.
- **Application** Make a conscious effort to apply what you are studying to your communication in the language.
- **Perspective** As an intermediate- or advanced-level student of the language, you are on a lifelong journey. Remember that learning a language is a process that will not end with one more year of study. It is natural for you not to know everything, and to make mistakes, even in areas that you have covered a number of times. Do not allow frustration to become an obstacle. Be patient with your own needs, and keep trying. The more you seek to understand and practice, the richer your journey will be.

AS A REFERENCE TOOL

In this program, we provide a variety of contexts you may use as reference when you are expressing yourself in Spanish, such as explanations, examples, tables, and contextualized exercises. Familiarize yourself with all of the features of the book so you can make the most effective use of it as a tool. Locate the table of contents, the index at the end, and the mini-index of verbs and the accompanying verb tables; mark the pages with useful tables for you (verb conjugations, reflexive verbs, false cognates), and the pages referring to areas where you have noted weaknesses. Refer to these frequently as you write.

Note also that the print text includes cross-references from explanations to exercises, and vice-versa. If you are doing an exercise and fail to understand the reasons for your mistakes, look for the header prior to the exercise: you will find beneath it a reference to the pages of the text containing the relevant rules and explanations.

The Answer Key for the sixth edition is available below the eBook on the learning path for self-directed learners.

We hope that you find this book as useful a means of increasing your accuracy of the Spanish language as others have before you, and that you find ways to enjoy this process by making it one of your own design.

USING *MANUAL DE GRAMÁTICA* IN MINDTAP

The online learning path in MindTap guides you through the material in each chapter, step by step.

Ready? is a short introduction to the main points of each section. This activity encourages you to begin engaging with the new grammar topic.

Learn it! activities present new topics through text, visuals, audio, and video.

Practice it! activities make up the majority of your online work. Your instructor may assign these activities for a grade or ask you to complete them on your own.

Use it! activities encourage you to apply what you are learning.

Got it! activities show you how well you have mastered one or more grammar topics. If these activities are assigned, your instructor will get the results.

Cengage Mobile App: Free access to this course on your mobile device allows you to read the text offline, study with flashcards, set reminders, and view your grades. Download the free Cengage Mobile App from the app store on your mobile device.

LANGUAGE CHOICES

For reasons of personal preference in some cases, and to avoid confusion in other instances, we have made the following choices.

1. We opted for the use of **lo** as direct object, human or not, and of **le** in the case of human direct objects with the impersonal **se**. We have tried to avoid situations where other dialects may be in conflict.

2. We use the verb tense and mood nomenclature closest to English, so it is more recognizable for students. Students wishing to become familiar with the standard terminology used in texts in the Spanish-speaking world should take note of the following differences.

English Terminology	*Manual* Terminology	Spanish Terminology
Imperfect	Imperfecto	Pretérito imperfecto
Preterite	Pretérito	Pretérito indefinido
Pluperfect	Pluscuamperfecto	Pretérito pluscuamperfecto
Present perfect	Presente perfecto	Pretérito perfecto
Conditional	Condicional	Potencial
Conditional present	Condicional presente	Potencial simple
Conditional perfect	Condicional perfecto	Potencial compuesto

REFERENCES

Following is an intentionally skeletal bibliography of those published texts that we consider indispensable reference tools. To this list need to be added the articles published continually in professional journals, which contribute to our evolving perspective of the field, as well as the unpublished dialogue with friends and colleagues, which informs our thinking on the subject of communication in different languages.

Bello, A. *Gramática*. Caracas: Ediciones del Ministerio de Educación, 1972.
Bull, W. *Spanish for Teachers*. Ronald, 1965.
Campos, H. *De la oración simple a la oración compuesta*. Georgetown University Press, 1993.
de Bruyne, J. *A Comprehensive Spanish Grammar*. Blackwell, 1995.
Gili Gaya, S. *Curso superior de sintaxis española*. Barcelona: Vox, 1964.
King, L.D. and Suñer, M. *Gramática española: Análisis y práctica*. McGraw-Hill, 1999.
Lázaro, F. *Curso de lengua española*. Madrid: Ediciones Anaya, 1983.
Llorach, E., et al. *Lengua española*. Madrid: Santillana, 1981.
Moliner, María. *Diccionario de uso del español*. Madrid: Editorial Gredos, 1998.
Real Academia Española. *Gramática de la lengua española*. Madrid: Espasa-Calpe, 1931.
Real Academia Española. *Esbozo de una nueva gramática española*. Madrid: Espasa-Calpe, 1991.
Real Academia Española, Asociación de Academias de la Lengua Española. *Diccionario panhispánico de dudas*. Madrid: Santillana, 2006.
Real Academia Española, Asociación de Academias de la Lengua Española. *Nueva gramática de la lengua española*. Madrid: Espasa Libros, 2009.
Real Academia Española, Asociación de Academias de la Lengua Española. *Ortografía de la lengua española*. Madrid: Espasa Libros, 2010.

Real Academia Española. *Diccionario de la lengua española*. Madrid: Espasa, 2014. Also available online at rae.es, and as an application: DRAE Diccionario de la Lengua Española.

Seco, R. *Diccionario de dudas y dificultades de la lengua castellana*. Madrid: Espasa-Calpe, 1986.

Seco, R. *Manual de gramática española*. Aguilar, 1998.

REVIEWERS

Carla Aguado Swygert, *University of South Carolina*
Jonathan Arries, *College of William & Mary*
Melvin Arrington, *University of Mississippi*
Ann Baker, *University of Evansville*
Michelle Bettencourt, *University of North Carolina-Asheville*
Esther Castro, *San Diego State University*
Chyi Chung, *Northwestern University*
Vilma Concha, *Meredith College*
Ava Conley, *Harding University*
Maite Correa, *Colorado State University*
John Deveny, *Oklahoma State University*
Paula Ellister, *University of Oregon*
Adriana Gutiérrez, *Harvard University*
Denise Hatcher, *Aurora University*

Johanna Liander, *Harvard University*
Dallas Malhiwsky, *University of Nebraska at Omaha*
Marina Martin, *St. John's University*
Geoff Mitchell, *Maryville College*
Lisa Nalbone, *University of Central Florida*
Gayle Nunley, *University of Vermont*
Maria Paniagua-Tejo, *Rollins College*
Alejandro Puga, *DePauw University*
Jennifer Rathbun, *Ashland University*
Roman Santos, *Mohawk Valley Community College*
Nancy Smith, *Allegheny College*
Diana Spinar, *Dakota Wesleyan University*
Helen Tarp, *Idaho State University*
Leslie Veenstra, *Oregon State University*

ACKNOWLEDGMENTS

For this edition, we owe thanks to Beth Kramer and to Martine Edwards, for the opportunity to work on this sixth edition. We would like to also thank Dan Cruse and other members of the enthusiastic and dedicated Cengage team, and in particular Esther Marshall for her attention to detail, and for her prompt and thorough feedback. We are also sincerely grateful for the constructive comments of reviewers of the previous and current editions.

We would especially like to thank Aileen Mason, Esther Marshall, Nancy Kindraka, Lori Mele Hawke, Kim Beuttler, Lara Semones, Elyssa Healy, Garegin Yesayan, Mary Reynolds, Jessica Quila, Sarah Cole, and valued consultants Rachael Gulish, Verónica Esteban, and Gabriela Ferland for their dedicated work on the MindTap course.

Eleanor Dozier
Zulma Iguina

CHAPTER 1

Overview

A Sentence Components

B Verb Structure

C Sentence Structure

D Subject–Verb Agreement

A SENTENCE COMPONENTS

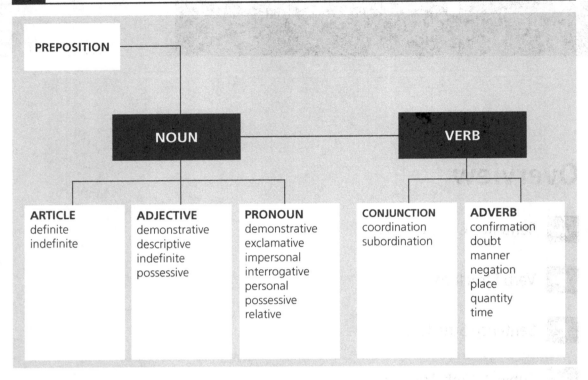

A sentence is a self-contained unit of communication that may be formed with combinations of the following eight types of words: nouns, verbs, prepositions, articles, adjectives, pronouns, conjunctions, and adverbs. Each of these types of words has a particular function to perform in a sentence:

NOUN: may serve as the subject of a verb, its direct or indirect object, or the object of a preposition. In Spanish, equivalents of nouns (i.e., words or groupings of words that may have the same grammatical functions as nouns) are pronouns, infinitives, and nominalized words or groups of words.

VERB: the grammatical core of a sentence; expresses an action or state. Its form changes in agreement with subject, tense, mood, aspect, and voice.

ARTICLE: accompanies and modifies a noun or its equivalent as to specificity.

ADJECTIVE: accompanies and modifies a noun or its equivalent.

ADVERB: modifies a verb, an adjective, another adverb, or a sentence.

PRONOUN: is used to avoid repeating a noun whose reference is clear.

PREPOSITION: relates a noun or its equivalent to another noun, to the verb, or to the rest of the sentence.

CONJUNCTION: joins two parts of a sentence. Conjunctions of subordination introduce subordinate clauses.

The following table expands on what we have just covered and gives the Spanish terms. Refer to the index at the end of the *Manual* to locate additional information on specific topics.

SENTENCE COMPONENTS AND THEIR FUNCTIONS				
WORD TYPE	TIPO DE PALABRA	SUBCATEGORÍAS Y EJEMPLOS	GRAMMATICAL FUNCTION	FUNCIÓN GRAMATICAL
Noun or nominalized word or phrase	**Nombre o sustantivo; palabra o locución nominalizada**	Propio (**España**, la **Inmaculada**...)	Subject; direct / indirect object; prepositional object	Sujeto; objeto directo / indirecto; objeto de preposición
		Común (el **libro**, el **bien**, la **de azul**...)		
Pronoun	**Pronombre**	Personal (**yo, me, mí**...)	Same as the noun	Igual que el nombre
		Impersonal (**se, uno**...)		
		Demostrativo (**eso, esto**...)		
		Posesivo (**el mío, el tuyo**...)		
		Interrogativo (**¿qué?, ¿quién?**...)		
		Exclamativo (**¡qué!, ¡quién!**...)		
		Indefinido (**alguien, algo**...)		
		Relativo (**que, el que, cuyo**...)	Replaces a noun and introduces a relative clause; subject or object of verb in subordinate clause, or prepositional object	Reemplaza el nombre e introduce una cláusula relativa; sujeto u objeto del verbo de la cláusula subordinada, u objeto de preposición

(continued)

WORD TYPE	TIPO DE PALABRA	SUBCATEGORÍAS Y EJEMPLOS	GRAMMATICAL FUNCTION	FUNCIÓN GRAMATICAL
Article	**Artículo**	Definido (**el, la; los, las**)	Accompanies and modifies the noun or its equivalent	Acompaña y modifica el nombre o su equivalente
		Indefinido (**un[a]; unos[as]**)		
Adjective	**Adjetivo**	Calificativo (**verde, grande**…)	Accompanies and modifies the noun or its equivalent	Acompaña y modifica el nombre o su equivalente
		Demostrativo (**ese, esta**…)		
		Posesivo (**mi, tu, su**…)		
		Indefinido (**algún, ningún**…)		
Preposition	**Preposición**	(**a, de, en, con, desde, por, para, sin, sobre**…)	Introduces the noun or its equivalent	Introduce el nombre o su equivalente
Verb	**Verbo**	Transitivo / Intransitivo	Provides action or description; is the core of the sentence	Proporciona acción o descripción; es el núcleo de la oración
		1.ª, 2.ª, 3.ª conjugación		
Adverb	**Adverbio**	(**aquí, bajo, bien, cuando, mal, muy, no, rápidamente**…)	Modifies a verb, an adjective, an adverb, or a sentence	Modifica un verbo, un adjetivo, un adverbio o una oración
Conjunction	**Conjunción**	De coordinación (**y, o, pero, sino**…)	Links two parts of speech or clauses	Une dos palabras o grupos de palabras
		De subordinación (**que, aunque**…)	Introduces a subordinate clause	Introduce una cláusula subordinada

Ejercicios 1.1–1.2, página 382

B. VERB STRUCTURE

VERB STRUCTURE					
MODO	MOOD	TIEMPO O ASPECTO	TENSE OR ASPECT	EJEMPLO	EXAMPLE
Infinitivo	Infinitive	Presente	Present	**estudiar**	*to study*
		Perfecto	Perfect	**haber estudiado**	*to have studied*
Participio	Participle	Presente	Present	**estudiando**	*studying*
		Pasado	Past	**estudiado**	*studied*
Indicativo	Indicative	Presente	Present	**estudio**[1]	*I study*
		Presente perfecto	Present Perfect	**he estudiado**	*I have studied*
		Futuro	Future	**estudiaré**	*I will study*
		Futuro perfecto	Future Perfect	**habré estudiado**	*I will have studied*
		Pretérito	Preterite	**estudié**	*I studied*
		Imperfecto	Imperfect	**estudiaba**	*I studied, would study, was studying*
		Pluscuamperfecto	Pluperfect	**había estudiado**	*I had studied*
Condicional[2]	Conditional	Presente	Present	**estudiaría**	*I would study*
		Perfecto	Perfect	**habría estudiado**	*I would have studied*
Subjuntivo	Subjunctive	Presente	Present	**estudie**	*(translation varies with context)*
		Presente perfecto	Present Perfect	**haya estudiado**	
		Imperfecto	Imperfect	**estudiara**	
		Pluscuamperfecto	Pluperfect	**hubiera estudiado**	
Imperativo	Imperative	(solo una forma)	(only one form)	**¡Estudien!**	*Study!*

Ejercicio 1.3, páginas 382–383

---

[1] The examples for the indicative, conditional, and subjunctive are given in the first-person singular (**yo**). The example for the imperative is given in the **ustedes** form.

[2] Some grammarians consider the conditional to be a tense of the indicative mood, not a mood in itself. Because it is used for contexts that are modally different from those in which other moods are used, and because it has two tenses itself, we have chosen to consider it a mood. The only situation in which it could be considered a tense of the indicative is when it is used as a future of the past.

C SENTENCE STRUCTURE

A sentence may be composed of one or many clauses. A clause can be identified by the fact that it has a verb that is conjugated (i.e., not in the infinitive or participle form).

When you look at a sentence, you can tell exactly how many clauses it has by the number of conjugated verbs:

¡**Llegué**! (1)	*I arrived!*
¿**Estás** estudiando? (1)	*Are you studying?*
Había caído tanta nieve / que **era** difícil caminar sin resbalarse. (2)	*So much snow had fallen that it was hard to walk without slipping.*
Ven / y te **doy** dinero / para que me **compres** la medicina / que me **recetó** el médico. (4)	*Come and I'll give you money so you can buy me the medicine the doctor prescribed me.*

Note in the above sentences that the conjugated verbs are in bold, and clauses are separated by a slash. The number in parentheses at the end of each sentence indicates how many clauses there are in the sentence.

> Ejercicios 1.4–1.6, páginas 383–384

1 Independent Clauses

Independent clauses are not dependent upon one another, nor do they have other clauses depending on them. They can stand alone:

Querían ahorrar dinero en gasolina.	*They wanted to save money on gas.*

or they may be attached to one another by means of conjunctions of coordination (**y** in the following sentence):

Querían ahorrar dinero en gasolina y estaban considerando un coche de energía alternativa.	*They wanted to save money on gas and were considering an alternative energy car.*

2 Main or Principal Clauses

A main clause is a clause that could be independent according to its meaning but that has one or more clauses that are its dependents. In the following sentence, the main clause is **Soltaron a los presos:**

Soltaron a los presos para que estuviera clara su intención de cumplir con los derechos humanos.	*They released the prisoners so that their intention to comply with human rights was clear.*

3 Dependent or Subordinate Clauses

In Spanish, a subordinate or dependent clause is introduced by a conjunction of subordination or adverbial phrase (**que, porque, cuando, tan pronto como...**) or by a relative pronoun (**que, el que, lo que, cuyo...**). As its name indicates, a dependent clause depends on a main clause. The relationship of the dependent clause to the main clause varies according to the type of dependent clause it may be: nominal, adverbial, or adjectival. We define each below:

Nominal clause: one that behaves like a noun and can serve the function of subject, direct object of the verb of the main clause, or object of a preposition. In the following two sentences, the noun **pan** and the nominal clause **que me ayudes** have the same grammatical function as the direct object of the main verb **Quiero:**

Quiero **pan.**	*I want bread.*
Quiero **que me ayudes.**	*I want you to help me.*

Adverbial clause: one that behaves like an adverb and modifies the verb of the main clause by indicating manner (how?), purpose (what for?), reason (why?), time (when?), condition (under what condition?), etc. In the following two sentences, the adverb **rápidamente** and the adverbial clause **tan pronto como pudo** both modify the main verb **Salió** by indicating the manner in which (how?) the action took place:

Salió **rápidamente.**	*She left quickly.*
Salió **tan pronto como pudo.**	*She left as soon as she could.*

Adjectival clause: one that behaves like an adjective and modifies a noun. Adjectival clauses are also called relative clauses: they each begin with a relative pronoun, which replaces a noun in the main clause (its antecedent) and introduces the subordinate clause that modifies the antecedent.

Quiero leer una novela **divertida.**	*I want to read a fun novel.*
Quiero leer una novela **que me haga reír.**	*I want to read a novel that will make me laugh.*

In the preceding two sentences, the adjective **divertida** and the adjectival clause **que me haga reír** both modify the noun **novela.**

We provide below a list of basic terminology for discussions regarding sentence structure:

SPANISH / ENGLISH TERMINOLOGY	
SPANISH	ENGLISH
cláusula	clause
cláusula independiente	independent clause
cláusula principal	main clause
cláusula relativa	relative clause
cláusula subordinada	subordinate or dependent clause
depender de	to depend on
expresión, locución	phrase
frase, oración	sentence
función	function
palabra	word
relación	relationship, rapport
término	term
tipo	type, sort

The following chart compares diverse types of clauses as to the types of words that introduce them, and their grammatical functions within the sentence:

CLAUSE TYPES			
TYPE OF CLAUSE	SUBCATEGORY	INTRODUCED BY	FUNCTION
Independent		(nothing)	(exists on its own)
Main clause		(nothing)	(could exist on its own)
Subordinate	Nominal	Conjunction of subordination	Subject or direct object of verb of main clause
	Adverbial	Conjunction of subordination or adverbial phrase	Modifies the verb of the main clause by describing manner, purpose, reason, time, condition, etc.
	Adjectival	Relative pronoun	Modifies the antecedent of the relative pronoun

The following chart gives examples of main and dependent or subordinate clauses:

CLAUSE EXAMPLES		
MAIN CLAUSE	SUBORDINATE CLAUSE	
	INTRODUCED BY	CLAUSE TYPE
	Conjunction	Nominal clause
Le dije a Elsa *I told Elsa*	**que** *(that)*[3]	**me gustaba la universidad.** *I liked the university.*
	Conjunction	Adverbial clause
Nos fuimos *We left*	**porque** *because*	**hacía mucho frío.** *it was very cold.*
	Relative pronoun	Adjectival or relative clause
Fuimos a una fiesta *We went to a party*	**que** *(that)*[4]	**dieron nuestros amigos.** *our friends gave.*

Sentence Analysis

Split Main Clause. In some complex sentences, one clause may be broken into two parts with another, subordinate, clause inserted within it:

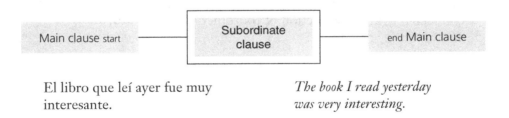

El libro que leí ayer fue muy interesante.

The book I read yesterday was very interesting.

Main clause: **El libro (...) fue muy interesante.**
Subordinate clause: **que leí ayer** [relative clause]

---

[3] This conjunction is in parentheses because in English, the conjunction may be omitted. In Spanish, however, all conjunctions must be stated.

[4] This relative pronoun is in parentheses because in English, the relative pronoun may be omitted within certain contexts. In Spanish, however, the relative pronoun is always stated.

Subordinate as Secondary Main Clause. In some complex sentences, a subordinate clause may serve as a main clause to yet another subordinate (sub-subordinate) clause:

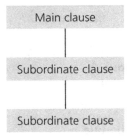

La clase de español que me recomendaste que tomara me ha interesado mucho.

The Spanish class (that) you recommended (to me) (that) I take has interested me a lot.

Main clause: **La clase de español (...) me ha interesado mucho.**
Subordinate clause #1: **que me recomendaste** [relative or adjectival clause]
Subordinate clause #2 (subordinate clause #1 serves as its main clause): **que tomara** [nominal clause]

Multiple Subordinates. One main clause may have two subordinates of equal value connected with a conjunction of coordination (**y, o, pero, sino**):

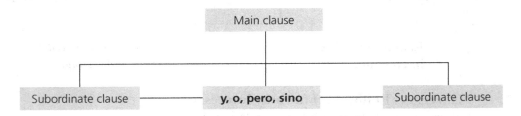

Me dijo que lo haría y que[5] me lo daría.

She told me (that) she would make it and (that she would) give it to me.

Main clause: **Me dijo**
Subordinate clause #1: **que lo haría** [nominal]
Subordinate clause #2: **que me lo daría** [nominal]
Conjunction of coordination: **y**

---

[5] This conjunction may be omitted because it is a repetition of the previous one: **Me dijo que lo haría y me lo daría.**

Yo sabía que Juan lo había hecho
o que había ayudado a sus amigos
a hacerlo.

*I knew that Juan had done it, or that
he had helped his friends do it.*

Main clause: **Yo sabía**
Subordinate clause #1: **que Juan lo había hecho** [nominal]
Subordinate clause #2: **que había ayudado a sus amigos a hacerlo** [nominal]
Conjunction of coordination: **o**

Me dijo que vendría, pero que
llegaría tarde.

*He told me that he would come, but
that he would arrive late.*

Main clause: **Me dijo**
Subordinate clause #1: **que vendría** [nominal]
Subordinate clause #2: **que llegaría tarde** [nominal]
Conjunction of coordination: **pero**

No le dije que viniera, sino
que me llamara.

*I did not tell her to come, but
rather to call me.*

Main clause: **No le dije**
Subordinate clause #1: **que viniera** [nominal]
Subordinate clause #2: **que me llamara** [nominal]
Conjunction of coordination: **sino**

Multiple Main Clauses with Subordinates. One sentence may have two main clauses connected by conjunctions of coordination, each main clause having its own subordinate clause(s):

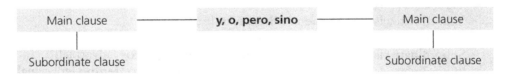

Lamento que no puedas venir, pero
estoy contento de que tus amigos te
hayan invitado a cenar.

*I am sorry you cannot come,
but I am glad (that) your
friends have invited you to dinner.*

Main clause #1: **Lamento**
Subordinate clause #1: **que no puedas venir** [nominal]
Main clause #2: **estoy contento de**
Subordinate clause #2: **que tus amigos te hayan invitado a cenar** [nominal]
Conjunction of coordination: **pero**

Me dijo que necesitábamos boletos y luego llamó para que nos reservaran dos.

She told me that we needed tickets, and then she called so that they would reserve two for us.

Main clause #1: **Me dijo**
Subordinate clause #1: **que necesitábamos boletos** [nominal]
Main clause #2: **luego llamó**
Subordinate clause #2: **para que nos reservaran dos** [adverbial]
Conjunction of coordination: **y**

Multiple Sub-subordinates. The complexity of a sentence is practically limitless. The following diagram is an example of a sentence with one main clause and four subordinates, three of which are subordinated to the first subordinate clause:

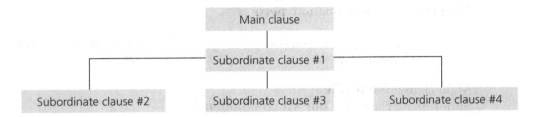

Mis amigos me habían dicho que cuando regresaran de las vacaciones me llamarían para que pudiéramos salir juntos a pesar de que tuviéramos poco tiempo.

My friends had told me that when they returned from vacation they would call me so that we could go out in spite of the fact that we might have little time.

Main clause: **Mis amigos me habían dicho**
Subordinate clause #1: **que me llamarían** [nominal]
Subordinate clause #2: **cuando regresaran de las vacaciones** [adverbial]
Subordinate clause #3: **para que pudiéramos salir juntos** [adverbial]
Subordinate clause #4: **a pesar de que tuviéramos poco tiempo** [adverbial]

Ejercicios 1.7–1.11, páginas 384–386

D SUBJECT–VERB AGREEMENT

A verb agrees in number and in person with the subject:

Tú cami**nas** rápido.	*You walk fast.*
Ellos no contest**aron**.	*They did not answer.*

The subject is always implicit in the ending of the verb in Spanish, whether the subject is stated in the sentence or not. (For more on the need for the subject pronouns, see Chapter 3, section 2, pages 53–56.)

Lleg**amos**.	*We arrived.*

A verb will usually agree in number with a plural subject:

Esos actores **son** estoicos.	*Those actors are stoic.*

When a plural subject includes the speaker, the verb will take the first-person plural ending:

Los españoles nos consider**amos** europeos.	*We Spaniards consider ourselves (to be) European.*

When the verb **ser** is used with a first- or second-person subject in the main clause, followed by a relative clause, the verb of the relative clause will be conjugated in the third person, based on its agreement with the relative pronoun as the subject:

Fui yo la que lleg**ó** primero.	*It was I who arrived first.* (OR: *I was the one who arrived first.*)
Eres tú el que mient**e**.	*You are the one who lies.*

Collective nouns are singular in principle: **gente, grupo, infinidad, muchedumbre, multitud, número, pareja, pueblo, vecindario,** etc.

La gente comprenderá.	*People will understand.*
La pareja salió por atrás.	*The couple went out the back.*
Un grupo de estudiantes se manifestó en contra del cambio.	*A group of students protested against the change.*

The combination of a collective (in the following sentences: **mitad, mayor parte, gran número**) with a plural noun (**familias, exiliados, ciervos**) will permit a choice of singular or plural verb:

> La mitad de las familias no tien**e(n)** comida.
> *Half of the families have no food.*

> La mayor parte de los exiliados viv**ía(n)** en campos de refugiados.
> *Most of the exiled people lived in refugee camps.*

> Un gran número de ciervos se acerc**aba(n)** a la casa.
> *A large number of deer came close to the house.*

The same choice occurs when the collective subject (in the following sentence: **gente**) is separated from one of its verbs:

> La **gente** se espant**ó** con la explosión, y poco a poco se **fueron** (OR: **fue**) amontonando en las escaleras.
> *The people were frightened by the explosion, and little by little, they crowded together in the stairway.*

When the first person or the second person is included in the collective (in the following sentences: **todos, los cuatro, algunos**), the verb will indicate this agreement:

> Todos lleg**amos** al mismo tiempo.
> *We all arrived at the same time.*

> Los cuatro salt**asteis** a la vez.
> *All four of you jumped at once.*

> Algunos sab**íamos** la respuesta.
> *Some of us knew the answer.*

When a subgroup (in the following sentence: **aquel grupo**) is being distinguished from the plural whole (**todos los manifestantes**), a singular verb is required to avoid confusion:

> Aquel grupo, entre todos los manifestantes, ten**ía** los mayores carteles.
> *That group, among all the protesters, had the largest signs.*

Impersonal verbs are always singular. They have no subject; the entities that follow them (in the sentences below: **niños, sillas, años**) function as direct objects:

> **Hay** tres niños en la calle.
> *There are three children in the street.*

> **Había** veinte sillas en la clase.
> *There were twenty chairs in the class.*

> **Hace** dos años que vivimos aquí.
> *We have been living here for two years.*

Verbs relating to the time and weather are normally impersonal (**amanecer, anochecer, llover, nevar, lloviznar, granizar, relampaguear, tronar...**):

Nieva mucho en febrero.	*It snows a lot in February.*
Llovería cuarenta días.	*It would rain for forty days.*
Amaneció nublado.	*It was cloudy at daybreak.*

When one of these verbs is used figuratively, with a noun as its figurative subject, it will agree with the subject:

Parecía que **llovían** desgracias sin cesar.	*It seemed to be raining misfortunes incessantly.*
Amanezco feliz en verano.	*I get up feeling happy in summertime.*

In contexts that present attributes, with verbs like **ser, estar,** and **parecer,** the verb sometimes agrees with its attribute instead of with its subject. In the first of the following sentences, **es** is singular because the subject **lo que dices** is neutral. In the second sentence there is a plural attribute, **mentiras,** which takes over the agreement of the verb:

Lo que dices **es** cierto.	*What you say is true.*
Lo que dices **son** mentiras.	*What you say are lies.*

When there are multiple subjects, the verb is plural:

El amor y la locura siempre **van** juntos.	*Love and madness always go together.*

If the group is considered a unit, the verb is singular:

La compra y venta de drogas **estaba** prohibida.	*Buying and selling drugs was forbidden.*
El constante **ir y venir** de la gente me **molestaba.**	*The constant coming and going of people bothered me.*

In combinations of first-, second-, and/or third-person subjects, the first person takes precedence over the second, and the second person takes precedence over the third. Thus, if the first person is one of the subjects, the verb is conjugated in the first-person plural:

Tú y yo **somos** amigos.	*You and I are friends.*
Ustedes y yo **somos** amigos.	*You and I are friends.*
Vosotros y yo **somos** amigos.	*You and I are friends.*
Ellos y yo **somos** amigos.	*They and I are friends.*

If the second person is combined with second- or third-person subjects, the verb is conjugated in second-person plural in the **ustedes** or **vosotros** form, depending on the dialect in use and the degree of formality. The variations in the following sentences reflect differences in dialect between Spain and Latin America. In both regions, **usted** is formal and **tú** is informal, but for the plural, Latin America uses **ustedes** for both formal and informal, whereas in Spain **vosotros** is informal, and **ustedes** is formal. All three of the following sentences translate as *Both you and he are responsible*:

Informal:

    Ambos tú y él **son** responsables. (Latin America)

    Ambos tú y él **sois** responsables. (Spain)

Formal:

    Ambos usted y él **son** responsables. (Latin America and Spain)

With *either / or* combinations (in Spanish **o / o**), or *neither / nor* (**ni / ni**), the singular or the plural can be used:

O Luis o Eva lo hará(**n**) por mí.	*Either Luis or Eva will do it for me.*
Ni Luis ni Eva lo hará(**n**) por mí.	*Neither Luis nor Eva will do it for me.*

With combinations of first- and second-person subjects, the verb is usually in the plural, and the first person takes precedence over second, and second over third:

O tú o yo lo har**emos**.	*Either you or I will do it.*
Ni tú ni yo lo har**emos**.	*Neither you nor I will do it.*
O tú o él lo har**án**. (OR: har**éis**)	*Either you or he will do it.*
Ni tú ni él lo har**án**. (OR: har**éis**)	*Neither you nor he will do it.*

When the verb precedes the subject, it often agrees only with the first subject, and a pause is felt between the two subjects, as if the second were an afterthought:

No estaba caliente la carne, ni la salsa.	*The meat was not hot, nor (was) the sauce.*

Infinitives and clauses that function as subjects are singular:

Me gusta **soñar**.	*I like to dream.*
Convien**e que digas la verdad**.	*It is best that you tell the truth.*

Even when there are multiple infinitives and clauses, the main verb is usually invariable:

Me gusta **bailar y cantar.**	*I like to dance and sing.*
Es mejor **que vengas a casa y te acuestes.**	*It is best that you come home and go to bed.*

With titles such as **usted, señoría, excelencia, eminencia, alteza,** and **majestad,** agreement varies according to the gender of the person to whom they apply:

Usted es muy generos**o**.	*You are very generous.* (masculine)
Usted es muy generos**a**.	*You are very generous.* (feminine)
Ustedes son honrad**os**.	*You are honest.* (masculine)
Ustedes son honrad**as**.	*You are honest.* (feminine)
¿Su Alteza está cansad**o**?	*Is your Highness tired?* (masculine)
¿Su Alteza está cansad**a**?	*Is your Highness tired?* (feminine)

In the case of terms of endearment used as epithets (such as **alma, amor, cariño, corazón, vida,** etc.), the verb and other modifiers agree in gender and in person with the individual addressed, not with the term of endearment. Only modifiers of the epithet itself will agree with it in gender.

¿Est**ás** cansad**o** esta mañana, vida mía?	*Are you tired this morning, my love?*

In the preceding sentence, notice that the term of endearment **vida** is feminine, as is the possessive that accompanies it, **mía.** However, the person being addressed is second-person singular (est**ás**) and masculine (cansad**o**).

Similarly, in the following sentence, note that **amor** is masculine; however, the person being addressed is a woman, as can be seen in the agreement of **guapa:**

¡Qué guap**a** estás hoy, mi amor!	*You look so beautiful today, my love!*

Note that in the above sentence, the verb is second-person singular, marking the subject.

After a percentage, the verb may be singular or plural:

78% de los hombres tien**e**(**n**) barba.	*78% of the men have a beard.*
El veinte por ciento de los habitantes no trabaj**a**(**n**).	*Twenty percent of the inhabitants do not work.*

Ninguno uses a singular verb, except if it is qualified by a plural noun or pronoun, in which case the verb may be singular or plural:

    No me gusta ninguno.   *I don't like any of them.*

    Ninguno de nosotros lo sab**e**   *None of us knows.*
    (OR: sab**emos**).

> Ejercicios 1.12–1.14, página 386

CHAPTER 2

Nouns and Noun Determiners

A Nouns and Their Equivalents

B Noun Determiners

A NOUNS AND THEIR EQUIVALENTS

1 Introduction

a. Definition

Nouns: words that can take on the grammatical function of the subject of a verb.

In the following sentence, **soldado** is a noun, and it is the subject of the verb **sabe:**

Ese **soldado** sabe mucho de armas. — *That soldier knows a lot about weapons.*

b. Noun equivalents

Other words that can have the basic function of the subject of a verb are pronouns, infinitives, and any nominalized words or phrases.

Pronouns: words that replace nouns and have the same gender and number as the nouns to which they refer.

Ellas me lo dijeron. — *They told me.*

¿**Cuál** es **el mío**? — *Which one is mine?*

El mío costó menos que **el tuyo.** — *Mine cost less than yours.*

El que vino ayer fue Juan. — *The one who came yesterday was Juan.*

Esa casa es **mía.** — *That house is mine.*

Infinitives: (See Chapter 6.H, pages 237–239, on the use of the infinitives and the present participles.)

Caminar es bueno para la salud. — *To walk (Walking) is good for one's health.*

Me gusta **bailar.** — *I like to dance. (Dancing is pleasing to me.)*

Nominalized words and phrases: words and phrases converted into nouns.

El azul del Mediterráneo siempre me sorprende. — ***The blue** of the Mediterranean always surprises me.*

Note that often in the case of nominalized adjectives in Spanish, the person or object being referred to is included in the meaning of the adjective. In English this reference is stated, often in the form of nouns such as *man, woman, people,* or when the reference is more specific, in the form of the pronoun *one:*

Esa refugiada tiene ojos azules.	*That refugee <u>woman</u> has blue eyes.*
Ese moreno es mi hermano.	*That dark-complexioned <u>man</u> is my brother.*
Los indígenas resisten la pérdida de su territorio.	*The indigenous <u>people</u> resist the loss of their territory.*
Este jabón no sirve. Tengo que encontrar **el bueno**.	*This soap is no good. I have to find the good <u>one</u>.*

Any adjective can be nominalized. Remember this when you want to write something equivalent to the preceding contexts, in which *one* or *people,* or other equivalents, are involved in English:

El primero en terminar gana.	*The first **one** to finish wins.*
El último en irse cierra las ventanas.	*The last **one** to leave closes the windows.*
Deberíamos respetar a **los mayores**.	*We should respect **older people**.*
Es una batalla en que no hay ni **buenos** ni **malos**.	*It's a battle in which there are neither **good guys** nor **bad guys**.*

The placement of the neuter **lo** in front of a nominalized adjective is also frequently used in Spanish, and alters the meaning of the adjective to make it a generalization or a characteristic:

Lo interesante es el silencio.	***What is interesting** is the silence.*
Lo mejor sería una tregua.	***The best** thing would be a truce.*
Lo bueno y **lo malo** se confunden.	***Good** and **evil** become confused.*
Eso es **lo absurdo** de la situación.	*That is **the absurdity** of the situation.*
Lo violento en las noticias me deprime.	***The violence** in the news depresses me. (OR: It always depresses me **how violent** the news is.)*
Me encanta **lo dulce** combinado con **lo agrio**.	*I love the combination of **sweet** (foods, things, flavors . . .) and sour (foods, things, flavors . . .).*

Notice the different uses of the nominalized adjective **extranjero**:

El extranjero llegó ayer.	*The **foreigner** arrived yesterday.*
Viajarán **al extranjero**.	*They will travel **abroad**.*
Evita **lo extranjero**.	*He avoids **what is foreign**.*

Nominalized phrases are also frequent in Spanish:

La del velo es mi prima.	*The **woman with the veil** is my cousin.*
El de azul es mi hermano.	*The **one in blue** is my brother.*
Los de al lado siempre hacen ruido.	*The **people next door** always make noise.*
Me caen bien **los que respetan a los demás**.	*I like **people who respect others**.*

c. Noun companions

Articles and adjectives are words that accompany and modify nouns. They agree with the nouns they modify:

la casa **blanca**, **las** casas **rojas**	*the white house, the red houses*
el árbol, **los** árboles	*the tree, the trees*
una mesa, **unas** mesas	*a table, some tables*[1]
esa casa, **esas** casas	*that house, those houses*
este libro, **estos** libros	*this book, these books*
nuestra casa, **vuestras** ideas	*our house, your ideas*
mis libros, **tus** cuadernos	*my books, your notebooks*
una niña **lista**, **unas** niñas **listas**	*a clever girl, some clever girls*

Prepositions are words that show a relationship between a noun or its equivalent and another noun, the verb, or the rest of the sentence:

Te llamo **con** mi celular.	*I'll call you **on** my cell phone.*
La devastación **del** huracán fue una sorpresa **para** todos.	*The destruction **of** the hurricane was a surprise **for** everyone.*
Después **de** rescatar al perro, lo llevaron adentro **a** secarlo.	*After rescuing the dog, they took him inside to dry him off.*

Ejercicios 2.1–2.2, página 387

---

[1] In the plural, **unos** and **unas** mean *some*.

2 Nouns: Gender and Number

a. Gender (Género)

All Spanish nouns are either masculine or feminine.

Most nouns ending in **-o, -l,** and **-r** are masculine:

    el libro *book*   el barril *barrel*   el actor *actor*

Exceptions:

la foto *photo*	la capital *capital*	la moral *morale*
la mano *hand*	la cárcel *jail*	la piel *skin*
la moto *motorcycle*	la catedral *cathedral*	la sal *salt*
la radio *radio*	la miel *honey*	la señal *sign, signal*

Most nouns ending in **-a, -d, -ción, -sión, -umbre,** and **-z** are feminine:

la trama *plot*	la libertad *liberty*
la costumbre *custom, habit*	la luz *light*
la condición *condition*	la decisión *decision*

Exceptions:

el día *day*	el arroz *rice*
el tranvía *streetcar*	el lápiz *pencil*
el ataúd *coffin*	el maíz *corn*
el césped *lawn*	el matiz *shade of color*
el huésped *guest*	el pez *fish*
el clima *climate*	el poema *poem*
el crucigrama *crossword puzzle*	el poeta *poet*
el drama *drama*	el problema *problem*
el fantasma *ghost*	el programa *program*
el idioma *language*	el síntoma *symptom*
el mapa *map*	el sistema *system*
el panorama *panorama*	el telegrama *telegram*
el planeta *planet*	el tema *theme, topic*

Languages, days of the week, mountains, rivers, and oceans are masculine:

el español	el lunes	los Pirineos
Spanish	*Monday*	*the Pyrenees*

Letters of the alphabet are feminine:

la a	la hache	la jota
(the letter) a	*(the letter) h*	*(the letter) j*

Infinitives are masculine when nominalized:

el amanecer *dawn* el poder *power*

Many Spanish nouns referring to humans and animals occur in pairs, sometimes similar in form, sometimes not, but gender is always distinguished:

el hombre *man* ⟷ la mujer *woman*

el actor *actor* ⟷ la actriz *actress*

el rey *king* ⟷ la reina *queen*

el toro *bull* ⟷ la vaca *cow*

Some Spanish nouns referring to humans are identical in form—only the modifier shows the gender:

el/la estudiante *student*	el/la demócrata *democrat*
el/la joven *young man / woman*	el/la ciclista *cyclist*
el/la modelo *model*	el/la comunista *communist*
el/la turista *tourist*	el/la pianista *pianist*
el/la atleta *athlete*	el/la guía *guide*

Some nouns can change meaning with a change in gender:

el policía ⟷ BUT: la policía
policeman   *policewoman / the police*

el guía ⟷ BUT: la guía
guide (e.g., *tour guide*)   *guide (woman) / guidebook*

el papa ⟷ BUT: la papa
pope   *potato*

el cura ⟷ BUT: la cura
priest   *cure*

Some nouns exist only in one gender, but serve for both sexes. The following examples can refer to women as well as to men:

Mi tía es **un ángel**.	*My aunt is an angel.*
Esa niña es **un amor**.	*That little girl is a sweetheart.*
Mi padre es **una persona** encantadora.	*My father is a charming person.*
Ese hombre fue **una víctima** de la sociedad.	*That man was a victim of society.*

b. Number (Número)

A noun ending in a vowel adds **-s** to form the plural:

casa *house* ⟶ casas *houses*

A noun ending in a consonant, in **-y,** or in a stressed vowel adds **-es** to form the plural:

amor *love* ⟶ amores *loves*

ley *law* ⟶ leyes *laws*

rubí *ruby* ⟶ rubíes *rubies*

francés *Frenchman* ⟶ franceses[2] *Frenchmen*

examen *exam* ⟶ exámenes[2] *exams*

A noun ending in **-z** has a plural ending in **-ces:**

lápiz ⟶ lápices

A noun ending in an unstressed vowel with final **-s** does not change for the plural:

el lunes ⟶ los lunes

el tocadiscos ⟶ los tocadiscos

la crisis ⟶ las crisis

Ejercicios 2.3–2.5, páginas 387–389

---

[2] Notice the accents on **francés** and **exámenes**. A plural can acquire or lose a written accent so that the stress can remain on the same syllable as in the singular.

3 Personal a

In Spanish, direct object nouns referring to human beings are preceded by the personal **a**. The reason for the addition of the personal **a** is that without it, the direct object could be confused with the subject.

The use of the personal **a** with human direct objects extends to all contexts, no matter what the subject of the verb may be. However, as a rule, the personal **a** is used with persons, as its name indicates, and not with things:

Vi[3] el libro en tu casa.	*I saw the book in your house.*
Vi **a** Carmen en la clase.	*I saw Carmen in class.*
Conocemos ese barrio.	*We are familiar with that neighborhood.*
Conocemos **al** tío de Juan.	*We know Juan's uncle.*

If the persons referred to are not specific, and are thus dehumanized to the point of being perceived for all practical purposes as objects, omit the personal **a**:

Buscan secretarios bilingües.	*They are looking for bilingual secretaries.*
Busco **a** mi secretaria.	*I am looking for my secretary.*

Conversely, if the nonhuman direct object is a live being (real or fictitious), it is preceded by the personal **a**. This is the case for animals and personified concepts:

El cazador mató **al** león.	*The hunter killed the lion.*
El científico vio **a** la Muerte.	*The scientist saw Death.*

In both of the above sentences, the direct object is an animate being, and as such, could take on the action of the verb: the lion could kill the hunter, and Death (personified) could see the scientist.

When the verb **tener** is used with human direct objects, do not use the personal **a** in contexts that are objective, in which the simple fact of possession is being stated:

Tengo cuatro tíos.	*I have four uncles.*

However, if **tener** is used in a context that is subjective, in which the subject is affected by the context in some personal manner, or some additional meaning of keeping or holding is implied rather than merely having, the personal **a** is used. In these contexts the direct object is more specifically identified than in the contexts

---

[3] Note the absence of subject pronoun in this sentence and the following ones. In Spanish, the norm is for an unstressed subject to be embedded in the verb form, and not expressed explicitly. For more information on subject pronoun usage, see Chapter 3, page 53.

in which no personal **a** is used. The direct object may be a proper noun or may be preceded by a possessive adjective:

> Tenemos **a** nuestro abuelo *We have our grandfather in*
> en una residencia de ancianos. *a retirement home.*

(In other words, our grandfather is living in a retirement home, and we are responsible for this, or are feeling helpless or sorry about it.)

> Tengo **a** mi suegra de visita. *I have my mother-in-law visiting.*

(In other words, my mother-in-law is visiting, and this affects my daily routine in some manner.)

> Esa mujer tenía **a** mi bebé en sus brazos. *That woman had my baby in her arms.*

(In other words, my baby was in her arms: she was holding him there.)

> —No tengo **a** nadie que me acompañe *"I don't have anyone to go with me*
> al baile. ¿Y tú tienes **a** alguien? *to the dance. Do you have someone?"*
> —Sí, yo tengo **a** Rita. *"Yes, I have Rita."*

(In this context, the first speaker is pointing to a significant absence, implying a certain degree of self-pity, perhaps. It may be that the second speaker is feeling a special sense of security or pride at having Rita to go with.)

Because the pronouns **alguien, nadie,** and **quien** refer to persons, they are preceded by the personal **a** when they function as direct objects:

> Oí **a** alguien llorando. *I heard someone crying.*
> No conozco **a** nadie aquí. *I do not know anyone here.*
> ¿**A** quién viste? *Whom did you see?*

Direct object pronouns (**lo, la, los,** and **las**) are never accompanied by the personal **a** although they may refer to persons. The pronoun form used would be the stressed form:

> Lo vi **a** él ayer. *I saw him yesterday.*
> La llamé **a** ella anoche. *I called her last night.*
> **A ellos** no los entiendo nunca. *I never understand them.*
> **A ellas** las regañé ayer. *I scolded them yesterday.*

(Notice that the above sentences contain examples of repetitive object pronouns, used for emphasis or clarification. If there is no doubt as to reference, the only required pronoun in each of the four sentences above is the unstressed **lo, la, los,** or **las.**)

Ejercicios 2.6–2.8, páginas 389–390

B NOUN DETERMINERS

Noun determiners are the words that accompany and modify nouns.

1 Articles

a. Definite articles

DEFINITE ARTICLES		
	SINGULAR	PLURAL
Masculine	**el**	**los**
Feminine	**la**	**las**

Agreement: The definite article agrees with the noun it accompanies:

| **el** hombre *(the) man* | **la** mujer *(the) woman* |
| **los** libros *(the) books* | **las** clases *(the) classes* |

Definite articles are also used in the case of nominalization of words or expressions, such as adjectives, pronouns, infinitives, and expressions with **de** used for characteristics:

Me gusta **el azul**.	*I like **blue** (OR: **the blue one**).*
El alto es mi padre.	***The tall one** is my father.*
La rubia ganó.	***The blond woman** won.*
Los ricos no entienden.	***Rich people** do not understand.*
Todo se olvida con **el correr del tiempo**.	*Everything is forgotten with **the passing of time**.*
La del sombrero es mi hermana.	***The one with the hat** is my sister.*
Ya llegaron **los míos**.	***Mine** already arrived.*

When a feminine singular noun starts with a stressed **a** or **ha**, to avoid the hiatus, **la** is changed to **el**:

el **agua** *water*	el **aula** *classroom*
el **alma** *soul*	el **ave** *bird*
el **ama de casa** *housewife*	el **hacha** *axe*
el **águila** *eagle*	el **hambre** *hunger*

The use of **el** instead of **la** in the above examples does not alter the gender of the noun. All other modifiers remain feminine:

el agua frí**a**	*the cold water*
el alma tranquil**a**	*the tranquil soul*

For the plural, use **las: las aguas, las almas, las amas de casa,** etc.

A feminine noun beginning with an unstressed **a** or **ha** uses the standard feminine article **la.** Note that in the following two words, the stress falls on the second syllable, and the initial syllable is unstressed:

la ab**e**ja *bee*	la har**i**na *flour*

Ejercicios 2.9, página 390

Definite articles have two functions in Spanish—they may refer to a specific item or a group of specific items:

La conferencia le gustó **al** público.	*The audience liked the speech.*

or they may refer to a generalized concept (English uses no article here):

Las conferencias de ese tipo son muy buenas para **la** gente, porque aumentan **los** conocimientos humanos.	*Speeches of that type are very good for people, because they increase human knowledge.*

(1) Subjects

As a rule, sentences in Spanish do not begin with unaccompanied subject nouns, as they might in English. Compare the following:

La gente es así. (OR: Así es **la gente**.)	***People*** *are like that.*
El amor es eterno.	***Love*** *is eternal.*

In the preceding examples, the noun being used as subject also happens to be a generalized concept (all people, all love), and therefore it is natural in Spanish to add the definite article. However, in cases in which generalization does not apply (not all people, but some people), you may choose to alter the word order in Spanish, and place the subject after the verb:

Venía **gente** a verlo.	***People*** *came to see him.*
Llegaron **noticias** de Juan esta mañana.	***News*** *from Juan arrived this morning.*

NOTE: It would be an error (an anglicism) to say ⊠ ~~Gente venía...,~~ ⊠ ~~Noticias llegaron....~~

In some contexts you can work around this type of difficulty of translation by altering the context and adding *there were*, thus converting the subject into an object of a new clause:

Había gente que venía a verlo.	*There were people who came to see him.*

With *people* in particular, when it is not a generalized concept, you can omit the subject entirely, and let a plural of the verb serve as the impersonal subject *they*:

Venían a verlo.	*They came to see him.*

(2) Titles
Use the definite article when speaking <u>about</u>, not <u>to</u>, someone you address with a title (**señor, señora, señorita, profesor, profesora, doctor, doctora**):

La señora Gómez le explicó a **la** profesora Ruiz por qué su hijo había faltado.	*Mrs. Gómez explained to Professor Ruiz why her son had missed (class).*

Exceptions: don, doña, san, santo, santa

Don Jesús Gamboa es un ranchero muy conocido de esta región.	*Don Jesús Gamboa is a very well-known rancher in this region.*

When addressing someone directly, no article is used:

—Profesora Ruiz, perdone la ausencia de mi hijo: estuvo enfermo.	*"Professor Ruiz, forgive my son's absence: he was ill."*
—No se preocupe, señora Gómez, le ayudaré a repasar.	*"Do not worry, Mrs. Gómez, I will help him review."*

(3) Languages
The definite article is used before the names of languages, except when the name of the language follows **en** or the verb **hablar**:

Escribe **el** español con facilidad.	*She writes Spanish easily.*
Hablo español.	*I speak Spanish.*
Me lo dijo **en** español.	*She told me that in Spanish.*

---

[4] The symbol ⊠ is used before grammatically incorrect structures.

Omit the article after **de** when two nouns are used, one to modify the other:

mi profesora **de** español	*my Spanish professor*
el libro **de** ruso	*the Russian book*

With **aprender, entender, comprender, enseñar, leer,** and other verbs relating to activities with language, the article is optional:

Aprendí (el) español a los seis años.	*I learned Spanish when I was six.*
Mi madre **enseña** (el) inglés.	*My mother teaches English.*

The article is necessary if an adverb is used between the verb and the name of the language:

Aprendí **fácilmente el** español cuando tenía seis años.	*I learned Spanish easily when I was six.*

(4) Possessives vs. articles

With parts of the body, articles of clothing, and anything that pertains to the person in situations in which there could be no ambiguity, the possessive is not necessary; a definite article is most frequently used:

El estudiante levantó **la** mano.	*The student raised his hand.*

In sentences in which the part of the body, article of clothing, etc., is the direct object of the verb, and the indirect object indicates the possessor, an article is used instead of a possessive:

El dentista me sacó **el** diente.	*The dentist extracted my tooth.*
Nos compró **el** coche.	*He bought our car.*

With reflexive verbs, the definite article is used with parts of the body and articles of clothing:

Me lavé **las** manos.	*I washed my hands.*
Se quitaron **el** abrigo.	*They took off their coats.*

In most cases, the definite article accompanies a prepositional object:

Lo llevaron **a la cárcel.**	*They took him to jail.*
Salimos **de la mezquita** a esa hora.	*We left the mosque at that time.*
Estaban **en el salón.**	*They were in the room.*

When **casa, clase,** or **misa** are objects of **a, de,** or **en,** omit the article:

Voy **a clase** a las ocho.	*I go to class at eight.*
Saldremos **de misa** a las once.	*We will leave church at eleven.*
No está **en casa** ahora.	*She is not at home now.*

With days of the week, always use the article, even after **hasta** and **para:**

El lunes tenemos una prueba.	*On Monday we have a test.*
¡**Hasta el martes**!	*See you on Tuesday!*
Esta tarea es **para el viernes.**	*This assignment is for Friday.*
La prueba **es el** lunes.	*The test is on Monday.*

After **ser,** only use the article before days of the week when the sentence translates into English with *on,* as in the last example above. Otherwise, omit the article:

Hoy **es** miércoles.	*Today is Wednesday.*

Ejercicios 2.10–2.11, páginas 390–391

b. Indefinite articles

INDEFINITE ARTICLES		
	SINGULAR	**PLURAL**
Masculine	**un**	**unos**
Feminine	**una**	**unas**

Agreement: The indefinite article agrees with the noun it accompanies. **Una** is changed to **un** when a feminine noun starts with a stressed **a** or **ha:**

¡Tengo **un** hambre!	*I am so hungry! (I have such a hunger!)*

The indefinite article is used much less in Spanish than in English. Note that **un** and **una** may also represent the number *one.* In the plural, **unos** and **unas** mean *some.* The basic rules of usage and omission of the indefinite article follow.

Omit the indefinite article after **ser** when an unmodified noun referring to profession, religion, nationality, or marital status is used:

    Es estudiante. *She is a student.*   Es mexicana. *She is (a) Mexican.*

    Soy católico. *I am (a) Catholic.*   Eres soltero. *You are a bachelor.*

If the noun is modified, use the article:

    Es **una** estudiante muy aplicada.   *She is a very hardworking student.*

    Es **un** dentista joven.   *He is a young dentist.*

    Es **una** mexicana famosa.   *She is a famous Mexican.*

Omit the indefinite article before or after **cierto, cien, mil, otro, medio, semejante, tal,** and **¡qué... !**:

    Había **cierta** duda en su voz.   *There was a certain (some) doubt in her voice.*

    Hay **cien** invitados.   *There are a hundred guests.*

    Necesito **mil** dólares.   *I need a thousand dollars.*

    ¿Puede darme **otro** ejemplo?   *Can you give me another example?*

    Pesa cinco kilos y **medio.**   *It weighs five and a half kilos.*

    ¿Puedes creer **semejante** mentira?   *Can you believe such a lie?*

    Nunca dije **tal** cosa.   *I never said such a thing.*

    ¡**Qué** problema!   *What a problem!*

Omit the indefinite article in negative sentences after **haber** used impersonally and **tener:**

    No hay respuesta.   *There is no answer.*

    No tiene coche.   *He has no car.*

If you use the singular article, it has the meaning of the number *one*:

    No tiene **un** coche; tiene dos.   *He does not have one car—he has two.*

    No tengo ni **un** centavo.   *I do not have a single cent.*

Omit the indefinite article after **sin:**

    Salió **sin** abrigo.   *She went out without a coat.*

Omit the indefinite article after **con**:

> Escriban **con** pluma, por favor. *Please write with a pen.*

If the object is specific or the number *one* is present, use the article:

> Pudo hacerlo con **una** mano. *He was able to do it with one hand.*

> Ejercicios 2.12–2.13, página 391

2 Adjectives

a. Demonstrative adjectives[5]

DEMONSTRATIVE ADJECTIVES		
	SINGULAR	PLURAL
Masculine	este	estos
Feminine	esta	estas
Masculine	ese	esos
Feminine	esa	esas
Masculine	aquel	aquellos
Feminine	aquella	aquellas

este = *this*, **ese** = *that* (near you),
aquel = *that* (over there, far from you)

Agreement: The demonstrative adjective agrees in gender and in number with the noun it accompanies. As a rule, this adjective precedes the noun:

> **Esta** [*adj.*] mañana [*noun*] vi al médico. *This morning I saw the doctor.*
>
> ¿Recuerdas **aquellos** días? *Do you remember those days?*

> Ejercicios 2.14–2.15, página 392

---

[5] See Chapter 3.C.1, pages 78–79, on demonstrative pronouns.

b. Possessive adjectives[6]

SHORT POSSESSIVE ADJECTIVES		
	SINGULAR	PLURAL
1st person singular	mi	mis
2nd person singular	tu	tus
3rd person singular	su	sus
1st person plural	nuestro, nuestra	nuestros, nuestras
2nd person plural	vuestro, vuestra	vuestros, vuestras
3rd person plural	su	sus

Agreement: The possessive adjective agrees in gender and in number with the thing possessed, <u>not</u> with the possessor:

No tengo **mis** libros hoy. — *I do not have my books today.*

Me gustan **vuestras** ideas. — *I like your ideas.*

Sus manos siempre están limpias. — *His hands are always clean.*

Ellos me regalaron **su** coche. — *They gave me their car.*

LONG POSSESSIVE ADJECTIVES		
	SINGULAR	PLURAL
1st person singular	mío, mía	míos, mías
2nd person singular	tuyo, tuya	tuyos, tuyas
3rd person singular	suyo, suya	suyos, suyas
1st person plural	nuestro, nuestra	nuestros, nuestras
2nd person plural	vuestro, vuestra	vuestros, vuestras
3rd person plural	suyo, suya	suyos, suyas

Long possessive adjectives are used when the possessive follows the noun, in contexts in which English would use *of* + possessive:

Es una amiga **mía**. — *She is a friend of mine.*

---

[6] See Chapter 3.C.2, pages 79–80, on possessive pronouns (**el mío, el tuyo**, etc.).

They are also used after the verb **ser:**

Este libro es **mío.**	*This book is mine.*
Esta caja es **mía.**	*This box is mine.*

Suyo in certain contexts may cause ambiguity, since it can refer to *his, hers, yours,* or *theirs*. In such a case, it is best to use **de él, de ella, de usted, de ellos, de ellas,** or **de ustedes** instead:

Aquí están sus cosas: creo que esta bufanda es **de él;** este abrigo es **de ella;** este sombrero es **de usted.** ¿No es así?	*Here are your things: I think this scarf is his; this coat is hers; this hat is yours. Am I right?*

> Ejercicios 2.16–2.17, página 392

c. Forms of descriptive adjectives

Descriptive adjectives (e.g., **rojo, viejo,** etc.) are those that modify nouns.

Agreement: The descriptive adjective agrees in number and in gender with the noun it modifies.

(1) Common adjective endings

An adjective ending in **-o** changes to **-a** for the feminine:

un lugar remot**o**	*a distant place*
una probabilidad remot**a**	*a remote chance*

An adjective ending in a consonant, **-e,** or **-ista** does not generally change for gender:

un hombre **joven,** una mujer **joven**	*a young man, a young woman*
un final **triste,** una mirada **triste**	*a sad ending, a sad look*
un vestido **azul,** una túnica **azul**	*a blue dress, a blue tunic*
un joven **terrorista,** una célula **terrorista**	*a young terrorist, a terrorist cell*

Exceptions: An adjective that ends in a consonant and refers to nationality, religion, or origin does change for gender:

español, española, españoles, españolas	*Spanish*
alemán, alemana, alemanes, alemanas	*German*
francés, francesa, franceses, francesas	*French*
inglés, inglesa, ingleses, inglesas	*English*
libanés, libanesa, libaneses, libanesas	*Lebanese*
andaluz, andaluza, andaluces, andaluzas	*Andalusian*
musulmán, musulmana, musulmanes, musulmanas	*Muslim*

Note that the following adjectives do not change for gender, only for number:

belga, belgas	*Belgian*
iraní, iraníes	*Iranian*
iraquí, iraquíes	*Iraqi*
israelí, israelíes	*Israeli*
marroquí, marroquíes	*Moroccan*
pakistaní, pakistaníes	*Pakistani*

(2) Adjectives with short and long forms

Bueno and **malo** drop the final **-o** before singular masculine nouns:

un **buen** libro / un libro **bueno**	*a good book*
el **mal** tiempo / el niño **malo**	*the bad weather / the bad child*

Grande becomes **gran** before a singular noun of either gender:

un **gran** evento	*a great event*
una **gran** amiga	*a great friend*

Santo becomes **San** before any masculine name, unless it begins with **To-** or **Do-**:

San Juan de la Cruz	**Santo** Tomás
San Nicolás	**Santo** Domingo

An adjective ending in a consonant adds **-es** for the plural, and an accent may be added or deleted to maintain the stress on the same syllable as the singular:

j**o**ven, j**ó**ven**es**   *young*

> Ejercicio 2.18, página 393

d. Position of descriptive adjectives

There are a few adjectives, principally quantitative in nature, that always precede nouns; to this group belong all ordinal numbers such as **primer, segundo, tercer,** etc., as well as **algún, varios, ambos, mucho, poco, tanto, otro:**

Era mi **primer viaje** a México.	*It was my first trip to Mexico.*
Algún día volveré.	*Some day I'll go back.*
Tengo **varios amigos** aquí.	*I have several friends here.*
Sueño en **ambas lenguas.**	*I dream in both languages.*
Muchas gracias.	*Thank you very much. (Many thanks.)*
Tiene **poca paciencia.**	*He has little patience.*
No necesito **tanto dinero.**	*I don't need so much money.*
Quiero **otro café.**	*I want another coffee.*

Nonquantitative descriptive adjectives in Spanish usually follow the nouns they modify; as a rule, they serve the purpose of restricting which person, thing, or place is being referred to:

Viene a hablarnos un profesor **famoso.**	*A famous professor is coming to talk to us.*
Me gusta la casa **verde.**	*I like the green house.*

In the preceding sentences, a contrast is being established between the mentioned nouns and others that do not have the same qualities indicated by the adjectives: A famous professor is coming, not an unknown one; I like the green house, not the white one or the others.

A descriptive adjective will precede the noun if this noun indicates someone or something that is already identified, known, or otherwise restricted. When an adjective precedes the noun, its function is explicative, not restrictive. It adds to the already identified thing or person, describes it, colors it, decorates it, or defines it with innate or inherent characteristics or traits. Often, the adjective itself is already associated with the noun.

This is the case, for example, with proper nouns, but also with nouns describing things or relations of which we only have one (a nose, a navel, a mother, a father, a husband, a wife, etc.):

>el **extravagante** Dalí
>*the extravagant Dalí* [Salvador Dalí was extravagant by nature]
>
>el **elegante** Museo del Prado
>*the elegant Prado Museum* [elegance is an inherent quality of the museum]
>
>la **conocida** profesora Sainz
>*the famous Professor Sainz* [her fame precedes her]
>
>la **simbólica** torta de manzanas
>*the symbolic apple pie* [apple pie is symbolic in the United States]
>
>tu **pequeño** ombligo
>*your small navel* [smallness is an inherent quality of your navel]
>
>su **gigantesca** nariz[7]
>*his gigantic nose* [gigantic is a characteristic of his nose]
>
>mi **hermosa** madre
>*my beautiful mother* [my mother is innately beautiful]

A common noun that refers to a specific person, place, or thing would also fit in the category described above:

>nuestra **adorada** maestra
>*our adored teacher* [we know her name]
>
>el **utilísimo** manual
>*the very useful manual* [we know it by title]
>
>los **impresionantes** avances de la tecnología moderna
>*the impressive advances of modern technology* [**de la tecnología moderna** clearly specifies the progress to which we are referring]

---

[7] If you want to describe something already identified as big or large, avoid using **gran**, which, when placed before the noun, means *great;* other possibilities: **gigantesco, enorme, voluminoso,** etc.

If an identified or proper noun is followed by an adjective, the implication is that there are two or more such things or people:

> el Museo del Prado **moderno**
> *the modern Museo del Prado* [either the museum was renovated, or there are two parts to the museum, one modern, one not]

> el vaso **lleno**
> *the full glass* [not the others, which are not full]

When an adjective is used to describe an inherent quality of something, it may have poetic or oratorial overtones, especially when it is universally redundant:

> La **blanca** nieve cubría los montes.
> *The white snow covered the hills.* [snow is inherently white; this construction is poetic]

Adjectives of nationality always follow the noun:

> Esa novela es de un autor **argentino**.
> *That novel is by an Argentine author.*

Fifteen common descriptive adjectives change meaning depending on their location. These fifteen adjectives and examples of their use can be found in the chart on the following page.

ADJECTIVE	BEFORE THE NOUN	AFTER THE NOUN
alto	el <u>alto</u> funcionario *the high official*	el funcionario <u>alto</u> *the tall official*
antiguo	el <u>antiguo</u> contrato *the old [former, not current] contract*	la mesa <u>antigua</u> *the old [not new] table*
bueno	un <u>buen</u> estudiante *a good student [studious]*	un hombre <u>bueno</u> *a good man [moral]*
cierto	<u>cierto</u> tono *a certain tone [indeterminate]*	una declaración <u>cierta</u> *a true statement*
diferente	<u>diferentes</u> lugares *various or several places*	lugares <u>diferentes</u> *different or distinct places*
grande	un <u>gran</u> hombre *a great man*	un hombre <u>grande</u> *a big man*
medio	<u>medio</u> litro *half a liter*	la clase <u>media</u> *the middle class* temperatura <u>media</u> *average temperature*
nuevo	el <u>nuevo</u> contrato *the new [latest] contract*	un coche <u>nuevo</u> *a [brand] new car*
pobre	el <u>pobre</u> hombre *the poor [unfortunate] man*	un hombre <u>pobre</u> *a poor [not rich] man*
puro	<u>pura</u> suerte *sheer luck, just luck*	agua <u>pura</u> *pure [uncontaminated] water*
raro	la <u>rara</u> habilidad *the rare ability*	una voz <u>rara</u> *a strange voice*
simple	un <u>simple</u> adiós *just a simple good-bye [nothing more]*	un hombre <u>simple</u> *a simpleton*
triste	una <u>triste</u> manzana *just one humble, insignificant apple*	una empleada <u>triste</u> *a sad employee*
único	mi <u>único</u> problema *my only problem*	un problema <u>único</u> *a unique problem*
viejo	un <u>viejo</u> amigo *an old [longtime] friend*	un amigo <u>viejo</u> *an old [aged] friend*

When these special adjectives are used with nouns referring to specific, already identified people, things, or places, they lose some of their variety of meaning:

mi **viejo** padre
my old father [obviously not former or longtime]

las **pobres** obreras de esa fábrica
the poor workers of that factory [they may be pitiful or penniless, or both]

Some adjectives are fixed in certain expressions by sheer usage:

idea **fija** *set idea*	la **pura** verdad *the basic truth*
sentido **común** *common sense*	**libre** albedrío *free will*
Semana **Santa** *Holy Week*	**alta** fidelidad *high fidelity*

Bueno and **malo** are two special adjectives that follow the general rules, but because of the possible ambiguities of *goodness* and *badness*, there are probably more subtleties regarding placement than with other adjectives. In many cases, these adjectives exist in ready-made expressions:

buena suerte *good luck*	**mala** suerte *bad luck*
un **buen** día *one day, unexpectedly*	**mal** dormir *sleeplessness*
de **buena** familia *from a good family*	**malos** pensamientos *evil thoughts*
¡**Buenos** días! *Good morning!*	

Some nouns have been formed incorporating the adjective:

la hierbabuena *spearmint*	el malhumor *ill temper*
la buenaventura *good fortune*	el malparto *miscarriage*

Ultimately, the dictionary is the best place to check special usage of common adjectives.

Ejercicios 2.19–2.21, páginas 393–394

e. Comparisons

(1) Comparisons of inequality

(a) With adverbs, adjectives, and nouns

COMPARISON OF INEQUALITY • ADVERBS, ADJECTIVES, NOUNS					
Object of comparison: NOUN, PRONOUN, OR EQUIVALENT A & B					
NOUN, PRONOUN, OR EQUIVALENT A	verb	más / menos	adverb adjective noun	que	NOUN, PRONOUN, OR EQUIVALENT B

Marta comprende **más** fácilmente **que** yo.
Marta understands more easily than I do.

Esa novela es **más** larga **que** esta.
That novel is longer than this one.

José tiene **menos** dinero **que** yo.
José has less money than I do.

(b) With a numerical expression, use **de** instead of **que**

COMPARISON OF INEQUALITY • NUMERICAL EXPRESSION			
Object of comparison: NOUN, PRONOUN, OR EQUIVALENT			
CLAUSE	más de / menos de	numerical expression	NOUN, PRONOUN, OR EQUIVALENT

Leí que había **más de treinta** rehenes en un solo cuarto.
I read there were more than thirty hostages in a single room.

Nos quedan **menos de veinte** minutos.
We have less than twenty minutes left.

Te di **más de la mitad.**
I gave you more than half.

Conocí a **menos de diez** personas nuevas.
I met fewer than ten new people.

No invitó a **más de treinta** personas.
He did not invite more than thirty people.

Special use of **más que**

In negative sentences, **más que** is the equivalent of *only* in English, or some other exclusive type expression, and is not comparative in meaning:

No tengo **más que** tres pesos.	*I have only three dollars.*
No invitó **más que** a tres personas.	*She invited only three people.*
Nunca come **más que** fruta.	*He eats only fruit.* [He never eats anything but fruit, anything other than fruit.]
Nunca viaja **más que** a España.	*She only travels to Spain.* [She never travels to any other place than Spain, nowhere but to Spain.]

Irregular comparatives

mejor(es) *better, best*	**mayor(es)** *older, oldest*
peor(es) *worse, worst*	**menor(es)** *younger, youngest*

(**Más bueno** and **más malo** are used only occasionally, when the emphasis is on character traits of people, especially in idiomatic expressions. **Más viejo** and **más joven** are often interchangeable with **mayor** and **menor**.)

Mi clase es **mejor que** la tuya.	*My class is better than yours.*
Yo canto **peor que** tú.	*I sing worse than you do.*
Yo soy **mayor que** tú. Yo soy **más viejo que** tú.	*I am older than you.*
Tú eres **menor que** yo. Tú eres **más joven que** yo.	*You are younger than I.*

(c) With a verb or clause as second part of comparison

With a noun as the focus of the comparison, and a verb or clause as the second part of the comparison, use the variable phrase **del que, de la que, de los que,** or **de las que,** in agreement with the gender and number of the noun.

COMPARISON OF INEQUALITY • CLAUSE 2nd part Object of comparison: NOUN				
verb	más / menos	NOUN	[masc. sing.]	del que	clause
			[fem. sing.]	de la que	
			[masc. pl.]	de los que	
			[fem. pl.]	de las que	

Alquilamos más películas **de las que** pudimos ver.   *We rented more movies than we could watch.*

Yo le di muchos menos regalos **de los que** me dio él a mí.   *I gave him a lot fewer gifts than he gave me.*

Me serví más comida **de la que** me puedo comer.   *I served myself more food than I can eat.*

The noun may also be referred to from a prior context, as in the following sentence, in which wedding photos (**las fotos de la boda**) are being talked about, and thus, the feminine plural is used for the variable phrase **de las que**:

[. . .] Sacaron más **de las que** habíamos pedido.   *[. . .] They took more than we had ordered.*

When there is less specificity intended in the comparison, the neuter invariable phrase **de lo que** is used instead of the variable form:

Aquí hay más libros **de lo que** creía.   *There are more books here than I thought.*

When the focus of the comparison is not a noun but a verb, an adjective, or an adverb, use the invariable neuter phrase **de lo que**.

COMPARISON OF INEQUALITY • CLAUSE 2nd part Object of comparison: VERB, ADJECTIVE, OR ADVERB			
VERB	más / menos		de lo que	clause
clause	más / menos	ADJECTIVE ADVERB		

Nevó más **de lo que** nos hubiera gustado.	*It snowed more than we would have liked.*
La guerra fue más **larga de lo que** esperaban.	*The war was longer than they expected.*
El taxi llegó más **rápidamente de lo que** anticipábamos.	*The taxi arrived more quickly than we expected.*

(2) Comparisons of equality

(a) Tanto(-a, -os, -as)... como

With a noun, use the variable **tanto(-a, -os, -as)... como,** in agreement with the noun:

Tengo **tantos problemas como** tú.	*I have as many problems as you do.*

(b) Tanto como

Alone as an adverb, use the invariable **tanto como:**

Ella no come **tanto como** yo.	*She does not eat as much as I do.*

(c) Tan... como

With an adverb or an adjective, use **tan... como:**

Ese coche está **tan brillante como** el nuestro.	*That car is as shiny as ours.*
Ellos hablan **tan bien como** tú.	*They speak as well as you do.*

f. Superlatives

The superlative in Spanish is formed with a definite article + **más / menos** + adjective + **de** (if a group is being indicated):

Iris es **la más lista de** la clase.	*Iris is the smartest in the class.*
Esas flores son **las más rojas de** todas.	*Those flowers are the reddest of all.*
Mi tío es **el menos presumido de** todos.	*My uncle is the least conceited of all.*
Julio es **el más alto.**	*Julio is the tallest.*
Esa noche fue **la más oscura.**	*That night was the darkest.*

El más grande and **el más pequeño** become **el mayor** and **el menor** when referring to age:

> Jorge es **el mayor** y Juan es **el menor.**
>
> *Jorge is the oldest and Juan is the youngest.*

> Ejercicios 2.22–2.23, página 394;
> Ejercicios de repaso 2.24–2.26, páginas 395–396

CHAPTER 3

Pronouns

A Personal Pronouns

B Se

C Demonstrative and Possessive Pronouns

D Interrogatives

E Exclamatives

F Indefinites and Negatives

G Relative Pronouns

A | PERSONAL PRONOUNS

Personal pronouns are differentiated by their grammatical function: subject, object (direct, indirect, prepositional), and by their stress: stressed or unstressed. They may refer to first person (**yo, me, mí; nosotros/as, nos**), second person (**tú, te, ti; usted, le; ustedes, les; vosotros/as, os**), or third person (**él/ella/ellos/ellas, lo/la/le/se/sí, los/las/les/se/sí**).

1 Grammatical Functions of Personal Pronouns

a. Subject

The subject carries out the action of the verb. The verb of a sentence may suffice in and of itself to express everything that we need to say about the subject, with no additional complements:

María llegó.	*María arrived.*
Pepa salió.	*Pepa went out.*
Nosotros pagamos.	*We paid.*
Ella ya jugó.	*She already played.*

b. Direct object complement

A direct object complement specifies who or what receives the action of the verb directly. It may be a person, an animal, or a thing:

[subj.[1]: **yo**; d.o.: **las noticias / las**]:
    Oí las noticias.   *I heard the news.*
    Las oí.   *I heard them.*

[subj.: **nosotros**; d.o.: **la película / la**]:
    Vimos la película.   *We saw the movie.*
    La vimos.   *We saw it.*

[subj.: **yo**; d.o.: **tu hermana / la**]:
    Vi a[2] tu hermana.   *I saw your sister.*
    La vi.   *I saw her.*

---

[1] The subject pronoun in Spanish is used mostly for emphasis or clarification. In these examples, the subject pronoun is not necessary.

[2] The personal **a** is used with a human or personified direct object noun.

c. Indirect object complement with direct object

An indirect object complement is affected by the action of the verb.

[subj.: **nosotros**; d.o.: **los dulces / los**; i.o.: **su abuelita / se(le)**]:

Le regalamos los dulces a[3] su abuelita.	*We gave the sweets to her grandmother.*
Se los regalamos.	*We gave them to her.*

[subj.: **tú**; d.o.: **el mensaje / lo**; i.o.: **tu consejera / le / se**]:

¿Le enviaste el mensaje a tu consejera?	*Did you send the message to your advisor?*
¿Se lo enviaste?	*Did you send it to her?*

[subj.: **ella**; d.o.: **la niña / la**; i.o: **los padres / les / se**]:

Les dio la niña[4] a los padres adoptivos.	*She gave the child to the adoptive parents.*
Se la dio.	*She gave her to them.*

d. Indirect object complement without direct object

The verb **gustar** is used generally as a model of this type of verb (one which cannot have a direct object, but does have an indirect object). (See Chapter 6.I, pages 239–244, on verbs like **gustar**.) For many of these verbs, the translation to or from English is tricky because the subject in English is the indirect object in Spanish, and the object in English is the subject in Spanish.

[Spanish—subj.: **este cuadro / ∅** *pron.*; i.o.: **me**]

Me gusta este cuadro.
Me gusta.

[English—subj.: **I**; d.o.: **this painting / it**]

I like this painting.
I like it.

[Spanish—subj.: **tú**; i.o.: **a mi hermano / le**]

Le caes bien a mi hermano.
Le caes bien.

[English—subj.: **My brother / He**; d.o.: **you**]

My brother likes you.
He likes you.

[Spanish—subj.: **Sevilla / ∅** *pron.*; i.o.: **nos**]

Nos encanta Sevilla.
Nos encanta.

[English—subj.: **We**; d.o.: **Seville / it**]

We love Seville.
We love it.

---

[3] The preposition **a** is used to introduce an indirect object.

[4] In case of possible ambiguity, the personal **a**, usually required before the human direct object, **la niña**, is eliminated. Here, there is an indirect object, **los padres**, introduced by the preposition **a**. If the personal **a** were used before **la niña**, it wouldn't be clear who is being given to whom.

In the preceding sentences, note the absence of a pronoun for *it* in the first set (**cuadro**) and last set (**Sevilla**): the reason for this is that in Spanish, there is no personal pronoun for a subject which is a thing (not a person).

e. Transitivity

Transitive: A transitive construction is one in which the verb has a direct object complement.

Intransitive: An intransitive construction is one in which the verb has no direct object complement.

Understanding transitivity is of particular advantage to the learner when using the dictionary. A close look at the dictionary for many of the verbs listed in our examples will reveal additional uses. If you look up the verb **encantar,** for example, you will see it has one set of meanings or translations for the intransitive use (e.g., to love or thoroughly enjoy something), and another for the transitive use (e.g., to place a spell on, to bewitch). Most dictionaries indicate transitive vs. intransitive use by the abbreviations "vt" or "v.t." and "vi" or "v.i." immediately following the verb.

It is important to notice that there are often significant differences between the English and Spanish languages with regard to verbs and their transitive or intransitive usage; these are principally lexical distinctions that directly affect the choice of pronouns. It is part of the lifelong process of learning a language to become familiar with these distinctions. Some students find it helpful to keep a list of intransitive and transitive structures, verbs with multiple uses, and differences between English and Spanish verb usage. This list should be based on your experience with the language, and, more specifically, include areas where you have had difficulty with your writing—where an instructor has corrected you, for example—or details you have noted while studying. Your list might be subdivided into the following five categories:

1. No object complement, either direct or indirect (e.g., **Llegamos.**)
2. Direct object only (e.g., **Comimos pan.**)
3. Direct object and indirect object (e.g., **Le dio un anillo.**)
4. Indirect object only (e.g., **Me gusta ese color.**)
5. Problem verbs (this will be a very long entry—some samples follow):

   - **RETURN:** In English, the verb *to return* can be transitive or intransitive, but Spanish uses two different verbs:

     | **Volví** ayer. | *I returned* yesterday. |
     | **Devolví** el libro. | *I returned* the book. |

- **LOOK AT:** In Spanish this is expressed by **mirar**. The function of the English preposition *at* is embedded in the verb **mirar,** and **el libro** is the direct object in Spanish:

    Miro el libro.   *I look at the book.*

- **LOOK FOR:** In Spanish this translates into **buscar**. Here too, the function of the English preposition *for* is embedded in the verb **buscar,** and **el libro** is the direct object in Spanish:

    Busco el libro.   *I look for the book.*

> Ejercicio 3.1, página 399

2 Subject Pronouns

SUBJECT PRONOUNS		
PERSON	SINGULAR	PLURAL
1st	yo	nosotros
2nd	tú	vosotros
3rd	él[5]/ella/usted*	ellos/ellas/ustedes*

***Usted** is used to directly address someone else and is therefore a second, rather than a third, person pronoun (the first person is the speaker, the second person is the one addressed, and the third person is the one talked about or referred to). However, the forms of object pronouns and of verbs that correspond to **usted** are all in the third person, and for that reason, in this table and in all of the related tables on object pronouns that follow, forms relating to **usted** are placed under the third person. For more on the usage of **usted, tú, vosotros,** and **vos,** see pages 56–57.

Subject Pronoun Usage

The subject pronoun in Spanish is most often absent. Normally, the reference to the subject is contained in the verb ending, and the context is clear enough without the subject pronoun. This is true even for the third person, as long as the context is unambiguous:

Juan se levantó y caminó a la ventana. Miró afuera y suspiró: "Otro día de nieve".

Juan got up and walked to the window. He looked outside and sighed, "Another day of snow."

---

[5] In this table of subject pronouns, why are **tú** and **él** the only two pronouns with accent marks? For more on these accents, see Chapter 9, page 351.

Notice in the preceding series of sentences that **caminó, miró,** and **suspiró** do not require the use of **él**; it is understood that the verbs that follow the first one (with Juan as the subject) will also have Juan as the subject, unless it is otherwise indicated. However, such absolute clarity is not really required in Spanish. You will frequently run across narratives that begin without any subject specificity and clarify it only later in the context of the story:

> Se levantó y caminó a la ventana. Miró afuera y suspiró: "Otro día de nieve". Entonces oyó la voz de su compañero de cuarto que le gritaba: "¡Juan!".

In order to translate this text, you must read it completely before you know the actual subject of the first verb. You can't tell if the subject is *she* or *he* until you read the name **Juan**.

There are essentially four reasons to use the subject pronoun: focus, contrast, change of subject, and with **usted**.

Focus: The subject pronoun is used when the subject is the focus. Compare the two following brief dialogues:

—¿Cuántos hermanos tienes?	*"How many brothers do you have?"*
—Tengo tres hermanos.	*"I have three brothers."*
—¿Quién hizo esto?	*"Who did this?"*
—Lo hice **yo**.	*"I did it."*

In the first dialogue above, the question relates to the object of the verb, the brothers, and not to the subject of the verb. Given that **tienes** and **tengo** indicate without a doubt who the subject is, there is no reason to add **tú** or **yo**. However, in the second dialogue, the question relates to the subject of the verb. For that reason, the subject must be stated in the response, either as a noun or as a pronoun.

Contrast: The subject pronoun is used to mark a contrast between two different subjects:

> **Yo** resumo el informe, y **tú** lo lees.   *I will summarize the report, and **you** will read it.*

Change of subject: In paragraphs where you change from one subject to another, you must use the new subject either in pronoun or in noun form:

Caminaron juntos hasta el borde del lago. **Él** la abrazó, y le dijo que la quería. **Ella** se quedó callada.	*They walked together to the edge of the lake. He put his arms around her and told her he loved her. She remained quiet.*

In the above series of sentences the subject changes from *they* to *he* to *she*.

Notice, however, that you would not need to add the subject if there were no change of subject:

Héctor caminó con ella hasta el borde del lago. La abrazó y le dijo que la quería. Esperó una respuesta, pero no oyó nada.	*Hector walked with her to the edge of the lake. He put his arms around her and told her that he loved her. He waited for an answer, but heard nothing.*

With usted: The use of **usted** as a subject pronoun conveys an idea of formality or courtesy:

¿Desea **usted** algo más?	*Would you like something else?*
Usted conoce a mi prima, ¿verdad?	*You know my cousin, don't you?*

The third person subject pronouns **él, ella, ellos,** and **ellas**[6] refer only to persons, never to things. There is no subject pronoun for *it* (or its plural *they*) in Spanish:

Esa mesa es de madera.	*That table is made of wood.*
Es de madera.	*It is made of wood.*
Me gusta[7] esa película.	*I like that movie.*
Me gusta mucho.	*I like it a lot.*
Se venden[8] muchas PC ahora.	*Many PCs are sold now.*
Se venden rápido.	*They are sold quickly.*

---

[6] These pronouns cannot be used as subjects when they refer to things; however, they can be used as prepositional objects referring to things: **¿Y esos tomates? ¿Qué vas a preparar con ellos?** *And those tomatoes? What are you going to prepare with them?*

[7] For **gustar** and similar verbs, the subject in English is the indirect object in Spanish, and the object in English is the subject in Spanish.

[8] With the impersonal **se** construction with inanimate objects, the inanimate object functions as the subject of the verb. This translates frequently as the passive voice in English.

Usage of usted, tú, vosotros, and vos

Ustedes is the plural of **tú** or **usted** in Latin America, but in Spain, **vosotros** is the plural of **tú**, and **ustedes** is only the plural of **usted**.

Usted and **ustedes** are often seen in the abbreviated forms **Ud.** and **Uds.**

Usted is used to varying degrees in different dialects[9]. As a general rule, you will notice that its usage is more common in Latin America than it is in Spain. It is used to mark difference of some sort, either of age or of status. For example, an adolescent would address an adult of equal or higher status with **usted**; the parents in a household would possibly address the servants with **tú**, but a servant would use **usted** to address them. In some families, **usted** is used between parents and children; in others, **tú** is more common. However, at times you might hear a scolding parent switch to **usted** as the form of address for a son or daughter in order to establish some distance and achieve a more effective scolding.

As for deciding whether to use **usted** or **tú** for a given situation, the local use should help determine your choice, but while you wait, the following rule of thumb might come in handy: in a workplace or in a government office, it is safest to use **usted** as a general rule; in social contexts, it is generally safe to use **tú** with anyone your age or younger; and it is safest to use **usted** with anyone else.

If you have spent any time in Central or South America, or among people from this part of the world, you are probably well aware of the **voseo**. **Voseo** refers to the use of the pronoun **vos** as an alternative second person singular, used instead of, or along with, **tú/ti**. Its acceptance varies from region to region, as does its usage.

In Argentina, Paraguay, and Uruguay, the **voseo** is accepted in most registers[10], but it can be restricted to informal registers in some instances. In Uruguay, although **vos** is more common, **tú** may also be heard concurrently. In both cases, the verb is conjugated in **vos** form (**Vos tenés/Tú tenés**, rather than **Vos tenés/Tú tienes**).

In other regions, **vos** is used mostly among individuals who perceive themselves as social equals, and who have an informal relationship.

Some examples of the use of **vos** follow:

Vos as subject:

    Vos no sabés nada del asunto.   *You know nothing about the matter.*

Vos as prepositional object:

    Siempre lo hago todo <u>por</u> **vos**.   *I always do everything for you.*

    Si ella sale <u>con</u> **vos**, se va a divertir.   *If she goes out with you, she'll have fun.*

---

[9] For more information on dialects, see Chapter 9, pages 376–378.
[10] For more information on language registers, see Chapter 9, page 379.

Note that **vos** does not have an alternate form for **te, tu,** and **tuyo,** which can be found in combination with it:

Vos te dormiste en clase.	*You fell asleep in class.*
Abrí **vos** tu libro.	*Open your book.*
No amo a nadie como te amo a **vos**.	*I don't love anyone the way I love you.*

Verb conjugation

Although there are instances of **voseo** usage in different tenses, the present indicative and the imperative are by far the most accepted. The **vos** form resembles the **vosotros** form, with minor changes:

Present indicative—note the loss of the **i** of the **vosotros** ending diphthong:
  Vosotros: habláis/coméis/sois
  Vos: hablás/comés/sos
  NOTE: Where there is no diphthong in the **vosotros** form, as in -**ir** verbs (e.g., **partís**), the same form is used for both **vos** and **vosotros**.

Imperative—note the loss of the **-d** ending of the **vosotros** verb form:
  Vosotros: hablad/comed/partid/decid/oíd
  Vos: hablá/comé/partí/decí/oí
  NOTE: In the imperative, for the **voseo**, the verb **andar** (**andá, andate**) is used instead of the verb **ir.**

Ejercicios 3.2–3.4, página 399

3 Direct Object Pronouns

a. Formation and usage

DIRECT OBJECT PRONOUNS		
PERSON	SINGULAR	PLURAL
1st	me	nos
2nd	te	os
3rd	lo/la*	los/las*

*Object pronouns that correspond to **usted** are listed under third person because their verb form is the same.

Direct object pronouns receive the direct action of the verb.

Me ven.	*They see **me**.*
Te conocen.	*They know **you**.*
Nos escuchan.	*They listen to **us**.*
Os entiendo.	*I understand **you**.*
Lo vi ayer.	*I saw **him/you** (usted) yesterday.*
Las conozco bien.	*I know **them/you** (ustedes) well.*

In most of Spain, but not in most of Latin America, **le(s)** is used instead of **lo(s)** for males:

No **lo** conozco. (Latin America)	*I do not know him.*
No **le** conozco. (Spain)	*I do not know him.*

The use of **le** for the human direct object is called **leísmo**; those who speak this way are called **leístas**. Learners of Spanish should adopt this use of **le** only when they adopt the rest of the dialectal traits of the region, which include the use of **vosotros**.

Os is used only in Spain, for the plural of **te**:

	LOS vs. OS	
	LATIN AMERICA *(I saw you.)*	**SPAIN** *(I saw you.)*
Singular	**Te vi.**	**Te vi.**
Plural	**Los vi (a ustedes).**	**Os vi.**

The direct object pronoun replacing an inanimate object will reflect the gender and number of the noun it replaces:

Miro la televisión. ¿Tú **la** miras?	*I watch television. Do you watch it?*
—¿Dónde pusiste los libros? —**Los** puse en la mesa.	*"Where did you put the books?"* *"I put them on the table."*

b. Stressed and unstressed object pronouns (Direct or indirect object)

It is important to note the difference between the unstressed (clitic) pronoun forms **me, te, lo, la, le, se, nos, os, los, las, les,** and the stressed (tonic) forms **a mí, a ti, a él, a ella, a usted, a sí, a nosotros, a vosotros, a ellos, a ellas, a ustedes**. The first set of unstressed pronouns is used in most standard reference conditions; the second set is added to the first if there is a special focus, if additional stress is required, or if clarification is needed in the case of the third person. Consider the following contexts:

Focus: To answer questions specifically about the object:

—¿A quién llamó?   *"Whom did he call?"*
—**A mí.** (OR: **Me** llamó **a mí**.)   *"Me."*

Stress: English adds stress by pronouncing pronouns (or other words) more emphatically, whereas Spanish cannot. In Spanish, we add words to indicate stress. In the example below, capitalized words are pronounced emphatically. Notice the need in Spanish for additional words. In this case, the additional words (which are boldfaced in the following examples) are the stressed forms of the pronouns:

No te escribió **a ti**, me escribió **a mí**,   *He didn't write **you**, he wrote **me**, so*
así que me quiere **a mí** y no **a ti**[11].   *he loves **me** and not **you**.*

Clarification: When the third-person pronoun is used, and ambiguity of reference exists, the stressed form is added to clarify:

—¿Viste a Ricardo y a Luisa?   *"Did you see Ricardo and Luisa?"*
—Sí, los vi. Pero la vi **a ella** primero,   *"Yes, I saw them. But I saw **her** first,*
y no lo vi **a él** hasta después.   *and did not see **him** until later. They*
No estaban juntos. Quería   *were not together. I wanted to ask them*
preguntarles por qué, pero no   *why, but didn't dare."*
me atreví.

A frequent mistake made by English-speaking learners of Spanish is to use the stressed form instead of the unstressed form of the pronouns in full sentences: [⊠[12]~~Vi a ella.~~ ⊠~~Quería preguntar a ellos.~~] The stressed form can only exist alone when there is no verb present, and in such cases, the unstressed form cannot be used: it cannot stand alone.

---

[11] In this sentence, why does **mí** have an accent mark, but **ti** does not? For more on this use of the accent, see Chapter 9, page 351.

[12] The symbol ⊠ indicates a grammatically incorrect structure.

c. Lo: The neuter (invariable) pronoun

The neuter **lo** refers to an idea or situation that is not specific enough to be either masculine or feminine:

—Nos queda poco tiempo.	*"We have little time left."*
—Sí, ya **lo** sé.	*"Yes, I know it."*

Lo is used as a complement to replace adjectives, pronouns, or nouns with **ser**, **estar**, and **parecer**; notice that in English the equivalent of **lo** in most cases is merely represented by emphasis on the verb when it is spoken:

—Creo que ella es muy lista.	*"I think she is very clever."*
—Yo no creo que **lo** sea.	*"I do not think she **is**."*
—Esa mujer es la tía de Juan.	*"That woman is Juan's aunt."*
—Sé que no **lo** es porque conozco a su tía.	*"I know she **is not** because I know his aunt."*
—¿Estas llaves son tuyas?	*"Are these keys yours?"*
—No, no **lo** son.	*"No, they **are not**."*
—¿Estás frustrada?	*"Are you frustrated?"*
—Sí, **lo** estoy.	*"Yes, I **am**."*
—Parece que está nervioso.	*"He looks nervous."*
—Quizá **lo** parezca, pero no **lo** está.	*"Maybe he **looks** that way, but he **isn't**."*

> Ejercicios 3.5–3.8, páginas 400–401

4 Indirect Object Pronouns

INDIRECT OBJECT PRONOUNS		
PERSON	SINGULAR	PLURAL
1st	me	nos
2nd	te	os
3rd	le*	les*

*When combined with **lo(s)** or **la(s)**, **le(s)** becomes **se**. Note also that object pronouns corresponding to **usted** are listed under third person because their verb form is the same.

| **Le** dio **la** manzana a la maestra. | ⟶ | **Se la** dio. |
| *He gave the apple to the teacher.* | | *He gave it to her.* |

| **Les** regaló **el** coche. | ⟶ | **Se lo** regaló. |
| *She gave them the car.* | | *She gave it to them.* |

The indirect object is used to indicate the person(s) receiving the direct object or to indicate the person or thing that is affected in some way by the action of the verb:

Me regaló sus guantes.	*He gave me his gloves.*
¿**Te** dijo su secreto?	*Did she tell you her secret?*
Les mandó el recado.	*She sent them the message.*

There are many possible translations into English of indirect objects in Spanish, with a variety of prepositions used in the English versions:

Le hiciste la merienda.	*You made the snack **for her**.*
Les quitó la llave.	*He took the key **away from** them.*
Nos pidió ese favor.	*He asked that favor **of us**.*

Verbs commonly used with indirect objects may be verbs like **gustar**[13]:

Le gustaron los regalos.	*She liked the gifts.* (literal translation: *The gifts were pleasing **to her**.*)
¿**Te** cayó bien mi tía?	*Did you like my aunt?* (literal translation: *Was my aunt pleasing **to you**?*)
Nos faltan diez pesos.	*We are missing ten pesos.* (literal translation: *Ten pesos are lacking **for us**.*)

---

[13] See Chapter 6.I, pages 239–244, for full explanation of verbs like **gustar**.

Below are some verbs that can change meaning if used with a direct object or an indirect object:

No **le** creo.
I do not believe him (or her).
[i.e., he is lying.]

No **lo** creo.
I do not believe it.
[He may be telling what he believes to be the truth, but I think the truth is different, i.e., he is not lying.]

¿**Le** pagaste?
Did you pay him (or her)?

¿**La** pagaste?
Did you pay it? (e.g., la cuenta)

Le gané.
I beat him (or her) [at a game].

Lo gané.
I won it.

Le pegué duro.
I hit him (or her) hard.

Lo pegamos.
We glued it.

Le di en la cara.
I hit him (or her) in the face.

Me **lo** dio.
He gave it to me.

Le robaron.
They robbed him (or her).

Lo robaron.
They stole it.

Le extraña que hagas eso.
It surprises him (her) that you do that.

Lo extraña mucho.
She misses him a lot.

Ejercicios 3.9–3.12, páginas 401–402

5 Required Repetitive Object Pronouns

The following object pronouns must be used, however redundant they may sound.

a. Direct object pronouns

Direct object pronouns must be used when the object noun precedes rather than follows the verb:

La salida la encontrará a su derecha.
You will find the exit to the right.

A todos los convidados los critica.
She criticizes all of her guests.

A ella no **la** conozco.
I don't know her.

Direct object pronouns must also be used whenever the pronoun **todo (toda, todos, todas)** is used as a direct object:

Lo vendieron **todo**.	*They sold it all.*
La cantaron **toda**. (e.g., la canción)	*They sang it all.*
Nos invitaron a **todos**.	*They invited all of us.*

b. Indirect object pronouns

These are almost always used even though their referent appears in the sentence:

Le dije **a Maira** que venías.	*I told Maira you were coming.*
Le cedió el poder **a su hermano**.	*He transferred the power to his brother.*
Les caes bien **a mis hijos**.	*My children like you.*
Le caes bien **a él**.	*He likes you.*
Le caes bien.	*He likes you.*
Les hace falta **a sus padres**.	*Her parents miss her.*
Les hace falta **a ellos**.	*They miss her.*
Les hace falta.	*They miss her.*

Ejercicio 3.13, páginas 402–403

6 Order of Object Pronouns when Combined

ORDER OF OBJECT PRONOUNS WHEN COMBINED			
#1 SE	#2 2ND PERSON	#3 1ST PERSON	#4 3RD PERSON
se	te	me	lo(s)
	os	nos	la(s)
			le(s)

Examples:

Se te cayeron los libros.	*You dropped your books.*
Se os dirá cuando llegue el momento.	*You will be told when it is time.*
Se me dijo la verdad.	*I was told the truth.*
Se nos acabaron las ideas.	*We ran out of ideas.*
Se lo expliqué.	*I explained it to him/her.*
Se los regalé.	*I gave them to him/her.*
Se la mandaron.	*They sent it to them.*
Se le olvidó.	*He/She forgot it.*
Te lo dije.	*I told you (so/it).*
Te la regalé.	*I gave it to you.*
Me lo dijeron.	*They told me (so/it).*
Me la enseñaron.	*They showed it to me.*
Nos lo contaste.	*You told us (so/it).*
Nos la enseñaron.	*They showed it to us.*

Ejercicio 3.14, página 403

7 Position of Object Pronouns

Direct and indirect object pronouns must be placed before or after their related verbs, depending upon the forms of the verbs themselves. There is no choice as to the position after the verb with the affirmative command. There is no choice as to the position before the verb with every other form except the infinitive and the present participle; with these last two, pronouns may be placed before or after the verb phrase, as long as all pronouns relating to the same verb are placed in the same position.

POSITION OF OBJECT PRONOUNS		
VERB FORM	PRONOUN POSITION	EXAMPLES
Conjugated verb	before	**La** vi ayer. *I saw her yesterday.*
Compound tense	before auxiliary (**haber**)	Nunca **la** he visto. *I have never seen her.*
Infinitive	before auxiliary or after infinitive[14]	**Me la** quiero comprar. Quiero comprár**mela**. *I want to buy it (for myself).*
Present participle	before auxiliary or after present participle[14]	**Lo** estaba mirando. Estaba mirándo**lo**. *I was looking at it.*
Affirmative command	after[14]	Mírа**la**. *Look at it.* Cómpra**telos**. *Buy them (for yourself).*
Negative command	before	No **la** mires. *Do not look at it.* No **te los** compres. *Do not buy them (for yourself).*

In sentences combining more than one verb, the object pronoun must be placed near the verb that governs it:

Viajaremos para conseguir**lo**.	*We will travel to get it.*
Salieron persiguiéndo**la**.	*They left pursuing her.*
Vaya a comprar**lo**.	*Go and buy it.*
Sigue estudiándo**lo**.	*Continue studying it.*
Sígue**me** tomando apuntes.	*Follow me, taking notes.*
La oyeron decír**telo**.	*They heard her tell it to you.*
Nos dejó gritándo**nos**.	*She left us yelling at each other.*

Ejercicio 3.15, página 403

---

[14] When pronouns are attached to the end of an infinitive, a present participle, or a command, an accent may be needed to maintain the original stress within the verb: **vender—venderlos—vendérselos; vendiendo—vendiéndolos; vende—véndelos**. For more information on accents, see Chapter 9, pages 349–350.

8 Prepositional Object Pronouns

PREPOSITIONAL OBJECT PRONOUNS		
PERSON	SINGULAR	PLURAL
1st	mí	nosotros
2nd	ti	vosotros
3rd	él/ella	ellos/ellas
Formal	usted	ustedes
Reflexive	sí	sí

Prepositional object pronouns are used after prepositions:

Lo hizo **por mí**.	*She did it because of me.*
Puedes contar **con nosotros**.	*You can count on us.*
Se fue **sin ella**.	*He left without her.*
Lo guardó **para sí**.	*He kept it for himself.*
Lo guardó **para él**.	*She kept it for him.*
Estaba sentado **frente a vosotros**.	*He was sitting in front of you.*
Corrió **tras ella**.	*He ran after her.*
Estaba **cerca de ti**.	*He was near you.*
No encuentro mi diccionario; ayer trabajé **con él**.	*I cannot find my dictionary; yesterday I worked with it.*
La gorra de Roberto es parte **de él**; nunca sale **sin ella**.	*Roberto's cap is a part of him; he never leaves without it.*

The following prepositions take the subject pronoun forms for **yo** and **tú**:

entre:

Estaba sentado **entre tú y yo**.	*He was sitting between you and me.*

según:

Según tú, esto es incorrecto.	*According to you, this is incorrect.*

Como, excepto, and **menos** take **yo** and **tú**, unless they are followed by other prepositions. Use the pronoun that goes with the last preposition.

como:

Mis amigos piensan **como yo.**	*My friends think like me.*
A mí no me duele **como a ti.**	*It does not hurt me the way it hurts you.*

excepto:

Todos lo vieron **excepto yo.**	*They all saw it except me.*
Les dieron **a** todos **excepto a mí.**	*They gave to everyone but me.*
Se lleva bien **con** todos **excepto conmigo.**	*He gets along with everyone but me.*

menos:

Todos **menos tú** comieron postre.	*They all ate dessert except you.*
Hubo una carta **para** todos **menos para ti.**	*There was a letter for everyone but you.*

The preposition **con** with **mí, ti,** and **sí** becomes **conmigo, contigo,** and **consigo:**

Ven **conmigo.**	*Come with me.*
Pensé que estaba **contigo.**	*I thought he was with you.*
Se lo llevó **consigo.**	*He took it along (with him).*

Consigo is used when the subject of the verb is the same as the object of **con,** as in the previous example. In situations where the subject is different from the object of **con,** use the standard third-person prepositional pronoun:

Fuimos al cine con Juan. Fuimos al cine **con él.**	*We went to the movies with Juan.* *We went to the movies with him.*
Quiero bailar con María. Quiero bailar **con ella.**	*I want to dance with Maria.* *I want to dance with her.*
Me gusta hablar con mis vecinos. Me gusta hablar **con ellos.**	*I like to talk with my neighbors.* *I like to talk with them.*
Nunca he ido al cine con mis hermanitas. Nunca he ido al cine **con ellas.**	*I have never gone to the movies with my little sisters.* *I have never gone to the movies with them.*

> Ejercicios 3.16–3.17, páginas 403–404;
> Ejercicios de repaso 3.18–3.19, páginas 404–405

B Se

1 Introduction

The pronoun **se** in Spanish can have different usages, depending upon the context in which it is used:

- The indirect object pronouns **le** and **les** change to **se** when followed by direct object pronouns such as **lo** or **la**. (See Chapter 3.A.4, pages 60–64.)
- **Se** is also the third-person singular and plural form of the reflexive pronoun.
- In its function as a reflexive pronoun, **se** can be used in constructions with things as subjects and people as indirect objects to describe accidental occurrences. In **Se me olvidó la tarea,** the subject of the verb is **tarea** and the person is the indirect object. In this type of sentence the thing is doing the action to itself (thus the reflexive), and the person appears as an innocent bystander or victim, indirectly affected by the event.
- In the impersonal usage of **se,** the action is being done with no subject mentioned—clearly someone is doing it, but this fact is irrelevant to the context. When you read **Se habla español** on the door of a store, it indicates that Spanish is spoken in that store in case of need. It is irrelevant to state who speaks the language.

OVERVIEW OF USES OF **SE**
1. **Le** or **les** transformed before **lo(s)** or **la(s)** **Le di la flor.** → **Se la di.** *I gave her the flower.* → *I gave it to her.*
2. Third-person reflexive **Ella se levanta temprano.** *She wakes up early.* Third-person reciprocal **Ellos se odian.** *They hate each other.*
3. Accidental **Se me cayó el libro.** *I dropped the book.*
4. Impersonal **Se habla español.** *Spanish is spoken.*

2 Reflexive Pronouns

a. Reflexives

REFLEXIVE PRONOUNS		
PERSON	SINGULAR	PLURAL
1st	me	nos
2nd	te	os
3rd	se	se

A reflexive construction occurs when the subject and the object of a verb are the same person. In some cases, the object of the verb is direct:

> **Me** lavo.   *I wash myself.*

In other cases, the object of the verb is indirect:

> **Se** escribían todos los días.   *They wrote (to) each other every day.*

Certain verbs that refer to daily personal habits are most frequently used in the reflexive construction. (See Chapter 6.J, pages 245–247, on reflexive verbs.)

> bañarse *to bathe (oneself)*   lavarse *to wash (oneself)*
>
> despertarse *to wake (oneself) up*   levantarse *to get (oneself) up*

These verbs can be used nonreflexively, in a standard transitive construction, with the object different from the subject:

Nonreflexive:

> La madre bañó a su bebé. ⟶ **Lo** bañó.
> *The mother bathed her baby.*   *She bathed him.*

Reflexive:

> Ella se bañó a las seis. ⟶ **Se** bañó.
> *She bathed (herself) at six.*   *She bathed (took a bath).*

In reflexive constructions, definite articles are used with parts of the body or articles of clothing, rather than possessives:

> **Me** lavé **las** manos.   *I washed my hands.*
>
> **Me** puse **el** abrigo.   *I put on my coat.*

To stress or emphasize the reflexive pronouns, the following reflexive prepositional or stressed object pronouns are used:

REFLEXIVE PREPOSITIONAL OBJECT PRONOUNS		
PERSON	SINGULAR	PLURAL
1st	mí	nosotros
2nd	ti	vosotros
3rd	sí	sí[15]

These pronouns are used to mark stressed pronouns after prepositions, and sometimes in constructions in which the verb itself is not reflexive, but the action is:

Es muy codicioso. Se lo guarda todo **para sí (mismo)** y no deja nada para los demás.	*He is very greedy. He keeps everything for himself and leaves nothing for the rest.*
Lo hago **por mí**.	*I do it for myself.*
Lo compró **para sí**.	*She bought it for herself.*
Trajo el paraguas **consigo**.	*She brought the umbrella (with her.)*

b. Reciprocals

The plural pronouns can be used for reciprocal actions as well:

Ellos **se** conocen bien.   *They know each other well.*

In case of ambiguity, the following may be added:

RECIPROCAL = *each other*		
	SINGULAR	PLURAL
Masculine	el uno al otro	unos a otros
Feminine	la una a la otra	unas a otras

---

[15] In this table, why do **mí** and **sí** have accents, but not **ti**? For more on this use of the accent, see Chapter 9, page 351.

REFLEXIVE = *myself, yourself*, etc.		
PERSON	SINGULAR	PLURAL
1st	a mí mismo(a)	a nosotros(as) mismos(as)
2nd	a ti mismo(a)	a vosotros(as) mismos(as)
3rd	a sí mismo(a)	a sí mismos(as)

Nos conocemos **el uno al otro**.   *We know each other.* (reciprocal)

Nos conocemos **a nosotros mismos**.   *We know ourselves.* (reflexive: each one of us knows him- or herself.)

Ejercicios 3.20–3.22, páginas 405–406

3 Se me Construction: Accidental se

In Spanish there is a structure that is very commonly used when dealing with accidental, chance, or unplanned situations. This is often the case with such actions as forgetting, dropping, burning, breaking, etc. In these situations, the thing involved in the accident becomes the subject of the verb, and the verb is used in a reflexive format. The person, or victim of the accident, becomes the indirect object of the verb. Therefore, it might appear misleading to name this **se** differently from any other reflexive **se**—the only reason it is invariable is because things are always third-person singular or plural, never first- or second-person singular or plural, forms that are reserved for humans.

Examples:

Se rompieron mis lentes.   *My glasses broke.*
[subj.: **mis lentes**; d.o.: none]

Se rompió tu regla.   *Your ruler broke.*
[subj.: **tu regla**; d.o.: none]

Se me rompieron los lentes.[16]   *I (accidentally) broke*[17] *my glasses.*
[subj.: **los lentes**; i.o.: **a mí**)   [subj.: *I*; d.o.: *my glasses*]

Se me rompió tu regla.   *I (accidentally) broke your ruler.*
[subj.: **tu regla**; i.o.: **a mí**]

---

[16] The nouns in these sentences that function as the subjects or indirect objects may be placed before or after the verbs:

Se me rompieron los lentes. = Los lentes se me rompieron.

[17] If the action of breaking was done on purpose, the verb and pronouns follow the norm in Spanish, with the person being the subject of the verb:

Ese chico me puso tan furioso que le rompí los lentes. (subj.: **yo**; d.o.: **lentes**)
That kid made me so angry that I broke his glasses.

In English, as in Spanish, there are a number of verbs that can be used in such a way that the thing to which the accident occurred is the subject of the verb: things break, fall, tear, close, open, go out (like a light), wrinkle, get dirty, get wet, go bad, etc.

The difference in structure in Spanish is that you can include the person to whom this accidental occurrence happened. Notice in the following examples that the possessive changes to a definite article when referring to a part of the body or an article of clothing or personal possession:

Se me rompieron los lentes.	*My glasses broke.*
Se te rompieron los lentes.	*Your* (tú) *glasses broke.*
Se le rompieron los lentes.	*His/Her/Your* (Ud.) *glasses broke.*
Se nos rompieron los lentes.	*Our glasses broke.*
Se os rompieron los lentes.	*Your* (vosotros) *glasses broke.*
Se les rompieron los lentes.	*Their/Your* (Uds.) *glasses broke.*

Notice that **rompieron** is third-person plural because the subject of the verb is plural: **los lentes**. If the subject were singular, the verb would be singular too:

Se me rompió la uña.	*My fingernail broke.*

If you wish to state the person to whom the accident happened, remember that the grammatical function of the person is the indirect object, introduced with the preposition **a**:

Se le olvidó la cita **al presidente**.	*The president forgot the quote.*
A Quico se le perdieron los boletos.	*Quico lost the tickets.*
Se le rompió el paraguas **a Carmelita**.	*Carmelita's umbrella broke.*

If it is not necessary to state the subject of this type of sentence because it has already been mentioned before in the context, remember the basic rule that in Spanish there is no subject pronoun equivalent to *it* in English (or *they* as the plural of *it*):

—¿Qué pasó con tu lente?	*"What happened to your lens?"*
—Se me rompió.	*"It broke."*

The following verbs can be used with this construction:

quemársele a uno *to burn*

> On purpose: **Quemaron los libros.** *They burned the books.*
> Accidental (no victim): **Los libros se quemaron.** *The books burned (up).*
> Accidental (with victim): **Se nos quemaron los libros.** *We accidentally burned up our books.*

caérsele a uno *to drop; to fall* (The phrase **dejar caer** is used for the purposeful action, and means, literally, *to let fall*.)

> On purpose: **Dejó caer el vaso.** *He dropped the glass. (He let it fall.)*
> Accidental (no victim): **El vaso se cayó.** *The glass fell.*
> Accidental (with victim): **Se le cayó el vaso.** *He dropped the glass.*

olvidársele a uno *to forget*

> On purpose: **Olvidemos nuestros problemas.** *Let's forget our problems.*
> Accidental (no victim): impossible in Spanish
> Accidental (with victim): **Se nos olvidó el libro.** *We forgot the book.*

In Spanish, a variety of unfortunate accidental occurrences can be described with this construction:

Se me cerró la puerta en la mano.	*The door closed on my hand.*
Se nos apagó el fuego.	*The fire went out (on us).*
Se nos fue la luz.	*The electricity went out (on us).*
Los temblores no se me van.	*My shivering will not go away.*
Se te arrugó la falda.	*Your skirt got wrinkled.*
Se les ensuciaron los pantalones.	*Their pants got dirty.*
Se me cierran los ojos.	*My eyes are closing.*
El frío no se te va a quitar si no te pones los calcetines.	*The cold you feel is not going to go away if you do not put on your socks. (You will not warm up . . .)*
Siempre se te ocurren las ideas más raras.	*You always come up with the strangest ideas. (They come to your mind unexpectedly.)*
Se nos pasó la hora; ya son las nueve.	*We are running late; it is already nine. (We lost track of time . . .)*
Se me quedaron las muletas en casa.	*I left my crutches at home. (They stayed at home.)*
Se me quitó el apetito.	*I lost my appetite.*
Se me pararon los pelos.	*My hair stood on end. (I got goose bumps.)*
Se le dobló la foto.	*She accidentally folded the picture. (Her picture got folded.)*

Notice that this construction cannot be used with every accident or involuntary action, even if the word *accidentally* or another indication of accident is added:

Me robaron el coche.	*They stole my car.*
Leímos el libro equivocado.	*We read the wrong book.*
Me caí.	*I fell down.*
Lo vi sin querer.	*I saw it by accident (unintentionally).*
Chocamos.	*We crashed (had a car accident).*

> Ejercicios 3.23–3.27, páginas 406–407;
> Ejercicio de repaso 3.28, páginas 408–409

4 Impersonal se

a. Introduction

The impersonal **se** is used for actions with no specific subject. These sentences correspond to the English passive voice or the impersonal *they, you, people,* or *one*:

En el Senado **se rechazó** una medida que hubiera elevado el salario mínimo.	*At the Senate they voted down a measure that would have raised the minimum wage.*
No entiendo por qué **se dicen** tantas mentiras.	*I do not understand why people tell so many lies.*
Eso implica que **se abandonó** la prohibición de llevar equipaje de mano en todos los vuelos.	*That implies that they lifted the ban on hand baggage on all flights.*
Hay indicios de que **se avanza** en el desarrollo de fuentes alternas de energía.	*There is evidence that they are making progress in the development of alternative sources of energy.*

There are other ways of expressing impersonal sentences in Spanish:

En España usan el "vosotros" como plural de "tú".	*In Spain **they** use "vosotros" as the plural of "tú."*
En época de sequía **la gente** come lo que haya.	*In times of drought, **people** eat whatever there is.*
Uno nunca sabe lo que el futuro puede traer.	***One** never knows what the future might bring.*

b. The passive voice and the impersonal se

The passive voice (See Chapter 7.B.4, pages 270–272 for more information.) is used much more in English than in Spanish, where it is found mostly in literary contexts. The passive voice in Spanish is used with increasing frequency in journalistic prose, but this is considered the result of literal translation from English. For those who are not yet experts in the language, it is best to avoid the passive voice in Spanish; instead, use the active voice if the action of the verb has a subject or agent, and an impersonal structure if there is no subject. The stronger the degree of impersonality, the more Spanish tends to use the impersonal **se**.

(1) Agent present (Subject of the action: Stated)

Agent present ⟶ Spanish: active
She was awakened by the dog. ⟶ El perro la despertó.

Here the active voice is preferred in Spanish since the agent *(dog)* is stated. Although it is grammatically acceptable, there is no reason to use a passive construction here in Spanish because there is an agent, or subject, for the action of the verb (the dog). However, it is grammatically incorrect to use the impersonal **se** to render this sentence into Spanish, given the presence of an agent (or subject of the action).

(2) No agent: Not impersonal (Subject of the action: Absent but implied)

No agent: not impersonal ⟶ Spanish active: nonspecific subject
She was found. ⟶ La encontraron. Alguien la encontró.

In the preceding context the subject is omitted, either because it is not the focus of the sentence, or because it is unknown. If you tried to visualize the person who is doing the finding, you would imagine a specific individual or individuals, rather than a generalized "people." The most common translation into Spanish would be the active voice with a nonspecific subject such as *they* or *somebody*.

(3) No agent: Impersonal (Subject of the action: Absent and irrelevant)

No agent: impersonal ⟶ Spanish: impersonal **se**
Spanish is spoken. ⟶ Se habla español.

The impersonal **se** is ideal for a context such as the one above, where there is no agent. If you thought about the implied subject of the verb, you would see that it is impersonal, since it can be replaced with *people*, rather than a specific individual. This example has a greater degree of impersonality than the implied subject of the previous sentence.

PASSIVE • SPANISH vs. ENGLISH		
SUBJECT OF THE ACTION	SPANISH PREFERENCE	ENGLISH PREFERENCE
Stated	ACTIVE	ACTIVE or PASSIVE
Absent but implied	ACTIVE	ACTIVE or PASSIVE
Absent and irrelevant	Impersonal **se**	PASSIVE

c. Impersonal **se** with inanimate objects

When referring to inanimate objects, the inanimate object functions grammatically as the subject of the verb (i.e., the verb agrees in number with the inanimate object[s]):

Se habla kurdo en Irak.	*Kurdish is spoken in Iraq.*
Se hablan muchas lenguas en Suiza.	*Many languages are spoken in Switzerland.*

If the subject of the verb has been stated previously in the context, and you wish to replace it with a pronoun, remember that there is no subject pronoun for an inanimate object (it/they):

Sí, **se** habla.	*Yes, it is spoken.*
Se hablan.	*They are spoken.*
¿Cómo **se** dice eso?	*How does one say that?*
¿Cómo **se** dice?	*How does one say it?*
¿Cómo **se** prepara ese platillo?	*How does one prepare that dish?*
Se prepara con huevos y leche.	*One prepares it with eggs and milk.*

d. Impersonal **se** with persons

When an impersonal **se** structure refers to a human being and not an inanimate object, the grammatical function of the human being is that of the direct object of the verb. For this reason, the verb remains singular. In addition, the personal **a** is needed to mark the human as the direct object:

Se castiga **a** los criminales.   *Criminals are punished.*

If the verb agreed with the human, and no personal **a** were used, you would have a reflexive construction rather than an impersonal one (**Se castigan los criminales** = *Criminals punish themselves*).

The impersonal **se** can be used in conjunction with all persons and with all verb tenses, according to contextual needs. Some examples follow—note that **se** is always invariable and that the verb is always in the third-person singular:

Se **te** notificará por correo electrónico.	*You will be notified by e-mail.*
No se **nos** había visto allí antes.	*We had not been seen there before.*
Ojalá se **os** hubiera premiado.	*I wish you had been rewarded.*

To refer to human beings in the third person in impersonal **se** contexts (in most dialects[18]), **le** is used rather than the standard direct object form **lo, la.**

¿Y a los niños?	*What about the children?*
¿Se **les** avisó de los peligros?	*Were they warned of the dangers?*

The object pronoun is used in this structure similarly to others, in that it is omitted when the actual object is present in the sentence, and is needed only either when the object is absent, or when it precedes the verb. (See "Required Repetitive Object Pronouns," in this chapter, 3.A.5, pages 62–63.) Both of the sentences below translate as *The parents will be invited tomorrow*; note that **les** is added in the second sentence because of the changed word order (the direct object precedes the verb):

Se invitará a los padres mañana.

A los padres se **les** invitará mañana.

In rare cases where the persons are being perceived as a category, and not as specific individuals, they are treated in this construction as if they were things:

Se buscan empleados.	*Help needed. Now hiring.* (literally: *Employees are being sought.*)

Notice that no article is used with **empleados**, since they are nonspecific.

e. Impersonal **se** with both human and inanimate objects

In sentences with impersonal **se** and both human and inanimate objects, the person is the <u>indirect object</u> of the verb, and the inanimate object continues to function as the grammatical subject of the verb:

No se me dio un ejemplar.	*I was not given a copy.*
No se nos anunciaron los cambios.	*The changes were not announced to us.*
Se les envió una solicitud a las universidades.	*The universities were sent an application.* (OR: *An application was sent to the universities.*)

---

[18] For more information on dialects, see Chapter 9, pages 376–379.

Notice that in the third example **les** is a repetitive indirect object pronoun referring to **las universidades.**

f. Impersonal reflexive construction: uno

It is not possible to use both the reflexive and the impersonal **se** together. Use **se** as a reflexive pronoun and **uno** as an impersonal pronoun. Notice the variations of position in the following sentences:

Uno se levanta temprano en el ejército. *One gets up early in the army.*
Se levanta **uno** temprano en el ejército.

Uno se broncea rápido con ese sol. *With that sun, one tans quickly.*
Con ese sol **se** broncea **uno** rápido.

> Ejercicios 3.29–3.34, páginas 409–413

C DEMONSTRATIVE AND POSSESSIVE PRONOUNS

1 Demonstrative Pronouns

In their form demonstrative pronouns are identical to demonstrative adjectives. (See page 34.) The accent mark that used to be required is no longer required, even in cases of ambiguity. (See Chapter 9, page 353 for the use of the accent.)

DEMONSTRATIVE PRONOUNS		
	SINGULAR	PLURAL
Masculine	**este**	**estos**
Feminine	**esta**	**estas**
Masculine	**ese**	**esos**
Feminine	**esa**	**esas**
Masculine	**aquel**	**aquellos**
Feminine	**aquella**	**aquellas**

este = this one; **ese** = that one (near you);
aquel = that one (over there, far from you)

Examples:

Esta mesa es más grande que **esa**, pero más pequeña que **aquella**.
This table is larger than that one, but smaller than that one over there.

Mañana terminaré **esta**.
I'll finish this one tomorrow.

When there is no noun as referent for the pronoun, the neutral pronoun is used.

NEUTRAL DEMONSTRATIVE PRONOUNS	
esto	this
eso	that
aquello	that

Examples:

Esto es riquísimo. — *This is delicious.*

¿Qué es **eso**? — *What is that?*

Aquello fue aburrido. — *That was boring.*

2 Possessive Pronouns

Possessive pronouns are formed with the long forms of the possessive adjectives (See Chapter 2.B.2.b, pages 35–36.), with an added definite article that agrees with the possessed item, not with the possessor.

POSSESSIVE PRONOUNS	
el mío, la mía, los míos, las mías	mine
el tuyo, la tuya, los tuyos, las tuyas	yours (tú)
el nuestro, la nuestra, los nuestros, las nuestras	ours
el vuestro, la vuestra, los vuestros, las vuestras	yours (vosotros)
el suyo, la suya, los suyos, las suyas	yours (Ud./Uds.) his hers its theirs

Examples:

Mi mochila pesa más que **la tuya**.	*My backpack weighs more than yours.*
—¿Cuál es mi café?	*"Which is my coffee?"*
—Este es **el suyo**.	*"This one is yours."*
—Mis abuelos están en Florida.	*"My grandparents are in Florida."*
—¿Y **los vuestros**?	*"And yours?"*
—**Los nuestros** están en California.	*"Ours are in California."*

With **ser** the article is omitted.

Esa llave es **mía**.	*That key is mine.*

The article is used when there is a choice between items.

—¿Cuáles son tus llaves?	*"Which keys are yours?"*
—Estas son **las mías** y esas son **las tuyas**.	*"These are mine and those are yours."*

Whenever there may be ambiguity regarding the reference of **suyo**, you can clarify the context by specifying with **de él, de ella, de usted, de ellos, de ellas, de ustedes.**

—¿Cuál es mi café?	*"Which is my coffee?"*
—Este es el **de usted**, este otro es el **de él**, ese es el **de ella** y aquel es el **de ustedes**.	*"This one is yours, this other one is his, that one is hers, and that one over there is yours." (plural in Latin America, formal plural in Spain)*

When the possessed item is not specific, but general (my things, my part, etc.), the neutral form **lo** is used instead of the article:

Quiero **lo mío** y nada más.	*I want what is mine, and nothing else.*

Ejercicios 3.35–3.36, página 413

D INTERROGATIVES

INTERROGATIVES	
¿Qué?	What? (before a noun—Which?)
¿Cuál(es)?	Which? (before **ser**—What?)
¿Cuánto(a)(s)?	How much? How many?
¿Quién(es)?	Who?
¿Dónde?	Where?
¿Cómo?	How?
¿Por qué?	Why?
¿Cuándo?	When?

1 ¿Qué?

This interrogative can be used either before a verb or before a noun.

¿Qué quieres?	*What do you want?*
¿Qué es esto?	*What is this?*
¿Qué película prefieres ver?	*Which movie do you prefer to see?*

2 ¿Cuál(es)?

This interrogative can also be used before a verb, and before **de** and a noun phrase, but not before a noun.

¿Cuál prefieres?	*Which one do you prefer?*
¿Cuál de estos libros es tuyo?	*Which one of these books is yours?*
¿Cuáles son los tuyos?	*Which ones are yours?*

3 ¿Qué? vs. ¿Cuál? with **ser**

¿Qué? + **ser** asks for a definition or the meaning of words.

¿Cuál? + **ser** asks for a pinpointing or specification.

Here are a few sets of dialogues for you to compare:

—¿**Qué es** "La Bamba"?	*"What is 'La Bamba'?"*
—Es un baile folklórico mexicano.	*"It is a Mexican folkloric dance."*
—¿**Cuál es** "La Bamba"?	*"Which one is 'La Bamba'?"*
—Es la que están tocando ahora.	*"It's the one they are playing now."*

In the previous two dialogues, the context is completely different. The person asking the first question might have heard the words **"La Bamba"** for the first time and is asking the other person to explain what they mean. In the second dialogue, the person asking the question knows what **"La Bamba"** is and is asking the other person to let him or her know when it is played.

—¿**Cuál es** tu apellido?	*"What is your last name?"*
—Gómez.	*"Gómez."*
—¿**Cuál es** tu apellido?	*"Which one is your last name?"*
—Es este.	*"It's this one."*

Such a question with **¿Qué?** would be one inquiring about the meaning of the two words **tu** and **apellido,** or about the origin of the name:

—¿**Qué es** "tu apellido"?	*"What is 'tu apellido'?"*
—Es tu nombre de familia.	*"It's your family name."*
—¿**Qué es** tu apellido?	*"What is your last name?"*
—Es turco.	*"It's Turkish."*

If you want to ask about the difference between two things, you would ask the following:

¿**Cuál es** la diferencia?	*What is the difference?*

A child wanting to know what the word *difference* means would use **¿Qué?** for this question.

¿**Qué es** "diferencia"?	*What is "difference"?*

¿Cuál es? is used when you have a set of items in front of you and you want someone to select a specific one:

—¿**Cuál es** el tuyo?	*"Which one is yours?"*
—Este.	*"This one."*

Following are some more examples of the use of **¿Cuál es?** Think about the implications these same questions would have if they were asked with **¿Qué es?**:

¿Cuál fue el problema?	*What was the problem?*
¿Cuál era la fecha?	*What was the date?*
¿Cuál es tu número de teléfono?	*What is your phone number?*

When a noun follows the interrogative instead of the verb, **¿Qué?** is preferred:

¿Qué <u>color</u> te gusta más?	*What color do you prefer?*
¿Cuál <u>es</u> tu color favorito?	*Which is your favorite color?*

Who? has a singular and a plural form in Spanish: **¿Quién? ¿Quiénes?**

¿Quién te dijo eso?	*Who told you that?*
¿Quiénes fueron a la fiesta?	*Who (all) went to the party?*

Whose? is translated with the preposition **de** preceding **¿quién(es)?**:

¿De quién es esto?	*Whose is this?*

In Spanish, the preposition must always precede the interrogative:

¿De dónde sale esa idea?	*Where does that idea come from?*
¿Para qué sirve esto?	*What is this for?*
¿Con cuál lo escribiste?	*Which one did you write it with?*

4 How?

The translation into Spanish of questions starting with *How?* will vary depending upon what follows the interrogative—a verb, an adjective, or an adverb.

a. How? + verb = ¿Cómo?

¿Cómo estás?	*How are you?*
¿Cómo lo hiciste?	*How did you do it?*
¿Cómo llegaron?	*How did they get here?*

Be aware of the following questions:

¿Cómo te llamas?	*What is your name?*
¿Cómo es?	*What is he/she/it like?*

b. *How?* + *adj.* or *adv.* ≠ **¿Cómo?**

Never use **¿cómo?** to translate *how?* followed by an adjective or adverb.

HOW? + *ADJECTIVE* OR *ADVERB*			
ENGLISH QUESTION	FOCUS	SPANISH QUESTION	LITERAL MEANING
How tall is he?	height **estatura**	¿Qué <u>estatura</u> tiene?	What height does he have?
		¿Cuánto mide de <u>estatura</u>?	What does he measure in height?
How important is it?	importance **importancia**	¿Qué <u>importancia</u> tiene?	What importance does it have?
		¿Cuál es su <u>importancia</u>?	What is its importance?
How far is it?	distance **distancia**	¿A qué <u>distancia</u> queda?	At what distance is it?
How big is it?	size **tamaño**	¿De qué <u>tamaño</u> es?	What size is it?
How old is she?	age **edad**	¿Qué <u>edad</u> tiene?	What age does she have?
How fast do you run?	speed **velocidad**	¿A qué <u>velocidad</u> corres?	At what speed do you run?
How often do you see him?	frequency **frecuencia**	¿Con qué <u>frecuencia</u> lo ves?	With what frequency do you see him?

In Mexico, *How tall is he?* is translated as **¿Qué tan alto es?** and in the Caribbean as **¿Cuán alto es?** but neither of these forms is used in many other Spanish-speaking countries. This type of question must be reformulated using a noun instead of the adjective or adverb by saying, for example, *What is his height?* If you learn to reformulate the question following the provided models, you'll be best equipped for communicating in any Spanish-speaking country.

These questions may also be asked as follows:

¿Es muy alto? ¿Cómo es de alto? ¿Es de nuestra edad?

¿Es muy importante? ¿Corres muy rápido?

¿Queda muy lejos? ¿Lo ves a menudo / frecuentemente?

¿Es muy grande? ¿Cómo es de grande?

c. *How much / many?* = **¿Cuánto(a)(s)...?**

¿**Cuánto** dinero tienes?	*How much money do you have?*
¿**Cuántos** huevos compraste?	*How many eggs did you buy?*

5 Word Order

In questions beginning with interrogative words the standard word order is inverted: the verb precedes the subject.

¿**Qué** vio Rafael?	*What did Rafael see?*
¿**Cuándo** salió Silvana?	*When did Silvana leave?*
¿**Por qué** gritaron los niños?	*Why did the children yell?*

This rule applies in indirect discourse as well. (Notice the difference from English.)

No sé **qué** vio Rafael.	*I don't know what Rafael saw.*
No sé **cuándo** salió Silvana.	*I don't know when Silvana left.*
No sé **por qué** gritaron los niños.	*I don't know why the children yelled.*

> Ejercicios 3.37–3.39, páginas 413–414

E EXCLAMATIVES

EXCLAMATIVES	
¡Qué! + *noun, adj., or adv.*	What (a)(an)... ! How ... !
¡Cómo! + *verb*	(How)... !
¡Cuánto! + *verb or noun*	How much ... !
¡Cuántos(as)! + *noun*	How many ... !
¡Quién(es)! + *verb*	Who ... !

1 ¡Qué! + *noun*

Please notice in the following examples that Spanish does not use an article in this construction as English does when the noun is singular:

¡Qué alivio!	*What **a** relief!*
¡Qué problema!	*What **a** problem!*
¡Qué lío!	*What **a** mess!*
¡Qué desastre!	*What **a** disaster!*

In some cases the Spanish noun is translated as an adjective in English, with a variety of constructions:

¡Qué asco!	*Ugh! Gross! How disgusting!*
¡Qué calor (hace)!	*It is so hot!*
¡Qué frío (hace)!	*It is so cold!*
¡Qué cansancio (tengo)!	*I am so tired!*
¡Qué hambre (tengo)!	*I am so hungry!*

2 ¡Qué! + *modified noun*

Here are examples of the adjective preceding the noun:

¡Qué buena idea!	*What a good idea!*
¡Qué lindos ojos!	*What beautiful eyes!*

If the adjective follows the noun, it is often preceded by **más** or **tan**:

¡Qué explosión más/tan horrible!	*What a terrible explosion!*
¡Qué final más/tan sorprendente!	*What a surprising end!*

3 ¡Qué! + *adj.*

¡Qué interesante!	*How interesting!*

Some of the exclamations that follow are very idiomatic, geographically or historically marked, and translate very differently depending upon the context or the period.

¡Qué rico!

This exclamation can be used in many situations. Essentially, it is a positive comment on practically anything, and means something like *"How nice!"* If referring to food, it could mean *"Mmm! Delicious!"*

Other similar expressions are as follows:

¡Qué bueno!	*Good! Great!*
¡Qué chévere![19] ¡Qué padre![20]	*Wow!* (other equivalents: *Cool!*
¡Qué guay![21] ¡Qué bestial![22]	*Excellent! Awesome! Rad!*)

4 ¡Qué! + adv.

¡Qué rápido acabaste!	*You finished so fast! How quickly you finished! That was fast!*
¡Qué bien bailas!	*How well you dance! You dance so well! You are such a good dancer!*
¡Qué mal me siento!	*I feel so sick!*

5 ¡Cómo! + verb

¡Cómo gritan!	*How they scream!*
¡Cómo te miraban!	*How they looked at you!*

6 ¡Cuánto! + verb

¡Cuánto lo siento!	*I am so sorry!*
¡Cuánto me gusta este pan!	*I like this bread so much!*
¡Cuánto gastan!	*They spend so much!*
¡Cuánto quisiera ser así!	*How I wish I could be like that!*

7 ¡Cuánto(a)! + noun

¡Cuánta paciencia tienes!	*How patient you are! You are so patient!*
¡Cuánto vino producen!	*They produce so much wine!*

---

[19] The adjective **chévere** is used in Puerto Rico and other Caribbean countries.
[20] The adjective **padre** is used in Mexico.
[21] The adjective **guay** is used in Spain.
[22] The adjective **bestial** is used in Bolivia, Ecuador, and other South American countries.

8 ¡Cuántos(as)! + *noun*

¡Cuántos heridos hubo!	*There were so many who were injured!*
¡Cuántas islas hay en el Caribe!	*There are so many islands in the Caribbean!*

9 ¡Quién(es)! + *verb*

¡Quién pudiera bailar como ella!	*If only I could dance the way she does!*

> Ejercicios 3.40–3.41, página 414

F INDEFINITES AND NEGATIVES

INDEFINITE PRONOUNS	
AFFIRMATIVE	**NEGATIVE**
alguien someone	**nadie** nobody, no one, not anyone
alguno(a) anyone, one	**ninguno(a)** none, neither (of two)
algunos some **unos** some	**ninguno** nobody, no one, none, not any, not anyone
algo something	**nada** nothing, not anything
cualquiera anybody, any	**nadie** nobody, no one, not anyone

Examples:

Alguien te llamó.	*Someone called you.*
No conozco a **nadie** aquí.	*I do not know anyone here.*
—¿Quieres **algo** de beber? —No, no quiero **nada**, gracias.	*"Do you want something to drink?"* *"No, I do not want anything, thank you."*
—No sé de dónde es. —¿Lo sabrá **alguno** de tus abuelos? —No, **ninguno** de ellos lo sabe.	*"I do not know where he is from."* *"Would one of your grandparents know?"* *"No, none of them knows."*
Cualquiera podría cantar mejor.	*Anybody could sing better.*

| INDEFINITE ADJECTIVES ||
AFFIRMATIVE	NEGATIVE
algún *some*	**ningún*** *not any, no*
todo *all of*	

*The plural forms **ningunos** and **ningunas** are very rarely used.

Examples:

Algún libro tendrá eso.	*Some book will have that.*
Algunas manzanas son agrias.	*Some apples are bitter.*
Aquí no hay **ningún** niño.	*There is no little boy here.*
Todo el público aplaudió.	*All of the audience applauded.*

NOTE: Do not use **de** after **todo**.

No regó **ninguna** flor.	*He did not water any flowers.*

| INDEFINITE ADVERBIALS ||
AFFIRMATIVE	NEGATIVE
también *also*	**tampoco** *neither, not . . . either*
en alguna parte *somewhere*	**en ninguna parte** *nowhere, not anywhere*
de algún modo *somehow*	**de ningún modo** *no way, by no means*
alguna vez *ever, at some (any) time* **algunas veces** *sometimes* **una vez** *once* **algún día** *some day, ever* **siempre** *always*	**nunca, jamás** *never, not . . . ever*

Examples:

—Tú **también** lo hiciste.	*"You did it too."*
—Yo no lo hice. ¿Y tú?	*"I did not do it. Did you?"*
—Yo **tampoco** lo hice.	*"I did not do it either."*
—¿Dónde estará mi libro? No lo encuentro **en ninguna parte**.	*"Where is my book? I cannot find it anywhere."*
—Tiene que estar **en alguna parte**.	*"It has to be somewhere."*

—No puedo convencerlo **de ningún modo**.	*"I cannot convince him at all."*
—**De algún modo** lo convencerás.	*"Somehow you will convince him."*
—Cantó **una vez** en Buenos Aires.	*"She sang in Buenos Aires once."*
—Yo **nunca** la oí cantar.	*"I never heard her sing."*
—**Algún día** comprenderás.	*"Some day you will understand."*
—No comprenderé **nunca**.	*"I will never understand."*
—**Siempre** cometes el mismo error.	*"You always make the same mistake."*
—Y tú **nunca** cometes errores…	*"And you never make mistakes…"*

In questions, **alguna vez** and **algún día** mean *ever*, the first for the standard meaning of *ever*, the second for a distant future:

—¿Has ido a Chile **alguna vez**?	*"Have you ever been to Chile?"*
—No, **nunca** he ido a Chile.	*"No, I have never been to Chile."*
—¿Irás a Chile **algún día**?	*"Will you ever go to Chile?"*

If the negative precedes the verb, it is used alone; if it follows the verb, **no** or **ni** must precede the verb:

Nadie te llamó. **No** te llamó **nadie**.	*No one called you.*
Nada le gusta. **No** le gusta **nada**.	*He does not like anything.*
Nunca lo vi. **No** lo vi **nunca**.	*I never saw it.*
Tampoco lo vi. **No** lo vi **tampoco**.	*I did not see it either.*

Multiple negatives are frequent in Spanish:

Nunca entiendes **nada**.	*You never understand anything.*
Nunca le digas **nada** a **nadie**.	*Never tell anything to anyone.*

Ningún (Ninguna) is used for emphatic negatives:

No tengo interés.	*I have no interest. I am not interested.*
No tengo **ningún** interés.	*I have no interest whatsoever. I am not interested at all.*

NOTE: *Any*, *anything*, and *anyone* in English can be either negative or indefinite and translate differently into Spanish depending upon the usage:

| ANY • ANYTHING • ANYONE ||
NEGATIVE	INDEFINITE
No veo <u>ninguno</u>. *I do not see <u>any</u>.*	**Podríamos usar <u>cualquiera</u>.** *We could use <u>any</u>.*
No quiero <u>nada</u>. *I do not want <u>anything</u>.*	**<u>Cualquier cosa</u> serviría.** *<u>Anything</u> would work.*
No traigas a <u>nadie</u>. *Do not bring <u>anyone</u>.*	**<u>Cualquiera</u> podría hacer eso.** *<u>Anyone</u> could do that.*

Certain negative words occasionally carry no negative meaning, as seen in the following examples:

—With impersonal expressions indicating futility, impossibility (note in the first example the use of the personal **a** with **nadie** as human direct object):

Era imposible convencer a **nadie**.   *It was impossible to convince anyone.*

Es inútil decirle **nada** cuando llora.   *It is useless to tell him anything when he cries.*

—With comparatives or superlatives:

Es la mejor película que **jamás** haya visto.   *It is the best movie I have ever seen.*

Mi hermano comió más que **nadie**.   *My brother ate more than anyone.*

Hablas menos que **ninguno** de tus compañeros.   *You speak less than any of your classmates.*

—With certain restrictive terms:

Llegamos **antes que nadie**.   *We arrived before anyone.*

Apenas comimos **nada**.   *We barely ate anything.*

Se lo tragó **sin nada** de beber.   *He swallowed it without anything to drink.*

Ejercicios 3.42–3.43, página 415

G RELATIVE PRONOUNS

1 Formation and Usage

RELATIVE PRONOUNS	
que	*(invariable)*
el que	(la que, los que, las que)
el cual	(la cual, los cuales, las cuales)
lo que	*(invariable)*
lo cual	*(invariable)*
quien	(quienes)
cuyo	(cuya, cuyos, cuyas)
donde	*(invariable)*

A relative pronoun refers to a noun (its antecedent) from the main clause and introduces a subordinate clause: a relative or adjectival clause. It joins two references to the same noun: (See Chapter 6.G.3, pages 213–214, on the use of the subjunctive in adjectival clauses.)

1.	El estudiante se especializa en español.	*The student is a Spanish major.*
2.	El estudiante vino a verme.	*The student came to see me.*
1. + 2.	El estudiante **que** vino a verme se especializa en español.	*The student who came to see me is a Spanish major.*

In English, the relative pronoun is often not expressed:

The house we saw yesterday is too big.

In Spanish, however, the relative pronoun cannot be omitted:

La casa **que** vimos ayer es demasiado grande.

The relative pronoun follows its antecedent immediately; only a few structures, such as prepositions, can come between them:

Se quemó la **casa en que** nos criamos.	*The house we grew up in burned down.*

The antecedent (**casa**) and its relative pronoun (**que**) are separated by the preposition **en.**

A relative pronoun may hold the same variety of grammatical functions in a sentence that a noun can; it can be the subject of the verb of the relative clause, or its direct object, or its indirect object, or it can be the object of the preposition that precedes it:

>La autora **que** nos habló ayer es famosa en Chile.
>*The author who spoke to us yesterday is famous in Chile.*
>Function of **que:** subject of **habló**

>El perro **que** vimos es de los vecinos.
>*The dog (that) we saw is the neighbors'.*
>Function of **que:** direct object of **vimos**

>El hombre **al que** le preguntamos no sabía la respuesta.
>*The man (whom) we asked did not know the answer.*
>Function of **al que:** indirect object of **preguntamos**

>La ventana al lado de **la cual** trabajo no cierra bien.
>*The window next to which I work does not close well.*
>Function of **la cual:** object of the preposition **al lado de**

You may often use a variety of relative pronouns depending upon the grammatical structure of the sentence. To simplify your task in learning to use these pronouns, here is a simple set of options that are always grammatically correct.

RELATIVE PRONOUN OPTIONS		
	WITHOUT PREPOSITION	**WITH PREPOSITION***
ANTECEDENT = ONE NOUN	**que**	**el cual / el que****
ANTECEDENT = CLAUSE	**lo que / lo cual**	
ENGLISH = *the one...*	**el que**	
ENGLISH = *what*	**lo que**	
ENGLISH = *whose*	**cuyo****	

*__A, de, en,__ and **con** may take **que** alone when the antecedent is an inanimate object.
__El/La que__ and **el/la cual agree with their antecedents; **cuyo** agrees with the noun that follows it.

2 Relative Pronouns with no Preposition

Que can always be used, whether the antecedent is an inanimate object or a human being. **Quien** is <u>never</u> correct in this type of sentence (a sentence with no preposition or comma before the relative pronoun):

La casa **que** tengo en Ithaca es vieja. (a thing)	*The house (that) I have in Ithaca is old.*
El amigo **que** vive en Ithaca es viejo. (a person)	*The friend who lives in Ithaca is old.*

3 Relative Pronouns with a Preposition

a. El cual / el que[23]

The forms **el/la cual, los/las cuales, el/la que,** and **los/las que** can always be used. NOTE: Always place the preposition before the relative pronoun.

La compañía para **la cual / la que** trabajo es japonesa.	*The company for which I work (I work for) is Japanese.*
La mujer para **la cual / la que** trabajo es puertorriqueña.	*The woman for whom I work (I work for) is Puerto Rican.*

b. Que after a/de/en/con

The following prepositions[24] may be used with **que** alone when the antecedent is an inanimate object (not human): **a, de, en, con.**

La iglesia **a que** voy está en el centro.	*The church I go to is downtown.*
El tifón **de que** me habló ha sido el peor.	*The typhoon he told me about has been the worst.*
La silla **en que** me senté estaba pegajosa.	*The chair I sat in was sticky.*
El lápiz **con que** escribo se me rompió.	*The pencil I write with broke.*

---

[23] There is dialectal variation in the use of these pronouns: in many areas, **el que** is preferred to **el cual**.
[24] **A, de, en** and **con** can also be used with **el que** or **el cual**.

4 Additional Uses

a. Lo que / lo cual (Invariable)

If the antecedent is an entire clause, both **lo que** and **lo cual** are possible:

El examen fue difícil, **lo que / lo cual** nos sorprendió.
The exam was hard, which surprised us.

b. El que[25]

When used with **ser**, this pronoun means *the one, the one who, the one (that), the one (which)*:

Margarita es **la que** me regaló estas flores.
Margarita is the one who gave me these flowers.

Ese libro es **el que** me gusta.
That book is the one (that) I like.

Esas mujeres, **las que** están vestidas de traje (y no las otras), son abogadas.[26]
Those women, the ones wearing suits (not the other ones), are lawyers.

Mi coche, **el que** está en el garaje, es un Ford.
My car, the one that is in the garage, is a Ford. (I have another one.)

La que me gustó fue la verde.
The one I liked was the green one.

Los que no tenían eran los azules.
The ones they did not have were the blue ones.

La que me cae bien es Nilda.
The one I like is Nilda.

In structures such as these, **quien** is only required if the sentence is a proverb.

Quien bien te quiera te hará llorar.
Whoever loves you a lot will make you cry.

---

[25] **El que** followed by the subjunctive means *whoever* or *whomever*.

Regálaselo al que quieras. *Give it to whomever you want.*

La que le gane a Sánchez se hará famosa. *Whoever beats Sánchez will become famous.*

[26] If you were to use **la que** instead of **que** in the following sentence, it would translate as *the one who* and would sound absurd—in most cases:

Mi madre, que vive en México, nunca viaja. *My mother, who lives in Mexico, never travels.*

c. Lo que

When used without an antecedent at the beginning of a sentence, **lo que** means *what*:

Lo que no entiendo es por qué lo hicieron. Eso es **lo que** me molesta.	*What I do not understand is why they did it. That is what bothers me.*
Lo que dijiste no es verdad.	*What you said is not true.*
Contrario a **lo que** pueden pensar los que solo lo conocen por los periódicos, es un personaje complejo.	*Contrary to what those who only know him through the papers may think, he is a complicated person.*

NOTE: **Lo que** followed by the subjunctive means *whatever*.

Haré **lo que** digas.	*I will do whatever you say.*

d. Cuyo

This is a word that joins the attributes of a relative and a possessive: it means *whose*. It functions like an adjective, and agrees with the noun referring to the possessed element, not with the possessor:

Es un árbol **cuyas** ramas proveen buena sombra.	*It's a tree whose branches provide good shade.*

NOTE: The interrogative *Whose?* is translated into Spanish with **¿De quién(es)?** (notice the accent mark).

¿De quién es ese anuncio? (direct discourse)	*Whose ad is that?*
No me dijo **de quién** era el anuncio. (indirect discourse)	*He did not tell me whose ad it was.*

e. Donde

Donde means *where* and is invariable:

Prefiero las oficinas **donde** entra mucha luz del día.	*I prefer offices where there is a lot of daylight.*

NOTE: The interrogative *Where?* is translated into Spanish with **¿Dónde?** with an accent mark:

¿Dónde están los archivos?	*Where are the files?*

Remember that the interrogative in indirect discourse can be distinguished from the relative pronoun because of the absence of an antecedent.

Quería saber dónde estabas.	*He wanted to know where you were.*

f. *Who*

Who in a question translates as **quién,** but it translates as **que** in a relative clause.

(1) Interrogative pronoun: ¿Quién?

¿**Quién** te dio eso? (direct discourse)	***Who*** *gave you that?*
No sé **quién** lo hizo. (indirect discourse)	*I do not know* ***who*** *did it.*

(2) Relative pronoun: Que

Please be aware of the danger of translating *who* with **quien** in a relative clause, especially when there is no preposition before it.
Que translates as *who* when there is no preposition.

El candidato **que** copie perderá. (<u>Never</u> use **quien** here.)	*The candidate* ***who*** *copies will lose.*

(3) El cual / el que

El cual and **el que** are always possible with prepositions.

La estudiante con **la cual** llegaste es nueva. (*also:* con **la que,** con **quien**)	*The student with whom you arrived is new.*

g. *What*

What in a question translates as **qué,** but in a relative clause it is **lo que.**

Questions:

¿**Qué** dijo? (direct discourse)	***What*** *did he say?*
No sé **qué** hacer. (indirect discourse)	*I do not know* ***what*** *to do.*

Relative clause:

    Eso es **lo que** me gusta. *That is **what** I like.*
    (antecedent = that)

    Lo que hizo fue horrible. ***What** he did was horrible.*
    (relative clause without an antecedent)

    ¿Sabes **lo que** dijo durante la tregua? *Do you know **what** he said during the truce?*

> Ejercicios 3.44–3.46, páginas 415–416;
> Ejercicios de repaso 3.47–3.48, páginas 416–418

CHAPTER 4

Prepositions, Adverbs, Conjunctions, and Transitions

A Prepositions

B Adverbs

C Conjunctions

D Transitions

A PREPOSITIONS

1 Function of Prepositions

A preposition relates a noun or its equivalent to another noun, to the verb, or to the rest of the sentence.

With nouns:

    Salí **con Ana**. *I went out with Ana.*

    Esta comida es **para mi perro**. *This food is for my dog.*

With pronouns:

    Vete **con ellos**. *Go with them.*

    Entremos **en esta**. *Let's go into this one.* (e.g., **tienda**)

    Vamos **en el mío**. *Let's go in mine.* (e.g., **coche**)

    ¿Esta tortilla es **para alguien**? *Is this tortilla for someone?*

    No, no es **para nadie**. *No, it isn't for anyone.*

    ¿**Con quién** saliste? *With whom did you go out?*

    Ese es el hombre **con el cual** llegó. *That is the man she arrived with.*

With infinitives:

    Terminé rápido **para salir**. *I finished quickly so as to (so I could) go out.*

When used in combination, prepositions may be grouped with adverbs or with other prepositions to form a single prepositional expression:

a por	Voy **a por** leche. [a por is used in Spain] *I'm going to get milk.*
debajo de	Se escondió **debajo de** la mesa. *He hid under the table.*
delante de	Ella se sienta **delante de** mí. *She sits in front of me.*
dentro de	La pluma está **dentro de** mi chequera. *The pen is inside my checkbook.*

detrás de	Yo me siento **detrás de** ella. *I sit behind her.*
encima de	Pon las llaves **encima de** mi mochila. *Put the keys on top of my backpack.*
enfrente de	Está **enfrente de** usted. *It is in front of you.*
frente a	Me senté **frente a** la estatua. *I sat in front of the statue.*
fuera de	Eso está **fuera de** mi alcance. *That is out of my reach.*
para con	Su actitud **para con**migo ha cambiado. *His attitude toward me has changed.*
por delante de	El desfile pasa **por delante de** la casa. *The parade passes in front of the house.*
por encima de	El avión voló **por encima de** mi casa. *The plane flew over my house.*

(See the section on adverbs of place, page 133, and the table on "Related Adverbs and Prepositions," page 137.)

Ejercicio 4.1, página 419

2 Verbs Used without Prepositions

The following verbs are transitive in Spanish, whereas in English they are used with prepositions. The difference is that in Spanish, the preposition is part of the meaning of the verb itself, and the thing or person you are waiting for, looking for, etc., is the direct object of the verb:

agradecer *to be grateful for*	Te agradezco la ayuda. *I am grateful to you **for** your help.*
buscar *to look for*	—¿Qué buscas? —Estoy buscando mis llaves, pero no las encuentro. *"What are you looking **for**?" "I am looking **for** my keys, but I cannot find them."*
esperar *to wait for*	Esos niños siempre esperan el autobús en la esquina. *Those children always wait **for** the bus on the corner.*
pedir + *thing* *to ask for (something)*	Siempre me piden dinero cuando no tengo. *They always ask me **for** money when I do not have any.* (See also **preguntar por** + *person*, under "Verbs with **por**.")
pensar + *inf.* *to plan to / on*	Pensamos ir a Sudamérica el verano entrante. *We are planning **to** go / **on** going to South America next summer.* (See also **pensar en** and **pensar de**, under "Verbs with **en**" and "Verbs with **de**.")

3 Individual Prepositions

a. A

(1) Usage

A	
USAGE	**EXAMPLES**
To introduce the indirect object	**Se lo dio a Jorge.** *He gave it to Jorge.*
To indicate direction toward something or some place, after a verb of movement (**ir, venir, bajar, subir, dirigirse, acercarse...**)	**Fueron a la cabaña.** *They went to the cabin.* **Subieron al tren.** *They got on the train.*
To indicate the time at which something happens	**Me levanté a las ocho.** *I got up at eight.*
To indicate the period of time after which something happened	**Se divorciaron a los dos años.** *They divorced after two years.*
To indicate the distance at which something is	**Mi auto está a una cuadra.** *My car is one block away.*
Al + *infinitive*: To indicate simultaneous actions	**Al entrar, lo vi.** *When I went in, I saw it.*

(2) Personal a[1]

PERSONAL a	
USAGE	**EXAMPLES**
To introduce a human or personified direct object	**Veo a Juan.** *I see Juan.* **Veo a mi perro.** *I see my dog.*
With indefinite pronouns **alguien, nadie, alguno, ninguno, cualquiera,** when referring to humans	**No veo a nadie.** *I don't see anyone.*
OMISSION	**EXAMPLES**
After **tener**	**Tengo una hermana.** *I have a sister.*
With indefinite direct objects	**Buscan secretarias.** *They are looking for secretaries.*

---

[1] See Chapter 2.A.3, pages 26–27, for more on the personal **a**.

(3) Expressions with **a**

a caballo	Llegaron **a caballo**. *They arrived on horseback.*
a causa de + *noun*	No pudimos ir **a causa de** la tormenta. *We were unable to go because of the storm.* (NOTE: *because* + conjugated verb = **porque**: No pudimos ir **porque** había una huelga. *We were unable to go because there was a strike.*)
a eso de	Llegaron **a eso de** las tres. *They arrived at about (around) three.* (NOTE: **a eso de** is used only with time, not with space: *It is about two miles away.* = **Está a unas dos millas**.)
a fondo	Quiero que estudies esto más **a fondo**. *I want you to study this more in depth.*
a fuerza de	**A fuerza de** trabajar día y noche, lo terminé. *By (dint of) working day and night, I finished it.*
a la vez[2]	No puedo hacer dos cosas **a la vez**. *I cannot do two things at the same time.* (NOTE: *at the time* translates as **en esa época** and not **a la vez**.)
al final	Eso se va a resolver **al final**. *That will be resolved in the end.*
al menos	Nos quedan **al menos** dos horas. *We have at least two hours left.*
al principio	**Al principio** no se sabe quién es el narrador. *In the beginning we don't know who the narrator is.*

---

[2] See Chapter 8.B.26, pages 303–304, for more on expressing matters related to time.

a lo mejor	¿Qué es eso? No sé; **a lo mejor** es el viento. *What is that? I do not know; maybe it is the wind.*
a mano	Está hecho **a mano**. *It is handmade.*
a menudo	Visito a mi abuela **a menudo**. *I visit my grandmother frequently (often).*
a ojo	No tengo cinta métrica; tendré que calcular la distancia **a ojo**. *I do not have a measuring tape; I will have to calculate the distance by eye (roughly, by guessing).*
a pesar de	Me gusta jugar en la nieve **a pesar del** frío. *I like to play in the snow in spite of the cold.*
a pie	Prefiero ir **a pie** por el ejercicio. *I would rather go on foot (walk) for the exercise.*
a tiempo[2]	La clase siempre termina **a tiempo**. *Class always finishes on time.*
a veces[2]	**A veces** no sé qué decir. *Sometimes I do not know what to say.*

(4) Verbs with a[3]

acostumbrarse a + *inf.*	**Me acostumbré a** bañarme con agua fría. *I got used to bathing with cold water.*
aprender a + *inf.*	Quiero **aprender a** patinar. *I want to learn how to skate.*
apresurarse a + *inf.*	**Se apresuró a** ayudar a las víctimas. *She rushed to help the victims.*

---

[3] Some verbs, like **aprender**, use **a** only to link to a following infinitive; others, like **acostumbrarse**, use **a** with any object including an infinitive; still others, like **asistir**, govern **a**, but do not take infinitives.

asistir a + *noun (not inf.)*	**Asistieron a** clase ayer. *They attended class yesterday.*
atreverse a + *inf.*	**Se atrevió a** hablar. *He dared to speak.*
ayudar a + *inf.*	Me **ayudaron a** conseguir seguro médico. *They helped me get medical insurance.*
comenzar a + *inf.*	**Comencé a** estudiar el caso hace dos años. *I began to study the case two years ago.*
detenerse a + *inf.*	Los turistas **se detuvieron a** admirar la estatua. *The tourists stopped to admire the statue.*
empezar a + *inf.*	Los pájaros **empiezan a** cantar al amanecer. *The birds begin to sing at dawn.*
enseñar a + *inf.*	¿Quién te **enseñó a** cantar así? *Who taught you to sing like that?*
invitar a + *inf.*	Te **invito a** cenar fuera. *I invite you to eat dinner out.*
ir a + *inf.*	**Vamos a** lograr la paz. *We are going to achieve peace.*
negarse a + *inf.*	La víctima **se negó a** identificar al criminal. *The victim refused to identify the criminal.*
ponerse a + *inf.*	De repente, **se puso a** gritar. *Suddenly, he began to scream.*
resignarse a + *inf.*	Tendrás que **resignarte a** ganar menos dinero. *You will have to resign yourself to earning less money.*
volver a + *inf.*	Tu amigo te **volvió a** llamar. *Your friend called you again.*

b. Con

(1) Usage

CON	
USAGE	EXAMPLES
To express accompaniment	**Vengan <u>con</u> nosotros al cine.** *Come with us to the movies.*
Followed by a noun in adverbial expressions	**Lo visitamos <u>con</u> frecuencia.** *We visit him frequently.*
To indicate adherence, content, possession	**El hombre <u>con</u> la guitarra se llama José.** *The man with the guitar is named José.*
Followed by an instrument or tool	**Tendremos que cortarlo <u>con</u> el serrucho.** *We will have to cut it with the saw.*
To indicate relation	**Habló <u>con</u> su novia.** *He spoke with his girlfriend.*
To indicate concession	**<u>Con</u> todo el dinero que tiene, más vale que no se queje.** *With all the money he has, he'd better not complain.*

(2) Expressions with **con**

con respecto a	No sé qué hacer **con respecto a** mi abuela. *I do not know what to do regarding (about) my grandmother.*
con tal (de) que	Te ayudaré **con tal (de) que** me pagues. *I will help you provided that you pay me.*

(3) Verbs with **con**

casarse con	**Se casó con** un arborista. *She married an arborist.*
encontrarse con	**Me encontré con** mis compañeros en el centro. *I met my friends downtown.*
enojarse con	Creo que **se enojó conmigo**. *I think she got mad at me.*

meterse con	No **te metas con** esa pandilla. *Do not get involved (mixed up) with that gang.*
quedarse con	**Se quedó con** mi diccionario. *She kept my dictionary.*
soñar con	Anoche **soñé con** la luna. *Last night I dreamed about the moon.*

c. De

(1) Usage

DE	
USAGE	**EXAMPLES**
Possession	El suéter **de** María es lindo. *Maria's sweater is pretty.*
Origin, nationality	Jorge es **de** Colombia. *Jorge is from Colombia.*
Material something is made of	La mesa es **de** madera. *The table is (made of) wood.*
With noun complements functioning as adjectives	Me encanta la clase **de** español. *I love Spanish class.*
Followed by a noun, to describe condition or state	**De** niña, me dormía fácilmente. *As a child, I fell asleep easily.*
With **estar** to signify *acting as*	Está **de** directora este año. *She's working (acting) as director this year.*
With **estar** in typical expressions: **de pie, de rodillas, de luto, de acuerdo con, de buen humor, de mal humor, a favor de, en contra de, de huelga, de vacaciones, de viaje, de visita, de vuelta, de regreso**	No estoy **de** acuerdo contigo. *I do not agree with you.* Los obreros están **de** huelga. *The workers are on strike.*
To indicate the place of something or someone	La farmacia **de** la esquina cerró. *The corner drugstore closed.* Conozco a la gente **del** barrio. *I know the people in the neighborhood.*
To describe people by something physical or worn	¿Ves al hombre **del** bigote? *Do you see the man with the mustache?* Es la mujer **de** ojos azules. *It's the woman with blue eyes.*

(2) Expressions with de[4]

de buena / mala gana	Lo hizo **de buena gana**. *He did it willingly.*
de esta manera	Mira, se hace **de esta manera**. *Look, this is the way you do it.*
de modo que	Habló rápido **de modo que** no la interrumpieran. *She spoke quickly so that they would not interrupt her.* **De modo que** no me vas a decir tu secreto, ¿eh? *So, you are not going to tell me your secret, are you?*
de nuevo	El partido quedó **de nuevo** en empate. *The game was tied again.*
de pie	He estado **de pie** todo el día. *I have been standing all day long.*
de repente	**De repente** empezó a llover a cántaros. *Suddenly it started pouring.*
de veras	**De veras** que no sé la respuesta. *I really do not know the answer.*
de vez en cuando	**De vez en cuando** se aparece sin avisar. *Once in a while he shows up without warning.*

(3) Verbs with de

acabar de + *inf.*	**Acabo de** comer. *I just ate.* **Acababa de** comer. *I had just eaten.* **Acabé de** comer. *I finished eating.*
acordarse de	**Me acordé de** ponerme el reloj. *I remembered to put on my watch.*
alegrarse de	**Me alegro de** verte. *I am glad to see you.*

---

[4] See Chapter 7.D, page 274, for expressions with **estar** + **de**.

arrepentirse de	**Se arrepintió de** haberse burlado de ella. *He regretted having made fun of her.*
avergonzarse de	**Me avergüenzo de** mis estupideces. *I am ashamed of my stupidities.*
burlarse de	¡No **se burlen de** él! *Do not make fun of him!*
darse cuenta de	**Me di cuenta de** mi error. *I realized my mistake.*
dejar de	**Dejen de** molestar al perro. *Stop bothering the dog.*
depender de	—¿Cuál es la verdad? —**Depende de** quién habla. *"Which is the truth?"* *"It depends on who is speaking."*
despedirse de	**Nos despedimos de** nuestros padres en el aeropuerto. *We said good-bye to our parents at the airport.*
enamorarse de	**Se enamoró de** ella. *He fell in love with her.*
enterarse de	¿**Te enteraste de** las noticias? *Did you hear (find out about) the news?*
estar enamorado(a) de	**Estamos enamorados de** la misma chica. *We are in love with the same girl.*
irse de + *place*	**Se fueron de** la universidad ayer. *They left the university yesterday.*
olvidarse de	No **te olvides de** sacar la basura. *Do not forget to take out the garbage.*
pensar de	¿Qué **piensas de** este libro? *What do you think about this book?* *(i.e., Do you like it?)*
quejarse de	**Se quejaron de** la duración del vuelo. *They complained about the duration of the flight.*

reírse de	Me gusta que **te rías de** mis chistes. *I like it that you laugh at my jokes.*
terminar de + *inf.*	**Terminaron de** comer y se fueron. *They finished eating and left.*
tratar de + *inf.*	**Trataron de** ayudarme, pero no pudieron. *They tried to help me, but could not.*
tratarse de	—Me gustó esa película. —¿**De** qué **se trata**? —**Se trata de** una familia durante la Segunda Guerra Mundial. *"I liked that movie."* *"What is it about?"* *"It is about a family during the Second World War."*

d. En

(1) Usage

EN	
USAGE	EXAMPLES
To indicate where something takes place or is located	**Estábamos en la playa.** *We were at the beach.*
Signifying *in, inside*	**Ese cuaderno está en mi mochila.** *That notebook is in my backpack.*
Signifying *on, on top of*	**Tu libro está en mi escritorio.** *Your book is on my desk.*
With time expressions—months, years, and other expressions of time (but not days of the week: **Lo haré el lunes.** *I will do it on Monday.*)	**La visité en enero.** *I visited her in January.* **No quería verlo en ese momento.** *I did not want to see him at that moment.*
With ordinal numbers followed by the infinitive	**Fue el primero en irse.** *He was the first to leave.*

(2) Expressions with **en**

en cambio	Yo no hablaba su idioma; ellos, **en cambio**, sí hablaban inglés. *I did not speak their language; they, however, did speak English.*
en cuanto	Llámame **en cuanto** llegues a casa, por favor. *Call me as soon as you get home, please.*
en cuanto a	**En cuanto a** la comida india, no sé mucho. *In regard to Indian food, I do not know much.*
enfrente de	Se sentó **enfrente de** mí en el cine. *She sat in front of me at the movies.*
enseguida	Vendrá **enseguida**. *He will come right away (immediately).*
en vez de	**En vez de** llorar, deberíamos reír. *Instead of crying, we should laugh.*

(3) Verbs with **en**
Some of these may take the infinitive, others not.

consentir en	Ella nunca **consentirá en** casarse contigo. *She will never consent to marrying you.*
consistir en	¿**En** qué **consiste** este programa? *What does this program consist of?*
convenir en	**Convinimos en** encontrarnos a las diez. *We agreed to meet at ten.*
convertirse en	Estas semillas pronto **se convertirán en** plantitas. *These seeds will soon become little plants.*
empeñarse en	**Se empeñó en** pagarme lo que me debía. *He insisted on paying me what he owed me.*

entrar en	**Entró en** la sala cantando. *He entered the room singing.*
especializarse en	Ella **se especializa en** ingeniería. *She is majoring in engineering.*
fijarse en	No **me había fijado en** sus ojos. *I had not noticed his eyes.*
influir en	La enseñanza **influye en** nuestras decisiones. *Education influences our decisions.*
insistir en	**Insistimos en** pagar. *We insist on paying.*
pensar en	**Pienso en** ti a menudo. *I often think of you.*
tardar en	**Tardaron** mucho **en** responder. *They took a long time to respond.*

Ejercicios 4.2–4.7, páginas 419–421

e. Para

(1) Usage

PARA	
USAGE	EXAMPLES
Destination	**Lo escribí para la profesora de historia.** *I wrote it for the history professor.*
Purpose	**Lo hice para ti.** *I did it for you.* (e.g., to give it to you) **Fue a la tienda para comprar pan.** *He went to the store to (in order to) buy bread.* **¿Para qué sirve esto?** *What is this for?* **Es un buen libro para leer.** *It is a good book to read.* **Necesita una mesa para estudiar.** *He needs a table to study.*
Destination in time, deadline	**Lo terminaré para las diez.** *I will finish by ten.*
Destination in space	**Salimos para Europa.** *We left for Europe.* **Ven para acá.** *Come over here.*
Comparison with the norm	**Para extranjero, habla muy bien.** *For (Considering he is) a foreigner, he speaks very well.*
To indicate an employer	**Ella trabaja para el gobierno.** *She works for the government.*

(2) Expressions with **para**

no estar para bromas	**No estoy para bromas** hoy. *I am not in the mood for jokes today.*
no ser para tanto	¡No llores! **No es para tanto.** *Do not cry! It is not that bad.*
para siempre	Pensé que la conferencia duraría **para siempre.** *I thought the lecture would last forever.*

f. Por

(1) Usage

POR	
USAGE	**EXAMPLES**
To introduce the agent of the passive voice	**Esa novela fue escrita por Cervantes.** *That novel was written by Cervantes.*
Reason	**Lo hice por ti.** *I did it because of you.*
Cause	**Por comer tanto, le dio dolor de estómago.** *He got a stomachache from eating so much.* **No fuimos por la lluvia.** *We did not go because of the rain.*
Through time	**Trabajó por dos horas.** *She worked for two hours.*
Through space	**Pasamos por el parque.** *We went through the park.* **Los vi por aquí.** *I saw them somewhere around here.*
Means of communication	**Te llamaron por teléfono.** *They called you on the phone.*
Means of transportation	**Lo mandaron por avión.** *They sent it (via) airmail.*
Exchange *(in exchange for)*	**Te daré un dólar por tu ayuda.** *I will give you a dollar (in exchange) for your help.*
Indicating substitution *(instead of)*	**Ella trabajó por mí porque estaba enfermo.** *She worked for (instead of) me, because I was ill.*
With verbs of movement, introducing a noun, signifying *to get* or *to fetch*	**Fue a la tienda por pan.** *He went to the store for (to fetch) bread.*
With *estar*, meaning *to be about to* (in Latin America) or *to be in favor of*	**Estamos por salir.** *We are about to leave.* **Yo estoy por la libertad de expresión.** *I am in favor of freedom of speech.*
With *quedar*, followed by the infinitive meaning *(yet) to be done*	**Me quedan dos tareas por hacer.** *I have two assignments (yet) to be done.*

(2) Expressions with por

por eso	Llueve. **Por eso** llevo el paraguas. *It is raining. That is why I am taking my umbrella.*
por fin	**Por fin** me dejaron jugar. *They finally let me play.*
por lo general	**Por lo general** estudio de noche. *As a rule, I study at night.*
por lo menos	Me dijo que tardaría **por lo menos** una hora. *He told me that it would take him at least an hour.*
por otra parte	No me gusta el clima aquí. **Por otra parte,** sí me gusta el pueblo. *I do not like the climate here. On the other hand, I do like the town.*
por poco	¡**Por poco** me caigo! *I almost fell!*
por... que + *subjunctive*	**Por más que** trate, no puedo alzarlo. *However much I try, I cannot lift it.* **Por más** sed **que** tenga, no bebe. *However thirsty she may be, she will not drink.* **Por** evidente **que** fuera el peligro, nadie lo reconoció a tiempo para evitar el desastre. *However evident the danger was, nobody recognized it in time to prevent the disaster.*
por supuesto	—¿Te gustaría ir al cine conmigo? —¡**Por supuesto**! *"Would you like to go to the movies with me?" "Of course!"*

(3) Verbs with **por**

esforzarse por	Ella **se esfuerza por** darles lo mejor a sus hijos. *She makes an effort to give her children the best.*
interesarse por	**Me intereso por** tu futuro. *I am interested in your future.*
preguntar por + *person*	Llamó Carlos y **preguntó por ti.** *Carlos called and asked for you.*
preocuparse por	No **te preocupes por** mí. *Do not worry about me.*
tomar por	Lo **tomaron por** idiota. *They took him for an idiot.*

Ejercicios 4.8–4.10, páginas 421–422

4 List of Expressions with Prepositions (English–Spanish)

The following list incorporates all of the expressions from the section on prepositions. You may find it useful for studying, or for focused practice.

EXPRESSIONS WITH PREPOSITIONS

again: **de nuevo**
agree to: **convenir en**
almost: **por poco**
as soon as: **en cuanto**
ask a question: **hacer una pregunta**
ask for someone: **preguntar por alguien**
ask for something: **pedir algo**
at about, around (time): **a eso de**
at least: **al menos, por lo menos**
at the same time: **a la vez**
be about, deal with (e.g., a story): **tratarse de**
be ashamed of: **estar avergonzado(a) de, avergonzarse de**
be glad that: **alegrarse de**
be in love with: **estar enamorado(a) de**
because of something: **a causa de**
because of that: **por eso**
begin to: **comenzar a, empezar a, ponerse a**
by dint of: **a fuerza de**
complain about: **quejarse de**
consent to: **consentir en**

consist of: **consistir en**
conversely, however: **en cambio**
dare to: **atreverse a**
delay in (doing): **tardar en**
depend on: **depender de**
do again: **volver a**
fall in love with: **enamorarse de**
finally: **por fin**
find out about: **enterarse de**
finish: **terminar de**
fire someone: **despedir a alguien**
forever: **para siempre**
forget about: **olvidarse de, olvidar** (no prep.), **olvidársele a uno**
get angry with: **enojarse con**
get used to: **acostumbrarse a**
have just (done): **acabar de**
help to: **ayudar a**
however much . . . : **por... que...** + subjunctive
hurry to: **apresurarse a**
immediately: **enseguida**
in depth: **a fondo**
in front of: **enfrente de**
in general, as a rule: **por lo general**

in regard to: **en cuanto a**
in spite of: **a pesar de**
in such a way that: **de modo que**
in that way: **de esa manera**
influence: **influir en**
insist on: **empeñarse en, insistir en**
instead of: **en vez de**
intend (to do something): **pensar** + inf. (no prep.)
interest oneself in, become interested in: **interesarse por**
invite to: **invitar a**
keep: **quedarse con**
laugh at: **reírse de**
learn to: **aprender a**
look for: **buscar** (no prep.)
major (specialize) in: **especializarse en**
make an effort to: **esforzarse por**
make fun of: **burlarse de**
marry, get married to: **casarse con**
maybe: **a lo mejor**
meet: **conocer, encontrarse con**
not to be up for jokes: **no estar para bromas**

(continued)

EXPRESSIONS WITH PREPOSITIONS

not to exaggerate: **no ser para tanto**	*realize:* **darse cuenta de**	*take for:* **tomar por**
notice: **fijarse en**	*really:* **de veras**	*teach to:* **enseñar a**
of course: **por supuesto**	*refuse to:* **negarse a**	*thank (someone) for:* **agradecer** (no prep.)
often: **a menudo**	*regarding:* **con respecto a**	*that is why:* **por eso**
on foot: **a pie**	*remember:* **acordarse de**	*think about:* **pensar en, pensar de**
on horseback: **a caballo**	*repent, regret:* **arrepentirse de**	*try to:* **tratar de**
on the other hand: **por otra parte**	*say good-bye to:* **despedirse de**	*wait for:* **esperar** + *noun* (no prep.)
on time: **a tiempo**	*sometimes:* **a veces**	*willingly / unwillingly:* **de buena / mala gana**
once in a while: **de vez en cuando**	*standing:* **de pie**	*worry about:* **preocuparse por**
plan (to do something): **pensar** + *inf.* (no prep.)	*stop* (to do something): **detenerse a**	
provided that: **con tal (de) que**	*suddenly:* **de repente**	

5 Review of Expressions with Prepositions

por	(más) + *adj.* / *adv.* + que	**a**	lo mejor	**a**	pie
de	buena gana	**por**	lo menos	**de**	pie
en	cambio	**de**	mala gana	**por**	poco
en	cuanto	**al**	menos	**de**	repente
por	eso	**por**	más + *noun* + que	**para**	siempre
de	esta manera	**por**	más que	**por**	supuesto
por	fin	**a**	menudo	**con**	tal (de) que
a	fondo	**de**	modo que	**a**	tiempo
a	la vez	**de**	nuevo	**a**	veces
por	lo general	**por**	otra parte	**de**	veras

(continued)

no estar	**para**	bromas
no ser	**para**	tanto

de	vez	**en**	cuando

a	causa	**de**
a	eso	**de**
a	fuerza	**de**
a	pesar	**de**
con	respecto	**a**
en	cuanto	**a**
en	vez	**de**

acabar	**de** *(+ inf.)*	depender	**de**	olvidar	**Ø**
acordarse	**de**	despedirse	**de**	olvidarse	**de**
acostumbrarse	**a**	detenerse	**a** *(+ inf.)*	pedir *(+ thing)*	**Ø**
agradecer	**Ø**	empeñarse	**en**	pensar	**en**
alegrarse	**de**	empezar	**a** *(+ inf.)*	pensar	**Ø** *(+ inf.)*
aprender	**a** *(+ inf.)*	enamorarse	**de**	pensar *(opinion)*	**de**
apresurarse	**a** *(+ inf.)*	encontrarse	**con**	ponerse	**a** *(+ inf.)*
arrepentirse	**de**	enojarse	**con**	preguntar *(+ person)*	**por**
atreverse	**a** *(+ inf.)*	enseñar	**a** *(+ inf.)*	preocuparse	**por**
avergonzarse	**de**	enterarse	**de**	quedar	**por** *(+ inf.)*
ayudar	**a** *(+ inf.)*	esforzarse	**por**	quedarse	**con**
burlarse	**de**	especializarse	**en**	quejarse	**de**
buscar *(+ thing)*	**Ø**	esperar	**Ø**	reírse	**de**
casarse	**con**	estar enamorado(a)	**de**	resignarse	**a**
comenzar	**a** *(+ inf.)*	fijarse	**en**	soñar	**con**
consentir	**en**	influir	**en**	tardar	**en**
consistir	**en**	insistir	**en**	terminar	**de**
convenir	**en**	interesarse	**por**	tomar	**por**
convertirse	**en**	invitar	**a** *(+ inf.)*	tratar	**de** *(+ inf.)*
darse cuenta	**de**	irse	**de**	tratarse	**de**
dejar *(to let, leave)*	**Ø**	meterse	**con**	volver	**a** *(+ inf.)*
dejar *(to stop)*	**de** *(+ inf.)*	negarse	**a** *(+ inf.)*		

Ejercicios 4.11–4.22, páginas 422–426

B ADVERBS

1 Definition

An adverb is a word that modifies a verb, an adjective, another adverb, or a sentence. The following are examples of adverbs:

Hazlo **bien**.	*Do it right.*
Tienen un nivel de vida **muy** alto.	*They have a very high standard of living.*
Tu perro menea la cola **muy lentamente**.	*Your dog wags its tail very slowly.*

Adverbs and prepositions have much in common; what distinguishes them is their grammatical function in the sentence. A preposition introduces a noun or its equivalent, whereas an adverb does not. (See page 137 for a table contrasting these two functions.)

2 Adverbs Ending in **-mente**

An adverb ending in **-mente** is formed with the feminine of the adjective:

Adjective	→	**Feminine**	→	**+ -mente**
lento	→	lenta	→	lentamente

If an adjective does not have a different feminine form, the adverb is formed with the base of the adjective:

Adjective	→	**Adverb**
alegre	→	alegremente
vil	→	vilmente

An adjective with an accent maintains the accent when transformed into an adverb:

Adjective	→	**Adverb**
fácil	→	fácilmente

When placed in a series, adverbs ending in **-mente** drop the ending except for the last of the series:

El presidente habló discreta, elegante y apasionadamente.	*The president spoke discreetly, elegantly, and passionately.*

This rule may be ignored if the effect desired is one of monotony:

> El profesor presentaba sus explicaciones detalladamente, pausadamente, aburridamente.
>
> *The professor presented his explanations in detail, slowly, tediously.*

Note that one adverb ending in **-mente** may not modify another adverb ending in **-mente**. It would be incorrect to say:

> ⊠5 ~~Lo presentó sorprendentemente claramente.~~
>
> *He presented it surprisingly clearly.*

You would have to say:

> Lo presentó muy claramente. OR . . . con una claridad sorprendente.

3 Word Order

In Spanish the adverb is best placed close to the word it modifies. Notice the difference from English.

> Raúl se disculpó **elocuentemente** en su presentación.
>
> *Raúl apologized eloquently during his talk.*

> Habla **bien** el quechua.
>
> *She speaks Quechua well.*

4 Multiple-Function Words

There are words that serve as adjectives, as pronouns, or as adverbs depending upon their function in the sentence: **mucho, poco, bastante, tanto, cuanto, algo, nada,** etc. Compare the following sentences.

> **a.** Comen **mucho** pan.   *They eat a lot of bread.*
>
> **b.** Comen **mucho.**   *They eat a lot.*
>
> **c.** Corren **mucho.**   *They run a lot.*

In sentence *a.*, **mucho** modifies **pan,** and is an adjective. Notice that this is confirmed by the fact that if you changed **pan** to a plural, the adjective would also change. This is one distinction between adjectives and adverbs: adverbs are invariable, whereas adjectives change according to the nouns they modify, as the following sentence illustrates.

> **d.** Comen **muchas** frituras.   *They eat a lot of fried foods.*

---

[5] The symbol ⊠ indicates a grammatically incorrect structure.

In sentence *b.*, **mucho** can be a pronoun, which incorporates **pan,** or it could be an adverb, which is invariable and modifies the verb **comen** and does not relate to any particular food. Similarly, if you wanted **mucho** to refer to the previously mentioned **frituras,** you would say **Comen muchas.** If you are dealing with a transitive verb such as **comer,** only context can determine whether or not an object is being referred to.

In sentence *c.*, the verb is intransitive, and therefore **mucho** is an adverb.

Some adjectives are frequently used as adverbs:

Habla **claro.**	*Speak clearly.*
Caminen **derecho.**	*Walk straight ahead.*
Lo pronuncian **distinto.**	*They pronounce it differently.*
Pégale **duro.**	*Hit it hard.*
Respira **hondo.**	*Breathe deeply. (Take a deep breath.)*
Lo hice **igual.**	*I did it the same way.*
Juega **limpio.**	*Play fairly (cleanly). (Don't cheat.)*
Corro **rápido.**	*I run fast.*
Hablan **raro.**	*They speak in a strange fashion.*

In some cases, a word can have different meanings, depending upon whether it is used as an adjective or as an adverb, or whether it ends in **-mente** or not. Consider the following differences:

Es un hombre **alto / bajo.**	*He is a tall / short man.* (adjective)
Ella habla **alto / bajo.**	*She speaks loudly / quietly.* (adverb)
Es un hombre **altamente** moral.	*He is a very moral man.*
Lo hizo **bajamente.**	*He did it meanly.*

Ejercicios 4.23–4.24, páginas 426–427

5 Adverbs of Time

ADVERBS OF TIME			
ahora	now	luego	afterwards, then, thus
anoche	last night	mañana	tomorrow
anteayer	day before yesterday	mientras	while
antes	before	nunca	never
aún	still	siempre	always
ayer	yesterday	tarde	late
cuando	when	temprano	early
después	later, after	todavía	still
entonces	then	todavía no	not yet
hoy	today	ya	already
jamás	never (absolutely)	ya no	no longer

Some Examples of Usage

Aún

Aún is a synonym of **todavía**. This word exists also without an accent, in which case it means *even* and is a synonym of **incluso** (note that **aun** is not an adverb of time):

| **Aún** no la he visto. | *I have not seen it yet.* |
| **Aun** de adulto se me antojan. | *Even as an adult I crave them.* |

Nunca, jamás

Jamás is stronger than **nunca**. The two can be combined for an even stronger negative (note that, in combination, **nunca** always precedes **jamás**):

Nunca volveré.	*I shall never return.*
Jamás volveré.	*I shall **never** return.*
Nunca jamás volveré.	*I shall never, ever return.*

Tarde, temprano

Tarde and **temprano** can be used with the verb **ser** only in the very limited context of the impersonal expression of time of day, *it is late* or *it is early*, where *it* does not refer to anything specific, but is an impersonal subject similar to *it* in *it is three o'clock*:

Es **tarde**.	*It is late*. (time of day)
Es **temprano**.	*It is early*.

If the subject of *to be late / early* is a specific person or thing, you cannot use **ser** in Spanish. The most common way of making these statements is with the verb **llegar**:

Llegó tarde.	*It is late*. (the package)
Llegué tarde.	*I am late*.
Llegaste temprano.	*You are early*.

Tarde and **temprano** are commonly used with action verbs:

Comen **tarde** en España.	*They eat late in Spain.*
Me levanto **temprano**.	*I get up early.*

Tarde o temprano means *sooner or later*:

Tarde o temprano ganaremos.	*We'll win sooner or later.*

Ya, ya no, todavía, todavía no

Beware of these expressions: they are very useful if you learn their meanings, but they tend to cause confusion. Compare the following pairs of sentences:

Ya comí.	*I **already** ate.*
Todavía no he comido.	*I have **not** eaten **yet**.*
Todavía anda en triciclo.	*He **still** rides a tricycle.*
Ya no anda en triciclo.	*He **no longer** rides a tricycle.*

Ya can also be used emphatically; English would emphasize the pronunciation of specific words to indicate the same emphasis, and some dialects in English might use *already*:

¡**Ya** voy!	*I am coming!* (already, or right away)
Ya sé.	*I know (already).*

Other Examples of Adverbs of Time

Ahora tengo hambre.	*Now I am hungry.*
Anoche no pude dormir.	*I could not sleep last night.*
Llegaron **anteayer**.	*They arrived the day before yesterday.*
Lo había practicado **antes**.	*I had practiced it beforehand.*
Ayer lavé el baño.	*Yesterday I cleaned the bathroom.*
Habla **cuando** quiere.	*He speaks when he wants to.*
Nos vemos **después**.	*We shall meet afterwards.*
Entonces lo vi.	*Then I saw it.*
Hoy es mi cumpleaños.	*Today is my birthday.*
Luego la felicitaron.	*Then they congratulated her.*
Mañana será otro día.	*Tomorrow is (will be) another day.*
Lo hice **mientras** dormías.	*I did it while you were sleeping.*
Nunca he bailado tanto.	*I have never danced so much.*
Pronto se abrirán las tiendas.	*The stores will open soon.*
Son **recién** casados.	*They are newlyweds.*
Siempre te querré.	*I shall always love you.*

Ejercicios 4.25–4.26, página 427

6 Adverbs of Manner

ADVERBS OF MANNER			
así	like this, like that	**¿cómo?**	how?
bien	well	**mal**	poorly, badly
como	like, as	**según**	according to, depending on

Some Examples of Usage

Así

Así is used to signify *like this* or *like that;* English-speaking students often add **como** before it, which is a mistake. Consider the following sentences:

—¿Cómo lo hiciste? *"How did you do it?"*
—**Así.** *"Like this."*

Así can also be used as an adjective to modify a noun:

Estudiamos los adverbios, y cosas **así.** *We studied the adverbs, and things like that.*

Bien

Bien can have two meanings: when it modifies a verb it means *well;* when it modifies another adverb or an adjective, it intensifies it, and means *really* or *very*:

Cocinas **bien.** *You cook well.*

Está **bien** lindo el día. *The day is really beautiful.*

Bien used with **estar** can have different meanings:

—¿Cuál quieres? *"Which one do you want?"*
—El rojo está **bien.** *"The red one is okay (OR: good)."*

Su hija está **bien** ahora. *Your daughter is well now.*

Bien can also be used as an adjective:

Viene de una familia **bien.** *He is from a well-to-do family.*

> Ejercicio 4.27, página 428

7 Adverbs of Quantity

ADVERBS OF QUANTITY			
algo	somewhat, rather	medio	half
apenas	barely, scarcely	menos	less
bastante	rather, enough, quite, really	mucho, muy	very
casi	almost	nada	not at all
cuanto	as much	poco	little
¿cuánto?	how much?	solo*	only
demasiado	too much	tanto	so much

***Solo** as an adverb used to have an accent mark: this accent is no longer required, not even when there is possible confusion with the adjective.

Some Examples of Usage

Demasiado, mucho, muy

Demasiado is not used as frequently as *too* or *too much* are in English. The indication of excess can be in the context of the sentence, or in words such as **mucho** or **muy**, rather than in **demasiado**:

Es temprano para que vuelva.	*It is too early for him to be back.*
Ya es tarde para ti.	*It is too late for you.*
Es **muy** joven para beber.	*He is too young to drink.*
Hace **mucho** calor para salir.	*It is too hot to go out.*

If there is any ambiguity as to the indication of excess, **demasiado** would be used:

Hablas **demasiado**.   *You talk too much.*

Beware of the common mistake of combining **demasiado** and **mucho**.

Other Examples of Adverbs of Quantity

Estoy **algo** incómoda.	*I am slightly uncomfortable.*
Apenas llegamos.	*We just made it.*
Apenas si me habló.	*He barely spoke to me.*
No comes **bastante**.	*You don't eat enough.*

Es **bastante** tarde.	*It is quite late.*
Casi lo compré.	*I almost bought it.*
Come **cuanto** quiere.	*She eats as much as she wants.*
Gritan **demasiado**.	*They shout too much.*
Trabajas **mucho**.	*You work a lot (too much).*
Es **muy** fuerte.	*It is very strong.*
No estoy **nada** seguro.	*I am not at all sure.*
Se ejercita **poco**.	*He exercises little.*
Solo irá allí.	*He will only go there.*
¡Nieva **tanto**!	*It snows so much!*

Ejercicio 4.28, página 428

8 Adverbs of Confirmation, Doubt, or Negation

ADVERBS OF CONFIRMATION • DOUBT • NEGATION			
acaso	by chance	**sí**	yes
bueno	okay, all right, well	**tal vez**	perhaps, maybe
no	no, not	**también**	also, as well
¿no?	no? right? isn't it?	**tampoco**	neither
quizá(s)	perhaps, maybe	**ya**	already, enough already, I know, of course

Some Examples of Usage

Acaso

Acaso has a variety of uses, most of which carry an implication of chance:

¿**Acaso** dudas de mí?	*Perhaps you doubt me?*
¿**Acaso** compraste pan?	*By any chance did you buy bread?*
Llamemos primero, por si **acaso**.	*Let's call first, just in case.*
Si **acaso** te llaman, yo te aviso.	*If by chance they call you, I'll let you know.*

When followed by the subjunctive, **acaso** is synonymous with **quizá** and **tal vez**:

Acaso necesite tu ayuda.	*I may need your help.*

Quizá, tal vez

These two words have a similar meaning of doubt, but have uses that are slightly different. The use of the subjunctive adds to the doubt of the context, or indicates future action. Consider the following examples:

Quizá es Roberto.	*Maybe it is Roberto.*
Quizá sea Roberto.	*Maybe it might be Roberto.*
Tal vez era de noche.	*Maybe it was nighttime.*
Tal vez salgamos.	*Maybe we'll go out.*

Bueno

You are familiar with the word **bueno** as an adjective. When used adverbially in conversation, it means something like *okay*:

—¿Te llamo mañana?	*"Shall I call you tomorrow?"*
—**Bueno.**	*"Okay."*

It can also be used as a transition or pause in speech, similar to *"well . . ."* in English:

Bueno... y ahora... ¿qué hacemos?	*Well . . . and now . . . what shall we do?*

In Mexico, **¿bueno?** is used to answer the telephone. Spanish speakers from other countries might say **¿diga?** or **¿aló?**

No

No must precede the verb it modifies:

No puedo comer.	*I cannot eat.*
Puedo **no** comer.	*I can go without eating.*
No puedo **no** comer.	*I cannot go without eating.*

No is often used in the interrogative "**¿no?**" after a sentence to mean *"right?"* or something similar; a frequent mistake is to use "**¿sí?**" instead:

Fueron al cine, **¿no?**	*They went to the movies, right?*

Sí

Sí is often used to emphasize the affirmative:

—Yo no quiero ir al cine.	*"I don't want to go to the movies."*
—Pues yo **sí** (quiero).	*"Well, I do."*
Ahora **sí** que vamos a gozar.	*Now we really are going to have fun.*
Ah, no, ¡eso **sí** que no!	*Oh, no. No way! (Not a chance!)*

También, tampoco

Tampoco is the negative of **también**:

—Tengo hambre.	*"I'm hungry."*
—Yo **también**.	*"Me too."*
—Pero no quiero comer tacos.	*"But I don't want to eat tacos."*
—Yo **tampoco**.	*"Me neither."*

Ya

The colloquial interjection **"Ya"** is used as an affirmative response to indicate remembering, or completion of an action. In this usage, **"Ya"** is not synonymous with the simple affirmative **"Sí."** There is no satisfactory translation for the term in English. Below are some examples:

—¿Terminaste tu trabajo?	*"Did you finish your work?"*
—**Ya.**	*"Yes, I already finished it."*
—Marta está enferma.	*"Marta is sick."*
—**Ya.**	*"I know this already."*
—¡Apúrate! ¡Vamos a llegar tarde!	*"Hurry up! We're going to be late!"*
—**Ya ya.**	*"Okay, okay, enough already, I'm coming!"*

Ejercicios 4.29–4.30, página 429

9 Adverbial Phrases

Some of these expressions are also listed in this *Manual* under the prepositions they include.

ADVERBIAL PHRASES	
a gusto	at ease, comfortably, (to feel) at home
a medias	halfway, half
a menudo	often, frequently
al final	at the end, in the end
alguna vez	sometime, ever
en alguna parte, en algún lugar	somewhere
en fin	finally, in the long run, oh well
en resumen	in summary, all in all
no… hasta	not until
por cierto	actually, as a matter of fact, by the way
por fin	finally, at last
por poco	almost

Some Examples of Usage

Viven muy **a gusto** aquí.	*They live very comfortably here.*
No lo hagas **a medias.**	*Don't do it halfway.*
Viajan **a menudo.**	*They travel often.*
Al final de la película, lo vi.	*At the end of the movie, I saw him.*
¿Lo has visto **alguna vez**?	*Have you ever seen it?*
Lo vi **en alguna parte.**	*I saw it somewhere.*
En fin, así fue.	*Well, that's how it was.*
En resumen, me divertí.	*In summary, I had fun.*
No iré **hasta** enero.	*I won't go until January.*

Por fin llegamos.		*We finally arrived.*	
Por cierto, nevó.		*By the way, it snowed.*	
Por poco me caigo. (With **por poco**, notice the idiomatic use of the present tense to refer to the past.)		*I almost fell down.*	

> Ejercicio 4.31, páginas 429–430

10 Adverbs of Place

ADVERBS OF PLACE			
abajo	below, downstairs	cerca	close
acá	here (over here)	debajo	underneath, beneath
adelante	ahead, forward	delante	in front
adentro	inside	dentro	within, inside
adonde	where [to]	detrás	behind
¿adónde?	where [to]?	donde	where [at]
afuera	outside	¿dónde?	where [at]?
allá	there (over there)	encima	on top
allí (ahí)	there (right there)	enfrente	in front, across
aquí	here	fuera	out, outside
arriba	above, upstairs	lejos	far
atrás	behind, in back		

Some Examples of Usage

¿Adónde?, ¿dónde?, donde, adonde

¿**Adónde?** and **adonde** are used to refer to movement toward a spatial location, whereas ¿**dónde?** and **donde** are used to refer to a spatial location:

¿**Dónde** viste esa casa?	*Where did you see that house?*
No sé **dónde** está.	*I do not know where it is.*
¿**Adónde** fue?	*Where did he go?*
No me dijo **adónde** iba.	*He did not tell me where he was going.*
Está **donde** lo dejaste.	*It is where you left it.*
Iremos **adonde** nos digas.	*We shall go where you tell us to.*

Acá, allá; aquí, allí

Acá and **allá** are generally used with verbs of movement, whereas **aquí** and **allí** tend to be used with verbs of state:

Vengan **acá** primero y luego vayan **allá**.	*Come here first and then go there.*
Están **aquí** ahora.	*They are here now.*

Aquí and **allí** refer to a more specific spot or location, whereas **acá** and **allá** refer to a general area close to or far from the speaker:

—No sé dónde puse mis libros. Pensé que estaban **aquí**.	*"I don't know where I put my books. I thought they were here."*
—Creo que los vi **allá**, en el otro cuarto. Ah, no, mira: **allí** están, en el estante cerca de ti.	*"I think I saw them over there, in the other room. Oh, no, look: there they are, on the shelf next to you."*

You may also find the use of **aquí** and **allí** for contexts with movement, as in **Ven aquí** (*Come here*), or **Ponlo allí** (*Put it there*), when a more precise location is intended.

Abajo, arriba, debajo, encima

These adverbs refer to a location above or below an understood reference point within the context.

Abajo and **arriba** can translate in certain contexts as upstairs or downstairs, or up or down a street:

Ellos viven **arriba**.	*They live upstairs.*
Nosotros vivimos **abajo**.	*We live downstairs.*
Esa casa está más **arriba**.	*That house is farther up the street.*

They can also serve as exclamations to express support, opposition, or a hold-up:

¡**Arriba** la libertad!	*Long live liberty!*
¡**Abajo** el terrorismo!	*Down with terrorism!*
¡**Arriba** las manos!	*Hands up!*
OR: ¡Manos **arriba**!	

Debajo and **encima** refer to the specific, relative location of things that are on top of or underneath others:

Pon esa caja **encima**.	*Put that box on top.*
Pon la otra **debajo**.	*Put the other one underneath.*

Abajo and **arriba** can also be used similarly to **debajo** and **encima**, referring to the specific, relative location of things that are on top of or underneath others, but there can be ambiguity:

Pon esa caja **arriba**.	*Put that box on top (or upstairs).*
Pon la otra **abajo**.	*Put the other one underneath (or downstairs).*

(For uses of the preposition **bajo**, and the prepositional phrases **encima de** and **debajo de**, see the table on "Related Adverbs and Prepositions," page 137.)

Adentro, afuera; dentro, fuera

Although there is flexibility in the usage of these adverbs, **adentro** and **afuera** are most often used with literal physical location, understood in relation to a particular context. They are frequently used to refer to inside and outside a house or a building:

Ven **adentro**.	*Come inside.*
Vamos **afuera**.	*Let's go outside.*
Afuera hay un patio.	*Outside (the house) there is a patio.*

Dentro and **fuera** may refer to a figurative location:

Sufría por **dentro**, pero por **fuera** logré mantener la calma.	*I suffered inside, but on the outside I managed to stay calm.*

(For uses of the prepositional phrases **dentro de** and **fuera de**, see the table on "Related Adverbs and Prepositions," page 137.)

Adelante, atrás; delante, detrás; enfrente

The adverbs **adelante** and **atrás** will often be used with verbs of movement, in space or in time:

Vete **adelante**.	*Go to the front (forward, ahead).*
¡**Adelante**!	*Come on in!* (answering a knock at the door)
Dio un paso para **atrás**.	*He stepped back (backward).*
De aquí en **adelante** todo será diferente.	*From here on in, everything will be different.*
Años **atrás** se habían conocido en la universidad.	*Years before, they had met at the university.*

Delante and **detrás** are used in more static situations, often with implied specifics that only the rest of the context can clarify (note that **adelante** and **atrás** could also be used in these contexts, whereas **delante** and **detrás** would not be used for the previous examples):

Lo tengo **delante**.	*I have it in front (of me).*
Tiene el motor **detrás**.	*It (the car) has the engine in the back.*

Enfrente is used to indicate a location across (the street, the hall, etc.) from the speaker's point of reference:

Eva vive **enfrente**.	*Eva lives across the street.*
	Eva lives across the hallway.

> Ejercicio 4.32, página 430

(For uses of the preposition **tras**, and the prepositional phrases **delante de, detrás de, frente a,** and **enfrente de**, see the table on "Related Adverbs and Prepositions," on the following page.)

11 Related Adverbs and Prepositions

Compare the sentences in the chart on page 137, and notice the addition of **de** for certain prepositional structures.

> Ejercicio 4.33, página 431

\multicolumn{4}{c}{RELATED ADVERBS AND PREPOSITIONS}
ADVERB	EXAMPLE	PREPOSITION	EXAMPLE
abajo *below, downstairs*	**Los niños están abajo, en la cocina.** *The children are downstairs, in the kitchen.*	**bajo** *below, under (not physically underneath)*	**Nos sentamos bajo los árboles.** *We sat under the trees (not underneath their roots, however).*
(a)delante *in front, ahead*	**Sigan adelante.** *Continue ahead.*	**delante de** *in front of, ahead of*	**Ella se sienta delante de mí.** *She sits in front of me.*
(a)dentro *inside*	**Prefiero trabajar adentro.** *I prefer to work inside.*	**dentro de** *inside*	**Mi cuaderno está dentro de la gaveta.** *My notebook is inside the drawer.*
(a)fuera *outside*	**Vamos afuera a jugar.** *Let's go outside to play.*	**fuera de** *out(side) of*	**Estaba fuera de nuestro alcance.** *It was out of reach.*
alrededor *around*	**Miraron alrededor, pero no vieron nada.** *They looked around but did not see anything.*	**alrededor de** *around*	**Corrimos alrededor de la casa.** *We ran around the house.*
atrás *behind, back*	—¿Dónde están los niños? —**Están atrás, jugando a la pelota.** *"Where are the children?"* *"They are in the back, playing ball."*	**detrás de, tras** *behind, after*	**Venían detrás de nosotros.** *They were coming behind us.* **Venían tras nosotros.** *They were coming after (pursuing) us.*
cerca *near, nearby*	**Viven cerca.** *They live nearby.*	**cerca de** *near, close*	**Ese árbol está muy cerca de la casa.** *That tree is very close to the house.*
debajo *below, underneath*	**Lo pusieron debajo.** *They put it underneath.*	**debajo de** *below, under(neath)*	**El perro duerme debajo de la casa.** *The dog sleeps underneath the house.*
encima *on top*	**Cayó encima.** *It fell on top.*	**encima de** *on top of, above*	**Ponga la fruta encima de las latas de conserva.** *Put the fruit on top of the canned foods.*
enfrente *facing, in front, across the street*	**La casa de enfrente es linda.** *The house across the street is pretty.*	**enfrente de, frente a** *in front of, facing*	**Hay tres árboles frente a la casa.** *There are three trees in front of the house.*
lejos *far away*	**¿Vives lejos?** *Do you live far away?*	**lejos de** *far from*	**No está muy lejos de la casa.** *It is not very far from the house.*

C CONJUNCTIONS

1 Usage

A conjunction is a word that is used to join two parts of speech. This union may be of equal parts, or the second half of the union may be subordinated to the first. If the union is one of two equal parts, conjunctions of coordination are used; if the second part is subordinated to the first, conjunctions of subordination are used.

2 Conjunctions of Coordination

Conjunctions of coordination join any two parts of speech: nouns, adjectives, adverbs, pronouns, etc., or two clauses of equal value.

CONJUNCTIONS	
SPANISH	ENGLISH
y/e	and
o/u	or
pero	but
sino	but rather
ni… ni	neither . . . nor

Y becomes **e** before words beginning with **i** or **hi**:

| España **e** Italia están en el sur de Europa. | *Spain and Italy are in the south of Europe.* |
| Mis materias favoritas son geografía **e** historia. | *My favorite subjects are geography and history.* |

O becomes **u** before words beginning with **o** or **ho**:

| No importa que sea mujer **u** hombre. | *It does not matter whether it is a man or a woman.* |
| Siempre me preocupo por una cosa **u** otra. | *I am always worried by one thing or another.* |

Pero is used to indicate something contrary to what precedes it:

| Sé que hace frío, **pero** yo tengo calor. | *I know it is cold, but I am hot.* |
| No hace calor, **pero** yo estoy sudando. | *It is not hot, but I am sweating.* |

Sino is used after a negative to indicate alternate (rather, instead):

No fue Marta **sino** Juana la que me lo dijo.
It was not Marta, but (rather) Juana who told me.

Sino becomes the conjunction **sino que** before a conjugated verb:

No me lo vendió **sino que** me lo regaló.
She did not sell it to me, but rather gave it to me.

No solo... sino también is translated as **not only . . . but also**:

No solo trajeron flores, **sino también** una botella de vino.
They not only brought flowers, but also a bottle of wine.

Note that **también** can be omitted, and merely implied, as seen in the following sentence:

La fuerza de sus esculturas radica **no solo** en la perfección de su técnica **sino** en la forma en que el artista utiliza la pose, los gestos y la escala para transmitir emociones.
The power of his sculptures resides not only in the perfection of the artist's technique but also in the manner in which he utilizes pose, gestures, and scale to transmit emotions.

Ejercicios 4.34–4.36, páginas 431–432

3 Conjunctions of Subordination

Conjunctions of subordination introduce subordinate clauses. **Que** is the most common conjunction of subordination:

Veo **que** estás cansada.
I see (that) you are tired.

In English, the conjunction *that* may be omitted, but in Spanish it must be stated:

Dice **que** viene.
He says he is coming.

Most prepositions combine with the conjunction **que** to introduce clauses. This is usually the case when the subject of the main verb and the subject of the subordinate clause are different. Compare the following two sentences: the one on the left has the same subject **(yo)** for the main verb **(llamé)** and for the second verb **(avisarte)**; the preposition **para** is used here to introduce the infinitive, which functions as a noun. The sentence on the right has two different subjects: the subject of the main verb **(llamé)** is **yo**, whereas the subject of the subordinate verb **(vinieras)** is **tú**; here, the conjunction **que** is needed after the preposition **para** to introduce the subordinate clause:

Te llamé **para** avisarte. ⟶ Te llamé **para que** vinieras.
I called you to warn you. *I called you so (that) you would come.*

> Ejercicios 4.37–4.38, página 432

D TRANSITIONS

The following are expressions that may be useful in writing narrative or analytical essays:

con respecto a en cuanto a en lo tocante a por lo que se refiere a	*regarding / concerning / as for / as far as x is concerned*

Con respecto a su pedido, enviaré el libro esta tarde. — *Regarding your order, I will send the book this afternoon.*

En cuanto al precio, le cobraré luego. — *As for the price, I shall charge you later.*

En lo tocante al diccionario que pide, no lo tenemos. — *Concerning the dictionary you ask for, we do not have it.*

Por lo que se refiere a lo demás, me comunicaré con los interesados. — *As for the rest, I will get in touch with the interested parties.*

según	*according to*

Según el patrón, no hay fondos. — *According to the boss, there are no funds.*

por lo general	*in general / as a rule*

Por lo general, yo gano. — *In general, I win.*

al principio	*in the beginning / at first*
al final	*in the end*

Al principio, los personajes parecen inocentes, pero **al final** uno se da cuenta de lo contrario. — *In the beginning, the characters appear to be innocent, but in the end one realizes that it is the opposite.*

| en primer lugar | in the first place |
| en segundo lugar | in the second place |

En primer lugar, no tengo tiempo. *In the first place, I don't have time.*
En segundo lugar, no quiero. *In the second place, I don't want to.*

por ejemplo	for example
casi siempre	almost always
casi nunca	almost (n)ever
en gran parte	for the most part

Por ejemplo, casi siempre comen arroz blanco. *For example, they almost always eat white rice.*

| cada vez más
de más en más | more and more |
| cada vez menos
de menos en menos | less and less |

Hay **cada vez más** guerras y **cada vez menos** humanidad. *There are more and more wars and less and less humanity.*

| acaso | by chance, perhaps, maybe |
| a lo mejor
quizás
tal vez | maybe, perhaps |

¿**Acaso** no ves que lo hago por tu bien? *Don't you see that I am doing this for your own good?*

Quizás algún día comprendas: **a lo mejor** cuando te cases o **tal vez** cuando seas madre. *Maybe someday you will understand: possibly when you get married, or perhaps when you are a mother.*

| por suerte | luckily, fortunately |
| por desgracia | unfortunately |

Por desgracia, tuvo un accidente. *Unfortunately, he had an accident.*
Por suerte, nadie se hizo daño. *Luckily, nobody got hurt.*

a su vez por su parte	in turn
por otro lado	on the other hand

Mi padre, **por su parte,** nos llevaba al cine los sábados.

Por otro lado, era mi madre la que luchaba con nuestros problemas cotidianos.

My father, in turn, would take us to the movies on Saturday.

On the other hand, it was my mother who struggled with our daily problems.

entonces por consiguiente por lo tanto	thus, therefore, then
por eso por ese motivo por esa razón	for that reason
como consecuencia como resultado	as a result

Estaba harto del gobierno. **Por consiguiente,** decidió mudarse con la familia a otro país. **Por eso** terminamos viviendo en México, y **como resultado,** todos hablamos español.

He was fed up with the government. Therefore, he decided to move with his family to another country. For that reason we ended up living in Mexico, and as a result, we all speak Spanish.

de hecho	in fact, as a matter of fact
en realidad	actually
actualmente hoy en día	nowadays

En realidad, no sé cuándo empezó todo. **Actualmente** no quedan rastros de la lucha. **De hecho,** tenemos muy pocos datos.
(Notice that **actualmente** and *actually* are false cognates.)

Actually, I don't know when it all began. Nowadays there are no traces left of the struggle. As a matter of fact, we have very little information.

sin embargo no obstante	nevertheless, yet, however
a pesar de	in spite of

Somos pobres. **No obstante,** venceremos **a pesar de** todo.

We are poor. Nevertheless, we shall prevail in spite of it all.

desde	since (time)
como	since (because)

Desde el día en que llegué aquí, la vida ha sido más fácil.

Since the day I arrived here, life has been easier.

Como tenía hambre, comí.

Since I was hungry, I ate.

Certain expressions are used as transitions between related thoughts in the same sentence:

... pero / sino...	... but ...
... y / e...	... and ...
... también...	... also ...
... porque...	... because ...

To introduce a less closely connected thought, often at the beginning of a new sentence, the following expressions may be used:

Sin embargo	However But Yet
Además	In addition Also
Como **Puesto que** **Ya que** **Debido a que**	Since Because

A frequent error is the use of **pero** at the beginning of a sentence, followed by a comma. When a comma is used to separate it from what follows, the emphasis on the meaning of **pero** is such that it would be better to replace it with the stronger **sin embargo**. The same is true for **también**, which is awkward when followed by a comma: the best term in such a context would be **además**.

Consider the following informal statement:

> Ayer llamé a Luisa. **Como** ella no me llamaba, la llamé yo. **Pero** no le dije por qué llamaba **porque** no quería que supiera lo que siento. **Sin embargo,** sí quería oír su voz, y **también** contarle de la visita de mis padres. **Además,** no quería dejar pasar más tiempo sin comunicarme con ella.
>
> *Yesterday I called Luisa. Since she wouldn't call me, I called her. But I didn't tell her why I was calling because I didn't want her to know what I feel. However, I did want to hear her voice and also to tell her about my parents' visit. Besides, I didn't want to let more time go by without getting in touch with her.*

(Notice that the third sentence begins with **pero**. However, if you look closely, you will see that the third sentence is different from the fourth sentence. The third sentence is not a new thought, but is a continuation of the second sentence. It could have followed a comma or a period. The fourth sentence, on the other hand, has a different focus.)

The following expressions might be useful when concluding:

en conclusión	in conclusion

En conclusión, es mejor tratar de vivir bien. — *In conclusion, it is best to try to live well.*

para resumir en resumen en resumidas cuentas	in short, to summarize

En resumen, es un cuento de amor tradicional. — *In short, it's a traditional love story.*

Para resumir, diría que es un cuento de amor tradicional. — *To summarize, I would say it is a traditional love story.*

de lo anterior, se puede concluir que	from the above, it can be concluded that

De lo anterior, se puede concluir que no es oro todo lo que reluce. — *From the above, it can be concluded that all that glitters is not gold.*

de todos modos	*anyway*
en todo caso	*in any case*
después de todo	*after all*
a fin de cuentas	*in the end, all in all*

De todos modos, siguieron siendo amigos.

Anyway, they continued being friends.

En todo caso, nadie se mudó.

In any case, nobody moved.

Después de todo, se conocían desde la primaria.

After all, they had known each other since primary school.

A fin de cuentas, todos salieron ganando.

In the end, everyone ended up winning.

> Ejercicios 4.39–4.40, páginas 433–434;
> Ejercicios de repaso 4.41–4.42, páginas 434–436

CHAPTER 5

Verbs: Formation

A Indicative Mood

B Conditional Mood

C Subjunctive Mood

D Imperative Mood

E Infinitive

F Participle

> **NOTE:** For full conjugations of verbs, see Appendix A: Verb Tables. Appendix A also provides an index of verbs listing the table to which each conjugation corresponds.
>
> For information regarding the use of accent marks and spelling changes in verb forms, see Chapter 9, pages 346–356.

A INDICATIVE MOOD

1 Present Indicative

[For contextualized usage of the present indicative, see Chapter 6.A: Present Indicative, pages 178–179.]

a. Regular verbs

	-ar hablar	-er comer	-ir vivir
yo	hablo	como	vivo
tú	hablas	comes	vives
él, ella, usted	habla	come	vive
nosotros	hablamos	comemos	vivimos
vosotros	habláis	coméis	vivís
ellos, ellas, ustedes	hablan	comen	viven

b. Stem-changing verbs

	-ar cerrar	-er perder	-ir sentir
	cierro	pierdo	siento
	cierras	pierdes	sientes
	cierra	pierde	siente
	cerramos	perdemos	sentimos
	cerráis	perdéis	sentís
	cierran	pierden	sienten

Other verbs with **e → ie** change:

-ar	-er	-ir
comenzar	defender	mentir
empezar	encender	preferir
negar	entender	
pensar	querer	

e → i

pedir
pido
pides
pide
pedimos
pedís
piden

Other verbs with **e → i** change: **conseguir, impedir, seguir, elegir, repetir, servir**

o → ue

-ar	-er	-ir
contar	**volver**	**dormir**
cuento	vuelvo	duermo
cuentas	vuelves	duermes
cuenta	vuelve	duerme
contamos	volvemos	dormimos
contáis	volvéis	dormís
cuentan	vuelven	duermen

Other verbs with **o → ue** change:

-ar	-er	-ir
costar	devolver	morir
encontrar	llover	
mostrar	mover	
probar	poder	
recordar		

Other verbs with **o → ue** change, with some variation:

oler	jugar
huelo	juego
hueles	juegas
huele	juega
olemos	jugamos
oléis	jugáis
huelen	juegan

c. Spelling-changing verbs

Spelling changes are made to preserve the consistency of sound throughout the verb. For example, in the conjugation of verbs ending in **-ger** or **-gir,** to retain the pronunciation of /j/ in the verb stem, **g** changes to **j** before verb endings in **a** or **o.** (For more information on these spelling / pronunciation concerns, see Chapter 9, pages 320–345.)

escoger
escojo
escoges
escoge
escogemos
escogéis
escogen

Other verbs with **g → j** change:

-er	-ir
coger	corregir
proteger	dirigir
	elegir
	exigir
	fingir

$$gu \rightarrow g$$

distinguir
distingo
distingues
distingue
distinguimos
distinguís
distinguen

Other verbs with **gu → g** change: **seguir, conseguir**

> **c → zc**

Before -o: **parecer**
parezco
pareces
parece
parecemos
parecéis
parecen

Other verbs with **c → zc** change:

-er	-ir
agradecer	conducir
aparecer	introducir
conocer	producir
merecer	traducir
obedecer	
ofrecer	
permanecer	
reconocer	

> **c → z**

Before -o: **convencer**
convenzo
convences
convence
convencemos
convencéis
convencen

Other verbs with **c → z** change: **vencer, torcer, ejercer, mecer**

d. Classified irregular verbs

i → í	u → ú
enviar	**continuar**
envío	continúo
envías	continúas
envía	continúa
enviamos	continuamos
enviáis	continuáis
envían	continúan

Other verbs with **i → í / u → ú** change:

-iar	-uar
confiar	acentuar
criar	actuar
guiar	graduar

Reunir is similar:

reunir
reúno
reúnes
reúne
reunimos
reunís
reúnen

ui → uy

concluir
concluyo
concluyes
concluye
concluimos
concluís
concluyen

Other verbs with **ui → uy** change: **construir, distribuir, contribuir, huir, destruir, incluir**

e. Other irregular verbs

caer	hacer	poner*	salir	traer**	valer
caigo	hago	pongo	salgo	traigo	valgo
caes	haces	pones	sales	traes	vales
cae	hace	pone	sale	trae	vale
caemos	hacemos	ponemos	salimos	traemos	valemos
caéis	hacéis	ponéis	salís	traéis	valéis
caen	hacen	ponen	salen	traen	valen

*Like **poner**: componer, disponer, proponer, suponer
Like **traer: atraer, distraer

decir*	tener**	venir‡
digo	tengo	vengo
dices	tienes	vienes
dice	tiene	viene
decimos	tenemos	venimos
decís	tenéis	venís
dicen	tienen	vienen

*Like **decir**: desdecir, maldecir
Like **tener: atenerse, contener, detener, mantener, obtener, sostener
‡Like **venir**: convenir, prevenir

dar	estar	haber*	ir
doy	estoy	he	voy
das	estás	has	vas
da	está	ha	va
damos	estamos	hemos	vamos
dais	estáis	habéis	vais
dan	están	han	van

*Not included in the traditional conjugation, **haber** has a special third-person form—**hay,** which is used for both singular and plural and means *there is* or *there are.* (e.g., **Hay una carta.** *There is a letter.* **Hay varios ejemplos.** *There are several examples.*)

oír	saber	ser	ver
oigo	**sé**[1]	**soy**	**veo**
oyes	sabes	**eres**	ves
oye	sabe	**es**	**ve**
oímos	sabemos	**somos**	vemos
oís	sabéis	**sois**	veis
oyen	saben	**son**	ven

Ejercicios 5.1–5.9, páginas 437–442

2 Aspects of the Past Indicative

[For contextualized usage of the past indicative, see Chapter 6.B: Aspects of the Indicative Past Tense: Preterite vs. Imperfect and Pluperfect, pages 179–190.]

a. Imperfect indicative

Regular:

-ar	-er	-ir
hablar	**comer**	**vivir**
habl**aba**	com**ía**	viv**ía**
habl**abas**	com**ías**	viv**ías**
habl**aba**	com**ía**	viv**ía**
habl**ábamos**	com**íamos**	viv**íamos**
habl**abais**	com**íais**	viv**íais**
habl**aban**	com**ían**	viv**ían**

Irregular:

ir	ser	ver
iba	era	veía
ibas	eras	veías
iba	era	veía
íbamos	éramos	veíamos
ibais	erais	veíais
iban	eran	veían

Ejercicios 5.10–5.13, páginas 442–445

---

[1] Why does this word have an accent mark? For more information on accents with monosyllables, see Chapter 9, pages 441–443.

b. Preterite

Regular:

-ar	-er	-ir
hablar	**comer**	**vivir**
habl**é**	com**í**	viv**í**
habl**aste**	com**iste**	viv**iste**
habl**ó**	com**ió**	viv**ió**
habl**amos**	com**imos**	viv**imos**
habl**asteis**	com**isteis**	viv**isteis**
habl**aron**	com**ieron**	viv**ieron**

PRETERITE (Irregular Stems with "u")		
INFINITIVE	STEM	ENDINGS
andar	anduv-	
caber	cup-	-e
estar	estuv-	-iste
haber	hub-	-o
poder	pud-	-imos
poner	pus-	-isteis
saber	sup-	-ieron
tener	tuv-	

PRETERITE (Irregular Stems with "i")	
INFINITIVE	STEM
hacer[2]	hic-
querer	quis-
venir	vin-

---

[2] For the preterite of **hacer**, in third person, **hic-** changes to **hiz-** to retain the /s/ or /z/ sound before /o/, rather than /k/. For more information on this type of spelling change, see Chapter 9, page 325.

A Indicative Mood

Dar has **-ir** endings.

d**i**
d**iste**
d**io**
d**imos**
d**isteis**
d**ieron**

Ir and **ser** are identical in the preterite.

fui
fuiste
fue
fuimos
fuisteis
fueron

Irregular: stem change **c → j** (including all verbs ending in **-ducir**):

decir	producir	traer
dije	produje	traje
dijiste	produjiste	trajiste
dijo	produjo	trajo
dijimos	produjimos	trajimos
dijisteis	produjisteis	trajisteis
dijeron	produjeron	trajeron

All **-ir** verbs with stem changes in the present show stem changes in the third-person singular and plural of the preterite:

e → i			o → u
pedir	**reír**	**sentir**	**dormir**
pedí	reí	sentí	dormí
pediste	reíste	sentiste	dormiste
pidió	rio*	sintió	durmió
pedimos	reímos	sentimos	dormimos
pedisteis	reísteis	sentisteis	dormisteis
pidieron	rieron	sintieron	durmieron

*Note the absence of accent on **rio**. For information on this, see Chapter 9.I. *Summary of 2010 Ortografía Changes*, page 380.

Spelling changes:

i → y

caer	creer	leer	oír	concluir*
caí	creí	leí	oí	concluí
caíste	creíste	leíste	oíste	concluiste
cayó	creyó	leyó	oyó	concluyó
caímos	creímos	leímos	oímos	concluimos
caísteis	creísteis	leísteis	oísteis	concluisteis
cayeron	creyeron	leyeron	oyeron	concluyeron

*Applies to verbs ending in **-uir** with the same spelling change in the present tense.

c → qu **g → gu** **z → c**

buscar	llegar	alcanzar
busqué	llegué	alcancé
buscaste	llegaste	alcanzaste
buscó	llegó	alcanzó
buscamos	llegamos	alcanzamos
buscasteis	llegasteis	alcanzasteis
buscaron	llegaron	alcanzaron

Other verbs with **c → qu / g → gu / z → c** changes[3]:

-car	-gar	-zar
explicar	apagar	almorzar
sacar	colgar	comenzar
tocar	entregar	empezar
	jugar	
	negar	
	pagar	

Ejercicios 5.14–5.18, páginas 445–448

---

[3] For more information on these spelling changes, see Chapter 9, pages 325–330.

c. Present perfect indicative

[For contextualized usage of the present perfect indicative, see Chapter 6.B.13, page 189, and Chapter 6.C.2, page 192]

The present perfect indicative is formed with the present indicative of the auxiliary **haber** + *past participle* ending in **-o**:

> **he**
> **has**
> **ha**   (hablado)
> **hemos**
> **habéis**
> **han**

Ejercicio 5.19, página 448

d. Pluperfect indicative

[For contextualized usage of the pluperfect indicative, see Chapter 6.B.13, page 189, and Chapter 6.C.2.c, page 192.]

The pluperfect indicative is formed with the imperfect indicative of the auxiliary **haber** + *past participle* ending in **-o**:

> **había**
> **habías**
> **había**   (hablado)
> **habíamos**
> **habíais**
> **habían**

Ejercicio 5.20, página 449

3 Future

[For contextualized usage of the future, see Chapter 6.C.2.b, page 192, Chapter 6.D, page 199, and Chapter 6.F, pages 201–203.]

a. Simple future

The future tense is formed with the infinitive plus endings that are identical for all verbs:

-ar	-er	-ir
hablar	**comer**	**vivir**
hablaré	comeré	viviré
hablarás	comerás	vivirás
hablará	comerá	vivirá
hablaremos	comeremos	viviremos
hablaréis	comeréis	viviréis
hablarán	comerán	vivirán

FUTURE TENSE (Irregular Stems)

INFINITIVE	STEM	INFINITIVE	STEM
caber	cabr-	querer	querr-
decir*	dir-	saber	sabr-
haber	habr-	salir	saldr-
hacer**	har-	tener†	tendr-
poder	podr-	valer	valdr-
poner‡	pondr-	venir	vendr-

Verbs derived from these have the same irregularity: *desdecir, **deshacer, ‡suponer, †mantener, etc.

Ejercicios 5.21–5.23, páginas 449–450

b. Future perfect

The future perfect tense is formed with the future of the auxiliary **haber** + *past participle* ending in **-o**:

habré	
habrás	
habrá	(hablado)
habremos	
habréis	
habrán	

Ejercicio 5.24, página 450

B CONDITIONAL MOOD

[For contextualized usage of the conditional, see Chapter 6.E, pages 200–201, Chapter 6.F, pages 201–203, and Chapter 6.G.6, pages 228–230.]

1 Present Conditional

The present conditional is formed with the infinitive plus endings that are identical for all verbs:

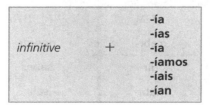

-ar	-er	-ir
hablar	**comer**	**vivir**
hablaría	comería	viviría
hablarías	comerías	vivirías
hablaría	comería	viviría
hablaríamos	comeríamos	viviríamos
hablaríais	comeríais	viviríais
hablarían	comerían	vivirían

CONDITIONAL (Irregular Stems)			
INFINITIVE	STEM	INFINITIVE	STEM
caber	cabr-	querer	querr-
decir*	dir-	saber	sabr-
haber	habr-	salir	saldr-
hacer**	har-	tener†	tendr-
poder	podr-	valer	valdr-
poner‡	pondr-	venir	vendr-

Verbs derived from these have the same irregularity: ***desdecir,** ***deshacer,** ‡**suponer,** †**mantener,** etc.

Ejercicios 5.25–5.26, página 451

2 Conditional Perfect

The conditional perfect is formed with the present conditional of the auxiliary **haber** + *past participle* ending in **-o:**

habría	
habrías	
habría	(hablado)
habríamos	
habríais	
habrían	

Ejercicio 5.27, páginas 451–452;
Ejercicio de repaso 5.28, página 452

C SUBJUNCTIVE MOOD

[For contextualized usage of the subjunctive, see Chapter 6.G, pages 203–218.]

1 Present Subjunctive

a. Regular verbs

The present subjunctive is formed by dropping the **o** of the first-person singular present indicative and adding the "opposite" vowel endings: **e** for **-ar** verbs and **a** for **-ir / -er** verbs:

	-ar **hablar**	-er **comer**	-ir **vivir**
yo	hable	coma	viva
tú	hables	comas	vivas
él, ella, usted	hable	coma	viva
nosotros	hablemos	comamos	vivamos
vosotros	habléis	comáis	viváis
ellos, ellas, ustedes	hablen	coman	vivan

b. Stem-changing verbs

If the verb is stem-changing in the present indicative, the present subjunctive will show the same changes:

cerrar	**perder**	**contar**	**volver**
cierre	pierda	cuente	vuelva
cierres	pierdas	cuentes	vuelvas
cierre	pierda	cuente	vuelva
cerremos	perdamos	contemos	volvamos
cerréis	perdáis	contéis	volváis
cierren	pierdan	cuenten	vuelvan

Exceptions: In the first- and second-person plural forms of stem-changing **-ir** verbs, the **e** of the stem changes to **i**, and the **o** of the stem changes to **u**:

pedir	**sentir**	**dormir**
pida	sienta	duerma
pidas	sientas	duermas
pida	sienta	duerma
pidamos	sintamos	durmamos
pidáis	sintáis	durmáis
pidan	sientan	duerman

c. Irregular verbs

If the verb is irregular in the present indicative, the present subjunctive will show the same irregularities:

decir	oír	tener
diga	oiga	tenga
digas	oigas	tengas
diga	oiga	tenga
digamos	oigamos	tengamos
digáis	oigáis	tengáis
digan	oigan	tengan

enviar	continuar	reunir
envíe	continúe	reúna
envíes	continúes	reúnas
envíe	continúe	reúna
enviemos	continuemos	reunamos
enviéis	continuéis	reunáis
envíen	continúen	reúnan

parecer	conducir	concluir
parezca	conduzca	concluya
parezcas	conduzcas	concluyas
parezca	conduzca	concluya
parezcamos	conduzcamos	concluyamos
parezcáis	conduzcáis	concluyáis
parezcan	conduzcan	concluyan

The following verbs also maintain the irregularity throughout all persons:

PRESENT SUBJUNCTIVE (Irregular Stems)			
INFINITIVE	1st Person	INFINITIVE	1st Person
caber	quepa	salir	salga
caer	caiga	traer	traiga
hacer	haga	valer	valga
poner	ponga	venir	venga

Even **dar, estar, haber, ir, saber,** and **ser,** all of which have a first-person singular present indicative that does not end with **-o,** remain regular in their endings:

dar[4]	**estar**	**haber**
dé	esté	haya
des	estés	hayas
dé	esté	haya
demos	estemos	hayamos
deis	estéis	hayáis
den	estén	hayan

ir	**saber**	**ser**
vaya	sepa	sea
vayas	sepas	seas
vaya	sepa	sea
vayamos	sepamos	seamos
vayáis	sepáis	seáis
vayan	sepan	sean

If the verb has spelling changes in the present indicative, the present subjunctive will show the same irregularities:

$g \rightarrow j$

escoger	**dirigir**
escoja	dirija
escojas	dirijas
escoja	dirija
escojamos	dirijamos
escojáis	dirijáis
escojan	dirijan

$gu \rightarrow g$

distinguir
distinga
distingas
distinga
distingamos
distingáis
distingan

$c \rightarrow z$ $c \rightarrow qu$ $g \rightarrow gu$ $z \rightarrow c$

convencer	**buscar**	**llegar**	**alcanzar**
convenza	busque	llegue	alcance
convenzas	busques	llegues	alcances
convenza	busque	llegue	alcance
convenzamos	busquemos	lleguemos	alcancemos
convenzáis	busquéis	lleguéis	alcancéis
convenzan	busquen	lleguen	alcancen

---

[4] The first- and third-person singular forms of **dar** have an accent to differentiate them from the preposition **de.** For more on accents of this nature, see Chapter 9, page 351.

All verbs ending in:

-ger are like **escoger** (g → j)	**-car** are like **buscar** (c → qu)
-gir are like **dirigir** (g → j)	**-gar** are like **llegar** (g → gu)
-guir are like **distinguir** (gu → g)	**-zar** are like **alcanzar** (z → c)

Most verbs ending in a vowel plus **-cer** and **-cir** and all verbs ending in **-ducir** are like **parecer**. Verbs ending in **-ncer** and **-ncir** are like **convencer** (c → z).

(For more information on the above spelling changes, see Chapter 9, pages 325–330.)

> Ejercicios 5.29–5.34, páginas 452–454

2 Imperfect Subjunctive

The imperfect subjunctive of all verbs without exception is formed by dropping **-ron** from the third-person plural preterite and adding **-ra, -ras, -ra, -´ramos*, -rais, -ran** or **-se, -ses, -se, -´semos*, -seis, -sen.** In most of Latin America, the **-ra** forms predominate. (*The accent before **nosotros** endings [-´ramos / -´semos] indicates that the preceding syllable requires an accent mark.)

	-ar **hablar**	-er **comer**	-ir **vivir**
yo	habla**ra**	comie**ra**	vivie**ra**
tú	habla**ras**	comie**ras**	vivie**ras**
él, ella, usted	habla**ra**	comie**ra**	vivie**ra**
nosotros	hablá**ramos**	comié**ramos**	vivié**ramos**
vosotros	habla**rais**	comie**rais**	vivie**rais**
ellos, ellas, ustedes	habla**ran**	comie**ran**	vivie**ran**

OR:

yo	habla**se**	comie**se**	vivie**se**
tú	habla**ses**	comie**ses**	vivie**ses**
él, ella, usted	habla**se**	comie**se**	vivie**se**
nosotros	hablá**semos**	comié**semos**	vivié**semos**
vosotros	habla**seis**	comie**seis**	vivie**seis**
ellos, ellas, ustedes	habla**sen**	comie**sen**	vivie**sen**

C Subjunctive Mood

All verbs with an irregular stem in the preterite show the same irregularities in the imperfect subjunctive:

IMPERFECT SUBJUNCTIVE (Irregular Stems)			
INFINITIVE	1st Person	INFINITIVE	1st Person
andar	anduviera	poder	pudiera
caber	cupiera	poner	pusiera
caer	cayera	poseer	poseyera
concluir	concluyera	preferir	prefiriera
conducir	condujera	producir	produjera
dar	diera	querer	quisiera
decir	dijera	reír	riera
dormir	durmiera	saber	supiera
estar	estuviera	seguir	siguiera
haber	hubiera	sentir	sintiera
ir	fuera	ser	fuera
leer	leyera	tener	tuviera
oír	oyera	traer	trajera
pedir	pidiera	venir	viniera

Ejercicios 5.35–5.36, páginas 455–456

3 Present Perfect Subjunctive

The present perfect subjunctive is formed with the present subjunctive of the auxiliary **haber** + *past participle* ending in **-o:**

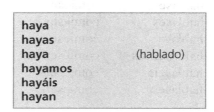

Ejercicio 5.37, página 456

4 Pluperfect Subjunctive

The pluperfect subjunctive is formed with the imperfect subjunctive of the auxiliary **haber** + *past participle* ending in **-o:**

> **hubiera**
> **hubieras**
> **hubiera**   (hablado)
> **hubiéramos**
> **hubierais**
> **hubieran**

OR:

> **hubiese**
> **hubieses**
> **hubiese**   (hablado)
> **hubiésemos**
> **hubieseis**
> **hubiesen**

> Ejercicio 5.38, página 457;
> Ejercicio de repaso 5.39, página 457

D IMPERATIVE MOOD

1 Direct Commands

a. Tú

Affirmative informal commands are formed with the third-person singular of the present indicative:

Examples: habla, come, vive, cierra, abre

There are eight exceptions:

TÚ IMPERATIVE (Irregular Affirmative Forms)			
INFINITIVE	FORM	INFINITIVE	FORM
decir	di	salir	sal
hacer	haz	ser	sé[5]
ir	ve	tener	ten
poner	pon	venir	ven

Object pronouns are attached to the endings of the affirmative imperative (enclitic), and a written accent is added when it is necessary to maintain stress on the same syllable of the stem. (For more information on this use of the accent mark, see Chapter 9, page 350.)

Háblame.	*Talk to me.*
Ciérrala.	*Close it.* (**la** = **la puerta**)
Ábrelo.	*Open it.* (**lo** = **el sobre**)
Dímelo.	*Tell it to me.* (**lo** = **el secreto**)
Hazlo.	*Do it.* (**lo** = **el trabajo**)
Vete.	*Go away.* (**irse** is reflexive)
Póntelo.	*Put it on.* (**lo** = **el abrigo**; **ponerse** is reflexive)

Negative **tú** commands are formed with the second-person singular of the present subjunctive:

Examples: no hables, no comas, no vivas, no cierres, no abras

Those irregular in the affirmative are regular in the negative:

TÚ IMPERATIVE (Negative Forms)			
INFINITIVE	FORM	INFINITIVE	FORM
decir	no digas	salir	no salgas
hacer	no hagas	ser	no seas
ir	no vayas	tener	no tengas
poner	no pongas	venir	no vengas

---

[5] For more information on accents with monosyllables, see Chapter 9, pages 351–352.

Pronouns are placed before the imperative in the negative:

No me hables.	*Do not talk to me.*
No la cierres.	*Do not close it.*
No lo abras.	*Do not open it.*
No me lo digas.	*Do not tell it to me.*
No lo hagas.	*Do not do it.*
No te vayas.	*Do not go away.*
No te lo pongas.	*Do not put it on.*

> Ejercicios 5.40–5.43, páginas 458–459

b. Usted / ustedes

The imperative of **usted / ustedes** is formed with the third-person singular and plural of the present subjunctive, for both the affirmative and the negative:

hable	coma	viva	cierre	abra
no hable	no coma	no viva	no cierre	no abra
hablen	coman	vivan	cierren	abran
no hablen	no coman	no vivan	no cierren	no abran

The formal command may be followed by **usted / ustedes** to be more polite:

Hable usted con la gerencia.	*Speak with the management.*
Pidan ustedes lo que deseen.	*Order whatever you wish.*

Examples of affirmative **usted / ustedes** imperatives with pronouns:

USTED(ES) IMPERATIVES (Affirmative Forms)		
USTED	**USTEDES**	**TRANSLATION**
hábleme	**háblenme**	*talk to me*
ciérrela	**ciérrenla**	*close it*
ábralo	**ábranlo**	*open it*
dígamelo	**díganmelo**	*tell it to me*
hágalo	**háganlo**	*do it*
váyase	**váyanse**	*go away*
póngaselo	**pónganselo**	*put it on*

Note in the above table the use of accent marks on these combinations of verb + attached pronoun. For more information on this use of the accent, see Chapter 9, page 350.

Examples of negative **usted / ustedes** imperatives with pronouns:

USTED(ES) IMPERATIVES (Negative Forms)		
USTED	USTEDES	TRANSLATION
no me hable	no me hablen	*do not talk to me*
no la cierre	no la cierren	*do not close it*
no lo abra	no lo abran	*do not open it*
no me lo diga	no me lo digan	*do not tell it to me*
no lo haga	no lo hagan	*do not do it*
no se vaya	no se vayan	*do not go away*
no se lo ponga	no se lo pongan	*do not put it on*

Ejercicio 5.44, página 459

c. Vosotros

The affirmative **vosotros** command is formed with the infinitive, minus the **r**, plus **d**:

hablad	decid
cerrad	haced
abrid	id

Examples of affirmative **vosotros** imperatives with pronouns:

Habladme.	*Talk to me.*
Cerradla.	*Close it.*
Abridlo.	*Open it.*
Decídmelo.	*Tell it to me.*

With the reflexive pronoun **os**, the **d** of the ending is dropped. (The only exception is **ir: idos**.)

Levantaos.	*Get up.*
Callaos.	*Be quiet.*
Laváoslas.	*Wash them.* (**las = las manos**)
Ponéoslo.	*Put it on.*

Note that although it is not grammatically correct, in colloquial speech, the final **-d** is replaced by **-r** for the affirmative commands. Thus, **venir** or **escuchar** are used in place of **venid** or **escuchad.** For imperatives of reflexives, an **-r** is often added prior to the pronoun at the end, not only for **iros,** but also for the rest, that would normally omit the **-d** entirely. Thus, **callaros** and **acercaros** are used in place of **callaos** and **acercaos.**

(For more information on the use of the accent mark with these forms, see Chapter 9, pages 347–348.)

The negative **vosotros** imperative is formed with the second-person plural of the present subjunctive:

No me habléis.	*Do not talk to me.*
No la cerréis.	*Do not close it.*
No me lo digáis.	*Do not tell it to me.*
No lo hagáis.	*Do not do it.*
No os vayáis.	*Do not go away.*
No os lo pongáis.	*Do not put it on.*

Ejercicios 5.45–5.48, páginas 460–461

d. Nosotros

Affirmative commands are formed with the first-person plural of the present subjunctive:

hablemos	digamos
comamos	hagamos
abramos	pongamos

Exception: Ir and **irse** in the affirmative imperative become **vamos** and **vámonos.** With pronouns[6]:

Hablémosle.	*Let's talk to him.*
Cerrémosla.	*Let's close it.*
Abrámoslo.	*Let's open it.*
Hagámoslo.	*Let's do it.*

---

[6] Note the use of accent marks on these combinations of verb + attached pronoun. For more information on this use of the accent, see Chapter 9, page 350.

With **nos** and **se,** drop the final **-s** of the verb:

Digámoselo.	*Let's tell it to him.*
Levantémonos.	*Let's get up.*
Callémonos.	*Let's be quiet.*
Lavémonoslas.	*Let's wash them.*
Pongámonoslo.	*Let's put it on.*

In the negative imperative, pronouns precede the verb:

No le hablemos.	*Let's not talk to him.*
No la cerremos.	*Let's not close it.*
No lo hagamos.	*Let's not do it.*
No nos levantemos.	*Let's not get up.*
No nos las lavemos.	*Let's not wash them.*

> Ejercicios 5.49–5.50, página 461

2 Indirect Commands

When a command is being given to one person, but is meant to be carried out by another, use **que** + *present subjunctive* in third-person singular or plural:

Que venga.	*Let him come. Have him come. Tell him to come.*
Que lo haga Regina.	*Let Regina do it. Have her do it. Tell her to do it.*
Que pague Elena.	*Let Elena pay. Have her pay. Tell her to pay.*

> Ejercicios 5.51–5.52, página 461;
> Ejercicios de repaso 5.53–5.57, páginas 462–463

E INFINITIVE

1 Present Infinitive

This is the standard form used as identification of any verb:

    hablar *to speak*

    comer *to eat*

    vivir *to live*

2 Perfect Infinitive

This is formed with the infinitive of the auxiliary **haber** + *past participle*:

haber hablado	*to have spoken*
haber comido	*to have eaten*
haber vivido	*to have lived*

F PARTICIPLE

[For contextualized usage of the participle, see Chapter 6.H, pages 234–239.]

1 Present participle or gerund

Regular present participles are formed with **-ando** and **-iendo**:

    hablar: hablando

    comer: comiendo

    vivir: viviendo

Stem-changing verbs ending in **-ir** have stem changes in the present participle too: **e → i, o → u:**

    sentir: sintiendo

    pedir: pidiendo

    dormir: durmiendo

The ending **-iendo** becomes **-yendo** when added to a stem that ends in a vowel:

    concluir: concluyendo   leer: leyendo

    caer: cayendo   oír: oyendo

Other irregular present participles:

    decir: diciendo   poder: pudiendo

    ir: yendo   venir: viniendo

> Ejercicios 5.58–5.60, páginas 463–464

2 Past Participle

Regular past participles are formed by adding **-ado** and **-ido** to the stem of the infinitive:

    hablar: hablado

    comer: comido

    vivir: vivido

IRREGULAR PAST PARTICIPLES			
INFINITIVE	PAST PARTICIPLE	INFINITIVE	PAST PARTICIPLE
abrir	abierto	morir	muerto
cubrir*	cubierto	poner‡	puesto
decir†	dicho	resolver	resuelto
escribir**	escrito	romper	roto
hacer***	hecho	volver††	vuelto

Verbs derived from the preceding infinitives have the same irregularity: *descubrir, ††devolver, and ‡suponer are examples. There are many more such verbs, such as *recubrir, *encubrir, †desdecir, ††envolver, ††revolver, **reescribir, ***rehacer, ***deshacer, ‡posponer, ‡anteponer, ‡deponer, ‡reponer, etc.

Some verbs have two past participles—one regular, used in compound tenses with **haber**, and one irregular, used as an adjective:

verb:	he bendecido	*I have blessed*
adjective:	bendito (un lugar bendito)	*holy, blessed (a holy place)*
verb:	he freído	*I have fried*
adjective:	frito (papas fritas)	*fried (french fries)*
verb:	he maldecido	*I have cursed*
adjective:	maldito (maldito examen)	*awful, accursed (accursed exam)*
verb:	he prendido	*I have arrested*
adjective:	preso (un hombre preso)	*prisoner (a male prisoner)*
verb:	he soltado	*I have released*
adjective:	suelto (pelo suelto)	*loose (flowing hair)*
verb:	he imprimido	*I have printed*
adjective:	impreso (la palabra impresa)	*printed (the printed word)*

Ejercicios 5.61–5.63, página 464

CHAPTER 6

Verbs: Usage

- **A** Present Indicative
- **B** Aspects of the Past Indicative Tense: Preterite vs. Imperfect and Pluperfect
- **C** Compound Tenses
- **D** Ways of Expressing the Future
- **E** Conditional
- **F** Probability
- **G** Subjunctive
- **H** Infinitives and Present Participles
- **I** Verbs Like **gustar**
- **J** Reflexive Verbs
- **K** Indirect Discourse

PRELIMINARY DEFINITIONS

Mood is a characteristic of verbs that indicates whether the action or situation is regarded as a fact (indicative), as potential (conditional), as affected by doubt, desire, emotion, etc. (subjunctive), as a command (imperative), etc.

Tense refers to when a given action or situation occurs: present, past, or future.

Aspect provides nuances as to whether the action or situation is seen as completed (perfective), unfinished or in process (imperfective), repetitive (iterative), habitual, progressive, starting (inchoative), ending (terminative), etc.

A PRESENT INDICATIVE

[To review the formation of the present indicative, see Chapter 5.A.1, pages 148–154.]

The present indicative in Spanish is equivalent to the present or present progressive in English:

Hablo español.	*I speak Spanish.*
Viven en España.	*They are living in Spain.*

In the interrogative, it is equivalent to the English *do* or *does* + verb:

¿Hablas español?   *Do you speak Spanish?*

In addition to this, it can be translated as:

¿Lo compro?   *Shall I buy it? Should I buy it?*

It is used with **si** meaning *if*:

Si lo hace Iris, le pago.   *If Iris does it, I'll pay her.*

With **si** meaning *whether*, the future is used in Spanish:

No sé **si** lloverá.   *I don't know if (whether) it will rain.*

The present is used for polite commands:

Nos da la cuenta, por favor.   *Give us the check, please.*

Acabar + de in the present means *to have just*. (See pages 280–281 for more on **acabar**.)

> Acabo de comer.   *I just ate. (I have just eaten.)*

The present progressive in Spanish is formed with the present indicative of **estar** + *present participle*. It is used to express ongoing actions in the present, as in English:

> Estamos estudiando.   *We are studying.*

Never use the present progressive in Spanish to refer to the future:

> Josefina se va mañana a las diez.   *Josefina is leaving tomorrow at ten.*

Other auxiliary verbs used occasionally in the progressive are **andar, ir,** and **seguir:**

> Anda buscando a su perro.   *He is looking for his dog. (He is going around looking for his dog.)*
>
> Poco a poco vamos comprendiendo.   *We are understanding little by little.*
>
> Siguen durmiendo.   *They are still sleeping. (They continue sleeping.)*

> Ejercicios 6.1–6.3, páginas 465–467

B | ASPECTS OF THE PAST INDICATIVE TENSE: PRETERITE VS. IMPERFECT AND PLUPERFECT

The distinction between these two aspects of the past tense (note that they are not tenses, but aspects of the past tense) is one of the most difficult points for learners to master. The following table summarizes the basic functions of each (the numbers in parentheses refer to the segments following the table):

PRETERITE	IMPERFECT
• Changed Past Conditions, Reactions (2)	• Past Conditions, Beliefs (1)
• Actions, Single or Consecutive (3)	• Habitual Actions (4)
• Habitual Actions Limited in Time (5)	• Actions—Middle, in Progress, Interrupted (6b)
• Repeated Actions (5)	• Actions—Parallel to the Present (7)
• Actions—Beginning and / or End (6a)	• Projected Actions—Indirect Discourse (8)

Notice in the preceding table the terms *action*, *reaction*, and *condition*. Understanding the difference between these is essential to grasping the subtle differences between preterite and imperfect. The primary difference resides in the meanings of the verbs themselves:

ACTIONS are depicted by verbs that denote doing (rather than being), such as **decir, ver, hacer**; also in this group are verbs that denote movement, such as **caminar, saltar, correr**.

CONDITIONS (or states) are depicted by verbs that denote being, having or appearing (rather than doing), such as **ser, estar, parecer, tener**. To this group also belong verbs that depict (unchanged) opinion, belief, preference, liking: **pensar, creer, gustar**.

Each of these two groups of verbs can be found in preterite or imperfect: if you can identify the type of verb you are working with (action vs. condition or state), you will have succeeded in the first step of the process.

The next step is to see within the context of the sentence how the action or condition is being perceived by the speaker: whether the focus is on the middle, the beginning or the end, on repetition or habit, on change or reaction, etc. We elaborate on these distinctions in the following sections.

1 Past Conditions, Beliefs—Imperfect

The imperfect serves to illustrate a condition or custom in the past, as contrasted with the present, explicitly or implicitly:

Yo **tenía** quince años en esta foto.	*I was fifteen years old in this picture.*
Antes le **gustaba** lo picante.	*He used to like hot (spicy) food.*
Mi madre solo **tenía** dos hijos en esa época.	*My mother only had two children at the time.*
Creíamos que éramos inmortales.	*We thought we were immortal.*

2 Changed Conditions, Reactions—Preterite

The preterite is used to depict changes in beliefs, conditions, or feelings in the past, typically as reactions to some events:

Me **gustó** la película que vimos anoche.   *I liked the movie we saw last night.*

Mi madre **tuvo** su tercer hijo en este hospital.   *My mother had her third child in this hospital.*

En ese instante, **creí** que me iba a desmayar.   *At that instant, I thought I was going to faint.*

IMPERFECT	PRETERITE
No implication of change, reaction or action, or time limitation	To indicate a sudden change, a reaction, or time limitation
Eran las dos de la tarde. *It was two o'clock.*	**De repente, fueron** las dos de la tarde. *Suddenly it was two o'clock in the afternoon.* (Here, the expression **de repente** is altering the standard way of seeing time.)
Jorge **tenía** catorce años. *Jorge was fourteen years old.*	Jorge **cumplió** catorce años ese día. *Jorge turned fourteen that day.* (NOTE: You do not use **tener** here.)
Mi madre **creía** en Dios. *My mother believed in God.*	En ese instante **creyó** en Dios. *In that instant, he believed in God.* (sudden conversion)
Hacía mucho frío ayer. *It was very cold yesterday.*	Todo ese invierno **hizo** mucho frío. *All that winter it was very cold.* (time limit: **Todo ese invierno**)
Había diez sillas en la clase. *There were ten chairs in the classroom.* (NOTE: These are objects, not events.)	**Hubo** una tormenta, una huelga, una pelea, un incendio, etc. *There was a storm, a strike, a fight, a fire, etc.* (events or actions)
Estaba en Río cuando ganó. *I was in Río when he won.*	**Estuve** en España por dos años. *I was in Spain for two years.* (time limit: **dos años**)

3 Actions, Single or Consecutive—Preterite

The preterite is used to depict actions or events, single or consecutive:

Ayer **vimos** a Juan.	*Yesterday we saw Juan.*
Corrió diez millas.	*She ran ten miles.*
Se levantó, se bañó, desayunó, y **fue** al trabajo.	*She got up, bathed, ate breakfast, and went to work.*

One confusing point for many learners is the fact that it does not matter how long an action or event lasts—if it is a single event, it will be in the preterite:

Estudió los idiomas durante toda su vida.	*He studied languages all of his life.*

4 Habitual Actions or Events—Imperfect

Habitual actions are stated in the imperfect:

Mi hermano me **acompañaba** a la escuela.	*My brother used to accompany me to school.*

5 Finite Habitual and Repeated Actions—Preterite

Habitual actions limited in time or frequency are stated in the preterite:

Mi hermano me **acompañó** a la escuela durante seis años.	*My brother accompanied me to school for six years.*
Mi hermano me **acompañó** a la escuela tres veces.	*My brother accompanied me to school three times.*

6 Actions—Beginning, Middle, End

Actions can be perceived from a variety of angles, either at the beginning, middle, or end. The preterite is used for actions seen at their origin or at their end, or as begun and ended in the past; the imperfect is used for actions perceived in the middle, or in progress, with no vision of their beginning or their end.

a. Preterite: Beginning and/or end

```
Beginning |————— - - - - - -
```

Empecé a trabajar a las tres.	*I started to work at three.*

```
End - - - - - —————|
```

Trabajé hasta las cuatro de la tarde.	*I worked until four in the afternoon.*
Estuve en México hasta la edad de veinte años.	*I was in Mexico until the age of twenty.*

```
Beginning and end |—————|
```

Trabajé desde las tres hasta las cuatro.	*I worked from three to four.*
Estuve en España por dos meses.	*I was in Spain for two months.*

b. Imperfect: Middle, in progress, interrupted

```
Middle - - - - - - ————— - - - - - -
```

Cuando entré, las dos **hablaban** de sus clases.	*When I entered, both were speaking about their classes.*

(I don't know when they began speaking; the action was in progress when I entered. The action of speaking could be seen as interrupted by the action of entering, which occurred at a specific point in time while the act of speaking was in progress.)

7 Imperfect as Parallel to the Present

The imperfect is parallel to the present when it refers to actions that are ongoing, customary or future in relation to another point in time. Compare the examples in the following table:

PARALLELS BETWEEN IMPERFECT AND PRESENT	
IMPERFECT	PRESENT
1. Ongoing event in the past **Leía** una novela. He read (was reading) a novel.	1. Ongoing event in the present **Lee** una novela. He reads (is reading) a novel.
2. Customary event in the past Siempre me **despertaba** al amanecer. I always woke up (OR: used to wake up, would wake up) at dawn.	2. Customary event in the present Siempre me **despierto** al amanecer. I always wake up at dawn.
3. Future event from a point in the past **Salía** en una hora. He was leaving in an hour.	3. Future event from the present **Sale** en una hora. He is leaving in an hour.

8 Projected Actions / Indirect Discourse—Imperfect

In Spanish, the present tense can refer to an event that is projected in the future in relation to the context, but that has not yet occurred at the moment of speech:

Dice que **llega** pronto. *He says **he will arrive** soon.*

The imperfect serves as backshift of the present, and in contexts of indirect discourse, may refer to actions that are projected or planned (not yet finished):

Dijo que **llegaba** pronto. *He said **he would arrive** soon.*

The same logic applies to modal auxiliary **ir a** + *infinitive*, used to denote a near future. When shifted to the past, this expression is always in the imperfect:

Dicen que **va a** llover. *They say it's going to rain.*

Dijeron que **iba a** llover. *They said it was going to rain.*

(NOTE: when **ir a** is used in the preterite, it is no longer an auxiliary, but becomes the verb of action *to go*, as in: **Fuimos a** comer. *We went to eat.*)

Disconcerting to many learners is the fact that the imperfect can be used to refer to an event that is projected beyond the actual present, to the future (See Chapter 6.K pages 252–258 for more information on the indirect discourse.):

    Dice que su vuelo **sale** mañana.   *He says his flight leaves tomorrow.*

    Dijo que su vuelo **salía** mañana.   *He said his flight leaves tomorrow.*

9 *Would*—Contexts and Translations

In English, habitual actions can be expressed by using the auxiliaries *used to* or *would* before the verb, or simply the verb in the past; all of these can be translated by the imperfect in Spanish:

    Cuando era niño, mis padres   *When I was a child, my parents*
    me **llevaban** al cine una vez   ***would take** me* (OR: *used to take me*)
    por semana.   *to the movies once a week.*

It must be noted that *would* has other uses in English for which the imperfect in Spanish cannot be used; one of them is the conditional, for which Spanish also uses the conditional:

    Si fuera rico, me **compraría** una isla.   *If I were rich, I **would buy** an island.*

A third use of *would* is in the negative, *would not*, to indicate refusal. For this, Spanish could use the preterite of **querer:**

    No quiso decirme el secreto,   *He **would not** tell me the secret,*
    por más que yo insistiera.   *no matter how much I insisted.*

This is not to be confused with a negative of a habit (the context will indicate whether it was a habit or a refusal at one particular moment).

    Mi hermano **no me decía** nunca   *My brother **would** never **tell***
    nada triste.   *me anything sad.*

10 **Saber** and **conocer**

The verbs **saber** and **conocer** change meaning when used in the preterite and the imperfect. Consider the following differences:

SABER

    Imperfect—to know

        Sabía español cuando era niño.   *He knew Spanish as a child.*

Preterite—to find out, or become informed, or realize

    Supo que ella había muerto.   *He found out that she had died.*

CONOCER

Imperfect—to know

    Conocíamos a los Gómez.   *We knew the Gomezes.*

Preterite—to meet (for the first time, as in being introduced)

    Conocí a Marta en la fiesta.   *I met Marta at the party.*

(NOTE: To say *to meet* for someone you know already, when it means to get together with that person, use **encontrarse con**. [See Chapter 8.B.16, page 294.])

11 Modal Auxiliaries in the Past

Modal auxiliaries (**acabar de, deber, ir a, poder, querer, tener que**) follow the same general principles as those indicated above for the preterite and imperfect, and often change meaning:

a. Acabar de + *infinitive* (See more on this verb in Chapter 8.B.1, pages 280–281.)

Imperfect—to have just done something

    Acababa de comer cuando llegaste.   *I had just eaten when you arrived.*

Preterite—to finish

    Acabé de comer y me fui.   *I finished eating and left.*

b. Deber + *infinitive*

Imperfect—to have an obligation, or be due (not completed)

    Debíamos cenar juntos.   *We were supposed to have dinner together.*

    Debía tener el bebé esa semana.   *She was due to have the baby that week.*

Preterite—should (not) have, ought (not) to (contrary to reality)

    Debimos haber hablado de eso.   *We should have spoken about that.*

    No **debiste** haberme dicho.   *You should not have told me.*

c. Ir a + *infinitive*

Imperfect—to be about to (not completed)

Íbamos a cenar juntos.	*We were going to eat dinner together.*
Parecía que no **iba a** parar nunca.	*It seemed she was never going to stop.*

Preterite—to go (completed action)

Fuimos a trabajar.	*We went to work.*
No **fue** a practicar.	*He did not go to practice.*

(NOTE: when you want to say an event *was going to* happen, you should use the imperfect of **ir a.** Otherwise, if you use the preterite, the verb **ir a** takes on the meaning of *went to:* a verb of action, instead of an auxiliary.)

d. Poder + *infinitive*

Imperfect—to be able, can

Podían trabajar juntos.	*They could work together.*

Preterite—affirmative: to succeed, be able, manage; negative: to fail

Después de mucho esfuerzo, **pudieron** abrir la ventana.	*After a lot of effort, they succeeded in opening the window.*
No pudieron salir.	*They could not (failed to) get out.*

e. Querer + *infinitive*

Imperfect—to want

Queríamos viajar.	*We wanted to travel.*

Preterite—affirmative: to attempt, try; negative: to refuse to

Quiso escapar, pero no pudo.	*He tried to escape, but failed.*
No quiso ayudarme.	*He would not (refused to) help me.*

Note carefully this use of *would* in English, which is different from the habitual and the conditional.

f. Tener que + *infinitive*

Imperfect—obligation not necessarily fulfilled

Tenía que trabajar, pero fui al cine.   *I had to work, but I went to the movies.*

Preterite—fulfilled obligation

Tuve que trabajar anoche.   *I had to work last night [and did].*

12 Ser in Sentences with Relative Clauses

The verb **ser**, typically used in the imperfect to depict a state in the past, behaves differently in sentences with relative pronouns, in which the identification of a subject is at stake. In such sentences, there are necessarily two verbs (one for the main clause, and one for the relative clause), and what normally determines the aspect of the verb **ser** in such contexts is the aspect of the other verb:

La que me **reconoció fue** Lupe.   *The one who recognized me was Lupe.*

In the above sentence, **fue Lupe** is the main clause, and **La que me reconoció** is the relative clause. The act of recognition, which was a single action viewed as finished in the past, is in the preterite. The verb **ser**, in the main clause, identifies the subject of the act of recognition, in the same aspect as the act (preterite).

Similarly, if the act of the relative clause is presented as ongoing or habitual, in the imperfect, the verb **ser** used to identify the subject of that action will be in the imperfect too:

El que siempre me **saludaba era** Jorge.   *The one who always used to greet me was Jorge.*

When the verb **ser** is not being used to identify the subject of the action of the relative clause, but rather to describe something about that subject, **ser** will be in the imperfect. This follows the norm for unchanging or uninterrupted description in the past, regardless of the aspect of the verb of the relative clause. Consider the following examples:

La que **me reconoció era** joven.   *The one who recognized me was young.*

El que siempre me **saludaba era** cortés.   *The one who always used to greet me was courteous.*

13 The Preterite and the Present Perfect

The present perfect in English typically coincides with the uses of the present perfect in Spanish: both refer to actions that extend to the present, or relate to the present directly.

Ya **he visto** esa película.	*I have already seen that movie.*
No **he tomado** mis vitaminas en tres días.	*I haven't taken my vitamins for three days.*

There are, however, some cases in which the present perfect in Spanish does not translate into English as present perfect. Note, for example, that in some areas of Spain, actions that refer to a recent past are stated in the present perfect:

Esta mañana **me he levantado** a las seis.	*This morning I got up at six.*
Anoche **hemos ido** al cine.	*Last night we went to the movies.*

In Latin America and some regions of Spain, the preterite is preferred for the above actions:

Esta mañana **me levanté** a las seis.	*This morning I got up at six.*
Anoche **fuimos** al cine.	*Last night we went to the movies.*

> Ejercicios 6.4–6.12, páginas 467–470

14 The Pluperfect

[To review the formation of the pluperfect indicative, see Chapter 5.A.2.d, page 158.]

When narrating or reporting something from the past, one of the actions often precedes the others. In such a case, the pluperfect is used. Pluperfect comes from "plus" which means "more," and "perfect" which means "completed." This is a verb aspect that is used to report actions that ended before the basic past timeline that the narrator is using.

An extreme example of this would be to say that if an historian is telling the story of the Second World War, and wants to refer back to events in the First World War, (s)he would use the pluperfect. However, the distance between the two pasts does not have to be so great. It could be a matter of minutes; as long as there is a reference back to an action completed prior to the basic past timeline, the pluperfect would be used.

The use of the pluperfect exists in English as well, but is not used as frequently as it is in Spanish. Consider the following sentences:

El príncipe vio que a Cenicienta se le **había caído** un zapato al salir corriendo.	*The prince saw that one of Cinderella's shoes had fallen off while she was running away.*

The basic timeline here is the moment when the prince appeared on the scene outside the palace, after midnight. He ran outside to look for Cinderella, saw that she was gone, and noticed her shoe on the steps. He immediately assumed that her shoe had fallen off while she was running away. The loss of her shoe occurred prior to the prince seeing the shoe. Note that if we were narrating this tale in the present, you would have the following set of verbs (notice the tenses): the prince runs out, looks for Cinderella, sees she is gone, notices her shoe on the steps, and assumes it fell off while she was running away. The only past tense verb in this series is *fell*. Roughly speaking, you could say that the pluperfect is to the past what the preterite or present perfect is to the present.

Note that if the story is told from a different perspective, the tenses may change:

Mientras corría escaleras abajo, se le cayó un zapato. Después el príncipe lo encontró y lo usó para encontrar a la misteriosa desconocida.	*While she ran down the stairs, one of her shoes fell off. Later the prince found it and used it to find the mysterious stranger.*

The point of view for the preceding narration is different. Here Cinderella is seen first while (as) she is running away. She loses her shoe as she descends the stairs. The prince comes in afterwards and follows the timeline in a logical way. There is no referring back to prior events; there is no pluperfect.

> Ejercicio 6.13, página 470;
> Ejercicios de repaso 6.14–6.20, páginas 471–474

C COMPOUND TENSES

1 Introduction

In the table that follows, the verbs in bold are what we call "compound tenses," because they are formed with more than one part. Notice that for the progressive form, **estar** is used with the present participle. For the perfect forms, **haber** is used as auxiliary with the past participle. Progressive perfect forms combine **estar** in the perfect form (conjugated auxiliary **haber + estado**) and the present participle of the verb being conjugated.

	MOOD	TENSE	NONPROGRESSIVE	PROGRESSIVE
S I M P L E	Indicative	Present	camino	**estoy caminando**
	Indicative	Future	caminaré	**estaré caminando**
	Indicative	Imperfect	caminaba	**estaba caminando**
	Indicative	Preterite	caminé	**estuve caminando**
	Conditional	Present	caminaría	**estaría caminando**
	Subjunctive	Present	camine	**esté caminando**
	Subjunctive	Imperfect	caminara	**estuviera caminando**
P E R F E C T	Indicative	Present Perfect	**he caminado**	**he estado caminando**
	Indicative	Future Perfect	**habré caminado**	**habré estado caminando**
	Indicative	Pluperfect	**había caminado**	**había estado caminando**
	Conditional	Perfect	**habría caminado**	**habría estado caminando**
	Subjunctive	Present Perfect	**haya caminado**	**haya estado caminando**
	Subjunctive	Pluperfect	**hubiera caminado**	**hubiera estado caminando**

2 Perfect Tenses

As a rule, perfect tenses are used to focus on the completion of an action in relation to a particular point in time, present, past, or future.

PERFECT TENSES			
Formation	Auxiliary **haber**	+	Past Participle
Example	Hemos		llegado.
Translation	We have		arrived.

a. Present perfect indicative

[To review the formation of the present perfect indicative, see Chapter 5.A.2.c, page 158.]

This form is used to express completed events in relation to the present:

Hemos regresado del museo.   *We have returned from the museum.*

Todavía no **ha terminado** la guerra.   *The war still has not ended.*

b. Future perfect

[To review the formation of the future perfect, see Chapter 5.A.3.b, page 160.]

This form is used to express a future event that will have been completed by a specific time or after another event in the future:

Habremos acabado para las cinco.   *We will have finished by five.*

The future perfect can also be found in contexts expressing probability, for actions that were probably completed in the past:

—¿Adónde crees que fue Roberto?   *"Where do you think Roberto went?"*

—No sé. **Habrá ido** a la peluquería.   *"I don't know. I guess he went to the barbershop."*

c. Past perfect (pluperfect) indicative

[To review the formation of the pluperfect indicative, see Chapter 5.A.2.d, page 158.]

This form is used to express an event prior to another one in the past:

Ya se **había apagado** el fuego cuando llegaron los bomberos.   *The fire had already gone out when the firemen arrived.*

d. Conditional perfect

[To review the formation of the conditional perfect, see Chapter 5.B.2, page 161.]

This form is used to express a future event in relation to another event in the past:

> Todos pensaban que la guerra **habría terminado** para entonces.
>
> *Everyone thought that the war would have ended by then.*

This form can also be found in probability structures, referring to an action in the past prior to another one in the past:

> —¿Por qué piensas que esa estudiante se aburría en clase el semestre pasado?
>
> *"Why do you think that student was bored in class last semester?"*
>
> —No sé. Ya **habría leído** los mismos libros para otra clase.
>
> *"I don't know. Maybe she had already read the same books for another class."*

e. Present perfect subjunctive

[To review the formation of the present perfect subjunctive, see Chapter 5.C.3, page 166.]

This form describes an event that is completed in relation to the present:

> Me sorprende que **hayan publicado** el secreto.
>
> *It surprises me that they published the secret.*

f. Pluperfect subjunctive

[To review the formation of the pluperfect subjunctive, see Chapter 5.C.4, page 167.]

This form describes an event that was completed before another one in the past:

> Nos sorprendió que **hubiera cenado** antes de venir.
>
> *It surprised us that he had eaten before coming.*

3 Simple Progressive Tenses

a. Introduction

The progressive is used to express an ongoing action.

	PROGRESSIVE TENSES		
Formation	Auxiliary **estar**	+	Present Participle
Example	Estamos		estudiando.
Translation	We are		studying.

Exception:

Ir and **venir** are never used in the progressive in Spanish:

| Vamos a Ginebra. | *We're going to Geneva.* |
| Adivina quién viene a cenar. | *Guess who's coming to dinner.* |

Spanish, unlike English, does not use the progressive for states or conditions. Compare the following sentences:

Llevaba una chaqueta de cuero.	*She was wearing a leather jacket.*
Tengo zapatos puestos.	*I'm wearing shoes.*
Estoy sentado.	*I'm sitting.*
Faltaban dos sillas.	*Two chairs were missing.*
Dime si se me ve el tirante.	*Tell me if my strap is showing.*

b. Present progressive

This tense is formed with the present of **estar** and refers to ongoing actions in the present:

| **Estoy trabajando** en este momento y no podré ayudarte. | *I'm working at this moment and won't be able to help you.* |
| Pronto comeremos; **están preparando** la cena. | *We will eat soon; they're preparing dinner.* |

The present progressive is never used in Spanish to refer to the future, as it often is in English:

| Mañana van a tumbar el árbol. | *Tomorrow they are going to cut down the tree.* |

c. Future progressive

This tense is formed with the future of **estar** and refers to ongoing actions in the future:

Mañana, domingo, a las siete de la tarde, Asunción **estará jugando** al sudoku. Lo sé porque siempre hace lo mismo.	*Tomorrow, Sunday, at seven in the evening, Asunción will be playing sudoku. I know that because she always does the same thing.*

The future progressive is also used to express probability in the present:

—¿Qué hace Regina?	*"What is Regina doing?"*
—No lo sé. **Estará cortando** el césped.	*"I don't know. She must be mowing the lawn."*

d. Past progressive

This tense is formed with the imperfect or preterite of **estar** and refers to an action that was ongoing in the past and is now completed:

Estaba pensando en Citlali cuando me llegó su mensaje electrónico.	*I was thinking about Citlali when her e-mail arrived.*
Jeannine **estuvo viajando** todo el verano.	*Jeannine was traveling all summer long.*

The past progressive in Spanish can never be used to refer to a future action in the past, as it can in English:

Iba a llover.	*It was going to rain.*

e. Conditional present progressive

This tense, formed with the present conditional of **estar**, refers to an ongoing action that is future (has yet to take place) in the past, a backshift from the future progressive (see section **c** above):

Cecilia me dijo que el día siguiente, domingo, a las siete de la tarde, se **estaría mudando**.	*Cecilia told me that the next day, Sunday, at seven in the evening, she would be moving.*

The conditional progressive is also used to express probability for an ongoing action in the past:

—¿Por qué no fue Brisa a la fiesta anoche?	*"Why didn't Brisa go to the party last night?"*
—Quién sabe. **Estaría corrigiendo** exámenes.	*"Who knows. Maybe she was grading exams."*

f. Subjunctive present progressive

This tense is formed with the present subjunctive of **estar** and refers to an ongoing action in the present, colored by the subjunctive:

Temo que mi hijo no **se esté cuidando**.	*I fear that my son is not taking care of himself.*

g. Subjunctive imperfect progressive

This tense is formed with the imperfect subjunctive of **estar** and refers to an ongoing action in the past, colored by the subjunctive:

No podía creer que **estuvieran peleando** todavía.	*I could not believe they were still fighting.*

4 Perfect Progressive Tenses

a. Introduction

This combination serves to focus on the completion of an ongoing action in relation to another moment, present, past, or future.

PERFECT PROGRESSIVE TENSES				
FORMATION	AUXILIARY **haber**	+	PAST PARTICIPLE **estar**	+	PRESENT PARTICIPLE MAIN VERB
Example	**Hemos**		estado		corriendo.
Translation	*We have*		*been*		*running.*

b. Indicative present perfect progressive

Mi madre **ha estado llamándome** todos los días.	*My mother has been calling me every day.*

c. Indicative future perfect progressive

Para cuando llegue, **habré estado manejando** durante doce horas sin parar.

By the time I get there, I will have been driving for twelve hours nonstop.

This form can also serve for probability, when referring to a completed ongoing action in the past:

—¿Por qué está tan cansada Ana?

"Why is Ana so tired?"

—No sé. **Habrá estado trabajando** toda la noche.

"I don't know. She was probably working all night."

d. Indicative pluperfect progressive

Cuando por fin me dejaron entrar, **había estado esperando** tres horas.

When they finally let me in, I had been waiting for three hours.

e. Conditional perfect progressive

La policía **habría estado vigilando** la casa si se lo hubieras pedido.

The police would have been watching the house if you had asked them.

This form can also be used for probability, when referring to a completed ongoing action in the past prior to another:

—¿Por qué crees que tardó tanto en abrir la puerta?

"Why do you think he took so long to open the door?"

—**Habría estado escondiendo** las pruebas.

"He must have been hiding the evidence."

f. Subjunctive present perfect progressive

Use this form in a subordinate clause in which the main verb is in the present set and to refer to a completed ongoing action in the past:

Dudo que **haya estado haciendo** lo que decía.

I doubt that he was doing what he said.

g. Subjunctive pluperfect progressive

Use this form in a subordinate clause to refer to a completed ongoing action at a particular time in the past, prior to another action also in the past:

Nos chocó que **hubieran estado usando** escucha electrónica sin consultar con nadie primero.	*It shocked us that they had been wiretapping without first consulting with anyone.*

5 Modal Auxiliaries

It should be noted that there are other auxiliaries in addition to **haber** and **estar**, each of which is used with a main verb and alters its value in one way or another. These are called modal auxiliaries. They can each exist as the main verb of a sentence and have a different meaning or weight. Among modal auxiliaries, the following are used with the present participle: **ir, venir**; the following are used with the infinitive: **ir a, tener que, poder, haber de, deber.** Some examples follow:

Vamos preparándonos poco a poco.	*We are preparing ourselves little by little.*
Vengo planeando esto desde hace ya varios años.	*I have been planning this for several years now.*
Van a darme la respuesta mañana.	*They are going to give me the answer tomorrow.*
Ustedes **tienen que** decirnos la verdad.	*You have to tell us the truth.*
Tuve que llamar a casa.	*I needed to call home.*
	(Note that to translate *I needed to do something* or *I had to do something* you would use **tuve que** and not **necesité**. **Necesitar** is not used in the preterite as a modal auxiliary.)
No **podemos** nadar.	*We can't swim.*
Han de saber la verdad.	*They must* know the truth.* (*probability)
Deberías comer más.	*You should eat more.*

Ejercicios 6.21–6.23, páginas 474–475

D. WAYS OF EXPRESSING THE FUTURE

[To review the formation of the future, see Chapter 5.A.3, pages 159–160.]

The future in Spanish can be expressed with the simple future:

    Mañana **iremos** al cine.   *Tomorrow we will go to the movies.*

It can also be expressed with the present of **ir** + **a** + *infinitive*:

    Mañana **vamos a ir** al cine.   *Tomorrow we are going to go to the movies.*

It can also be expressed with the present tense:

    Mañana **vamos** al cine.   *Tomorrow we are going to the movies.*

NOTE: The future cannot be expressed in Spanish with the progressive, as it can in English. This is a very common error that should be avoided. Note carefully in the following sentence how the progressive future in English is translated into Spanish:

    Esta tarde **vamos a comer**   *This afternoon we <u>are eating</u> here.*
    (OR: **comemos**) aquí.

Remember that the progressive in Spanish can only be used for actions that are occurring at the moment. **Estamos comiendo** can only refer to the ongoing action of eating, now, in the present. Notice that the following context is not future, and, for that reason, can be translated with the progressive:

    No puede venir al teléfono ahora: *He cannot come to the phone now:*
    está comiendo.   *he <u>is eating</u>.*

> Ejercicios 6.24–6.26, página 475

E CONDITIONAL

[To review the formation of the conditional, see Chapter 5.B, pages 160–161.]

1 Introduction

The conditional is used to express the following:
- Courtesy with conditional of modal auxiliaries
- Hypothetical situations implied or stated
- Future of the past
- Probability in the past

2 Courtesy with Conditional of Modal Auxiliaries

This is merely a softening of the indicative, as in English; the difference between *can you* and *could you*, *must not* and *should not*, *I want* and *I would like*, etc.

¿**Podría** Ud. ayudarme, por favor?	*Could you help me, please?*
No **deberías** decir eso.	*You should not say that.*

Note that the verb **querer** tends to be used in the imperfect subjunctive rather than the conditional to express courtesy:

Quisiera que me ayudaras.	*I would like you to help me.*

> Ejercicio 6.27, página 476

3 Hypothetical Situations Implied or Stated

[See Chapter 6.G.6, pages 228–230, on si ("if") clauses.]

En esa situación, yo **tendría** mucho miedo.	*In that situation, I would be very frightened.*
Yo en tu lugar no le **pagaría** por grosero.	*If I were you I would not pay him because he was rude.*
Si me atreviera, **saltaría** en paracaídas.	*If I dared, I would skydive.*

4 Future of the Past

[See Chapter 6.K, pages 252–258, on indirect discourse.]

> Se anunció que para esta noche **se sabría** su identidad.
>
> *They announced that by tonight his identity would be known.*

> Ejercicio 6.28, página 476

5 Probability in the Past

[See Chapter 6.F, pages 201–203, on probability.]

> ¿Dónde **estaría** el enemigo?
>
> *I wonder where the enemy was.*

> ¿Dónde se **habría** escondido?
>
> *Where could he have hidden?*

> Ejercicio de repaso 6.29, página 476

F PROBABILITY

[To review the formation of the tenses in this section, see Chapter 5.A.3, pages 159–160, on simple future and future perfect, and Chapter 5.B, pages 160–161, on present conditional and conditional perfect.]

English has many ways of expressing probability. Here is a list of some of the many possibilities of expressing doubt with the question *Who is it?*

I wonder who it is.	*Who do you suppose it is?*
Who can it be?	*Who do you think it is?*
Who in the world is it?	

Spanish uses a variety of tenses to express probability.

The future is used to express probability in the present:

> ¿Quién **será**?

(All of the variations of the English above would be translated like this.)

The future progressive form is frequently used with verbs of action:

> ¿Qué **estarán haciendo**?
>
> *I wonder what they are doing.*

The future perfect is used to express probability in the preterite or the present perfect:

Habrá ido al cine. *He probably went to the movies.*
I guess he went to the movies.
He has probably gone to the movies.
I suppose he went ... etc.

The conditional present is used to express probability in the imperfect aspect of the past:

Estaría en el cine. *He probably was at the movies.*
He must have been at the movies.
I guess he was ... etc.

The conditional progressive form is used for probability with verbs of action:

Estaría bañándose. *He was probably bathing.*

The conditional perfect is used to express probability in the pluperfect:

Habría salido temprano. *He probably had gone out early.*
He must have gone out early.
I guess he went out ... etc.

The following parallel columns show how probability is expressed in Spanish. On the left, the sentences are formed with the adverb **probablemente** and the standard form of the verb, whereas the column to the right gives you the altered verb tense that expresses probability without the need for the adverb.

EXPRESSIONS OF PROBABILITY		
STANDARD	PROBABILITY	TRANSLATION
Probablemente está en casa.	Estará en casa.	He must be home.
Probablemente está bañándose.	Estará bañándose.	He must be bathing.
Probablemente estaba en casa.	Estaría en casa.	He must have been home.
Probablemente estaba comiendo.	Estaría comiendo.	He must have been eating.
Probablemente murió.	Habrá muerto.	He must have died.
Probablemente lo ha visto.	Lo habrá visto.	He must have seen it.
Probablemente había regresado.	Habría regresado.	He must have returned.

In English, the first sentence in the preceding chart could also be: *He's probably at home, I guess he's at home, I suppose he's at home,* etc. Each sentence in the chart could thus have a variety of translations in English.

> Ejercicios 6.30–6.31, páginas 476–477

G SUBJUNCTIVE

[To review the formation of the tenses of the subjunctive, see Chapter 5.C, pages 162–167.]

1 Introduction

The subjunctive is used in subordinate clauses and in some independent clauses introduced by **ojalá, quizá(s),** and **tal vez.**

Ojalá que se logre la paz.	*I hope peace will be achieved.*
Quizá pase este año.	*Maybe it will happen this year.*
Tal vez sea muy tarde.	*Maybe it's too late.*

The primary use of the subjunctive is in subordinate clauses. There are three types of subordinate clauses in which the subjunctive might be necessary.

- Nominal
- Adjectival
- Adverbial

Each type of clause has its own set of rules to determine whether or not you need to use the subjunctive. Therefore, you need to be able to recognize the three types.

2 Nominal Clauses

a. Definition and usage

Definition: A nominal clause is one that has the same function as a noun would (i.e., it may be the subject of the main verb or its direct object).

Quiero **pan.**	*I want bread.*
Quiero **que me ayudes.**	*I want you to help me.*

Both **pan** and **que me ayudes** have the same function in the sentence, that of direct object of the main verb; **que me ayudes** is called a nominal clause because it behaves like a noun. In the sentence **Me gusta que canten** the subordinate clause is the subject of the main verb.

Use of the subjunctive: What determines whether or not you need to use the subjunctive in the nominal clause is the verb of the main clause. If this verb indicates fact or truth, the subordinate clause will be in the indicative. This would be the case for such verbs as *to see, to notice, to observe, to be clear, to be obvious, to be true*.

Es obvio que no me entiendes.	*It's obvious that you don't understand me.*
Es cierto que viajé a Rusia.	*It's true that I traveled to Russia.*
Veo que tienes bastante dinero.	*I see you have enough money.*
Me fijé que era hora de irnos.	*I noticed it was time to leave.*

However, if the verb of the main clause indicates anything other than a mere statement of fact, such as emotion, doubt, desire, approval, feeling, volition, influence, etc., the verb of the nominal clause must be in the subjunctive:

Me encanta que **vengan.**	*I am delighted that they are coming.*
Dudo que ellos **puedan** hacerlo.	*I doubt that they can do it.*
Quiero que me **des** un beso.	*I want you to give me a kiss.*
Me gusta que **participen** mucho.	*I like them to participate often.*

Parecer, creer, and **pensar** in the negative or interrogative take the subjunctive only when there is doubt in the mind of the speaker. Also, **parecer** followed by an adjective takes the subjunctive:

Parece que **va** a llover.	*It seems like it's going to rain.*
No parece que **vaya** a llover.	*It doesn't seem like it's going to rain.*
¿Parecía que **fuera** culpable?	*Did he seem guilty?*
Parece **increíble** que **hagan** eso.	*It seems incredible that they do that.*
Creo que **puede** hacerlo.	*I believe he can do it.*
No creo que **pueda** hacerlo.	*I don't believe he can do it.*
¿Crees que **pueda** hacerlo?	*Do you think he can do it?*
Pienso que **vendrá.**	*I think he will come.*
No pienso que **venga.**	*I don't think he will come.*

Sentir will change meaning if followed by the subjunctive:

Siento que **voy** a estornudar.	*I feel like I am going to sneeze.*
Siento que **estés** enferma.	*I am sorry that you are ill.*

b. Subjunctive after expressions of emotion

If the main clause contains a verb or an expression of emotion, this affects the verb of the subordinate clause. In this case, the subjunctive must be used, whether or not the action of the subordinate has occurred or will occur:

Estás aquí.	*You are here.*
Sé que **estás** aquí.	*I know you are here.*
Me alegro de que **estés** aquí.	*I am glad you are here.*

Following is a list of commonly used verbs of emotion:

esperar *to hope*	Espero que lo encuentren. *I hope they find him.*
lamentar *to regret*	Lamento que te hayan engañado. *I regret that they deceived you.*
sentir *to be sorry, regret*	Siento que no puedas entrar al país. *I am sorry you can't get into the country.*
temer *to fear*	Temo que sea muy tarde. *I fear it's too late.*
tener miedo *to be afraid*	Tengo miedo de que haya una bomba. *I am afraid there will be a bomb.*

Reflexive verbs:

alegrarse de *to be happy, glad*	Me alegro de que hayan llegado a un acuerdo. *I am glad they have arrived at an agreement.*
avergonzarse de *to be ashamed*	Se avergüenza de que sus hijos no usen ropa tradicional. *He is ashamed that his children don't wear traditional clothing.*

Verbs like gustar:

encantarle a uno *to delight, "love"* (not romantic)	Me encanta que toques el piano. *I'm delighted that you play the piano.* Nos encantaría que vinieran. *We would love you to come.*
enojarle a uno *to anger, make angry, be angry*	Nos enoja que nos griten. *It makes us angry that they yell at us.* *We are angry that they yell at us.*
gustarle a uno *to please, like*	Le gusta que ganen. *It pleases him that they win.* *He likes them to win.*
molestarle a uno *to annoy, be annoyed*	¿Te molesta que haga ruido? *Does it annoy you that I make noise?*
sorprenderle a uno *to surprise, be surprised*	Les sorprende que seamos malabaristas. *They are surprised that we are jugglers.*

Use of the infinitive in the subordinate clause:

For verbs of emotion, if the subject is the same in both clauses, use an infinitive for the second verb:

Sentimos no **poder** ir a la fiesta.	*We're sorry we can't go to the party.*
Me alegro de **ver**te.	*I am glad to see you.*
Adela odia **comer** fuera.	*Adela hates to eat out.*

For verbs like **gustar**, if the indirect object of the verb like **gustar** is the same as the subject of the second verb, use an infinitive for the second verb:

| Me encantó **bailar** contigo. | *I loved dancing with you.* |
| Me gustó **visitar** a mis abuelos. | *I enjoyed visiting my grandparents.* |

c. Subjunctive after expressions of volition and influence

If the main clause contains a verb or an expression of volition or influence, the subjunctive must be used in the subordinate clause:

| Quiero que **cantes** conmigo. | *I want you to sing with me.* |

Commonly used verbs of volition:

desear *to want*	¿Desea que le traiga algo de beber? *Do you want me to bring you something to drink?*
empeñarse en *to insist*	Se empeña en que la respeten. *She insists that they respect her.*
insistir en *to insist on*	Insistieron en que les pagáramos. *They insisted on our paying them.*
necesitar *to need*	Necesito que me escuches. *I need you to listen to me.*
oponerse a *to object to*	Se oponía a que le abrieran la maleta. *He objected to their opening his suitcase.*
preferir *to prefer*	Prefiero que me hables en español. *I prefer that you speak to me in Spanish.*
querer *to want*	Queremos que llegue la primavera. *We want spring to arrive.*

Use of the infinitive in the subordinate clause: For verbs of volition, if the subject is the same in both clauses, use an infinitive in the subordinate clause:

Deseamos **ir** solos.	*We want to go alone.*
Se empeña en **gritar**.	*He insists on yelling.*
Insisto en **llamar** primero.	*I insist on calling first.*
Necesitas **tomar** vitaminas.	*You need to take vitamins.*
Me opongo a **votar** por él.	*I'm against voting for him.*
Prefieren **viajar** en barco.	*They prefer to travel by ship.*
Quiero **dar**te un recuerdo.	*I want to give you a souvenir.*

Verbs of communication such as **decir** and **escribir** may be followed by the indicative or the subjunctive; if they are used with the subjunctive, they imply a command:

| Dijo que quería irse. | *He said he wanted to leave.* |
| Me dijo que me fuera. | *He told me to leave.* |

Verbs of influence commonly used with direct objects:

dejar* to let, allow	Dejé que pasara. I let him in.
hacer* to make	Hizo que soltaran las armas. He made them drop their weapons.
invitar a* to invite	La invito a que cene con nosotros. I invite you to eat dinner with us.
obligar a* to force	Los obliga a que hablen. He forces them to talk.

Verbs of influence commonly used with indirect objects:

aconsejar to advise	Le aconsejo que se calle. I advise you to be quiet.
advertir to warn	Les advierto que presten atención. I warn you to pay attention.
exigir to demand	Exigen que liberen a los presos políticos. They demand that they free the political prisoners.
impedir* to prevent	Impidieron que pasara la frontera. They prevented him from crossing the border.
mandar* to order	Mandó que nadie dijera nada. He ordered that nobody say anything.
pedir to ask	Nos pide que tengamos paciencia. He asks us to be patient.
permitir* to allow	Le permiten que regrese tarde. They allow him to return late.
prohibir* to forbid	Te prohíbo que salgas con ellos. I forbid you from going out with them.

recomendar* *to recommend*	Nos recomiendan que tomemos aspirina. *They recommend that we take aspirin.*
rogar *to beg*	Le ruego que me disculpe. *I beg you to forgive me.*
sugerir *to suggest*	Sugieren que nos quedemos aquí. *They suggest that we stay here.*

***Dejar, hacer, invitar a, obligar a, impedir, prohibir, recomendar, mandar,** and **permitir** are commonly used with infinitives, even if there is a change of subject, and with direct or indirect object pronouns: **Lo dejé pagar. Las hizo limpiar su cuarto. Te mandó callarte. Le permiten regresar tarde.** (See Chapter 6.H, pages 234–237, on the infinitive.)

Impersonal expressions:

bastar *to be enough*	Basta que me lo pidas. *It's enough that you ask me for it.*
convenir *to be suitable, a good idea*	Conviene que te prepares con antelación. *It's a good idea that you prepare in advance.*
importar *to matter*	No importa que no tengas los medios. *It doesn't matter that you don't have the means.*
más valer *to be better*	Más vale que me pague pronto. *He had better pay me soon.*

d. Subjunctive after expressions of doubt and negation of reality

If the main clause contains a verb or an expression of doubt, or a negation of reality, the subjunctive must be used in the subordinate clause:

Dudo que sea verdad.   *I doubt that it's true.*

Niega que él lo haya visto.   *She denies that he saw it.*

Commonly used verbs of doubt and negation of reality:

dudar *to doubt*	Dudo que el usuario haga copias digitales. *I doubt that the user will make digital copies.*
negar *to deny*	Negó que fuera verdad. *He denied that it was true.*
puede ser *it may be*	Puede ser que llueva hoy. *It may be that it will (it might) rain today.*
no creer *not to believe*	No creo que el avión pueda despegar a tiempo. *I don't believe that the plane will be able to take off on time.*
no decir *not to say*	No digo que seas culpable. *I don't say that you are guilty.*
no pensar *not to think*	No piensa que tú le creas. *He doesn't think you believe him.*
no ser *not to be*	No es que no quiera, es que no puedo. *It isn't that I don't want to, it's that I can't.*
no significar *not to mean*	Eso no significa que no te quiera. *That doesn't mean that he doesn't love you.*

e. Subjunctive after impersonal expressions with ser

If the main clause contains an impersonal expression with **ser** + *adjective* or *noun*, and the adjective or noun denotes anything but truth or certainty, the subjunctive must be used in the subordinate clause.

Indicative:

| **Es verdad** que se **fue** temprano. | *It's true that he left early.* |
| **Es cierto** que **hace** frío. | *It's true that it's cold.* |

Subjunctive:

| **Es posible** que **pueda** hacerlo. | *It's possible that he can do it.* |
| **No es cierto** que lo **haya visto**. | *It isn't true that he saw it.* |

Commonly used impersonal expressions taking the subjunctive:

(ser) bueno *(to be) good*	Es bueno que sepas hacerlo sola. *It's good you know how to do it alone.*
malo *bad*	Fue malo que se lo dijeras. *It was bad for you to tell him.*
mejor *better*	Es mejor que nos vayamos temprano. *It's better that we leave early.*
curioso *curious, odd*	Es curioso que no haya correo. *It's odd that there is no mail.*
extraño *strange*	Fue extraño que se estrellara contra esa pared. *It was strange that he crashed into that wall.*
fantástico *fantastic*	Es fantástico que puedas venir. *It's fantastic that you can come.*
raro *strange, odd*	Es raro que no haga frío. *It's strange that it isn't cold.*
triste *sad*	Es triste que se haya complicado tanto la situación. *It's sad that the situation has gotten so complicated.*
deseable *desirable*	Es deseable que pague al contado. *It's desirable that you pay cash.*

importante *important*	Es importante que apoyemos a los que tienen una minusvalía. *It's important that we support those who have a handicap.*
necesario *necessary*	Es necesario que estudies más. *It's necessary that you study more.*
difícil *unlikely*	Es difícil que llegue a tiempo con esta tormenta. *It's unlikely that she will arrive on time with this storm.*
fácil *likely*	Es fácil que venga hoy el convoy de la OTAN. *It's likely that the NATO convoy will come today.*
imposible *impossible*	Es imposible que se lo haya dicho. *It's impossible that she told him.*
posible *possible*	Es posible que haya sido un atentado suicida. *It's possible that it was a suicide attempt.*
probable *probable*	Es probable que haya una inundación. *It's probable that there will be a flood.*
(una) lástima *a pity*	Es una lástima que rechazara ser nuestro portavoz. *It's a pity that he didn't agree to be our spokesperson.*
(una) maravilla *a wonder*	Es una maravilla que el terremoto no los afectara. *It's a wonder that the earthquake didn't affect them.*
(una) pena *a pity*	Es una pena que no hagan caso al alto el fuego. *It's a pity that they don't respect the cease-fire.*

Notice that these expressions parallel the categories of verbs of emotion, volition, influence, and doubt or uncertainty. All impersonal expressions take the subjunctive, except those that denote absolute certainty:

Es evidente, obvio, cierto, claro, etc.

> Ejercicios 6.32–6.39, páginas 477–480;
> Ejercicio de repaso 6.40, página 480

3 Adjectival Clauses

a. Definition

An adjectival clause is one that modifies a noun as an adjective would.

Quiero leer una novela **divertida.**	*I want to read a fun novel.*
Quiero leer la novela **que me regalaste.**	*I want to read the novel you gave me.*
Quiero leer una novela **que me haga reír.**	*I want to read a novel that will make me laugh.*

b. Usage

Notice that **que** in the above sentences is a relative pronoun (See Chapter 3.G, pages 92–98.) and not a conjunction, as is the case in nominal clauses. The antecedent of the relative pronoun is **novela.** To determine whether or not to use the subjunctive in an adjectival or relative clause, you must find the antecedent and see whether it is within the context of the main clause. You will only use the subjunctive if the antecedent is nonexistent, or if its existence is unknown or uncertain.

Tengo una casa que **tiene** dos pisos.	*I have a house that has two floors.*
Quiero una casa que **tenga** dos pisos.	*I want a house that has two floors.*

Notice that in the first sentence above, the fact that *I have a house* means that the house exists. Thus, you must use the indicative in the subordinate clause. However, in the second sentence, the house I want has not been found, so I do not know if it exists. For this reason, the verb of the subordinate must be in the subjunctive. Compare the following sentences:

Conozco a una mujer que **es** ingeniera.	*I know a woman who is an engineer.* (existent)
No conozco a nadie que **sea** brasileño.	*I don't know anyone who is Brazilian.* (existence unknown)
Hay alguien aquí que **está fumando** una pipa.	*There is someone here who is smoking a pipe.* (existent)
¿Hay alguien aquí que **sea** doctor?	*Is there someone here who is a doctor?* (existence unknown)

Lo que is followed by the subjunctive when the implied antecedent is totally unknown and the implication is *whatever it might be*. If the antecedent is known by the speaker, the indicative is used.

Haré lo que me digas.	*I'll do what (whatever) you tell me to do.*
Haré lo que me dijiste.	*I'll do (specifically) what you told me to do.*

NOTE: When a long adjectival clause complements the subject of the main verb, English places the subject plus its clause first, but Spanish would tend to place it last:

Esta mañana llamó [**el reportero al que querías entrevistar sobre el artículo**].	*[The reporter (whom) you wanted to interview about the article] called this morning.*

In the preceding sentence, the reporter is the subject of the main verb *called*.

Ejercicios 6.41–6.42, página 481

4 Adverbial Clauses

a. Definition

An adverbial clause is one that modifies the verb in the main clause in the same manner as an adverb would, by indicating how, when, for what purposes, or under what circumstances the action of the main clause takes place:

Salió **rápidamente**.	*He left quickly.*
Salió **tan pronto como pudo**.	*He left as soon as he could.*

b. Usage

Use of the subjunctive: If the action of the subordinate clause has not been accomplished at the time indicated in the main verb, the subjunctive is used. This rule permits us to subdivide conjunctions into two categories, according to their meanings. Some conjunctions, such as **para que** and **antes de que,** will always introduce actions that have not yet taken place at the time of the main clause:

Lo hago para que tú no tengas que hacerlo.	*I'm doing it so that you won't have to.*
Vino antes de que lo llamáramos.	*He came before we called him.*

Other conjunctions, such as **cuando,** can refer to situations that already occurred or that have not yet occurred. If they refer to a situation that already took place, the verb of the subordinate clause will be in the indicative; if not, it will be in the subjunctive:

Mi perro viene cuando lo llamo.	*My dog comes when I call him.*
Mi perro vendrá cuando lo llame.	*My dog will come when I call him.*

Some conjunctions take the indicative and not the subjunctive because they generally refer to situations that already occurred: **así que, porque,** and **desde que** are some examples:

La obra me aburrió, así que me fui temprano.	*The play bored me, so I left early.*
Se lo regalé a Luis porque él me lo pidió.	*I gave it to Luis because he asked me for it.*
No lo he visto desde que se graduó.	*I haven't seen him since he graduated.*

Following is a table of conjunctions that take the subjunctive, either always or occasionally. (See examples of usage on pages 217–218.)

ALWAYS SUBJUNCTIVE	OCCASIONALLY SUBJUNCTIVE
a fin de que	mientras
salvo que	apenas
a no ser que	cuando
en caso de que	hasta que
sin que	en cuanto
con tal de que	tan pronto como
a menos que	aunque
para que	después de que
antes de que	a pesar de que

When the subject of the main verb is the same as the subject of the subordinate verb, some of these conjunctions change into prepositions.

Obligatory change:

antes de que → antes de	Antes de salir, me puse el abrigo. *Before going out, I put on my coat.*
para que → para	Para preparar esto, necesitas dos huevos. *To prepare this, you need two eggs.*
sin que → sin	Se fue sin despedirse. *He left without saying good-bye.*
después de que → después de	Después de cenar, jugaron a la baraja. *After eating dinner, they played cards.*

Optional change:

| hasta que → hasta | No se irá hasta haberse acabado la comida. (OR: No se irá hasta que se acabe la comida.) *He won't leave until he has finished his food.* |

The conjunctions in the chart on the following page always take the subjunctive, or the infinitive if the subject is the same for both the main verb and the subordinate; however, they would never be followed by the indicative.

CONJUNCTION	MEANING	EXAMPLES
para que a fin de que	so that	SUBJUNCTIVE: **Preparé la comida para que la <u>comieras</u>.** *I prepared the food so that you would eat it.* INFINITIVE (same subject for both verbs): **para que → para** **a fin de que → a fin de** **Se vistió para <u>salir</u>.** *He got dressed to go out.* **Estudia a fin de <u>mejorarte</u>.** *Study to improve yourself.*
a menos que salvo que a no ser que	unless	SUBJUNCTIVE: **Iremos al parque a menos que <u>llueva</u>.** *We will go to the park unless it rains.*
antes de que	before	SUBJUNCTIVE: **Lo preparé todo antes de que <u>llegaran</u> los invitados.** *I prepared everything before the guests arrived.* INFINITIVE: **antes de que → antes de** **Se despidió antes de <u>irse</u>.** *He said good-bye before leaving.*
con tal de que con tal que	provided (that)	SUBJUNCTIVE: **Haré la cena con tal de que tú <u>laves</u> los platos.** *I'll make dinner provided that you wash the dishes.* INFINITIVE: **con tal de que → con tal de** **Iré al cine con tal de <u>poder</u> ir con ustedes.** *I'll go to the movies provided that I can go with you.*
sin que	without	SUBJUNCTIVE: **Salí sin que ellos me <u>oyeran</u>.** *I left without their hearing me.* INFINITIVE: **sin que → sin** **Salí sin <u>hacer</u> ruido.** *I left without making any noise.*
en caso de que	in case (that)	SUBJUNCTIVE: **Traje abrigo en caso de que <u>hiciera</u> frío.** *I brought a coat in case it was cold.*

The conjunctions in the chart on the following page take the subjunctive only when the situation referred to has not been experienced or if there is an implication of the future in the main clause.

CONJUNCTION	MEANING	EXAMPLES
cuando	when	SUBJUNCTIVE: **Vendré cuando <u>pueda</u>.** *I'll come when I can. (whenever that might be)* INDICATIVE: Vino cuando <u>pudo</u>. *He came when he could.*
apenas en cuanto tan pronto como	as soon as	SUBJUNCTIVE: **Vendré en cuanto <u>pueda</u>.** *I'll come as soon as I can.* INDICATIVE: **Vino en cuanto <u>pudo</u>.** *He came as soon as he could.*
aunque a pesar de que aun cuando	even though (subj.) although (indic.)	SUBJUNCTIVE: **Vendrá aunque no lo <u>invites</u>.** *He will come even though you don't invite him.* INDICATIVE: **Vino aunque no lo <u>invitaste</u>.** *He came although you did not invite him.*
después de que	after	SUBJUNCTIVE: **Llegaré después de que tú te <u>hayas ido</u>.** *I'll arrive after you have left.* INDICATIVE: **Llegó después de que tú te <u>fuiste</u>.** *He arrived after you had left.* INFINITIVE: después de que → después de **Llamó después de <u>irse</u>.** *He called after leaving.*
mientras	provided (that), as long as (subj.) while (indic.)	SUBJUNCTIVE: **Mientras no <u>digas</u> la verdad, no te escucharé.** *As long as you don't tell the truth, I will not listen to you.* INDICATIVE: **Yo miraba la televisión mientras ella <u>trabajaba</u>.** *I watched TV while she worked.*
hasta que	until	SUBJUNCTIVE: **No me iré hasta que me <u>digas</u> tu secreto.** *I will not leave until you tell me your secret.* INDICATIVE: **No me fui hasta que me <u>dijo</u> su secreto.** *I did not leave until he told me his secret.* INFINITIVE: hasta que → hasta **No me iré hasta <u>saber</u> la verdad.** *I will not leave until I know the truth.*

Ejercicios 6.43–6.45, páginas 481–482

5 Sequence of Tenses

a. Introduction

The relationship between the action of the main clause and that of the subordinate clause will determine which tenses you may use. We will present three perspectives; in general, the first is more applicable than the other two, which relate to specific formats only.

- Chronological relativity
- Aspect relativity
- Tense relativity from indicative to subjunctive

b. Chronological relativity

The first perspective we will present is the one that uses one basic concept for all combinations: the relativity of occurrence of the actions in the sentence.
The first question would be: What is the tense of the verb of the main clause? There are two general subdivisions of tenses for the verb of the main clause:

- The present set (present, present perfect, future, or imperative)
- The past set (imperfect, preterite, pluperfect, conditional present, or conditional perfect)

The next question is: When did the action of the subordinate clause occur in relation to the action of the verb of the main clause? After? At the same time? Before? Before another action in the past? We will name the four relationships as follows:

- Subsequent
- Simultaneous
- Prior
- Prior to prior

The last question is: Which tense of the subjunctive must be used? There are four tenses of the subjunctive:

- Present
- Present perfect
- Imperfect
- Pluperfect

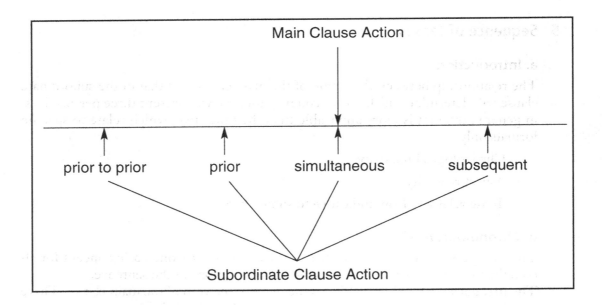

The following sentences might serve as examples of cases in which the main clause action and the subordinate clause action are simultaneous:

Both actions present:

No **creo** que **esté** lloviendo en este momento.

I don't think it's raining at this moment.

Both actions past:

Me **molestaba** que me **mirara** de esa manera.

It bothered me that he would look at me that way.

The following chart indicates which tense could be used for each situation:

MAIN VERB TENSE	CHRONOLOGICAL RELATIVITY OF SUBORDINATE TO MAIN	SUBORDINATE CLAUSE: TENSES OF THE SUBJUNCTIVE	EXAMPLES	REF. #
Present set	1. Subsequent OR: 2. Simultaneous	a. Present	Dudo que <u>llueva</u> mañana.	1a
			Dudo que <u>esté</u> enfermo.	2a
	3. Prior	b. Present perfect	Dudo que ya <u>haya comido</u>.	3b
		c. Imperfect	Dudo que <u>estuviera</u> verde.	3c
	4. Prior to another prior action	d. Pluperfect	Me sorprende que no <u>hubiera llamado</u> antes de venir.	4d
Past set	1. Subsequent OR: 2. Simultaneous	c. Imperfect	Dudaba que se <u>acabara</u> pronto la conferencia.	1c
			Dudaba que <u>estuviera</u> enfermo.	2c
	3. Prior	d. Pluperfect	Dudaba que <u>hubiera dicho</u> esa mentira.	3d

Please note that the present and present perfect subjunctive cannot be used in sentences in which the main clause is in the past set.

Explanation and further contextualization of the examples in the table:

1a. Dudo que **llueva** mañana.   *I doubt (now) that it **will rain** tomorrow.*

The act of raining is subsequent to the moment of doubt; I am having doubt now, the rain has not yet occurred.

2a. Dudo que **esté** enfermo.   *I doubt (now) that he **is** ill (now).*

The (possible) illness and my doubt are happening simultaneously.

3b. Dudo que ya **haya comido**.   *I doubt (now) that he **has eaten** (OR: ate) already.*

I have doubts about whether he has eaten already. Has he already eaten? Did he eat already? I doubt it.

3c. Dudo que **estuviera** verde.   *I doubt (now) that it **was** green (yesterday).*

I was just told that the apple I ate yesterday was green and that is what caused my stomachache. I doubt now that the apple was green (or unripe). I think my stomachache was due to something else.

4d. Me sorprende que no **hubiera llamado** antes de venir.   *I'm surprised that **he had not called** before he came.*

Yesterday, David came to visit me. He did not call before coming. Now that I think about it, it surprises me that he had not called before coming.

1c. Dudaba que se **acabara** pronto la conferencia.   *I doubted that the lecture **would end** soon.*

I was having doubts (during the lecture) that the lecture was going to end soon.

2c. Dudaba que **estuviera** enfermo.   *I doubted that he **was** ill.*

I was at a party, and a friend of mine arrived and told me that my roommate could not come because he was sick. I doubted at that moment that my roommate was sick at that moment. The two actions are simultaneous.

3d. Dudaba que **hubiera dicho** esa mentira.   *I doubted that he **had told** that lie.*

I was told yesterday that my younger brother had lied about his age a few days before. When I was told this, I doubted it. His alleged lie preceded my doubt.

More examples:

1a. Subsequent to a main verb in the present set:

No quiero que **vayas** al cine.   *I don't want you to go to the movies.*

Dile a Natalia que me **llame**.   *Tell Natalia to call me.*

Nunca te lo he dicho para que no te **enojes**.   *I have never told you so you wouldn't get angry.*

2a. Simultaneous to a main verb in the present set:

Me sorprende que la manzana ya **esté** madura.   *I'm surprised the apple is already ripe.*

Encontraré una casa que **tenga** invernadero.   *I'll find a house that has a greenhouse.*

3b. Prior to a main verb in the present set:

¿Conoces a alguien que **haya viajado** a Chile?	*Do you know someone who has traveled to Chile?*
Me iré cuando **haya terminado**.	*I'll leave when I have finished.*
Llámala, a menos que ya lo **hayas hecho**.	*Call her, unless you have already done so.*

3c. Prior to a main verb in the present set:

Es extraño que no **supiera**.	*It's strange that she didn't know.*
Me sorprende que no **pudiera** hacerlo.	*It surprises me that he wasn't able to do it.*

4d. Prior to another action prior to a main verb in the present set:

Carlota vino a cenar a casa anoche.	*Carlota came to dinner last night.*
Antes de venir, había llamado para averiguar si podía traer algo.	*Before coming, she had called to find out whether she could bring something.*
Me sorprende que **hubiera llamado** antes de venir ayer.	*It surprises me that she had called before coming yesterday.*
Los empleados se quejan de que los patrones nunca les **hubieran pedido** su opinión antes de cambiar esa regla.	*The employees complain that the bosses never asked their opinion before changing that rule.*
Lamentamos que no **hubieran recibido** nuestro mensaje antes de salir de viaje.	*We're sorry that they had not received our message before they left on their trip.*
La adivina sabe el pasado de Raúl sin que nadie se lo **hubiera contado** antes.	*The soothsayer knows Raúl's past without anyone having told her before.*

1c. Subsequent to a main clause in the past set:

Dudaba que mi hermana **viniera** a visitarme para Navidad.	*I doubted that my sister would come to visit me for Christmas.*
Mi hermana me lo dio en caso de que lo **necesitara** más tarde.	*My sister gave it to me in case I needed it later.*
Querían una compañía de seguros que **cumpliera** en caso de accidente.	*They wanted an insurance company that would pay in case of an accident.*
Preferiría que te **fueras**.	*I would prefer that you left.*

2c. Simultaneous to a main clause in the past set:

Me encantó que **llegaran** a tiempo.	*I was delighted that they arrived on time.*
La artista lo pintó sin que nadie la **viera**.	*The artist painted it without anyone seeing her.*
No había nada allí que le **gustara**.	*There was nothing there that she liked.*

3d. Prior to a main verb in the past set:

Dudaba que Miguel **hubiera dicho** esa mentira. (I doubted, when I was told yesterday, that he had told the lie the week before.)	*I doubted that Miguel had told that lie.*
Salió corriendo en caso de que no le **hubieran quitado** la pistola al ladrón.	*He ran out in case they had not taken the gun away from the thief.*
Buscaban una casa a la que ya le **hubieran hecho** todas las reparaciones necesarias.	*They were looking for a house that would have already had all the necessary repairs.*
Se habían hablado sin que nadie los **hubiera presentado**.	*They had talked to each other without anyone having introduced them.*
Los bomberos habrían llegado antes de que la casa se **hubiera quemado** si ese accidente no hubiera ocurrido en la carretera.	*The firemen would have arrived before the house had burned down if that accident hadn't happened on the highway.*

c. Aspect relativity

The second perspective we will present elaborates on the distinction between the use of the imperfect and the present perfect subjunctive when the main clause is in the present set (3b and 3c from the preceding table).

Aspect: This term refers to the internal temporal constituency of an event or state (e.g., ongoing vs. completed; beginning vs. middle vs. end), or the way a verb's action is distributed in time (e.g., habitual, repetitive), as opposed to tense, which is a term that refers only to a point in time (e.g., past, present, future).[1]

Use the present perfect subjunctive when the action of the verb of the subordinate clause is perceived as completed or beginning in the past.

Completed:

Es extraño que Luis no **haya venido** a clase.	*It's strange that Luis has not come to class.*
¿Has conocido a alguien que **haya viajado** a Chile?	*Have you met anyone who has traveled to Chile?*
Me iré cuando **haya terminado**.	*I'll leave when I've finished.*
Llámala, a menos que ya lo **hayas hecho**.	*Call her, unless you have already done so.*

Beginning:

Dudo que el vuelo **haya salido** a tiempo.	*I doubt that the flight left on time.* (focus on the beginning of the flight)
Me sorprende que todavía no **hayan empezado** a leer la novela.	*I'm surprised that they still haven't begun to read the novel.*

Use the imperfect subjunctive when the action of the verb of the subordinate clause is perceived as ongoing in the past, or habitual.

---

[1] This is the same difference that applies to preterite and imperfect in the indicative. (See Chapter 6.B: "Aspects of the Indicative Past Tense: Preterite vs. Imperfect and Pluperfect," page 179.)

Ongoing:

Jorge dice que **era** tímido de niño. Dudo que **fuera** tímido.

Jorge says he used to be shy as a child. I doubt that he was shy.

Estaban jugando cuando entré. Me sorprende que **estuvieran** jugando.

They were playing when I entered. It surprises me that they were playing.

Habitual:

Nunca he conocido a nadie que **cantara** así de niño.

I've never met anyone who sang that way as a child.

Se avergüenza de que sus padres nunca **pagaran** impuestos.

She is ashamed that her parents never paid taxes.

d. Tense relativity from indicative to subjunctive

This explanation runs parallel to the previous two explanations, but might be easier to understand.

(1) Main clause in the present set

In the chart below, notice the change in the original verb forms once **Dudo** is inserted.

MAIN CLAUSE IN THE PRESENT SET		
INDICATIVE	MAIN CLAUSE	SUBJUNCTIVE
Irá al cine.	Dudo	que <u>vaya</u> al cine.
Va al cine.	Dudo	que <u>vaya</u> al cine.
Iba al cine.	Dudo	que <u>fuera</u> al cine.
Fue al cine.	Dudo	que <u>haya ido / fuera</u> al cine.
Ha ido al cine.	Dudo	que <u>haya ido</u> al cine.
Habrá ido al cine.	Dudo	que <u>haya ido</u> al cine.
Había ido al cine.	Dudo	que <u>hubiera ido</u> al cine.

The preceding sentences translate as follows:

I doubt that he   *will go*   *to the movies.*
　　　　　　　　　　　goes / is going
　　　　　　　　　　　used to go / was going
　　　　　　　　　　　went
　　　　　　　　　　　has gone
　　　　　　　　　　　will have gone
　　　　　　　　　　　had gone

Table of tense conversions with **dudo:**

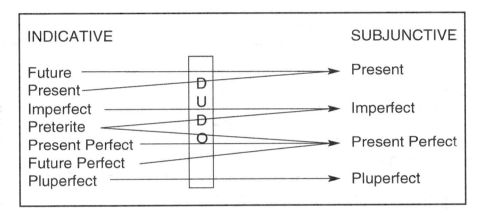

(2) Main clause in the past set

MAIN CLAUSE IN THE PAST SET		
INDICATIVE	MAIN CLAUSE	SUBJUNCTIVE
Irá al cine.	Dudaba	que <u>fuera</u> al cine.
Va al cine.		
Iba al cine.		
Fue al cine.		
Fue al cine.	Dudaba	que <u>hubiera ido</u> al cine.
Ha ido al cine.		
Habrá ido al cine.		
Había ido al cine.		

The preceding sentences translate as follows:

I doubted that he	*would go*	*to the movies.*
	went / was going	
	used to go	
	went	
I doubted that he	*went / had gone*	*to the movies.*
	had gone	
	would have gone	
	had gone	

Table of tense conversions with **dudaba:**

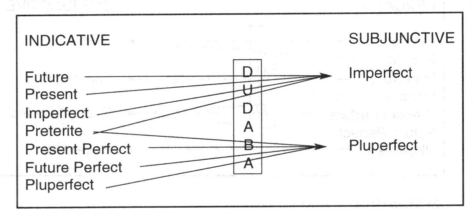

Ejercicios 6.46–6.54, páginas 482–485

6 *If* (**si**) Clauses

a. Sequence of tenses

In Spanish, a sentence that contains a clause with **si** *(if)* or an implication of a condition follows a rigid construction pattern that must always be followed. Memorize the following three types of sentences and remember that they are essentially unchanging, as long as the time frame is the same for both clauses (for example, if both refer to the past):

SI CLAUSE		MAIN CLAUSE
1. Indicative	↔	Indicative or Imperative
2. Imperfect Subjunctive	↔	Present Conditional
3. Pluperfect Subjunctive	↔	Past (Perfect) Conditional or Pluperfect Subjunctive

Sentence type 1 from the above chart refers to situations that are possible. For example, one could say:

1a. Si llueve, me llevo el paraguas. *If it rains, I take my umbrella.*

1b. Si llueve, llévate el paraguas. *If it rains, take your umbrella.*

1c. Si llovía, me llevaba el paraguas. *If it rained, I used to take my umbrella.*

Notice that in each case we are speaking about the possibility of it raining. Just about any tense of the indicative can be used, and usually the same tense is used for both clauses. In the main clause (the one that does not begin with **si**), you can also find the imperative (sentence type **1b**).

The future does not occur in conditional *if* clauses; it does occur when **si** means *whether*.

No sé si lloverá o no. *I don't know whether it will rain or not.*

Sentence types 2 and 3 refer to situations that are contrary to the truth. Type 2 refers to a situation contrary to the present truth. For example:

2a. Si estuviera lloviendo, no saldría. *If it were raining (now), I would not go out.*

2b. Si fuera rico, me compraría un coche deportivo. *If I were rich (now), I would buy myself a sports car.*

Sentence type 3 refers to a situation contrary to past reality:

3a. Si hubiera estudiado más, habría pasado el examen. *If I had studied more (last week), I would have passed the exam.*

There exist exceptions to the rule, as can be seen when a situation in the past affects the present:

Si no hubiera llovido anoche, hoy todo estaría seco. *If it had not rained last night, everything would be dry today.*

All of these sentences can be inverted in order of clauses, beginning with the main clause instead of the **si** clause. For example: **No saldría si estuviera lloviendo.** Note the removal of the comma for this word order.

b. Como si *(As if)*

The expression **como si** is always followed by the past subjunctive—either the imperfect subjunctive to speak of an action simultaneous with the main verb, or the pluperfect subjunctive to speak of an action prior to the main verb:

Habla como si te **conociera**.	*He speaks as if he knew you.*
Te saluda como si te **hubiera visto** antes.	*He greets you as if he had seen you before.*

> Ejercicios 6.55–6.57, páginas 485–486

7 Ojalá

Sentences with **ojalá** can be translated into English as either *I hope* or *I wish*. When you *hope (for)* something, the implication is that you don't know what the reality of the situation is or will be. Consider the following sentences:

1. *I hope that it will not rain tomorrow.* (hope for the future)
2. *I hope that it isn't raining.* (hope for the present)
3. *I hope that our team won.* (hope for the past)

In these sentences, the speaker does not know: 1. whether it will rain, 2. whether it is raining, or 3. whether the team won or lost.

On the other hand, when you *wish (for)* something, it is contrary to the actual reality. Consider the following sentences:

4. *I wish it were not raining.* (it is in fact raining; wish for the present)
5. *I wish our team had won.* (actually, they lost; wish for the past)

To translate this difference in Spanish, you use **ojalá** with different tenses of the subjunctive:

Present subjunctive—hope for the future and the present:

Ojalá que no llueva mañana.	*I hope it will not rain tomorrow.*
Ojalá que no esté lloviendo.	*I hope it isn't raining.*

Present perfect subjunctive—hope for the past:

    Ojalá que nuestro equipo haya ganado.   *I hope our team won.*

Imperfect subjunctive—wish for the present and the future:

    Ojalá que no estuviera lloviendo.   *I wish it weren't raining.*

    Ojalá que pudiera venir mañana.   *I wish he could come tomorrow.*

Pluperfect subjunctive—wish for the past:

    Ojalá que nuestro equipo hubiera ganado.   *I wish our team had won.*

> Ejercicios 6.58–6.59, página 486

8 Expressions of Leave-Taking

The most common expressions of leave-taking in Spanish are **adiós, chao, nos vemos,** and **hasta luego (hasta mañana, hasta el lunes, hasta el 2 de mayo, hasta entonces,** etc). When saying good-bye, you might also want to wish your interlocutor well in some immediate context, such as getting over an illness, having a good trip, enjoying an event, etc. For such expressions of well-wishing, in English, the imperative is used: *Have a good day, Get well, Have a good trip, Have fun,* etc. In Spanish, however, the imperative is not used in this context. Note on the following page how to express good wishes in Spanish (you can think of these phrases as having an unexpressed **Ojalá** or **Espero** before the conjunction **Que**, which would help to remind you to use the subjunctive).

For someone whom you address as:

Tú:

Que[2] te vaya bien.	*Have a good day / trip / etc.* (literally: *"May it go well for you."* in which *it* is determined by the context.)
Que te mejores.	*Get better (Get well).*
Que te alivies.	*Get well.*
Que tengas (un) buen viaje.	*Have a good trip.*
Que te diviertas.	*Have fun.*
Que Dios te acompañe.	*May God accompany you.* (for someone leaving on a trip)
Que la / lo pases bien.	*Have a good one.*
Que tengas (un) buen fin de semana.	*Have a good weekend.*

Usted:	**Ustedes:**
Que le vaya bien.	Que les vaya bien.
Que se mejore.	Que se mejoren.
Que se alivie.	Que se alivien.
Que tenga (un) buen viaje.	Que tengan (un) buen viaje.
Que se divierta.	Que se diviertan.
Que Dios lo / la acompañe.	Que Dios los / las acompañe.
Que la / lo pase bien.	Que la / lo pasen bien.
Que tenga (un) buen fin de semana.	Que tengan (un) buen...

Notice that these verbs are of different constructions.

---

[2] Notice that this **que** does not have an accent mark, even if you choose to place the expression in an exclamation. This is because it is not the exclamative **que**, but a conjunction. For more information on accents, see Chapter 9, pages 353–355.

In a standard construction, with a subject and a direct object, the verb agrees with the person being addressed:

VERB	DIRECT OBJECT	EXAMPLE		
pasar	fin de semana	Que	pases pase pasen paséis	(un) buen fin de semana.
		*May **you** have a good weekend.*		
pasar	lo la	Que lo / la	pases pase pasen paséis	bien.
		*May **you** have a good one.*		
tener	fin de semana viaje	Que	tengas tenga tengan tengáis	(un) buen fin de semana. (un) buen viaje.
		*May **you** have a good weekend / trip.*		

With reflexive verbs, when the same word serves as both subject and object, the verb agrees with the person being addressed:

VERB	REFLEXIVE PRONOUN	EXAMPLE	
divertirse	te se os	Que	te diviertas. se divierta(n). os divirtáis.
		Have fun.	
aliviarse	te se os	Que	te alivies. se alivie(n). os aliviéis.
		Get well.	
mejorarse	te se os	Que	te mejores. se mejore(n). os mejoréis.
		Get well (OR: *Get better*).	

When a verb like **gustar** is used with a subject and an indirect object, the verb itself remains invariable, because the subject is impersonal, as in **irle bien a uno**:

VERB	INDIRECT OBJECT	EXAMPLE		
ir	te le(s) os	Que	te le(s) os	vaya bien.
		May it go well for you.		

With **Dios** as the subject and the person being addressed as the direct object, the verb agrees with the subject **Dios**:

VERB	DIRECT OBJECT	EXAMPLE		
acompañar	te la(s) lo(s) os	Que Dios	te la(s) lo(s) os	acompañe.
		May God accompany (OR: *be with*) *you.*		

Ejercicios 6.60–6.63, páginas 486–487

H INFINITIVES AND PRESENT PARTICIPLES

1 Infinitives

a. Present infinitive

The infinitive functions like a noun in Spanish, and, like a noun, it can be the subject or object of a verb or the object of a preposition. In English, the present participle is frequently used in these roles.

The infinitive as subject (sometimes preceded by the article **el**):

Caminar es bueno para la salud.	*Walking is healthy.*
Me gusta **montar** a caballo.	*I like riding (to ride) horseback.*
Les encanta **perder** el tiempo.	*They love wasting time.*
El **haber ganado** el Pichichi se le subió a la cabeza.	*Winning the Pichichi went to his head.*

The infinitive as direct object:

Quiero **aprender** español.	*I want to learn Spanish.*
No sé **hacer** eso.	*I don't know how to do that.*
Pienso **respaldar** la resolución.	*I'm planning to back the resolution.*
Debemos **estudiar** la lección.	*We must study the lesson.*
Decidimos **ir** al cine.	*We decided to go to the movies.*
¿Desea **comprar** algo?	*Do you wish to buy something?*
Logré **convencerla**.	*I succeeded in convincing her.*
Parece **estar** triste.	*He seems to be sad.*

Verbs used with direct object pronouns and infinitives (**dejar, hacer**):

No lo dejan **jugar**.	*They don't let him play.*
Lo hizo **recitar** el poema.	*She made him recite the poem.*

Verbs used with indirect object pronouns and infinitives (**permitir, aconsejar, impedir, prohibir, recomendar, rogar**):

No le permiten **salir**.	*They don't let him go out.*
Les aconsejo **llegar** temprano.	*I advise you to arrive early.*
Le impidieron **hablar**.	*They prevented him from speaking.*
Les prohíbe **beber** cerveza.	*He forbids them to drink beer.*
Le recomiendo **ver** esa película.	*I recommend that you see that movie.*
Les ruego **escucharme**.	*I beg you to listen to me.*

Verbs of perception used with direct objects and infinitives (**ver, oír**):

La vi **llegar** hace una hora.	*I saw her arrive an hour ago.*
Los oí **cantar** anoche.	*I heard them sing (singing) last night.*

The infinitive as an object of a preposition:

Se fue sin **despedirse**.	*He left without saying good-bye.*
Lo hice para **ayudarte**.	*I did it to help you.*
Eso te pasa por **comer** tanto.	*That happens to you because you eat so much.*
Antes de **salir**, siempre desayuna.	*Before going out, he always eats breakfast.*
Estoy cansada de **estudiar**.	*I'm tired of studying.*

The infinitive after **que** (**hay que, tener que, algo que, nada que, poco que**):

Hay que **tener** confianza.	*It's necessary to have confidence.*
Tuvieron que **disolverlo** por falta de patrocinadores.	*They had to dissolve it for lack of sponsors.*
Eso no tiene nada que **ver** con el asunto.	*That doesn't have anything to do with the matter.*
Tenemos poco que **hacer**.	*We have little to do.*

The infinitive after **de** with **fácil, difícil, posible,** and **imposible**:

Ese sonido es difícil de **pronunciar**.	*That sound is difficult to pronounce.*

In the preceding sentence, the subject of the verb **ser** is **sonido**. However, if the infinitive itself is the subject of **ser**, the preposition **de** must be omitted.

Es difícil **pronunciar** ese sonido.	*It's difficult to pronounce that sound.*

The same construction is used with **fácil, posible,** and **imposible**.

The construction **al** + *infinitive* is used for an action that occurs at the same time as the main verb:

Al **entrar**, los saludaron a todos.	*When they entered (Upon entering), they greeted everyone.*
Al **verlos**, los saludé.	*When I saw them, I greeted them.*

The infinitive in advertising, signs, commands, questions:

No **fumar.**	*No smoking.*
Prohibido **tirar** basura.	*No littering.*
¿Por qué **engordar**? Con nuestro sistema puede usted adelgazar sin ningún esfuerzo.	*Why gain weight? With our system, you can lose weight effortlessly.*

The infinitive with passive meaning after **oír, ver, mirar, escuchar, dejar, mandar, hacer:**

Lo he oído **decir.**	*I have heard it (being) said.*
Hice **copiar** las pruebas.	*I had the tests copied.*
Mandé **enviar** flores.	*I ordered flowers to be delivered.*

b. Perfect infinitive

The perfect infinitive (formed with the auxiliary **haber** in the infinitive, plus the past participle of the verb) is used to express an action that occurred before the action of the main verb, when the subject is the same for both:

Debes de **haberlos dejado** en el coche.	*You must have left them in the car.*
Creo **habérselo dicho.**	*I think I told him that.*
Se fue sin **haber comido** nada.	*He left without having eaten anything.*
Se cansó de la película después de **haberla visto** tres veces.	*He got tired of the movie after having seen it three times.*

2 Present Participles

[To review the formation of the present participle, see Chapter 5.F.1, pages 173–174. See also "Simple Progressive Tenses" pages 194–196, and "Perfect Progressive Tenses" pages 196–198.]

The present participle, when not used with auxiliaries such as **estar,** functions in Spanish like an adverb and refers to an action occurring at the same time as or prior to the main action, indicating manner, cause, or condition. In this usage, it is also a gerund.

Manner:

Entró **gritando.**	*He entered yelling.*

Cause:

    Siendo persona sencilla, nunca pensó que otros no fueran honrados.
    Being a simple person, he never thought that others wouldn't be honest.

Condition:

    Estando los padres en casa, él no llamará.
    With the parents at home, he won't call.

In Spanish, the present participle may be used to indicate that two actions are happening simultaneously:

    Preparó la cena **escuchando** la radio.
    He prepared dinner while he listened to the radio.

As a rule, the present participle follows the main verb. However, in cases in which it describes a cause or condition related to the main verb, it may be placed before:

    Explicándoselo claramente de antemano, no habrá ambigüedad.
    By explaining it clearly to them in advance, there will be no ambiguity.

In English the present participle can be used as an adjective. In these cases, Spanish uses:

    an adjective (not formed with the present participle form):

una persona **interesante**	*an <u>interesting</u> person*
un interés **creciente**	*a <u>growing</u> interest*
los problemas **existentes**	*the <u>existing</u> problems*

    de + *noun or infinitive:*

papel **de escribir**	*<u>writing</u> paper*
dolores **de crecimiento**	*<u>growing</u> pains*

    a clause:

Vio un pájaro **que volaba**.	*She saw a bird <u>flying</u>.*
Es una niña **que está creciendo**.	*She's a <u>growing</u> girl.*

    a preposition:

el libro **con** fotos de España	*the book <u>containing</u> pictures of Spain*
lo **de** ella	*those things <u>belonging</u> to her*

a past participle for postures and other conditions:

parado *standing, still*	aburrido *boring*
sentado *sitting*	divertido *amusing*
acostado *lying down*	entretenido *entertaining*

Eduardo está **sentado** en mi silla.	*Eduardo is sitting in my seat.*
Estaba **acostado** cuando llamaste.	*I was lying down when you called.*

In idiomatic expressions, the present participle of some verbs of motion indicates location.

Mi cuarto se encuentra **entrando** a la izquierda.	*My room is to the left of the entrance.*
Esa tienda está **pasando** el museo.	*That store is beyond the museum.*

In summary, never use the present participle form in Spanish as if it were a noun (i.e., as subject, object, or object of preposition) or as an adjective. In Spanish, it functions only as an adverb.

> Ejercicios 6.64–6.72, páginas 487–489

VERBS LIKE GUSTAR

1 Formation

The grammatical structure of Spanish sentences with **gustar** is different from that of English sentences with *to like*. The subject in English is the indirect object in Spanish. The direct object in English is the subject in Spanish:

Me gustan las películas mexicanas.	*I like Mexican movies.*

In the Spanish sentence above, **me** is the indirect object of the verb, and **las películas mexicanas** is the subject. (Notice the agreement of the verb with the plural of its subject.) To illustrate more clearly the fact that **me** is the indirect object, notice that if you wished to give emphasis to the person, you would add **a mí** to the basic sentence (and *not* **yo**):

A mí me gustan las películas mexicanas.	*I like Mexican movies.*

For further emphasis on this structure, look at the subject, **películas mexicanas.** If you wished to replace the subject with a pronoun, it would be impossible. The rule in this structure is that a thing that is a subject cannot be replaced by a pronoun, because subject pronouns refer to people. If you do not wish to repeat the noun because, for example, you have already mentioned it in the context preceding the sentence, you would simply omit it:

Me gustan.	*I like them.*

Another way to emphasize this construction is to see what happens when the question is asked: "Who likes Mexican movies?" In English, the answer is "I (do)." Observe what happens in Spanish:

—¿A quién le gustan las películas mexicanas?	*"Who likes Mexican movies?"*
—**A mí.**	*"I do."*

You would never answer **yo** to this question, because the person is the indirect object, not the subject of the verb.

2 Word Order

For verbs like **gustar,** the subject, when it is a noun or other nominalized form, is most commonly placed after the verb. In the following sentences, the subject is in bold (note in the translation that the subject is different in English):

Te gustaban **las películas de misterio.**	*You used to like mystery movies.*
Me encantó **bailar** contigo.	*I loved dancing with you.*
A Beto le hacen falta **sus padres.**	*Beto misses his parents.*
Te caerá bien **Juanita.**	*You will like Juanita.*

With **faltar, sobrar,** and **quedar,** always place the subject after the verb:

Le falta **un trofeo** para tener la colección completa.	*She needs one trophy to have the whole collection.*
Nos sobró **comida.**	*We had food left over.*

3 Verbs Similar to **gustar**

There is a group of verbs that behaves like **gustar:**

caer bien / mal	*to like / to dislike*
encantar	*to "love"* (as on bumper stickers)
faltar	*to lack*
hacer falta	*to miss; to need*
quedar	*to have remaining, left*
sobrar	*to have in excess, left over*

Some of these verbs have other uses and meanings; for example, **caer** and **caerse** mean *to fall, fall down,* and **faltar** can mean *to be absent.* Also, the verb **quedarse** used reflexively means *to stay, remain.* Thus, depending upon the grammatical construction you give the sentence, its meaning can change dramatically.

Caer bien / mal	*to like / to dislike (a person)*
Mis amigos **me caen bien.**	*I like my friends.*
Creo que **les caigo bien** a tus padres.[3]	*I think your parents like me.*
El novio de mi hermana **me cae mal.** (OR: El novio de mi hermana **no me cae bien.**)	*I don't like my sister's boyfriend.*

Gustar is used with things or with people who are perceived as professionals, such as professors, presidents, etc. In this use of **gustar,** you mean that you respect their work, not necessarily that you like them personally:

Me gusta mi profesor de historia. Es excelente, y siempre viene preparado.	*I like my history professor. He's excellent and he always comes prepared.*
Me cae bien mi profesor de historia. Es muy simpático.	*I like my history professor. He's very nice.*

---

[3] The majority of these verbs are used exclusively in the third-person singular or plural, but those that may have people as subjects can be used in any person. The two most common verbs of this category are **caer bien** and **hacer falta.**

Me haces falta.   *I miss you.*
Le caigo bien.   *She likes me.*

Given the meanings of **gustar** in certain dialects, it is best to avoid using it with a human being as its subject, or to make certain it is being used with its intended meaning.

If you use the verb **gustar** with an individual whose relationship to you is other than professional, the implication may be that you are attracted to that person:

Me gusta Silvia.	*I am attracted to Silvia.*

Caer bien / mal with food:

Le cayó muy **mal** la cena.	*Dinner disagreed with her.*

Encantar   *to love* (as in "I love New York")

"Bumper-sticker" love is different from sentimental love. Once you understand its meaning, you can use it, as bumper stickers do, with almost anything except sentimental love:

Me encanta Nueva York, me **encantan** los perros, los bebés, etc.	*I (just) love New York (I ❤ NY), I love dogs, babies, etc.*

Sentimental love is expressed with **querer**:

Te **quiero**. Te **quiero** mucho.	*I love you. I love you a lot.*

Te amo is more literary, more poetic, than **te quiero**:

"**Te amo**", le dijo Romeo a Julieta.	*"I love you," Romeo told Juliet.*
Quiero mucho a mis padres, a mi perro...	*I love my parents, my dog . . .*

Faltar   *to lack*

A esta baraja le **faltan** dos cartas.	*This deck of cards lacks (is missing) two cards.*

Hacer falta   *to miss (a person), to need (a thing)*

Me **haces falta**.	*I miss you.*
Te **hace falta** un abrigo.	*You need a coat.*

Quedar   *to have left*

Nos **quedan** cinco minutos.	*We have five minutes left.*

Sobrar   *to have left over, in excess*

Les **sobró** mucha comida.	*They had a lot of food left over.*

There are other verbs that are used in the same type of construction, but these behave in essentially the same way in English. These other verbs are:

bastarle a uno	to be enough	parecerle a uno	to seem
convenirle a uno	to be convenient	pasarle a uno	to happen
dolerle a uno[4]	to hurt	sentarle bien a uno	to suit
importarle a uno	to matter	sucederle a uno	to happen
interesarle a uno	to interest	tocarle a uno	to be one's turn

Examples:

Me **bastan** cinco minutos.	*Five minutes are enough for me.*
No nos **conviene** esa hora.	*That time isn't convenient for us.*
¿Te **duele** la pierna?	*Does your leg hurt?*
No nos **importa** si llueve.	*It doesn't matter to us if it rains.*
Me **interesaría** participar.	*I would be interested in participating.*
Me **parece** increíble.	*It seems incredible to me.*
Siempre me **pasan** cosas así.	*Things like that always happen to me.*
Te **sienta** bien el azul.	*Blue suits you.*
¿Qué te **sucedió**?	*What happened to you?*
A mí me **toca** jugar.	*It's my turn to play.*

4 Articles

Remember to use definite articles in Spanish with **gustar, caer bien,** and **encantar** when their subjects are general in nature. (See Chapter 2.B, pages 28–32.)

Me gusta **el** chocolate semiamargo.	*I like semisweet chocolate.*
Me caen bien **los** hijos de Juana.	*I like Juana's sons.*
Me encantan **las** playas.	*I love beaches.*

---

[4] The subject of **doler** can only be a body part:
   Me duele la pierna. *My leg hurts.*
If you want to say *That shoe hurts*, you need the verb **lastimar**:
   Ese zapato me lastima.
The translation of *hurt* with human direct objects is **hacer daño**:
   ¿**Te hizo daño?** *Did he hurt you?*
   ¿**Te hiciste daño?** *Did you hurt yourself?*

5 Changes in Meaning

Some verbs can have other meanings if used in different grammatical constructions:

convenir en *to agree to*	**Convinimos** en encontrarnos en la plaza a las dos. *We agreed to meet in the plaza at two o'clock.*
importar + *d.o.* *to import*	Los EE. UU. **importan** automóviles del Japón. *The U.S. imports cars from Japan.*
interesarse por / en *to be interested in*	Ella **se interesa** en la política. *She's interested in politics.*
parecerse a *to look like*	Tú **te pareces a** tu mamá. *You look like your mother.*
pasar + *d.o.* *to pass*	**Pasa** la sal, por favor. *Pass the salt, please.*
sentar / sentarse *to seat / to sit*	La mamá **sentó** al niño en la silla. *The mother sat the child on the chair.* **Te sentaste** en mi silla. *You sat on my chair.*
tocar *to touch* OR: *to play* (a musical instrument)	Los turistas lo **tocaban** todo. *The tourists touched everything.* **Tocamos** la guitarra. *We play the guitar.*

Ejercicios 6.73–6.79, páginas 489–490

J REFLEXIVE VERBS

Grammatically speaking, the reflexive construction implies that the subject of the verb receives the action of the verb as well. In other words, the subject and the object are the same. (See Chapter 3.B.2, pages 69–71, on reflexive pronouns.)

Nonreflexive:

    Miro el cielo.   *I look at the sky.*

    subject **= yo;** object **= el cielo**

Reflexive:

    Me **miro** en el espejo.   *I look at myself in the mirror.*

    subject **=** object **= yo**

In many cases, Spanish uses a reflexive when no reflexivity appears to exist in the English translation. This is why we perceive this section as a lexical rather than a grammatical one, and offer a list that may help you remember when the reflexive is used.

Notice that in Spanish, the reflexive almost always indicates a change of state or the beginning of an action. Consider the differences between the following sentences:

Me **dormí** a las siete.	*I fell asleep at seven.*
Dormí siete horas.	*I slept seven hours.*
Estaba dormido.	*I was asleep.*
Me **estaba durmiendo** cuando llamaste.	*I was falling asleep when you called.*
Se **sentó** frente a nosotros.	*He sat down in front of us.*
Está sentado frente a nosotros.	*He is sitting in front of us.*
Me **enamoré** de él.	*I fell in love with him.*
Estoy enamorada de él.	*I am in love with him.*

Change of emotional state, or emotional reaction to something:

aburrirse	*to get bored*	divertirse	*to have fun*
alegrarse	*to rejoice, be glad*	enojarse	*to become or be angry*
asustarse	*to become or be frightened*	enorgullecerse	*to feel or be proud*
avergonzarse	*to be ashamed, embarrassed*	entristecerse	*to become or be sad*
calmarse	*to calm down*	preocuparse	*to worry*

Change of physical state:

acostarse	*to lie down*	moverse	*to move (physically)*
despertarse	*to wake up*	mudarse	*to move (residences)*
dormirse	*to fall asleep*	secarse	*to dry off, dry out*
levantarse	*to get up*	sentarse	*to sit down*
mojarse	*to get wet*	volverse	*to turn around*

Change of mental state or level of consciousness or memory:

acordarse	*to remember*	equivocarse	*to be mistaken*
darse cuenta	*to realize*	fijarse	*to notice*
enterarse	*to find out*	olvidarse	*to forget*

Verbs with more than one usage: Some verbs may or may not be used in the reflexive construction. The basic meaning of the verb may change depending upon the construction used:

Los soldados **marcharon** por una hora.	*The soldiers marched for an hour.*
Los invitados **se marcharon**.	*The guests left.*

Other verbs of this type are:

bajar	*to go down*	dormir	*to sleep*
bajarse	*to get down from, get off*	dormirse	*to fall asleep*
caer	*to fall*	ir	*to go (somewhere)*
caerse	*to fall down*	irse	*to leave*
despedir	*to fire (a person)*		
despedirse	*to say good-bye*		

Reflexive pronouns are also used in situations in which the subject is somehow affected by the action of the verb; with verbs of consumption, such as eating and drinking, the implication in the reflexive is one of enjoyment or thoroughness of the consumption:

Comí a las cuatro.	*I ate at four.*
¿**Te comiste** todo el desayuno?	*Did you eat all of your breakfast?*

Other verbs of this type:

aprender	to learn	saber	to know
aprenderse	to learn (thoroughly, by heart)	saberse	to know (thoroughly, by heart)
beber	to drink	tomar	to drink, eat, take
beberse	to drink (up, completely)	tomarse	to drink, eat (up, completely)

The verbs in the nonreflexive form have more general meanings, while the verbs in the reflexive form have more specific meanings:

Aprender es fácil. *It's easy to learn.*

Aprenderse el vocabulario es difícil. *Learning vocabulary is difficult.*

Obligatory reflexives: The following verbs exist exclusively in the reflexive form:

acordarse	to remember	jactarse	to brag, boast
arrepentirse	to regret, repent	quejarse	to complain
atreverse	to dare	rebelarse	to rebel
equivocarse	to make a mistake	suicidarse	to commit suicide

Following are two lists of verbs (one English–Spanish, the other Spanish–English) that are frequently or always used in the reflexive construction. You may find these lists useful for studying, or for focused practice.

Ejercicios 6.80–6.82, páginas 491–492

J Reflexive Verbs

REFLEXIVE VERBS • ENGLISH–SPANISH

address someone: **dirigirse a alguien**

approach something / someone: **acercarse a algo / alguien**

be angry with someone: **enojarse con alguien**

be ashamed of something: **avergonzarse de algo**

be called: **llamarse**

be frightened of something: **asustarse de algo**

be glad about something: **alegrarse de algo**

be interested in something: **interesarse por / en algo**

be mistaken: **equivocarse**

be named: **llamarse**

be proud: **enorgullecerse**

be quiet: **callarse**

become (by physical or metaphysical transformation): **convertirse en algo**

become (describing mood): **ponerse** (+ *adj.*)

become (describing undesired state [blind, crazy…]): **volverse** (+ *adj.*)

become (through one's efforts [a lawyer, doctor…]): **hacerse** (+ *noun*)

become ill: **enfermarse**

become sad: **entristecerse**

begin to do something: **ponerse a hacer algo**

brush (one's teeth, hair…): **cepillarse**

calm down: **calmarse, tranquilizarse**

comb one's hair: **peinarse** (el pelo)

commit suicide: **suicidarse**

complain about something: **quejarse de algo**

confront something or someone: **encararse con / enfrentarse a algo / alguien**

dare to do something: **atreverse a hacer algo**

die: **morirse**

dry off, dry out: **secarse**

face something or someone: **encararse con / enfrentarse a algo / alguien**

fall asleep: **dormirse**

fall behind, be late: **atrasarse**

fall down: **caerse**

fall in love with someone: **enamorarse de alguien**

feel (+ *adj.*): **sentirse** (+ *adj.*)

fight with someone: **pelearse con alguien**

find out about something: **enterarse de algo**

forget something: **olvidarse de algo**

get ahead: **adelantarse**

get along (not get along) *with someone:* **llevarse bien (mal) con alguien**

get bored: **aburrirse**

get divorced: **divorciarse**

get down from something, get off (bus, train, tree…): **bajarse de algo**

get lost: **perderse**

get married to someone: **casarse con alguien**

get near something / someone: **acercarse a algo / alguien**

get onto something, get on (bus, train…): **subirse a algo**

get rid of something: **deshacerse de algo**

get sick: **enfermarse**

get up: **levantarse**

get used to something: **acostumbrarse a algo**

get well: **aliviarse, curarse**

get wet: **mojarse**

get worse: **empeorarse**

go to bed: **acostarse**

graduate: **graduarse**

have fun: **divertirse**

improve (one's condition): **mejorarse**

insist on doing something: **empeñarse en hacer algo**

(continued)

REFLEXIVE VERBS • ENGLISH–SPANISH

interfere with someone: **meterse con alguien**

keep something: **quedarse con algo**

laugh at: **reírse de**

leave: **marcharse, irse**

lie down: **acostarse**

look like someone / something: **parecerse a alguien / algo**

make an appointment / a date with someone: **citarse con alguien**

make an effort to do something: **esforzarse por hacer algo**

make a mistake: **equivocarse**

make fun of someone: **burlarse de alguien**

major in something: **especializarse en algo**

make up one's mind to: **decidirse a**

meet someone (not for the first time): **encontrarse con alguien**

miss out on something: **perderse algo**

move (change residences): **mudarse**

move (one's body, objects): **moverse**

move away from something: **alejarse de algo**

notice: **fijarse en**

object to something: **oponerse a algo**

prepare to do something: **disponerse a hacer algo**

put on something (article of clothing): **ponerse algo**

realize something: **darse cuenta de algo**

rebel: **rebelarse**

refer to something: **referirse a algo**

refuse to do something: **negarse a hacer algo**

regret (doing) *something:* **arrepentirse de algo**

rejoice about something: **alegrarse de algo**

remember something: **acordarse de algo**

remove something (article of clothing): **quitarse algo**

resign oneself to something: **resignarse a algo**

rub: **frotarse**

say good-bye to someone: **despedirse de alguien**

scratch oneself: **rascarse**

shut up: **callarse**

sit down: **sentarse**

specialize in something: **especializarse en algo**

stay: **quedarse**

take off something (article of clothing): **quitarse algo**

take something away / with oneself: **llevarse algo**

trust someone: **fiarse de alguien**

wake up: **despertarse**

worry about something: **preocuparse por algo**

J Reflexive Verbs

REFLEXIVE VERBS • SPANISH–ENGLISH

aburrirse: *get bored*

acercarse a algo / alguien: *approach, get near something / someone*

acordarse de algo: *remember something*

acostarse: *lie down, go to bed*

acostumbrarse a algo: *get used to something*

adelantarse: *get ahead*

alegrarse de algo: *rejoice / be glad about something*

alejarse de algo: *move away from something*

aliviarse: *get well*

arrepentirse de algo: *regret (doing) something*

asustarse de algo: *be frightened of something*

atrasarse: *fall behind, be late*

atreverse a hacer algo: *dare to do something*

avergonzarse de algo: *be ashamed of something*

bajarse de algo: *get down from something, get off (bus, train, tree…)*

burlarse de alguien: *make fun of someone*

caerse: *fall down*

callarse: *be quiet, shut up*

calmarse: *calm down*

casarse con alguien: *get married to someone*

cepillarse: *brush (one's teeth, hair…)*

citarse con alguien: *make an appointment / a date with someone*

convertirse en algo: *become (by physical or metaphysical transformation)*

curarse: *get well*

darse cuenta de algo: *realize something*

decidirse a hacer algo: *make up one's mind to do something*

deshacerse de algo: *get rid of something*

despedirse de alguien: *say good-bye to someone*

despertarse: *wake up*

dirigirse a alguien: *address someone*

disponerse a hacer algo: *prepare to do something*

divertirse: *have fun*

divorciarse: *get divorced*

dormirse: *fall asleep*

empeñarse en hacer algo: *insist on doing something*

empeorarse: *get worse*

enamorarse de alguien: *fall in love with someone*

encararse con algo / alguien: *face / confront something or someone*

encontrarse con alguien: *meet someone (not for the first time)*

enfermarse: *get sick, become ill*

enfrentarse a algo / alguien: *face / confront something / someone*

enojarse con alguien: *be angry with someone*

enorgullecerse: *be proud*

enterarse de algo: *find out about something*

entristecerse: *become sad*

equivocarse: *be mistaken, make a mistake*

esforzarse por hacer algo: *make an effort to do something*

especializarse en algo: *specialize / major in something*

fiarse de alguien: *trust someone*

fijarse en algo: *notice something*

frotarse: *rub*

graduarse: *graduate*

hacerse (+ noun): *become (through one's efforts [a lawyer, doctor…])*

interesarse por / en: *be interested in*

irse: *leave*

levantarse: *get up*

llamarse: *be called, named*

llevarse algo: *take something away / with oneself*

(continued)

REFLEXIVE VERBS • SPANISH–ENGLISH

llevarse bien (mal) con: *get along (not get along) with*

marcharse: *leave*

mejorarse: *improve* (one's condition)

meterse con alguien: *interfere with someone*

mojarse: *get wet*

morirse: *die*

moverse: *move* (one's body, objects)

mudarse: *move* (change residences)

negarse a hacer algo: *refuse to do something*

olvidarse de algo: *forget something*

oponerse a algo: *object to something*

parecerse a alguien / algo: *look like someone / something*

peinarse (el pelo): *comb one's hair*

pelearse con alguien: *fight with someone*

perderse: *get lost*

perderse algo: *miss out on something*

ponerse (+ *adj.*): *become* (describing mood)

ponerse a hacer algo: *begin to do something*

ponerse algo: *put on something* (article of clothing)

preocuparse por algo: *worry about something*

quedarse: *stay*

quedarse con algo: *keep something*

quejarse de algo: *complain about something*

quitarse algo: *take off / remove something* (article of clothing)

rascarse: *scratch oneself*

rebelarse: *rebel*

referirse a algo: *refer to something*

reírse de: *laugh at*

resignarse a algo: *resign oneself to*

secarse: *dry off, dry out*

sentarse: *sit down*

sentirse (+ *adj.*): *feel* (+ *adj.*)

subirse a algo: *get onto, get on* (bus, train…)

suicidarse: *commit suicide*

tranquilizarse: *calm down*

volverse (+ *adj.*): *become* (describing undesired state [blind, crazy…])

REFLEXIVE VERBS WITH CHARACTERISTIC PREPOSITIONS

a	con	de	en	por
acercarse a	casarse con	acordarse de	convertirse en	esforzarse por
acostumbrarse a	citarse con	alegrarse de	empeñarse en	interesarse por
atreverse a	encararse con	alejarse de	especializarse en	preocuparse por
decidirse a	encontrarse con	arrepentirse de	fijarse en	
dirigirse a	enojarse con	asustarse de	interesarse en	
disponerse a	llevarse bien con	avergonzarse de		
enfrentarse a	meterse con	bajarse de		
negarse a	pelearse con	burlarse de		
oponerse a	quedarse con	darse cuenta de		
parecerse a		deshacerse de		
ponerse a		despedirse de		
referirse a		enamorarse de		
		enterarse de		
		fiarse de		
		olvidarse de		
		quejarse de		
		reírse de		

K INDIRECT DISCOURSE

1 Introduction

Indirect discourse is the relating of oral statements without quoting them directly.

DIRECT DISCOURSE	INDIRECT DISCOURSE	
	PRESENT	PAST
—Te <u>llamaré</u> mañana. *"I'll call you tomorrow."*	**Dice que me <u>llamará</u> mañana.** *He says that he will call me tomorrow.*	**Dijo que me <u>llamaría</u> al día siguiente.** *He said that he would call me the following day.*

Notice the three possible types of changes in indirect discourse:
- Verb [will → would]
- Person [I → he; you → me]
- Time reference [tomorrow → the following day]

As logic indicates, these changes do not always occur, or only some of them might occur. For example, if I am quoting what I just said today about today, there will be no change *("It's cold today." "I am saying it's cold today.")*. However, when there is a change of person or of time reference between the direct quote and the indirect quote, there will be changes, as in English. If the communication verb is in the past, there is a change in most tenses.

2 Verb-Tense Changes

DIRECT DISCOURSE	INDIRECT DISCOURSE
Present Indicative →	**Imperfect Indicative**
Lo **hago**. *I do it.*	Dijo que lo **hacía**. *He said he used to do it.*
Present Subjunctive →	**Imperfect Subjunctive**
Quiere que **vaya**. *He wants me to go.*	Dijo que quería que **fuera**. *He said he wanted me to go.*
Present Perfect Indicative →	**Pluperfect Indicative**
Nos **han visto**. *They have seen us.*	Dijeron que nos **habían visto**. *They said they had seen us.*
Present Perfect Subjunctive →	**Pluperfect Subjunctive**
Dudo que lo **hayan visto**. *I doubt that they saw it.*	Dijo que dudaba que lo **hubieran visto**. *He said that he doubted they'd seen it.*
Preterite →	**Pluperfect Indicative**
Lo **vi**. *I saw it.*	Dijo que lo **había visto**. *He said he had seen it.*

Future	→	**Present Conditional**

Iré mañana.
I'll go tomorrow.

Dijo que **iría** al día siguiente.
He said he would go the next day.

Future Perfect	→	**Perfect Conditional**

Para el lunes **habré acabado.**
By Monday I will have finished.

Dijo que para el lunes **habría acabado.**
He said that by Monday he would have finished.

Imperative	→	**Imperfect Subjunctive**

Cómete la fruta.
Eat your fruit.

Me dijo que me **comiera** la fruta.
She told me to eat my fruit.

3 No Verb-Tense Changes

The following verb tenses never change in indirect discourse, even if the communication verb is in the past (notice, however, changes in pronouns):

- Imperfect indicative or subjunctive
- Pluperfect indicative or subjunctive
- Conditional present or perfect

DIRECT DISCOURSE → **INDIRECT DISCOURSE**

Íbamos a comer.
We were going to eat.

Dijeron que **iban** a comer.
They said they were going to eat.

Ya **habíamos comido.**
We had already eaten.

Contesté que ya **habíamos comido.**
I answered that we had already eaten.

Dudo que me **estuvieras** mintiendo.
I doubt that you were lying to me.

Me dijo que dudaba que le **estuviera** mintiendo.
He told me that he doubted that I was lying to him.

Si **fuera** rico, me lo **compraría.**
If I were rich, I would buy it.

Pensó que si **fuera** rico, se lo **compraría.**
He thought that if he were rich, he would buy it.

Verb changes in a nutshell (when the communication verb is in the past):

Present*	→	Imperfect
Preterite	→	Pluperfect
Future**	→	Conditional
Imperative	→	Imperfect Subjunctive

*Present indicative becomes imperfect indicative, present subjunctive becomes imperfect subjunctive, present perfect indicative becomes pluperfect indicative (i.e., present of auxiliary becomes imperfect of auxiliary), present perfect subjunctive becomes pluperfect subjunctive (i.e., present of auxiliary becomes imperfect of auxiliary).
**Future becomes conditional present, future perfect becomes conditional perfect (i.e., future of auxiliary becomes conditional of auxiliary).

4 Person Changes

Logic rules here, just as it does in English. Any reference to an individual that is altered by a change of a point of view will affect all references to the individual. Read the following transformations carefully:

DIRECT DISCOURSE		INDIRECT DISCOURSE
Vamos a visitar a **nuestros** padres. *We are going to visit our parents.*	→	Dijeron que iban a visitar a **sus** padres. *They said they were going to visit their parents.*
Te di **tu** libro. *I gave you your book.*	→	Ella le dijo que **le** había dado **su** libro. *She told him she had given him his book.*
No voy con**tigo**. *I am not going with you.*	→	Ella me dijo que no iba con**migo**. *She told me she was not going with me.*

5 Time Changes

In indirect discourse in the past, time expressions will change unless the reporting of the statement occurs within the same day or pertinent amount of time. (If I say something today about tomorrow, and you repeat my words before the day is over, there is no change; the same logic applies here as in English.) If the reporting of the direct statement is made on a different day than when the statement was made, *yesterday* becomes *the day before* and *tomorrow* becomes *the next day*. In Spanish, some common changes are:

DIRECT DISCOURSE		INDIRECT DISCOURSE
ahora	→	**entonces**
Ahora sí puedo. *Now I can.*		Dijo que **entonces** sí podía. *He said that he could then.*
ayer	→	**el día anterior**
Lo hice **ayer.** *I did it yesterday.*		Confesó que lo había hecho **el día anterior.** *He confessed that he had done it the day before.*
anoche	→	**la noche anterior**
La vi **anoche.** (La = la película) *I saw it last night.*		Dijo que la había visto **la noche anterior.** *He said that he had seen it the night before.*
mañana	→	**al día siguiente**
Iré **mañana.** *I'll go tomorrow.*		Anunció que iría **al día siguiente.** *He announced that he would go the following day.*
la semana pasada	→	**la semana anterior**
La vi **la semana pasada.** (La = *her*) *I saw her last week.*		Admitió que la había visto **la semana anterior.** *He admitted that he had seen her the week before.*
la semana entrante	→	**la próxima semana**
Te llamaré **la semana entrante.** *I'll call you next week.*		Me prometió que me llamaría **la próxima semana.** *He promised me he would call me the following week.*

6 Other Changes

a. Connectives

When the quotes are of questions requiring a yes / no answer, connect them with **si** (*whether*). When the quotes are for *"yes"* and *"no"* responses, use **que** before **sí** or **no**.

Example:

DIRECT DISCOURSE	INDIRECT DISCOURSE
—¿Quieres ir al cine conmigo? — No. *"Do you want to go to the movies with me?"* *"No."*	Me preguntó si quería ir al cine con él. Yo le contesté que no. *He asked me whether I wanted to go to the movies with him.* *I said "no."*

b. *This, that,* and the other

When the speaker changes location from the moment of direct speech to the moment of reported speech, other things change referentially as well.

DIRECT DISCOURSE		INDIRECT DISCOURSE
—¿Quieres **esto**?	→	Me preguntó si quería **eso**.
*"Do you want **this**?"*	→	*He asked me if I wanted **that**.*

c. Verbs of communication

- For questions: **preguntar**
- For statements: **exclamar, agregar, contestar, responder, insistir, confesar, admitir,** etc.
- For requests or commands: **rogar, pedir, suplicar, decir, insistir,** etc.

d. A note about word order with indirect interrogatives

In English you would say:

> *I don't know what Rafael saw.*

In the combination *what + Rafael + saw*, notice that *Rafael* is placed before the verb. The word order of these elements in Spanish is different. The subject is placed after the verb when dealing with an indirect interrogative:

> No sé qué vio Rafael.

The same applies to any indirect question:

Me pregunto cuándo vienen los invitados.	*I wonder when the guests are coming.*
No puedo imaginar dónde están mis llaves.	*I can't imagine where my keys are.*

> Ejercicios 6.83–6.86, páginas 492–493;
> Ejercicios de repaso 6.87–6.88, páginas 494–497

CHAPTER 7

Ser, estar, haber, hacer, and tener

A Overview

B Ser vs. estar

C Estar vs. haber

D Expressions with estar and tener

E Time Expressions

A OVERVIEW

The verb *to be* in English can be translated into Spanish in different ways, depending upon the context. The study of the different translations of *to be* is broken down into categories of verbs and expressions: **ser** vs. **estar**; idiomatic expressions with **estar** and **tener**; passive voice with **ser** vs. resultant condition with **estar**; **hacer** with time expressions, etc.

Examples of **ser, tener,** and **haber** *(there is / are)* with nouns and pronouns:

Ángela **es** mi prima.	*Angela is my cousin.*
Este **es** Javier.	*This is Javier.*
Jaime **es** piloto.	*Jaime is a pilot.*
Es católica.	*She is a Catholic.*
Es soltero.	*He is a bachelor.*
Ese libro **es** mío.	*That book is mine.*
Fue Gema la que lo hizo.	*It was Gema who did it.*
Tengo veinte años.	*I am twenty years old.*
La niña **tiene** sed / calor / hambre / etc.	*The little girl is thirsty / hot / hungry / etc.*
Hay una ardilla en la mesa.	*There is a squirrel on the table.*
Hay granizo en el césped.	*There is hail on the grass.*

Examples of **hacer** + *noun* and **estar** + *adjective* or *present participle* in descriptions of the weather:

Hace calor hoy.	*It is hot today.*
Hace frío hoy.	*It is cold today.*
Hace viento.	*It is windy.*
Hace buen tiempo.	*The weather is good. (We are having good weather.)*
Hace mal tiempo.	*The weather is bad. (We are having bad weather.)*
Está nublado.	*It is cloudy.*
Está lloviendo / nevando / lloviznando.	*It is raining / snowing / drizzling.*

Examples of **ser** (inherent characteristic) and **estar** (condition subject to change) with adjectives:

Jorge **es** peruano.	*Jorge is Peruvian.*
Es alto / delgado.	*He is tall / slender.*
Rosa **está** emocionada.	*Rosa is excited.*
Berta **está** triste.	*Berta is sad.*

Examples of **ser** and **estar** with prepositions:

Soy de Guatemala.	*I am from Guatemala.*
Estoy de pie / de rodillas / de luto / etc.	*I am standing / kneeling / in mourning / etc.*
Estoy por salir.	*I am about to go out.*

Example of **estar** with present participle:

Están leyendo / cantando.	*They are reading / singing.*

Examples of **ser, estar,** and **haber** with past participles:

Passive—**ser:**

Esa novela **fue** escrita por Cervantes.	*That novel was written by Cervantes.*

Resultant condition—**estar** (past participle = adjective):

Sus camisas ya **están** planchadas.	*Your shirts are already ironed.*

Perfect tenses—**haber** (*to have* as an auxiliary verb):

He escrito, **había** escrito...	*I have written, I had written . . .*

B   SER VS. ESTAR

We have broken down the uses of these two verbs based on the type of word that follows or precedes the verb: in some cases only one of the two can be used; in other cases there are choices.

1   With Equal Elements: ser

The verb **ser** is used when the verb *to be* serves to make an equation between two grammatically similar elements, such as two nouns, pronouns, adverbs, or clauses, or two noun equivalents, such as a noun and a relative clause, or a pronoun and a noun, or a noun or pronoun and an infinitive, etc.:

El hombre **es** un animal. (noun = noun)	*Man is an animal.*
Esto **es** mío. (pronoun = pronoun)	*This is mine.*
Aquí **es** donde nos reuniremos. (adverb = adverb clause)	*Here is where we will meet.*
Trabajar así **es** volverse loco. (infinitive = infinitive)	*To work like that is to go mad.*
Lo que yo digo **es** lo que vale. (clause = clause)	*What I say is what counts.*
Héctor **es** el alto. (noun = nominalized adjective)	*Hector is the tall one.*
Esa mujer **es** la que te presenté ayer. (noun = clause)	*That woman is the one I introduced to you yesterday.*
Eso **es** vivir. (pronoun = infinitive)	*That is living.*

The verb **ser** is also used for telling time:

—¿Qué hora **es**? "*What time is it?*"
—**Es** la una. / **Son** las tres y media. "*It is one o'clock. / It is three thirty.*"

2   With Adjectives

a. Predicate adjectives

The contrast between the norm and a change of norm is the contrast we find most useful in understanding the different uses of **ser** and **estar** with adjectives.

When the adjective describes an aspect of the subject that is considered the norm universally, the verb **ser** is used:

El hielo **es** frío.   *Ice is cold.*

For an object that is not by definition cold, the verb **estar** would be used:

> La superficie **está** fría. *The surface is cold.*

The concept of "norm" is one that can vary depending upon the speaker. For example, the following sentence was spoken by a loving son or daughter:

> Mi madre **es** maravillosa. **Es** bellísima, joven y muy simpática. *My mother is marvelous. She is very beautiful, young, and very nice.*

The same woman, perceived by someone else, might be thought of differently. An acquaintance might say of her:

> **Es** madura y muy severa. *She is older and very strict.*

Any change in the norm, or subjective reaction, would take the verb **estar:**

> **Está** pálida hoy porque **ha estado** enferma. *She is pale today, because she has been sick.*

Over time, the norm might change as well. Imagine you have just met someone, and you perceive him as being active. You describe him as follows:

> **Es** activo. *He is active.*

Yet, someone else knew him before, when he was idle, and perceives his currently being active as a change from the norm:

> Siempre **fue** ocioso. Ahora **está** activo. *He was always idle. Now he is active.*

As you see, there is a choice between the two verbs based on the perception of norm or of change, a choice that could mean a lot depending upon the context. If you want to tell someone how beautiful he / she is, in Spanish you must decide whether you want to make a statement about that person's beauty in general, or a statement about that person's beauty at the moment:

> ¡Qué bella **eres**!

> ¡Qué bella **estás**!

In English, the first would be: *"You are so beautiful (in general)!"* The second might best be translated: *"You look so beautiful (right now)!"* The implications of this difference are the same in the two languages.

If you are describing an object to someone who does not know about it, and want to paint a picture that you would consider a standard for the object, you would use **ser**:

    Los girasoles **son** grandes.   *Sunflowers are big.*

If you are growing sunflowers, and observing their daily changes, or if you find something to be different from what you expected, you would use **estar**:

    Este girasol **está** grandísimo.   *This sunflower is very large.*

    ¡Qué grandes **están** los girasoles este año!   *The sunflowers are so big this year!*

Certain adjectives tend to indicate conditions rather than standard attributes and therefore tend to be used mostly with **estar**. This is the case with adjectives indicating illness, reactions such as joy or sadness, and changes in weight, size, or other aspects. **Enfermo, contento, harto,** and **bien** are most always used with **estar**:

    Mi padre **está enfermo**.   *My father is sick.*

    Estoy contenta de verte.   *I am happy to see you.*

    Están hartos de tanto ataque aéreo.   *They are tired of (fed up with) so many air raids.*

    ¿Estás bien?   *Are you okay?*

Other adjectives may vary in their meanings depending upon which verb is used. Some of the more dramatically altering adjectives follow:

(1) Aburrido (*boring* vs. *bored*)

    Esa película **fue** aburrida.   *That movie was boring.*

    El público **estaba** aburrido.   *The audience was bored.*

(2) Bueno (*good* vs. *in good health, tasty*)

    La fruta **es** buena para la salud.   *Fruit is good for your health.*

    ¡Qué buena **está** esta manzana!   *This apple is so good (tasty)!*

NOTE: To avoid ridicule, it may be best to avoid the combination of **estar** and **bueno** when describing people. In some countries, such as Mexico, some **piropos** (compliments men pay women on the streets) allude to how good a woman **está**; a typical one would be: "**¡Qué buena estás!**" Culturally, this does not translate; it is a comment on physical attraction.

In other countries, **"Estoy bueno"** simply means *"I am feeling okay now."* If you want to refer to health, you can always use expressions such as **sentirse bien, sentirse mejor, estar bien, estar mejor.**

(3) Callado (*quiet by nature* vs. *silent now*)

Francisco **es** muy callado.	*Francisco is very quiet (by nature).*
Ustedes que siempre hablan tanto, ¿por qué **están** tan callados ahora?	*You who always talk so much, why are you so quiet now?*

(4) Ciego (*blind* vs. *blinded figuratively or momentarily*)

Lázaro sirve a un limosnero que **es** ciego.	*Lázaro serves a beggar who is blind.*
¡**Estoy** ciega!	*I am blind!* (Context: *Suddenly I can't see a thing, although my eyesight is normal.*)

NOTE: **Mudo** *(mute)* and **sordo** *(deaf)* behave similarly.

(5) Cómodo (*comfortable object* vs. *comfortable person*)

Esta butaca **es** cómoda.	*This armchair is comfortable.*
Estoy cómodo.	*I am comfortable.*

(6) Frío (*cold as norm or not, used with objects*)

El invierno **es** frío.	*Winter is cold.*
Tu mano **está** fría.	*Your hand is cold.*

NOTE: Remember the uses of **tener** and **hacer** with nouns for temperatures. Note that **frío** can be an adjective or a noun, whereas **caliente** is the adjective for the noun **calor**. **Tener** is used with people, while **hacer** is used impersonally for weather:

Tengo frío (calor).	*I am cold (hot).*
Hace frío (calor) afuera.	*It is cold (hot) out.*

(7) Listo (*clever [person or animal]* vs. *ready*)

Mi hermana **es** muy lista.	*My sister is very clever.*
¿Ya **están** listos?	*Are you ready?*

NOTE: To speak of a clever idea or concept, you could use the adjective **inteligente** or **genial** (note that **genial** is stronger than **inteligente**).

(8) Maduro (*mature* vs. *ripe*)

Ese niño **es** muy maduro.	*That boy is very mature.*
El aguacate **está** maduro.	*The avocado is ripe.*

(9) Rico (*wealthy* vs. *delicious*)

Mi tío **es** rico.	*My uncle is rich.*
La comida **estuvo** rica.	*The meal was delicious.*

(10) Verde (*green* vs. *unripe*)

Los aguacates **son** verdes.	*Avocados are green.*
El aguacate **está** verde.	*The avocado is unripe.*

(11) Vivo (*smart, bright person* vs. *alive*)

Son muy vivos tus hermanos.	*Your brothers are very bright.*
Mi abuela todavía **está** viva.	*My grandmother is still alive.*

NOTE: Both **vivo** *(alive)* and **muerto** *(dead)* are used with the verb **estar**. (e.g., **Mi abuelo está vivo / muerto.**) The usage of **estar** with **vivo** is understandable because of the impermanence of life, but with **muerto** it may seem contradictory, especially if you think of death as permanent. Yet, it makes sense if you think of death focusing on its outset, as a change from the state of living.

b. Expressions with *to be*

Some frequent errors occur with the following expressions with *to be*. Note the correct translations:

I am cold.	Tengo frío.
It is cold.	Hace frío. [weather]
	Es frío. [Something is always cold. Cold here is the norm.]
	Está frío. [Something is cold now. Cold here is not the norm.]
I am dead (dead-tired).	Estoy muerto(a) (de cansancio). Estoy agotado.
I am done.	Terminé. He terminado. Ya acabé. (etc.)

It is done.	Está terminado. Ya está. (etc.)
I am finished.	Terminé. He terminado. Ya acabé. (etc.)
It is finished.	Está terminado / hecho. Se terminó. Ya está. (etc.)
I am excited.	Estoy emocionado.
I am glad / happy that . . .	Me alegro* que…
I am happy (satisfied) with the results.	Estoy contento con los resultados.
I am happy (in my life).	Soy feliz.

(*NOTE: to signify *to be glad*, the verb **alegrarse** is preferred to the adjective **alegre** used with **ser** or **estar**. Alegre has a meaning that is closer to *joyful, lighthearted* than to *glad* or *satisfied* or *happy*.
Hoy traes cara alegre. La música caribeña es una música alegre.)

I am hot.	Tengo calor.
It is hot.	Hace calor. [weather] Está caliente. [the soup, for example]

(NOTE: **Estar caliente**, when used to describe a person, can mean **estar ardiente sexualmente** in colloquial usage. In other words, unless you want to refer to yourself as sexually hot, don't say **estoy caliente**.)

I am hungry.	Tengo hambre.
I am interested.	Me interesa.
I am late.	Llegué tarde.
It is late.	Es tarde.
I am sad to hear that.	Me apena mucho oír eso. Me da mucha pena oír eso.
I am sorry.	Lo siento.
I am short [not tall].	Soy bajo.
I am short (of money).	No tengo suficiente dinero.

It [the line] is short.	Es / Está corta.
I am sitting.	Estoy sentado.
It is working.	Está funcionando.
I am working.	Estoy trabajando.

(NOTE: See more on the distinctions between people and things working, running, starting, etc. in Chapter 8, pages 296–297.)

I was born.	Nací.
That is the problem.	He allí el problema.

(NOTE: This expression is used when pointing to or presenting something. **He** is invariable and serves as a verb. Other English renderings: *There's the rub.* **He allí la dificultad.** *Here's the situation:* ... **He aquí la situación:... .**)

c. Impersonal expressions

Generally, impersonal expressions are formed with **ser**:

Es bueno dormir mucho.	*It is good to sleep a lot.*
Es interesante viajar.	*It is interesting to travel.*
Fue maravilloso estar allí.	*It was marvelous to be there.*

Use **estar** with **bien** and **claro**:

Está **bien** que vengan tus amigos.	*It is okay for your friends to come.*
Está **claro** que ya no me quieres.	*It is clear that you do not love me anymore.*

3 With Prepositions and Adverbs

a. De

Use **ser** to indicate origin, the material of which something is made, or possession:

Soy de Cuba.	*I am from Cuba.*
El edificio **era** de ladrillo.	*The building was made of bricks.*
Este paraguas **es** de Tito.	*This umbrella is Tito's.*

Use **estar** with set expressions, which indicate opinion, temporary condition or position, or change of location (See tables under "Expressions with **estar** and **tener**," page 274.), such as **estar de acuerdo, de buen humor, de luto, de pie, de rodillas, de viaje, de vuelta:**

Estoy de acuerdo contigo.	*I agree with you.*
Mis padres **están de buen humor** hoy.	*My parents are in a good mood today.*
Estoy de luto por la muerte de mi padre.	*I am in mourning for the death of my father.*
Los niños **estuvieron de pie** todo el día.	*The boys were standing all day long.*
La mujer **estaba de rodillas**, rezando.	*The woman was kneeling, praying.*
La familia **está de viaje**.	*The family is away (on a trip).*
¿Cuándo **estarán de vuelta**?	*When will they be back?*

b. Time and place

To indicate location or time of an event, use **ser**; to indicate location of an object or a person, use **estar**:

La conferencia **es** a las diez en el auditorio.	*The lecture is at ten in the auditorium.*
El profesor **está** en su despacho.	*The professor is in his office.*
La sal **está** en la mesa.	*The salt is on the table.*

Note that some words can signify either an event or an object. For example, an exam can be the paper itself or the event; a movie can be a DVD or the actual showing of it:

El examen **es** esta noche en Morrill Hall.	*The exam is tonight in Morrill Hall.*
El examen **está** debajo del libro en la gaveta del centro.	*The exam is under the book in the middle drawer.*
La película **es** arriba.	*The movie is (being shown) upstairs.*
La película **está** al lado del televisor.	*The movie is next to the TV set.*

Adverbs of time and place and adverbial clauses function similarly:

La conferencia **es** cuando te dije.	*The lecture is when I told you.*
El libro no **está** donde lo dejé.	*The book is not where I left it.*

Ejercicios 7.1–7.8, páginas 498–501

4 With Past and Present Participles

a. With present participles

With the present participle, **estar** is used to indicate the progressive:

Estoy estudiando.   *I am studying.*

b. With past participles: Passive voice and resultant condition

With past participles, **ser** is used to indicate the passive voice, and **estar** to indicate a condition resulting from a completed action:

Passive voice:

Las ventanas **fueron** abiertas a las ocho.   *The windows were opened at eight. (Somebody opened them.)*

Los edificios **son** construidos por ingenieros.   *Buildings are built by engineers.*

Resultant condition:

Las ventanas **están** abiertas.   *The windows are open. (It does not matter who did it.)*

If what is being focused upon is not the action or who did it, but the result of the action, the verb **estar** is used with the past participle functioning as an adjective:

El edificio **está** terminado.   *The building is finished.*

(1) Formation of the passive voice

The passive voice in Spanish is formed essentially in the same way as in English:

ACTIVE vs. PASSIVE VOICE				
	SUBJECT	VERB	PREPOSITION	DIRECT OBJECT
ACTIVE	La tormenta	destruyó	ø	la casa.
	The storm	*destroyed*	*ø*	*the house.*
	SUBJECT	VERB	PREPOSITION	AGENT
PASSIVE	La casa	fue destruida	por	la tormenta.
	The house	*was destroyed*	*by*	*the storm.*

To change from active to passive voice:
- The subject of the active sentence becomes the agent (preceded by **por**) of the passive.
- The direct object of the active sentence becomes the subject of the passive sentence.
- The verb of the active sentence undergoes the following transformation: the verb itself becomes a past participle (variable in gender and number with its new subject) and is preceded by the verb **ser** in the same tense and mood as the verb of the original active sentence.

Examples:

ACTIVE	PASSIVE
Isabel Allende escribió esa novela. *Isabel Allende wrote that novel.*	Esa novela fue escrita por Isabel Allende. *That novel was written by Isabel Allende.*
Millones leerán el libro. *Millions will read the book.*	El libro será leído por millones. *The book will be read by millions.*
Ella había corregido las tareas. *She had corrected the homework.*	Las tareas habían sido corregidas por ella. *The homework had been corrected by her.*

(2) A note about the passive voice

The passive voice, which is very common in English, is rarely used in Spanish. It is seen more in journalism translated directly from English into Spanish, often online. If there is a subject, or an agent, or someone who does the action, whether present in the sentence or implied, Spanish prefers the active voice. If there is no agent implied, the impersonal **se** is the preferred construction. (See more about the impersonal **se** on pages 74–78.)

PASSIVE • SPANISH vs. ENGLISH		
SUBJECT OF THE ACTION	SPANISH PREFERENCE	ENGLISH PREFERENCE
Stated	ACTIVE	ACTIVE or PASSIVE
Absent but implied	ACTIVE	ACTIVE or PASSIVE
Absent but irrelevant	Impersonal **se**	PASSIVE

Stated subject:

    Los meseros sirvieron la cena.   *The waiters served dinner. / Dinner was served by the waiters.*

Although the second sentence in English is passive, and there could be an equivalent passive construction in Spanish, it would not be the choice of Spanish speakers. They tend to use the active whenever the doer of the action is stated.

Absent but implied subject:

    Sirvieron la cena a las diez.   *Dinner was served at ten (when I was at my neighbors' house last night).*

Here, the neighbors are the ones who served dinner at ten, but they are not mentioned in the English sentence. They are implied, however, and their role in the serving is relevant. For this reason, Spanish would use the active structure.

Absent and irrelevant subject:

    Se habla español.   *Spanish (is) spoken.*

When the doer of the action is not a part of the statement, not present, or even relevant to the focus of the sentence, Spanish uses the impersonal **se**.

NOTE: For more on the impersonal **se**, see Chapter 3.B.4, pages 74–78. When the grammatical subject of the English passive is an indirect object of the verb, it is impossible to use the passive in Spanish. Such structures can be translated with the impersonal **se** or other impersonal structures:

    A Eva no se le dijo la verdad.   *Eva was not told the truth.*
    OR: No le dijeron la verdad a Eva.

In the preceding sentence in English, Eva is the grammatical subject of the passive sentence, whereas in both Spanish examples, Eva is the indirect object of the verb *to tell*, and the subject of the verb *to tell* (who did not tell her?) is not relevant to the context. This is why the passive cannot be used in Spanish in this context.

> Ejercicio 7.9–7.11, páginas 501–506

C ESTAR VS. HABER

When indicating the existence or presence of people or things, **estar** and **haber** have different uses.

Estar means *to be* and has a specific subject:

    Los libros **están** en la mesa.   *The books are on the table.*

Whoever hears the preceding sentence knows which books are being referred to: they are specific books.

Haber (**hay, había,** etc.) means *there is, there are, there were, etc.*, and has no subject; it is impersonal:

    Hay libros en la mesa.   *There are books on the table.*

The focus of the preceding sentence is not the location of specific books, but the mere existence of unspecified books on the table.

Note that **hay** is invariable in number: it does not change to plural. When it is used in any tense or mood (**había, habrá, habría, hubo, haya, hubiera,** etc.), it remains invariable in number:

    Había más de mil musulmanes en la mezquita.   *There were more than a thousand Muslims in the mosque.*

    Hubo varios accidentes en esa esquina.   *There were several accidents on that corner.*

    No creo que **haya** suficientes movimientos ambientalistas.   *I don't think there are enough environmental movements.*

Ejercicio 7.12, página 506

D EXPRESSIONS WITH ESTAR AND TENER

1 Expressions with estar

EXPRESSIONS WITH ESTAR			
estar a favor de	to be for / in favor of	estar de luto	to be in mourning
estar ausente[1]	to be absent	estar de regreso, de vuelta	to be back
estar contento[2]	to be glad / pleased / happy	estar de rodillas	to be kneeling
estar de acuerdo con	to agree with	estar de vacaciones	to be on vacation
estar de buen (mal) humor	to be in a good (bad) mood	estar de viaje	to be traveling
estar de huelga	to be on strike	estar de visita	to be visiting
estar de pie[3]	to be standing	estar en contra de	to be against

2 Expressions with tener

Notice that **tener frío** and **tener calor** are used exclusively for people or animals. If you wish to say that an object is hot or cold, use **ser** or **estar**.

EXPRESSIONS WITH TENER			
tener ___ años	to be ___ years old	tener la culpa	to be guilty
tener calor	to be hot	tener lugar	to take place
tener cuidado	to be careful	tener miedo	to be afraid
tener en cuenta que	to bear in mind that	tener prisa	to be in a hurry[4]
tener éxito	to be successful / succeed	tener razón	to be right[5]
tener frío	to be cold	tener sed	to be thirsty
tener ganas de	to feel like / desire	tener sueño	to be sleepy[6]
tener hambre	to be hungry	tener vergüenza	to be ashamed

---

[1] This expression may only be used with **estar**; *to be late* = **llegar tarde**; *to be on time* = **llegar a tiempo**.
[2] This expression may only be used with **estar**.
[3] The expression used for *to be sitting* is **estar sentado**, whereas sentarse means *to sit down* (the process of changing from the standing to the sitting position).
[4] *to hurry up* = **apurarse**
[5] *to be wrong* = **estar equivocado / equivocarse**
[6] *to have a dream* = **tener un sueño / soñar**

> Ejercicios 7.13–7.14, página 507;
> Ejercicios de repaso 7.15–7.17, páginas 507–508

E | TIME EXPRESSIONS

1 Introduction

a. Counting forward

In Spanish, as in English, time can be perceived in various ways—we can narrate a story from beginning to end, with a series of preterites and imperfects:

Me levanté, me bañé y desayuné. Mientras desayunaba, sonó el teléfono.	*I got up, I bathed, and I had breakfast. While I was eating breakfast, the phone rang.*

We can state the duration of an action in a variety of ways:

Estudié por cuatro horas.	*I studied for four hours.*
Viví en España por seis meses.	*I lived in Spain for six months.*

b. Counting backward

If you want to say how long something has lasted by counting back from the present, as you do in English with *I have been studying for four hours* or *I had been studying for four hours when you called* (counting back from a moment in the past, *when you called*), in Spanish you most frequently use expressions with **hacer que** and **llevar**.

2 Duration

a. Counting back from the present

COUNTING BACK FROM THE PRESENT: HACER			
EXPRESSION (INVARIABLE)	AMOUNT OF TIME	EXPRESSION	ACTION VERB FORM (VARIABLE)
Hace (invariable)	x horas, meses, etc.	**que**	Present indicative (**yo, tú,** etc.)

COUNTING BACK FROM THE PRESENT: LLEVAR		
EXPRESSION (VARIABLE)	AMOUNT OF TIME	ACTION VERB FORM (INVARIABLE)
Llevo (Llevas, Lleva, etc.)	x horas, meses, etc.	1. Affirmative: Present participle
		2. **Estar:** Ø (no verb)
		3. Negative: **sin** + infinitive

Affirmative—The sentence *I have been studying for three hours* (implication: and continue to do so) could be translated as:

> **Hace** tres horas **que estudio.**
> OR: **Llevo** tres horas **estudiando.**

Notice where the person is expressed in these two sentences: with **hace... que** the person doing the action is perceived in the second verb **(estudio [yo]),** whereas with **llevar** the person is seen in the verb **llevar** itself **(Llevo [yo])** and not in the action verb **estudiando.**

With *estar*—If the "action" verb is **estar,** the expression with **llevar** does <u>not</u> state the verb:

> **Hace** tres horas **que estamos** aquí.
> OR: **Llevamos** tres horas aquí.

In other words, <u>never</u> use **estando** in sentences like **Llevamos tres horas aquí.**

Negative—The sentence *We have not slept for two nights* (i.e., the last two nights) could be translated as:

> **Hace** dos noches **que no dormimos.**
> OR: **Llevamos** dos noches sin dormir.

In the negative, the sentence with **llevar** does not take the <u>present participle</u> for its action verb, but the <u>infinitive</u> preceded by **sin.**

b. Counting back from a moment in the past

COUNTING BACK FROM THE PAST: **HACER**			
EXPRESSION (INVARIABLE)	AMOUNT OF TIME	EXPRESSION	ACTION VERB FORM (VARIABLE)
Hacía (invariable)	x horas, meses, etc.	**que**	Imperfect indicative (**yo, tú,** etc.)

COUNTING BACK FROM THE PAST: **LLEVAR**		
EXPRESSION (VARIABLE)	AMOUNT OF TIME	ACTION VERB FORM (INVARIABLE)
Llevaba (Llevabas, Llevaba, etc.)	x horas, meses, etc.	1. Affirmative: Present participle
		2. **Estar:** Ø (no verb)
		3. Negative: **sin** + infinitive

Affirmative—The sentence *I had been studying for three hours* (implication: when something interrupted my work), would be translated as:

Hacía tres horas **que estudiaba.**
OR: **Llevaba** tres horas **estudiando.**

Here, **hacer** and **llevar** are in the imperfect, as is the main verb of the first sentence. In the second sentence, the action verb is still in the present participle.

With *estar*—If the "action" verb is **estar,** the expression with **llevar** does not state the verb:

Hacía tres horas **que estábamos** allá.
OR: **Llevábamos** tres horas allá.

Negative—The sentence *We had not gone to the movies in a long time* would translate as follows:

Hacía mucho tiempo **que no íbamos** al cine.
OR: **Llevábamos** mucho tiempo **sin ir** al cine.

As you see, the same rules apply for the negative in the past as did in the present. The only difference is that the verbs must be kept in the imperfect (all but the infinitive, of course).

3 Ago

Another type of sentence that counts time in reverse relates to finished actions in the past, as opposed to actions that have been going on and continue to go on (duration). In English, this reverse counting uses the expression *ago*, as in the example *I did that two hours ago* (as opposed to *I did it at three o'clock*). To translate sentences with *ago*, you cannot use **llevar**, only **hace** [present]... **que** + *preterite*.

Hace tres años **que** se fue.	*He left three years ago.*
OR: Se fue **hace** tres años.	

This same situation shifted into a past context would use the following structure:

Hacía tres años **que** se había ido.   *He had left three years before.*

We can also refer to things that *were happening* some time ago. For these actions, Spanish uses the imperfect of the main verb, usually with the progressive form for action verbs, and nonprogressive for non-action verbs:

¿Qué estabas haciendo **hace** dos horas?	*What were you doing two hours **ago**?*
Me estaba bañando **hace** dos horas.	*I was bathing two hours **ago**.*
OR: **Hace** dos horas, me estaba bañando.[7]	
¿Dónde estaba usted **hace** treinta minutos?	*Where were you thirty minutes **ago**?*

> Ejercicios 7.18–7.20, páginas 508–509;
> Ejercicios de repaso 7.21–7.22, páginas 509–510

---

[7] Notice the absence of **que** from the expression.

CHAPTER 8

Lexical Variations

A Introduction

B Terms and Expressions

C False Cognates and False Friends

A INTRODUCTION

The contents of this chapter are not technically grammatical in nature: they are lexical. Then again, some of the most commonly covered grammatical points focus more on lexical differences. For this reason, we are not concerned that this chapter may be out of place in a grammar manual. In fact, we include this list of terms here because they represent some of the most common areas of difficulty for students. We consider a focused practice of them to be useful to improve accuracy of expression.

In some cases, the terms have been covered in grammatical chapters and are consolidated and reviewed in this chapter from the point of view of vocabulary. **Acabar** was covered under preterite and imperfect and then under accidental **se;** *what* was covered previously under interrogatives and under relative pronouns; here we consolidate the two for a brief, focused review. Some of these points have been touched upon under reflexives, such as *become* or *get;* here we present the most common terms more thoroughly by elaborating on some of their subtle lexical distinctions. Other expressions on this list are shown here for the first time, and may be false cognates *(apply, attend, exit, realize)*, or differences in perception *(come* and *go, take)*.

This list of terms and expressions is by no means exhaustive: it should serve merely as a stepping stone, followed by careful consultation of a good translation dictionary and a good Spanish–Spanish dictionary.

B TERMS AND EXPRESSIONS

For an easy, quick reference, we have arranged these terms in alphabetical order (rather than in conceptual or other types of groupings).

1 Acabar

acabar = *to finish*

    Acabé la tarea.   *I finished the homework.*

acabar de (+ *inf.*) = *to finish doing something*

The meaning of this expression changes depending upon the context in which it is used:

    Acabé de poner la mesa.   *I finished setting the table.*

    Cuando **acabes de lavar** los platos, sécalos y guárdalos.   *When you finish washing the dishes, dry them and put them away.*

When used in the present and imperfect indicative, it may mean *to have just (done something)*:

Present Indicative:

    Acabo de <u>comer</u>.   *I just ate.*

Imperfect Indicative:

    Acabábamos de <u>terminar</u>.   *We had just finished.*

acabarse = *to end, finish, use up, or eat up* [reflexive]; *to be no more, run out of* (accidental **se**)

Me acabé el pan.	*I ate up all the bread.*
Se acabó el azúcar.	*There is no more sugar.*
Se acabaron los limones.	*There are no more lemons.*
Se nos acabó la leche.	*We have no more (ran out of) milk.*
Se nos acabaron los cacahuates.	*We have no more (ran out of) peanuts.*

> Ejercicios 8.1–8.2, página 511

2 Apply

aplicar = *to apply* (e.g., an ointment)

    Instrucciones: **aplicar** la crema sobre la herida cuatro veces al día.   *Instructions: Apply the cream to the injury four times a day.*

aplicación (f.) = *application* (of a theory, of one's efforts, of a medication, etc.)

    Estudia con **aplicación**.   *He/She studies with application (diligence).*

solicitar = *to apply for or to* (a job, loan, fellowship, university acceptance, etc.)

    Solicité el puesto de subgerente.   *I applied for the job of assistant manager.*

    Le dieron la beca que **solicitó**.   *They gave him the fellowship he applied for.*

    Solicitaré entrada a cuatro universidades.   *I'll apply to four universities.*

solicitud (f.) = *application* (form to fill out for a job, university, loan, etc.)

    Envié la **solicitud** a tiempo.   *I sent the application on time.*

> Ejercicios 8.3–8.4, páginas 511–512

3 Ask

pedir algo (without a preposition) = *to ask for something*

    Me **pidieron** dinero.   *They asked me for money.*

pedir que = *to ask to*

    Le **pedí que** me despertara.   *I asked him to wake me up.*

preguntar: "¿...?" = *to ask: "... ?"*

    Me **preguntó**: "¿Qué hora es?"   *He asked me, "What time is it?"*

preguntar si..., qué..., cuándo..., (etc.) = *to ask whether . . . , what . . . , when . . . , (etc.)*

    Se **preguntaban** si las pistas se vinculaban.   *They asked themselves (wondered) whether the clues were linked.*

    Nos **preguntaron** qué queríamos.   *They asked us what we wanted.*

hacer una pregunta = *to ask a question*

    ¿Me permite **hacerle una pregunta**?   *May I ask you a question?*

pedido (m.) = *request, order*

    ¿Cuál es el número de su **pedido**?   *What is your order number?*

cuestión (f.) = *matter, question*

    Es una **cuestión** de estética.   *It's a matter (question) of aesthetics.*

> Ejercicios 8.5–8.6, página 512

4 At

En is the usual equivalent of *at* referring to static location in space:

Estoy **en** casa.	*I'm **at** home.*
Estoy **en** la casa de mi hermano.	*I'm **at** my brother's house.*
Me quedé **en** su apartamento.	*I stayed **at** his apartment.*

This could extend to actions that take place within the confines of a certain location:

Comimos **en** ese restaurante.   *We ate **at** that restaurant.*

A would be used for movement *to* a destination:

Vamos **a** casa.   *We're going home.*

Viajamos **a** Puerto Rico.   *We traveled to Puerto Rico.*
(for travel within or throughout
the island, you would use **por**)

A is the usual equivalent of *at* when referring to time of day:

La clase es **a** las diez.   *Class is **at** ten.*

Other expressions with *at*:

at this moment	**en** este momento
at times	**a** veces
at the door	*(outside)* **a** la puerta
	(inside) **en** la puerta
at my side	**a** mi lado
to be at the table	estar **a** la mesa
to throw at	tirar **a**, lanzar **a**
to sell at a price	vender **a** un precio

Ejercicios 8.7–8.8, páginas 512–513

B Terms and Expressions

5 Attend

asistir a = *to attend* (a class, formal meeting, conference, etc.)

    Asistimos a una reunión esta tarde.   *We attended a meeting this afternoon.*

    Hoy no **asistí a** clase.   *Today I didn't attend class.*

asistencia (f.) = *attendance, audience*

    La **asistencia** a clase es un requisito.   *Attendance at class is a requirement.*

    Había un desconocido en la **asistencia**.   *There was a stranger in the audience.*

    NOTE: *audience* is more often translated as **público** than **asistencia**. **Audiencia** exists, and also means *court* or *hearing*.

asistencia social (f.) = *welfare*

    Muchos reciben **asistencia social**.   *Many receive welfare.*

atender = *to assist, serve* (a person), *pay attention, tend to* (something or someone)

    ¿En qué puedo **atenderlo**?   *How may I assist you?*

    Me **atendieron** de inmediato.   *They served me immediately.*

    Atiéndanme, por favor.   *Pay attention, please.*

    Atiende a tus amistades, Gregorio.   *Tend to your friends, Gregorio.*

    No **atiende** a la conferencia porque lo distraen los ruidos de afuera.   *He doesn't pay attention to the lecture because the outdoor noises distract him.*

atento(a) = *attentive, well-mannered, polite, kind*

    Su marido es muy **atento** con ella.   *Her husband is very considerate toward her.*

    Es un joven muy **atento**.   *He's a very polite young man.*

(See also Chapter 8.B.23, page 300.)

> Ejercicios 8.9–8.10, página 513

6 Because

Por and **a causa de** mean *because of* and are used with nouns. (**Por** can also have other meanings, such as *on account of, instead of,* etc. Context should indicate the meaning.)

Lo felicitaron **por** el hallazgo.	*They congratulated him because of (on account of) his discovery.*
No salimos **a causa de** la tormenta.	*We didn't go out because of the storm.*

Por is used with pronouns:

Dejó su carrera **por** ella.	*He gave up his career because of her.*
Vendrán temprano **por** eso.	*They'll come early because of that.*

Por can also be used with an infinitive [same subject], whereas **a causa de** cannot:

Me enfermé **por** comer tanto.	*I got sick because I ate so much.*

Porque is used only with a conjugated verb:

Reconocieron el caballo **porque** tenía una crin distintiva.	*They recognized the horse because it had a distinctive mane.*

Gracias a is used when there is a positive force involved:

Salí pronto del hospital **gracias a** tu ayuda.	*I got out of the hospital quickly because of (thanks to) your help.*

> Ejercicios 8.11–8.12, páginas 513–514

7 Become or Get

alegrarse = *to become happy, be glad*

Me alegro de que puedas venir.	*I'm glad you can come.*

callarse = *to become quiet, keep silent, shut up*

¡Cállate!	*Be quiet!*

B Terms and Expressions

calmarse = *to become calm, calm down*

    Al darse cuenta de que el ciempiés no representaba ningún peligro, **se calmaron**.

    When they realized that the centipede didn't represent a danger, they calmed down.

cansarse = *to get tired*

    Me cansé de trabajar.

    I got tired of working.

empobrecerse = *to become poor*

    Se fueron empobreciendo poco a poco.

    They became poor little by little.

enfermarse = *to get sick*

    Te vas a **enfermar** si sales así.

    You're going to get sick if you go out like that.

enfurecerse = *to become furious*

    Su padre **se enfureció** al oír las noticias.

    Her father became furious when he heard the news.

enloquecerse = *to go mad, become crazy*

    Al perderla, **se enloqueció**.

    When he lost her, he went crazy.

enojarse = *to get angry*

    No **te enojes** conmigo.

    Don't get angry with me.

enriquecerse = *to become or get rich*

    Pensaban **enriquecerse** con eso.

    They thought they could get rich with that.

entristecerse = *to become sad*

    Se entristecieron sus hijos más que él.

    His children became sadder than he did.

envejecerse = *to become or get old*

    Con este producto, nadie **se envejece**.

    With this product, nobody gets (or becomes) old.

mejorarse = *to get better, improve*

¡Que **te mejores** pronto! — *I hope you get better soon!*

tranquilizarse = *to become calm, calm down*

Con esa música, **se tranquilizaron.** — *With that music, they calmed down.*

ponerse (+ **serio, pálido, triste,** and other adjectives of involuntary and transient psychological or physical states) = *to become* (serious, pale, sad . . .)

Se puso triste al oír las noticias. — *He became sad upon hearing the news.*

hacerse (+ **abogado, médico,** and other nouns of profession) = *to become* (a lawyer, doctor . . .)

Mi hermana **se hizo** abogada. — *My sister became a lawyer.*

llegar a ser (+ *nouns* or *adjectives* expressing importance or high personal status) = *to become* (rich, famous . . .)

Llegó a ser famoso. — *He became famous.*

convertirse en = *to become or turn into* (by physical transformation)

El vino **se convirtió** en vinagre. — *The wine became (turned into) vinegar.*

De repente **se convirtió** en lobo. — *Suddenly he became a wolf.*

> Ejercicios 8.13–8.14, página 514;
> Ejercicio de repaso 8.15, páginas 514–515

8 But

pero = *but* (nevertheless)

Tengo suficiente dinero, **pero** no quiero ir. — *I have enough money, but I don't want to go.*

No tengo suficiente dinero, **pero** voy a ir. — *I don't have enough money, but I'm going to go.*

El nuevo gerente es eficaz, **pero** antipático. — *The new manager is efficient, but disagreeable.*

menos, excepto = *but*

    Tráelos todos **menos** los azules.   *Bring all but the blue ones.*

    Todos **excepto** Jeannine creyeron la amenaza.   *All but Jeannine believed the threat.*

sino = *but* (but rather, but instead—when contrasting with a negative in the first part)

    No es antipático, **sino** serio.   *He isn't disagreeable, but (rather) serious.*

    No fue a la tienda, **sino** al banco.   *He didn't go to the store, but (instead) to the bank.*

sino que = **sino** followed by a conjugated verb

    No se lo vendí, **sino que** se lo regalé.   *I didn't sell it to him, but gave it to him (instead).*

NOTE: A common mistake is to use **pero** at the beginning of a sentence, followed by a comma. This emphasis on **pero** is incorrect in Spanish: to translate an emphatic initial *but*, it would be best to use **Sin embargo**.

> Ejercicio 8.16, página 515

9 Come and Go

venir = *to come* (toward the speaker)

    Decidieron **venir** a vernos.   *They decided to come see us.*

    ¡**Ven** acá!   *Come here!*

ir = *to go* (away from the speaker)

NOTE: **Ir** is frequently translated as *to come*.

    Voy a tu casa esta tarde.   *I'll come to your house this afternoon.*

    ¡**Voy**!   *I'm coming!* (literally, in Spanish, "I'm going.")

NOTE: Do not confuse ¡**Voy**! *(I am coming!)* with ¡Me **voy**! *(I am leaving!)* They have opposite meanings. See more on this below under *Go* and *Leave* / **irse** and **salir**.

llegar = *to arrive, get someplace*
llegar tarde, temprano = *to be late, early*

Los huéspedes **llegaron** esta mañana.	*The guests arrived (got here) this morning.*
Llegamos al hotel a las tres.	*We got to the hotel at three.*
Llegaste temprano.	*You're early. (You arrived early.)*
Llegué tarde al trabajo.	*I was late to work.*
Lamento **haber llegado tarde.**	*I'm sorry I'm late.*

Ejercicios 8.17–8.18, páginas 515–516

10 Despedir

despedir = *to fire, dismiss*

Esa empresa **despidió** a veinte empleados.	*That firm fired twenty employees.*

despedirse = *to say good-bye*

Nos despedimos en el aeropuerto.	*We said good-bye at the airport.*

Ejercicios 8.19–8.20, página 516

11 *Exit* and *Success*

éxito = *success*

El **éxito** del hotel depende de la calidad del servicio.	*The success of the hotel depends upon the quality of service.*

tener éxito = *to be successful*

Si se esmeran, **tendrán éxito.**	*If you make an effort, you will be successful.*

B Terms and Expressions

salida = *exit*

 ¿Dónde se encuentra la **salida** de emergencia?   *Where is the emergency exit?*

suceso = *event*

 Fue un **suceso** de tal importancia que vinieron los reporteros.   *It was such an important event that the reporters came.*

> Ejercicios 8.21–8.22, página 516

12 Go and Leave

ir = *to go* (*toward* a specific destination)

 Ayer **fuimos** al museo.   *Yesterday we went to the museum.*

 ¡**Vamos**!   *Let's go!* (focus on the destination: i.e., *Let's get there.*)

Depending on the context, ¡**Vamos**! can also mean something like *Come on!* with an overtone of impatience or disbelief. A good dictionary will provide you with all of the subtleties of this verb, including the uses of ¡**Vaya**!

irse = **marcharse** = *to leave* (direction *away from* some understood location)

 El señor Cárdenas ya **se fue**.   *Mr. Cárdenas already left.*

 El gerente **se va** a las cinco.   *The manager leaves at five.*

 No está; **se marchó**.   *He isn't in; he left.*

 ¡**Me voy**!   *I'm leaving!*

 ¡**Vámonos**!   *Let's go!* (focus on the departure: i.e., *Let's leave / Let's get out of here / ...*)

salir = *to go out*

 Los niños **salieron** a jugar.   *The children went out to play.*

 Los huéspedes **salieron** a la playa.   *The guests went out to the beach.*

 Saldremos esta noche a las siete.   *We'll go out tonight at seven.*

salir vs. **irse** (intransitive) = *to leave*

Salir is used as a synonym for **irse** when the person leaving is also leaving an enclosed area, such as a building. **Irse** is more permanent than **salir**; for example, when a person is at home or in the office and leaves expecting to return, **salir** is used more frequently. At the end of the day, when a person leaves the office until the next day, **irse** would be more common. (Notice that these verbs are intransitive in Spanish, and do not take direct objects in the same manner as in English.)

In the following sentences **salir** would be preferable:

Elena **salió** de casa hace una hora.	*Elena left home an hour ago.*
La secretaria **salió** a almorzar.	*The secretary went out to lunch.*

In sentences like the following you could only use **irse**:

Estábamos en la playa platicando cuando de repente Luis se levantó y **se fue**.	*We were on the beach chatting when suddenly Luis got up and left.*
Lo siento, pero el gerente ya **se fue**.	*I'm sorry, but the manager has already left.*

Salir is commonly used with travel and with means of transportation. The logic here is that the enclosure from which the traveler departs is a particular geographical space:

Saldremos para España la semana entrante.	*We're leaving for Spain next week.*
El tren **sale** a las nueve.	*The train leaves at nine.*
Su vuelo **sale** de Madrid esta tarde.	*Your flight leaves Madrid this afternoon.*

NOTE: The parallel term **salida** is used to indicate the *departure* of a person, flight, etc.:

La **salida** del vuelo es a las cinco.	*The flight leaves at five.*

Partir and **partida** are also used for departures:

Siempre **partíamos** al amanecer.	*We always left at dawn.*
La próxima **partida** del AVE para Sevilla es al mediodía.	*The next departure of the AVE to Seville is at noon.* (The AVE—Alta Velocidad Española—is a high-speed train.)

dejar (+ *noun* or *pronoun*) (transitive) = *to leave* (something or someone)

    Dejé las maletas en el taxi.   *I left the suitcases in the taxicab.*

    Su hermano la **dejó** en el aeropuerto.   *Her brother left her at the airport.*

dejar (+ *inf.*) = *to let*

    No me **dejó** pagar nada.   *She didn't let me pay for anything.*

dejar de (+ *inf.*) = *to stop*

    De repente **dejaron de** hablar.   *Suddenly, they stopped talking.*

> Ejercicios 8.23–8.24, página 517

13 Guide

el guía = *guide* (person)

    El guía habló de la estatua.   *The guide spoke about the statue.*

la guía = *guide* (booklet or female guide)

    Está explicado en **la guía**.   *It's explained in the guidebook.*

    La guía hablaba catalán.   *The guide (fem.) spoke Catalan.*

> Ejercicios 8.25–8.26, página 517;
> Ejercicio de repaso 8.27, página 518

14 Know

conocer = *to know* (someone); *to meet* (someone) *for the first time* (make someone's acquaintance) [preterite]

    Conozco a Luis.   *I know Luis.*

    Ayer **conocí** a Luis.   *Yesterday I met Luis.*

(See Chapter 8.B.16, page 294, on *to meet*.)

conocer = *to be familiar with* (something)

    No **conozco** la ciudad.   *I don't know the city.*

saber = *to know* (something)

    Saben nuestra dirección.   *They know our address.*

saber (+ *inf.*) = *to know how* (to do something)

    Ella **sabe** hablar español.   *She knows how to speak Spanish.*

saber que..., qué..., si..., cuándo... = *to know that . . . , what . . . , whether/if . . . , when . . .*

    Sabíamos que hacía calor.   *We knew that it was hot.*
    No **sé qué** hacer.   *I don't know what to do.*
    ¿**Sabes si** llamó?   *Do you know if he called?*
    Nunca **sabemos cuándo** va a nevar.   *We never know when it's going to snow.*

Ejercicios 8.28–8.29, página 518

15 *Learn*

aprender = *to acquire knowledge or a skill*

    Aprendí el español.   *I learned Spanish.*

enterarse de = *to find out, discover* (something) *accidentally or intentionally*

    Se enteró de que nos íbamos.   *He found out we were leaving.*
    Se enteraron de la verdad.   *They discovered the truth.*

averiguar = *to find out* (to get information by investigation)

    Tengo que **averiguar** dónde está.   *I have to find out where it is.*

saber [preterite] = *to find out, learn about* (something) *by chance*

    Nunca supe que estabas enfermo.   *I never knew (heard) you were sick.*

Ejercicios 8.30–8.31, página 519

16 Meet

conocer [preterite] = *to meet, make* (someone's) *acquaintance*

    Lo **conocí** en la fiesta.   *I met him at the party.*

NOTE: When the verb **conocer** is conjugated in other tenses, it means *to know* (someone) or *to be familiar with* (something).

encontrarse (con) = *to meet* (planned or by chance)

    Me encontré con ella para almorzar.   *I met her for lunch.*

    Me encontré con él en el tren.   *I ran into him on the train.*

    Nos encontraremos en el restaurante.   *We'll meet at the restaurant.*

encontrar = *to find*

    Encontré cien pesos en la calle.   *I found a hundred pesos on the street.*

    Encontraron a la niña perdida.   *They found the lost child.*

toparse con = *to meet* (run into, meet by chance)

    Se topó con mi primo en la tienda.   *He met (ran into, met by chance) my cousin at the store.*

tropezar con = *to meet* (run into, run across, stumble upon)

    Tropezó con ellos en el cine.   *He ran into them at the movies.*

NOTE: In other contexts, **tropezar** or **tropezarse** means *to trip* or *to stumble* literally, not figuratively:

    Me tropecé y me caí.   *I tripped and fell.*

(See also Chapter 8.B.19, pages 296–298.)

Ejercicios 8.32–8.33, página 519

17 Order

el orden = *order, organization, neatness*

Es esencial que preparen este postre en el **orden** indicado.	*It's essential that you prepare this dessert in the order indicated.*
Por favor archíveme estos folletos en **orden** alfabético.	*Please file these brochures in alphabetical order for me.*

la orden = *order, request*

Recibirá sus **órdenes** del supervisor.	*You will receive your orders from the supervisor.*
¿Puedo tomarles la **orden** (el **pedido**)?	*May I take your order?*
Juan Rodríguez, a sus **órdenes.**	*Juan Rodríguez, at your service.*

> Ejercicios 8.34–8.35, páginas 519–520

18 Pensar

pensar en = *to think about* (someone or something)—intransitive

Siempre **pienso en** mi hermano cuando veo ese cuadro.	*I always think of my brother when I see that painting.*
¿**En** qué **piensas**?	*What are you thinking about?*

pensar *x* de = *to think* x *about something or someone* (x = direct object)—transitive

¿Qué **piensas de** la omnipresencia hoy en día de la telerrealidad?	*What do you think about the ubiquity of reality TV today?*
No quiso decirme lo que **pensaba de** la idea de ser el máximo goleador.	*He didn't want to tell me what he thought about being the top goal scorer.*

NOTE: In the above two sentences, **Qué** and **lo que** are the direct objects of **pensar.** This transitive use of **pensar + de** is only used in direct or indirect interrogatives.

pensar (+ *inf.*) = *to think about, plan to* (do something)—transitive

—¿Qué **piensas** hacer este verano?   *"What are you planning to do this summer?"*

—**Pienso** trabajar en un restaurante.   *"I'm planning to work in a restaurant."*

> Ejercicios 8.36–8.37, página 520

19 People vs. Machines

	PEOPLE VS. MACHINES	
	PEOPLE	**MECHANICAL DEVICES**
to run	**correr**	**andar / funcionar**
	Jorge corre. *Jorge runs.*	Mi coche anda. *My car runs.*
	PEOPLE	**MACHINES AND SYSTEMS**
to work	**trabajar**	**andar / funcionar**
	Jorge trabaja. *Jorge works.*	El reloj no funciona. *The clock is not working.* Este método funciona. *This method works.*
	PEOPLE AND EVENTS	**MOTORS**
to start	**comenzar / empezar**	**poner en marcha / arrancar**
	Empiezo a trabajar a las 7.00 h. *I start work at 7 o'clock.* Comienza a las 8.00 h. *It starts at 8 o'clock.*	Puse el auto en marcha. *I started the car.* Mi coche no arranca. *My car will not start.*
	PEOPLE	**THINGS**
to run out	**salir corriendo**	**acabársele a uno**
	Jorge salió corriendo. *Jorge ran out.*	Se nos acabó el tiempo. *We ran out of time.*
	PEOPLE	**LIGHTS**
to go out	**salir**	**apagarse / irse**
	Jorge salió. *Jorge went out.*	Se apagó (Se fue) la luz. *The light(s) went out.*

As a general rule, before translating an English expression containing a verb with a preposition, remember to think about the meaning of the English expression to avoid a literal and meaningless translation. The following are some other prepositional usages:

To work out:

- as in a person doing exercises: **hacer ejercicio**

    Hago ejercicio al levantarme por la mañana.   *I work out when I get up in the morning.*

- a problem: **resolver un problema**

    No pudieron **resolver el problema**.   *They were unable to work out the problem.*

To run across:

- something: **dar con, tropezar con**

    La busqué por todos lados hasta que al fin **di con** ella en la biblioteca.   *I looked for her everywhere until at last I ran across her in the library.*

- literally, a room, a place: **atravesar corriendo**

    Atravesó el cuarto **corriendo**.   *He ran across the room.*

To run down:

- as in a liquid running down a surface: **escurrir, gotear**

    El sudor le **goteaba** por la cara.   *The sweat ran down his face.*

- with batteries: **descargarse**

    La batería **se descargó** durante el invierno.   *The battery ran down during the winter.*

- with watches: **acabarse la cuerda**

    Se le acabó la cuerda al reloj y paró.   *The watch ran down and stopped.*

- the stairs: **bajar corriendo**

    Bajamos las escaleras **corriendo** para recibirla.   *We ran down the stairs to greet her.*

To run into:

- e.g., a tree with your car: **chocar con**

    Choqué con el árbol.   *I ran into the tree.*

- a person by chance: **tropezar con, toparse con, encontrarse con**

Tropezamos con / Nos topamos con / Nos encontramos con ella en la biblioteca.	*We ran into her at the library.*

To turn out:

- a light: **apagar**

Apaga la luz.	*Turn out the light.*

- right, wrong, etc. (a situation or thing): **las cosas salen bien, mal,** etc.

—¿Cómo **salió** todo?	*"How did everything turn out?"*
—Bien.	*"Okay."*

(See also Chapter 8.B.16, page 294.)

> Ejercicios 8.38–8.39, páginas 520–521

20 Play

jugar = *to play* (a game)

Me gusta **jugar** al ajedrez.	*I like to play chess.*

tocar = *to play* (an instrument)

Ella **toca** el piano.	*She plays the piano.*

a play = **una obra (de teatro)** [theater play], **una jugada** [a single game play in sports, cards, or board games]

to play a game = jugar **un juego** [any game], jugar **un partido** [sports], jugar **una partida** [board game, cards]

Examples:

El póquer es un **juego** de barajas.	*Poker is a card game.*
Vamos a un **partido** de fútbol este fin de semana.	*We're going to a soccer game this weekend.*
¿Quieres jugar un **juego** conmigo? No me importa de qué—escoge tú.	*Do you want to play a game with me? I don't care what kind of game—you choose.*

Mis padres vieron una **obra** de
Cervantes cuando fueron al teatro
en Salamanca.

*My parents saw a Cervantes play when
they went to the theater in Salamanca.*

Juguemos una **partida** de damas.

Let's play a game of checkers.

Están pasando una repetición de
las mejores **jugadas** del **partido**
de anoche.

*They're running a replay of the
highlights* (literally: *the best plays*)
from last night's game.

> Ejercicios 8.40–8.41, página 521;
> Ejercicio de repaso 8.42, página 521

21 Put

poner = *to put; to set* (the table)

    Pusimos la llave sobre la mesa.   *We put the key on the table.*

    Pongan la mesa.   *Set the table.*

guardar, ahorrar = *to put away*

    Guarden los platos.   *Put the plates away.*

    Necesito **ahorrar** algo de dinero.   *I need to put some money away.*

NOTE: There are many other uses of the expression "*to put* + preposition" in English: check the dictionary when you want to use it.

meter = *to put in*

    ¿**Metiste** el coche en el garaje?   *Did you put the car in the garage?*

    El niño **se metió** el dedo en la boca.   *The boy put his finger in his mouth.*

ponerse = *to put on* (+ noun); *to become* (+ adjective)

    Me puse el abrigo.   *I put my coat on.*

    Se puso triste.   *He became sad.*

aguantar, soportar = *to put up with, stand*

> Tengo que **aguantar** todas tus quejas.
> *I have to put up with all of your complaints.*

> ¡Ya no **aguanto** el calor!
> *I can't stand the heat anymore!*

> No sé cómo me **soporta**.
> *I don't know how he/she puts up with me.*

NOTE: *To support* someone morally is **apoyar**; financially it is **mantener**.

> Ejercicios 8.43–8.44, página 522

22 Realize

darse cuenta de = *to realize*

> No **me di cuenta de** la hora que era.
> *I didn't realize what time it was.*

> No **te das cuenta de** las implicaciones de tus actos.
> *You don't realize the implications of your actions.*

realizar = *to come true; to carry out*

> Ahora sí que se me **realizará** el sueño de viajar a Sudamérica.
> *Now my dream to travel to South America will really (**sí**) come true.*

> Ese empleado **realiza** sus funciones con mucha eficacia.
> *That employee carries out his duties very efficiently.*

> Ejercicios 8.45–8.46, página 522

23 Serve

servirle = *to serve* or *to help* (a person)

> ¿Le **sirvo** más vino?
> *Shall I serve you more wine?*

> ¿Le **serviste** agua a esa persona?
> *Did you serve that person water?*

> ¿En qué puedo **servirle**?
> *How may I help you?*

servirlo, servirla; servir algo = *to serve it; to serve something*

—Ya es hora de **servir** la comida.   *"It's time to serve the meal."*

—¿Dónde está la ensalada?   *"Where is the salad?"*

—Ya la **serví.**   *"I already served it."*

(See also Chapter 8.B.5, page 294.)

> Ejercicios 8.47–8.48, página 523

24 *Spend*

gastar = *to spend* (money)

     Gastamos mucho en ese viaje.   *We spent a lot on that trip.*

pasar = *to spend* (time)

     Pasó dos años tras las rejas bajo sospecha de espionaje.   *He spent two years behind bars under suspicion of espionage.*

desperdiciar = *to waste*

     No **desperdicies** dinero.   *Don't waste money.*

     No **desperdicien** mi tiempo.   *Don't waste my time.*

> Ejercicios 8.49–8.50, páginas 523–524

25 *Take*

We recommend that you look up *to take* in a good translation dictionary to get a full picture of all of its uses and translations into Spanish. Note that it is used in many phrases *(to take aback, after, along, apart, around, aside, away, back, down, for, from, in, off, on, out, over, through, to, up, upon)*—each of which may have several different meanings, depending on the context. We list here the uses that have presented our students with the most frequent difficulties:

tomar = *to take* (something [a bus, etc.]), *to drink*

Tomó la llave sin decir nada.	*He took the key without saying anything.*
Quiero **tomar** una cerveza bien fría.	*I want to drink a very cold beer.*
Tome el autobús.	*Take the bus.*

tomar, tardar, demorar(se) = *to take* (time)

¿Cuánto tiempo **tomará / (se) demorará / tardará**?	*How long will it take?*

Toma (Tome usted) is used when you hand someone something. (*"Here."*)

—¿Tienes un lápiz?	*"Do you have a pencil?"*
—Sí. **Toma.** (handing out the pencil)	*"Yes. Here."*
—Gracias.	*"Thanks."*

llevar = *to take* (someone or something [somewhere]) (English also uses *bring* in this case. Spanish distinguishes between movement *away from* the speaker's place **[llevar]** and *to* the speaker's place **[traer].**)

Llevamos a mis padres al aeropuerto.	*We took my parents to the airport.*
Llevaremos toallas a la playa.	*We will take towels to the beach.*
Tráigame un café, por favor.	*Bring me a coffee, please.*

llevarse = *to take* (something away, with oneself)

El mesero **se llevó** mi tenedor.	*The waiter took my fork away.*

apuntar / bajar = *to take down*

La operadora **apuntó** el mensaje.	*The operator took down the message.*
El botones **bajará** su equipaje.	*The bellboy will take (bring) your luggage down.*

subir = *to take up*

El botones **subirá** el equipaje.	*The bellboy will take the luggage up.*

admitir / alojar = *to take in* (as in *to lodge*)

    Esa casa de huéspedes solo **admite (aloja)** adultos.   *That guesthouse only accepts adults.*

sacar = *to take out*

    Sacaron a los niños a pasear.   *They took the children out for a stroll.*

quitarse = *to take off* (articles of clothing)

    Se quitó la ropa para bañarse.   *He took off his clothes to bathe.*

tener lugar = *to take place*

    El concierto **tendrá lugar** esta noche.   *The concert will take place tonight.*

traer = *to bring* (toward the speaker only)

    El mesero no nos **trajo** la cuenta muy rápido.   *The waiter didn't bring us the check very quickly.*

> Ejercicios 8.51–8.52, página 524

26 Time

tiempo = *time; weather*

    No tengo **tiempo** para ayudarte hoy.   *I do not have time to help you today.*

    Hace buen **tiempo** hoy.   *The weather is nice today.*

vez = *time* (countable)

    Toma café cuatro **veces** al día.   *He drinks coffee four times a day.*

    Esta **vez** yo pago.   *This time, I will pay.*

hora = *time* (chronological)

    —¿Qué **hora** es?   *"What time is it?"*

    —Es **hora** de irnos.   *"It is time to leave."*

rato = *time, while*
ratito = *a little while*

    Hace **rato** (**ratito**) que estoy esperando.   *I have been waiting for some time (a [little] while).*

divertirse = *to have a good time*

    Nos divertimos mucho en la fiesta ayer.   *We had a very good time at the party yesterday.*

BUT:

    Ayer tuvimos buen **tiempo**.   *Yesterday we had good weather.*

Idiomatic expressions:

a tiempo = *on time*
a la vez = *at the same time*
al mismo tiempo = *at the same time*
en esa época = *at the time* (general)
en ese momento = *at the time* (specific moment)
a veces = *at times, sometimes*
de vez en cuando = *once in a while*
al rato = *after a while*
en vez de = *instead of*

> Ejercicios 8.53–8.54, páginas 524–525

27 What

¿Qué es...? = *What is . . . ?* (asking for a definition)

    ¿Qué es un "cántaro"?   *What is a "cántaro"?*

¿Cuál es...? = *What is . . . ?* (asking for identification or specification)

    ¿Cuál es la diferencia entre los dos?   *What is the difference between the two?*

    ¿Cuál es el estacionamiento para minusválidos?   *Which is the handicapped parking space?*

¿**Qué** (+ noun)...? = *What, Which* (+ noun) . . . ?

 ¿**Qué** libro leíste anoche?   *What (Which) book did you read last night?*

 ¿**Qué** ciudades visitaste en Sudamérica?   *What cities did you visit in South America?*

 ¿**Qué** (comida) vamos a comer?   *What are we going to eat?*

 ¿**Qué** (ropa) te vas a poner esta noche?   *What are you going to wear tonight?*

¿**Cómo**? = *Excuse me?*

NOTE: ¿**Cómo**? is more polite in Spanish than ¿**Qué**? to mean *"What?"* when asking someone to repeat what he or she just said:

 ¿**Cómo**? OR: ¿**Cómo** dijo?

Lo que = *what* (relative pronoun, not used in interrogatives)

 Lo que me gusta de la película es el misterio.   *What I like about the movie is the mystery.*

 No me dijo **lo que** quería.   *He did not tell me what he wanted.*

> Ejercicios 8.55–8.56, página 525;
> Ejercicio de repaso 8.57, página 525

C FALSE COGNATES AND FALSE FRIENDS

A "cognate" is a word that has a common etymological origin in two languages. For example, given their shared etymological history, **abandonar** is a cognate of *to abandon*.

A "false cognate" is a word that appears to have a common etymological origin, but does not. For example, **mucho** and *much* would appear to be cognates but as a matter of fact they come from different etymological sources.

"False friends" is an expression that is used to describe words that sound alike or look alike, but do not have the same meaning. Some are actually cognates, but have evolved over time to have different meanings in different languages. An example of a false friend is the word **librería** which sounds like *library* but in fact means *bookstore*.

In the following table, we list the words that may be false friends, false cognates, or that have some uses that can lead to error, although some might have an area of overlap with English. For example, as we have seen already, the word *question* can be translated as **cuestión,** but only when it means *issue, matter,* and not when it relates to a *question* that one asks. In addition, you may find that some Spanish speakers do use some of these terms as borrowings from English (for example, some may say **americano** to signify someone from the United States rather than someone from anywhere in the American continent, North or South, the latter being its true meaning). For purposes of visual clarity and economy of space, we use only the masculine singular form of words even if they also have feminine and plural forms. A good English–Spanish dictionary coupled with a good Spanish–Spanish dictionary will be necessary to get a full sense of all of the nuances of these words.

*Words marked with asterisks in the following table are more thoroughly analyzed in this chapter under **B. Terms and Expressions.** Each asterisk is followed by the number indicating the subsection in which the word appears.

ENGLISH		SPANISH		POTENTIAL CONFUSION
to abuse [someone]	=	maltratar, abusar sexualmente	≠	abusar *(to take advantage of; to overuse)*
to accommodate	=	complacer	≠	acomodar *(to place; to arrange)*
actual	=	verdadero	≠	actual *(present)*
actually	=	en realidad	≠	actualmente *(nowadays; at the moment)*
advertisement	=	anuncio	≠	advertencia *(warning; reminder; preface)*
American	=	estadounidense	≠	americano *(from the American continent, either North or South)*
apology	=	disculpa	≠	apología *(defense)*
application	=	solicitud	≠	aplicación *(dedication)*
to apply for (a job)	=	solicitar	≠	aplicar*2 *(to apply [an ointment])*
to appreciate	=	agradecer	≠	apreciar *(to augment in value)*
arena	=	estadio	≠	arena *(sand)*
to assist	=	ayudar	≠	asistir*5 *(to attend)*
to assume	=	suponer	≠	asumir *(to take on)*
to attend	=	asistir	≠	atender*5 *(to pay attention to)*
bachelor	=	soltero	≠	bachiller *(high school graduate)*

(continued)

ENGLISH		SPANISH		POTENTIAL CONFUSION
camp	=	campamento	≠	campo (field; country [vs. city])
card	=	tarjeta	≠	carta (letter)
career	=	profesión	≠	carrera (race; row; beam; course of study at the university)
carpet	=	tapete, alfombra	≠	carpeta (folder)
character (literary)	=	personaje	≠	carácter (personality)
to choke	=	sofocar, ahogar	≠	chocar (to crash)
collar	=	cuello	≠	collar (necklace)
college	=	universidad, facultad	≠	colegio (private high school)
colored	=	de color	≠	colorado (red; reddish)
compromise	=	concesión recíproca, acuerdo mutuo	≠	compromiso (commitment, obligation; promise)
conductor (orchestra)	=	director	≠	conductor (electric conductor; driver; radio presenter)
conference	=	consulta	≠	conferencia (lecture)
constipated	=	estreñido	≠	constipado (congested with a cold)
to contest	=	contender	≠	contestar (to answer)
copy (of a book)	=	ejemplar	≠	copia (photocopy; duplicate copy)
courage	=	valor, valentía	≠	coraje (anger; rage)
cult	=	secta	≠	culto (refined; educated; cultured)
cup	=	taza	≠	copa (glass; alcoholic drink; trophy)
dance	=	baile	≠	danza (ritual or folkloric dance)
deception	=	engaño	≠	decepción (disappointment)
delight	=	placer, deleite	≠	delito (minor crime)
to demand	=	exigir	≠	demandar (to sue)
destitute	=	desamparado, indigente	≠	destituido (removed from office)
discussion	=	debate, deliberación	≠	discusión (argument; dispute)
disgrace	=	deshonra	≠	desgracia (mishap; misfortune)
disgust	=	asco, repugnancia	≠	disgusto (displeasure; misfortune)

(continued)

ENGLISH		SPANISH		POTENTIAL CONFUSION
disparate	=	[adj.] desigual, diferente	≠	disparate [noun] (nonsense; remark or act that is stupid; foolish; madness)
distinct	=	particular, marcado	≠	distinto (different)
education	=	formación, enseñanza	≠	educación (upbringing; good manners)
effective	=	eficaz	≠	efectivo (actual; cash)
embarrassed	=	avergonzado	≠	embarazada (pregnant)
equivocal	=	ambiguo, equívoco	≠	equivocado (wrong)
excited	=	emocionado	≠	excitado (aroused)
excitement	=	emoción	≠	excitación (arousal)
exit	=	salida	≠	éxito*[11] (success; hit)
fabric	=	tela	≠	fábrica (factory)
faculty	=	profesorado	≠	facultad (university department; mental ability)
fastidious	=	escrupuloso	≠	fastidioso (annoying)
fault	=	culpa (blame); defecto (imperfection)	≠	falta (lack; absence; shortage)
firm (noun)	=	empresa	≠	firma (signature)
football	=	fútbol americano	≠	fútbol (soccer)
gang	=	pandilla	≠	ganga (bargain)
goal (figurative)	=	meta, objetivo, fin	≠	gol (soccer goal; scored point)
to grab	=	asir, agarrar, arrebatar	≠	grabar (to record; to engrave)
gracious	=	cortés, amable	≠	gracioso (funny; cute)
grade	=	nota	≠	grado (degree; stage)
grocery (store)	=	abarrotería, bodega	≠	grosería (rudeness; vulgarity; curse word)
honest	=	honrado	≠	honesto (sincere; decent)
idiom	=	modismo	≠	idioma (language)
ingenuity	=	ingeniosidad	≠	ingenuidad (innocence)

(continued)

ENGLISH		SPANISH		POTENTIAL CONFUSION
to ignore	=	no hacer caso	≠	ignorar (to not know)
inhabitable	=	habitable	≠	inhabitable (uninhabitable)
to introduce someone	=	presentar	≠	introducir (to place, put; to begin; etc.)
labor	=	trabajo (actual work); mano de obra (the workers)	≠	labor (work; chores; etc.)
large	=	grande	≠	largo (long)
lecture	=	conferencia	≠	lectura (reading)
letter	=	carta	≠	letra (handwriting; letter of the alphabet; words of a song)
library	=	biblioteca	≠	librería (bookstore)
luxury	=	lujo	≠	lujuria (lewdness; lust; excess)
mark	=	señal, mancha	≠	marca (brand, make, label); marco (frame, setting, framework)
mass	=	misa	≠	masa (dough)
material (cloth)	=	tela	≠	material (material [but not cloth])
mayor	=	alcalde	≠	mayor ([adj] older; larger; major; main; [noun] ancestor)
money	=	dinero	≠	moneda (coin; currency)
to molest	=	abusar sexualmente de	≠	molestar (to bother; annoy)
notice	=	aviso	≠	noticia (news item; piece of news)
nude	=	desnudo	≠	nudo (knot)
number	=	número	≠	nombre (name)
office	=	despacho, oficina	≠	oficio (function; trade; religious service)
paper (term paper)	=	trabajo escrito	≠	papel (piece of paper; role)
parents	=	padres	≠	parientes (relatives)
patron	=	cliente, patrocinador	≠	patrón (boss; owner; pattern)
pain (physical)	=	dolor	≠	pena (sorrow, grief)
people	=	gente	≠	pueblo (nation; common people)
phrase	=	expresión	≠	frase (sentence)

(continued)

ENGLISH		SPANISH		POTENTIAL CONFUSION
policy	=	política	≠	policía (police)
politician	=	político	≠	política (politics; policy)
present (gift)	=	regalo	≠	presente (the present tense)
preservative	=	conservador	≠	preservativo (condom)
to pretend	=	fingir, simular	≠	pretender (to try; to claim; to expect)
to procure	=	obtener, conseguir	≠	procurar (to try)
question	=	pregunta	≠	cuestión (matter)
quiet	=	silencioso	≠	quieto (calm; still)
to quit	=	dejar de + inf. dimitir + noun	≠	quitar (to remove)
race (for speed)	=	carrera	≠	raza (ethnicity, race)
rare	=	excepcional, poco común	≠	raro (strange; weird; odd)
rate	=	velocidad, ritmo, paso, tasa	≠	rato (while)
real	=	verdadero	≠	real (royal)
to realize that . . .	=	darse cuenta de que…	≠	realizar algo*[22] (to make something come true)
receipt	=	recibo	≠	receta (recipe; prescription)
to record	=	grabar, inscribir, registrar	≠	recordar (to remember)
red	=	rojo	≠	red (network; net)
to register	=	inscribirse	≠	registrar a alguien (to search someone)
a relative	=	un pariente	≠	relativo ([adj.] not absolute)
rent	=	alquiler	≠	renta (income; annuity; interest)
to rest	=	descansar	≠	restar (to subtract; take away)
resort	=	balneario	≠	resorte (metal spring)
rope	=	soga, cuerda	≠	ropa (clothing)
rude	=	maleducado, grosero	≠	rudo (rough; coarse)
salary	=	sueldo	≠	salario (hourly wages)
sane	=	cuerdo	≠	sano (healthy)

(continued)

ENGLISH		SPANISH		POTENTIAL CONFUSION
school (as in Law)	=	facultad	≠	escuela (elementary school)
to sense	=	tener la impresión	≠	sentir (to feel)
sensible	=	sensato	≠	sensible (sensitive)
sentence	=	frase, oración	≠	sentencia (verdict)
soap	=	jabón	≠	sopa (soup)
to succeed	=	tener éxito	≠	suceder*[11] (to happen)
success	=	éxito	≠	suceso*[11] (event)
subject (of an article, class)	=	tema (de artículo), materia (clase)	≠	sujeto (a person) (individual; guy; character)
to support	=	mantener, apoyar	≠	soportar*[21] (to tolerate)
sympathetic	=	compasivo, comprensivo	≠	simpático (nice; friendly)
sympathy	=	compasión, pésame, etc.	≠	simpatía (charm; friendliness)
table	=	mesa	≠	tabla (board; plank)
tense (of a verb)	=	tiempo (verbal)	≠	tenso (tense [adj.])
torment	=	tormento	≠	tormenta (storm)
tramp	=	vagabundo	≠	trampa (trick; trap)
to translate	=	traducir	≠	trasladar (to move; to transfer)
tuna	=	atún	≠	tuna (cactus fruit; singing group of college students)
ultimate	=	fundamental	≠	último (last)
ultimately	=	a fin de cuentas	≠	últimamente (lately)
vase	=	florero, jarrón	≠	vaso (drinking glass)
to violate	=	violar	≠	violar (to violate; to rape)

CHAPTER 9

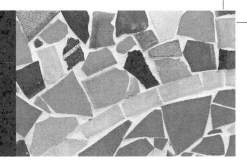

Orthography

A General Information

B Consonants: Spelling Issues

C Vowels and Accents

D Linking between Words: Synalepha

E Capitalization

F Numbers

G Punctuation

H Dialectal Variation, Norm, Register

I Summary of 2010 *Ortografía* Changes

A. GENERAL INFORMATION

Incorporated herein are the revised rules and recommendations published in the new *Ortografía de la lengua española*[1]. For a summary of the specific changes affecting this **Manual,** see Section I at the end of this chapter, pages 378–380.

1 The Alphabet

The alphabet in Spanish consists of the following letters, shown with their recommended names in Spanish:

	EL ALFABETO				
A	a	J	jota	R	erre
B	be	K	ka	S	ese
C	ce	L	ele	T	te
D	de	M	eme	U	u
E	e	N	ene	V	uve
F	efe	Ñ	eñe	W	uve doble
G	ge	O	o	X	equis
H	hache	P	pe	Y	ye
I	i	Q	cu	Z	zeta

Letters of the alphabet are feminine nouns, variable in number (singular, plural[2]). Following are some examples of their use in context:

"Uva" se deletrea **u, uve, a.**   *"Uva" is spelled u, v, a.*

Identificaron al criminal por su forma de escribir **la erre.**   *They identified the criminal by the way he wrote the r.*

"Buzo" se escribe con **be** y **zeta.**   *"Buzo" is spelled with b and z.*

---

[1] *Ortografía de la lengua española*, Real Academia Española, Asociación de Academias de la Lengua Española, Espasa Libros, 2010.

[2] The plurals of the letters of the alphabet are formed by adding an s to the end of the name of each letter, with the exceptions of the vowels (**aes, ees, íes, oes, úes**).

The letters **b** and **v**[3] have had over time a number of different names: you may have heard these two letters referred to as **be grande, larga,** or **alta** and **ve chica, corta,** or **baja**. You may also have heard **i griega** for the letter **y**. The latest revised rules of Spanish orthography recommend the use of the simpler names of the letters **b, v, w,** and **y**: respectively, **be, uve, uve doble,** and **ye**.

Note that **ch (la che)** and **ll (la elle)** are no longer part of the Spanish alphabet. Current Spanish dictionaries place the **ch** under **c**, and the **ll** under **l**, as do English dictionaries. As for the **rr (la doble erre o erre doble)**, it is less of an issue because there are no words that begin with two **rs**, and for this reason it does not need a separate section in the dictionary.

There is still a separate section in the dictionary for the **ñ**, after the **n** section, for the few words that begin with this letter. If you are looking up a word with an **-ñ-** inside it, you will find it after all the entries for **-n-** (e.g., **maña** is not found after **mana**, but after **manzano**).

We provide below a brief glossary of useful terms for Chapter 9:

CHAPTER 9 GLOSSARY	
acento [m] *(accent)*	**letra** [f] *(letter, as in a, b, c)*
alfabeto [m] *(alphabet)*	**oír**[4] *(to hear)*
cognado [m] *(cognate)*	**ortografía** [f] *(orthography)*
confundir *(confuse)*	**palabra** *(word)*
consonante [f] *(consonant)*	**pronunciación** [f] *(pronunciation)*
deletrear *(to spell)*	**pronunciar** *(to pronounce)*
deletreo [m] *(spelling)*	**sílaba** [f] *(syllable)*
dialectal *(dialectal)*	**sonar**[5] *(to sound)*
dialecto [m] *(dialect)*	**sonido** [m] *(sound)*
énfasis [m] *(stress)*	**vocal** [f] *(vowel)*

Ejercicio 9.1, página 526

---

[3] You may also hear v referred to as **la ve labiodental**; this is a reference to the pronunciation of the **v** as in English. It is considered to be incorrect in Spanish to pronounce the letter **v** differently from the letter **b**. For more on this see Section B.1. of this chapter, pages 319–320.

[4] For the conjugation of oír, see verb table #40, Appendix A, page 16.

[5] **Sonar** is conjugated like **contar**. See verb table #17, Appendix A, page 8. Note that it is used with the preposition **a** (e.g., En ese contexto la ge **suena a** jota. *In that context g **sounds like** j.*)

2 Representation of Letters by Sound

Intermediate or advanced learners of the Spanish language are well aware of the relationship of its sound with its spelling. It is a common fallacy to say that Spanish is pronounced as it is written. Indeed, although pronunciation and spelling in Spanish are much closer than in English, even in Spanish different letters may have different sounds depending on what surrounds them. Knowing how to spell what you hear requires the knowledge of some rudimentary guidelines.

Following is a chart of symbols used to represent the basic sounds of letters in standard Spanish, adapted from the 2010 *Ortografía*. Note that we are deliberately avoiding traditional phonetic transcription systems, because our focus is not to teach phonetics, but rather to provide readily available tools to help the learner identify basic sounds and relate them to the spelling of words.

We do not include in this chart much detail on regional pronunciation other than the very generalized Spanish-speaking areas of Spain and Latin America. Each of these areas has a variety of regional pronunciation features. For more on this, see later in this chapter, Section H, pages 374–378.

Note that in this chart a letter or combination of letters is indicated without markers, the sound of a letter or combination of letters is between slashes, and the pronunciation of whole words is between brackets.

SOUND REPRESENTATION OF LETTERS			
LETTER[6]		SOUND SYMBOL	ENGLISH SOUND	SPANISH EXAMPLE
a	/a/	father	favor
b	/b/	**b**in	**b**ien
c	c + a, o, u	/k/	cat	**c**al, **c**oche, **c**uesta
	c + cons.[7]			**c**lase, **c**rema, a**c**to
	-c			blo**c**, fra**c**
	c + e, i	/s/ (seseo[8]), /z/	**s**ip, **th**in	**c**ero, **c**inta
ch	/ch/	**ch**in	mu**ch**acho
d	/d/	**d**en	**d**ar
e	/e/	p**e**n	p**e**lo
f	/f/	**f**eat	**f**oto
g	g + a, o, u	/g/	**g**oat	**g**ala, re**g**uero
	g + ü			**g**üiro
	g + cons.			**g**lobo, si**g**no
	-g			zig**z**ag
	g + e, i	/j/	**ch** in Ba**ch**	**g**ente, **G**inebra
h	Ø (silent)	**h**our	**h**ora [óra]
i	/i/	s**ee**n	s**i**n
j	/j/	**ch** in Ba**ch**	**j**inete
k	/k/	**c**at, **k**id	**k**araoke
l	/l/	**l**id	**l**avo
ll	/y/ (yeísmo[9]), /ll/	**y**et; **ll** in mi**ll**ion	**ll**ave
m	/m/	**m**ost	**m**atar
n	/n/	**n**ib	**n**oche
ñ	/ñ/	the **-ni-** in o**ni**on	ni**ñ**o, **ñ**ame
o	/o/	n**o**se	**o**so

(continued)

---

[6] In this first column, a hyphen before a consonant = a word ending with that consonant, a hyphen after a consonant = a word starting with that consonant, a hyphen on both sides = an intervocalic consonant (between vowels).

[7] In this column, cons. = consonant.

[8] For information on the **seseo**, see Section B.2.b. of this chapter, page 322.

[9] For information on the **yeísmo**, see Section H.1.a. of this chapter, page 376.

LETTER		SOUND SYMBOL	ENGLISH SOUND	SPANISH EXAMPLE
p		/p/	s*p*in	**p**an
q		/k/	*c*ap	**q**ueso
r	-r-, -r	/r/	similar to the **tt** sound in *matter*	pe**r**o, cami**n**a**r**
	br, cr, dr, fr, gr, kr, pr, tr			b**r**azo, af**r**enta, ing**r**ediente
	r-, -rr-	/rr/	rolled or trilled **r**	**r**ápido, pe**rr**o
	lr, nr, sr			al**r**ededor, en**r**edo, is**r**aelí
s		/s/	*s*top	**s**anto
t		/t/	s*t*ep	**t**ú
u	u	/u/	b*oo*t	**u**n
	gue, gui, que, qui	Ø (silent)	g*u*itar	**g**u**e**rra [gérra], **q**u**i**so [kíso]
v		/b/	*b*in	**v**alor
w		/b/ /u/, /gu/	*b*in *w*ay, g*u*ano	**W**agner [bágner] ki**w**i [kíui], **w**eb [guéb]
x	x-	/s/	*s*top	**x**enofobia [senofóbia]
	-x	/ks/	ta*x*	tóra**x** [tóraks]
	x + cons.	/ks/, /s/	a*cc*ept, *s*top	e**x**tra [ékstra, éstra]
	-x-	/ks/	a*cc*ept	e**x**iste [eksíste], ta**x**i [taksi]
	-x-[10]	/j/	*ch* in *Bach*	Mé**x**ico [méjiko]
y		/y/	*y*et	**y**a
z		/s/ (seseo), /z/	*s*ip, *th*in	**z**apato, a**z**ul, bi**z**co

B CONSONANTS: SPELLING ISSUES

In this segment we focus on consonants (**las consonantes**) that are problematic in relation to spelling. These are especially problematic for heritage learners of Spanish who have greater familiarity with the language in an oral/aural context, and have not had ample opportunities to see the language in written form.

---

[10] For more on this regional pronunciation of x, see Section B.5.c. of this chapter, pages 334–335.

NOTE: We enclose in brackets ([ ]) the pronunciation of the word, with the stressed vowel marked with an accent mark. This accent mark does not translate into the actual spelling of the word, unless it coincides with a syllable that requires a written accent mark[11]:

Examples:

español	[españól]
familia	[família]
académico	[akadémiko]

1 B, V

These two consonants vary only in writing, but sound the same in Spanish[12]. Thus, for example, **botar** *(to kick out)* and **votar** *(to vote)* are homophones (sound the same), and if you are hearing one of these, only the context can let you know which one it is:

Antes de dejar **votar** a los que estaban esperando pacientemente su turno en la cola, decidieron **botar** a los manifestantes.

Before allowing to vote those who were patiently waiting in line, they decided to kick out the protesters.

Following are some common homophones:

varón	*male*	≠	**barón**	*baron*
vienes	*you come*	≠	**bienes**	*goods*
votar	*vote*	≠	**botar**	*throw away/kick out*
bobina	*bobbin*	≠	**bovina**	*bovine*
revelar	*reveal*	≠	**rebelar**	*rebel*
tubo	*tube*	≠	**tuvo**	*had*
bello	*beautiful*	≠	**vello**	*soft down-like body hair*

Between vowels, the sound of the letter **b** is softened, but remains bilabial (articulated with both lips), never labiodental (never articulated with the lower lip against the upper teeth; the English **v** is labiodental). Note in the following sentence the words with this softened **b** sound (in bold):

I**b**a a la**v**ar las sá**b**anas, pero no tu**v**e tiempo.

I was going to wash the sheets, but I didn't have time.

---

[11] See section 9.C of this chapter, for rules of written accentuation.
[12] For more on these two letters, see Section A.1. at the beginning of this chapter, page 315.

The following table lists the most common uses of **b** and **v** in spelling.

B • V	
SPELLED WITH B	**SPELLED WITH V**
verbs ending in **-bir, -buir** (e.g., **escribir, contribuir**…) **Exceptions: hervir, servir, vivir,** and composites	verbs ending in **-olver** (e.g., **volver, devolver, disolver**…)
the verbs **beber, caber, deber, saber, haber**	the verbs **estar, andar, tener** in preterite indicative and imperfect subjunctive (e.g., **estuve, anduviera, tuvo**…)
imperfect indicative of **-ar** verbs: **-aba, -abas**… and of the verb **ir: iba, ibas**…	the verb **ir** in the present indicative, imperative, and present subjunctive. (e.g., **voy, ve, vaya**…)
words starting with the prefixes: **bene-, bien-** (good, well) (e.g., **beneficio, bienvenida**…) **biblio-** [book], and the syllables **bu-, bur-, bus-** (e.g., **biblioteca, bula, burlar, busca**…) **Exception: vudú** (voodoo) and derivatives **bi-, bis-, biz-** (two) (e.g., **bilateral, bisabuelo, bizcocho**…) **bio-, -bio** (life) (e.g., **biología, biosfera, microbio**…)	words starting with: **eva-, eve-, evi-, evo-** (e.g., **evadir, evento, evitar, evolución**…) **Exception: ébano** and derivatives **vice-, viz-, vi-** (instead of) (e.g., **vicepresidente, vizconde, virrey**…)
when the sound /b/ precedes another consonant or ends the word (e.g., **obtener, amable, brazo, baobab**…) **Exception: OVNI** (UFO) Note that although both spellings are accepted, **-s-** is preferred to **-bs-** in the following words and their derivatives: **obscuro (oscuro), subscribir (suscribir), substancia (sustancia), substitución (sustitución), substraer (sustraer).**	when the sound /b/ is preceded by **ad-, sub-, ob-** (e.g., **advertir, subvenir, obvio**…) words ending in **-viro, -vira** that are stressed on the next to last syllable (e.g., **triunviro, Elvira**…) words ending in **-ívoro, -ívora** (e.g., **carnívoro, omnívora**…) **Exception: víbora**
words ending in **-bilidad** (e.g., **disponibilidad, posibilidad**…) **Exceptions: movilidad, civilidad** words ending in **-bundo(a)** (e.g., **vagabundo, abunda**…)	adjectives ending in **-avo(a), -evo(a), -eve, -ivo(a)** that are stressed on the next to last syllable (e.g., **esclavo, nueva, leve, decisivo, activo**…) **Exceptions: suabo, mancebo**

Ejercicios 9.2–9.4, páginas 526–527

2 K, C, Qu, S

a. The sound /k/

The sound /k/ in Spanish can be represented in writing by the letter **k, c,** or **q**, as follows:

In a few words, the letter **k** itself is found, for example:

karate	[karáte]	*(karate)*
kermés	[kermés]	*(bazaar, kermess)*
kilo	[kilo]	*(kilo)*
kimono	[kimóno]	*(kimono)*
kiosco	[kiósko]	*(kiosk)*
koala	[koála]	*(koala)*
kurdo	[kúrdo]	*(Kurdish)*

The letter **c**, followed by **a, o,** or **u,** is pronounced /k/:

casa	[kása]	*(house)*
cola	[kóla]	*(tail, line)*
cuesta	[kuésta]	*(slope)*

The letter **q** is pronounced /k/. When **q** is followed by **e** or **i**, a silent **u** is required (see section 3.a., page 325, for more on the silent **u**):

que	[ke]	*(that)*
quechua	[kéchua]	*(Quechua)*
quiquiriquí	[kikirikí]	*(cock-a-doodle-doo)*

Foreign words with the sound /k/ are to be spelled as normal Spanish words would (e.g., **cuásar, cuórum, Catar**). It is also possible to quote foreign words from their original language, in which case they need to be in italics and with no accent (e.g., *quasar, quorum, Qatar*). An exception to this rule is **Irak**, historically spelled with a **k** in Spanish rather than a **q.** Note however that the adjective **iraquí** reverts to standard rules of Spanish spelling for the /k/ sound.

b. The sounds /s/ and /z/; seseo

(1) The letter s
The letter **s** is pronounced /s/ in Standard Spanish[13]. There are numerous variants to this norm in the Spanish-speaking world, which we will not cover here (e.g., the aspiration of the /s/, its omission, the **ceceo**[14] or pronunciation of **s** as /z/, etc.).

(2) The letter c + e, i
When the letter **c** is followed by **e** or **i**, it is pronounced /s/ in Latin America and other regions of **seseo** (see box below), and /z/ in Spain.

A Note about the <u>SESEO</u>

The term **seseo** (verb: **sesear**) refers to the pronunciation as /s/ of the letter **c**, followed by **e** or **i**, and of the letter **z**. In Spain[15] these are pronounced /z/ (like the *th* in *thin*). The **seseo** is standard in Latin America.

	SESEO		
	LATIN AMERICA (SESEO)	SPAIN	
cesta	[sésta]	[zésta]	*basket*
cinta	[sínta]	[zínta]	*tape*
zapato	[sapáto]	[zapáto]	*shoe*
zorro	[sórro]	[zórro]	*fox*
pe**z**	[pes]	[pez]	*fish*
pe**c**es	[péses]	[pézes]	*fish*

In this chapter, we provide both pronunciations, to help learners identify the /z/ sound when they hear it, and associate it with proper spelling. When it comes to usage, we recommend the learner use the **seseo** (except for heritage speakers of the regions that use /z/, or individuals who intend to adopt the rest of the dialectal traits of the regions that use /z/, which include the use of **vosotros** and of the **leísmo**). For more on this, see Chapter 3.A.3.a, pages 57–58).

---

[13] Standard Spanish is that which is considered the educated norm throughout the Spanish-speaking world. For more on this, see in this chapter the introduction to Section H, page 374.

[14] For more on the **ceceo**, see in this chapter, Section H.1.a., page 375.

[15] This is true with the exceptions of certain regions: Canarias, Andalucía, some areas of Murcia and Badajoz, in informal speech in Valencia, Cataluña, Mallorca, and el País Vasco, along with certain rural areas of Galicia. In these regions, when Spanish is spoken, the **seseo** can be heard.

(3) Stem changes for verbs ending in -cer or -cir: c → z

In the conjugations of certain verbs ending in **-cer** or **-cir**, to retain the pronunciation of /s/ or /z/ in the verb stem, **c** changes to **z** before verb endings **a** and **o**:

Hacer[16]: [asér]/[azér]

hi**c**e   →   hi**z**o

(If the **c** were maintained in the spelling of the third person singular of the preterite, it would be mispronounced [íko] rather than [íso] / [ízo].)

Examples:

Ha**c**emos lo que podemos.	*We do what we can.*
Lo hi**z**o ella.	*She did it.*

Vencer[17]: [bensér] / [benzér]

ven**c**e   →   ven**z**o (1st pers. pres. ind.)
                ven**z**a, -s, -mos, -n (pres. subj.)

(If the **c** were maintained in the spelling of these endings, they would be mispronounced [-énko], [-énka], etc.)

Other verbs like **vencer:** convencer, torcer, ejercer, mecer

Examples:

Vine, vi y ven**c**í.	*I came, I saw, and I conquered.*
No te tuer**z**as el tobillo.	*Don't twist your ankle.*

Not all verb conjugations ending in **-cer** or **-cir** function in the same manner. Other alterations are made with verbs like **parecer**[18] and **lucir**[19] where **c** changes to **zc** before **a** or **o**.

c. Words ending in -ción, -sión, -tión, -xión

Most words that end in *-tion* in English end in **-ción** in Spanish; English words ending in *-sion,* or *-ssion,* end in **-sión** in Spanish:

association	asocia**ción**	[asosiasión] / [asoziazión]
direction	direc**ción**	[direksión] / [direkzión]

---

[16] See verb table #32, Appendix A, page 13; note that there are other irregularities with this verb, such as the **g** in the first person present indicative **hago,** and in the present subjunctive **haga, hagas,** etc.

[17] See verb table #64, Appendix A, page 24; see also verb table #12, Appendix A, page 6 for similar changes in the verb **cocer** et al.; see also verb table #28, Appendix A, page 12, for similar changes in the verb **esparcir** et al.

[18] See verb table #42, Appendix A, page 16. See also verb table #70, Appendix A, page 26, for the stem changes in the verb **yacer.**

[19] See verb table #36, Appendix A, page 14.

*deci**si**on*	deci**sió**n	[desisión] / [dezisión]
*pos**se**ssion*	pose**sió**n	[posesión]

There are a few words in Spanish that end in **-tión** or **-xión,** for example:

*ques**tion***	cues**tió**n	[kuestión]
*diges**tion***	diges**tió**n	[dijestión]
*connec**tion***	cone**xió**n	[koneksión]
*reflec**tion***	refle**xió**n	[refleksión]

Derivatives follow suit (*-tion-, -sion-,* and *-xion-* become, respectively, **-cion-, -sion-,** and **-xion-** within words):

cues**tion**able	[kuestionáble]
profe**sion**al	[profesionál]
refle**xion**ar	[refleksionár]

> Ejercicios 9.5–9.6, páginas 527–528

3 G, Gu, Gü, J

a. The sound /g/; silent u; ü

The letter **g** can be pronounced differently in Spanish depending on its context in the word.

Followed by **a, o,** or **u,** the letter **g** is pronounced /g/, similar to the English pronunciation of **g** in *goat:*

gato	[gáto]	*(cat)*
gorila	[goríla]	*(gorilla)*
gusto	[gústo]	*(taste, pleasure)*

To produce the sound /g/ in front of **e** or **i,** a silent **u (u muda)** follows the **g:**

guerrilla	[gerríya]	*(guerrilla)*
gueto	[géto]	*(ghetto)*
guiso	[gíso]	*(stew)*

When the **u** after **g** is not silent before **e** or **i,** a diaeresis, or umlaut, is added:

a**gü**ero	[agüéro]	*(omen)*

U • Ü
NOTE ABOUT THE SILENT U AND THE DIAERESIS, OR UMLAUT

The **u** is silent (<u>not</u> pronounced) in the following combinations:
  gue /ge/   gui /gi/   que /ke/   qui /ki/
 	
Following a **g,** the **u** <u>is</u> pronounced only if it has a diaeresis **(diéresis),** or umlaut, over it:
  güe /gue/   güi /gui/
 	
Examples:
  Quiero **que** me **gu**íen en ling**üí**stica.   [**kié**ro**ke**megíenenling**uí**stika]
  Averi**güé que** la **gu**erra estallaba.   [aberi**gué**ke la **gé**rraestayába]

b. The sound /j/

The sound /j/, which sounds like the **ch** in *Bach*, is produced in two contexts:

- With the letter **j** in any context:

ad**j**etivo	[adjetíbo]	*(adjective)*
a**j**o	[ájo]	*(garlic)*
a**j**ustar	[ajustár]	*(adjust)*
bara**j**a	[barája]	*(deck of cards* or *card)*
beren**j**ena	[berenjéna]	*(eggplant)*
jamás	[jamás]	*(never)*
jefe	[jéfe]	*(boss, head, chief)*
jinete	[jinéte]	*(horseback rider)*
joven	[jóben]	*(young)*
junta	[júnta]	*(meeting, committee)*
vie**j**o	[biéjo]	*(old)*

- With the letter **g** when it is followed directly by **e** or **i**:

a**g**ente	[ajénte]	*(agent)*
gelatina	[jelatína]	*(gelatin)*
gitano	[jitáno]	*(gypsy)*
vi**g**ilar	[bijilár]	*(watch, guard)*

The following table lists the most common uses of **g** and **j** in the spelling of words with the sound /j/:

G • J	
SPELLED WITH G	**SPELLED WITH J**

words starting with
    gest-   **geo-**
    (e.g., **gesto, geografía**...)
	words derived from those with
	j before **a, o, u**
	(e.g., **caja** → **cajero, cajita**
	          cojo → **cojear**
	           ojo → **ojear**
	           rojo → **rojizo**...)

words ending in
    -gélico   **-genio**   **-ginal**
    -genario   **-génito**   **-gíneo**
    -géneo   **-gesimal**   **-ginoso**
    -génico   **-gésimo**   **-gírico**
    -giénico   **-gético**
    -gia   **-gión**
    -gio   **-gional**
    -gioso   **-gionario**
    -gente   **-ígeno(a)**
    -gencia   **-ígero(a)**
    -logía
    -gogia   **-gogía**
    -algia
(e.g., **angélico, homogéneo, fotogénico, primogénito, vigésimo, higiénico, virginal, magia, regio, vigente, indígena, pedagogía, neuralgia**...)
Exceptions: **aguajinoso**, words ending in **-plejía** or **-plejia** (e.g., **apoplejía**), and **ejión**
	words ending in
	    -aje
	    -eje
	    -jería
	(e.g., **coraje, garaje, hereje, conserjería**...)

	the preterite and imperfect subjunctive of
	    traer
	    decir
	and verbs ending in
	    -ducir
	(e.g., **traje, dijera, condujéramos**...)

verbs ending in
    -igerar
    -ger
    -gir
and their forms with **i** and **e** following the /j/ sound, except forms with **a** and **o**, in which the **g** changes to **j** to retain the pronunciation /j/.
(e.g., **aligerar, proteger, fingir, protegemos, protegíamos**, but: **protejo, finjamos**...)
Exceptions: **tejer, crujir,** and their derivatives
	verb forms of infinitives ending in
	    -jar
	    -jer
	    -jir
	    -jear
	(e.g., **trabajar** → **trabaje, trabajemos**
	        tejer → **tejimos**
	        crujir → **crujía**
	        cojear → **cojeo**...)

c. Verb spelling changes to maintain the /j/ or /g/ sound of the stem

(1) Verbs ending in -ger /jer/ or -gir /jir/: g → j

In the conjugations of certain verbs ending in **-ger** and **-gir,** to retain the pronunciation /j/ in the verb stem, **g** changes to **j** before verb endings **a** and **o**:

Escoger[20]: [eskojér]

escoge → escojo (1st pers. pres. ind.)
escoja, -s, -mos, -n (pres. subj.)

(If the **g** were maintained in the spelling of these forms, they would be mispronounced ⊠[21][eskógo], ⊠[eskóga], etc.)

Examples:

Escoge el color que prefieras.	*Choose the color you prefer.*
Siempre escojo lo mejor.	*I always choose the best.*

Dirigir[22]: [dirijír]

dirigir → dirijo (1st pers. pres. ind.)
dirija, -s, -mos, -n (pres. subj.)

(If the **g** were maintained in the spelling of these forms, they would be mispronounced ⊠[dirígo], ⊠[diríga], etc.)

Examples:

No pudo dirigir el globo.	*He couldn't guide the balloon.*
Dudo que se dirija hacia acá.	*I doubt she'll come this way.*

(2) Verbs ending in -guir /gir/, -gar /gar/, -guar /guar/:

gu → g; gu → gü

In the conjugations of verbs ending in **-guir /gir/,** to avoid a pronounced **u,** the **u** is dropped before **a** or **o**:

Distinguir[23]: [distingír]

distinguir → distingo (1st pers. pres. ind.)
distinga, -s, -mos, -n (pres. subj.)

---

[20] See verb table #13, Appendix A, page 7 for similar verbs.

[21] We use the symbol ⊠ before a word or sentence or pronunciation to indicate a usage that is incorrect.

[22] See verb table #22, Appendix A, page 10 for similar verbs.

[23] See verb table #24, Appendix A, page 10 for similar verbs; see also verb table #56, Appendix A, page 21 for similar changes in the verb **seguir** et al.

(If the **g** were maintained in the spelling of these forms, they would be mispronounced ⊠[distínguo], ⊠[distíngua], etc.)

Examples:

¿Los bebés distin**gue**n colores?	*Do babies distinguish colors?*
No distin**go** nada.	*I can't distinguish a thing.*

Conversely, verbs ending in **-gar,** to retain the pronunciation /g/ in the verb stem, add silent **u** after the **g** before the verb ending **e:**

Jugar[24]: [jugár]

jug**a**r → jue**gue**, -s, -n (pres. subj.)

(If the **g** were maintained without a silent **u** in the spelling of this form, it would be mispronounced ⊠[juéje], etc.)

Examples:

Ayer ju**ga**mos al ajedrez.	*Yesterday we played chess.*
Ju**gue**mos a las damas.	*Let's play checkers.*

In the conjugations of verbs ending in **-guar,** to retain the pronunciation of the **u** in the verb stem, **gu** changes to **gü** before the verb ending **e:**

Averiguar[25]: [aberiguár]

averi**gu**ar → averi**güe**, -s, -mos, -n (pres. subj.)

(If **u** were used instead of **ü** in the spelling of this form, it would be silent, and the verb would be mispronounced ⊠[aveíge], etc.)

Examples:

El espía averi**guó** los secretos.	*The spy found out the secrets.*
Averi**güe**n la verdad.	*Find out the truth.*

Ejercicios 9.7–9.10, páginas 528–529

---

[24] See verb table #34, Appendix A, page 14; see also verb table #39, Appendix A, page 15, and #53, Appendix A, page 20, for the same change in the verbs **negar, rogar,** and similar verbs.

[25] See verb table #6, Appendix A, page 4 for similar verbs.

4 H

a. Pronunciation of the letter h

The **h** is never pronounced in Spanish. Consider the pronunciations of the following words:

ahí	[aí]	*(there)*	habla	[ábla]	*(speak)*
ahijado	[aijádo]	*(godson)*	hispano	[ispáno]	*(Hispanic)*
ahora	[aóra]	*(now)*	hospital	[ospitál]	*(hospital)*
ahorrar	[aorrár]	*(save)*	huevo	[uébo]	*(egg)*
alcohol	[alkól]	*(alcohol)*	prohibir	[proibír]	*(forbid)*

b. Spelling with the letter h

As a rule, aside from foreign borrowings, Spanish has no combination of the letter **h** with other consonants, other than the **ch**. In other words, there are no Spanish words (other than foreign borrowings) spelled with **gh, ph, th,** or **sh**. (For more on spelling in Spanish of cognate words with English **ch, th,** and **ph,** see below, section 8, pages 342–343).

The following table lists the most common uses of **h** in spelling:

H
SPELLED WITH H
all forms of the conjugations of   **haber   habitar   hablar   hacer   hallar** (e.g., **hay, hace, hablamos…**)
composites of words with **h,** for example: **humano → inhumano   hueso → deshuesar**
words starting with the sounds   **/ia/   /ie/   /ue/   /ui/** (e.g., **hiato   hiena   huevo   huir…**)

words starting with
    hect- *(hundred)*   **hidro-, hidra-** *(water)*
    helio- *(sun)*   **hiper-** *(over, excessive)*
    hema-, hemo- *(blood)*   **hipo-** *(under, insufficient)*
    hemi- *(half)*   **holo-** *(all)*
    hepta- *(seven)*   **homeo-** *(like)*
    hetero- *(other)*   **homo-** *(same)*
(e.g., **hectárea, hidrógeno, hipócrita…**)

in general, words starting with   **herm-   hern-   histo-   hog-   holg-   horm-   hosp-   hum-** (e.g., **hermandad, hernia, historia, hospital, hormiguero, holganza, hogareño, humedad…**)
some interjections: **bah, eh**

c. Homophones

The following are homophones; when you hear them, they can only be distinguished by their context:

a ver	let's see	≠	haber	to have	[abér]
halla	finds	≠	haya	have	[áya]
hecho	done	≠	echo	I throw	[écho]
hala	he pulls	≠	ala	wing	[ála]
hola	hello	≠	ola	wave	[óla]
hay	there is	≠	ay	ouch	[ái]
ha habido	there has been	≠	habido	been	[abído]
he estado	I have been	≠	estado	been	[estádo]
huno	Hun	≠	uno	one	[úno]

The following words sound identical in regions of **seseo**:

has	you have	≠	haz	do	[as]
hace	he does	≠	ase	he seizes	[áse]

A VER, HABER [abér]

A ver is the combination of the preposition **a** and the verb **ver**.

Vamos **a ver** una película.	*We're going to see a movie.*
A ver si podemos resolver esto.	*Let's see if we can resolve this.*
—Mira lo que encontré.	*"Look at what I found."*
—¿**A ver**?	*"Let's see?"*

Haber is the infinitive of the verb, which, as any infinitive, can be used as a noun equivalent. It is frequently found after a modal auxiliary (**acabar de, deber, ir a, poder, querer, tener que, haber de**):

El **haber** perdido lo tiene deprimido.	*He's depressed from having lost.*
Parece **haber** un secreto en esa familia.	*There seems to be a secret in that family.*
Tiene que **haber** terminado.	*He has to have finished.*
Ha de **haber** oído.	*She must have heard.*
Haberlo dicho antes.	*If only you had said it beforehand.*
Eso le pasó por **haber** robado.	*That happened to him for having stolen.*

Compare the following two sentences, which sound identical:

Va a haber una película hoy.	*There is going to be a movie today.*
Va a ver una película hoy.	*He is going to see a movie today.*

HALLA, HAYA [áya][26]

Halla is a conjugated form of the verb **hallar** (synonym of **encontrar**). It can be the third person singular present indicative or the affirmative imperative of **tú**:

Jorge no **halla** su iPad.	*Jorge can't find his iPad.*
Halla el tesoro.	*Find the treasure.*

Haya is a form of the verb **haber**. It's the present subjunctive, third person singular:

Ojalá que no **haya** problemas.	*I hope there aren't any problems.*
Dudo que **haya** comido.	*I doubt that he has eaten.*

HAS, HAZ (with **seseo**) [as]

Has is the verb **haber** in the present indicative for the second person singular (**tú**)[27]. It is used as an auxiliary of any verb in the present perfect, or as a modal auxiliary (with **de**):

¿**Has** viajado a España?	*Have you traveled to Spain?*
Has de saber que eso no se permite.	*You must know that that is not allowed.*

---

[26] Note that these two words are homonyms only in areas of **yeísmo** (which constitute the majority of the Spanish-speaking world). For more on **yeísmo**, see page 376 at the end of this chapter.

[27] See the full conjugation of the present indicative of **haber** in Chapter 5, page 153 and its full conjugation in verb table #31, Appendix A, p. 13.

Haz is the verb **hacer** in the affirmative imperative for the second person singular (**tú**). It is one of eight exceptions to the regular form of the imperative[28].

    Haz tu tarea.   *Do your homework.*

When in doubt as to the correct spelling, it helps to imagine these words in the negative. For **has** there would be no change, but for **haz**, the change is significant:

AFFIRMATIVE	NEGATIVE
Has visto el resultado.	**No has** visto el resultado.
Haz lo que te digo.	**No hagas** lo que te digo.

ECHO, HECHO [écho]

Echo is the verb **echar** in the present indicative, first person singular (**yo**). **Echar** is a regular -ar verb (**echo, echas, echa, echamos, echáis, echan**). Depending on the context in which it is used, it can be synonymous with **tirar** *(throw)*, **poner** *(put)*, or **despedir** *(fire)*. It is also used in idiomatic phrases like **echar de menos, echarle la culpa a alguien,** and as a modal auxiliary (**echar a** + *inf.*).

¿Te **echo** la pelota?	*Shall I throw you the ball?*
Yo no le **echo** chile a la salsa.	*I don't put chile in the sauce.*
Hoy **echo** a ese empleado.	*Today I am firing that employee.*
Echo de menos a mis padres.	*I miss my parents.*
Si salgo, me **echo** a estornudar.	*If I go outside, I start sneezing.*

Hecho is the verb **hacer** in the past participle, or the noun **un hecho** *(a fact)*.

¿Has **hecho** la tarea?	*Have you done your homework?*
El **hecho** es que no tengo tiempo.	*The fact is that I don't have time.*

There are other forms of these verbs that sound the same: **echa/hecha** and **echas/hechas**. Consider the following sentences:

La cama está **hecha**.	*The bed is made.*
Echa eso a la basura.	*Throw that in the garbage.*
Las galletas están **hechas**.	*The cookies are done.*
Siempre me **echas** la culpa a mí.	*You always blame me.*

> Ejercicios 9.11–9.13, páginas 529–530

---

[28] See the forms of the affirmative imperative of **tú** in Chapter 5, pages 167–169, and its full conjugation in verb table #32, Appendix A, page 13.

5 X

a. The letter x pronounced /s/

The letter **x** is most commonly pronounced /s/ in two contexts:

- when it starts the word:

xenofobia	[**s**enofóbia]	*(xenofobia)*
xerografía	[**s**erografía]	*(xerography)*
xileno	[**s**iléno]	*(xylene)*
xilófono	[**s**ilófono]	*(xylophone)*

- when it is followed by a consonant that does not sound like /s/:

e**x**clamar	[e**s**klamár]	*(exclaim)*
e**x**plicar	[e**s**plikár]	*(explain)*
e**x**perto	[e**s**pérto]	*(expert)*
e**x**plotar	[e**s**plotár]	*(explode)*
e**x**terior	[e**s**teriór]	*(exterior)*

b. The letter x pronounced /ks/

The letter **x** is most commonly pronounced /ks/ in two contexts:

- when it is between vowels:

a**x**ial	[a**ks**iál]	*(axial)*
e**x**amen	[e**ks**ámen]	*(exam)*
pró**x**imo	[pró**ks**imo]	*(next)*

  —this category includes an **h** following the **x**, since the **h** is not pronounced:

e**x**halar	[e**ks**alár]	*(exhale)*
e**x**haustivo	[e**ks**austíbo]	*(exhaustive)*
e**x**hibir	[e**ks**ibír]	*(exhibit)*
e**x**hortar	[e**ks**ortár]	*(exhort)*
e**x**humar	[e**ks**umár]	*(exhume)*

- in final position in a word:

tórax	[tóra**ks**]	*(thorax)*
clímax	[klíma**ks**]	*(climax)*
cóccix	[kóksi**ks**]	*(coccyx)*
fénix	[féni**ks**]	*(phoenix)*
ónix	[óni**ks**]	*(onyx)*

- when it is followed by **ce** or **ci**:

excelente	[e**ks**elénte, e**ks**zelénte]	*(excellent)*
excepción	[e**ks**epsión, e**ks**zepzión]	*(exception)*
exceso	[e**ks**éso, e**ks**zéso]	*(excess)*
excitar	[e**ks**itár, e**ks**zitár]	*(excite)*

c. The letter x pronounced /j/

In Mexican words spelled with **x**, frequently derived from Mayan or Náhuatl, the **x** is most often pronounced /j/:

México	[méjiko]	*(Mexico)*
mexicano	[mejikáno]	*(Mexican)*
Xavier	[jabiér]	*(Xavier)*
Oaxaca	[oajáka]	*(Oaxaca)*
Texas	[téjas]	*(Texas)*

Note that these words may have been spelled in the past in certain contexts with **j** rather than **x** (e.g., **Méjico, mejicano**): Current orthography rules recommend that they be spelled with **x**.

There are other pronunciations of the letter **x** in words of Mexican origin:

- pronounced /s/: **Xochimilco** [sochimilko] *(lake near Mexico City)*, **xóchil** [sóchitl] *(flower)*…

- pronounced /sh/: **xocoyote** [shokoyote] *(youngest son)*, **xola** [shola] *(head or turkey hen)*…

d. Spelling with the letter x

X
SPELLED WITH X
words beginning with the following prefixes: 　　　**xeno-** (foreign)　　**xero-** (dry)　　**xilo-** (wood) (e.g., **xenofobia, xerografía, xilófono…**)
words beginning with the syllable **ex-** followed by **-pr-** (e.g., **expresar, expresivo, expresión, exprimir…**)
words beginning with the prefixes **ex-** (out, beyond, without) and **extra-** (beyond, outside) (e.g., **excavar, excéntrico, exclamar, exculpar, extracurricular, extrajudicial, extramuros, extraterrestre…**)
many words beginning with the syllable **ex-** followed by **-pl-** (e.g., **explicar, explorar, explotar…**) **Exceptions: esplendor, espléndido, espliego,** and derivatives
many words of Mexican (usually Mayan or Náhuatl) origin: (e.g., **Ixtapa, ixtle, México, Nuevo México, mexicano, mexicanismo, taxcal, Texas, texano, texcoqueño, Xochimilco, xóchil…**)

Ejercicio 9.14, página 530

6　Ll, Y, Í

a. The sound /y/

In most of the Spanish-speaking world, when you hear the sound /y/, only the context can let you know whether a word is spelled with **ll**[29], **y,** or some combination of vowels with **í. Examples:**

callado	[kayádo]	(*quiet*)
cayado	[kayádo]	(*crozier* or *crook*)
cayo	[káyo]	(*key* – as in *Florida Keys*)
callo	[káyo]	(*callus*, or first person singular of present indicative **callar**)
ardilla	[ardíya]	(*squirrel*)
ardía	[ardía]	(*burned*)

---

[29] For more on **yeísmo,** see page 376 at the end of this chapter.

Beware of mispronouncing words ending in **-ia** as if they ended in **-ía**. This happens with words like **gracias** [grásias, grázias] (misspelled and mispronounced ⌧gracías; the correct stress is on gra) and **familia** [família] (misspelled and mispronounced ⌧familía; the correct stress is on mi). This type of error comes from a false association[30] with verbs ending in **-ía**.

b. Spellings for the sound /y/

Verbs with **ll** in the infinitive are the only ones that will have **ll** in their conjugations.
Examples:

    callar *(to quiet)*   callo, callas, calla

    estallar *(to burst)*   estallaba, estallaran

The /y/ sound in verbs without **ll** in the infinitive is spelled with **y**. This includes the following:

- verbs ending in **-aer, -eer, -oer:**

  caer *(to fall)*   cayó, cayeron

  leer *(to read)*   leyeron, leyera

- verbs ending in **-uir** (e.g., **atribuir, contribuir, distribuir**):

  atribuir *(attribute)*   atribuyo, atribuyeron, atribuya

- the final **y** in the present tense of **dar, estar, haber, ir,** and **ser:**

  doy, estoy, hay, voy, soy

- the present subjunctive of **ir** and **haber:**

  vaya, vayas, vayamos… (pres. subj. of **ir**)

  haya, hayas, hayamos… (pres. subj. of **haber**)

c. Lists of common words ending in -ia, -illa, and -ía

Given the high number of words ending in **-ia, -illa,** and **-ía,** and the possible confusion in spelling for these, we provide here a list of the most commonly used words with each ending.

---

[30] A similar spelling problem occurs with some endings of the preterite. Learners often apply the accentuation of the endings of regular verbs to those of irregular verbs. This simplification of the rule leads to frequent errors, such as ⌧dijó for **dijo**, ⌧hizó for **hizo**, etc. To avoid such errors, review the endings of the preterite of irregular verbs (see Chapter 5.A.2.b., pages 155–156).

Common words ending in **-ia:**

-ia		
SPANISH	PRONUNCIATION	ENGLISH
academia	[akadémia]	academia
ciencia	[siénsia, ziénzia]	science
correspondencia	[korrespondénsia, korrespondénzia]	correspondence
democracia	[demokrásia, demokrázia]	democracy
distancia	[distánsia, distánzia]	distance
envidia	[embídia]	envy
familia	[família]	family
farmacia	[farmásia, farmázia]	pharmacy
gloria	[glória]	glory
gracia(s)	[grásia(s), grázia(s)]	grace, thanks
historia	[istória]	history
importancia	[importánsia, importánzia]	importance
injusticia	[injustísia, injustízia]	injustice
inteligencia	[inteligénsia, inteligénzia]	intelligence
lluvia	[yúbia]	rain
materia	[matéria]	matter
memoria	[memória]	memory
secretaria	[secretária]	secretary

Common words ending in **-ía**[31]:

-ía		
SPANISH	PRONUNCIATION	ENGLISH
alegría	[alegría]	*joy*
anatomía	[anatomía]	*anatomy*
armonía	[armonía]	*harmony*
bahía	[baía]	*bay*
compañía	[kompañía]	*company*
cortesía	[kortesía]	*courtesy*
día	[día]	*day*
economía	[ekonomía]	*economy*
energía	[enerjía]	*energy*
espía	[espía]	*spy*
fotografía	[fotografía]	*photography*
geografía	[jeografía]	*geography*
librería	[librería]	*bookstore*
poesía	[poesía]	*poetry*
policía	[polisía, polizía]	*police*
teoría	[teoría]	*theory*
todavía	[todabía]	*still*

---

[31] Note that we do not include here verb forms ending in **-ía**.

Common words ending in **-illa**[32]:

-illa		
SPANISH	PRONUNCIATION	ENGLISH
ardilla	[ardíya]	squirrel
cajetilla	[kajetíya]	cigarette pack
capilla	[kapíya]	chapel
colilla	[kolíya]	cigarette butt
comilla	[komíya]	quotation mark
costilla	[kostíya]	rib
mantequilla	[mantekíya]	butter
maravilla	[marabíya]	marvel
mejilla	[mejíya]	cheek
milla	[míya]	mile
orilla	[oríya]	edge
pandilla	[pandíya]	gang
parrilla	[parríya]	grill
pesadilla	[pesadíya]	nightmare
rodilla	[rodíya]	knee
semilla	[semíya]	seed
silla	[síya]	chair
tortilla	[tortíya]	tortilla, omelette
vainilla	[bainíya]	vanilla

Ejercicios 9.15–9.16, página 530

---

[32] Note that we do not include in this list diminutives ending in **-illa** except those that have become commonly used terms, no longer considered diminutives. Note also that it is only in areas of **yeísmo** (most of the Spanish-speaking world) that **-illa** is pronounced /-íya/ rather than /-ílla/. For more on **yeísmo**, see page 376 at the end of this chapter.

7 R, Rr

The letter **r** in Spanish can be pronounced like the sound of *-tt-* in the word *matter*, or like a trilled **r**, depending on where the **r** is in the word.

a. The sound /r/

The first sound (not trilled) is that in words with an intervocalic **r** (between vowels), or when the **r** follows **b, c, d, f, g, k, p,** or **t**. It is also the sound for words ending in **r**. This sound corresponds to a single **r** in spelling.

Examples of the non-trilled /r/ sound:

caro	[káro]	*(expensive)*
brillo	[bríyo]	*(shine)*
lucro	[lúkro]	*(gain)*
ladrar	[ladrár]	*(bark)*
fruta	[frúta]	*(fruit)*
grado	[grádo]	*(degree)*
Kremlin	[krémlin]	*(Kremlin)*
pronto	[prónto]	*(soon)*
atributo	[atribúto]	*(attribute)*
calor	[kalór]	*(heat)*

b. The sound /rr/

The letter **r** in Spanish is pronounced like a trilled **r** /rr/ when it starts a word, or when it follows **n, l,** or **s**. In these contexts, the trilled **r** /rr/ sound corresponds to a single **r** in spelling.

Examples:

rabia	[rrábia]	*(rage)*
honrado	[onrrádo]	*(honest)*
alrededor	[alrrededór]	*(around)*
Israel	[isrraél]	*(Israel)*

The double **rr** is always pronounced trilled. It is only found in an intervocalic position (between vowels).

Examples:

a**rr**eglar	[arreglár]	*(fix)*
e**rr**or	[errór]	*(error)*
i**rr**eal	[irreál]	*(unreal)*
ho**rr**ible	[orríble]	*(horrible)*
bu**rr**o	[búrro]	*(donkey)*

c. Spelling with r and rr

The following table lists the most common uses of **r** and **rr** in spelling.

R / RR	
SPELLED WITH R AND PRONOUNCED /R/	**SPELLED WITH RR**
words with the sound /r/ between vowels (e.g., **cara, duro, farol, garantía, loro…**) words with the sound /r/ after **b, c, d, f, g, k, p, t** (e.g., **brote, incremento, Andrés, fruta, grande, kriptón, prado, trama…**)	words with a trilled **r** /rr/ between vowels (e.g., **perro, carro, ferrocarril…**)
words ending in **r** (e.g., **caminar, amor…**)	
SPELLED WITH R AND PRONOUNCED /RR/	
words beginning with **r** (e.g., **raya, rezo, rima…**)	
words with **r** after **n, l,** or **s** (e.g., **honra, Israel, enriquece, alrededor…**)	

d. Soft d, r

Sometimes in their efforts to learn to pronounce the Spanish /r/ sound, students of Spanish confuse it with a soft **d** sound.

Indeed, the letter **d** has two basic sounds in Spanish:

- at the beginning of a word, and following **n** or **l**, the **d** in Spanish sounds similar to the English **d** in *den* (e.g., **d**amos, an**d**o, al**d**ea…).

- in other contexts within a word, and at the end of a word, the letter **d** in Spanish is softer; it sounds something like *-th-* in *father* (e.g., mira**d**a, Ma**d**ri**d**…).

Confusion of sounds is not a grave problem, unless it interferes with understanding. Below are sets of words that are often pronounced the same by learners of the language. These words are <u>not</u> homophones and should maintain their proper distinct pronunciations to avoid misunderstanding:

ca**r**a *(face)*	ca**d**a *(each)*
ce**r**o *(zero)*	ce**d**o *(I concede)*
du**r**a *(hard)*	du**d**a *(doubt)*
du**r**o *(hard)*	du**d**o *(I doubt)*
pe**r**o *(but)*	pe**d**o *(fart)*
vi**r**a *(turn)*	vi**d**a *(life)*

> Ejercicio 9.17, página 531

8   Ch, Ph, Th → **C/Qu, F, T**

Words of Greek origin spelled in English with **ch** (pronounced in English /k/), **ph**, and **th**, are spelled in Spanish, respectively, with **c** /k/ or **qu, f,** and **t**:

a. Ch → **C/Qu**

The English cognates of the following words are all spelled with **ch**:

ar**c**aico(a)	**c**arácter	**C**risto	matriar**c**a
ar**c**ángel	**c**arisma	**c**ristiano(a)	patriar**c**a

When in English **ch** (pronounced /k/) is followed by **e** or **i**, in Spanish **qu** is used rather than **c** to retain the /k/ sound. Note the following cognates:

anar**qu**ía	ar**qu**itecto	**qu**iropráctico	oligar**qu**ía
ar**qu**eología	**qu**iromancia	monar**qu**ía	

b. Ph → **F**

Words of Greek origin that in English are spelled with **ph**, in Spanish are spelled with **f**. Note the following cognates:

al**f**abeto	a**f**orismo	apóstro**f**e	as**f**ixiar
a**f**asia	a**f**rodisíaco	as**f**alto	ele**f**ante
peri**f**eria	**f**antasma	**f**ísico	**f**armacia
foto	**f**enómeno	**F**iladelfia	**f**onética

c. *Th* → **T**

Words of Greek origin that in English are spelled with **th**, in Spanish are spelled with **t**. Note the following cognates:

apoteosis	Atenas	teatro	tema
termómetro	termo	termostato	tesauro
Teseo	tesis	tórax	ortografía

9 Double Consonants

In English you will find many words spelled with double consonants that in Spanish almost always correspond to words with single consonants. Note the following cognates:

a**b**reviar	o**c**asión	o**c**ulto	ta**b**aco
a**d**icional	di**f**erencia	a**g**ravar	sí**l**aba
gramática	a**n**ual	o**p**ortunidad	a**s**ociar

In Spanish there are only four consonants used in duplicate. Two are each pronounced with a single sound:

| **rr** | /rr/ | carro [kárro] | *(car)* |
| **ll** | /y/ | calle [káye] | *(street)* |

and the other two are each pronounced with more than one sound:

| **cc** | /k/ + /s/ or /k/ + /z/ | acceso [akséso, akzéso] |
| **nn** | /n/ + /n/ | innovación [innobasión, innobazión] |

Note that *imm-* in English is **inm-** in Spanish:

inmortalidad *(immortality)*

inmigrante *(immigrant)*

Ejercicio 9.18, página 531

C VOWELS AND ACCENTS

Vowels **(las vocales)** are, with few exceptions, pronounced similarly in all Spanish-speaking regions. Worth noting is that in Spanish each vowel is a single sound, whereas in English, a single vowel is more often than not pronounced with more than one sound (e.g., in Spanish, the **a** in **casa** is pronounced /a/; in English, the **a** in *case* is pronounced /ei/; in Spanish, the **i** in **tino** is pronounced /i/; in English, the **i** in *tide* is pronounced /ai/). Even in combination, Spanish vowels tend to retain their individual sounds[33]: the letters **e** and **a** in **vea** are pronounced /ea/, whereas in English, **e** and **a** merge to form a single sound in words like *beat* and *heat*.

In writing, Spanish vowels can have written accent marks. The decision of where to use an accent mark will require knowledge of syllabification (how the word is broken down into syllables), and of where the stress falls in the word.

1 Syllabification

The division of a word into syllables **(sílabas)**, or single uninterrupted sound units, aids in the application of accent rules. In this section we use periods (.) to mark syllable breaks within words.

a. Consonants: Their role in syllables

Single intervocalic consonants: one consonant between two vowels joins the following vowel to form a syllable. (Note that in Spanish **ch, ll,** and **rr** each represent one consonant.)

ta.za	**me.**sa	**mi.**sa	**ma.ce.**ta	**me.ch**a
ta.lla	**ba.rr**o	**ca.la.ba.**za	**fe.rro.ca.rri.le.**ro	

> Ejercicio 9.19, página 531

Two intervocalic consonants: these are separated (except **ch, ll,** and **rr**).

lám.pa.ra	**pan.ta.ll**a	**an.gus.**tia	**com.pu.ta.do.**ra
per.so.na	**en.ca.**rar	**dic.cio.na.**rio	

---

[33] This is true except in cases of linking between words: see below, Section D, pages 354–356.

Do not separate the consonant **b, c, f, g,** or **p** from a following **l** or **r**, or the combinations **dr** and **tr**.

    ta.**bl**a   fe.**br**e.ro   te.**cl**a   re.**cr**e.o   a.**fl**o.jar
    a.**fr**en.ta   re.**gl**a   a.**gr**io   re.**pl**e.to   de.**pr**i.mir
    po.**dr**i.do   re.**tr**a.to

> Ejercicio 9.20, página 531

Three or more intervocalic consonants: with three or more consonants between vowels, only the last consonant joins the next vowel (unless it is **l** or **r**).

    co**ns**.ta   i**ns**.pi.ra   i**ns**.tan.te   in.**gl**és   com.**pr**ar

> Ejercicio 9.21, página 532

b. Multiple vowels

When combined, vowels can form a single syllable, or more than one, depending on which vowels are combined, and which vowel is stressed. In combination, **a, e,** and **o** are categorized as strong vowels, whereas **i** and **u** are weak vowels.

MULTIPLE VOWELS		
STRONG VOWELS	WEAK VOWELS	VOWEL COMBINATIONS
a	i	**Hiato:** two vowels forming two syllables
e	u	**Diptongo:** two vowels forming one syllable
o		**Triptongo:** three vowels forming one syllable

Hiato *(Hiatus):* each strong vowel represents one syllable; when combined with another strong vowel, they are separated.

    ca.e.mos   le.en   em.ple.o   em.ple.a.do

If a weak vowel before or after a strong vowel is stressed, there is a separation; a stressed weak vowel in combination with a strong vowel will always have an accent mark.

ca.**í**.da	re.**í**.mos	ma.**ú**.lla	gra.**dú**.en	
tí.os	sa.**lí**.an	**rí**.en	**grú**.a	re.**ú**.no

Ejercicio 9.22, página 532

Diptongo *(Diphthong):* a combination into one syllable of two weak vowels or one strong and one weak represents a diphthong and is not separated.

I.ta.**lia**	**bai**.le	**vie**.nen	**rei**.no
re.me.**dio**	**vio**.lín	**cuan**.do	**au**.la
rue.da	**deu**.da	**rui**.do	es.ta.**dou**.ni.den.se
cuo.ta	**ciu**.dad		

Stressed strong vowel: the same is true even when there is an accent on the strong vowel of the diphthong.

diá.fa.no	tam.**bién**	na.**ció**	**cuó**.rum[34]
fué.ra.mos	**guár**.da.lo	bai.**láis**	die.ci.**séis**
ói.ga.me	**cáu**.sa.me	**Éu**.fra.tes	

Ejercicio 9.23, página 532

Triptongo *(Triphthong):* a triphthong is one syllable formed by three vowels.

a.ve.ri.**guáis**   lim.**piéis**

More than one syllable occurs if there is more than one strong vowel or a stressed weak vowel in the combination.

se.**áis**   ca.**í**.an   re.**í**.a.mos

Ejercicio 9.24, página 532

---

[34] Words imported from other languages follow the same accentuation rules as other Spanish words. Note that this word used to be written with a **q** in Spanish. It is now recommended for foreign words with the sound /k/ to be spelled as they would normally in Spanish (e.g., /ku/ = **cu**). It is also possible to spell the foreign word as it is in its original language, in which case it needs to be in italics and with no accent: *quorum*.

The **h** in Spanish is not pronounced; if it is enclosed between two vowels, these two vowels will interact as if they were next to each other.

No accent required:

    a.ho.rrar   re.**ha**.cer   re.**ho**.gar   ahi.**ja**.do
    re**hi**.lar   re**hun**.dir

Accent required:

    pro.**hí**.bo   **bú**.ho

> Ejercicio 9.25, página 532;
> Ejercicio de repaso 9.26, página 533

2 Stress

Every word with more than one syllable in Spanish has one syllable with more stress than the rest. Depending on the type of word it is, or where the stress falls, the word may or may not require a written accent.

a. Categorization of words by stress

In Spanish, words with more than one syllable are categorized as follows:

| WORD CATEGORIZATION BY STRESS |||
TYPE	STRESSED SYLLABLE	EXAMPLES
Aguda	Last (última)	ca.mi.**né**; ca.mi.**nar**
Llana	Next-to-last (penúltima)	**lá**.piz; ca.**mi**.no
Esdrújula	Third-to-last (antepenúltima)	**quí**.mi.ca
Sobresdrújula	Fourth-to-last (anteantepenúltima)	**cóm**.pre.me.lo

b. Rules for written accents

Agudas: this type of word needs a written accent only when the word ends in a vowel, **n,** or **s.**

Accent required:

    am**ó**   viv**í**   viv**ís**   fran**és**   caim**án**

No accent required:

    a**mar**   vi**vir**   espa**ñol**   ciu**dad**   Je**rez**

Llanas: this type of word needs a written accent only when the word ends in a consonant other than **n** or **s.**

Accent required:

    car**á**cter   im**bé**cil   **lá**piz   **tú**nel   ver**sá**til

No accent required:

    hablo   a**cen**to   nece**si**ta   conso**nan**te   **bai**las
    fran**ce**ses   **mar**gen   **lu**nes   e**xa**men   estu**dia**ron

Esdrújulas and **sobresdrújulas:** these types of words always require accent marks.

Esdrújulas:

    car**á**tula   es**tú**pido   lu**cié**rnaga

Sobresdrújulas:

    ven**dá**moselo   **dé**moselas   pon**gá**monoslas

> Ejercicios 9.27–9.30, página 533

c. Special cases

(1) Adverbs ending in -mente

Adverbs formed from adjectives + **mente** require accents only when their original adjectives had them:

rápido	is the adjective form of the adverb	rápidamente
fácil	is the adjective form of the adverb	fácilmente
lento	is the adjective form of the adverb	lentamente

> Ejercicio 9.31, página 534

(2) Monosyllables

Monosyllables (words consisting of only one syllable) must be left *without* written accent marks. There is only one part of the word that can be stressed: thus no accent is needed:

    a   al   ti   la   le   lo   di   da   me   fui   fue   dio   Dios

Some monosyllables are homonyms (words with the same spelling or pronunciation but with different meanings). One of each pair will have an accent mark to distinguish it from the other:

\multicolumn{8}{c}{MONOSYLLABLES WITH HOMONYMS}
el	the	mas	but	se	[pron.]	te	you, yourself
él	he	más	more	sé	I know	té	tea
de	of, from	mi	my	tu	your	si	if
dé[35]	give	mí	me	tú	you	sí	yes, itself, oneself

Me preguntó **el** nombre **de mi** profesora.	*She asked me the name of my professor.*
—¿A ti[36] **te** lo dijo?	*"Did she tell you?"*
—**Sí**, a **mí** me lo dijo.	*"Yes, she told me."*
¿**Tú** también necesitas que **te dé** la llave?	*Do you also need me to give you the key?*
El problema en **sí** no es tan grave.	*The problem in itself isn't so serious.*

---

[35] When the verb **dar** is conjugated in the imperative and has a pronoun attached, it loses the accent: **dele**. It is no longer a homonym of the preposition in this situation. Of course, it regains the accent when a second pronoun is added, due to the fact that the stress on the verb must be maintained and the new word is an **esdrújula: démelo**.

[36] Beware of the temptation to place an accent over **ti** just because **mí** has one; **ti** is not a homonym, as is **mí**.

Mas vs. más

With an accent, **más** means *more*. Without an accent, **mas** is used in literary contexts, and means *but*.

No **sé si él** quiere **más té**.	*I don't know if he wants more tea.*
Necesito **más** azúcar.	*I need more sugar.*
Lejos de ti, vivir no quiero, **mas** en aquel sombrío invierno, empecé el viaje sin rumbo, herida, y ahora regreso, tal cual ave perdida.	*Far from you, I do not wish to live, but in that somber winter, I began the journey with no end, injured, and I now return, just like a lost bird.*

Ejercicio 9.32, página 534

(3) Non-monosyllabic homonyms

Although they are not monosyllables, the following words are also homonyms: an accent mark is used in certain cases to distinguish one usage from another.

(a) Aun[37] vs. aún

The word **aún** requires an accent when it means *still* (**todavía**); however, when it means *even*, it has no accent mark (**aun**).

Aun de día hace frío.	*Even during the day it is cold.*
Aún no hemos llegado.	*We still have not arrived.*

(b) Solo

The word **solo** may be an adjective (*alone*) or an adverb (*only*). An accent is never required, but it may be used on the adverb to distinguish it from the adjective in cases of possible confusion as to the meaning of the sentence.

Vivo **solo**.	*I live alone.*
Mi hermana **solo** come fruta.	*My sister only eats fruit.*
Mi tío viaja **solo** en tren.	*My uncle travels alone by train.*
Mi tío viaja **solo/sólo** en tren.	*My uncle travels only by train.*

---

[37] Although **aun** is a monosyllable, we have placed it outside of the category because when it takes an accent, **aún**, it is not a monosyllable.

In this last sentence, the accent on **solo** may be used to avoid confusion with "alone" but it is not required. It would be preferable to clarify the context by changing the word order:

    Mi tío **solo** viaja en tren.   *My uncle only travels by train.*

(c) Demonstrative pronouns

The words **ese, esa, esos, esas; este, esta, estos, estas; aquel, aquella, aquellos,** and **aquellas** may be adjectives or pronouns[38]. An accent is never required, but it may be used on the pronouns in cases of possible confusion in the meaning of the sentence:

Lograremos las dos metas	*We'll achieve both goals*
en orden: **esta/ésta** mañana,	*in order: this one tomorrow,*
y **esa** el lunes.	*and that one on Monday.*

In the above sentence, there are two demonstrative pronouns (**esta** and **esa**), but there is only one whose meaning could be muddled by the lack of accent, and that is **esta** because of its combination with **mañana**. The reason for this is that **mañana** can be a noun *(morning)* or an adverb *(tomorrow)*. If **esta** were an adjective, **esta mañana** would mean *this morning*. For this reason, an accent on **ésta** would be allowed.

The neutral forms of the pronouns, **eso, esto,** and **aquello,** have no adjective equivalents and thus do not require accents.

    Mira **eso.**   *Look at that.*

(d) Exclamative and interrogative adjectives, pronouns, and adverbs

Exclamative and interrogative adjectives, pronouns, and adverbs take accents. In exclamations and interrogations, there is not always an interrogative or exclamative pronoun or adverb. You might, for example, ask: **¿Me dijiste la verdad?** or exclaim: **¡Bien dicho!** None of these words has an accent. You might also exclaim: **¡Que te vaya bien!** Here the **que** is a conjunction, not a pronoun or adjective, and has no accent.

Some examples of exclamative pronouns and adverbs follow:

¡**Qué** día!	*What a day!*
¡**Cómo** trabajas!	*How you work!*
¡**Cuánto** comes!	*How much you eat! (i.e., You eat a lot!)*

---

[38] For more information on demonstrative adjectives, see Chapter 2.B.2.a., page 34. For more on demonstrative pronouns, see Chapter 3.C.1., pages 78–79.

Some examples of interrogative adjectives, pronouns, and adverbs are found in the following chart:

INTERROGATIVES vs. NONINTERROGATIVES		
INTERROGATIVE[39] (ACCENT)		**NONINTERROGATIVE (NO ACCENT)**
DIRECT DISCOURSE[40]	INDIRECT DISCOURSE	
¿Qué? = *What?*		**Que** = *That, which, who*
¿Qué quieres? *What do you want?*	No sabía **qué** hacer. *I did not know what to do.*	Quiero **que** estudies. *I want you to study.* (literally: *I want that you study.*) [that = conjunction] El libro **que** quiero es azul. *The book that I want is blue.* [that = relative pronoun]
¿Por qué? = *Why?*		**Porque** = *Because*
¿Por qué llamaste? *Why did you call?*	No sé **por qué** llamó. *I do not know why he called.*	Llamé **porque** quise. *I called because I wanted to.*
¿Cómo? = *How?*		**Como** = *Like*
¿Cómo llegó? *How did she get here?*	No sé **cómo** llegó. *I do not know how she got here.*	Trabaja **como** yo. *He works like me.*
¿Cuánto? = *How much/many?*		**Cuanto** = *As much/many as*
¿Cuántos libros tienes? *How many books do you have?*	No sé **cuántos** tengo. *I do not know how many I have.*	Te di **cuantos** pude. *I gave you as many as I could.*
¿Dónde? = *Where?*		**Donde** = *Where, in which*
¿Dónde está? *Where is it?*	Me dijo **dónde** estaba. *He told me where it was.*	Es la casa **donde** me crie. *It is the house in which I grew up.*
¿Cuándo? = *When?*		**Cuando** = *When*
¿Cuándo llega? *When does it arrive?*	Me dijo **cuándo** venía. *She told me when she was coming.*	Lo vi **cuando** entró. *I saw him when he came in.*
¿Quién? = *Who(m)?*		**Quien** = *Who(m), he who*
¿Quién es? *Who is it?*	Me dijo **quién** era. *He told me who it was.*	Ese es el hombre con **quien** llegó. *That is the man with whom she arrived.*

---

[39] **Interrogative vs. noninterrogative.** This distinguishes words that are used in questions, whether directly stated or indirectly related, from words that are not interrogative at all, such as conjunctions, relative pronouns, and adverbial phrases.

[40] **Direct vs. indirect discourse.** This distinguishes questions that are asked directly (e.g., *What is your name?*) from reported questions (e.g., *He asked me what my name was.*).

Que

Please note that the "noninterrogative" column for **Que** contains conjunctions and relative pronouns that frequently have no translations into English, whereas the columns to the left, "interrogative," contain interrogative words that will always be stated in English. Notice the translations of the following sentences:

> Quiero **que** estudies. *I want you to study.*
>
> El libro **que** quiero es azul. *The book (that) I want is blue.*

Por qué vs. Porque • Cómo vs. Como • Cuánto vs. Cuanto

It is not difficult to remember when these words require accent marks because of their differences in meaning.

por qué = why	cómo = how	cuánto = how much/many
porque = because	como = as, like	cuanto = as much/many

Dónde vs. Donde

Whereas in most cases you can see that the translations of the accented and unaccented words are different, in the case of **dónde** and **donde** there is not always a difference. It would help perhaps to think of the unaccented word as a relative pronoun that requires an antecedent: a noun prior to it and to which it refers.

> Es la **casa donde** me crie. *It is the **house in which** I grew up.*
> OR: *It is the **house** I grew up in.*

The interrogative **dónde**, whether in direct or in indirect discourse, never has an antecedent.

> —¿**Dónde** está? *"Where is she?"*
> —No sé **dónde** está. *"I do not know **where** she is."*

Cuándo vs. Cuando

With these two words, the distinction is perhaps even harder to make; for there to be an accent mark, there must be an explicit or implicit question involved. The non-interrogative *when* might be replaced by *at the time* without much change in meaning, whereas the interrogative could be replaced by *at what time*. Compare the following sentences:

> No sé **cuándo** se fue. *I do not know **when** (at what time) she left.*
> Lloramos **cuando** se fue. *We cried **when** (at the time) she left.*

Frequently in indirect discourse in English, there is a greater stress on the word when it is interrogative in nature than when it is not; compare the following, reading them out loud.

Te vi **cuando** entraste.	*I saw you **when** you came in.*
No sé **cuándo** entraste.	*I don't know **when** you came in.*

Quién vs. Quien

Quién with an accent mark is used whenever there is a question, explicit or implicit. **Quien** without an accent mark is not interrogative. It is a relative pronoun, usually preceded by a noun (which is its antecedent). It may also be used with no antecedent at the beginning of a sentence. In such cases, it means "He who..." or "Whoever..."

¿**Quién** eres?	*Who are you?*
No sé **quién** eres.	*I don't know **who** you are.*
El hombre con **quien** habla es un espía.	*The man with **whom** she is talking is a spy.*
Quien busca encuentra.	*He **who** seeks shall find.*

> Ejercicios 9.33–9.40, páginas 534–536;
> Ejercicios de repaso 9.41–9.43, páginas 536–537

D LINKING BETWEEN WORDS: SYNALEPHA

In oral communication in Spanish, words are linked to each other following certain syllabification rules. This linking is called *synalepha* (in Spanish, **sinalefa**) from the Greek for *to melt together*. For learners of Spanish, linking of words can create considerable frustration as to listening comprehension, because individual words may be difficult to detect. Heritage learners of the language, many of whom may have learned Spanish primarily by listening to it, tend to write the way they speak, which, because of the synalepha, can cause frequent mistakes in spelling. For example, if you hear [bea-sér-lo][41], can you transcribe it into a meaningful sentence?

---

[41] In this section, the pronunciation of sentences between brackets uses hyphens to separate units of sound. Note that it does not coincide precisely with the syllabification of the individual words, due to the effects of linking.

Consider these three types of linking:

1 Same Letter

In a sentence, when a word ends with the same letter that begins the following word, the two letters merge into a single sound.

¿Qué es eso?

> would be pronounced [ke-sé-so]
> in which the **é** in **qué** links to the **e** in **es**.

Mis sobrinos son simpáticos.

> would be pronounced [mi-so-brí-no-son-sim-pá-ti-kos]
> in which the **s** in **mis** links to the first **s** in **sobrinos** and the final **s** in **sobrinos** links to the **s** in **son**.

2 Vowel + Vowel

In a sentence, when a word ending with a vowel is followed by a word beginning with a different vowel, the two vowels link into a single syllable.

Llegó la fea infanta.

> would be pronounced [ye-gó-la-fé-ain-fán-ta][42]
> in which the **a** in **fea** links to the **i** in **infanta**.

Es un coco entero.

> would be pronounced [é-sun-kó-koen-té-ro]
> in which the final **o** in **coco** links to the first **e** in **entero**.

Dijo que lo hiciera.

> would be pronounced [dí-jo-ke-loi-sié-ra] or [dí-jo-ke-loi-zié-ra]
> in which the **o** in **lo** links to the first **i** in **hiciera**.

---

[42] We are applying the pronunciation of regions of **yeísmo**. For more on this, see page 376 at the end of this chapter.

3 Consonant + Vowel

In a sentence, when a word ending in a consonant is followed by a word that begins with a vowel, the consonant at the end of the first word is linked to the vowel of the word that follows.

A veces‿iban bailando.

> would be pronounced [a-bé-se-sí-bam-bai-lán-do]
> or [a-bé-ze-sí-bam-bai-lán-do]
> in which the **s** in **veces** links to the **i** in **iban**. (Note that /n/ before /b/ is pronounced /m/.)

All this linking results in sentences in Spanish sounding like single words to non-Spanish speakers. This leads learners of the language, both heritage and not, to frequent spelling errors.

Consider the following three orders:

Vea hacerlo.	*See it being done.*
Ve a hacerlo.	*Go do it.*
Ve a serlo.	*Go be it.*

All three would be pronounced [bea-sér-lo] in regions of **seseo**. In regions that do not use the **seseo**, the first two sentences would be pronounced differently from the last: [bea-zér-lo] for the first two, and [bea-sér-lo] for the last.

Ejercicios 9.44–9.46, páginas 537–538

E. CAPITALIZATION

Capitalization in Spanish has some similarities with that in English, but is different in several ways. Following is a list of occurrences of capitalization:

- The first word in a sentence or of a title:

    La clase comienza a las diez.

    La novela se titula *Vivir para contarla*.

    Siempre consulto el *Diccionario de dudas*.

- Proper nouns, names of divinities, people's names, surnames, nicknames, pet names, personifications, etc:

    Juana, España, Gómez

    Acabo de leer el libro *La muerte de Artemio Cruz*.

    Alfonso el Sabio, Juana la Loca

    Dios, Alá, Júpiter

    la Muerte, el Mal

    —If a surname begins with a preposition, or a preposition and an article, these are not capitalized, unless the first name is omitted:

    María de Escovar, Juan de los Valles

    la señora De Escovar, el señor De los Valles

- Honorary titles of people, when used specifically in reference to individuals:

    El Papa estaba rezando.

    El Rey y la Reina estaban presentes.

    —When used generically, these words are not capitalized:

    Los papas no son santos.

    El rey es el jefe supremo de una monarquía.

- Abbreviations of titles of address and cardinal points are capitalized, whereas they are not normally capitalized when not abbreviated:

    Sr. (señor), Sra. (señora), Srta. (señorita)

    Ud. (usted), Uds. (ustedes)

N (norte)	NE (noreste)
S (sur)	NO (noroeste)
E (este)	SE (sureste)
O (oeste)	SO (suroeste)

- Nouns and adjectives that form the names of administrative institutions, entities, organisms, departments or divisions, buildings, monuments, public establishments, political parties, etc., are capitalized:

    la Iglesia

    el Estado

    el Tribunal Supremo

    el Museo del Prado

    —The above would not be capitalized if referring to them as places, not as institutions:

    La subasta tendrá lugar en la iglesia.

    Tenían que encontrarse en el tribunal.

    Ese museo fue mi favorito.

- Nouns and adjectives that are parts of the titles of periodicals, newspapers, or collections:

    La Vanguardia

    El Informador

    El País

    Nueva Revista

    La Gaceta de los Negocios

- Historical events:

    el Renacimiento

    la Primera Guerra Mundial

    la Reconquista

    —Adjectives accompanying **Revolución** or **Imperio** are not capitalized:

    la Revolución francesa

    el Imperio romano

- Geographical names:

    Estados Unidos

    Canadá

    —When the official name of the place includes an article, this article is capitalized:

    El Salvador

—Note that in these cases the correct written form is:
Vamos a El Salvador (and not ⊠Vamos al Salvador).

- Religious or civil holidays:
    Año Nuevo
    Feria de Abril
    Semana Santa

Note that the following, which are capitalized in English, are not capitalized in Spanish:

Adjectives referring to places and languages:

Es una palabra griega.	*It's a Greek word.*
Es alemán.	*He is German.*

Days of the week:

lunes, martes, etc.	*Monday, Tuesday, etc.*

Names of months and seasons:

mayo, verano	*May, Summer, etc.*

exceptions: historical events OR holidays: el Cinco de Mayo

Note about accents on capital letters: Capital letters obey the same rules as lowercase letters in relation to accentuation. Hence, the word **África** requires an accent, as does **PERÚ**. Acronyms, even those pronounced as if they were words, do not have accents (e.g., **la CIA** /lasía/, not **la ⊠CÍA**).

Ejercicio 9.47, página 538

F NUMBERS

1 Cardinal Numbers

	CARDINAL NUMBERS				
0	cero	30	treinta	1000[43]	mil
1	uno/un/una*	31	treinta uno/un/una*	1001	mil uno/un/una*
2	dos	32	treinta y dos	1002	mil dos
3	tres	33	treinta y tres	1010	mil diez
4	cuatro	40	cuarenta	1020	mil veinte
5	cinco	50	cincuenta	1021	mil veintiuno/-ún/-una*
6	seis	60	sesenta	1100	mil cien
7	siete	70	setenta	1101	mil ciento uno/un/una*
8	ocho	80	ochenta	1200	mil doscientos/-as*
9	nueve	90	noventa	2000	dos mil
10	diez	100	cien	10 000	diez mil
11	once	101	ciento uno/un/una*	20 000	veinte mil
12	doce	102	ciento dos	21 000	veintiún/-una mil*
13	trece	103	ciento tres	100 000	cien mil
14	catorce	110	ciento diez	200 000	doscientos/-as mil *
15	quince	120	ciento veinte	1 000 000	un millón
16	dieciséis	121	ciento veintiuno/-ún/-una*	1 000 001	un millón uno/un/una*
17	diecisiete	200	doscientos/-as*	1 000 100	un millón cien
18	dieciocho	300	trescientos/-as*	2 000 000	dos millones
19	diecinueve	400	cuatrocientos/-as*	10^7**	diez millones
20	veinte	500	quinientos/-as*	10^8**	cien millones
21	veintiuno/-ún/-una*	600	seiscientos/-as*	10^9**	mil millones
22	veintidós	700	setecientos/-as*	10^{10}**	diez mil millones
23	veintitrés	800	ochocientos/-as*	10^{11}**	cien mil millones
24	veinticuatro	900	novecientos/-as*	10^{12}**	un billón[44]

* The numbers with asterisks in the above table are variable, and agree with the nouns to which they refer:

¿Amigas? Solo tengo **una** (veinti**una**, treinta y **una**, doscient**as**, etc.)

**This superscripted number is an exponent (ten multiplied by itself the number of times indicated in the superscripted number; in this case it indicates the number of zeroes that follow the 1). We use this format merely to save space in the table.

---

[43] In most Spanish-speaking countries, a period is used with numbers to separate thousands beyond four digits and a comma is used to separate decimals. However, international norms recommend that no period be used to separate thousands, and that spacing be used for legibility as seen in this table.

[44] Note that the translation of **billón** is *trillion*. *Billion* translates into Spanish as **mil millones.**

In the case of **uno,** when it is used as an adjective rather than as a pronoun (i.e., with a noun after it), it becomes **un** for the masculine:

> **un** libro, veinti**ún** libros, etc.

A common error is to make certain numbers plural, when they should remain invariable (as in ⊠ cuatros años, which should be **cuatro años**).

Only the following can be made plural:

> cien, cientos
> mil, miles
> millón, millones
> billón, billones

Note that with **cien** and **mil** there is no article:

Vinieron cien pájaros.	*A hundred birds came.*
Tengo mil problemas.	*I have a thousand problems.*

The indefinite article **un** is required with **millón** and **billón:**

Había un millón de invitados.	*There were a million guests.*
Ganó un billón de pesos.	*She won a trillion pesos.*

Note the addition of the preposition **de** with **millón** and **billón:**

un millón **de** habitantes	*a million inhabitants*

BUT:

Tienen mil opciones.	*They have a thousand choices.*

If there is an additional number before the noun, **de** is not used:

un millón trescientos habitantes	*1,000,300 inhabitants*

In Spanish, years are said in the same manner as any other number, whereas in English, *nineteen hundred* (or simply *nineteen*) is used rather than *one thousand nine hundred*:

1945	mil novecientos cuarenta y cinco
2001	dos mil uno
2020	dos mil veinte

Note that the definite article **el** may be used before a year within a context, especially from the year 2000 on; the article is required if the noun **año** is present:

> Esta mejora se espera para **el** 2015.
>
> Eso ocurrió en **el** año dos mil.

Decades are referred to differently in English and in Spanish. Compare the following:

Era un baile popular en la década de los noventa (OR: en los noventa [no **s** on **noventa**]).	*It was a popular dance in the nineties.*

Decimals are indicated with commas in most of the Spanish-speaking world, and are said as follows:

0,5 (cero coma cinco)	*.5 (point five)/0.5 (zero point five)*
1,16 (uno coma dieciséis)	*1.16 (one point sixteen)*

Phone numbers are usually stated broken down into pairs of numbers:

> 52 31 38 24 27 05   cincuenta y dos, treinta y uno, treinta y ocho, veinticuatro, veintisiete, cero cinco

If there is a set of three digits in the number, it is usually stated split 1-11, as follows:

> (212) 647-7016   dos, doce, seis, cuarenta y siete, setenta, dieciséis

Dates, when abbreviated, are listed in Spanish in the following order: day/month/year.

> 01/12/2012 = el primero de diciembre de/del 2012
>
> 12/01/2012 = el doce de enero de/del 2012

—¿Cuál es la fecha de hoy? OR: ¿A cuánto estamos?	*"What's today's date?"*
—Es el 15. (OR: Estamos a 15.)	*"It's the 15th."*

Telling age:

¿Cuántos años tienes?	*How old are you?*
¿Qué edad tienes?	
Tengo catorce años.	*I am fourteen.*
¿Cuándo cumples quince años?	*When will you be fifteen?*
Cumplió dos años la semana pasada.	*He was/turned two last week.*
Mañana cumplo veinte años.	*Tomorrow is my twentieth birthday.*
mi hija de ocho años	*my eight-year-old daughter*
una mujer de cuarenta años	*a forty-year-old woman*
Ingresó a la universidad a los dieciséis años.	*He entered the university at sixteen.*
Tendrá unos treinta años.	*She's about thirty.*
Tiene más de sesenta años.	*He's over sixty.*
Tiene treinta y pico años.	*She's thirty-something*
Tiene menos/más de treinta años.	*He's under/over thirty.*
Es un cincuentón/una cincuentona.	*(pejorative) He's a man in his fifties/ She's a woman in her fifties.*
Es cinco años mayor que yo. OR: Me lleva cinco años.	*He's five years older than me.*
Es dos años menor que yo. OR: Le llevo dos años.	*He's two years younger than me.*

Telling time: Numbers used in telling time in Spanish may vary from those used in English (note the agreement of the verb and the article with the number):

Es la una y media.	*It's one thirty.*
Son las dos y cuarto.	*It's two fifteen* (OR: *quarter past two*).

After the half hour, Spanish time tends to be told by deducting the minutes remaining before the next hour:

Son las seis menos veinte.	*It's 5:40.*
Faltan diez para las ocho.	*It's 7:50.*

To the time you may add specifications such as **de la mañana** (from sunrise to noon, or from midnight to noon), **de la madrugada** (from midnight to sunrise), **de la tarde** (from noon to sunset), **de la noche** (from sunset to midnight), **mediodía** (noon), **medianoche** (midnight):

las diez de la mañana/de la noche	*10 A.M./P.M.*
las doce de la mañana, del mediodía	*12 noon, 12 P.M.*
las doce de la noche, la medianoche	*12 A.M., midnight*

Qualifications of the time may be indicated with **alrededor de** (about), **hacia** (about), **casi** (almost), **a eso de** (about), **y pico** (shortly after), **pasadas** (after), or **en punto** (exactly):

la una en punto	*exactly at one*
las dos y pico de la tarde	*shortly after two P.M.*
las tres pasadas	*past three*
a eso de/alrededor de/hacia las cuatro	*at around four*
casi las cinco	*almost five*

If the 24-hour system is used, you say:

El tren sale a las 13.10 h (trece horas diez minutos, OR: trece diez).	*The train leaves at one ten in the afternoon (1:10 P.M.).*
las cero horas	*midnight*

Either numbers (separated by a period or a colon) or letters can be used to tell time; it is, however, considered bad form to mix the two formats:

10.30 A.M./10:30 A.M.	*10:30 A.M.*
15.30 h	*3:30 P.M.*

las diez de la noche (*not recommended:* las 10 de la noche)

Measurement systems will vary depending on the context. Most of the Spanish-speaking world uses the metric system. Following are some common conversions:

1 kilómetro = 0,62 millas *(miles)*

100 kilómetros por hora = 62 millas por hora *(miles per hour)*

1 metro = 1,09 yardas *(yards)* o 3,28 pies *(feet)*

1 centímetro = 0,38 pulgadas *(inches)*

1 metro cuadrado = 10,76 pies cuadrados *(square feet)*

Mide 1 metro 63 y pesa 54 kilos.   *She's 5' 6" and weighs 120 lbs.*

Idiomatic expressions, sayings, etc. with numbers:

ser un cero a la izquierda	*to be totally useless*
empezar de cero	*to start from scratch*
¡Qué casualidad ni qué ocho cuartos!	*Yeah, right, a coincidence!/ This is no coincidence!*
Nos fue de mil maravillas.	*We had a wonderful time.*
Matar dos pájaros de un tiro.	*To kill two birds with one stone.*
Más vale pájaro en mano que cien volando.	*A bird in hand is worth two in the bush.*
No hay dos sin tres.	*These things always come in threes.*
Donde caben dos caben tres.	*Where there is room for two, there is room for three.*
Hombre precavido vale por dos.	*Forewarned is forearmed.*
No le busques tres (o cinco) patas al gato.	*Don't complicate things unnecessarily. Don't split hairs.*
Quien roba una vez roba diez.	*Once a thief, always a thief.*
Más vale un hoy que diez mañanas.	*One today is worth ten tomorrows.*
Martes trece ni te cases ni te embarques.	*On Tuesday the 13th, don't get married or travel.*

Ejercicios 9.48–9.51, página 539

2 Ordinal Numbers

ORDINAL NUMBERS		
ENGLISH		SPANISH
1st	1.°, 1.er, 1.a	primero/primer/primera
2nd	2.°, 2.a	segundo/-a
3rd	3.°, 3.er, 3.a	tercero/tercer/tercera
4th	4.°, 4.a	cuarto/-a
5th	5.°, 5.a	quinto/-a
6th	6.°, 6.a	sexto/-a
7th	7.°, 7.a	séptimo/-a
8th	8.°, 8.a	octavo/-a
9th	9.°, 9.a	noveno/-a
10th	10.°, 10.a	décimo/-a
11th	11.°, 11.a	undécimo/-a; décimoprimer/-o/-a; onceno/-a
12th	12.°, 12.a	duodécimo/-a; décimosegundo/-a
13th	13.°, 13.er, 13.a	décimotercer/-o/-a
20th	20.°, 20.a	vigésimo/-a
21st	21.°, 21.er, 21.a	vigésimoprimer/-o/-a
30th	30.°, 30.a	trigésimo/-a
40th	40.°, 40.a	cuadragésimo/-a
50th	50.°, 50.a	quincuagésimo/-a
60th	60.°, 60.a	sexagésimo/-a
70th	70.°, 70.a	septuagésimo/-a
80th	80.°, 80.a	octogésimo/-a
90th	90.°, 90.a	nonagésimo/-a
100th	100.°, 100.a	centésimo/-a
101st	101.°, 101.a	centésimo primer/-o/-a
144th	144.°, 144.a	centésimo cuadragésimo cuarto/-a
200th	200.°, 200.a	duocentésimo/-a
300th	300.°, 300.a	tricentésimo/-a
400th	400.°, 400.a	cuadringentésimo/-a
500th	500.°, 500.a	quingentésimo/-a
600th	600.°, 600.a	sexcentésimo/-a
700th	700.°, 700.a	septingentésimo/-a
800th	800.°, 800.a	octingentésimo/-a
900th	900.°, 900.a	noningentésimo/-a
1000th	1000.°, 1000.a	milésimo/-a
2000th	2000.°, 2000.a	dosmilésimo/-a
3000th	3000.°, 3000.a	tresmilésimo/-a

Ordinal numbers usually precede nouns, and are variable in gender; **primero** and **tercero** drop the **-o** before masculine nouns:

>el **primer** libro, el **tercer** voluntario
>
>BUT: el **segundo** año
>
>la **primera** clase, la **tercera** vez, la **segunda** parte

In dates, the first day of the month is usually ordinal, the rest are cardinal:

>el primero de enero
>
>el dos de marzo, el cinco de abril, el veintiuno de agosto

When referring to pages, chapters, etc., either a cardinal or an ordinal number is possible, up to ten. From eleven up, cardinals are preferred:

>| | |
>|---|---|
>| el primer capítulo, el capítulo uno | *the first chapter* |
>| el décimo párrafo, el párrafo diez | *the tenth paragraph* |
>| el siglo quinto | *the fifth century* |
>| el siglo veintiuno | *the 21st century* |

For titles of kings, the definite article is not used in Spanish with the number:

>| | |
>|---|---|
>| Carlos V (Carlos quinto) | *Charles the Fifth* |

After the number ten, cardinal numbers are used in titles:

>| | |
>|---|---|
>| Alfonso XIII (Alfonso trece) | *Alfonso the Thirteenth* |

Note the translation of the following:

>| | |
>|---|---|
>| la Primera Guerra Mundial | *World War I* |
>| la Segunda Guerra Mundial | *World War II* |

When referring to the floors of a building, what is called in American English the first floor is called **la planta baja,** and the second floor is **el primer piso.** Following are some of the more common variations in the use of ordinals in English and in Spanish:

>| | |
>|---|---|
>| al alba | *at first light* |
>| primeros auxilios | *first aid* |
>| primogénito | *first born* |

primera, primera clase	*first class*
primo(a) hermano(a)	*first cousin*
primera dama	*first lady*
estreno	*first night (premiere)*
[persona que *(verbo)*] por primera vez	*first-time* (+ noun)
primerizo(a)	*first-timer*
interrogar, cuestionar	*give the third degree*
Noche de Reyes	*Twelfth Night*
estudiante de primer año	*freshman, first-year (student)*
estudiante de segundo año	*sophomore*
estudiante de tercer año	*junior*
estudiante de cuarto año	*senior*
primera infancia	*early childhood*
primera plana	*front page*
primer plano	*foreground, close-up*
segundo plano	*background*

Note the following familiar expression:

por enésima vez	*for the nth/umpteenth time*

3 Fractions

FRACTIONS	
1/2	una mitad; medio/-a (adj.)
1/3	un tercio, una tercera parte
2/3	dos tercios
1/4	un cuarto, una cuarta parte
3/4	tres cuartos
1/5	un quinto, una quinta parte
1/6	un sexto, una sexta parte
1/7	un séptimo, una séptima parte
1/8	un octavo, una octava parte
1/9	un noveno, una novena parte
1/10	un décimo, una décima parte
1/11	un onceavo o undécimo, una onceava parte
1/12	un doceavo o duodécimo, una doceava parte
1/13	un treceavo, una treceava parte
1/14	un catorceavo, una catorceava parte
1/20	un veinteavo o vigésimo, una veinteava o vigésima parte
1/30	un treintavo o trigésimo, una treintava o trigésima parte
1/100	un centésimo, una centésima parte
1/1000	un milésimo, una milésima parte
1/10 000	un diezmilésimo, una diezmilésima parte
1/100 000	un cienmilésimo, una cienmilésima parte
1/1 000 000	un millonésimo, una millonésima parte
1/10 000 000	un diezmillonésimo, una diezmillonésima parte
1/100 000 000	un cienmillonésimo, una cienmillonésima parte
1/1 000 000 000	un milmillonésimo, una milmillonésima parte

Note that fractions corresponding to the numbers three to ten, as well as those corresponding to one hundred, one thousand, and their multiples, as well as a million and its multiples, coincide in their forms with the feminines of ordinal numbers: **tercera, cuarta, quinta, [...] décima, centésima, milésima**, etc. The rest are currently formed with the cardinal number and the suffix **-avo(a)**:

    1/13 = un treceavo

    1/21 = un veintiunavo

Fractions corresponding to eleven and twelve, as well as those relating to tenths, allow two forms, although there is a general preference for the first:

    1/11 = un onceavo o undécimo

    1/12 = un doceavo o duodécimo

    1/20 = un veinteavo o vigésimo

    1/30 = un treintavo o trigésimo

Fractions of less common use are said as follows:

    5/32 = cinco sobre treinta y dos

    89/520 = ochenta y nueve sobre quinientos veinte

Examples of usage:

Nos vemos dentro de un cuarto (tres cuartos) de hora.	*See you in a quarter (three quarters) of an hour.*
Salimos en media hora.	*We're leaving in half an hour.*
Deme medio kilo.	*Give me half a kilo.*
Bajó de un tercio de su peso debido a la enfermedad.	*He lost a third of his weight due to illness.*
Reserve una tercera parte de la mezcla para la salsa.	*Save one third of the mix for the sauce (or gravy).*
El precio se redujo a la mitad.	*The price was reduced by half.*
Se desperdicia un cuarto del agua.	*A quarter of the water is wasted.*
Un kilómetro es casi cinco octavos de una milla.	*One kilometer is almost five eighths of a mile.*
Una pulgada es la doceava parte de un pie.	*One inch is a twelfth of a foot.*
dos quintas partes	*two fifths*

una milésima de segundo	*a thousandth of a second*
un veinteavo del grupo	*one twentieth of the group*
una doceava parte	*one twelfth*

Fractions as percentages:

El sesenta y dos por ciento del público estaba a favor.	*Sixty-two percent of the audience was in favor.*
Había un recargo del quince por ciento.	*There was a fifteen percent surcharge.*
Gana un porcentaje de las ventas.	*She earns a percentage of the sales.*

Ejercicio 9.52, página 540

G PUNCTUATION

1 Terminology

	SIGNOS DE PUNTUACIÓN[45]				
.	**punto**	*period*	[ ]	**corchetes**	*brackets*
,	**coma**	*comma*	{ }	**llaves**	*curly brackets*
;	**punto y coma**	*semicolon*	« »	**comillas**	*guillemets*
:	**dos puntos**	*colon*	" "	**comillas inglesas**	*quotation marks*
—	**raya**	*dash*	' '	**comillas simples**	*single quotation marks*
-	**guion**	*hyphen*	¿ ?	**signos de interrogación**	*question marks*
/	**barra**	*slash*	¡ !	**signos de exclamación**	*exclamation marks*
( )	**paréntesis**	*parentheses*	...	**puntos suspensivos**	*ellipsis*

---

[45] Please note the vocabulary of symbols for the electronic age: **arroba [@]** *(at)*, **barra inversa [\]** *(backslash)*, **guion bajo [_]** *(underscore)*, **punto com [.com]** *(dot com)*.

2 Differences between English and Spanish Punctuation

Spanish and English are similar in most regards when it comes to punctuation, but there are a few important differences.

a. Questions and exclamations

In Spanish, questions and exclamations begin with inverted symbols:

> Disculpe, señorita, ¿dónde se encuentran los servicios?
> *Excuse me, miss, where is the restroom?*

> Para que lo sepas, ¡no vuelvo a dirigirte la palabra!
> *Just so you know, I am never speaking to you again!*

> ¡¿Cómo te atreves?! (OR: ¿¡Cómo te atreves!?)
> *How dare you?!*

When an exclamation or an interrogation mark is followed by a parenthesis or a quotation mark at the end of a sentence, a period is needed to close the sentence in Spanish:

> Entonces oyó la voz de su compañero de cuarto que le preguntaba:
> "¿Eres tú, Juan?".
> *Then he heard his roommate's voice asking him: "Is that you, Juan?"*

> La arañó el gato (¡estaba furioso!).
> *The cat scratched her (he was furious!)*

b. Dialogue

In Spanish, a dash is used to mark each instance of speech; a dash or a comma is used after the quoted speech if secondary information is added.

> —¿Cómo estás?— susurró su madre.
> —Bien. Estoy bien. No te preocupes por mí.

> *"How are you?" her mother whispered.*
> *"Fine. I'm fine. Don't worry about me."*

> —Esto es intolerable, dijo el juez.
> *"This is intolerable," said the judge.*

In correspondence, a colon and return is used after the greeting:

> Querida Georgina:
> Te escribo con gran alegría para informarte que…

c. Quotations

In Spanish, guillemets are preferred for citing, and the other types of quotation marks are used for internal references. Compare in the examples below the locations of the periods after the quotation marks in Spanish, but before the quotation marks in English:

> «Sofía murmuró: "Vaya problema el que tenemos ahora con este 'cachivache' que nos metieron a la casa"».
> *"Sofía murmured: 'Some problem we have now with this 'junk' they put in our house.'"*

The example below illustrates how dashes may be used within a quotation to indicate the speaker:

> Los mineros, evidentemente agotados después de su experiencia, se pararon al lado de los reporteros mientras estos hablaban dirigiéndose a la cámara. : «No podemos ni empezar a imaginarnos lo que habrán sufrido estos hombres—dijo el reportero principal— los horrores que habrán pasado y que probablemente nunca querrán recordar»[1].

[1] Esta constatación tendría mayor pertinencia de lo que se imaginaba.

> *The miners, evidently exhausted after their experience, stood next to the reporters while these spoke facing the camera. "We cannot begin to imagine what these men must have suffered," said the main reporter, "the horrors they must have been through and that probably they will never want to remember."[1]*

[1] This statement would have greater significance than he thought.

Compare the locations of the note references (the superscript numbers that denote the footnotes) for the quote in the two examples above: in both cases the note reference is placed directly after the closing quotation mark. What is different is the placement of the period.

d. End of line word division

When writing in Spanish, a word at the end of a line is divided with a hyphen, according to a syllable break[46], with some exceptions. We summarize below the more notable exceptions:

- Never split a word leaving a single vowel at the end of a line, unless it is preceded by an **h**:

    ani- / mal (not ⊠a- / nimal)[47]
    BUT: he- / lenista

---

[46] For information on the rules of syllabification, see earlier in this chapter, Section C.1., pages 344–347.
[47] We indicate a line break in this section with a hyphen followed by a slash.

- Never separate two vowels at the end of a line, even if there is hiatus, unless it is a compound word (note than an internal **h** behaves as if it were not present):

    escribí- / ríais (not ⊠escribirí- / ais)

    al- / cohol (not ⊠alco- / hol)

    BUT: hispano- / americano

- Never allow the combination **nh, sh, rh,** or **hl** at the start of a line:

    en- / harinar (not ⊠e- / nharinar)

    des- / humanizar (not ⊠de- / shumanizar)

> Ejercicio 9.53, página 540

H DIALECTAL VARIATION, NORM, REGISTER

Before we end this chapter on orthography, we think it is important to reiterate that the Spanish language is not identical in all regions of the world where it is spoken. In each region it is marked by the local history and culture; it evolves and merges with native languages as well as neighboring languages over time. It is also affected by the communicative context (e.g., an oral exchange tends to use less formal language than a written one) and sociocultural level of the speakers (e.g., language tends to become increasingly formal as the educational level of the individual rises).

These continually evolving language subsets share a strong common homogeneous base which can be seen at the level of formal communication, with variations primarily at the level of pronunciation and vocabulary. This common base is sometimes called **Standard Spanish** and is what is taught in school, what is used for formal writing and speech, and what allows Spanish speakers throughout the world to share a common means of formal communication.

Heritage learners as well as learners of Spanish as a second language will want to take a step back and become familiar with their own discourse, to learn to distinguish between standard and non-standard uses of the language, and to find a personally relevant linguistic level for their communications with friends, family, and others.

Following are some useful terms for analyzing discourse, whether it be your own or that of others.

1 Dialectal Variation

The study of dialectal variation is a field in and of itself, which we do not intend to delve into here in any depth. We will only provide a very superficial sampling, and encourage the learner to seek more detailed information within ample existing resources.

Dialect can be roughly defined as a variant of a language that is observed as the norm within a specific region. Dialectal variation can be seen in pronunciation, vocabulary, and grammar. We provide examples of each below.

a. Pronunciation

Seseo.[48] One example of dialectal variation is the different pronunciation of the letter **c** (before **e** or **i**) and the letter **z**, which in regions of **seseo**[49] are pronounced /s/ (like the *s* in *stop*), and in the central peninsular region are pronounced /z/ (like the sound *th* in *thin*).

Ceceo. This is the pronunciation of the s as /z/ in certain areas of Andalucía (e.g., **casa** would be pronounced [káza] rather than [kása]). Unlike the **seseo**, which is considered perfectly acceptable, the **ceceo** is avoided by educated speakers.

Deletion and aspiration of /s/. This is a feature of Andalusian and Caribbean regions, as well as many parts of South America. It consists of omitting the /s/ sound at the end of syllables or words, or weakening it to the sound of an **h**. For example, in these regions, **gracias a la suerte** would be said /grásiahalasuérte/, **los niños hermosos** would be said /lohníñohermosoh/, **¿Qué es eso?** would be said /kehéso/. Note that the intervocalic /s/ and the initial /s/ are not affected.

Deletion of /d/. This is a feature of Andalusian and Caribbean regions, as well as parts of South America. It consists of reducing, for example, **anclado** to /ancláo/. The final /d/ may also be dropped; **usted** would be pronounced /uhté/, **amistad** /amihtá/. Similarly, in Andalucía, you might hear in flamenco singing (**cante flamenco**) the dropping of the /d/ sound in other parts of words: **madre** becomes /máre/, **quemadura** /kemaúra/.

Change of /l/ or /p/ to /r/. This occurs in Andalusian, in which **palmas** is pronounced /parmah/, **mi alma** /miárma/, **algo** /árgo/, and **precepto** may be pronounced /precérto/.

---

[48] For more information on the **seseo**, see earlier in this chapter, Section B.2.b., page 322.
[49] Regions of **seseo**: Latin America, Canarias, Andalucía, certain areas of Región de Murcia and Extremadura, and in informal Spanish speech in Comunidad Valenciana, Cataluña, Islas Baleares, País Vasco, as well as in certain rural areas of Galicia. Note that Basque, Catalan, and Galician are not dialects, but distinct languages.

Change of /r/ to /l/. This can be heard in the Spanish of Puerto Rico, where **puerto** may be pronounced /puélto/, **carne** /kálne/, **hablar** /ablál/.

Variations of the sound /y/. Words spelled with **ll** used to be pronounced /ly/ in Peninsular Spanish (e.g., **calle** sounds almost like /kálye/), and /y/ in most of the rest of the Spanish-speaking world. Nowadays, the /y/ pronunciation of **ll** (called **yeísmo**) has become predominant throughout the Spanish-speaking world, including in most Peninsular Spanish. In Argentina and Uruguay, the sound /y/ is pronounced almost like the English sound *sh*, and so a word like **calle** is pronounced /káshe/, **lleno** /shéno/.

b. Vocabulary

It is in vocabulary usage that the strongest distinctions between dialects can be felt. Indeed, indigenous languages and neighboring languages over time have entered into the local dialects, causing them to diverge from each other.

Following is a sampling of dialectal variations for some common words. A good translation dictionary will provide specifics as to the regions where each term is used. The learner, when abroad, will need to become familiar with local terminology in order to be understood (i.e., if you ask for **chícharos** in Spain, you will not be understood, unless the listener is familiar with Mexican Spanish; likewise, in Mexico, not everyone will understand **arveja**, only those familiar with Peninsular Spanish).

ENGLISH	SPANISH
apartment	apartamento, departamento, piso
bean	alubia, frijol, habichuela, judía, poroto
bus	autobús, bus, camión, colectivo, ómnibus, micro, guagua
cake	pastel, tarta, torta, bizcocho, queque
computer	ordenador, computadora
green bean	habichuela verde, judía verde, ejote, chaucha verde, vainita
jacket	chaqueta, chaqueta americana, saco
omelette	tortilla, omelette
pea	arveja, guisante, chícharo
potato	patata, papa
sweater	suéter, pulóver, jersey, buzo, chompa
tray	bandeja, azafate, charola, cubetera, placa, chapa

c. Grammar

In earlier chapters of the **Manual** we have already covered the major grammatical distinctions between dialects; below are the page references:

Leísmo, Chapter 3.A.3. Direct Object Pronouns, pages 57–60

Vosotros, Ustedes, Vos, Chapter 3.A.2. Subject Pronouns, pages 53–57

Present Perfect, Preterite, Chapter 6.B.13. The Preterite and the Present Perfect, page 189

Diminutives. Another feature of contrast is the more expansive use of diminutives in the Spanish of the Americas, as contrasted with Peninsular Spanish: in addition to using diminutives for nouns (e.g., **casita, amorcito…**) and adjectives (e.g., **blanquito, negrito…**), in Latin America even adverbs and interjections may be used in diminutive (e.g., **adiosito, ahorita, apenitas, despuesito…**).

2 Norm

This term, when referring to language, is used to describe what is of common usage within a particular group. This group may be anything from the residents of a particular region to the members of a specific societal echelon. When used with a qualifier such as *educated* (in Spanish, **la norma culta**) it refers to what is considered acceptable for formal communication, and coincides with **Standard Spanish.**

As an example of different applications of the term *norm*, note that whereas it has been observed to be the norm for large groups of native Spanish speakers to say ⊠~~comistes~~ for **comiste,** ⊠~~habían~~ **20 libros** for **había 20 libros,** ⊠~~cercas~~ for **cerca,** ⊠~~naide~~ for **nadie,** ⊠~~antier~~ for **anteayer,** and ⊠~~más mejor~~ for **mejor,** these expressions are grammatically incorrect, and therefore not deemed acceptable in educated speech (**norma culta**).

3 Register

Register, when related to language, refers to the range of formality of speech or writing, from the lowest vernacular to the highest formality.

The same individual may use a range of registers throughout a day, speaking in one register in informal settings with a spouse, another among friends of the same sex, yet another with friends of the opposite sex, a higher register with elders in the family, and then possibly switch to a more formal register at the place of business with employees, managers, etc. In the realms of academics, law, and religion can be found the registers of the highest formality.

The lower the level of formality used, the easier it is to identify an individual's dialectal background. The higher the level of formality used, the more similar is the Spanish of all regions.

4 Useful Websites

If you find yourself wondering about the applications of a specific term, or wish to learn more about different dialects, you may find the following web resources useful:

Real Academia Española, Diccionario de la lengua española and Diccionario panhispánico de dudas: www.rae.es

Asociación de Academias de la Lengua Española: www.asale.org

> Ejercicio 9.54, páginas 540–541

I SUMMARY OF 2010 *ORTOGRAFÍA* CHANGES

We provide here a summary of the revised rules and recommendations published in late 2010 in the new *Ortografía de la lengua española* by the Real Academia Española and the Asociación de Academias de la Lengua Española. We have selected only the most pertinent issues for this ***Manual:***

- **Ch** and **ll** are no longer letters of the alphabet (but they do remain in use as digraphs producing each a distinct phoneme).

- For purposes of clarity, simplicity, and unification throughout the Spanish-speaking world, names or spellings of certain letters of the alphabet are recommended above others. This recommendation is made specifically for academic communications and teaching contexts:

Letter or Digraph	Recommended Name or Spelling	Variations (not recommended for academic communications or teaching contexts)
b	**be**	be alta, be grande, be larga
v	**uve**	ve baja, ve corta, ve chica, ve pequeña
w	**uve doble**	doble u, doble ve, doble uve, ve doble
r	**erre**	ere
rr	**erre doble, doble erre**	erre
y	**ye**	i griega
z	**zeta**	ceta

- The letter **q** is only to be used in words in which it represents the sound /k/ followed by **e** or **i** (**queso, quiso**). Words thus far spelled **Iraq, Qatar, quórum** are now to be spelled **Irak, Catar, cuórum**. If one chooses to use the spelling with **q,** then the word needs to be italicized, as a foreign term, with no accent mark (e.g., **cuórum** or *quorum*).
- **Solo** and demonstrative pronouns (**este, ese,** and **aquel,** plus their feminine and plural forms) no longer require accents, even in cases of ambiguity. It will not be deemed an error to use an accent in ambiguous contexts, but it is not required.
- It is no longer recommended to accentuate the conjunction of coordination **o** *(or)* between numbers (e.g., **4 ó 5** is now **4 o 5**).
- Some words are pronounced by different speakers as either monosyllables or words with a hiatus (i.e., more than one syllable), and in their spelling were allowed with or without an accent mark. The 2010 rules state that, regardless of how these words are pronounced, the following combinations of vowels are considered single syllables (diphthongs or triphthongs), and spelled accordingly:
    - a strong vowel (**a/e/o**) followed or preceded by a weak vowel (**i/u**).
    - two weak vowels (**i/u**).
    - a strong vowel (**a/e/o**) surrounded by weak vowels (**i/u**).

Words affected by this new rule follow:

- Nouns like **guion** (*script, dash*), **ion** (*ion*), **truhan** (*knave*).
- Certain proper names like **Ruan** and **Sion**.
- The following forms of the verbs **criar** (*to raise*), **fiar** (*to trust*), **fluir** (*to flow*), **freír** (*to fry*), **guiar** (*to guide, to drive*), **huir** (*to flee*), **liar** (*to tie up, to complicate*), **reír** (*to laugh*):

2010 NEW MONOSYLLABIC SPELLING					
SPELLING	SOUND	SPELLING	SOUND	SPELLING	SOUND
crie	[krié]	flui	[fluí]	hui	[uí]
crio	[krió]	fluis	[fluís]	huis	[uís]
criais	[kriáis]	frio	[frió]	lie	[lié]
crieis	[kriéis]	friais	[friáis]	lio	[lió]
fie	[fié]	guie	[guié]	liais	[liáis]
fio	[fió]	guio	[guió]	lieis	[liéis]
fiais	[fiáis]	guiais	[guiáis]	rio	[rió]
fieis	[fiéis]	guieis	[guiéis]	riais	[riáis]

Even if the user chooses to pronounce the above verb forms with a hiatus, they are deemed to be monosyllables in their spelling, and therefore to spell them with an accent now constitutes an error.

EJERCICIOS

TO THE STUDENT: Unless otherwise indicated, the following exercises are designed for self-correcting. For information regarding access to the answer key, please refer to the following sections in the preface to this edition: *A Note about the Answer Key and Technology.* If you are enrolled in a course, consult with your instructor as to access to available online resources.

Chapter 1
Overview

A | SENTENCE COMPONENTS

Chapter 1.A, pages 2–4

Ejercicio 1.1 Identifique las palabras en negrilla **(boldfaced)** en las frases siguientes.

MODELO: Me gusta **el** café **negro**.

el: artículo definido; **negro:** *adjetivo calificativo*

1. Después **de** trabajar varias horas **en** la computadora, **se** me cansan los ojos.
2. **Cuando** estudio, me gusta escuchar música **clásica**.   3. **Ayer** fuimos al parque **a** jugar a la pelota con unos **amigos**.   4. **Mi** abuela me llamó **por** teléfono ayer a **las** ocho de la mañana.   5. Me gustan **tus** zapatos más que los **míos**.   6. **Este** juego es más interesante que **ese**.   7. **Algunos** profesores son más estrictos que **otros**.
8. El abrigo **que** compré ayer me costó **mucho** dinero.   9. Mi hermana me dijo **que** tú eras **un** futbolista famoso.   10. Tengo dos dólares **y** veinte centavos, **pero** no es suficiente para ir al cine.

Ejercicio 1.2 Haga un análisis gramatical de las siguientes oraciones.

MODELO: Juan estudia español.

Juan: *sustantivo propio, sujeto del verbo "estudia";* ***estudia:*** *verbo estudiar, 3ª persona singular del presente del indicativo;* ***español:*** *sustantivo común, masc. sing., objeto directo del verbo "estudia"*

1. Estos ejercicios son fáciles.   2. Los niños cantaron una canción.   3. Marta me regaló este libro.

B | VERB STRUCTURE

Chapter 1.B, page 5

Ejercicio 1.3 Identifique el modo (MAYÚSCULA) y el tiempo (minúscula) de los verbos en negrilla.

MODELO: El niño **llegó cantando** de la escuela; **estaba** contento porque le **habían dado** un premio por **portarse** bien.

llegó: INDICATIVO pretérito; cantando: PARTICIPIO presente; estaba: INDICATIVO imperfecto; habían dado: INDICATIVO pluscuamperfecto; portarse: INFINITIVO

Estábamos todos en la cocina **preparando** la cena cuando mi hermana **anunció** que tenía buenas noticias: **se había ganado** la lotería. Mi mamá le **dijo** que **pensara** con mucho cuidado en lo que quería **hacer** con el dinero, porque si no, lo **gastaría** todo y luego se arrepentiría. Pero mi hermana ya lo había planeado todo. —No te **preocupes**, Mami; a ti y a Papi les **daré** la mitad para que la **pongan** en el banco, y el resto lo usaré para comprarme ropa y otras cosas que **necesito.**

C SENTENCE STRUCTURE

Chapter 1.C, pages 6–12

Ejercicio 1.4 Subraye los verbos conjugados en el texto siguiente.

MODELO: Ayer mis hermanos y yo nos levantamos temprano.

Ayer mis hermanos y yo nos <u>levantamos</u> temprano.

Para las vacaciones de Navidad, mi padre, mi hermana y yo íbamos a San Blas, y nos quedábamos en un hotel en la playa. La noche de Navidad, cuando todos los demás estaban celebrando en el hotel, nos íbamos a un lugar ya seleccionado en la playa oscura y hacíamos un fuego con leña que habíamos recogido el día anterior. Llevábamos comida para cocinar en el fuego, y pasábamos la noche allí, oyendo las olas del mar y mirando las estrellas.

Ejercicio 1.5 Subraye los verbos conjugados en el texto siguiente, usando como modelo el del ejercicio 1.4.

Juan, el protagonista de la película española "Celda 211" (ganadora del premio Goya a la mejor película), es un funcionario que sufre un accidente que lo hace perder el conocimiento dentro de una prisión. Por eso se encuentra tendido en la cama de una celda cuando se desencadena un motín de prisioneros. Los carceleros desaparecen del área y lo dejan solo: para protegerse, finge ser prisionero, y así comienza una serie de inquietantes y sorprendentes eventos.

Ejercicio 1.6 Divida cada oración en cláusulas usando barras (/) y cuente el total de cláusulas en cada una.

MODELO: Tengo una hermana que vive en Costa Rica.

Tengo una hermana / que vive en Costa Rica. (2)

Pedro Soria López ganó el campeonato de la siesta al dormir a puro ronquido durante 17 minutos en medio de un ruidoso centro comercial madrileño.

El campeonato, organizado por la Asociación Nacional de Amigos de la Siesta, buscaba rescatar la costumbre de la siesta que muchos identifican con España pero que según los organizadores está en peligro de perderse por las presiones de la vida moderna.

Unas 360 personas participaron en el concurso, en que tenían 20 minutos para acostarse en un sofá e intentar dormir. Una médica les medía el pulso para determinar cuánto tiempo durmieron. Un juez en una silla elevada daba puntos extras por la posición, la capacidad de roncar y los pijamas más llamativos.

Soria dijo que su esposa lo convenció de que entrara al concurso y que lo ayudó mucho el almuerzo que acababa de comer antes de competir.

Ejercicio 1.7 Subraye todas las cláusulas independientes del texto siguiente.

MODELO: Me desperté a las tres y bajé a hacerme café sin que nadie me oyera.

<u>Me desperté a las tres</u> y bajé a hacerme café sin que nadie me oyera.

El invierno está casi terminado. Ya no hace frío, y la nieve se ha transformado en lluvia. Pronto tendremos que empezar a preparar el jardín para que podamos plantar las hortalizas. Estoy tan contento de que la primavera esté en camino porque me gusta el calor. El invierno aquí es tan gris y triste, y me canso de la ropa pesada que tengo que ponerme.

Ejercicio 1.8 Subraye todas las cláusulas principales del mismo texto.

MODELO: Me desperté a las tres y bajé a hacerme café sin que nadie me oyera.

Me desperté a las tres y <u>bajé a hacerme café</u> sin que nadie me oyera.

El invierno está casi terminado. Ya no hace frío, y la nieve se ha transformado en lluvia. Pronto tendremos que empezar a preparar el jardín para que podamos plantar las hortalizas. Estoy tan contento de que la primavera esté en camino porque me gusta el calor. El invierno aquí es tan gris y triste, y me canso de la ropa pesada que tengo que ponerme.

Ejercicio 1.9 Subraye todas las cláusulas subordinadas del mismo texto.

MODELO: Me desperté a las tres y bajé a hacerme café sin que nadie me oyera.

Me desperté a las tres y bajé a hacerme café <u>sin que nadie me oyera</u>.

El invierno está casi terminado. Ya no hace frío, y la nieve se ha transformado en lluvia. Pronto tendremos que empezar a preparar el jardín para que podamos plantar las hortalizas. Estoy tan contento de que la primavera esté en camino porque me gusta el calor. El invierno aquí es tan gris y triste, y me canso de la ropa pesada que tengo que ponerme.

Ejercicio 1.10 Haga el análisis lógico de las frases siguientes.

MODELO: Quiero que me ayudes a preparar la cena.

> ***Quiero:*** *cláusula principal;* ***que me ayudes… cena:*** *cláusula subordinada nominal, objeto directo de "quiero"*

1. Necesito un libro que describa la Revolución mexicana.   **2.** Te prestaré dinero a condición de que me pagues mañana.   **3.** Sé que siempre quieres participar.

Ejercicio 1.11 Haga el diagrama de las frases siguientes, siguiendo el formato del modelo. (Use también los diagramas del capítulo en las páginas 9–12 para inspirarse.)

MODELO: El presidente dijo que era esencial que todos participáramos, y que nos mantuviéramos siempre al tanto.

Análisis:

El presidente dijo: cláusula principal
que era esencial: cláusula subordinada #1
que todos participáramos: cláusula subordinada #2
y que nos… tanto: cláusula subordinada #3

Diagrama:

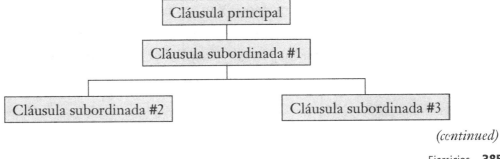

(continued)

1. Quiero que veas el libro que conseguí sobre la Revolución mexicana. **2.** Es necesario que los norteamericanos comprendan que estas tierras les pertenecían a los mexicanos originalmente, y que antes eran de los indios que vivieron en ellas por siglos. **3.** Me pidió que le comprara pan y le contesté que no tenía dinero.

D SUBJECT–VERB AGREEMENT

Chapter 1.D, pages 13–18

Ejercicio 1.12 Conjugue el verbo en el indicativo presente para concordar con el sujeto indicado.

1. Tú no (poder) imaginarte los problemas que (causar) cuando tu mal humor te (dominar). **2.** Los gatos (maullar) todas las noches cuando (haber) estrellas en el cielo y luna llena. **3.** Yo (ser) americano. Otros (decir) que los americanos (ser) inocentes en cuestiones de política internacional. ¿Tú y tus amigos (estar) de acuerdo? **4.** (Ser) yo la que les (dar) a sus amigos los mejores regalos. **5.** La pareja de recién casados (irse) de luna de miel al Caribe. (Ir/ellos) con ellos sus hijos de matrimonios anteriores. Algunos de nosotros (dudar) que la luna de miel fuera ideal. **6.** (Llover) todos los días en este lugar. **7.** Lo que tus amigos te (contar) (ser) chismes sin ninguna base en la realidad. **8.** Tú y yo (comprender) la situación mejor que nadie. **9.** Tú y ella (saber) la verdad. **10.** Me (encantar) jugar y reír.

Ejercicio 1.13 Conjugue en el pasado las frases 2, 4 y 5 del ejercicio 1.12.

Ejercicio 1.14 Complete el diálogo de enamorados según las indicaciones.

EVITA: Buenos días, mi amor.
HÉCTOR: Hola, cariño.
EVITA: Vida mía, ¿(**1.** *are you ready*) para la boda?
HÉCTOR: Claro que sí, mi amor. ¿Y tú, cariño adorado, (**2.** *are you ready*)?
EVITA: Hace años que (**3.** *I am ready*) para este día, mi vida.
HÉCTOR: Lo sé, corazón, pero (**4.** *you don't look very excited* [verse emocionado]).

Chapter 2
Nouns and Noun Determiners

A   NOUNS AND THEIR EQUIVALENTS

(Introduction)
Chapter 2.A.1, pages 20–22

Ejercicio 2.1   Conceptual questions

What is a noun? What types of grammatical functions can a noun have in a sentence? What other types of words can behave this way? What is a nominalized word? Give an example.

Ejercicio 2.2   Traduzca las oraciones siguientes, usando equivalentes de nombres para lo que está en **negrilla** *(boldfaced)*.

1. *"Which of these towels is mine?" "That one is **yours**."*   2. *I prefer **walking** in the morning.*   3. ***Tall people** and **blonde people** always stand out here.* (stand out = sobresalir)   4. *In the Hispanic world, **older people** live with their families.*   5. ***Decent people** often lose.*   6. ***The good guy** and **the bad guy** in this movie look alike* (se parecen).   7. ***Good** and **evil** are enemies.*   8. ***What is strange** is the color.*   9. ***That foreigner** speaks Spanish.*   10. *Sometimes **what is foreign** is frightening* (asusta) *because it's different.*   11. *In this picture, **the one in the grey suit*** (traje) *is my father, **the one with the hat** is my brother, and **the ones above** are my cousins.*

Nouns and Their Equivalents (Nouns: Gender and Number)
Chapter 2.A.2.a–b, pages 23–25

Ejercicio 2.3   Use un artículo definido con cada palabra para indicar si es masculina o femenina.

Esa mañana cuando vio **(1)** _____ amanecer, renació en ella brevemente **(2)** _____ amor por **(3)** _____ vida. Recordó **(4)** _____ cena de aquella última noche,

(continued)

(5) _____ sal y (6) _____ miel que había puesto en (7) _____ arroz exótico que había preparado para celebrar su aniversario; recordó (8) _____ poema que su marido le había leído; y también recordó (9) _____ metal helado de (10) _____ barandal en que se había recargado para no desmayarse, (11) _____ auto, (12) _____ barro, (13) _____ ataúd. Y luego revivió (14) _____ días que pasó en (15) _____ cama, sin salir nunca de (16) _____ casa en que habían vivido tantos años juntos; por (17) _____ mañana recogía (18) _____ periódico, hacía (19) _____ crucigrama, leía sobre (20) _____ problemas de (21) _____ capital, (22) _____ carril extra que iban a poner, (23) _____ catedral y (24) _____ cárcel que se tenían que reparar.

Miraba (25) _____ césped que no paraba de crecer, y todas (26) _____ hojas y (27) _____ ramas que se acumulaban porque había perdido (28) _____ costumbre de cuidar (29) _____ propiedad. Miraba (30) _____ televisión, buscaba (31) _____ dramas con (32) _____ tramas más simples, (33) _____ telenovelas, y (34) _____ programas sensacionalistas, como el que hablaba sobre (35) _____ hotel en que todos (36) _____ huéspedes tenían pesadillas. Se le estaba olvidando (37) _____ español, (38) _____ idioma que hablaba con él. Tenía frente a ella (39) _____ foto de su marido, y (40) _____ recorte de periódico con (41) _____ cara (42) _____ juez que le había dado (43) _____ libertad a (44) _____ asesino. Pasó (45) _____ mano por (46) _____ papel como para tocar de nuevo al ser que había perdido; acercó (47) _____ imagen a (48) _____ luz. Sintió (49) _____ piel que le ardía por (50) _____ rabia.

(51) _____ lunes iría a (52) _____ corte, y llevaría (53) _____ lápiz que había encontrado y que serviría posiblemente de prueba; les hablaría de (54) _____ ruido que había oído que era como (55) _____ señal (56) _____ radar de un coche. No podía aceptar que (57) _____ corrupción en (58) _____ sistema hubiera llegado a tal punto. No sabía si se atrevería a irse en (59) _____ moto de su marido, o si tomaría en vez (60) _____ tranvía. Miró (61) _____ mapa de (62) _____ ciudad para determinar (63) _____ distancia. Era increíble (64) _____ poder (65) _____ mal, y (66) _____ imposibilidad de elevar (67) _____ moral después de semejante lección. Después de luchar por (68) _____ justicia, se daría (69) _____ viaje que habían planeado darse juntos a (70) _____ Pirineos.

Ejercicio 2.4 Escriba el equivalente femenino de cada una de las siguientes palabras.

1. el hombre 2. el estudiante 3. el joven 4. el actor 5. el modelo 6. el turista 7. el rey 8. el policía 9. el comunista 10. los toros

Ejercicio 2.5 Indique en español la diferencia de significado entre el masculino y el femenino de los siguientes nombres.

1. el cura/la cura   2. el guía/la guía   3. el papa/la papa   4. el policía/la policía

Nouns and Their Equivalents (Personal a)

Chapter 2.A.3, pages 26–27

Ejercicio 2.6 Llene cada espacio en blanco con la **a** personal si se necesita.

1. Le gusta mirar _____ sus compañeros.   2. Vimos _____ nuestros vecinos en el centro.   3. No reconocieron _____ mi hermano.   4. ¿_____ quién viste hoy?   5. ¿_____ qué viste hoy?   6. Estoy buscando _____ mis llaves.   7. Esa compañía busca _____ empleados nuevos.   8. El jefe buscaba _____ su secretaria.   9. Tienen _____ tres gatos.   10. Tiene _____ su hijo en una escuela privada.   11. _____ ellas no las vieron hasta el final.   12. No oímos _____ nadie.   13. ¿Viste _____ alguien?   14. ¿Quieres _____ algo?

Ejercicio 2.7 Sustituya el objeto directo en negrilla con las palabras entre paréntesis, y añada la **a** personal cada vez que se necesite. Fíjese que los verbos **mirar** *(to look at)* y **esperar** *(to wait for, to expect)* en español toman un objeto directo.

1. Miro **el libro.** (el jardín, mi hermanito, tus ojos, la pantalla, la película, los vecinos, el periódico, el espejo) *[I look at the book, the garden, my little brother, your eyes, the screen, the movie, the neighbors, the newspaper, the mirror.]*

2. No oye **el teléfono.** (Juan, mi gato, nadie, el gallo, el profesor, la música, tu voz, los niños en la calle, nada) *[He doesn't hear the telephone, Juan, my cat, anybody, the rooster, the professor, the music, your voice, the children in the street, anything.]*

3. Jorge tiene **un apartamento.** (un hermano, una computadora, dos coches, su abuelo en un asilo de ancianos) *[Jorge has an apartment, a brother, a computer, two cars, his grandfather in a home.]*

4. Quiero **dinero.** (amigos, felicidad, amor, comida, mis padres, mi familia, vivir bien) *[I want money, friends, happiness, love, food; I love my parents, my family; I want to live well.]*

5. Espera **mi llamada.** (la alarma, Luis, su respuesta, tus hermanos, tu padre, alguien, ¿Quién?, ¿Qué?) *[Wait for my call, the alarm, Luis, his answer, your brothers, your father, someone, Whom is (s)he waiting for? What is (s)he waiting for?]*

6. Vio **una casa.** (una amiga, la pantalla, el reloj, mi perro, la carta, la gente que quería, gente) *[He saw a house, a friend, the screen, the watch, my dog, the letter, the people he wanted, people.]*

Ejercicio 2.8 Traduzca al español, usando la **a** personal cuando se necesite.

She looked at the mirror and then she looked at her fiancé (novio) out in the garden. Then, she checked (verificó) her makeup (maquillaje) and her hairdo (peinado) and admired her dress. She had two sisters who had gotten married before her. She had her mother waiting outside while she spent one last moment alone. She loved Rodolfo. She had never met anyone like him. She wanted this wedding, but she was afraid. She didn't want to lose her childhood. She didn't want to lose her family. Suddenly, she heard her name. She heard her mother. And she remembered her mother and her father and their happiness. And she felt ready.

B NOUN DETERMINERS

(Articles: Definite Articles)
Chapter 2.B.1.a, pages 28–32

Ejercicio 2.9 Póngale a cada nombre el artículo definido correcto. Todos los nombres de la lista son femeninos, pero ¿usan **la** o **el**?

1. agua 2. aguas 3. águila 4. aguja 5. alarma 6. alarmas 7. alma
8. almas 9. ama 10. aula 11. autonomía 12. avioneta 13. atracción
14. ave 15. avenida 16. avicultura 17. habichuela 18. habitación
19. hacha 20. hambre 21. hambres 22. hamburguesa 23. hartura

Ejercicio 2.10 Llene cada espacio en blanco con un artículo definido si se necesita.

1. _____ vida debe disfrutarse. 2. _____ señor Ruiz dice que _____ chocolate es malo para _____ salud, pero _____ doña Luisa sabe que él come _____ chocolate todos los días. 3. Ayer compramos _____ verduras, pero no tenían _____ verduras que tú pediste. 4. _____ Señorita Guzmán, ¿le gusta _____ chocolate?
5. _____ inglés es más difícil que _____ español. 6. Hablo _____ español, pero sueño en _____ inglés. 7. Mi clase de _____ español es la más divertida de todas.
8. _____ miércoles vamos a tener una prueba. 9. A mi padre le costó trabajo aprender _____ español. 10. Salieron temprano de _____ escuela y, como su padre había salido de _____ cárcel ese día, fueron a _____ iglesia a dar gracias.
11. Salimos de _____ clase y fuimos directamente a _____ casa porque teníamos que vestirnos para llegar a _____ misa a tiempo. 12. Aprendí _____ español cuando tenía seis años. 13. ¡Hasta _____ jueves! 14. Hoy es _____ viernes.

Ejercicio 2.11   Traduzca, usando artículos definidos donde se necesiten.

1. *Happiness is found in love.*   2. *Family and friends are the basis of a good life.*
3. *I speak Spanish. I read French easily.*   4. *Let's go home.*   5. *See you Monday!*
(Hasta…)   6. *People who need people are lucky.*   7. *When we came out of the
museum, we put on our gloves.*   8. *News in the papers is mostly bad news.*   9. *I told
Mr. Betancourt that we were able to remove the bullet* (bala).   10. *I washed my hands.*
11. *Digital journalism* (periodismo) *doesn't make* (ganar) *money.*   12. *They put him in
jail.*   13. *On Friday there's no class.*   14. *Wikileaks has shown how many have violated
human rights.*   15. *Democrats united to win the election.*   16. *According to that
economist, financial crises are creatures of habit.*   17. *Efforts to restore sanity* (cordura)
reveal an idealistic goal (meta).

Noun Determiners (Articles: Indefinite Articles)

Chapter 2.B.1.b, pages 32–34

Ejercicio 2.12   Llene cada espacio en blanco con un artículo indefinido si se necesita.

1. Jorge es _____ arquitecto.   2. Carlitos es _____ argentino.   3. Rafael es _____ hombre interesante.   4. Es _____ cantante mexicano.   5. Georgina es _____ protestante muy severa.   6. ¡Qué _____ dilema!   7. ¡Qué _____ lindo día!
8. Esa viejita acaba de cumplir _____ cien años.   9. Vamos a discutir _____ otro tema ahora.   10. —Tomaría _____ mil años corregir el daño que se ha hecho. —Lo dudo. Yo creo que tomaría _____ millón.   11. Dentro de _____ media hora nos iremos.   12. No tengo _____ bicicleta; tengo dos.   13. Ese pobre chico no tiene ni _____ amigo.   14. Se fue sin _____ gabardina.

Ejercicio 2.13   Traduzca.

Margarita was Puerto Rican. She was a student at the University of Puerto Rico. She was a hardworking student, and she had a certain style in the way she expressed herself that her professors considered original. She once won a prize of a hundred dollars for an analytic essay. She wrote one hundred words on one topic, with three and a half pages of references. She wrote without a computer; she didn't even have a typewriter. What a writer! Nobody had ever seen such a thing. There hasn't been another writer of her quality since she graduated.

Noun Determiners (Adjectives: Demonstrative Adjectives)

Chapter 2.B.2.a, page 34

Ejercicio 2.14 Llene cada espacio en blanco con todas las posibilidades.

este, esta, estos, estas, ese, esa, esos, esas, aquel, aquella, aquellos, aquellas

1. ¿De quién es _____ automóvil?   2. ¿Para quién son _____ mensajes?   3. ¿Por qué viajan por _____ carreteras?   4. ¿Te acuerdas de _____ mañana?   5. ¿Por qué no paramos en _____ gasolinera?   6. _____ mapa no nos sirve para nada: deberíamos conseguirnos un *GPS*.   7. ¿Ves _____ montañas? No paremos hasta llegar allá.

Ejercicio 2.15 Traduzca.

1. *Are those books new?*   2. *These apples are for you (fam. sing.).*   3. *That class does not cover these topics.*   4. *These students are very good.*   5. *That man is a friend.*   6. *Those days are unforgettable.*   7. *Temperatures will drop this week.*

Noun Determiners (Adjectives: Possessive Adjectives)

Chapter 2.B.2.b, pages 35–36

Ejercicio 2.16 Llene cada espacio en blanco con todas las posibilidades apropiadas.

**mi, mis, mío, mía, míos, mías;
tu, tus, tuyo, tuya, tuyos, tuyas;
su, sus, suyo, suya, suyos, suyas;
nuestro, nuestra, nuestros, nuestras;
vuestro, vuestra, vuestros, vuestras**

1. Esa es _____ casa.   2. _____ coche es más económico que el mío.   3. _____ problemas no se pueden resolver en un día.   4. _____ manos son más grandes que las mías.   5. ¿Tienes las llaves _____ ahí?   6. ¿Cuántos amigos _____ vienen?   7. Espero que _____ familia haya pasado un fin de semana fantástico.

Ejercicio 2.17 Traduzca.

1. *My cousins are coming today.*   2. *Did your brother call (fam. sing.)?*   3. *His theory is reasonable.*   4. *Each vote of ours is essential.*   5. *She gave me her ring.*   6. *She is a friend of mine.*   7. *This cell phone is mine.*

Noun Determiners
(Adjectives: Forms of Descriptive Adjectives)

Chapter 2.B.2.c, pages 36–38

Ejercicio 2.18   Haga los cambios necesarios para que el adjetivo concuerde con el nombre.

1. la casa (verde)   2. la casa (blanco)   3. la casa (azul)   4. el político (respetable)
5. el político (izquierdista)   6. el político (prometedor)   7. la profesora (severo)
8. la maestra (comunista)   9. los niños (feliz)   10. los vecinos (gritón)

Noun Determiners
(Adjectives: Position of Descriptive Adjectives)

Chapter 2.B.2.d, pages 38–42

Ejercicio 2.19   Vuelva a escribir las frases siguientes usando el adjetivo entre paréntesis para modificar el nombre en negrilla. Luego traduzca la frase al inglés.

1. Esa fue la **vez** que fui a San Juan. (primera)   2. ¡**Gracias**! (Mucho)   3. Luisito no tiene **dinero.** (tanto)   4. Somos **hermanos.** (medio)   5. Dame una **razón,** por favor. (otro)

Ejercicio 2.20   Vuelva a escribir las frases siguientes usando el adjetivo entre paréntesis para modificar el nombre en negrilla. Puede haber más de una posibilidad en algunos casos. Haga todos los cambios necesarios.

1. Ese hombre vende **muebles.** (antiguos)   2. La **gente** no siempre es infeliz. (pobre)   3. A esa **millonaria** la persiguen los periodistas. (pobre)   4. Te presento a Guzmán, un **amigo**; hoy es su cumpleaños: cumple dieciocho años. (viejo)
5. Desde que construyeron el **garaje,** ya no usan el viejo. (nuevo)   6. Te presento a mi **vecino.** (nuevo)   7. Mi **esposa** está de viaje. (linda)   8. Cornell es una **universidad.** (grande)   9. Charlie Chaplin fue un **actor.** (grande)   10. En esta tina, el **agua** se abre aquí. (caliente)   11. Subimos a la **torre** de la biblioteca. (alta)   12. Está enamorado de tu **hermana.** (bella)   13. Cruzaron el **río** Amazonas. (ancho)   14. Visitaron la **catedral** de Gaudí. (impresionante)
15. Esta es la **oportunidad** que tendremos. (única)   16. Me gustan las **casas.** (blancas)   17. Las **nubes** flotaban como algodón por el valle. (blancas)
18. Era un cielo extraño: abajo había **nubes (1),** y arriba **nubes (2).** [(1) blancas, (2) negras]   19. Esa película es de un **director.** (español)   20. Se le veía un **aire**

(continued)

de inseguridad. (cierto)   **21.** Sabían que eran **acusaciones.** (ciertas)   **22.** Tenía la **capacidad** de hacer que todos se sintieran a gusto. (rara)   **23.** Era un **sonido** que nadie podía identificar. (raro)   **24.** Te voy a decir la **verdad.** (pura)   **25.** Es un disco de **fidelidad.** (alta)   **26.** Querían estar en Sevilla para la **Semana.** (Santa)   **27.** La mejor solución es usar nuestro **sentido.** (común)

Ejercicio 2.21   Traduzca al inglés de una manera que explique claramente la diferencia entre los dos usos del adjetivo en cada caso.

1. Fuimos a diferentes lugares. Fuimos a lugares diferentes.   **2.** Es un buen político. Es un político bueno.   **3.** Tenemos raros momentos de satisfacción. Es un platillo raro.   **4.** Ese auto me causó puros problemas. Busca la vida pura.   **5.** Me tomó media hora. Eso se hacía en la Edad Media.   **6.** Es el único problema. Es un problema único.

Noun Determiners (Adjectives: Comparisons)

Chapter 2.B.2.e, pages 43–46

Ejercicio 2.22   Llene cada espacio en blanco con lo necesario para establecer una comparación. Cada espacio puede necesitar más de una palabra.

1. Beto come más ruidosamente _____ nadie.   **2.** Sabina es más lista _____ Raúl.   **3.** Elsa gana menos dinero _____ tú.   **4.** Hay más _____ veinte árboles aquí.   **5.** Me diste menos _____ la mitad.   **6.** Mi bicicleta es mejor _____ la tuya.   **7.** Hace más frío _____ esperaba.   **8.** Llovió menos _____ creíamos.   **9.** Nunca ganaré tanto dinero _____ Héctor.   **10.** Ese coche es _____ bello como este.   **11.** Esa niña grita más _____ las demás.   **12.** Había menos _____ cinco jugadores en la cancha.   **13.** Ese examen no fue tan fácil _____ los otros.   **14.** Compré más servilletas _____ necesitábamos.   **15.** Hay más servilletas _____ invitados.   **16.** Tengo menos trabajo _____ esperaba.   **17.** Elvira trabaja _____ como su hermano, pero no gana _____ dinero como él. Y a mí me parece que él no es _____ listo como ella.

Ejercicio 2.23   Escriba tres comparaciones para cada serie de dos elementos, una con **más,** otra con **menos** y otra de igualdad (con **tan** o **tanto**).

1. Argentina y Cuba   **2.** los Estados Unidos e Hispanoamérica   **3.** las culturas hispanas y las culturas anglosajonas   **4.** el amor y el odio   **5.** la televisión y el cine   **6.** la escuela y la universidad   **7.** los niños y los adultos   **8.** el periodismo electrónico y los periódicos   **9.** mi partido político y el tuyo   **10.** el verano y el invierno

Chapter 2 Review

Ejercicio 2.24 Complete el texto siguiente lógicamente, usando lo que está entre paréntesis como guía. Si no debe ponerse nada en un espacio en blanco, use el símbolo Ø.

Hace como veinte años yo fui a estudiar a **(1)** _____ *(the)* Estados Unidos para obtener **(2)** _____ (un/una/Ø) licenciatura en **(3)** _____ (un/una/Ø) universidad allá. **(4)** _____ *(The)* primer año lo pasé con muchísimos contratiempos causados por **(5)** _____ inglés *(caused by English)*, idioma que en **(6)** _____ entonces *(at that time, back then)* yo casi no comprendía y mucho menos hablaba. Tuve que tomar **(7)** _____ (un/una/Ø) examen para demostrar cuánto inglés sabía, y qué clases necesitaba tomar para poder comprender **(8)** _____ (los/las) conferencias y hacer todos **(9)** _____ (los/las) trabajos escritos durante **(10)** _____ *(my)* futuros estudios en **(11)** _____ *(that)* universidad. Se me hizo muy difícil comprender **(12)** _____ (estas/aquellas) conferencias de biología, dadas en **(13)** _____ (un/una/Ø) enorme salón con otros cientos de estudiantes que, al igual que yo, estaban en **(14)** _____ *(their)* primer año. Recuerdo que casi no podíamos ver **(15)** _____ *(the)* profesor si no teníamos **(16)** _____ *(the)* suerte de sentarnos hacia **(17)** _____ *(the)* frente del salón, cosa que yo siempre trataba de hacer pues se me facilitaba así entender mejor lo que él decía.

(18) _____ *(Some of my)* recuerdos más gratos de **(19)** _____ *(that first year)* fueron de **(20)** _____ *(my new friends)* allá, por medio de los cuales pude comprender y aprender un poco sobre **(21)** _____ *(the culture of that country)* donde iba a vivir durante **(22)** _____ *(so much time)*. No es por nada, pero de verdad que la mía fue **(23)** _____ *(a unique experience)* comparada con **(24)** _____ *(the one)* de muchos que **(25)** _____ *(were better prepared than I was)*. Imagínate **(26)** _____ *(that type)* de estudiante que se la pasa perdiendo el tiempo, yendo a fiestas cada semana, y dejando **(27)** _____ *(their)* trabajo para último minuto, **(28)** _____ (ese/este) mismo que se queja **(29)** _____ *(more strongly than anyone)*. En realidad puedo decir que aproveché **(30)** _____ *(my)* tiempo en Estados Unidos. El último año ya **(31)** _____ *(English)* era parte de **(32)** _____ *(my daily life)*; podía hacer todos los trabajos **(33)** _____ *(without a problem)* y salí **(34)** _____ *(as well as my friends)* en todas las clases que tomé.

¿Qué fue **(35)** _____ *(the best [thing])* de haber estudiado allá? Creo que fue el haber conocido **(36)** _____ *(another culture)* y el haber compartido **(37)** _____ *(mine)* con **(38)** _____ *(many other foreign students)* cuyos intereses y experiencias eran a veces diferentes y otras similares a los míos. **(39)** _____ (El/Lo) bueno fue

(continued)

haber visto en persona **(40)** _____ (the great melting pot [crisol]) de razas y culturas en un ámbito estudiantil y con todos nosotros llenos de esperanzas para **(41)** _____ (a better international future). Por eso, hija mía, yo estoy contentísima de **(42)** _____ (your) interés en estudiar **(43)** _____ (abroad) y apoyo tu decisión.

Ejercicio 2.25 Usando el texto en inglés como base, llene los espacios en blanco con un artículo definido (**el, la, los, las;** si hay contracción: **al, del**), o con un artículo indefinido (**un, una**). Si no se necesita nada, use el símbolo **Ø**.

I love dogs.

I remember when my family and I went to get my first dog. It was Sunday, and my parents took me to the park. Sundays the park had a special event for people who wanted to adopt animals that had been victims of some misfortune. What a surprise! There were more than a hundred animals in the park that Sunday.

In the first hour, I identified ten dogs I liked, but my parents told me I had to choose only one. After another half an hour I was sure I wanted either a small white one or a large black one. In the end, I chose the white one, and I called and I called him Coco because he seemed to be covered in shredded coconut. The only things that didn't look white were his ears; they looked a bit dirty.

When we were about to leave, we saw our neighbor, Mr. Ricardo, who was a bachelor, and wanted a dog to keep him company. He didn't like small dogs so he ended up adopting a big, caramel-colored, very sweet dog. Our neighbor looked happy with his new companion, who was wagging his tail non-stop.

As soon as my parents and I got home, we bathed Coco, and washed his ears well. He ended up all white and happy. And that's how life with Coco began.

Now I know that life without a dog would be sad, and I believe in the saying: "Dog is man's best friend."

Me encantan **(1)** _____ perros.

Recuerdo cuando mi familia y yo fuimos a conseguir mi primer perro. Era **(2)** _____ domingo, y mis padres me llevaron a **(3)** _____ parque. **(4)** _____ domingos, **(5)** _____ parque tenía **(6)** _____ evento especial para **(7)** _____ gente que quería adoptar animales que habían sido víctimas de alguna desgracia. ¡Qué **(8)** _____ sorpresa! Había más de **(9)** _____ cien animales en **(10)** _____ parque ese domingo. En **(11)** _____ primera hora, identifiqué a diez perros que me gustaban, pero mis padres me dijeron que tenía que escoger solo uno. Después de **(12)** _____ otra **(13)** _____ media **(14)** _____ hora estaba seguro de que quería ya sea uno pequeño blanco, o uno grande negro. En fin de cuentas, escogí **(15)** _____ blanco, y lo llamé Coco porque parecía estar cubierto de coco rallado. Lo único que no se le veía blanco eran **(16)** _____ orejas, que se le veían un poco sucias.

Cuando estábamos a punto de irnos, vimos a nuestro vecino, **(17)** _____ señor Ricardo, que era **(18)** _____ soltero, y quería **(19)** _____ perro que le hiciera compañía. No le gustaban **(20)** _____ perros chicos; terminó adoptando uno grande, de color caramelo, muy cariñoso. Se veía feliz con su nuevo compañero, que meneaba **(21)** _____ cola sin parar.

Tan pronto regresamos a **(22)** _____ casa, mis padres y yo le dimos un baño a Coco, y le lavamos bien **(23)** _____ orejas. Quedó todo blanquito y contento. Y así empezó **(24)** _____ vida con Coco.

Ahora sé que **(25)** _____ vida sin **(26)** _____ perro sería triste y creo en **(27)** _____ dicho: "**(28)** _____ perro es **(29)** _____ mejor amigo de **(30)** _____ hombre".

Ejercicio 2.26 Temas de ensayo y de práctica oral

a. Ensayo

Prestando atención al uso de artículos y adjetivos, y a la forma, género y número de los nombres, escriba un párrafo sobre uno de los temas siguientes:

1. describa a su mejor amigo
2. compare a dos de sus amigos
3. describa a su familia

b. Práctica oral

1. Hable con un amigo hispano, y pídale que le describa a los diferentes miembros de su familia. Preste atención para oír cómo los describe, qué adjetivos y artículos usa, cómo usa la **a** personal, y si nominaliza algunos adjetivos. Luego, hágale preguntas más específicas para comparar a los miembros de su familia, practicando sus adjetivos, comparativos y superlativos. Por ejemplo: De tus hermanos, ¿cuál es el más atlético (o la más atlética)? ¿qué deportes le gustan al (a la) menor? ¿y al (a la) mayor? ¿En tu familia, hay alguien que sea más valiente, más original, más listo, más orgulloso, etc. que los demás? ¿Qué miembro de tu familia baila/canta/cocina mejor? etc.

2. En clase, descríbales a sus compañeros la familia de su amigo hispano. Preste atención a los adjetivos, artículos, **a** personal, comparativos y superlativos.

3. Conversación informal: Comparen en grupos sus experiencias de viaje. Presten atención a los adjetivos, artículos, **a** personal, comparativos y superlativos.

(continued)

4. Debate: La mejor mascota. Hagan un debate en clase sobre los gatos y los perros. Comparen las cualidades de estos animales y lo que hace que unos sean mejores que otros como mascotas. Presten atención a los adjetivos, superlativos y comparativos.

5. Encuesta: Fuera de clase, haga una encuesta *(poll)* informal entre estudiantes y profesores hispanos sobre el racismo y el etnocentrismo que han presenciado en su vida. Tome apuntes para preparar un informe *(report)* para la clase. Preste atención a los adjetivos, artículos, **a** personal, comparativos y superlativos.

Chapter 3
Pronouns

A   PERSONAL PRONOUNS

(Grammatical Functions)

Chapter 3.A.1, pages 50–53

Ejercicio 3.1   Conceptual Questions

What is a pronoun? What is its relationship with a noun? What types of grammatical functions can it have in a sentence? What different types of pronouns exist?

Personal Pronouns (Subject Pronouns)

Chapter 3.A.2, pages 53–57

Ejercicio 3.2   Decida si se necesita pronombre sujeto o no.

1. —¿Cuándo salieron? —[Nosotros/Ø] salimos a las siete.   **2.** —¿Quién está ahí? —Soy [yo/Ø].   **3.** —¿Qué hacen? —[Ellos/Ø] están comiendo.   **4.** Mis vecinos sacaron la basura, pero [yo/Ø] no me acordé.   **5.** ¿Tendrías [tú/Ø] tiempo de ayudarme?   **6.** —¿Por qué no está Luis? —[Él/Ø] está enfermo.

Ejercicio 3.3   Traduzca, prestando atención al sujeto: ¿necesita pronombre en español? Para *you*, use el informal singular (tú).

1. *I bought a book.*   **2.** *It is in José's room.*   **3.** *We are going to study together this afternoon.*   **4.** *You have to start your assignments* (tareas) *for tomorrow.*   **5.** *They [your assignments] are long.*   **6.** *I know you studied, but I have not finished yet.*   **7.** *María is here; she wants to talk to you.*   **8.** *In Andalusia, they have access to stem cell research* (investigación con células madre).

Ejercicio 3.4   En el próximo párrafo hay varios momentos de ambigüedad y de repetición innecesaria. Añada *(Add)* los pronombres que faltan y tache *(cross out)* los innecesarios.

Mike y Luisa han sido novios desde hace ya cinco años. Ellos se quieren mucho y ellos se van a casar. Tiene seis años más que ella, pero parece más madura que él.

(continued)

Desde niña había soñado con una boda maravillosa, con toda su familia y sus amigos presentes. Pero no quiere lo mismo que ella: prefiere una boda muy privada, en que solo estén ellos dos, y dos testigos.

Personal Pronouns (Direct Object Pronouns)

Chapter 3.A.3, pages 57–60

Ejercicio 3.5 Reemplace **la comida** con un pronombre y vuelva a escribir cada frase.

1. Traigan la comida. (mandato)   2. Quiero guardar la comida.   3. He guardado la comida.   4. Están cocinando la comida.   5. Compramos la comida.   6. No toques la comida. (mandato)   7. Mira la comida y huele la comida, pero no quiere comer la comida.

Ejercicio 3.6 Vuelva a escribir cada frase reemplazando el objeto directo con un pronombre.

1. Veo a mi vecina por esta ventana.   2. Llevé a mis hijas al banco.   3. No conocen a la maestra.   4. Josefina es un poco extraña; nadie entiende a Josefina.   5. Los vecinos miraban a la muchacha mientras barría la calle.   6. El vendedor llamó a la clienta.   7. Oían a la niña cantar.   8. Oían a la niña cantar la canción.   9. Buscaron a la asesina.   10. Encontraron a la doctora.   11. Invitaron a Anita al baile.   12. Extraño a mi hermana.

Ejercicio 3.7 Vuelva a escribir cada frase reemplazando el objeto directo con un pronombre.

1. Veo a mi vecino por esta ventana.   2. Llevé a mis hijos al banco.   3. No conocen al maestro.   4. Roberto es un poco extraño; nadie entiende a Roberto.   5. Los vecinos miraban al muchacho mientras barría la calle.   6. El vendedor llamó al cliente.   7. Oían al niño cantar.   8. Oían al niño cantar la canción.   9. Buscaron al asesino.   10. Encontraron al doctor.   11. Invitaron a Panchito al baile.   12. Extraño a mi padre.   13. Lloraron al ver salir al primer minero.

Ejercicio 3.8 En el próximo párrafo hay mucha repetición innecesaria. Encuentre los nombres que son objetos directos, tache *(cross out)* los que son innecesarios y reemplácelos con pronombres.

Tengo la costumbre de observar a mis vecinos. Ayer vi a mis vecinos llegar en su coche: habían comprado plantas nuevas; sacaron las plantas del coche y dejaron las plantas en la tierra cerca de la casa porque no podían ponerse de acuerdo sobre dónde poner las plantas. Ella quería meter las plantas en la casa. Él le dijo que prefería las plantas afuera. Ella dijo que el frío de la noche iba a matar las plantas, y él le contestó que era necesario acostumbrar las plantas a los cambios de temperatura. La situación era típica, y terminó como siempre: ella miró mal a su marido y se fue, y él se encogió de hombros y siguió con lo que hacía como si nada. Después de una hora ella llamó a su marido para que entrara a cenar. Yo podía oír sus risas mientras platicaban durante la cena.

Personal Pronouns (Direct and Indirect Object Pronouns)

Chapter 3.A.3–4, pages 57–62

Ejercicio 3.9 Junte las partes para formar frases completas. Reemplace los nombres en negrilla con los pronombres adecuados.

1. los turistas / miraban / **a los indígenas**   **2.** el policía / dijo / **al vagabundo** / que se tenía que ir   **3.** regaló / **sus libros viejos / al asilo**   **4.** mandaron / **el paquete / a su familia**   **5.** el abuelo / contó / **el cuento / a sus nietos**   **6.** hicieron / **la cama / a los huéspedes**   **7.** el padre / quitó / **la llave / a su hijo**   **8.** mi amigo / pidió / **el dinero / a su tía**   **9.** otorgaron / **el premio / a Vargas Llosa**

Ejercicio 3.10 Traduzca lo que no está entre paréntesis.

1. *I beat him (in a game or competition).*   **2.** *I won it (it = the money* = el dinero). **3.** *They robbed him.*   **4.** *They stole it (it = the money* = el dinero).   **5.** *We believe him.*   **6.** *We believe it.*   **7.** *They hit him.*   **8.** *They glued it (it = the map* = el mapa).   **9.** *I paid her.*   **10.** *I paid it (it = the bill* = la cuenta).

Ejercicio 3.11 Siga escribiendo sobre el tema con el contexto indicado en la primera frase, usando los elementos entre paréntesis y haciendo las transformaciones necesarias para evitar la repetición.

MODELO: El candidato dio su presentación ayer. (observamos / al candidato mientras hablaba, / reconocimos / al candidato / como el mejor / y / dijimos / al candidato / que recomendaríamos / al candidato / para el puesto)

El candidato dio su presentación ayer. **Lo** *observamos mientras hablaba,* **lo** *reconocimos como el mejor y* **le** *dijimos que* **lo** *recomendaríamos para el puesto.*

1. Luisa es una amiga mía que va a Chile a estudiar durante un año. (conozco / a Luisa / desde hace cuatro años. / vi / a Luisa / ayer / y / hablé / a Luisa / de su año en el extranjero; prometí / a Luisa / que / escribiría / a Luisa / durante su ausencia)

(continued)

2. El hijo de la señora Ruiz no llegó a su casa en toda la noche. (La señora Ruiz / llamó / a su hijo / a su teléfono celular / y / preguntó / a su hijo / por qué no / había hablado / a ella / de sus planes; / regañó / a su hijo / por su irresponsabilidad; / él / pidió / a ella / que / perdonara / a él)

3. Su adorado perrito nuevo había desaparecido. (Habían estado buscando / al perrito / desde hacía varias horas / cuando por fin oyeron / al perrito / llorando / y / encontraron / al perrito / medio enterrado en el barro; / sacaron / al perrito / y / llevaron / al perrito / a casa donde / dieron / al perrito / un baño)

Ejercicio 3.12 Vuelva a escribir el próximo párrafo usando los pronombres correctos.

Conocí a Elena el primer día que llegué a la universidad, cuando vi (a ella) en el cuarto que íbamos a compartir como compañeras de cuarto. Saludé (a ella) y dije (a ella) que estaba contenta de conocer (a ella). Ella abrazó (a mí) y contó (a mí) con mucho entusiasmo sus planes para la universidad. Poco a poco llegué a conocer (a ella) y cada vez encontraba (a ella) más simpática. Hasta el día en que entró en nuestra vida Julio. Yo vi (a él) primero, un día de frío intenso, en la cafetería, y me enamoré a primera vista. Conté (a ella) de mi experiencia, y lo único que ella quería era conocer (a él), supuestamente por mi bien, para animarme más. Pues no fue así: cuando ella vio (a él) por primera vez, ella quiso (a él) también, y él parecía querer (a ella) de la misma manera. Yo me quedé congelada, mirando (a ella) primero, luego (a él), en unos segundos que parecieron durar una eternidad. Después, dije (a ella) que yo había visto (a él) primero, y que ella no tenía el derecho de quitarme (a él). Como yo nunca había dicho (a él) lo que sentía, sin embargo, y ellos dos evidentemente compartían el mismo sentimiento de amor, yo ya había perdido. Y lo sabía. Ahora, después de muchos años, quiero (a ellos) a los dos, y visito (a ellos) y a su familia cada vez que puedo: están casados y tienen cuatro hijos. Yo nunca me casé, y así me gusta.

Personal Pronouns (Required Repetitive Object Pronouns)

Chapter 3.A.5, pages 62–63

Ejercicio 3.13 Llene cada espacio en blanco con un pronombre repetitivo de objeto directo o indirecto si se necesita. Si no se necesita nada, use el símbolo Ø.

1. Ayer _____ compré el pan. 2. El pan _____ compré ayer. 3. Esta tarde _____ vi a Juan en la tienda. 4. A Juan _____ vi en la tienda esta tarde. 5. El correo _____ llegó hace media hora. 6. Hace media hora que _____ llegó el correo. 7. Marta _____ bañó al niño. 8. Al niño Marta _____ bañó. 9. Toda la gente

_____ vio el globo. **10.** Anoche _____ terminé todos. **11.** Mañana _____ enviaremos el regalo a Marieta. **12.** No _____ digas a Juan el secreto. **13.** Nunca _____ cuentes todo a tus amigos. **14.** Ese día _____ regañaron a todos nosotros. **15.** Con esa lluvia _____ crecerán todas las plantas. **16.** Dicen que a ese presidente _____ eligieron los jóvenes.

Personal Pronouns (Order of Object Pronouns When Combined)

Chapter 3.A.6, pages 63–64

Ejercicio 3.14 Conteste afirmativamente, reemplazando las palabras en negrilla con pronombres, y haciendo los demás cambios necesarios.

1. ¿Te dio **los regalos**? **2.** ¿Les enseñaste **la cosecha a los vecinos**? **3.** ¿Te contó **la noticia**? **4.** ¿Le dijiste **el secreto a Socorro**? **5.** ¿Se limpiaron ustedes **las botas**? **6.** ¿Os enviaron **la carta**?

Personal Pronouns (Position of Object Pronouns)

Chapter 3.A.7, pages 64–65

Ejercicio 3.15 Conteste las preguntas siguientes en el afirmativo, reemplazando las palabras en negrilla con el pronombre adecuado si se necesita pronombre. No use los nombres en negrilla en sus respuestas. No use pronombre si no se necesita.

1. ¿Están preparando **la cena**? **2.** ¿Le pudieron vender **la casa a ese cliente**? **3.** ¿Le va a hacer **los mandados a su suegra**? **4.** ¿Te has enviado **el mensaje a ti mismo**? **5.** ¿**La casa** está pintada? **6.** ¿Te gustó **el restaurante**? **7.** ¿**Joaquín** le dio **las flores a Marina**? **8.** ¿Se habla **español**?

Personal Pronouns (Prepositional Object Pronouns)

Chapter 3.A.8, pages 66–67

Ejercicio 3.16 Traduzca al español. Para *you*, use el informal singular (tú).

1. *This is for you.* **2.** *According to her, it was wrong.* **3.** *They were looking at him.* **4.** *They were looking for him.* **5.** *This is between him and me.* **6.** *Her children are like her.* **7.** *I am talking about you.* **8.** *Sing with me.* **9.** *I will sing with him.* **10.** *She took it away with her.* **11.** *Are you speaking for me?*

Ejercicio 3.17 Escoja la opción correcta entre paréntesis.

1. Elsa no quería ir con (yo, mí, -migo, me) al cine, pero sin (yo, mí, -migo, me) no tendría forma de llegar. A (yo, mí, -migo, me) no me molestaba su actitud, aunque prefería ir sola a ir con (ella, sí, -sigo, se).   **2.** Este dilema lo tendremos que resolver entre (tú y yo, te y me, ti y mí). Nadie más va a hacerlo por (nos, nosotros).   **3.** Tuvieron que presentarse en la corte con su abogado, porque según (él, lo, le, se, sí), si no lo hacían, terminarían en la cárcel.   **4.** No sé dónde está mi iPod. Ayer estuve jugando con (él, lo, le, -sigo) y pensé que lo había dejado aquí.   **5.** Parece que todos menos (tú, te, ti) se enteran de las noticias.   **6.** Mira, hazlo como (yo, me, mí): primero pon tus pies así, luego da un paso con el pie derecho.

Personal Pronouns (Review 1)

Ejercicio 3.18 El párrafo siguiente contiene mucha repetición: tache *(cross out)* los pronombres repetitivos innecesarios, ya sean sujeto, objeto directo u objeto indirecto.

Para Navidad yo siempre he querido ir a la playa, porque desde niña mi padre me acostumbró a mí a celebrar este día lejos de la sociedad materialista, en un rito de comunión con la naturaleza y el universo. Mi hermana, mi padre y yo nosotros íbamos a quedarnos una semana en la playa, y desde el día en que nosotros llegábamos, nosotros empezábamos a juntar leña en un lugar que mi padre escogía en la playa, donde hubiera un enorme tronco para descansar. Nosotros juntábamos leña por toda la playa cada día antes de la Nochebuena, y esa noche, cuando el resto de la gente en el hotel estaba celebrando con grandes banquetes y bailes, nosotros salíamos a escondidas por detrás, nosotros íbamos en la oscuridad a encontrar nuestro sitio escogido, y allí nosotros nos instalábamos para pasar la noche en la playa. Nosotros encendíamos la hoguera con la leña que nosotros habíamos juntado, y nosotros nos recargábamos contra el tronco a mirar el cielo y el mar. En el cielo brillaban las estrellas, y en el mar se veían las luces que echaban unos pececitos minúsculos. Era un espectáculo realmente impresionante. Las olas producían un ritmo que nos calmaba a nosotros. De vez en cuando mi padre rompía el silencio, y él nos contaba a nosotros de sus experiencias como vaquero, o él nos recitaba a nosotros uno de sus poemas, o él nos cantaba a nosotros una canción y él nos pedía a nosotros que nosotros cantáramos también. Son momentos que yo jamás olvidaré. Y por eso ahora que ya yo soy mayor y que mi padre ha muerto, cada vez que llega la época de Navidad, yo me dirijo hacia una playa.

Personal Pronouns (Review 2)

Ejercicio 3.19 El párrafo siguiente contiene mucha repetición: tache *(cross out)* los pronombres repetitivos innecesarios, ya sean sujeto, objeto directo u objeto indirecto.

En ese cuento de fantasía, la protagonista, una joven tímida y bella que se encuentra de visita en el pueblo de su padre, ella se enamora de un joven misterioso. En la escuela, todos sus compañeros ellos los tratan al joven misterioso y a sus hermanos como si ellos fueran extranjeros. De la misma manera, él y sus hermanos ellos se mantienen aparte del resto. La protagonista siente una atracción irreprimible hacia él, pero al principio él no parece tener los mismos sentimientos: la rechaza a ella, le huye a ella, hasta parece sentir repugnancia cuando ella se le acerca a él. Pero en fin de cuentas terminan los dos enamorados, y poco a poco se van desapareciendo los obstáculos y los secretos de la vida de cada uno de ellos. Ella descubre que la familia de él es diferente, es una familia de hijos adoptivos, y ellos tienen costumbres raras y poderes sobrenaturales. Ellos no parecen dormir ni comer nunca, y ellos no salen cuando está asoleado. Por fin ella se da cuenta de que ellos son vampiros, y que el joven a quien ella quiere le huye a ella por temor a sus sentimientos por ella, que podrían empujarlo más allá de los límites que él quiere respetar. Se complica la trama cuando ella descubre que un amigo de la infancia que él vive en el mismo pueblo, y que también él está enamorado de ella, él pertenece a un antiguo clan de licántropos, enemigo de los vampiros.

B Se

(Reflexive Pronouns)

Chapter 3.B.2, pages 68–71

Ejercicio 3.20 Traduzca, usando verbos reflexivos. Para *you*, use el informal singular (tú).

1. *We noticed his smile.*   2. *He fell in love with her.*   3. *We worry about you.*   4. *They found out about the accident the next day.*   5. *I took off my clothes.*   6. *She stayed there.*   7. *We complained about the time.*   8. *He said good-bye to his family.*   9. *They realized it was late.*   10. *They never got used to the weather.*   11. *He does not dare knock at the door.*   12. *They look like their mother.*

Ejercicio 3.21 Reemplace el nombre objeto directo de cada una de las siguientes frases con un pronombre, y luego añada una segunda parte de la frase que sea reflexiva. Use los pronombres que necesite para marcar el énfasis.

MODELO: Veo **a mi hermano.** (…y a mí también…)
Lo veo a él y me veo a mí mismo también.

1. Conocemos **a nuestros amigos.** (…pero a nosotros mejor…)   **2.** Oyes **al cantante.** (…y a ti al mismo tiempo…)   **3.** Roberto respeta **a sus padres.** (…y a Roberto también…)

Ejercicio 3.22 Escoja la opción correcta entre paréntesis. Un guion [-] antes de un pronombre significa que el pronombre va conectado al verbo anterior.

Esa mañana los pájaros (**1. Ø/la/se**) despertaron a Marisol. Después de estirar (**2. Ø/-la/-se/**), ella (**3. Ø/la/se**) levantó, (**4. Ø/la/se**) cepilló los dientes y (**5. Ø/la/se**) bañó. Después del baño, (**6. Ø/la/se**) secó (**7. Ø/a ella/a sí misma**), (**8. Ø/la/se**) maquilló con mucho cuidado, y (**9. Ø/la/se**) peinó (**10. Ø/a ella/a sí misma**) de la manera más sencilla. (**11. Ø/Ella/Se**) miró (**12. Ø/a ella/a sí misma**) en el espejo por buen rato, para asegurar (**13. Ø/-la/-se**) de que todo estuviera perfecto: este día iba a tener la entrevista de trabajo más importante de su vida, y (**14. Ø/la/se**) sentía muy nerviosa. (**15. Ø/Ella/Se**) conocía (**16. Ø/a ella/a sí misma**) muy bien, y (**17. Ø/la/se**) sabía que si no estaba perfectamente presentable, no estaría cómoda en la entrevista. La compañía que (**18. Ø/la/se**) iba a entrevistar (**19. Ø/la/se**) había llamado (**20. Ø/a ella/a sí misma**) la semana anterior para hacer cita para ese día. La madre de Marisol y la dueña de la compañía (**21. Ø/las/se**) conocían (**22. Ø/a ellas/a sí mismas/la una a la otra**) desde antes de que ella naciera, y fue así que Marisol consiguió la cita. Ahora tenía miedo de quedar mal con su madre, porque (**23. Ø/la/se**) sentía que si no conseguía el trabajo, iba a desilusionar (**24. Ø/-la/-se**). Ambas eran mujeres fuertes: Marisol y su madre (**25. Ø/las/se**) conocían bien a sí mismas, pero no (**26. Ø/las/se**) conocían (**27. Ø/a ellas/a sí mismas/la una a la otra**).

Se (Se me Construction: Accidental se)

Chapter 3.B.3, pages 71–74

Ejercicio 3.23 Vuelva a escribir estas frases usando el **se** accidental.

1. Olvidas que me quieres.   **2.** Quemé los plátanos.   **3.** Perdí la cadenita que me regalaste.   **4.** Mojaron su pelo.   **5.** Rompiste tu taza.

Ejercicio 3.24 Traduzca las frases siguientes usando el **se** accidental y los verbos indicados. Para *you*, use el informal singular (tú).

1. *He left his book.* (quedársele a uno)   2. *Our clothes got wet.* (mojársele a uno)
3. *I ran out of coffee.* (acabársele a uno)   4. *Your papers fell.* (caérsele a uno)
5. *She forgot her notes.* (olvidársele a uno)   6. *Their plates broke.* (rompérsele a uno)

Ejercicio 3.25 Llene cada espacio en blanco con lo que falta para completar la frase, usando el modelo como base.

MODELO: A Marta se **le** olvidó el libro.

1. A Jorge se _____ perdió el paraguas.   2. A mí se _____ rompió el jarro.   3. A ella se _____ cayó el guante.   4. Se _____ quemaron los frijoles a ti.   5. A los niños se _____ cierran los ojos.

Ejercicio 3.26 Conjugue cada verbo en la forma correcta del pretérito.

1. Se nos (olvidar) los regalos.   2. A ti se te (olvidar) las llaves.   3. A la niña se le (bajar) los calcetines.   4. A mí se me (romper) la silla.   5. A los vecinos se les (ir) la electricidad.   6. Se os (agotar) la pila.

Ejercicio 3.27 ¿Qué pasó? Describa las situaciones siguientes usando el **se** accidental.

MODELO: Ayer compraste un reloj, pero ahora no lo encuentras.

Se te perdió el reloj.

1. Ayer teníamos una cita, pero no fuimos porque no la habíamos marcado en el calendario.   2. El plato que compraste lo dejaste caer accidentalmente al piso y ahora está roto.   3. La cena que estaba preparando Beto está ahora toda negra, carbonizada.   4. Ayer no pude cargar la batería de mi computadora: no había electricidad en mi casa.   5. Estabas jugando al fútbol y ahora tus zapatos están todos sucios.   6. No tenemos nuestro paraguas: lo dejamos por error en casa.

Personal Pronouns (Review 3)

Ejercicio 3.28 *(Subject, Direct Object, Indirect Object, Prepositional Object, Reflexive, Accidental Se)* El siguiente texto está lleno de repetición excesiva: decida cuáles de las palabras en negrilla necesitan guardarse o no, o sustituirse con un pronombre. Tache *(cross out)* los pronombres innecesarios.

Yo fui estudiante de intercambio hace unos años en México, y cuando **yo** estuve allá, **yo** viví con los Rodríguez, una familia muy simpática y generosa que **yo** nunca olvidaré. Un día cuando **yo** estaba viviendo con **los Rodríguez**, **ellos se** ganaron la lotería, y la vida **se** puso de repente más compleja. Cada uno de **los Rodríguez** quería algo diferente.

Don Carlos, el padre, **él** quería jubilarse porque **él** quería poder pasar más tiempo con la familia; **a él se le** había ocurrido también comprar un yate para que todos pudieran divertir**se** paseándo**se** por el mundo.

Doña Julia, la madre, **ella** nunca había trabajado más que para su familia, y en realidad **ella** no tenía ambiciones. **Ella** deseaba que no **le** faltara nada a ninguno de sus hijos, y **ella** esperaba que el dinero sirviera ese propósito. **Ella** prefería no gastar **el dinero** en nada, sino más bien depositar **el dinero** en el banco. En realidad, **a ella** no **le** gustaba el dinero, **el dinero** representaba para **doña Julia** una maldición, y **ella** hasta **le** tenía un poco de miedo **al dinero**.

Los hijos, Carlitos, Matilde y Rosita, **ellos** tenían cada uno un plan distinto.

Carlitos, el mayor, **él** ya **se** había graduado de la universidad, y **él** estaba buscando trabajo en diferentes bufetes de abogados, pero **él** no había conseguido nada aún. **Él** seguía viviendo con la familia. **Él** se imaginaba que el dinero **le** podría servir **a él** para abrir su propio bufete, y así **él** podría empezar a trabajar solo y ganar suficiente dinero para poder casar**se**.

Matilde estaba todavía en la universidad: **ella** estudiaba medicina. **Ella** era modesta, y **ella** no tenía ningún plan personal para el dinero, sino que veía **el dinero** como un premio para sus padres. **Ella** esperaba que con **este dinero sus padres** pudieran vivir más a gusto. **Sus padres** habían sacrificado tanto para **Matilde** y sus hermanos, que ahora **ellos** se merecían un descanso. **Ella** siempre había sido muy generosa, y **ella** pensaba en los problemas de otros en vez de los suyos. Por ejemplo, una vez, cuando **ella** trabajaba de voluntaria en una escuela de niños pobres, un niño no tenía bastante dinero para comprar**se a sí mismo** los zapatos del uniforme de la escuela, y entonces **ella** usó su propio dinero para comprarle **los zapatos al niño**.

Rosita era la más ambiciosa de todos: para **Rosita** este dinero representaba la liberación posible de toda dependencia. **Ella** quería su parte del dinero para conseguir**se a sí misma** un apartamento y vivir lejos de la familia, independiente y libre. **Yo** conocía mejor **a Rosita** que a los demás, porque **ella** era compañera mía en el colegio y **nosotros** compartíamos la misma habitación en su casa. **Rosita me** contaba **a mí** sus planes de manera muy emocional. Cuando **yo la** escuchaba **a ella**, **yo** podía ver la pasión que **la** impulsaba **a ella**.

Se (Impersonal se)

Chapter 3.B.4, pages 74–78

Ejercicio 3.29 Traduzca usando el **se** impersonal.

1. *The house was sold. When was it sold?* 2. *If you make a mistake, it's not the end of the world.* 3. *The employees were fired. Why were they fired?* 4. *They were not told.*
5. *You do not say that in public.*

Ejercicio 3.30 Las frases que siguen usan la estructura impersonal; escoja la forma correcta del verbo.

1. En algunas partes del mundo hispano se (toma/toman) una siesta por la tarde. 2. En esa tienda se (habla/hablan) español. 3. A los niños se les (dijo/dijeron) que no salieran de noche. 4. En esa época, se (mataba/mataban) a los criminales. 5. Al presidente se le (recibió/recibieron) con gran aplauso. 6. A los estudiantes se les (mandó/mandaron) la información en verano. 7. Al gerente se le (anunció/anunciaron) los cambios hace mucho. 8. Se (vende/venden) libros.
9. Aquí no se (acepta/aceptan) cheques personales. 10. A la jefa ya se le (dio/dieron) las noticias.

Ejercicio 3.31 Traduzca haciendo los cambios necesarios para usar las estructuras más naturales en español.

1. *He was awakened by the noise.* 2. *Naps are taken at noon.* 3. *We were brought up* (criar) *by our mother.* 4. *You were rescued* (rescatar) *by the lifeguard* (salvavidas).
5. *I was moved by the speech.* 6. *She was sent to the hospital.* 7. *Bread was made at home in those days* (en aquel entonces). 8. *The passive is hardly ever* (casi nunca) *used in Spanish.* 9. *The pizza was just delivered.* 10. *A text message was left on her cell phone.*

Ejercicio 3.32 Complete el diálogo siguiente conjugando en el presente del indicativo los verbos entre paréntesis para el **se** impersonal según el contexto lo requiera.

JOSEFA: ¿Qué se (**1.** necesitar) para la cena de mañana? ¿Lo tienes todo? Pienso salir en unos minutos y puedo comprarte lo necesario.

MARTA: Creo que lo tengo todo pero no sé cómo se (**2.** preparar) una tortilla de patatas a la española.

JOSEFA: Bueno, pues se (**3.** necesitar) como ocho huevos, un kilogramo de patatas y poco menos de medio litro de aceite.

MARTA: ¿Cuánto es un kilogramo?

JOSEFA: Como 2.2 libras.

MARTA: Déjame apuntarlo todo en un papel.

JOSEFA: Según recuerdo, primero se (**4.** lavar) las patatas ya peladas, luego se (**5.** secar) y se (**6.** cortar) en láminas bien finitas. Se (**7.** poner) a calentar el aceite en tu sartén más grande y entonces se (**8.** freír) las patatas. Se les (**9.** poder) echar un poco de sal. Cuando ya estén fritas o casi doradas, se (**10.** separar) y se (**11.** poner) a escurrir en un colador. Se le (**12.** sacar) el aceite que sobre en el sartén.

MARTA: ¿Puedo usar otra sartén en vez?

JOSEFA: Seguro, si tienes más de uno. Continúo con la receta, en un tazón aparte se (**13.** batir) los huevos y se (**14.** poner) un poco de sal; en el mismo tazón de los huevos se (**15.** echar) las patatas y se (**16.** mover) con una cuchara o un tenedor. En la sartén que decidas usar se (**17.** poner) como siete cucharadas de aceite para que solo se cubra el fondo. Cuando se caliente la sartén, se (**18.** vertir) la mezcla de huevos y patatas. Se (**19.** mover) la sartén, y así no se (**20.** pegar) la tortilla. Cuando esté bien dorada, se (**21.** poner) una tapa encima, se (**22.** volcar) la sartén y se (**23.** escurrir) la tortilla de nuevo en la sartén. Hazlo poco a poco y con cuidado de no quemarte.

MARTA: Eso me suena difícil y se me puede caer la tortilla al suelo.

JOSEFA: Esa es la parte más difícil pero ve con cuidado y ya verás. ¿Por dónde iba?

MARTA: Cuando ya se (**24.** haber) cocinado por un lado.

JOSEFA: Bien, entonces se (**25.** volver) a mover la sartén y cuando la tortilla esté lista se (**26.** servir) en un lindo recipiente y eso es todo.

MARTA: Se (**27.** poder) servir fría, ¿verdad? porque la quiero preparar de antemano y guardarla.

JOSEFA: Sí, sí. ¿Tienes los ingredientes? Si quieres, regreso a ayudarte con la tortilla cuando termine lo que tengo que hacer.

Ejercicio 3.33 Traduzca lo que falta, usando el **se** impersonal. *(Note that the English verb forms are personal, whereas in Spanish they will be rendered by the impersonal. The translation will not be literal.)*

Questions and Answers about obtaining passports and official documents

Preguntas y Respuestas sobre la obtención de pasaportes y documentos oficiales

Q. Where **can I** get a passport application?

A. **You get them** at public offices like Post Offices, City Hall, or municipal offices where passport applications **are accepted.**

[Q] ¿Dónde (**1**) _____ conseguir una solicitud para un pasaporte?

[A] (**2**) _____ en las oficinas públicas, como el correo, el ayuntamiento u oficinas municipales donde (**3**) _____ solicitudes para pasaportes.

Q. Where **are** the instructions for filling out the passport forms?

A. They **are** on the back of the forms.

[Q] ¿Dónde (**4**) _____ las instrucciones para llenar los formularios?

[A] (**5**) _____ al dorso de los formularios.

Q. What **should I** do in case of a life or death emergency?

A. **Call** the National Passport Information Center (NPIC).

[Q] ¿Qué (**6**) _____ hacer en caso de emergencia de vida o muerte?

[A] (**7**) _____ al NPIC.

Q. How **do I renew** my passport?

A. **You bring in** your expired one, and **we prepare** a new one **for you.**

[Q] ¿Cómo (**8**) _____ un pasaporte?

[A] (**9**) _____ el caducado, y (**10**) _____ uno nuevo.

Q. My passport was lost or stolen. How **do I get** another one?

A. **You apply** in person. **You MUST** turn in Form DS-11. **Do not sign** the form until so **informed. You have to** submit a copy of a document of proof of U.S. citizenship.

(continued)

[Q] En caso de pérdida o de robo del pasaporte, ¿cómo (11) ____ otro?

[A] (12) ____ en persona. (13) ____ entregar el formulario DS11. (14) ____ hasta que (15) ____. (16) ____ entregar una copia de un documento de prueba de ciudadanía estadounidense.

Q. *How long does it take to get a new one?*

A. ***You can*** *get a new one in a day or two.*

[Q] ¿Cuánto tiempo toma conseguir uno nuevo?

[A] (17) ____ obtener uno nuevo en uno o dos días.

Q. *When **I renew** my passport, **do I get** the old one **back**?*

A. *Yes, **we give you** the old, cancelled passport. **It is a good idea** to keep it in a safe place as it is considered proof of your U.S. citizenship.*

[Q] Cuando (18) ____ un pasaporte, ¿ (19) ____ el viejo?

[A] Sí, (20) ____ el viejo pasaporte ya cancelado. (21) ____ mantenerlo en un lugar seguro pues sirve de prueba de su ciudadanía.

Q. *How **do I find out about** the status of my passport application?*

A. ***Contact*** *the NPIC.*

[Q] ¿Cómo (22) ____ el estado de la solicitud?

[A] (23) ____ en contacto con el NPIC.

Q. *How **do I get** a certified copy of my birth certificate?*

A. ***Call*** *the Vital Statistics office in the state in which you were born.*

[Q] ¿Cómo (24) ____ una copia certificada del acta de nacimiento?

[A] (25) ____ a la oficina del Vital Statistics de su estado natal.

Q. *What if there is an error in the passport **I just** received?*

A. *Passport Services **sends you** apologies for the error in your passport. **You must** return the new passport and evidence to document the correct information.*

[Q] ¿Qué pasa en caso de error en el pasaporte que (26) ____ de recibir?

[A] (27) ____ disculpas por los errores cometidos. (28) ____ devolver el pasaporte nuevo junto con toda evidencia necesaria como prueba para rectificar el error.

Ejercicio 3.34 Temas de ensayo y de práctica oral

a. Ensayo

Escriba un párrafo sobre algunos aspectos de su cultura, y cómo se contrasta con otra. Indique lo que se hace y lo que no se hace en su cultura, prestando atención al uso correcto del **se** impersonal. No use la voz pasiva con **ser**.

b. Práctica oral

Hable con un(a) compañero(a) sobre sus observaciones de diferencias culturales. Indique lo que se hace y lo que no se hace en su cultura, prestando atención al uso correcto del **se** impersonal. No use la voz pasiva con **ser**.

C DEMONSTRATIVE AND POSSESSIVE PRONOUNS

Chapter 3.C.1–2, pages 78–80

Ejercicio 3.35 Traduzca.

1. That application was more expensive than this one. 2. "Which printer do you prefer?" "I liked that one better." 3. "Give me that." "What? This?" 4. My sister is as brave as yours. 5. "My parents are coming for graduation. What about yours?" (What about = ¿Y... ?) "Mine are not coming." 6. That medicine is his. 7. "Which towel is yours?" "This one is mine and that one is yours." 8. "Whose keys are these?" "These are yours (formal sing.), these are his, and these are hers." 9. I'll take this pill today, and that one tomorrow.

Ejercicio 3.36 Indique las opciones entre paréntesis que NO podrían usarse.

1. Me gusta la otra casa más que (ésa, ésta, esa, esta, la suya, suya). 2. Ese programa no es tan divertido como (el mío, tuyo, éste, este). 3. No quiero esta computadora. Prefiero la pantalla de (aquélla, esa, la) que vimos en la otra tienda. 4. ¿Qué es (ese, eso) postre? Parece mejor que (éste, este, el nuestro, nuestros). 5. (Ese, Aquello, Eso) es algo que se vería en el Cirque du Soleil.

D INTERROGATIVES

Chapter 3.D, pages 81–85

Ejercicio 3.37 Traduzca usando los pronombres interrogativos. Para *you*, use el informal singular (tú).

1. How did they arrive? 2. How much sugar do you use? 3. Which color do you like? 4. Which one do you want? 5. How far is the store from here? 6. Which one is your name? (on a list) 7. What is your name? 8. How many books did you buy? 9. How often do you go?

Ejercicio 3.38 Siguiendo el modelo, haga una pregunta que tenga como respuesta la palabra o las palabras que aparecen en negrilla en cada una de las siguientes frases.

MODELO: Me llamo **Héctor**.
    ¿Cómo te llamas?

1. Es un **programa**.   2. Lo ganó **Vargas Llosa**.   3. Tengo **veinte** años.
4. Vivo en **Bolivia**.   5. Soy de **Perú**.   6. Cerré la ventana **porque tenía frío**.
7. Llegamos **a las diez de la noche**.   8. **Este** es el mío.   9. **La diferencia entre las dos películas** es que una es más vieja que la otra.   10. **Bien, gracias,** ¿y tú?

Ejercicio 3.39 Transforme las preguntas directas en indirectas, empezando la frase con lo que hay entre paréntesis. No se olvide de mantener el orden correcto de verbo y sujeto.

1. ¿De dónde son los aztecas? (Quieren saber…)   2. ¿Cuál es la religión? (Me pregunto…)   3. ¿Dónde vivían los incas? (Les interesa saber…)   4. ¿Cuánto dinero gana un arqueólogo? (Quieren averiguar…)   5. ¿Cómo conoció Romeo a Julieta? (Se le olvidó…)   6. ¿Quién era el actor? (No recordaba…)

E EXCLAMATIVES

Chapter 3.E, pages 85–88

Ejercicio 3.40 Traduzca, usando los exclamativos.

1. *What a scandal!*   2. *How original!*   3. *What an amusing game!*   4. *What good coffee!*   5. *How fast you run!*   6. *How the birds sing!*   7. *We loved her so much!*   8. *I am so hungry!*   9. *We visited so many countries!*   10. *I wish I could fly the way they do!*

Ejercicio 3.41 Llene cada espacio en blanco con el exclamativo correcto.

1. ¡_____ agua más fría!   2. ¡_____ se ríen!   3. ¡_____ delicioso!   4. ¡_____ ojos tan verdes tienes!   5. ¡_____ me alegro de que puedas venir a la fiesta!
6. ¡_____ hermanos tienes!   7. ¡_____ blanca se ve la nieve!   8. ¡_____ buena película!   9. ¡_____ comen esos niños!   10. ¡_____ suerte!

F INDEFINITES AND NEGATIVES

Chapter 3.F, pages 88–91

Ejercicio 3.42 Traduzca. Para *you*, use el informal singular (tú).

1. *Something fell.* 2. *Someone spoke.* 3. *I do not see anyone.* 4. *Do you need anything?* 5. *I do not want anything.* 6. "*Maybe one of the neighbors saw him.*" "*No, none of them saw him.*" 7. "*I went to the movies yesterday.*" "*I did too.*" 8. "*John could not see.*" "*We could not either.*" 9. "*Have you ever been to Peru?*" "*No, I have never been there. Someday I will go. My sister went there once and liked it.*" 10. *I cannot find my earphones anywhere. I know they are somewhere in this room.*

Ejercicio 3.43 Escoja la mejor opción de cada grupo entre paréntesis.

1. Jorge llamó esta mañana para preguntar si (alguien, algún, cualquiera, nadie) podría llevarlo al aeropuerto. 2. Me gustaría encontrar (algo, alguien, algún) para ponerme que no me dé calor. 3. Aquí no hay (alguien, cualquiera, nadie, ningún) que sepa bailar el tango. 4. Ese pintor es terrible; (alguien, cualquiera, nadie) podría hacer un mejor trabajo que él. 5. La fotógrafa de la boda sacó fotos maravillosas, pero yo no aparezco en (alguna, cualquiera, ninguna) de ellas.

G RELATIVE PRONOUNS

Chapter 3.G, pages 92–98

Ejercicio 3.44 Llene cada espacio en blanco con el pronombre relativo que mejor convenga.

1. Hay momentos en la vida _____ no se olvidarán nunca. 2. La mujer _____ vive ahí es famosa. 3. El libro _____ nosotros compramos era caro. 4. _____ me atrae de la universidad es el ambiente intelectual. 5. Natalia es _____ sabe bailar el merengue. 6. Esa es la casa en _____ filmaron la película. 7. El actor _____ aparece en esa película es muy arrogante en la vida real. 8. El político _____ fue elegido no era muy popular, _____ sorprendió a muchos extranjeros. 9. Llegó y apagó el televisor, _____ estaba a todo volumen. 10. La razón por _____ hice eso fue que sabía que no me iban a dejar en paz. 11. Esta es la estatua frente a _____ nos besamos por primera vez, ¿te acuerdas? 12. Ese es el pueblo _____ calles son las más limpias. 13. _____ busca, encuentra. 14. _____ me cae bien es Roberto. 15. Esa música es _____ tocaban en la película.

Ejercicio 3.45 Traduzca.

1. The person who called asked for you.   2. What he gave you was stolen.   3. I do not like what they do.   4. That is the result I was waiting for.   5. The one who sang that song was Lady Gaga.

Ejercicio 3.46 Elimine todos los paréntesis, y junte la información en frases completas, usando pronombres relativos cada vez que se necesite para evitar la repetición.

Un amigo mío (se llama Ernesto) me llamó de Florida. Me contó de su perrito (había comprado el perrito hacía tres semanas) (el perrito estaba dormido a su lado). Ernesto me contó que Chico (Ernesto le dio este nombre al perrito) estaba destruyendo el apartamento (¡Ernesto había conseguido el apartamento con tanta dificultad!) (Ernesto había gastado todo su dinero en el apartamento). Pero Ernesto no quería deshacerse de este perrito (el perrito ahora era su mejor amigo). Por eso Ernesto me pidió que le mandara el dinero (él me había prestado el dinero hacía más de un año).

Chapter 3 Review

Ejercicio 3.47 Vuelva a escribir el texto que sigue, llenando los espacios en blanco con pronombres personales, relativos, demostrativos, posesivos, interrogativos, negativos o indefinidos; si no necesita nada para un espacio en blanco, use el símbolo Ø; algunos espacios en blanco pueden tener más de una palabra. Si el pronombre va conectado al verbo anterior, escríbalo todo junto.

Los conquistadores llegaron a las Américas a partir del siglo XV. Al ver **(1)** _____ acercarse a sus costas, los indígenas salieron a recibir **(2)** _____ con los brazos abiertos. Nunca se imaginaron que las decoraciones que usaban para adornar sus cuerpos casi desnudos **(3)** _____ interesarían tanto a estos hombres blancos. Tampoco comprendieron por qué **(4)** _____ eran tan agresivos ni qué causaba esas fiebres que **(5)** _____ daban a tantos de los suyos y que **(6)** _____ mataban eventualmente.

Bajo el manto de la religión estos forasteros blancos **(7)** _____ dijeron a los indígenas que tenían que creer en otro Dios, **(8)** _____ obligaron a escuchar toda la retórica sobre el bien y el mal que **(9)** _____ imponía la religión católica a cambio de donaciones de sus metales preciosos.

Poco a poco los conquistadores **(10)** _____ llevaron todos los tesoros **(11)** _____ encontraron en su camino, **(12)** _____ destruyeron la naturaleza y el espíritu de los indígenas; a **(13)** _____ quitaron el poder **(14)** _____ tenían, la tierra en **(15)** _____ vivían, las creencias **(16)** _____ practicaban, y muchas veces hasta la vida. **(17)** _____ dejaron sin **(18)** _____, o peor aún, **(19)** _____ impusieron otra existencia, en **(20)** _____ de reyes se transformaban en esclavos y en **(21)** _____ tenían que construir iglesias para practicar una religión diferente a **(22)** _____, murallas para proteger los nuevos gobiernos establecidos por los conquistadores para dominar **(23)** _____ a ellos y edificios en **(24)** _____ estos nuevos gobernadores controlarían el continente que antes fue **(25)** _____.

El idioma **(26)** _____ hablaban los nuevos **(27)** _____ convirtió en el idioma **(28)** _____ todos debían hablar, y poco a poco los indígenas fueron perdiendo hasta su identidad con su lengua y la pureza de su raza.

Esta historia dejó marcado el espíritu de esta gente, **(29)** _____ se transformó de una gente saludable y fuerte con ideas claras sobre el universo en una gente **(30)** _____ único deseo era derrotar a los que **(31)** _____ habían derrotado a ellos. Los siglos fueron marcando la historia con guerras de independencia seguidas de gobiernos tiránicos **(32)** _____ imitaban al enemigo **(33)** _____ habían echado.

Hoy en día, cuando existe la posibilidad de que **(34)** _____ formen gobiernos pacíficos y tolerantes, la ambigüedad permanece muchas veces en el alma de estos pueblos **(35)** _____ nunca podrán olvidar por completo las crueldades a **(36)** _____ fueron sometidos.

En fin de cuentas, ¿**(37)** _____ somos? Algunos de nuestros antepasados fueron ya sea aztecas, o incas, o mayas, o tahínos o de algún otro pueblo; y **(38)** _____ fueron europeos de sangre conquistadora; y **(39)** _____ fueron africanos de sangre real convertida a la esclavitud. Ahora somos una mezcla, somos hispanos, latinos, americanos, hispanoamericanos, latinoamericanos, mestizos. Y con cada continente **(40)** _____ se añadía a la mezcla, venían sus cargas espirituales, sus tradiciones; y en la unión se formaba la multiplicidad de seres **(41)** _____ todos llevamos dentro.

Ejercicio 3.48 Temas de ensayo y de práctica oral

a. Ensayo

1. Escriba un brevísimo resumen de una película que trata de relaciones entre individuos.
2. Escríbale una cartita a un amigo (o amiga), contándole los chismes más recientes de un amigo (o amiga) de ambos.
3. Describa su relación con su(s) compañero(s) de cuarto, o con su(s) hermano(s) o con sus amigos.

(continued)

4. Escriba la biografía de un personaje famoso, como por ejemplo de un conquistador, de un libertador o de un gran revolucionario o político. Ejemplos: Cristóbal Colón, Hernán Cortés, Simón Bolívar, Che Guevara, Evita Perón.
5. Describa de manera paralela a dos individuos famosos, por ejemplo: Penélope Cruz y Salma Hayek, Juan Luis Guerra y Alejandro Sanz, Javier Bardem y Benicio del Toro.

b. Práctica oral

1. Pídale a un amigo hispano que le describa su película favorita. Preste atención, y escuche cómo usa los pronombres personales para referirse a los diferentes personajes, si usa pronombre relativo (el actor que…, el edificio en que…, no sabía lo que…, etc.), demostrativo (ese, aquel, etc.) o posesivo (la suya, el suyo, etc.), indefinido (alguien, unos, etc.) o negativo (nadie, ninguno, etc.). Usando los interrogativos y exclamativos, mientras su amigo describe la película, comente (¡qué extraño!, ¡qué horror! etc.), y hágale preguntas (¿qué edad tenía ese personaje? ¿de dónde era? etc.).
2. En clase, cuénteles a sus compañeros la película favorita de su amigo hispano. Preste atención a sus pronombres personales, relativos, demostrativos, posesivos, indefinidos y negativos.
3. Conversación informal: Hablen en grupos sobre sus héroes favoritos. Que cada quien cuente lo que le interesa de la vida de su héroe, y justifique por qué lo considera un héroe. Presten atención a todos sus pronombres.
4. Debate: La fama y la pérdida de privacidad. Discuta con sus amigos los problemas que tienen hoy en día los actores y la gente famosa con la persecución de los reporteros, usando ejemplos específicos. Presten atención a todos sus pronombres.
5. Encuesta: Películas hispanas favoritas. Fuera de clase, haga una encuesta *(poll)* informal entre estudiantes y profesores hispanos sobre sus películas hispanas favoritas, y sus actores favoritos. Pregúnteles sobre lo que consideran de mayor importancia hoy en día como progreso de la presencia hispana en los diferentes medios (cine, televisión, etc.). Tome apuntes para preparar un informe *(report)* para la clase. Preste atención a todos sus pronombres.

Analicen los diversos informes de sus compañeros, haciendo comparaciones y contrastes entre sus datos.

Chapter 4
Prepositions, Adverbs, Conjunctions, and Transitions

A PREPOSITIONS

(Function of Prepositions)
Chapter 4.A.1, pages 100–102

Ejercicio 4.1 Conceptual Questions

What is a preposition? Explain its name. What is its relationship with a noun? What is a conjunction? Explain its name. What is the difference between a conjunction of coordination and a conjunction of subordination?

Prepositions (Individual Prepositions: a, con, de, en)
Chapter 4.A.3.a–d, pages 103–113

Ejercicio 4.2 Llene cada espacio en blanco con **a, al, de, del, en, con** o **Ø** (nada), según parezca más lógico.

1. Asistiré _____ clase _____ cuanto me alivie.   2. Comenzaron _____ cocinar ayer.   3. Creo que _____ lo mejor se encuentre _____ Margarita _____ la ciudad.   4. Decidieron caminar _____ vez de manejar; nunca llegarán _____ pie.   5. Dudo que puedan influir _____ su decisión.   6. El mercado está _____ dos kilómetros.   7. El programa consiste _____ varios segmentos; en el primero, se trata _____ la Revolución mexicana.   8. Ella me gana _____ veces, y se burla _____ mí.   9. Este bordado está hecho _____ mano; este otro, _____ cambio, está hecho _____ máquina.   10. Fuimos _____ la tienda _____ el coche _____ mi padre _____ mis cuatro hermanitos.

Ejercicio 4.3 Llene cada espacio en blanco con **a, al, de, del, en, con** o **Ø** (nada), según parezca más lógico.

1. Iremos al trabajo _____ pesar de la tormenta.   2. La gente _____ barrio estaba _____ mal humor.   3. La mujer _____ ojos verdes trabaja _____ la tienda _____

(continued)

la esquina. **4.** Llegarán _____ eso de las cinco _____ tal de que no nieve.
5. Lo mediremos _____ ojo. **6.** Me detuve _____ echarle gasolina al carro.
7. Me acosté _____ las diez _____ coraje. **8.** Me enojé _____ ellos porque los dos estaban hablando _____ la vez. **9.** Me gusta montar _____ caballo _____ vez en cuando. **10.** Me invitaron _____ cenar _____ un restaurante que se especializa _____ comida mexicana.

Ejercicio 4.4   Llene cada espacio en blanco con **a, al, de, del, en, con** o Ø (nada), según parezca más lógico.

1. Nadie se había fijado _____ el cambio que ocurrió desde que se habían quejado _____ su horario. **2.** Necesitamos tratar esto más _____ fondo, pero _____ este momento no tengo tiempo. **3.** No veo _____ mis amigos _____ estos lentes.
4. Nos pusimos _____ llorar cuando nos enteramos _____ terremoto que hubo _____ Los Ángeles. **5.** Nunca se resignará _____ ser menos famoso. **6.** Por favor, lleguen _____ tiempo (*puntualmente*). **7.** Quisiera que se rieran _____ mis chistes, y no _____ mí. **8.** _____ cuanto empezó a ir a la escuela, Roberta aprendió _____ defenderse. **9.** Sabemos que tardan mucho _____ llegar a su destino.
10. Se casó _____ ella _____ los tres años de ser su novio.

Ejercicio 4.5   Llene cada espacio en blanco con **a, al, de, del, en, con** o Ø (nada), según parezca más lógico.

1. Se enamoró _____ ella cuando le enseñó _____ bailar el tango. **2.** Se negó _____ tomarse la píldora. **3.** Se quedaron _____ mis propuestas _____ vez de las suyas. **4.** Si esos niños no dejan _____ meterse _____ mi hijo, tendré que hablar _____ sus padres. **5.** Soñé _____ mi novia. **6.** Su hijo le pidió _____ dinero porque pensaba _____ comprarle un regalo a su madre. **7.** Subían _____ la montaña _____ frecuencia. **8.** Van _____ regalarle una novela _____ misterio. **9.** Ves a tus padres _____ menudo, y ellos siempre se alegran _____ verte. **10.** Volvieron _____ sentarse _____ frente de mí.

Ejercicio 4.6   Llene cada espacio en blanco con **a, al, de, del, en, con** o Ø (nada), según parezca más lógico.

1. Ya empezaron _____ salir las flores. **2.** _____ fuerza de hacer tanto ejercicio, bajó de peso. **3.** _____ niña, se acostumbró _____ desayunar temprano.
4. _____ repente tuvieron que entrar _____ causa de la tormenta. **5.** _____ respecto a ese asunto, parece que lo resolvieron ayer. **6.** ¿Me podrían ayudar _____ terminar este trabajo? **7.** —¿Qué haces? —Estoy buscando _____ mi libreta _____ direcciones. **8.** ¿Te atreverás _____ jugar? **9.** Le presté el libro _____ mi amigo _____ buena gana. **10.** Estudiamos _____ Miami.

Ejercicio 4.7 Llene cada espacio en blanco con **a, al, de, del, en, con** o **Ø** (nada), según parezca más lógico.

1. Iremos _____ tal de que no llueva.   2. —Anoche nevó. —¿_____ veras?
3. Mis hijos aprenderán _____ tocar el piano desde muy jóvenes.   4. Pienso _____ ti _____ menudo.   5. ¿Qué piensan tus padres _____ mis amigos?   6. No te olvides _____ traerte las llaves.   7. Nunca dejarán _____ quererte.   8. Pronto se acostumbrarán _____ la comida picante.   9. Decidí ir de compras _____ vez de estudiar.   10. La tormenta empezó _____ repente.   11. _____ veces es saludable no hacer nada.   12. ¿Tú te atreves _____ hablarle?   13. No pudimos ir _____ causa de la lluvia.   14. Mis padres nunca consentirán _____ dejarme ir contigo.

Prepositions (Individual Prepositions: **para, por**)

Chapter 4.A.3.e–f, pages 114–117

Ejercicio 4.8 Llene. cada espacio en blanco con **por, para** o **Ø** (nada), según parezca más lógico.

1. Fueron al centro _____ visitar el museo.   2. Fueron al mercado _____ verduras.   3. Toma: este regalo es _____ ti.   4. Viajaron _____ toda la isla.
5. Hay _____ lo menos quinientas personas aquí.   6. Prometieron que terminarían toda la construcción en el edificio _____ el semestre entrante.   7. Me gusta pasearme _____ la mañana.   8. Pasaremos _____ casa de tu abuelita en camino al partido.   9. Lo dijeron _____ que sus vecinos lo oyeran _____ lo que implicaba sobre sus hijos.   10. _____ fin llegó el cartero.

Ejercicio 4.9 Llene cada espacio en blanco con **por, para** o **Ø** (nada), según parezca más lógico.

1. Buscó _____ el documento en su disco duro, pero no lo encontró.   2. ¡Cálmate! ¡No es _____ tanto!   3. Necesito medicina _____ curarme.   4. Lo tomaron _____ idiota.
5. Espera _____ mi mensaje.   6. Fueron a la tienda _____ comprar lo necesario.   7. Te agradezco _____ la ayuda.   8. No pudieron salir _____ la tormenta.   9. La llamaremos _____ teléfono.   10. Saldrán _____ Madrid en la madrugada.

Ejercicio 4.10 Llene cada espacio en blanco con **por, para** o **Ø** (nada), según parezca más lógico.

1. —¿Quieres bailar? —¡_____ supuesto!   2. No estaba _____ bromas.
3. _____ lo general no me gusta levantarme tarde.   4. _____ más dinero que gane, no es feliz.   5. Tendremos que comprar _____ lo menos cuatro docenas.
6. Le queda un trabajo _____ escribir.   7. Se enfermó _____ comer tanto.

(continued)

8. _____ llegar al museo, hay que pasar _____ el parque. **9.** Acabo de entrar; _____ eso tengo frío. **10.** Jorge se esfuerza _____ sacar las mejores notas de la clase.

Prepositions (Review)

Ejercicio 4.11 Traduzca las oraciones, prestando atención a las preposiciones. Puede ser cualquier preposición, o ninguna. Para *you*, use el informal singular (tú).

1. *They worry about you.* 2. *He fell in love with her.* 3. *It consists of two sections.* 4. *The decision depends on all of us.* 5. *They laughed at him.* 6. *I dream about you every night.* 7. *They said good-bye to her.* 8. *I do not want my ideas to influence your decision.* 9. *She married my brother.* 10. *He stopped drinking.*

Ejercicio 4.12 Traduzca las oraciones, prestando atención a las preposiciones. Puede ser cualquier preposición, o ninguna. Para *you*, use el informal singular (tú).

1. *We arrived in Santa Cruz de Tenerife at two.* 2. *She opposes everything I say.* 3. *I try to help.* 4. *I realized my mistake.* 5. *She thanked me for the favor.* 6. *We got onto the bus.* 7. *Their house is five miles away.* 8. *I met my friends at the restaurant.* 9. *She studies at the university.* 10. *They will be the first to leave.*

Ejercicio 4.13 Traduzca las oraciones, prestando atención a las preposiciones. Puede ser cualquier preposición, o ninguna. Para *you*, use el informal singular (tú).

1. *We must think about the environment* (el medio ambiente) *every day.* 2. *The solution proposed by the president is debatable* (discutible). 3. *I noticed the change.* 4. *At this moment I am helping another customer.* 5. *They became angry at me because of my mistake.* 6. *We looked at the clock.* 7. *He saw his sister.* 8. *I asked you for money, not for advice.* 9. *I just ate.* 10. *They work for me.*

Ejercicio 4.14 Traduzca las oraciones, prestando atención a las preposiciones. Puede ser cualquier preposición, o ninguna. Para *you*, use el informal singular (tú).

1. *I sent it airmail.* 2. *They went to the store for bread.* 3. *I have two papers left to write.* 4. *We will have finished by ten.* 5. *For a child, he knows a lot.* 6. *They left for Guatemala yesterday.* 7. *They are looking for their keys.* 8. *They talked for three hours.* 9. *She worries about you.* 10. *What is this for?*

Ejercicio 4.15 Llene cada espacio en blanco con la preposición adecuada; si no se necesita nada, use el símbolo Ø.

Cuando primero llegué **(1)** _____ Guadalajara, viví **(2)** _____ un apartamento con mi esposa María y mis dos hijas. Fuimos **(3)** _____ esa ciudad porque María es **(4)** _____ allí, y **(5)** _____ esta manera ella podía estar cerca **(6)** _____ su familia.

Al principio yo daba clases **(7)** _____ el instituto cultural, pero el salario no era suficiente **(8)** _____ pagar el alquiler de una casa. **(9)** _____ eso empecé a buscar **(10)** _____ otros trabajos, y después de unos años alquilé una casa, y pudimos entonces vivir más cómodamente.

Ejercicio 4.16 Llene cada espacio en blanco con la preposición adecuada; si no se necesita nada, use el símbolo Ø. Si es necesaria una contracción de **a** o **de** con el artículo, ponga **al** o **del**.

Esta mañana llegué **(1)** _____ la cancha **(2)** _____ tenis **(3)** _____ mi mejor amiga, Sofía, porque queríamos practicar **(4)** _____ un poco antes **(5)** _____ tener que irnos **(6)** _____ el trabajo. Ambas trabajamos **(7)** _____ el centro y nos preocupamos **(8)** _____ llegar **(9)** _____ tiempo; **(10)** _____ eso tuvimos que empezar **(11)** _____ temprano nuestra práctica. **(12)** _____ poder jugar ahí tenemos que pagarle **(13)** _____ una mensualidad **(14)** _____ el club pero no es mucho. También, tenemos que vestirnos **(15)** _____ blanco porque así son las reglas **(16)** _____ el club. La cancha se encuentra **(17)** _____ una localidad muy lejos **(18)** _____ el centro. Hoy nos hubiera gustado quedarnos **(19)** _____ buena gana todo el día porque no teníamos ganas **(20)** _____ regresar **(21)** _____ el centro.

Ejercicio 4.17 Llene cada espacio en blanco con la expresión preposicional más apropiada para traducir lo que se encuentra entre paréntesis.

a caballo, a eso de, a la vez, a pesar de, a pie, de pie, a veces, al menos, en cambio, enseguida, por lo general

Los vecinos de la finca tenían toda clase de vehículos, y **(1)** _____ *(generally)* venían en camioneta, aunque **(2)** _____ *(sometimes)* también venían **(3)** _____ *(on foot)*, **(4)** _____ *(in spite of)* la distancia; ese día, **(5)** _____ *(however)*, vinieron a visitarnos **(6)** _____ *(on horseback)*. **(7)** _____ *(Around)* las cuatro de la tarde los vimos de lejos, todos **(8)** _____ *(at once)*, y **(9)** _____ *(immediately)* entramos a preparar algo de comer, porque así es en el campo, cuando viene alguien, hay que ofrecerle de beber y de comer, y darle la hospitalidad que se merece. **(10)** _____ *(At least)* hay que tener algo para ofrecerles. Entraron, y se sentaron en la sala. Algunos se quedaron **(11)** _____ *(standing)*, pero todos se veían muy contentos.

Ejercicio 4.18 Llene cada espacio en blanco con la expresión preposicional más apropiada para traducir lo que se encuentra entre paréntesis.

con tal de que, de esta manera, de vez en cuando, de modo que, con respecto a, de nuevo, de veras, de mala gana

(continued)

(1) _____ *(Regarding)* la cuestión de los salarios, el patrón está de acuerdo que se les aumente el salario a los empleados, **(2)** _____ *(so long as)* no se pase del tres por ciento, aunque en realidad tengo que decirle que el patrón aceptó esta idea **(3)** _____ *(unwillingly)*. En el futuro empleará gente nueva cada año, y **(4)** _____ *(this way)* se evitará tantos aumentos que **(5)** _____ *(really)* no se puede costear. **(6)** _____ *(Once in a while)* tendrá que aumentar **(7)** _____ *(again)* el sueldo de base **(8)** _____ *(so that)* no haya quejas demasiado extremas.

Ejercicio 4.19 Llene cada espacio en blanco con la expresión preposicional más apropiada para traducir lo que se encuentra entre paréntesis.

a tiempo, en cuanto, en cuanto a, enfrente de, en vez de, para siempre, por eso, por fin, por lo menos, por otra parte, por poco, por más que, por supuesto

¡**(1)** _____ *(Almost)* nos perdemos el concierto! **(2)** _____ *(Instead of)* tomar un taxi, decidimos viajar en autobús, y **(3)** _____ *(for that reason)* no teníamos ningún control sobre el tiempo. **(4)** _____ *(On the other hand, Besides)*, ninguno de nosotros había comprado boletos, **(5)** _____ *(however much)* hubiéramos discutido la necesidad de hacerlo temprano. **(6)** _____ *(In regard to, As far as . . . is concerned)* Roberto, pues **(7)** _____ *(of course)* no nos va a dejar olvidar que **(8)** _____ *(as soon as)* decidimos ir al concierto él nos dijo que consiguiéramos los boletos antes de ir porque si no tendríamos que esperar horas haciendo cola. **(9)** _____ *(Finally)* entramos justo **(10)** _____ *(on time)*, y pudimos disfrutar con el concierto. Pero tuve la mala suerte de tener **(11)** _____ *(in front of)* mí a un tipo con tanto pelo que yo no podía ver nada. Pero **(12)** _____ *(at least)* pude oír la música. Este será un recuerdo que guardaremos **(13)** _____ *(forever)*.

Ejercicio 4.20 Llene cada espacio en blanco con la preposición correcta o con el símbolo Ø (nada) si no se necesita preposición.

Acabo **(1)** _____ acordarme **(2)** _____ mi cita con el nuevo dentista. Le agradezco muchísimo **(3)** _____ la ayuda que me da. Él siempre se alegra **(4)** _____ verme, y se apresura **(5)** _____ atenderme con cuidado. Pero a fin de cuentas no me acostumbro **(6)** _____ este nuevo dentista: el problema es que no deja **(7)** _____ hablar, y yo, claro, no puedo contestar porque tengo la boca llena de instrumentos: hasta platica conmigo en español, se avergüenza **(8)** _____ sus errores, se burla **(9)** _____ sí mismo porque se da cuenta **(10)** _____ su falta de práctica. Aprendió **(11)** _____ hablar español en la universidad, y luego se casó **(12)** _____ una colombiana; convinieron **(13)** _____ hablar inglés la mayor parte del tiempo porque querían que sus hijos hablaran el idioma del país, y que no se convirtieran

(14) _____ extranjeros en su propio país. Sin embargo, cada vez que puede, ella lo ayuda **(15)** _____ practicar su español para que no se le olvide.

Yo lo dejo **(16)** _____ hablar porque no me queda otra opción, pero francamente ya no puedo más. Mis amigos creen que estoy exagerando, e insisten **(17)** _____ que no es para tanto. Pero yo quiero comenzar **(18)** _____ buscar **(19)** _____ otro dentista, pero no sé si me voy a atrever **(20)** _____ explicarle por qué me voy.

Ejercicio 4.21 Llene cada espacio en blanco con la preposición correcta, con la **a** personal o con el símbolo Ø si no se necesita nada.

Pensó que estaba enamorado **(1)** _____ Blanca hasta que se encontró **(2)** _____ Victoria y se enamoró **(3)** _____ ella a primera vista. Desde ese momento su vida dependía **(4)** _____ ella, y no se detuvo **(5)** _____ pensar en el efecto que tendría en Blanca el que él se despidiera **(6)** _____ ella así, sin motivo, sin siquiera enojarse **(7)** _____ ella.

Cuando Blanca supo lo que había pasado, se empeñó **(8)** _____ quedarse **(9)** _____ su novio, y empezó **(10)** _____ hacer planes de toda clase para enterarse **(11)** _____ todos los movimientos de ambos. La vida le había enseñado **(12)** _____ ser fuerte, y pensaba **(13)** _____ que si se esforzaba **(14)** _____ obtener algo, lo conseguiría. En la universidad, se había especializado **(15)** _____ sicología, y se había fijado **(16)** _____ las injusticias que podían surgir si uno no insistía **(17)** _____ conseguir lo mejor para uno mismo.

Decidió **(18)** _____ llamar **(19)** _____ Victoria y pedirle que no se metiera **(20)** _____ su novio. La invitó **(21)** _____ cenar con ella en un restaurante esa noche: llegó temprano y esperó **(22)** _____ el gran momento. Por fin, cuando hablaron, vio que Victoria se interesaba mucho **(23)** _____ su novio, y se negó **(24)** _____ dejarlo.

Pero ese no sería el final de sus esfuerzos. Pensaría **(25)** _____ otro plan.

Ejercicio 4.22 Llene cada espacio en blanco con la preposición correcta o con el símbolo Ø (nada) si no se necesita preposición.

¿Conoces el cuento que se trata **(1)** _____ un trencito que no podía subir la cuesta? Esta es una versión un poco modificada de la tradicional.

Había una vez un trencito que quería subir por una montaña y no podía: llegaba hasta la mitad de la cuesta y ya no podía más: tenía que volver **(2)** _____ bajar. Todos los otros trenes se burlaban **(3)** _____ él. Lo tomaban **(4)** _____

(continued)

incompetente. Su mamá le decía que no se preocupara **(5)** _____ lo que los otros pensaban **(6)** _____ él, pero él no podía resignarse **(7)** _____ una vida de mediocridad. Soñaba **(8)** _____ poder subir esa cuesta y llegar hasta la cima. Un día decidió tratar **(9)** _____ llegar hasta la cima, pero sabía que necesitaría toda la suerte del mundo **(10)** _____ lograr su sueño: **(11)** _____ eso fue a la casa del brujo, y cuando le abrió su hija, preguntó **(12)** _____ el brujo, y ella fue a buscarlo. Cuando llegó el brujo, el trencito le pidió **(13)** _____ un favor: que le diera un talismán o algo **(14)** _____ ayudarlo a subir hasta la cima. El brujo se rio **(15)** _____ él y le dijo que se olvidara **(16)** _____ talismanes, que no podría subir nunca.

El trencito se enfureció y le gritó: "¡Sí que puedo, ya verás!" Rabiando, fue a la base de la cima, y se puso **(17)** _____ correr con todo el coraje que le había causado esta última vergüenza. Llegó hasta la mitad de la cuesta, pero esta vez no paró: olvidó **(18)** _____ su miedo y siguió subiendo; cuando le quedaba solo un metro **(19)** _____ llegar a la cima, se sintió sin fuerzas, pero se dijo "¡Sí que puedo! ¡Yo sé que sí puedo!", y poco a poco, usando toda su energía para cada vuelta de sus ruedas, terminó **(20)** _____ subir la cuesta.

Y así fue que el trencito logró lo que quería: convirtió la energía de su rabia en fuerza positiva.

B ADVERBS

(Adverbs Ending in -mente, Word Order, Multiple-Function Words)

Chapter 4.B.2–4, pages 121–123

Ejercicio 4.23 Traduzca usando la palabra más apropiada de la lista en español y el orden correcto de palabras.

bien, derecho, distinto, duro, hondo, igual, limpio, rápido, raro

I used to get along (llevarse) *with my neighbors well, but the other day our relationship changed. I saw that their son wasn't playing fairly: whenever my daughter won, he would hit her, and he hit her hard. After seeing that twice, I decided I had to do something fast. I went straight to my neighbors' house, and told the mother what I had seen. She took a deep breath, and looked at me in a strange way. She told me she knew this: her son was short, but highly competitive. He couldn't play the same way as the rest: he had to play differently. It was natural.*

Ejercicio 4.24 Reescriba las oraciones siguientes con el adverbio que corresponda al adjetivo entre paréntesis.

1. Terminaron de preparar el salón para la fiesta. (rápido)   **2.** Mi abuela camina a la tienda y al correo. (lento)   **3.** Hablas el español. (bueno)   **4.** Lleva una vida moral. (alto)   **5.** Es necesario que el paciente respire. (hondo)

Adverbs (Adverbs of Time)

Chapter 4.B.5, pages 124–126

Ejercicio 4.25   Junte las oraciones usando adverbios de tiempo como transición.

(1) _____ *(Always)* he querido escribir una autobiografía, y **(2)** _____ *(the day before yesterday)* decidí que la iba a empezar. Sin embargo, **(3)** _____ *(when)* me senté a escribir, no podía decidir **(4)** _____ *(when)* debía comenzar la acción. Me preguntaba: ¿Empiezo **(5)** _____ *(now)*? ¿Empiezo en el pasado? Dieron las once de la noche y **(6)** _____ *(still not)* había escrito ni una palabra. **(7)** _____ *(So then)* decidí acostarme porque **(8)** _____ *(already)* era tarde.

(9) _____ *(Yesterday)* volví a sentarme para ver si podía inspirarme. Estuve tres horas tratando de escribir algo, pero no me gustaba nada. **(10)** _____ *(While)* escribía me sentía tonta, y sabía que **(11)** _____ *(never ever)* querría que nadie viera lo que estaba escribiendo. **(12)** _____ *(Soon)* decidí parar.

(13) _____ *(Last night)* soñé con mi autobiografía, y **(14)** _____ *(today)*, al despertarme, **(15)** _____ *(already)* estaba claro en mi mente lo que iba a escribir. **(16)** _____ *(Still not)* sabía las palabras exactas que usaría, pero sabía que escribiría sobre mis dudas. Y así fue que comencé a escribir mi autobiografía: estas son mis primeras palabras. Me siento como un **(17)** _____ *(newborn)* nacido, pero sé que **(18)** _____ *(tomorrow)*, cuando empiece a escribir de nuevo, me sentiré un poco más fuerte. Poco a poco, será lo más natural del mundo, y **(19)** _____ *(no longer)* tendré vergüenza ni dudas. **(20)** _____ *(Sooner or later)* saldrá una novela de todo esto.

Ejercicio 4.26   Llene cada espacio en blanco usando **ya, ya no, todavía** o **todavía no**.

(1) _____ *(Still)* recuerdo la primera noche en que vinieron a cenar mis suegros. Me dijeron que **(2)** _____ *(already)* habían comido, y claro que **(3)** _____ *(no longer)* tenían hambre. Yo no podía creerlo; pero como **(4)** _____ *(still not)* había terminado de preparar la cena, decidí no cocinar más, y sentarme a hablar con ellos sin comer nada. Esa noche mi marido no iba a poder llegar hasta la hora del postre, así que no importaba.

Adverbs (Adverbs of Manner)

Chapter 4.B.6, pages 126–127

Ejercicio 4.27 Llene cada espacio en blanco con el adverbio de modo correcto.

—¿Cómo se prepara una tortilla española?

—Mira, se prepara **(1)** _____ *(like this)*: bates **(2)** _____ *(well)* dos huevos, los pones a cocinar en un sartén con cebollas y papas cortadas en trozos y ya **(3)** _____ *(thoroughly)* cocinadas.

—Y ¿**(4)** _____ *(how)* la volteas?

—Esto es un arte. Tienes que hacerlo bien, porque si lo haces **(5)** _____ *(badly)*, la tortilla puede terminar en el piso. Necesitas algo del tamaño del sartén, **(6)** _____ *(like)* una tapa de olla.

—¿Y cuánto se cocina?

—Depende. A algunos les gusta más seca que a otros.

—Suena **(7)** _____ *(really)* fácil. ¿Hacemos una ahora?

—Está **(8)** _____. *(Okay.)*

Adverbs (Adverbs of Quantity)

Chapter 4.B.7, pages 128–129

Ejercicio 4.28 Llene cada espacio en blanco usando el adverbio de cantidad correcto.

Estoy **(1)** _____ *(rather)* cansada hoy. Dormí **(2)** _____ *(barely)* cuatro horas anoche, y no es **(3)** _____ *(enough)*. **(4)** _____ *(Almost)* no tengo fuerza. Además, hace **(5)** _____ *(too)* calor para trabajar, y me duele **(6)** _____ *(so much)* la cabeza que no puedo hacer nada. Quizás si camino **(7)** _____ *(a bit)*, me sienta mejor. Siempre como **(8)** _____ *(little)* para el desayuno, **(9)** _____ *(only)* pan o cereal, y por eso estoy **(10)** _____ *(half)* cansada todo el tiempo. El médico me dijo que debo ejercitarme **(11)** _____ *(more)* y tomar vitaminas. Me dijo que no debo tomar café, ni cenar **(12)** _____ *(too)* tarde. A veces creo que la salud exige **(13)** _____ *(too much)*, pero en realidad, si se pudieran ver los resultados de inmediato, no sería **(14)** _____ *(so much)*. ¿**(15)** _____ *(How much)* tengo que hacer para sentirme bien? Ahora mismo no estoy **(16)** _____ *(not at all)* satisfecha.

Adverbs (Adverbs of Confirmation, Doubt, or Negation)

Chapter 4.B.8, pages 129–131

Ejercicio 4.29 Traduzca usando el adverbio de confirmación, duda o negación correcto. Para *you*, use el informal singular (tú).

*"You are going to pay for our tickets, **aren't you**?"*
*"**Yes**, but I am missing one dollar. Tony, do you **by any chance** have one you can lend me?"*
*"**No**, I don't have a dollar, but **I do** have 75 cents. Do you want it?"*
*"Okay. **Maybe** Julio or Vicky has the other 25 cents. Julio, do you have 25 cents?"*
*"**No.**"*
"What about you, Vicky?"
*"No, I don't **either**."*
*"**Well**, then, **maybe** we won't go to the movies. Do you want to go for a walk in the park?"*
*"Oh, **no**! **No way!**"*

Ejercicio 4.30 Llene cada espacio en blanco con la palabra más apropiada de esta lista (use cada palabra solo una vez):

bueno, no, sí, tal vez, también, tampoco, ya

No sé por qué no puedo comer temprano en la mañana. Es un misterio. A todos mis hermanos les da hambre temprano y para cuando yo me levanto, ellos **(1)** _____ han desayunado. **(2)** _____ sea porque ceno muy tarde, pero ellos **(3)** _____ cenan tarde. **(4)** _____, el problema no es grave. ¿Acaso me estoy muriendo de hambre? ¡De ninguna manera! Como cuando quiero, y cuando **(5)** _____ tengo ganas, no como. Lo que **(6)** _____ he notado como diferencia entre mis hermanos y yo es que ellos tienen más energía que yo durante todo el día. Pero no voy a dejar que eso me preocupe, ni **(7)** _____ voy a dejar que me preocupe la falta de apetito. A cada quien lo suyo, como dicen.

Adverbs (Adverbial Phrases)

Chapter 4.B.9, pages 132–133

Ejercicio 4.31 Llene cada espacio en blanco usando la locución adverbial correcta.

Ayer fui al cine por primera vez en años y vi una película que me encantó. Había mucha gente y **(1)** _____ *(often)* había partes de mucho miedo y todos gritaban.

(continued)

Yo descansaba muy **(2)** _____ *(comfortably)* en mi butaca, tanto que **(3)** _____ *(almost)* me duermo. Me parece que la segunda mitad de la película solo la entendí **(4)** _____ *(halfway)*, y **(5)** _____ *(as a matter of fact)*, me perdí el final. Sin embargo, estoy seguro de que sé lo que pasó **(6)** _____ *(at the end)*, aunque no estaré satisfecho **(7)** _____ *(until)* verificarlo con alguien. **(8)** _____ *(Oh well)*, yo estoy contento porque **(9)** _____ *(finally)* fui al cine, y **(10)** _____ *(all in all)*, me gustó la experiencia. Solo quisiera encontrar **(11)** _____ *(sometime)* **(12)** _____ *(somewhere)* un cine que no fuera tan caro.

Adverbs (Adverbs of Place)

Chapter 4.B.10, pages 133–136

Ejercicio 4.32 Llene cada espacio en blanco con el adverbio de lugar correcto.

—Nos acabamos de mudar a un edificio de apartamentos de dos pisos: hay cuatro apartamentos, dos **(1)** _____ *(below)* y dos **(2)** _____ *(above)*; dos de estos están **(3)** _____ *(in front)* y dos **(4)** _____ *(in back)*. **(5)** _____ *(Outside)* hay un jardín precioso. ¿**(6)** _____ *(Where)* vives tú?

—Yo vivo **(7)** _____ *(here)*, en este edificio. Mi apartamento se encuentra **(8)** _____ *(inside)* a la derecha. ¿Quieren entrar?

—Sí, gracias.

—Vengan **(9)** _____, pues. Déjenme enseñarles el apartamento. **(10)** _____ *(There)* está la sala, **(11)** _____ *(across)* están las recámaras, **(12)** _____ *(over there)* está el baño.

—¡Qué bello apartamento! Bueno, gracias por todo. Ya nos tenemos que ir.

—¿**(13)** _____ *(Where)* van?

—Tengo una cita con el médico.

—¿Tienen que ir **(14)** _____ *(far)*? Si quieren, los llevo.

—No, muchas gracias. El consultorio del médico solo queda a dos cuadras.

Adverbs (Related Adverbs and Prepositions)

Chapter 4.B.11, pages 136–137

Ejercicio 4.33 Subraye la selección correcta para el contexto.

Mis vecinos de (**1.** abajo/bajo/debajo de) son recién casados y llevan una vida muy romántica, pero extraña a la vez. Los dos son estudiantes universitarios, y ella toma una clase conmigo. Siempre se sienta (**2.** adelante/delante de) mí. Ella y su marido se pasan los fines de semana (**3.** afuera/fuera de), trabajando (**4.** atrás/detrás de/tras) su garaje en motores de diferentes tipos. Es muy común verlos trabajar juntos en un mismo coche: recuerdo una mañana cuando él estaba parado (**5.** enfrente/frente a) un coche, trabajando con la cabeza metida (**6.** adentro/dentro de) el capó [*the hood*], y ella estaba acostada (**7.** abajo/bajo/debajo de) el mismo coche, haciendo algo con el aceite, creo. Yo tenía miedo que algo fuera a pasarles, pero nunca les pasa nada. A veces se pelean porque los dos quieren la misma herramienta, y terminan con carreras, en que uno corre (**8.** atrás/detrás de/tras) el otro para quitarle algo. De vez en cuando se sientan (**9.** abajo/bajo/debajo de) un árbol para descansar. El sábado pasado él salió solo; yo supuse que ella se había quedado (**10.** adentro/dentro de) porque estaría enferma, o algo así.

C CONJUNCTIONS

(Usage, Conjunctions of Coordination)

Chapter 4.C.1–2, pages 138–139

Ejercicio 4.34 Llene cada espacio en blanco con la conjunción de coordinación correcta: **y, e, o, u, pero, ni… ni, no solo** o **sino.**

Rafael Correa entró al cuartel donde los policías sublevados agredieron **(1)** _____ hirieron al presidente; su escolta tuvo que sacarlo para llevarlo al hospital. Él quiso salir del hospital de inmediato, **(2)** _____ su escolta se lo impidió. Cuando le preguntó un periodista si sintió miedo durante el incidente, el presidente contestó lo siguiente: "No sentí miedo, **(3)** _____ indignación y tristeza". Luego añadió: "No me creo **(4)** _____ héroe **(5)** _____ mártir: hice lo que creí que tenía que hacer en ese momento". Más tarde, explicó: "Para nosotros el golpe no ha terminado: tenemos que estar atentos porque hay muchos grupos que intentan atentar contra el proceso de cambio, **(6)** _____ en Ecuador, sino en toda la región". De un modo **(7)** _____ otro, el presidente se empeñaría en reducir la corrupción en su país.

Ejercicio 4.35 Traduzca, usando **pero, sino** o **sino que** para traducir *but*.

1. I was afraid but I did it. 2. It wasn't blue, but red. 3. It wasn't blue, but I bought it anyway. 4. I didn't buy a red car, but a blue one. 5. I didn't want a red car, but I bought one anyway. 6. I wanted a red car, but instead I bought a blue one. 7. I didn't buy the car, but rather I sold it.

Ejercicio 4.36 Junte la información que sigue para formar un párrafo; use conjunciones de coordinación donde se necesiten.

Norberto me llamó. Norberto me contó de su viaje a México. Me contó de su viaje a Puerto Rico. Le gustó mucho México. Se enfermó con la comida. Le encantó Puerto Rico. Sufrió del calor. El lugar que más le gustó no fue México: fue Puerto Rico. Le gustó más no solo porque tiene muchas playas; también porque es una isla. Pudo conocerla mejor en el poco tiempo que tenía.

Conjunctions (Conjunctions of Subordination)

Chapter 4.C.3, pages 139–140

Ejercicio 4.37 Llene cada espacio en blanco con la conjunción de subordinación **que** cuando se necesite. Si no se necesita nada, use el símbolo Ø.

Yo no sabía **(1)** _____ iban a venir todos juntos a **(2)** _____ cenar. Pensé **(3)** _____ solo venías tú, Julio, y **(4)** _____ los demás se encontrarían con nosotros en el bar para **(5)** _____ celebrar. Pero ahora **(6)** _____ están aquí, pues bienvenidos. No quiero **(7)** _____ se vayan sin **(8)** _____ comer. Creo **(9)** _____ tengo suficiente, y si no, entre todos preparamos algo. También Laura me dijo **(10)** _____ venía. Bueno, pues, déjenme **(11)** _____ servirles un vinito o algo para **(12)** _____ pueda ya empezar la fiesta.

Ejercicio 4.38 Traduzca las oraciones siguientes usando las conjunciones de coordinación y de subordinación apropiadas.

You said you were going to the store to buy milk. I told you we didn't need just milk, but bread as well. I see you bought neither bread nor milk, but instead you rented a video.

D TRANSITIONS

Chapter 4.D, pages 140–145

Ejercicio 4.39 Llene cada espacio en blanco con la transición correcta.

(1) _____ *(In general)*, me gusta más el teatro que el cine. **(2)** _____ *(In the first place)*, el teatro es más emocionante **(3)** _____ *(because)* los actores están allí mismo frente a uno; **(4)** _____ *(secondly)*, el acto de ir al teatro es un evento en sí. **(5)** _____ *(However)*, me parece que además de lo divertido que es ver una obra desarrollarse, existe un suspenso especial en el teatro, que es el de la posibilidad de que alguno de los actores cometa un error. **(6)** _____ *(In fact)*, a veces me pregunto si **(7)** _____ *(actually)* no vamos al teatro no tanto con el propósito de ver una obra maravillosa, sino **(8)** _____ *(perhaps)* para sentir una comunión humana con los actores que la representan. ¿**(9)** _____ *(By chance)* no sienten otros lo que siento yo, que al escuchar cada palabra que enuncian los actores, en vez de perderme en la ilusión de la obra, me la paso esperando bajo tensión la próxima palabra, siempre con la duda de que se le vaya a olvidar, o que se vea que solo es un acto? Cuando **(10)** _____ *(unfortunately)* un actor comete algún error, se confirma en mí la necesidad original de mi presencia allí: la de ser testigo de la humanidad que se esfuerza por alcanzar la perfección fuera de sí misma, pero que no siempre lo logra, y **(11)** _____ *(as a result)* nos recuerda nuestra propia humanidad. Si la obra tiene defectos, la aplaudo **(12)** _____ *(in spite of)* todo; aplaudo en ella el esfuerzo humano, y me siento un poco mejor, **(13)** _____ *(maybe)* por haber logrado ver estos defectos. **(14)** _____ *(On the other hand)*, cuando **(15)** _____ *(fortunately)* la obra sale perfecta, aplaudo más ruidosamente, aplaudo el logro de los actores; y **(16)** _____ *(yet)*, me queda una leve sensación de inferioridad, al menos hasta el momento en que pienso en la noche siguiente, cuando estos actores tendrán que volver a actuar con la misma perfección, y que existe todavía la posibilidad de que alguno de ellos se equivoque.

(17) _____ *(Regarding)* las películas, el placer es totalmente distinto: casi siempre logran eliminar los defectos antes de mostrar la película, y **(18)** _____ *(for the most part)* lo que queda está mecánicamente perfecto. Han perfeccionado **(19)** _____ *(more and more)* la tecnología visual y el arte de manipular al público. Como público de cine, ya no somos testigos de la humanidad de los actores, sino clientes que han comprado dos horas de distracción. Yo al menos me pierdo en la ilusión dramática de las películas, o **(20)** _____ *(in any case)* es lo que trato de hacer. No me concentro **(21)** _____ *(almost ever)* en las palabras que enuncian los actores ni en su arte. **(22)** _____ *(In the end)*, si una película no me deja disfrutarla sin distracciones, me da coraje, y no pienso para nada en la humanidad sino en el dinero que desperdicié.

Ejercicio 4.40 Añada la transición más lógica de la lista para cada espacio en blanco.

a fin de cuentas, a pesar de, además, casi siempre, con respecto a, de hecho, por consiguiente, por ejemplo, por eso, por lo tanto, por otro lado, porque, según, ya que

Mi sobrina acaba de cumplir los quince años: es muy bonita, y **(1)** _____ ha decidido tratar de hacerse modelo, **(2)** _____ los peligros que esa profesión conlleva. **(3)** _____ sus padres, es aceptable que se haga modelo, **(4)** _____ es una joven muy madura para su edad. **(5)** _____, puede reconocer la malicia de otros, y **(6)** _____ no cae en las trampas tradicionales como tantas jóvenes hoy en día.

(7) _____ el trabajo en sí, no es tan fácil como parece. **(8)** _____, es posible que sea uno de los más agotadores. Las sesiones de fotografía, **(9)** _____, pueden tomar hasta seis horas corridas, y las modelos deben mantenerse bellas y frescas, sin ningún rasgo de cansancio ni de mal humor. **(10)** _____, deben comer con muchísimo cuidado para mantener su cutis impecable. Y, **(11)** _____ los fotógrafos pueden pedirles en una misma sesión que se vean de playa o de románticas moribundas, deben evitar el sol y todo lo que pueda afectar su color.

(12) _____, el trabajo tiene aspectos divertidos. La modelo es el centro de atención, la visten y la maquillan para transformarla todo el día. Y **(13)** _____ tienen que viajar a diferentes partes del mundo.

(14) _____, la experiencia tiene que ser buena.

Chapter 4 Review

Ejercicio 4.41 Llene los espacios en blanco con preposiciones, conjunciones, adverbios o expresiones; si no necesita nada para un espacio en blanco, use el símbolo Ø; algunos espacios en blanco pueden tener más de una palabra.

El debate sobre la igualdad de los hombres **(1)** _____ las mujeres nunca va **(2)** _____ terminar, y en el mundo hispanohablante es un debate que para algunos lucha contra la cultura misma **(3)** _____ manera brutal. Hay dos preguntas básicas que nunca se han contestado bien: **(4)** _____, ¿qué hay de malo con que haya diferencias? **(5)** _____, ¿cuáles son las diferencias que realmente deberían de cambiar?

(6) _____ la primera pregunta, vamos a ver qué puede haber de malo. **(7)** _____ yo, es malo que haya dominación de cualquier individuo, mujer **(8)** _____ hombre. Es malo también que haya maltrato físico **(9)** _____ mental, y que algunos tengan más derechos humanos que otros. **(10)** _____, no sé si es malo reconocer que **(11)** _____ hay ciertas diferencias puramente físicas que no se pueden cambiar: la mujer tolera el dolor mejor que el hombre, **(12)** _____ puede alzar menos peso que él; la mujer tiene más aguante que el hombre en todos los sentidos, pero el hombre es probablemente mejor **(13)** _____ la guerra **(14)** _____ su agresividad. Claro que, en un mundo de paz, eso no importaría **(15)** _____ nada; **(16)** _____, uno se pregunta si habría tanta guerra si las mujeres gobernaran el mundo.

(17) _____ la segunda pregunta, **(18)** _____ empezamos a contestarla arriba: debemos insistir **(19)** _____ eliminar las diferencias que le quitan a la mujer los derechos humanos. Es fácil decir esto, **(20)** _____ las implicaciones son inmensas. En la cultura hispana, donde la mujer y el hombre tienen papeles **(21)** _____ claramente marcados en la vida cotidiana, uno pensaría **(22)** _____ un cambio de este tipo podría representar un peligro, y que habría que resignarse **(23)** _____ las diferencias con tal de no perder la base cultural que nos identifica. Algunos dicen que si la mujer se empeña **(24)** _____ ser igual al hombre en la vida profesional, y deja **(25)** _____ dedicarse al doble oficio de madre y cuidadora del hogar, **(26)** _____ el núcleo familiar, que **(27)** _____ es el centro de ese mundo, se desintegraría como ha pasado con la familia estadounidense. Pero hemos visto que **(28)** _____ existe en el mundo hispano una liberación femenina que no solo no ha destruido la cultura, **(29)** _____ la ha enriquecido: la mujer hispana moderna es profesional, instruida y madre y esposa **(30)** _____. El hombre hispano moderno **(31)** _____ es profesional, instruido y padre y marido. Ambos se esfuerzan **(32)** _____ apoyar al otro en estos cambios, y **(33)** _____ las dificultades, han logrado crear un nuevo mundo donde la cultura hispana, que **(34)** _____ de por sí era un modelo por el énfasis que le daba a la familia, se ha vuelto **(35)** _____ más poderosa internacionalmente.

(36) _____, este debate nunca se resolverá **(37)** _____ nunca se eliminarán las diferencias entre dos seres naturalmente diferentes. Lo que **(38)** _____ se puede resolver es lo que el ser humano creó como diferencias, y, **(39)** _____, eso es lo único que merece nuestra atención.

Ejercicio 4.42 Temas de ensayo y de práctica oral

a. Ensayo

Prestando atención al uso de preposiciones, adverbios, conjunciones y transiciones, escriba un párrafo sobre uno de los temas siguientes:

1. las aventuras de un gato que atrapa a un pájaro y lo mete en la casa de su dueño para jugar.

(continued)

2. las aventuras de un ratoncito que se encuentra un enorme queso suizo.

3. las aventuras de un niño que se pierde en el bosque.

4. una experiencia ambigua, que fue buena por ciertas razones pero mala por otras. Elabore al máximo la ambigüedad de sus sentimientos.

b. Práctica oral

1. Pídale a un amigo hispano que le cuente su cuento de niños favorito. Escuche con cuidado para ver cómo usa las preposiciones, los adverbios, las conjunciones y las transiciones. Usando preposiciones, adverbios, conjunciones y transiciones, haga algunas preguntas mientras su amigo cuenta, para aclarar más (por ejemplo: Y ¿el niño ya no estaba con ellos? ¿Todavía estaba de pie? Pero, ¿iban a pie o a caballo? ¿Cuánto se tardaron en llegar? Entonces, ¿se estaba burlando descaradamente de ella? Cuando llegó, ¿no se fijó en el cambio? Y después, ¿no preguntó por su padre? Según ellos, ¿la desconocida era mala o buena? ¿Es por eso que lo mató? etc.).

2. Pídale instrucciones a un amigo hispano para llegar a algún lugar (escoja un lugar al que usted ya sepa llegar, para asegurarse de comprender bien el uso de preposiciones, adverbios y conjunciones). Usando preposiciones, adverbios, conjunciones y transiciones, haga algunas preguntas para asegurarse de comprender las direcciones.

3. Conversación informal: Comparen entre ustedes sus lugares de residencia y su dormitorio en la casa de sus padres. Presten atención a su uso de preposiciones, adverbios, conjunciones y transiciones.

4. Debate: La mejor jugada. Comparen maldades o travesuras *(tricks, practical jokes)* que ustedes les han hecho a otros, o que saben que otros han hecho, y decidan cuál se gana el premio. Presten atención al uso de preposiciones, adverbios, conjunciones y transiciones.

5. Encuesta: Tradiciones culturales. Fuera de clase, haga una encuesta *(poll)* informal entre estudiantes y profesores hispanos sobre sus tradiciones culturales favoritas. Preste atención a su uso de preposiciones, adverbios, conjunciones y transiciones, y haga preguntas para practicar. Tome apuntes para preparar un informe *(report)* para la clase.

Chapter 5
Verbs: Formation

A INDICATIVE MOOD

(Present Indicative)
Chapter 5.A.1, pages 148–154

Ejercicio 5.1 Conjugue cada verbo en la primera persona singular del presente del indicativo **(yo)**.

Cariño mío, te (**1.** amar). Todos los días (**2.** escuchar) tu música, y solo (**3.** comer) lo que te gusta. Ahora (**4.** vivir) por ti; cuando (**5.** hablar) con otros, es contigo en mente; y si (**6.** caminar) por el pueblo, es contigo a mi lado. Ya no (**7.** hacer) nada para mí ni para nadie. Ya no (**8.** beber) más que agua fresca, tu bebida favorita. Cuando (**9.** abrir) la puerta para salir, estás ahí. Aún cuando (**10.** apagar) la luz en la noche, tu presencia me da fuerza.

Ejercicio 5.2 Conjugue cada verbo en la primera persona singular del presente del indicativo **(yo)**.

No sé por qué (**1.** mentir) tanto, y (**2.** seguir) mintiendo. Les (**3.** pedir) a mis amigos y a mi familia que me perdonen, pero luego (**4.** repetir) el mismo error. Siempre les (**5.** comentar) a ellos que (**6.** mezclar) la verdad con la fantasía, y así (**7.** impedir) que olviden mis mentiras. Si me critican, no (**8.** defenderse) nunca porque en realidad (**9.** querer) el castigo que me da su crítica. Cada vez que puedo, (**10.** elegir) criticarme yo mismo primero, y así (**11.** conseguir) mi propio castigo. Creo que es mejor si (**12.** revelar) mi crimen, y así me (**13.** servir) yo mismo de juez. Pero luego (**14.** cansarse) de tanto luchar conmigo mismo, y (**15.** cerrar) los ojos y (**16.** sentir) que (**17.** comenzar) a olvidarlo todo. A veces (**18.** pensar) que si (**19.** perderse) en el sueño, todo lo malo desaparecerá.

Ejercicio 5.3 Conjugue cada verbo en la tercera persona singular del presente del indicativo **(él/ella)**.

Como cada día al despertarse, este día especial del año, Roberto, que es un hombre de hábitos muy establecidos, (**1.** pensar) en lo que (**2.** querer) hacer. Antes de levantarse, se (**3.** hacer) la lista de sus actividades: (**4.** recordar) que este

(continued)

día siempre (**5.** recoger) las hojas y (**6.** podar) las ramas largas, luego, cuando ya le (**7.** doler) el cuello, va al pueblo y (**8.** votar), porque hoy (**9.** ser) el día de las elecciones. Después (**10.** volver) a su casa, va al patio que (**11.** oler) a aire fresco y (**12.** acostarse) en el sofá a tomar la siesta. Después de la siesta (**13.** ir) al club y (**14.** jugar) al tenis con sus amigos.

Pero cuando (**15.** levantarse) y (**16.** mirar) por la ventana, (**17.** ver) que hoy es diferente: (**18.** llover) sin parar. Roberto apenas (**19.** dominar) su frustración lo suficiente para llamar a su madre. Le (**20.** contar) de sus frustraciones, hasta que ella lo (**21.** interrumpir) para decirle del accidente de la noche anterior en que la tormenta destruyó el techo de su casa: ella (**22.** llorar), porque no (**23.** poder) imaginarse cómo se va a resolver su problema. Roberto (**24.** salir) corriendo a casa de su madre, bajo la lluvia que ni siquiera (**25.** sentir), y en camino, (**26.** jurar) ya no darle tanta importancia a sus pequeños hábitos y tratar de poner las cosas en perspectiva.

Ejercicio 5.4 Conjugue cada verbo en la tercera persona singular del presente del indicativo (**él/ella**).

Sentado en una silla central, con la pierna izquierda doblada sobre la derecha y con la sonrisa vivaracha del que (**1.** recordar) sus travesuras, el nonagenario les (**2.** contar) de su rutina diaria a unos quince párvulos del colegio infantil.

Antes de comenzar, (**3.** sentir) en el aire el interés de su público infantil que (**4.** jugar) nerviosamente con sus lápices y papeles. Los (**5.** mirar) cariñosamente y les (**6.** decir): "¿qué desean saber de mí?"

(**7.** Pensar) en sus biznietos mientras (**8.** ver) las manitas que se levantan tímidamente para llamar su atención. Cada uno (**9.** participar) a su debido tiempo: que si se (**10.** acostar) temprano, que si se (**11.** levantar) tarde, que si (**12.** poder) caminar sin ayuda del bastón, que si (**13.** salir) de noche, que si (**14.** dormir) a la intemperie, que si le (**15.** doler) la rodilla izquierda, que si (**16.** ser) de la ciudad, que si (**17.** oír) los pájaros, que si (**18.** oler) las flores, que si (**19.** asistir) a la escuela, que si (**20.** tener) que estudiar, y así se desarrolla su presentación, hasta el último alumno, que (**21.** recortar) una lámina de una revista mientras (**22.** hacer) su pregunta: "¿Por qué es imposible estornudar con los ojos abiertos?"

Así termina su mañana nuestro nonagenario, se (**23.** ir) a la biblioteca, (**24.** reanudar) su lectura y al terminar, (**25.** escoger) otro libro para mañana mientras (**26.** fingir) caminar bien sin bastón. (**27.** Merecer) todo nuestro respeto.

Ejercicio 5.5 Conjugue cada verbo en la primera persona singular del presente del indicativo **(yo)**.

1. Siempre (proteger) a mis hijos primero.   **2.** Sé que si (seguir) trabajando sin parar, voy a terminar a tiempo.   **3.** Creo que (obedecer) demasiado a mis superiores.   **4.** Cuando (traducir) del inglés al español, a veces uso anglicismos sin darme cuenta.   **5.** Cada vez que patino, me (torcer) un tobillo.   **6.** Si (recoger) mi ropa todos los días, hay menos desorden.   **7.** De vez en cuando (conseguir) lo que quiero, pero no siempre.   **8.** No sabes cuánto te (agradecer) tu ayuda.   **9.** Temprano en la mañana (producir) más.   **10.** No me (convencer) de la necesidad de comprar un auto nuevo.

Ejercicio 5.6 Conjugue cada verbo en la segunda persona singular del presente del indicativo **(tú)**.

1. Si (enviar) la carta esta mañana, te contestarán más rápido.   **2.** Veo que (continuar) con el mismo trabajo.   **3.** ¿No crees que (actuar) con demasiada precipitación?   **4.** ¿Siempre (reunir) a todos tus amigos en tu casa para celebrar el Año Nuevo?   **5.** Si no (criar) a tus hijos con amor, pueden tener problemas sicológicos más tarde en la vida.   **6.** ¿Cuándo (graduarse)?   **7.** Creo que (guiar) muy bien.   **8.** Me parece que (confiar) demasiado en la gente.   **9.** No siempre (concluir) lo mismo que yo.   **10.** Siempre (huir) de la verdad.

Ejercicio 5.7 Conjugue cada verbo en el presente del indicativo de la persona indicada por el contexto.

1. No nos gusta sacar la basura: por lo general, si no lo (hacer) yo, lo (hacer) él; pero a veces no lo (hacer/nosotros) para nada porque se nos olvida.   **2.** Mi hermana y yo tratamos de vestirnos de manera diferente. Yo la veo a ella vestirse y (ponerse/yo) algo diferente de ella, o si yo me visto primero, ella (ponerse) algo distinto a lo que yo me puse. Pero a veces no nos vemos y (ponerse / nosotros) lo mismo: es un problema muy grave.   **3.** Cuando (traer/yo) mi paraguas nunca llueve. A veces mi esposa (traer) el paraguas, y a veces los dos lo (traer/nosotros); siempre tratamos de tener al menos uno para que no llueva.   **4.** Hoy (venir/yo) con más hambre que nunca. Mi compañera también (venir) hambrienta hoy. Así que (venir/nosotros) las dos a comer con gusto y gana.   **5.** Nunca (decir / yo) más de lo que tengo que decir; si se (decir [impersonal]) más de lo necesario, a veces es peor. Si solo (decir) nosotros lo esencial, podemos mantener nuestra distancia.   **6.** No (tener / yo) suficiente dinero; si usted (tener) un par de pesos, creo que entre los dos (tener/nosotros) bastante para pagar la cuenta.   **7.** Si yo les (dar) diez pesos, y usted les (dar) quince, entre los dos les (dar/nosotros) el total

(continued)

de veinticinco. **8.** Yo no (ir) porque (ir) Juan. Nunca (ir/nosotros) los dos porque no es necesario. **9.** Creo que (ser/yo) responsable en cuanto a la ecología. (Ser [impersonal]) obvio que si todos (ser/nosotros) responsables, el mundo durará más. **10.** Yo (estar) triste porque se (estar [impersonal]) acabando el verano. Casi (estar / nosotros) a punto de volver a clases. **11.** (Haber / yo) de empacar las maletas para el viaje. No estoy segura pero creo que (haber [impersonal]) de hacer frío allá de noche. Nunca (haber / nosotros) viajado a esa parte del mundo. **12.** A veces no (oír / yo) bien lo que anuncian en los aviones. No se (oír [impersonal]) nada por el ruido de los motores, creo. Si no (oír / nosotros) los anuncios, ¿será grave? **13.** Yo (saber) hablar español, y si usted (saber) hablar francés, entre los dos (saber/nosotros) quizás lo suficiente para que el viaje sea cómodo. **14.** Es curioso que cuando yo (ver) una película y mi novio (ver) la misma película, nunca (ver/nosotros) exactamente lo mismo.

Ejercicio 5.8 Conjugue cada verbo en el presente del indicativo de la persona indicada.

1. Siempre (caminar/yo) en la madrugada. **2.** A veces (actuar/tú) diligentemente y a veces no. **3.** Nosotros (actuar) mejor juntos. **4.** Si (adquirir/yo) esa propiedad, estaré contenta. **5.** Siempre (adquirir/nosotros) propiedades que necesitan mejorarse. **6.** ¿En qué (andar/vosotros)? **7.** En la vida (aprender/nosotros) lo esencial si prestamos atención. **8.** Cuando se asusta, mi hermanito me (tomar) de la mano. **9.** Nunca me (avergonzar) mis padres. **10.** Creo que a veces nosotros (avergonzar) a nuestros padres. **11.** Si (averiguar/yo) el secreto, te lo cuento. **12.** ¿Te (decir/yo) lo que me contaron ayer? **13.** (Decir/él) Raúl que los nuevos vecinos son muy fiesteros. **14.** Parece que nunca les (decir/nosotros) a nuestros padres que los queremos. **15.** ¿Qué (buscar/ellos) esos hombres? **16.** Ya no (caber/yo) en esa sillita que usaba de niña. **17.** Esa ropa vieja ya no me (caber). **18.** Por suerte, no (caerse/yo) con tanta frecuencia como cuando era adolescente. **19.** Tu hermana me (caer) bien. **20.** ¿Siempre (cerrar/tú) la ventana de noche? **21.** ¿No (cerrar/vosotros) la casa con llave? **22.** Tengo un limonero en mi patio, y cada vez que quiero un limón, (escoger/yo) el más maduro. **23.** Mis padres no siempre (escoger) los mejores regalos. **24.** Nunca (comenzar/yo) a trabajar hasta las diez de la noche. **25.** Si (comenzar/nosotros) ahora, terminaremos antes de que lleguen. **26.** Creo que ella (contribuir) más de lo necesario. **27.** En verano siempre (construir/nosotros) algo nuevo, por pequeño que sea. **28.** (Conducir/yo) mejor cuando no estoy cansada. **29.** Es impresionante lo mucho que (producir/tú) cuando quieres. **30.** Esa mujer (contar) cuentos: es una cuentera profesional. **31.** Cuando tengo un resfriado, (sonarse/yo) la nariz sin parar. **32.** Nunca (recordar/nosotros) todo lo que tenemos que comprar si no preparamos una lista. **33.** (Creer/yo) que va a hacer calor hoy. **34.** Si les (leer/nosotros) libros a nuestros hijos, aprenderán más.

35. Las brujas (poseer) poderes especiales. 36. Nunca (cruzar/yo) esa calle porque es muy peligrosa. 37. ¿Siempre (almorzar/tú) solo? 38. Te (dar/yo) mi teléfono para que me llames. 39. Yo (decir) que no hace falta tanta atención. 40. Bueno, sí, a veces (contradecirse/yo), ¿y qué? 41. No siempre (elegir/yo) lo más fácil. 42. Me parece que (exigir/tú) demasiado de tus padres. 43. Creo que si (seguir/yo) caminando por aquí, voy a encontrar la catedral. 44. Ese niño siempre (conseguir) lo que quiere. 45. (Perseguir/nosotros) a los gatitos hasta que los agarramos. 46. Nunca (dormir/yo) bien. 47. ¿Y vosotros, (dormir/vosotros) bien? 48. Siempre (enviar/ellos) sus mensajes por correo electrónico. 49. A mi hermana le (enviar/nosotros) flores hoy. 50. (Escribir/yo) todos los días en mi diario. 51. (Estar/yo) muy orgullosa de ti. 52. Eventualmente los ladridos de mis perros me (forzar) a salir a investigar la causa de su alboroto. 53. (Hacer/yo) lo que puedo. 54. Estos programas (satisfacer) a los clientes, según entiendo. 55. (Ir/yo) al cine esta noche. 56. Mis amigos (ir) conmigo. 57. Mi hermanita (jugar/ella) muy bien al tenis. 58. Mis primos (llegar) hoy. 59. A veces un árbol (morir) por falta de agua. 60. Si (mover/tú) esa silla, cabremos. 61. Las víctimas (negar) haber dado permiso. 62. (Oír/yo) todo lo que dicen mis vecinos. 63. ¿(Oír/tú) la canción? 64. No (oír/nosotros) nada. 65. (Oler/yo) los melones antes de comprarlos. 66. Si los melones (oler) bien, los compro. 67. Dicen que (parecerse/yo) a mi madre. 68. Solo te (pedir/yo) este favorcito. 69. ¿Cuánto (pedir) usted por esta jarra? 70. Siempre (perder/tú) tus lentes. 71. Los estudiantes (poder) entender más de lo que crees. 72. Si (poner/yo) la mesa ahora, lo tendré todo listo. 73. A veces (reírse/yo) incontrolablemente. 74. Cuando (sonreírse) el profesor, sé que cometí un error interesante. 75. Siempre (reunir/ellos) suficiente dinero para los pobres. 76. Creo que si él le (rogar) un poco, ella aceptará. 77. ¡Qué hambre (tener/yo)! 78. ¿(Tener/tú) tiempo para ayudarme? 79. Me (torcer/yo) el tobillo. 80. Ese niñito (retorcerse) constantemente en su asiento. 81. (Traer/yo) buenas noticias. 82. Yo me (valer) de todos los recursos disponibles. 83. Si (convencer/yo) a mis padres, podré ir. 84. Hace tiempo que (venir/yo) planeando esto. 85. A mi amigo le molesta cuando sus padres (intervenir) en sus asuntos. 86. En esa clase, (ver/nosotros) una película por semana. 87. Luis (vivir) en Nicaragua. 88. Mi compañera (volver) mañana.

Ejercicio 5.9 Temas de ensayo y de práctica oral

a. Ensayo

Prestando atención a las formas verbales, escriba un párrafo sobre un día típico en su vida de hoy en día; use el presente del indicativo como base para su redacción,

(continued)

pero no es necesariamente el único tiempo verbal que puede necesitar: use su sentido común.

b. Práctica oral

1. Pídale a un amigo hispano que le cuente un día típico hoy en día para él. Preste atención a sus formas verbales.
2. Prestando atención a las formas verbales, cuéntele a un amigo un día típico en su vida hoy en día.

Indicative Mood
(Aspects of the Past Indicative: Imperfect)

Chapter 5.A.2.a, page 154

Ejercicio 5.10 Conjugue cada verbo en el imperfecto del indicativo de la persona indicada.

1. De niña (hablar/yo) cuatro idiomas.   2. ¿En la República Dominicana (comer/tú) comida picante?   3. Muchos (vivir) bajo el umbral de la pobreza en esa época.   4. Cuando estábamos en la playa, (caminar/nosotros) mucho.   5. ¿(Correr/vosotros) todas las mañanas?   6. Las dos hermanitas se (tomar) del brazo para caminar.   7. Los párpados (comenzar) a pesarle.   8. Siempre (decir/tú) lo mismo cuando me caía.   9. Mi padre (ver) el mundo de una manera muy diferente.   10. (Concluir/nosotros) el año con un brindis.

Ejercicio 5.11 Conjugue cada verbo en el imperfecto del indicativo de **yo** y **nosotros**.

1. Recuerdo que para la Navidad yo (ir) con mi familia a la playa; para la Nochebuena, (ir) todos a la playa a hacer una hoguera.   2. Cuando yo (ser) niño, mis dos hermanos y yo pensábamos que (ser) los tres mosqueteros.   3. En ese entonces no (ver/yo) que tú y yo no (ver) estas cosas de la misma manera.
4. Cuando trabajaba allí, nunca (pedir) favores, porque creía que si (pedir/nosotros) favores, terminábamos debiéndole demasiado a la gente.   5. Cuando vivía en la ciudad, siempre (cerrar) el carro con llave. De niña, en mi familia nunca (cerrar/nosotros) nada con llave.   6. De adolescente, (caerse/yo) todo el tiempo. De hecho, mi hermana y yo (caerse) todos los días.   7. Recuerdo que cuando (andar/yo) en Europa, mis amigos y yo (andar) sin parar.   8. Teníamos que escondernos, pero no pudimos hacerlo en la misma caja: yo (caber) pero no (caber/nosotros)

los dos.   **9.** Cuando yo (tener) hambre, no podía comer de inmediato. En mi familia (tener/nosotros) que esperar la hora exacta de la siguiente comida.   **10.** Nunca (hacer/yo) las tortillas sola: mi abuela y yo las (hacer) juntas.   **11.** Recuerdo que si yo le (dar) la espalda a mi amiguito Luis, él se enojaba, y eventualmente los dos nos (dar) de golpes hasta agotarnos.   **12.** Cuando estaba en la playa, yo siempre (dormir) a gusto. Todos (dormir/nosotros) en hamacas.   **13.** Cada vez que (reírse/yo), me sentía mejor; a veces (reírse/nosotros) horas sin parar.   **14.** Cuando vivía en ese apartamento, yo (oír) todas las discusiones de mis vecinos. A veces mi mejor amiga y yo (oír) peleas horribles, y no sabíamos si llamar a la policía o no.

Ejercicio 5.12   Conjugue cada verbo en el imperfecto del indicativo de la persona indicada. (Las palabras de vocabulario aparecen en el ejercicio con asterisco [*].)

> **Vocabulario*: a pesar de todo** *in spite of it all;* **alumno** *student;* **avergonzar** *to embarrass;* **avergonzarse** *to be embarrassed;* **castigar** *to punish;* **chillón** *shrill;* **competencia** *competition;* **darse por vencido** *to give up;* **enterarse** *to find out;* **enviar** *to send;* **fingir** *to pretend;* **ganarle** *to beat her (in a competition);* **gritar** *to scream;* **lograr** *to manage to;* **mandar** *to send;* **más bien** *instead;* **odiar** *to hate;* **platicar** *to chat;* **portarse** *to behave;* **quedarse** *to stay;* **regañar** *to scold;* **soportar** *to tolerate;* **travesura** *mischief, prank*

En la escuela, yo (**1.** tener) maestros muy severos, que siempre (**2.** insistir) en que mis compañeros y yo nos portáramos* muy bien. Recuerdo que cada día cuando yo (**3.** caminar) a la escuela, me (**4.** preguntar) si ese día algún maestro me regañaría* o me castigaría*. Yo siempre (**5.** avergonzarse*) fácilmente, especialmente cuando mis maestros me (**6.** sorprender) hablando con un compañero y me (**7.** regañar*) frente a todos. Al final de cada año ellos (**8.** evaluar) nuestro trabajo y nuestra conducta, y cada año nosotros (**9.** adquirir) nuevas estrategias para esconder nuestras travesuras*.

Cuando (**10.** ponerse/nosotros) a platicar* y a jugar y pasarnos notitas, la maestra de castellano nos (**11.** interrogar) en su voz chillona*: "¿Qué (**12.** hacer/vosotros)? ¿De qué (**13.** hablar/vosotros)?" Y nosotros le (**14.** contestar) que no (**15.** hacer) nada, que solo (**16.** hablar) de la tarea. Ella nos (**17.** creer), o (**18.** darse) por vencida* y nosotros (**19.** salir) ganando: eso (**20.** pensar/nosotros) entonces al menos.

A veces pienso que (**21.** aprender/nosotros) muy poco, justo lo suficiente para sobrevivir en la escuela. (**22.** Buscar/nosotros) siempre la manera de no

(continued)

concentrarnos en lo que el maestro (**23.** querer) que hiciéramos, y por lo general (**24.** lograr*/nosotros) divertirnos a pesar de todo.

Mi maestro de historia (**25.** ser) el peor de todos: cada vez que (**26.** poder/él), nos (**27.** avergonzar*/él). A veces nos (**28.** decir/él) que si no (**29.** portarse*/nosotros) bien, nos mandaría* a la oficina del director. Y casi cada semana, (**30.** enviar*/él) a uno a hablar con el director. Pero no (**31.** ser) grave: el alumno* que (**32.** deber) ir a la oficina del director no (**33.** ir): más bien*, (**34.** salir) al corredor y (**35.** tomar) agua, luego (**36.** meterse) en el baño y (**37.** quedarse*) allí hasta el final de la hora. Y el maestro nunca (**38.** enterarse*) de nada.

Recuerdo la travesura* favorita de los chicos más traviesos de la clase: les (**39.** gustar) poner una silla defectuosa en el escritorio de las maestras nuevas: ellas (**40.** llegar) muy serias y nerviosas con sus libros muy apretados contra su pecho, y a la hora de sentarse, (**41.** caerse). Casi siempre (**42.** gritar*/ellas), y siempre (**43.** sonrojarse). A veces hasta (**44.** llorar/ellas). Nosotros (**45.** reírse). ¡Qué vergüenza me da ahora!

(**46.** Tener/yo) una maestra de matemáticas que me (**47.** detestar) porque yo siempre (**48.** terminar) los ejercicios de práctica antes que ella. Cuando le (**49.** llevar/yo) mi respuesta, ella (**50.** ponerse) furiosa y me (**51.** preguntar/ella) por qué no (**52.** esperar/yo) a que ella terminara primero. No sé por qué (**53.** insistir) yo en ganarle: me imagino que (**54.** existir) un tipo de competencia* con los maestros.

Nosotros (**55.** creer) que (**56.** ser) invencibles. (**57.** Sentirse) superiores a los maestros, los (**58.** contradecir), y (**59.** rehusarse) a aprender las cosas como ellos (**60.** querer). Nosotros los (**61.** odiar*) a ellos, y ellos nos (**62.** odiar) a nosotros, o al menos, eso es lo que (**63.** fingir*). Porque en realidad, bajo la superficie de competencia, (**64.** saber/nosotros) muy bien que (**65.** ser) importante estudiar, y (**66.** reconocer/nosotros) el valor de los conocimientos. Lo que no (**67.** soportar* / nosotros) era la disciplina excesiva, los uniformes, la uniformidad reglamentaria de todo. Y por eso (**68.** rebelarse/nosotros).

Ejercicio 5.13 Temas de ensayo y de práctica oral

a. Ensayo

Prestando atención a las formas verbales, escriba un párrafo sobre un día típico en su vida en la escuela primaria o secundaria; use el imperfecto del indicativo como base para su redacción, pero no es necesariamente el único tiempo verbal que puede necesitar: use su sentido común.

b. Práctica oral

1. Pídale a un amigo hispano que le cuente un día típico en su vida cuando era niño. Preste atención a sus formas verbales.
2. Prestando atención a las formas verbales, cuéntele a un amigo un día típico en su vida cuando era niño.

Indicative Mood
(Aspects of the Past Indicative: Preterite)

Chapter 5.A.2.b, pages 155–157

Ejercicio 5.14   Conjugue cada verbo en el pretérito de la persona indicada.

1. ¿(Hablar/tú) con tus padres anoche?   **2.** Ayer (comer/nosotros) pescado.   **3.** Las víctimas (vivir) momentos de desespero.   **4.** Esta mañana (caminar/yo) cinco kilómetros.   **5.** ¿Por dónde (andar/tú)?   **6.** El niño trató de meterse en la caja, pero no (caber).   **7.** Este verano (estar/nosotros) en el campo.   **8.** Ayer (arrestar/nosotros) al sospechoso.   **9.** El año pasado (haber) menos crimen que el anterior.   **10.** Yo no (saber/yo) la respuesta.   **11.** ¿(Poder/tú) terminar tu trabajo?   **12.** Los iraníes (poner) en funcionamiento su central nuclear.   **13.** ¿A qué hora (salir/vosotros)?   **14.** Mis vecinos (tener) que mudarse.   **15.** Este fin de semana no (hacer/yo) nada porque hacía muchísimo calor.   **16.** ¿Qué (querer/tú) decir con eso?   **17.** Ese gran autor (venir) a nuestra clase para hablar con nosotros.

Ejercicio 5.15   Conjugue cada verbo en el pretérito de la persona indicada.

1. Le (dar/nosotros) flores a mi tía para su cumpleaños.   **2.** Blanca (hacer) las paces *(made up)* con su novio.   **3.** Anoche (ir/yo) al cine.   **4.** Nunca (ser/yo) tan atlético como mi hermano.   **5.** ¿Qué (decir/vosotros)?   **6.** Me sorprende lo mucho que (producir/tú) en tan poco tiempo.   **7.** Mis primas (traer) las tortillas.

Ejercicio 5.16   Conjugue cada verbo en el pretérito de **yo** y **él**.

1. (sentir) Después de comer, yo me _____ mal, pero él no _____ nada.   **2.** (empezar) Yo _____ a hablar español a los cinco años, pero mi padre no _____ hasta los treinta.   **3.** (reír) Yo me _____ mucho durante esa película, pero el resto del público no se _____ casi para nada.   **4.** (dormir) Yo _____ bien anoche, pero mi compañero de cuarto no _____ para nada.   **5.** (caer) Creo que yo le _____ bien a tu novio, pero no estoy segura de si él le _____ bien a mi familia.   **6.** (creer)

(continued)

Yo no le _____ nada a la gitana (*gypsy*), pero mi hermana sí le _____.   **7.** (leer) _____ ese libro el año pasado; el profesor lo _____ cuando tenía nuestra edad.   **8.** (oír) Yo no _____ nada, pero mi compañera de cuarto dice que _____ gritos (*screams*).   **9.** (concluir) Yo _____ algo muy diferente de lo que _____ él.   **10.** (buscar) Yo _____ mi anillo (*ring*) en todos lados, y mi mejor amigo también _____, pero no lo encontramos.   **11.** (llegar) Yo _____ ayer, pero mi hermano mayor _____ hace una semana.   **12.** (alcanzar *[to reach]*) Yo no _____ la guayaba en esa rama (*branch*), pero Juanito sí la _____.   **13.** (explicar) Yo le _____ mis razones y él me _____ las suyas.   **14.** (almorzar) Yo _____ más de lo que _____ el resto de la gente.   **15.** (apagar *[to turn off]*) A las diez, yo _____ todas las luces excepto la de la cocina; mi compañera de casa _____ esa antes de acostarse, a eso de la una de la mañana.   **16.** (sacar *[to take out]*) Yo _____ la basura (*garbage*) esta semana porque él la _____ la semana pasada.   **17.** (comenzar) Yo _____ a trabajar a las seis, y ella _____ a las diez.   **18.** (colgar *[to hang]*) Yo _____ ese cuadro (*painting*) en la sala, luego mi mamá lo _____ en el comedor.   **19.** (tocar) Yo _____ el piano para Navidades; mi primo _____ la guitarra para el Día de Reyes.   **20.** (pedir) Para la cena, yo _____ mejillones, y él _____ camarones.   **21.** (entregar *[to deliver]*) Yo le _____ el paquete al señor Ruiz, y él se lo _____ a la señora Gómez.   **22.** (pagar) Yo _____ las cuentas (*bills*) el mes pasado, y mi compañero de casa las _____ el mes anterior.

Ejercicio 5.17   Conjugue cada verbo en el pretérito de la persona indicada. Si no hay persona indicada, use el contexto para determinar cuál es el sujeto: puede ser impersonal, o tener el sujeto ya mencionado. (Las palabras de vocabulario aparecen en el ejercicio con asterisco [*].)

> **Vocabulario*: a la vez** *at the same time;* **acercarse** *to come near;* **agotado** *exhausted;* **alquilar** *to rent;* **apodo** *nickname;* **arena** *sand;* **averiguar** *to find out;* **de hecho** *as a matter of fact;* **a fin de cuentas** *all in all;* **encerrarse** *to lock oneself up;* **estadía** *stay (as in the duration of a trip);* **estrella** *star;* **fijarse** *to notice;* **grito** *scream;* **impresionadísimo** *very impressed;* **inerte** *lifeless;* **inolvidable** *unforgettable;* **médico** *doctor;* **pegar un grito** *to scream;* **pelando** *peeling;* **por detrás** *from behind;* **quedar impresionado** *to be impressed;* **quemarse** *to get burned;* **regresar** *to return;* **seguir** *to continue;* **sitio** *place;* **sombra** *shade;* **tipo** *character*

El año pasado (**1.** ir/yo) a Cancún por primera vez: (**2.** ser) una experiencia inolvidable*, y a la vez*, (**3.** haber) algunos incidentes que quisiera olvidar. Mi mejor amiga (**4.** ir) conmigo. El primer día (**5.** quedar*/yo) impresionadísima* cuando (**6.** ver/yo) la blancura de la arena* y la transparencia azul del agua; (**7.** acostarse/nosotros) al sol un ratito, y luego (**8.** entrar/nosotros) al hotel a bañarnos. (**9.** Cenar/nosotros), acompañadas de la música de los mariachis, y luego (**10.** salir/nosotros) a pasear en la noche llena de estrellas*.

De repente mi amiga (**11.** sentirse) muy mal, y (**12.** regresar*/nosotros) al hotel. (**13.** Tener/yo) que preguntar en la recepción si había un médico*. Por fin (**14.** venir) uno, la (**15.** ver/él), y le (**16.** decir/él) que tenía gastroenteritis, causada por el cambio de bacterias en el agua o la comida. Nos (**17.** contar/él) que esta enfermedad era tan común que tenía un apodo*: le decían "la venganza de Moctezuma", o "el turista". Le (**18.** traer/él) un té caliente que habían inventado en el hotel para curar este mal, y le (**19.** recomendar/él) un medicamento que luego yo le (**20.** poder) comprar en la farmacia del hotel. (**21.** Fijarse*/yo) que era el producto que más se vendía.

Mi amiga (**22.** sufrir) con esta enfermedad por dos días enteros: no (**23.** volver/ella) a ver el sol ni la playa, (**24.** encerrarse*) en el cuarto con las cortinas cerradas, y no (**25.** hacer) nada más que dormir. Yo (**26.** estar) sola todo este tiempo, y (**27.** pasarse) el rato leyendo con la luz de una lámpara, y también (**28.** escribir) unas veinte tarjetas postales: no quería dejar a mi amiga sola, por si necesitaba algo. Además, ese primer día de sol (**29.** quemarse*) por completo: la mañana siguiente, cuando (**30.** ir) a bañarme y (**31.** mirarse), (**32.** pegar) un grito* de horror al ver que toda la piel de la cara, y del cuerpo, se me estaba pelando*. Por dos días más, (**33.** pedir) que me trajeran la comida al cuarto.

El cuarto día de nuestra estadía* en Cancún, como no podíamos ir a la playa, (**34.** decidir/nosotros) hacer un poco de turismo. (**35.** Ir) a ver las ruinas de los antiguos mayas; para llegar allá, (**36.** alquilar*/nosotros) un coche. Yo (**37.** tener) que manejar porque mi amiga estaba un poco débil. (**38.** Estar/nosotros) manejando como una hora, en un cochecito sin aire acondicionado, bajo un sol implacable, y para cuando (**39.** llegar), estábamos ya agotadas* por el calor sofocante. Nunca se nos (**40.** ocurrir) que haría tanto calor. (**41.** Sentarse/nosotros) en la sombra* de un árbol y (**42.** beber) un refresco. De lejos, inertes, (**43.** mirar/nosotros) las ruinas. Un tipo* (**44.** acercarse*) a nosotros por detrás* y nos (**45.** ofrecer/él) ayuda. Yo (**46.** hablar) un poco con él y (**47.** averiguar*/yo) todo lo que (**48.** poder/yo) sobre las ruinas: en primer lugar, el hombre me (**49.** corregir) con un tono muy severo: me (**50.** decir/él) que no les dicen "ruinas", sino "edificios". Francamente, me (**51.** caer) bastante mal su actitud; el tipo (**52.** ofenderse) con mi ignorancia, lo cual me (**53.** parecer) un poco absurdo. Le (**54.** dar/yo) las gracias por su oferta de ayuda, pero no la (**55.** aceptar/nosotros). De hecho*, (**56.** irse/nosotros) rápidamente de allí, (**57.** ver/nosotros) superficialmente lo que (**58.** poder/nosotros) del sitio*, y (**59.** conducir/nosotros) de vuelta al hotel. En el coche, de repente, mi amiga (**60.** reírse), luego (**61.** reírse) yo, y (**62.** seguir*/nosotros) riendo todo el camino por lo ridículo de la situación.

A fin de cuentas*, nuestra visita a Cancún (**63.** ser) una experiencia que nunca olvidaremos.

Ejercicio 5.18 Temas de ensayo y de práctica oral

a. Ensayo

Prestando atención a las formas verbales, escriba un párrafo sobre su primer día o su primera noche en algún lugar especial (una casa nueva, una ciudad nueva, la escuela secundaria, la universidad, etc.). Use el pretérito del indicativo como base para su redacción, pero no es necesariamente el único tiempo verbal que puede necesitar: use su sentido común.

b. Práctica oral

1. Pídale a un amigo hispano que le cuente su primer día en este país o en esta universidad. Preste atención a sus formas verbales.
2. Prestando atención a las formas verbales, cuéntele a un amigo su primer día en la universidad o en un país hispano.

Indicative Mood (Aspects of the Past Indicative: Present Perfect)

Chapter 5.A.2.c, page 158

Ejercicio 5.19 Conjugue cada verbo en el presente perfecto del indicativo de la persona indicada.

1. Nunca _____ (caminar/yo) por ahí.   2. ¿_____ (hacer/tú) algo hoy?   3. Todavía no me _____ (devolver/él) todas las cosas que le presté. *(He has still not returned to me all of the things I lent him.)*   4. _____ (andar/nosotros) casi tres kilómetros.   5. ¿Qué _____ (aprender/vosotros) en vuestro viaje?   6. Creo que no _____ (tomar/ellos) agua en horas.   7. Nunca _____ (traer/yo) tanto.   8. ¿_____ (averiguar/tú) algo sobre los horarios nuevos? *(Have you found out anything about the new schedules?)*   9. Todavía no _____ (buscar/ella) alojamiento *(lodging)* en ese barrio.   10. Nunca _____ (caber *[to fit]*/nosotros) todos en este coche.   11. ¿_____ (cerrar/vosotros) la puerta con llave? *(Did you lock the door?)*   12. Ya _____ (recoger/ellas) las hojas tres veces. *(They already picked up the leaves three times.)*

Indicative Mood (Aspects of the Past Indicative: Pluperfect)

Chapter 5.A.2.d, page 158

Ejercicio 5.20 Conjugue cada verbo en el pluscuamperfecto del indicativo de la persona indicada.

1. Estaba agotada *(exhausted)* porque _____ (correr/yo) por una hora para llegar.   2. No vieron nada porque _____ (taparse/ellas) los ojos *(they had covered their eyes)*.   3. Cuando yo llegué, él ya *(already)* se _____ (ir).   4. No les _____ (decir/nosotros) a nuestros padres que nos queríamos casar.   5. ¿_____ (ver/vosotros) esa película antes?   6. Ellos ya *(already)* _____ (volver) de su viaje a Paraguay.   7. Yo te _____ (escribir/yo) seis cartas antes de que tú me contestaras.   8. Yo creía que ya *(already)* le _____ (poner/tú) baterías nuevas al reloj.   9. Cuando por fin llegó la policía, ella ya _____ (resolver) el crimen.   10. Nunca _____ (abrir/nosotros) esa puerta antes.   11. ¿_____ (cerrar/vosotros) las ventanas antes de que empezara a llover?   12. Pensé que nunca _____ (graduarse/tú) de la escuela secundaria.

Indicative Mood (Future: Simple Future)

Chapter 5.A.3.a, page 159

Ejercicio 5.21 Conjugue cada verbo en el futuro para la persona indicada.

1. Te _____ (amar/yo) para siempre.   2. ¿Dónde _____ (vivir/tú) cuando estés allá?   3. Sé que _____ (entender/él) el problema cuando yo se lo explique.   4. ¿A qué hora _____ (comer/nosotros) allá?   5. ¿En qué año os _____ (graduar/vosotros)?   6. _____ (Tomar/ellos) el autobús para llegar a la ciudad.   7. Me _____ (despedir/yo) pronto porque ya me voy. *(I'll say good-bye because I'm leaving now.)*   8. ¿Cómo _____ (averiguar *[to find out]*/tú) lo que necesitas si no preguntas?   9. Estoy seguro que ella nos _____ (buscar) en este lugar.   10. Esta noche _____ (cantar/nosotros) juntos.   11. Con este sol, os _____ (calentar/vosotros) pronto.   12. Sé que ellas _____ (escoger *[to choose]*) lo mejor.

Ejercicio 5.22 Conjugue cada verbo en el futuro para la persona indicada.

1. Si sigo comiendo tanto, no _____ (caber) dentro de mi ropa. *(If I continue to eat so much, I will not fit into my clothes.)*   2. ¡Tú _____ (decir)! *(It's up to you!)*   3. ¿Cuántos estudiantes _____ (haber) en esta universidad?   4. Siempre te _____ (querer/yo).   5. Vosotros _____ (poder) venir también.   6. Sé que ellos se _____ (poner) furiosos cuando se enteren.   7. Nosotros _____ (hacer) lo posible por ayudar.   8. ¿Cuándo _____ (saber/tú) si te van a aceptar?   9. Su vuelo _____ (salir) mañana por la noche.   10. _____ (Tener/nosotros) muchas horas libres.   11. ¿Cuánto _____ (valer) esa camisa? *(I wonder how much that shirt costs.)*   12. ¿_____ (Venir/vosotros) con nosotros?

Ejercicio 5.23   Temas de ensayo y de práctica oral

a. Ensayo

Prestando atención a las formas verbales, escriba un párrafo sobre sus planes para mañana. Use el futuro como base para su redacción, pero no es necesariamente el único tiempo verbal que puede necesitar: use su sentido común.

b. Práctica oral

1. Pídale a un amigo hispano que le cuente sus planes para mañana. Preste atención a sus formas verbales.
2. Prestando atención a las formas verbales, cuéntele a un amigo sus planes para mañana.

Indicative Mood (Future: Future Perfect)

Chapter 5.A.3.b, page 160

Ejercicio 5.24   Conjugue cada verbo en el futuro perfecto para la persona indicada.

1. _____ (Decir/yo) lo mismo veinte veces.   2. ¿Cuántas veces _____ (ver/tú) la misma película?   3. Supongo que él se _____ (cubrir) la cabeza.   4. Nosotros _____ (volver) para entonces.   5. Me imagino que vosotros _____ (hacer) este ejercicio antes.   6. ¿_____ (Beber/ellos) agua sucia?   7. No sé dónde _____ (poner/yo) mis lentes.   8. _____ (Experimentar/tú) con esto antes.   9. _____ (Buscar/ella) por todos lados antes de darse por vencida.   10. Antes de que se acabe la noche, _____ (cantar/nosotros) todo nuestro repertorio.   11. ¿_____ (Envejecer/vosotros) tanto?   12. Ellas _____ (escribir) primero.   13. Yo me _____ (ir) antes de que tú llegues.   14. ¿Cuánto dinero _____ (gastar/tú)?   15. Mi prima se _____ (graduar) antes que yo.

B CONDITIONAL MOOD

(Present Conditional)

Chapter 5.B.1, pages 160–161

Ejercicio 5.25 Conjugue cada verbo en el condicional presente para la persona indicada.

1. Si pudiera, _____ (secar *[to dry]*/yo) mi ropa al sol.   2. Pensé que no te _____ (preocupar/tú) tanto esta vez.   3. Él no _____ (vivir) aquí si no fuera por ella.   4. Me pregunto si _____ (llover) anoche.   5. ¿Cómo _____ (pronunciar/vosotros) esto?   6. Estoy segura que ellas _____ (pagar) si pudieran.   7. Si fuera yo, me _____ (organizar) primero.   8. Si te lo pidieran, _____ (atestiguar *[to testify]*/tú), ¿verdad?   9. ¿_____ (Leer/ella) el libro antes de ver la película?   10. No nos _____ (quejar *[to complain]*/nosotros) si no hicieran tanto ruido.   11. Vosotros _____ (sonreír) también con ese chiste *(joke)*.   12. Sabíamos que allá todo el mundo nos _____ (tutear). *(We knew that over there everyone would address us with **tú**.)*

Ejercicio 5.26 Conjugue cada verbo en el condicional presente para la persona indicada.

1. Yo no _____ (caber *[to fit]*) por esa ventana aunque quisiera.   2. ¿Qué _____ (decir) tú en mi lugar?   3. ¿Cuánta gente _____ (haber) en el público *(audience)*?   4. Nosotros lo _____ (hacer) de manera diferente.   5. ¿_____ (Poder/vosotros) venir a eso de las nueve?   6. ¿Dónde _____ (poner/ellos) las llaves *(keys)*?   7. ¿Qué _____ (querer) esos clientes?   8. Si te ocurriera a ti, estoy seguro que _____ (saber/tú) cómo reaccionar.   9. ¿Cuánto les _____ (costar) el viaje?   10. ¿_____ (Tener) usted tiempo para ayudarme, por favor?   11. ¿Cuánto _____ (valer) eso?   12. Si la invitáramos, _____ (venir/ella).

Conditional Mood (Conditional Perfect)

Chapter 5.B.2, page 161

Ejercicio 5.27 Conjugue cada verbo en el condicional perfecto para la persona indicada.

1. Si no me hubieran llevado a México, yo no _____ (hablar/yo) el español desde los cinco años *(since I was five years old)*.   2. Nunca _____ (comer/tú) eso si hubieras sabido lo que era.   3. Él _____ (vivir/él) muchos años más si no se hubiera enfermado.   4. Si hubiéramos sabido lo que había en ese cuarto, no _____

(continued)

(abrir/nosotros) la puerta.   **5.** Si no les hubiéramos preguntado, no _____ (decir/ellos) nada.   **6.** Sé que no lo _____ (hacer/tú) solo.   **7.** Nunca _____ (resolver/vosotros) el caso sin la ayuda de la policía.   **8.** Usted _____ (volver) en taxi si no lo hubiéramos llevado.

Ejercicio 5.28   Temas de ensayo y de práctica oral

a. Ensayo

Si no estuviera ahora en la universidad (o en la escuela secundaria), ¿en qué sería diferente su vida? ¿Le gustaría a usted este cambio? ¿Por qué? Prestando atención a las formas verbales, escriba un párrafo sobre este tema; use el condicional para indicar los cambios hipotéticos en su vida.

b. Práctica oral

1. Pídale a un amigo hispano que le cuente lo que estaría haciendo ahora si no hubiera venido a los Estados Unidos. Preste atención a sus formas verbales.
2. Prestando atención a las formas verbales, cuéntele a un amigo lo que usted estaría haciendo ahora si no fuera estudiante.

C SUBJUNCTIVE MOOD

(Present Subjunctive)

Chapter 5.C.1, pages 162–165

Ejercicio 5.29   Conjugue cada verbo en el presente del subjuntivo para la persona indicada.

1. Es posible que yo _____ (caminar) hoy.   **2.** Te prohíben que _____ (hablar/tú).   **3.** Me sorprende que él _____ (estudiar) tanto.   **4.** Se nos quitará el frío cuando _____ (bailar/nosotros).   **5.** Dudo que vosotros _____ (remar [*to row*]) tan rápido como ellos.   **6.** Tan pronto _____ (preparar/ellos) la cena, comeremos.   **7.** Es imperativo que usted _____ (tolerar) las diferencias de los demás.   **8.** Si no pueden cantar, les digo que _____ (tararear [*to hum*]/ustedes) la canción.

Ejercicio 5.30   Conjugue cada verbo en el presente del subjuntivo para la persona indicada.

1. Es imposible que yo _____ (comer) tanto.   **2.** Te traigo esto para que lo _____ (leer/tú).   **3.** ¿Crees que él _____ (ver) la diferencia?   **4.** Cuando ella _____ (vivir) allá, se acostumbrará (*she will get used to it*).   **5.** Espero que no _____ (toser [*to cough*]/nosotros) durante la obra.   **6.** No se va a ver bien a menos que lo _____ (coser [to sew]/vosotros) con hilo del mismo color.   **7.** Dale ánimo (Encourage him) para que _____ (correr/él) más rápido.   **8.** Es esencial que _____ (compartir [to share]/ellos) su comida con sus compañeros.   **9.** Le recomiendo que no _____ (tomar/usted) ninguna bebida alcohólica con esta medicina.   **10.** Es admirable que _____ (escribirse/ustedes) tan frecuentemente.

Ejercicio 5.31   Conjugue cada verbo en el presente del subjuntivo para yo y nosotros.

1. (cerrar) Primero me dice a mí que _____ al salir, y luego nos dice a los dos que _____: ¿creerá que soy irresponsable?   **2.** (perder) Para que yo me _____, es necesario que _____ el mapa primero.   **3.** (contar) No importa que yo _____ el cuento sola o que lo _____ juntos.   **4.** (volver) Es imposible que yo _____ y que no _____ los dos.   **5.** (sentir) Cuando yo _____ frío, ya será de noche. Entonces es probable que los dos _____ frío.   **6.** (dormir) Es una lástima que yo no _____ bien cuando hay visita. De hecho, dudo que _____ lo suficiente cuando hay gente en la casa.   **7.** (enviar) Es esencial que _____ este paquete hoy. Espero que lo _____ con el resto del correo al mediodía.   **8.** (evaluar) Me dicen que _____ a mis compañeros; es obligatorio que todos _____ a los demás.

Ejercicio 5.32   Conjugue cada verbo en la tercera personal singular del presente del subjuntivo.

1. Me encanta que usted me _____ (pedir) favores.   **2.** Dudo que Germán les _____ (decir) a sus padres.   **3.** Espero que mi hermano no _____ (oír) esta música.   **4.** Cuando Rosita _____ (tener) quince años, la dejarán salir con él.   **5.** Ojalá que esto _____ (concluir) todos los debates sobre el asunto.   **6.** ¿Se podrá arreglar sin que _____ (parecer) un remiendo?   **7.** Le prohíben ir a menos que _____ (conducir) su hermano mayor.   **8.** No creo que eso me _____ (caber).   **9.** Ojalá que Carlos le _____ (caer) bien a esa gente.   **10.** Es increíble que _____ (hacer) tanto calor.   **11.** No dejan que _____ (ponerse/yo) esos zapatos.   **12.** Espero que todo _____ (salir) bien.   **13.** ¿Quieres que Yolanda _____ (traer) algo?   **14.** Ojalá que este trabajo _____ (valer) la pena.   **15.** Me gusta que Paco _____ (venir) a visitar a su padre.

Ejercicio 5.33   Conjugue cada verbo en el presente del subjuntivo.

1. Es necesario que yo _____ (dar) dinero para esta causa.   **2.** No es que _____ (estar/tú) gordo: es que la ropa se encogió.   **3.** Tengo miedo de que no _____ (haber) suficiente tiempo.   **4.** Le molesta que _____ (irse/nosotros) tan pronto.   **5.** No importa que no _____ (saber/vosotros) la respuesta.   **6.** Conviene que _____ (ser/ellas) tolerantes.   **7.** Más vale que yo _____ (escoger)

(continued)

el número ganador.   **8.** No significa que tú no los _____ (dirigir) bien: son ellos los que no te hacen caso.   **9.** Es una lástima que no _____ (distinguir/ellos) esos colores.   **10.** No irán a menos que los _____ (convencer/nosotros) de que no hay peligro.   **11.** Es necesario que lo _____ (buscar) vosotros mismos.   **12.** No abran la puerta hasta que _____ (llegar/yo).   **13.** Te presto mi auto para que _____ (alcanzar/tú) el tren en la próxima estación.

Ejercicio 5.34   Repaso del subjuntivo presente. Conjugue cada verbo en el presente del subjuntivo.

1. Ojalá que _____ (dominar/yo) el idioma para entonces.   **2.** Es increíble que les _____ (temer/él) a los demás.   **3.** Te ruego que te _____ (defender/tú).   **4.** Es mejor que les _____ (dar/nosotros) nuestro número de teléfono ahora.   **5.** Espero que _____ (estar/vosotros) cómodos.   **6.** No creo que _____ (haber) más de cien personas en el público.   **7.** Es importante que yo _____ (ir) a la biblioteca hoy.   **8.** Aunque _____ (saber/tú) la verdad, no la digas.   **9.** Para que la fiesta _____ (ser) perfecta, vamos a poner música de salsa.   **10.** A menos que _____ (recoger/nosotros) a los niños, no van a llegar a tiempo.   **11.** Es curioso que no _____ (corregir/tú) errores tan graves.   **12.** Ojalá que _____ (seguir/vosotros) gozando de vuestro viaje.   **13.** Espero que pronto _____ (vencer/ella) esa enfermedad.   **14.** Me dice que no me _____ (rascar/yo).   **15.** Lo hará sin que le _____ (rogar/tú).   **16.** Más vale que _____ (rezar/él).   **17.** No puedo creer que realmente _____ (entender/ella).   **18.** Espero que usted _____ (encontrar) lo que busca.   **19.** Se lo presto con tal de que me lo _____ (devolver/ellos) mañana.   **20.** Espero que no lleguen antes de que _____ (envolver/nosotros) los regalos.   **21.** Es imposible que yo _____ (confiar) en esa gente.   **22.** Es deseable que _____ (criar/nosotros) a nuestros hijos de una manera responsable.   **23.** Te dejo para que _____ (continuar/tú) con tu ensayo.   **24.** No nos darán nada hasta que nos _____ (graduar/nosotros).   **25.** Parece imposible que ellas _____ (creerse) semejantes mentiras.   **26.** Ojalá que _____ (ver/yo) a mis amigos allá.   **27.** Le daremos la mano para que _____ (poder/ella) subir sin bastón.   **28.** Me sorprende que ellas lo _____ (hacer) todo tan bien.   **29.** No les ganarán a menos que los _____ (dividir/ellos).   **30.** Es importante que usted _____ (investigar) este asunto con cuidado.   **31.** A veces me molesta que ustedes lo _____ (analizar) todo de esa manera.   **32.** Prefiero que no _____ (discutir/tú) tanto.   **33.** Insiste en que su hijo no _____ (pelear) con sus amigos.   **34.** Ojalá que ella _____ (llegar) tarde hoy: no estoy listo aún.   **35.** Vendrán con sus amigos aunque no lo _____ (querer/nosotros).   **36.** Insisto en que vosotros _____ (entrar) primero.   **37.** No se irán hasta que ellas _____ (salir).   **38.** La profesora se empeña en que ellos lo _____ (repetir) todo.   **39.** Lamentamos que usted no _____ (oír) la música.   **40.** Esperaremos hasta que ustedes _____ (volver).

Subjunctive Mood (Imperfect Subjunctive)

Chapter 5.C.2, pages 165–166

Ejercicio 5.35 Conjugue cada verbo en el imperfecto del subjuntivo.

1. El doctor me recomendó que _____ (caminar/yo) todos los días un poco.
2. Preferiría que _____ (hablar/tú) conmigo primero.   3. Quería darle un libro que _____ (estudiar/él) con gusto.   4. Ojalá que ella _____ (cantar) esta vez.
5. Nos pusieron esa música para que _____ (bailar/nosotros).   6. No significa que no _____ (escuchar/vosotros).   7. Era imposible que ellas los _____ (amar).
8. Pedí que me _____ (preparar/ellos) una paella.   9. Le dieron esa droga para que _____ (tolerar/usted) mejor el dolor.   10. Solo les pedía que _____ (tararear/ustedes) la canción una vez.   11. No podían encontrar nada que yo _____ (comer) sin enfermarme.   12. Me sorprendió que _____ (leer/tú) su diario.   13. Esperaba que él _____ (ver) lo que yo había visto.   14. Tenía miedo que ella no _____ (vivir) en esa dirección.   15. Se avergonzaban de que nosotros _____ (toser) durante toda la obra.   16. Si vosotros _____ (coser) vuestra propia ropa, no tendríais este problema.   17. Teníamos que apurarnos en caso de que ellas _____ (correr).   18. Se lo dimos a condición de que lo _____ (compartir/ellos) entre ellos.   19. Escondimos todas las bebidas alcohólicas para que no _____ (beber/él).   20. Antes de que ustedes nos _____ (escribir), nosotros ya les habíamos escrito.   21. No dejaría de mojarse hasta que yo _____ (cerrar) las ventanas.
22. Era imposible que yo ganara sin que tú _____ (perder) como consecuencia.
23. Le pedimos que nos _____ (contar/ella) de su viaje.   24. Nos enteraríamos en cuanto _____ (volver/nosotros).   25. No nos creerían hasta que ellos mismos _____ (sentir) el temblor.   26. Les había conseguido este cuarto de atrás para que _____ (dormir/ustedes) mejor.   27. Nunca llegaría a menos que él lo _____ (enviar) por correo aéreo.   28. Me dijo que te daría un auto cuando te _____ (graduar/tú).

Ejercicio 5.36 Conjugue cada verbo en el imperfecto del subjuntivo.

1. Se sorprendieron de que yo _____ (andar) por esos lares.   2. Nadie pudo creer que tú _____ (caber) por esa ventana.   3. No lo aceptaría a menos que les _____ (caer/él) bien a sus padres.   4. Si ella no _____ (concluir) lo mismo que nosotros, tendríamos que cambiar el plan.   5. No irían a menos que usted _____ (conducir).   6. Nos pidieron que _____ (dar/nosotros) una presentación.   7. Si vosotros les _____ (decir) eso, no lo creerían.   8. Les dieron café para que no _____ (dormirse/ellos).   9. Hablaban como si _____ (estar/ellas) de acuerdo.
10. No podía creer que _____ (haber) tantos problemas en ese pueblito.

(continued)

11. Resolvieron el caso antes de que yo _____ (irse).   12. Te lo di a fin de que _____ (leer/tú) algo interesante.   13. Entré sin que nadie me _____ (oír).   14. Ojalá que mis abuelos no _____ (pedir/ella) tanto de mí.   15. Si usted _____ (poder) ayudarme, se lo agradecería.   16. Era esencial que _____ (poner/nosotros) el despertador.   17. No podíamos creer que vosotros _____ (poseer) esos poderes.   18. Queríamos encontrar una playa que ellos _____ (preferir).   19. No trabajaría en la película a menos que ellas la _____ (dirigir).   20. Traje el auto en caso de que ustedes _____ (querer) salir hoy.   21. Por suerte se calló antes de que yo _____ (reírse).   22. Si tú _____ (saber) lo que siento, no hablarías de esa manera.   23. Cambió su número para que él no la _____ (seguir) llamando.   24. Me encantó que ella _____ (sentir) lo mismo que yo.   25. No podíamos encontrar una casa que _____ (ser) tan barata como queríamos.   26. Dudo que nosotros _____ (ser) tan inocentes como ellos a su edad.   27. Os comportáis como si no _____ (tener/vosotros) nada que hacer.   28. Les pedimos que _____ (traer/ellos) pan.   29. No empezaríamos hasta que ellas _____ (venir) a ayudarnos.

Subjunctive Mood (Present Perfect Subjunctive)

Chapter 5.C.3, page 166

Ejercicio 5.37   Conjugue cada verbo en el presente perfecto del subjuntivo.

1. Ojalá que él _____ (ganar).   2. Tan pronto como _____ (graduarse/tú) iremos a Europa.   3. Haremos la sopa con tal de que él _____ (conseguir) los ingredientes.   4. No pueden creer que _____ (andar/nosotros) tanto.   5. Espero que _____ (aprender/vosotros) algo nuevo.   6. Esperamos que ellos no _____ (tomar) el agua.   7. Es posible que yo los _____ (avergonzar) sin darme cuenta.   8. Parece imposible que tú _____ (averiguar) tanto en tan poco tiempo.   9. Me alegro de que no _____ (buscar/ella) aquí.   10. Ahora les sorprende que nosotros _____ (cantar) esa canción.   11. Les dio coraje que vosotros _____ (cerrar) la puerta con llave.   12. Ojalá que ellas _____ (recoger) el correo hoy.   13. Todavía les sorprende que no me _____ (caber) esa camisa.   14. Lamentamos que no _____ (poder/tú) venir a la fiesta.   15. Puede ser que ella ya _____ (vender) el coche.   16. No importa que no _____ (viajar/nosotros) a ese país antes.   17. No creen que vosotros _____ (salir) anoche.   18. Basta que ellos _____ (tener) razón una vez.   19. No puedo creer que esos aretes _____ (costar) tanto.   20. ¡Qué bueno que yo _____ (venir) a tiempo!

Subjunctive Mood (Pluperfect Subjunctive)

Chapter 5.C.4, page 167

Ejercicio 5.38 Conjugue cada verbo en el pluscuamperfecto del subjuntivo.

1. No podían creer que yo les _____ (escribir) tantas veces. **2.** Si no me _____ (decir/ellos) eso ellos, no lo habría creído. **3.** Lo decían como si lo _____ (ver/ellos) en persona. **4.** Me parecía raro que no _____ (llegar/nosotros) todavía. **5.** No nos gustó que nos _____ (tratar/ellos) de esa manera. **6.** Era probable que nadie lo _____ (oír) antes. **7.** Dudaban que yo _____ (hacer) el trabajo en solo un mes. **8.** Nos bastaba que nuestros vecinos _____ (limpiar) su patio. **9.** Si me _____ (llamar/tú), no me habría preocupado tanto. **10.** Habría sido preferible que mi abuelo _____ (enterarse) desde un principio. **11.** Le molestó que tú no lo _____ (considerar). **12.** Ojalá que nunca _____ (lavar/vosotros) esa ropa en cloro. **13.** Si no _____ (volver/ellos) antes de la medianoche, habríamos llamado a la policía. **14.** Era imposible que _____ (resolver/él) el caso tan rápidamente. **15.** Estarías más cómoda si _____ (ponerse/tú) ropa de algodón. **16.** A veces me pregunto cómo sería mi vida si mi padre no _____ (morirse). **17.** Si _____ (abrir/nosotros) las ventanas, no haría tanto calor ahora. **18.** Ojalá que no _____ (comer/yo) tanto para la cena. **19.** Nos lo iban a decir tan pronto como _____ (confesar/nosotros) lo del robo. **20.** Les quitó el plato antes de que _____ (terminar/ellos) de comer.

Subjunctive Mood (Review)

Ejercicio 5.39 Temas de ensayo y de práctica oral

a. Ensayo

Prestando atención a las formas verbales, describa su relación con sus padres; piense en lo que ellos le dicen que haga o no haga, le piden que haga o no haga; en lo que usted les pide que hagan o no hagan. Use el subjuntivo cuando el contexto lo requiera.

b. Práctica oral

1. Pídale a un amigo hispano que le describa su relación con sus padres, y en particular lo que ellos le dicen que haga o no haga, lo que le aconsejan, lo que le piden, lo que los asusta, lo que los enorgullece, etc. Preste atención a sus formas verbales.

2. Prestando atención a las formas verbales, cuéntele a un amigo su relación con sus padres, y en particular lo que ellos le dicen que haga o no haga, lo que le aconsejan, lo que le piden, lo que los asusta, lo que los enorgullece, etc.

D IMPERATIVE MOOD

(Direct Commands: Tú)

Chapter 5.D.1.a, pages 167–169

Ejercicio 5.40 Conjugue en el imperativo de **tú**.

1. (Hablar) más alto, por favor.   2. (Comer) todo lo que tienes en el plato.
3. (Vivir) como se debe.   4. (Cerrar) las puertas con llave al salir.   5. (Abrir) esa ventana, por favor.   6. (Saltar) un poco.   7. (Escuchar) lo que te dicen tus padres.   8. (Volver) antes de las diez.   9. (Pedir) lo que tú quieras.   10. (Buscar) esta información en la red.   11. (Repetir) varias veces el mismo ejercicio, hasta memorizarlo.   12. (Mentir) solo si al mentir puedes hacer bien.   13. (Comenzar) ahora.   14. (Comentar) sobre el libro que leíste.   15. (Defender) a tus amigos.
16. (Seguir) trabajando.   17. (Pensar) en mí.   18. (Servir) la sopa, por favor.
19. (Elegir) el color que tú prefieras.   20. (Votar) por el mejor candidato.
21. (Envolver) los regalos antes de que lleguen los niños.   22. (Contar) conmigo.
23. (Cortar) el césped mientras yo barro.   24. (Apostar) poco dinero cada vez.
25. (Podar) los rosales con cuidado.   26. (Llorar) para desahogarte.   27. (Recordar) lo que te digo.   28. (Recortar) los anuncios que te interesen.   29. (Oler) esta rosa.   30. (Jugar) con nosotros.   31. (Jurar) decir la verdad.   32. (Proteger) a los animalitos indefensos.   33. (Seguir) caminando.   34. (Obedecer) a tus padres.   35. (Traducir) este documento.   36. (Producir) más si quieres ganar más.   37. (Enviar) el paquete por correo aéreo.   38. (Continuar) con el trabajo.
39. (Confiar) en mí.   40. (Reunir) a todos tus compañeros aquí esta tarde.
41. (Criar) a tus hijos como yo te crie a ti.   42. (Evaluar) este ensayo usando los mismos criterios.   43. (Concluir) tu trabajo.   44. ¡(Huir)!   45. (Callar) a esos niños ruidosos.   46. (Traer) una ensalada, si quieres.   47. (Dar) dos pasos para adelante.   48. (Oír), ¿vienes a la fiesta?

Ejercicio 5.41 Conjugue en el imperativo de **tú**.

1. (Decir) la verdad siempre.   2. (Hacer) lo mejor que puedas.   3. (Ir) a la tienda a comprar pan.   4. (Poner) la mesa.   5. (Salir) ahora a regar las matas.   6. (Ser) bueno.   7. (Tener) valor.   8. (Venir) conmigo.

Ejercicio 5.42 Conjugue en el imperativo de **tú**.

1. (Cantar), pero (no bailar).   2. (Estudiar), pero (no hablar) en voz alta.   3. (Beber) mucho jugo, y (no comer) nada artificial.   4. (Leer) el artículo, pero (no creer) todo lo que dice.   5. (Volver) a casa, pero (no correr).

6. (Descoser) el bolsillo, y (no coser) la bastilla.   **7.** (Escribir) una carta, pero (no describir) lo que pasó.   **8.** (Contar) lo que debes, y (no descontar) nada.   **9.** (Dormir) al bebé, pero (no dormirse) tú.   **10.** (Pedir) favores, y (no impedir) que te ayuden.   **11.** (Regalar) tu amistad y (no prestar) nada. **12.** (Buscar) el ungüento y (no rascarse) la picada.   **13.** (Escoger) la película que quieras ver, pero por favor (no escoger) una en inglés.   **14.** (Leer) tu correo electrónico, pero (no abrir) nada sospechoso.

Ejercicio 5.43   Conjugue en el imperativo de **tú**.

1. (Decir) la verdad y (no decir) mentiras.   **2.** (Hacer) la lectura para mañana, pero (no hacer) la tarea.   **3.** (Ir) a la tienda, pero (no ir) al correo.   **4.** (Poner) tu abrigo aquí y (no poner) tus zapatos en la mesa.   **5.** (Salir) a recoger el periódico, pero (no salir) por esa puerta.   **6.** (Ser) bueno, pero (no ser) tonto.   **7.** (Tener) hijos, pero (no tener) tantos como ella.   **8.** (Venir) a casa, pero (no venir) temprano.

Imperative Mood (Direct Commands: Usted/ustedes)

Chapter 5.D.1.b, pages 169–170

Ejercicio 5.44   Conjugue en el imperativo de **usted**.

1. (Seguir) caminando una cuadra más.   **2.** (No hablar) tan alto.   **3.** (Estudiar) solo.   **4.** (No cantar) ahora, por favor.   **5.** (Bailar) con nosotros.   **6.** (Tararear) la canción, a ver si la reconocemos.   **7.** (Comer) un poco para ver si le gusta. **8.** (No leer) ese periódico.   **9.** (Vivir) feliz.   **10.** (No toser) durante la obra, por favor.   **11.** ¡(Correr)! ¡Se le va a ir el tren!   **12.** (No beber) agua de la llave.   **13.** (Escribir) tarjetas postales.   **14.** (Cerrar) la ventana, por favor. **15.** (No perder) su mapa.   **16.** (Contar) el vuelto que le dan.   **17.** (No volver) a ese restaurante.   **18.** (Dormir) con la ventana abierta.   **19.** (No pedir) favores. **20.** ¿(Decir)?   **21.** (Oír), ¿sabe qué hora es?   **22.** (No tener) miedo. **23.** (Conducir) con cuidado.   **24.** (No caer) en la trampa.   **25.** (Hacer) la tarea. **26.** (Poner) la mesa, por favor.   **27.** (No salir) después de la medianoche. **28.** (Traer) el dinero mañana.   **29.** (Venir) pronto.   **30.** (No dar) nada.   **31.** (Ir) con ellos.   **32.** (No ser) ridículo.   **33.** (Dirigir) al grupo.   **34.** (Buscar) el tesoro. **35.** (No llegar) tarde.

Imperative Mood (Direct Commands: **Vosotros**)

Chapter 5.D.1.c, pages 170–171

Ejercicio 5.45 Conjugue en el imperativo de **vosotros**.

1. (Hablar) más claramente, por favor. 2. (Comer) un poco de todo.
3. (Exprimir) el jugo de los limones. 4. (Cerrar) las puertas. 5. (Abrir) los ojos. 6. (Saltar) por encima de los charcos. 7. (Escuchar) con cuidado.
8. (Volver) a tiempo. 9. (Pedir) lo que queráis. 10. (Conseguir) el mapa antes del viaje. 11. (Repetir) conmigo. 12. (Mentir) si es necesario. 13. (Comenzar) ahora. 14. (Comentar) sobre el artículo. 15. (Defender) a vuestra familia. 16. (Seguir) tratando. 17. (Pensar) en lo positivo. 18. (Servir) primero a los invitados. 19. (Elegir) el que prefiráis. 20. (Votar) hoy. 21. (Decir) solo lo necesario. 22. (Hacer) el trabajo. 23. (Ir) a visitar a vuestros abuelos.
24. (Poner) esas cosas aquí. 25. (Salir) temprano. 26. (Ser) discretos.
27. (Tener) paciencia. 28. (Venir) a verme.

Ejercicio 5.46 Conjugue en el imperativo de **vosotros**.

1. ¡(Despertarse)! ¡Ya es tarde! 2. (Levantarse) más temprano. 3. (Lavarse) las manos antes de comer. 4. (Irse) con los demás. 5. (Acostarse) temprano.
6. ¡(Dormirse) ya! 7. (Marcharse) con ellos. 8. (Despedirse) de la visita.
9. ¡(Callarse)!

Ejercicio 5.47 Conjugue en el imperativo de **vosotros**.

1. (Cantar), pero (no bailar). 2. (Estudiar), pero (no hablar) en voz alta.
3. (Beber) mucho jugo, y (no comer) nada artificial. 4. (Leer) el artículo, pero (no creer) todo lo que dice. 5. (Volver) a casa, pero (no correr). 6. (Descoser) el bolsillo, y (no coser) la bastilla. 7. (Escribir) una carta, pero (no describir) lo que pasó. 8. (Contar) lo que debéis, y (no descontar) nada. 9. (Dormir) al bebé, pero (no dormirse) vosotros. 10. (Pedir) favores, y (no impedir) que os ayuden. 11. (Regalar) vuestra amistad, y (no prestar) nada. 12. (Buscar) el ungüento, y (no rascarse) la picada. 13. (Escoger) la película que queréis ver, pero por favor (no escoger) una en inglés.

Ejercicio 5.48 Conjugue en el imperativo de **vosotros**.

1. (Decir) la verdad, y (no decir) mentiras. 2. (Hacer) la lectura para mañana, pero (no hacer) la tarea. 3. (Ir) a la tienda, pero (no ir) al correo. 4. (Poner) vuestro abrigo aquí, y (no poner) vuestros zapatos en la mesa. 5. (Salir) a recoger el periódico, pero (no salir) por esa puerta. 6. (Ser) buenos, pero (no ser) tontos.

7. (Tener) hijos, pero (no tener) tantos como ellos.   8. (Venir) a casa, pero (no venir) temprano.   9. (Apagar) el ventilador, pero (no apagar) la luz.

Imperative Mood (Direct Commands: **Nosotros**)

Chapter 5.D.1.d, pages 171–172

Ejercicio 5.49   Conjugue en el imperativo de **nosotros**.

1. (Caminar) por esta calle.   2. (No hablar) para que no nos oiga nadie.
3. (Estudiar) un poco antes de ir.   4. (No cantar) por favor.   5. (Bailar), ¿quieres?   6. (Tararear) la canción a ver si la reconocen.   7. (Comer) aquí.
8. (No leer) más.   9. (Vivir) en la Costa del Sol.   10. (No toser) sin taparnos la boca.   11. ¡(Correr)!   12. (No beber) tequila esta noche.   13. (Escribir) unas cartas antes de salir hoy.   14. (Cerrar) las ventanas antes de prender el aire acondicionado.   15. (No perder) de vista lo esencial.   16. (Contar) nuestro dinero antes de salir.   17. (No volver) a entrar aquí.   18. (Dormir) afuera hoy.
19. (Hacer) la tarea.   20. (Poner) las flores aquí.   21. (No salir) esta noche.
22. (No dar) nada.   23. (Ir) con ellos.   24. (No ser) tontos.   25. (Dirigir) al grupo.   26. (Buscar) su dirección.   27. (No llegar) tarde esta vez.

Ejercicio 5.50   Conjugue en el imperativo de **nosotros**.

1. (Despertarlas) antes de que sea muy tarde.   2. (No levantarse) tan temprano hoy.   3. (Lavarlo) con cloro.   4. (Marcharse) ya.   5. (No acostarse) en la arena esta vez.   6. ¡(Dormirse) ya!   7. (Irse) de aquí.   8. (No irse) hasta que nos traigan la cuenta.   9. (Vestirse) para la fiesta.

Imperative Mood (Indirect Commands)

Chapter 5.D.2, page 172

Ejercicio 5.51   Traduzca usando mandatos indirectos.

1. *I do not want to cook; let them cook today.*   2. *Have the manager call me.*   3. *If you do not have the money, let Mirta pay.*   4. *Have them send it to me.*

Ejercicio 5.52   Vamos a hacer los preparativos para una fiesta. Cada quien tiene algo que hacer. Usando los elementos indicados, formule un mandato para la persona indicada: Yo preparo la música.

1. Luisa / limpiar / el apartamento   2. Sara / enviar / las invitaciones   3. las vecinas / conseguir / globos   4. Pepe / pedir / pizza   5. todos / traer / de beber

Imperative Mood (Review)

Ejercicio 5.53 Conteste las preguntas, usando el imperativo familiar (**tú**) en el afirmativo y en el negativo. Transforme los nombres en pronombres cada vez que se pueda.

1. ¿Les digo el secreto?   2. ¿Hago los mandados?   3. ¿Le mando el mensaje?
4. ¿Voy al mercado?   5. ¿Le pongo los zapatos al niño?

Ejercicio 5.54 Conteste las preguntas, usando el imperativo formal (**Ud.** o **Uds.**) en el afirmativo y en el negativo. Transforme los nombres en pronombres cada vez que se pueda.

1. ¿Cantamos la canción?   2. ¿Le digo lo que pasó?   3. ¿Les enviamos las cartas?
4. ¿Vamos al cine?   5. ¿Me quito los zapatos?

Ejercicio 5.55 Conteste las preguntas, usando el imperativo de **nosotros** en el afirmativo y en el negativo. Transforme los nombres en pronombres cada vez que se pueda.

1. ¿Cantamos las canciones juntos?   2. ¿Vamos al cine?   3. ¿Le damos el dinero?
4. ¿Nos vamos ahora?   5. ¿Nos ponemos el abrigo?   6. ¿Jugamos el juego ahora?

Ejercicio 5.56 Traduzca la parte en negrilla usando el mandato indirecto (**Que** + subjuntivo).

1. *Have them prepare it.*   2. *I don't want to do it.* **Let Guillermo do it.**   3. *Have her come see me.*   4. *Have them call me.*   5. *If they're hungry,* **let them eat.**

Ejercicio 5.57   Temas de ensayo y de práctica oral

a. Ensayo

Prestando atención a las formas verbales, escriba un diálogo, usando el imperativo al máximo para la siguiente situación: es de noche, y de repente Luisito huele humo *(smoke):* va corriendo a despertar a su padre y a su madre.

b. Práctica oral

1. Pídale a un amigo hispano que le enumere los mandatos más comunes que recuerde de su infancia, de órdenes que le daban sus hermanos cuando jugaban, o sus padres a la hora de comer, sus abuelos o parientes cuando había reuniones de familia o sus maestros en la escuela. Preste atención a sus formas verbales.

2. Enumere los mandatos más comunes que recuerde de su infancia, de órdenes que le daban sus hermanos cuando jugaban, o sus padres a la hora de comer, sus abuelos o parientes cuando había reuniones de familia o sus maestros en la escuela.

F PARTICIPLE

(Present Participle)
Chapter 5.F.1, pages 173–174

Ejercicio 5.58 Llene cada espacio en blanco con el participio presente del verbo indicado.

1. Yo estaba _____ (hablar) por teléfono.   **2.** Estábamos _____ (comer) cuando llamaste.   **3.** En esa época estábais _____ (vivir) con vuestros abuelos.   **4.** Mi padre se estaba _____ (sentir) mejor.   **5.** No te estoy _____ (pedir) nada.
6. ¿Estás _____ (dormirse)?   **7.** Siempre estaban _____ (concluir) lo mismo.
8. Los niños estaban _____ (caer).   **9.** Estabas _____ (leer) el libro.   **10.** ¿Usted me está _____ (oír)?   **11.** Estaba _____ (decir) la verdad.   **12.** Nos fuimos _____ (ir) poco a poco.   **13.** _____ (Venir) por este camino se llega más rápido.
14. Creo que estaba _____ (poder).

Ejercicio 5.59 Llene cada espacio en blanco con el participio presente del verbo indicado.

1. Llegué _____ (caminar).   **2.** Estaba _____ (actuar).   **3.** Se fueron _____ (andar).   **4.** Habíamos estado _____ (estudiar) el idioma desde hacía tiempo.
5. No sabía qué estaban _____ (decir).   **6.** Andaban _____ (buscar) a su tío.   **7.** _____ (Ser) extranjero, no sentía que tuviera los mismos derechos.
8. La vi _____ (cerrar) el portón.   **9.** Estaban _____ (construir) un puente.
10. Iba _____ (conducir) a paso de tortuga.   **11.** Ese año estaban _____ (producir) más que nunca.   **12.** Iban _____ (recordar) poco a poco su pasado.   **13.** _____ (Creer) en su fuerza, lograrán más.   **14.** Estábamos _____ (almorzar).   **15.** Les iban _____ (dar) las respuestas una tras otra.   **16.** Se la pasaban _____ (elegir) a los candidatos más improbables.   **17.** Ellos iban _____ (seguir) el tren.

Ejercicio 5.60 Llene cada espacio en blanco con el participio presente del verbo indicado.

1. Venían _____ (llegar) poco a poco.   **2.** Estaban _____ (morirse) todas las plantas.   **3.** Lo iban _____ (mover) muy lentamente.   **4.** Nadie les estaba _____

(continued)

(negar) nada.   5. ¿Por qué estabais _____ (sonreírse)?   6. El perro seguía _____ (oler) la flor.   7. Los andaban _____ (despedir) uno tras otro.   8. ¿Quién estaba _____ (poner) esas cartas allí?   9. Los iban _____ (reunir) poco a poco.   10. _____ (Tener) el dinero, se podría hacer.   11. Los están _____ (traer) ahora mismo.   12. Siempre se la pasan _____ (intervenir) en los asuntos de otros.   13. Los estamos _____ (ver).   14. La estás _____ (volver) loca.

Participle (Past Participle)

Chapter 5.F.2, pages 174–175

Ejercicio 5.61   Llene cada espacio en blanco con el participio pasado del verbo indicado.

1. Había _____ (hablar) con tu padre.   2. Nunca hemos _____ (comer) aquí.   3. Su tía ha _____ (vivir) en Argentina.   4. He _____ (caminar) cuatro cuadras.   5. Juan: te has _____ (quedar) callado.   6. ¿Habéis _____ (aprender) a bailar el merengue?   7. Ojalá que no haya _____ (conducir) el abuelo.   8. Hemos _____ (almorzar) ya.   9. No habían _____ (dar) las tres todavía.   10. No te has _____ (sentar) en horas.   11. Nunca había _____ (oler) ese perfume antes.   12. Los Gómez han _____ (venir) a nuestra casa varias veces.

Ejercicio 5.62   Llene cada espacio en blanco con el participio pasado del verbo indicado.

1. Esa ventana nunca se ha _____ (abrir).   2. El pasto estaba _____ (cubrir) de granizo.   3. Nadie me había _____ (decir) eso antes.   4. ¿Les has _____ (escribir) a tus padres?   5. ¿Has _____ (hacer) tu cama?   6. No han _____ (morirse) los peces.   7. Ya habíamos _____ (ponerse) el traje de baño.   8. Si hubieran _____ (resolver) el caso, todos estarían satisfechos.   9. Ojalá que ya haya _____ (volver) Jorge.   10. ¿Qué pasaría si nunca hubieran _____ (descubrir) América?   11. Nunca había _____ (devolver) ese libro a la biblioteca.   12. Era imposible que hubieran _____ (suponer) eso.

Ejercicio 5.63   Traduzca.

1. *This is holy water.*   2. *They have blessed the food.*   3. *I want fried potatoes.*   4. *He had fried the fish.*   5. *Cursed luck!*   6. *I have never cursed anyone.*   7. *She wore her hair loose.*   8. *They have released the bulls.*   9. *The printed word is very important.*   10. *Have you printed your paper?*

Chapter 6
Verbs: Usage

A. PRESENT INDICATIVE

Chapter 6.A, pages 178–179

(To practice the present indicative forms, see Exercises 5.1–5.8. We recommend that you do those exercises before attempting these.)

Ejercicio 6.1 Usando sus conocimientos de los usos del presente del indicativo, traduzca los verbos de las oraciones siguientes.

1. La familia Gómez _____ *(live)* aquí. **2.** Profesora, ¿cuántos idiomas _____ *(do you speak)*? **3.** Mi auto está muy viejo. ¿Lo _____ *(should I sell it)* para poder comprarme uno nuevo? **4.** Si _____ *(it rains)*, no _____ *(we don't have to)* regar. **5.** ¿Me _____ *(Would you bring me)* un vaso de agua, por favor? **6.** —¿Tienes sueño? —Sí, _____ de despertarme *(I just . . .)*. **7.** Mañana _____ *(we are leaving* [salir]*)* temprano.

Ejercicio 6.2 Temas de ensayo y de práctica oral

a. Ensayo

Prestando atención al uso del presente del indicativo y usando una variedad de verbos, escriba una cartita informal:

1. de un amigo(a) a otro(a) que ya no vive en el mismo lugar, describiendo su vida estos días, lo que hace como rutina solo(a) y con sus amigos, y lo que hace con su tiempo libre, solo(a) y con sus amigos. Compare y contraste lo que prefieren hacer sus amigos y las actividades que usted prefiere. Haga preguntas sobre el otro amigo (o amiga).

2. respuesta a la carta del #1.

3. de un(a) novio(a) a otro(a) que vive lejos, contándole de su amor y describiendo su vida en su ausencia. No tenga miedo de ser melodramático(a). Haga preguntas sobre la vida del otro o la otra.

4. respuesta a la carta del #3.

5. de un(a) ex-novio(a) a otro(a) que le hace mucha falta y que quiere que vuelva. Use su imaginación para dramatizar la situación. Haga promesas sobre cómo va a cambiar su comportamiento si regresa ("Solo pienso en ti. No como. No duermo. Mis amigos no saben cómo consolarme…").

6. respuesta a la carta del #5.

7. de un(a) amigo(a) "electrónico(a)" a otro(a) conocido(a) a través de la red; prepare preguntas sobre la vida presente del individuo y de su familia, y haga lo posible por hacer preguntas detalladas, personales pero no indiscretas. Prepare un mínimo de diez preguntas.

8. respuesta a la carta del #7.

b. Práctica oral

Prestando atención al uso del presente del indicativo y usando una variedad de verbos, hable con un(a) compañero(a) sobre uno de los temas siguientes:

1. un día típico, lo que hace como rutina solo(a) y con sus amigos.

2. sus actividades favoritas en su tiempo libre.

3. sus añoranzas de familia y amistades de antes. ¿Quién le hace falta de su familia o de sus amistades, y por qué?

Ejercicio 6.3 Temas de ensayo y de práctica oral

a. Ensayo

Diario: En su diario personal, escriba un párrafo sobre uno de los temas que siguen, prestando atención al uso del presente del indicativo. Use un máximo de verbos diferentes.

1. Describa una costumbre que tiene usted o alguien que conoce y que le causa frustración.

2. Describa una virtud que usted admira en otra persona y que usted quisiera tener.

3. Describa en detalle un objeto nuevo que acaba de obtener y que le gusta mucho.

4. Describa en detalle un lugar donde usted se encuentra muy a gusto.

b. Práctica oral

1. Pídale a un(a) compañero(a) que le describa una relación amorosa típica entre jóvenes de su país. Que enumere las actividades que la sociedad requiere o permite, y las que prohíbe, lo que se recomienda, lo que se ve bien y mal frente a los demás y lo que se considera aceptable o no con los padres. Preste atención a sus formas verbales.

2. Prestando atención a las formas verbales, descríbale a un(a) amigo(a) una relación amorosa típica entre jóvenes norteamericanos. Describa las actividades que la sociedad requiere o permite, y las que prohíbe, lo que se recomienda, lo que se ve bien y mal frente a los demás y lo que se considera aceptable o no con los padres.

3. Hable con un(a) amigo(a) de los sucesos de hoy en día que más los frustran, los enojan y les da coraje.

4. Hable con un(a) amigo(a) de las cosas que les gustan que otros hagan o no hagan y digan o no digan.

B ASPECTS OF THE INDICATIVE PAST TENSE: PRETERITE VS. IMPERFECT AND PLUPERFECT

Chapter 6.B, pages 179–190

(See the corresponding exercises in Chapter 5 to practice the forms of the imperfect indicative [5.10–5.12] and the preterite [5.14–5.17]. We recommend that you do those exercises before these.)

Ejercicio 6.4 Conjugue cada verbo en el tiempo correcto (pretérito o imperfecto); para los verbos reflexivos, recuerde usar el pronombre apropiado.

1. Esta mañana Paco (levantarse) temprano, (bañarse) y (bajar) a la cocina a desayunar.   2. Ese hombre (ser) un cantante muy famoso, (tener) unos cincuenta años y (estar) casado con una modelo.   3. Todos los días mi padre (salir) para el trabajo a las cinco de la mañana y (volver) a la hora de la cena.   4. Yo (ver) esa película cuatro veces y cada vez me (gustar) por razones diferentes.   5. Mis amigos y yo (estar) en el parque cuando de repente (empezar) a caer granizo: todos juntos (correr) al árbol más cercano y (sentarse) a esperar a que pasara la tormenta; durante media hora (estar) ahí sin poder escaparnos.   6. Esta mañana Juanita me (decir) que (venir) a verme a las seis.   7. Cuando yo (ser) niño, (creer) en Santa Claus; luego cuando (tener) seis años, (descubrir) que (ser) un mito creado por la sociedad; me (molestar) mucho descubrir este engaño, y la vida no (ser) igual para mí de ese momento en adelante.   8. Cuando yo (entrar) al salón, (ver) que algunos de los estudiantes (comer), otros (hablar) y algunos (tratar) de estudiar.   9. La vida (parecer) más fácil en mi niñez: mis padres lo (decidir) todo por mí, y yo solo (hacer) lo que me (decir/ellos) o lo que (querer/yo).   10. Nadie (poder) creerlo: un boxeador le (morder) la oreja al otro dos veces. El público (ponerse) furioso porque el árbitro (interrumpir) la pelea.

Ejercicio 6.5 Transforme el párrafo siguiente al pasado, empezando con "En esa época,…".

Vivo bien. Tengo tres gatos y un perro, y una casa que me encanta. A mi esposa y a mí nos gusta lo mismo, y nos hacemos compañía en todo. Ganamos suficiente dinero para sobrevivir, y un poco más que ahorramos para jubilarnos y para algunos lujos. Una vez al año viajamos a algún lugar exótico.

Ejercicio 6.6 Conjugue cada verbo entre paréntesis en el tiempo correcto: pretérito o imperfecto. Para los verbos reflexivos, use el pronombre apropiado. Antes de comenzar, lea todo el párrafo.

Nunca olvidaré el invierno de 1995, cuando mis padres (**1.** irse) de vacaciones, y mi hermana y yo (**2.** quedarse) solas en casa durante una semana entera. Entre las dos, (**3.** planear) con cuidado una fiesta con todos nuestros amigos. Claro que no (**4.** pensar/nosotros) decirles nada a nuestros padres, porque siempre nos (**5.** regañar/ellos) cuando (**6.** invitar/nosotros) a más de un par de amigos a casa: no les (**7.** gustar) a mis padres que hiciéramos ruido. Así que en secreto (**8.** invitar/nosotros) a unos treinta amigos, y (**9.** venir) como cincuenta. La fiesta (**10.** ser) muy divertida: todos (**11.** beber) y (**12.** bailar) sin parar, y se (**13.** oír) la risa constante de los amigos por toda la casa. (**14.** Haber) tanta gente bailando en la sala en un momento que (**15.** parecer) que el piso se (**16.** ir) a romper. Y (**17.** ser) tantos que no (**18.** saber/nosotros) dónde (**19.** estar/ellos) a todas horas: en un momento yo (**20.** entrar) al cuarto de mis padres y (**21.** ver) a una docena de chicos que (**22.** beber) y (**23.** saltar) en la cama, y a otros tantos que (**24.** bailar) en el baño. En fin de cuentas, la fiesta nos (**25.** encantar) a todos, pero para mi hermana y para mí (**26.** ser) un desastre cuando mis padres (**27.** enterarse).

Ejercicio 6.7 Temas de ensayo y de práctica oral

a. Ensayo

Actos simultáneos o interrumpidos: Escriba un párrafo en el pasado para cada una de las situaciones que siguen. Elabore usando su imaginación.

1. Después de estudiar hasta las diez de la noche en la biblioteca, llegó usted a su cuarto esa noche, y al abrir la puerta vio que su compañero(a) de cuarto tenía varios amigos que estaban haciendo cosas diferentes: describa la escena.

2. Describa la escena que vio un viajero al entrar a un avión que lo iba a llevar a una isla del Caribe para las vacaciones de Navidad: cada uno de los pasajeros del avión estaba haciendo algo diferente.

3. Encuentre entre sus fotos de familia y de amigos algunas que tengan acciones en proceso. Fotocopie cada foto en una hoja aparte, y en la misma hoja, describa la escena, usando el pasado. (¿Cuándo se tomó esta foto? ¿quién tomó la foto? ¿qué estaba haciendo usted cuando se tomó esa foto? Y su hermano o amigo, ¿qué estaban haciendo?)

b. Práctica oral

Que cada compañero lleve a clase una foto de familia o de vacaciones. En parejas, hablen de sus fotos, describiendo lo que estaba pasando en cada contexto. Presten atención a sus formas verbales.

Ejercicio 6.8 Futuro en el pasado: La semana pasada, yo estaba con mi amiga Luisa en una discoteca, y ella me dijo muchas cosas. Ayer, Gregorio me pidió que le dijera lo que Luisa me había dicho. Como Gregorio está enamorado de Luisa, decidí contestar su pregunta: ¿Qué dijo? Aquí siguen las frases de Luisa. Dígale a Gregorio lo que dijo Luisa, empezando cada frase con: "Luisa dijo que…".

1. Mañana comemos en el restaurante mexicano. **2.** Esta noche bailo tango. **3.** Después de esta canción, bailo. **4.** El mes entrante mi familia va a Argentina. **5.** Mis vecinos se mudan pronto. **6.** Mañana llueve. **7.** Esta noche termino de leer mi novela.

Ejercicio 6.9 ¿Actos consecutivos o simultáneos (en proceso)? Indique para los actos entre paréntesis cuáles son los actos consecutivos [AC] (uno después de otro) y cuáles son los simultáneos [AS] (al mismo tiempo, en proceso). Luego escriba oraciones en el pasado usando los elementos dados.

> **Vocabulario***: **becerrito** *little calf*; **brillar** *to shine*; **brisa** *breeze*; **cola** *tail*; **menearse** *to move*; **monte** *hill*; **oler** *to smell*; **pájaro** *bird*; **rama** *branch*; **sol** *sun*; **vaca** *cow*

1. Esta mañana yo (despertarse), (levantarse), (bañarse), (vestirse) y (desayunar). **2.** Esta mañana cuando me desperté, los pájaros* (cantar), el sol* (brillar*) y yo (oler*) el pan tostado que (preparar/ellos) en la cocina. **3.** El espectáculo era hermoso: las vacas* (comer) pacíficamente en el monte*, los becerritos* (correr) para todos lados con la cola* en el aire, las ramas* de los árboles (menearse*) suavemente con la brisa* y hasta los insectos (cantar) de manera melodiosa. **4.** El profesor (entrar) al salón y les (anunciar) a los estudiantes la tarea para la semana siguiente. Luego (empezar) a hablarles del tema del día.

Ejercicio 6.10   Conjugue cada verbo entre paréntesis en el tiempo más lógico del pasado. Luego explique la diferencia entre los actos de las frases siguientes: 1 y 2; 3, 4 y 5; 6 y 7.

1. Cuando yo estaba en la escuela primaria, (sentarse) en una silla del frente.   **2.** Ayer (sentarse/yo) por accidente en un chicle.   **3.** Esta mañana (ir/yo) a mi primera clase cuando vi un accidente.   **4.** Anoche (ir/yo) al cine.   **5.** En esa época, (ir/yo) todos los días a visitar a mi abuelo que estaba en el hospital.   **6.** Abrí la puerta de mi cuarto y vi el desastre: las ardillas *(squirrels)* se habían metido; una de ellas (comer) cacahuates *(peanuts)* en mi escritorio, otra (buscar) algo entre las colchas *(blankets)* de mi cama y una tercera (correr) como loca por las paredes.   **7.** Esta mañana me levanté tarde porque mi despertador no funcionó. (Comer/yo) rápidamente, (buscar/yo) mis llaves a toda velocidad y (correr/yo) al trabajo.

Ejercicio 6.11   Traduzca las palabras en negrilla de las oraciones siguientes, prestando atención a los usos diferentes de *would*.

1. *I avoided the presence of my parents, because they **would say** the most embarrassing things about me.*   **2.** *If my mother were here, she **would say** she had told you so.*   **3.** *I know you **would not say** a word against me even if you were paid.*   **4.** *I insisted, but the boy **would not say** who had given him the money.*   **5.** *My mother **would not say** anything to anyone about our family's difficulties: she was that way.*

Ejercicio 6.12   Traduzca el verbo en negrilla, usando el verbo entre paréntesis. Para *you*, use el informal singular (tú).

1. *Yesterday I **met** your brother.* (conocer)   **2.** *We **met** at a party.* (conocer)   **3.** *I **knew** everyone there.* (conocer)   **4.** *When you were an adolescent, **could** you go to parties?* (poder)   **5.** *The prisoner **wanted** to get out, but he **knew** it was impossible so he did not even try.* (querer/saber)   **6.** *I **wanted** to tear the curtain (and tried), but I **was unable to**.* (querer/poder)   **7.** *My sister **did not want** to go with us (refused to), in spite of our insistence.* (querer)   **8.** *My sister **did not want** to go with us, but my father made her go.* (querer)   **9.** *When **did** you **find out** about the accident?* (saber)

Ejercicio 6.13   Pluscuamperfecto: Conjugue cada verbo en el imperfecto, el pretérito o el pluscuamperfecto.

1. Los indígenas les (tener) terror a los conquistadores porque nunca (ver) caballos antes.   **2.** No (comer/yo) nada en el cine porque (cenar) antes de ir.   **3.** Esta mañana me (doler) los ojos porque (trabajar/yo) en la computadora toda la noche.

Ejercicio 6.14 ¿Pretérito, imperfecto o pluscuamperfecto? Complete con la forma apropiada de cada verbo indicado.

Vocabulario*: alumbrar *to light;* **balde** *bucket;* **caballo** *horse;* **ensillar** *to saddle;* **ganado** *cattle;* **guiándose por el sonido** *being led by sound;* **leña** *firewood;* **madrugada** *early morning hours;* **ojo de agua** *water hole;* **vela** *candle*

El rancho de mi padre

Nunca olvidaré las semanas que (**1.** pasar/nosotros) en el rancho de mi padre. En esa época yo (**2.** tener) unos doce o trece años, y mi hermana unos catorce. En el rancho no (**3.** haber) ni electricidad ni agua corriente: todo se (**4.** alumbrar*) con velas o linternas, y mi hermana y yo (**5.** ir) a buscar agua en baldes* al ojo de agua* cerca de la casa. (**6.** Cocinar/nosotros) las tortillas y los frijoles con leña*. La rutina (**7.** ser) la siguiente: (**8.** levantarse/nosotros) a las cuatro de la mañana, y mientras una de nosotras (**9.** salir) a la oscuridad de la madrugada* a buscar los caballos*, guiándose por el sonido* nada más, la otra (**10.** preparar) el desayuno. (**11.** Terminar/nosotros) de desayunar, (**12.** ensillar*/nosotros) los caballos y (**13.** irse/nosotros) antes de que saliera el sol. Para cuando (**14.** llegar/nosotros) adonde (**15.** estar) el ganado*, ya el sol (**16.** salir) con todo su poder.

Ejercicio 6.15 ¿Pretérito, imperfecto o pluscuamperfecto? Complete con la forma apropiada de cada verbo indicado.

Una visita a la Alhambra

Para nuestro tercer viaje de grupo con el programa de Sevilla, (**1.** ir/nosotros) a visitar la Alhambra. Temprano en la mañana (**2.** tomar/nosotros) el autobús a Granada, que (**3.** tardar) unas tres horas y media en llegar.

El guía nos (**4.** decir) que la Alhambra (**5.** ser) uno de los monumentos más impresionantes del mundo, y que en ella se (**6.** poder) ver los últimos alientos del arte hispanomusulmán. La construcción de la Alhambra se (**7.** iniciar) a partir de la ocupación de Granada por Mohamed-Ben-Nazar, en el siglo XIII. No (**8.** ser) hasta 1492, con la reconquista de Granada por los Reyes Católicos, que la Alhambra (**9.** pasar) a ser palacio real.

En todo, (**10.** quedar/yo) impresionada con la belleza de los elementos decorativos, con las cúpulas y arcos, con las imponentes estructuras de defensa, y con los hermosos jardines llenos de plantas exóticas y bellas fuentes.

(continued)

Al entrar en una de las habitaciones, (**11.** ver/yo) una placa que (**12.** decir) que Washington Irving (**13.** escribir) "Cuentos de la Alhambra" en ese lugar.

Uno de mis lugares favoritos ese día en la Alhambra (**14.** ser) el Patio de los Leones, que en los tiempos musulmanes (**15.** ser) el refugio privado del sultán, de su familia y su harén.

De todos los lugares que (**16.** visitar/nosotros) durante nuestro año en Sevilla, la Alhambra (**17.** ser) el más impresionante.

Ejercicio 6.16 ¿Pretérito, imperfecto o pluscuamperfecto? Complete con la forma apropiada de cada verbo indicado.

Recuerdo la noche del incendio en nuestro pueblo. (**1.** Estar/nosotros) todos dormidos cuando de repente se (**2.** oír) golpes y gritos en la puerta. Eran los vecinos que (**3.** venir) a decirle a mi padre que (**4.** haber) fuego en una casa cerca de la nuestra. En ese pueblo no (**5.** haber) bomberos. (**6.** Vestirse/nosotros) a la carrera y (**7.** ir/nosotros) corriendo a ayudar a apagar el fuego que se (**8.** ver) de lejos. Una vez que llegamos allí, (**9.** unirse/nosotros) y así (**10.** empezar) una batalla que (**11.** durar) hasta el día siguiente. (**12.** Pasarse/nosotros) baldes de agua en cadena desde una casa vecina hasta la del incendio. (**13.** Lograr/nosotros) apagar el fuego, y salvar a la familia. Luego (**14.** enterarse/nosotros) que los mismos hijos adolescentes de la familia (**15.** provocar) el incendio accidentalmente con un cigarrillo.

Ejercicio 6.17 ¿Pretérito o imperfecto? Complete con la forma apropiada de cada verbo indicado.

> **Vocabulario*: acostumbrarse** *to get used to;* **chiquitito** *tiny;* **escalones** *steps;* **herido** *injured;* **leche** *milk;* **maullido** *meowing;* **platito** *little plate;* **por todos lados** *everywhere;* **tener terror** *to be terrified*

Gato

En mi casa, (**1.** ser/nosotros) gente de perros y no de gatos; de hecho, los gatos nos (**2.** caer) mal, quizá porque les (**3.** tener/nosotros) algo de miedo y no nos (**4.** respetar/ellos) como los perros. Pero un día del verano pasado todo eso (**5.** cambiar). (**6.** Estar/nosotros) sentados en la terraza tomando café cuando de repente (**7.** empezar/nosotros) a oír los maullidos* insistentes de un gatito perdido. Los maullidos eran tan fuertes que nos (**8.** imaginar/nosotros) que el gatito estaría atrapado en algún lugar, herido*. Lo (**9.** buscar/nosotros) por todos lados*, y por fin lo (**10.** encontrar/nosotros), debajo de los escalones* del frente de la casa.

(**11.** Ser) un gato tan chiquitito* que no (**12.** parecer) posible que esos maullidos salieran de él. (**13.** Ser) una cría, y nos (**14.** tener/él) terror*. (**15.** Estar/él) debajo de los escalones, pero (**16.** poder/él) salir. (**17.** Parecer) que su mamá lo (**18.** abandonar) y que no (**19.** saber) adónde ir. Nos (**20.** tomar) toda la mañana lograr que saliera de debajo de los escalones para tomar el platito* de leche* que le (**21.** ofrecer/nosotros). Muy lentamente (**22.** acostumbrarse/él) a nosotros y nos (**23.** adoptar/él). Desde entonces, somos gente de perros y de gatos.

Ejercicio 6.18   Temas de ensayo y de práctica oral

a. Ensayo

Escriba un párrafo sobre una costumbre cultural o una fiesta típica de su infancia.

b. Práctica oral

Cuéntele a un(a) amigo(a) de una costumbre cultural o una fiesta típica de su infancia. Preste atención a sus formas verbales.

Ejercicio 6.19   Temas de ensayo y de práctica oral

a. Ensayo

Imagínese que usted tiene un hermanito y que este le pide que le cuente un cuento. Cuéntele en el pasado uno de los cuentos siguientes, prestando atención al uso correcto del pretérito y del imperfecto: La Cenicienta (*Cinderella*); Caperucita Roja (*Little Red Riding Hood*); Los Tres Cerditos (*The Three Little Pigs*); Romeo y Julieta.

> **Vocabulario*: ceniza** *ashes;* **balcón** *balcony;* **baile** *ball;* **canasta** *basket;* **ladrillo** *brick;* **carroza** *carriage;* **enemigo** *enemy;* **hada madrina** *fairy godmother;* **fraile** *friar;* **cristal** *glass, crystal;* **abuelita** *granny, grandmother;* **caballo** *horse;* **cerdito** *little pig;* **leñador** *lumberjack;* **baile de disfraces** *masked ball;* **ratón** *mouse;* **palacio** *palace;* **cerdo** *pig;* **veneno** *poison;* **príncipe** *prince;* **calabaza** *pumpkin;* **rival** *rival;* **madrastra** *stepmother;* **hermanastra** *stepsister;* **paja** *straw;* **el lobo malo** *the big bad wolf;* **soplar** *to blow;* **exiliar** *to exile;* **tumbar** *to make something fall down;* **para verte mejor** *to see you better;* **parecer muerto** *to seem dead;* **¡Qué ojos más grandes tienes!** *What big eyes you have!;* **lobo** *wolf;* **madera** *wood;* **bosque** *woods*

b. Práctica oral

Usando la clase como público, cuente oralmente, en el pasado, uno de los cuentos sugeridos en el tema de ensayo.

Ejercicio 6.20 Temas de ensayo y de práctica oral

a. Ensayo

Cuente en el pasado uno de sus recuerdos de infancia favoritos.

b. Práctica oral

Hable con un(a) compañero(a) sobre sus recuerdos de infancia favoritos.

C COMPOUND TENSES

Chapter 6.C, pages 191–198

(To practice the forms of compound tenses and the present and past participle forms, see Exercises 5.19–5.20; 5.24; 5.27; 5.37–5.38; and 5.58–5.63. We recommend that you do those exercises before these.)

Ejercicio 6.21 Traduzca. Para *you*, use el informal singular (tú).

1. *I am writing a letter.*   2. *They have been working there since last week.*   3. *I was eating when you arrived.*   4. *He had been in the sun for three hours.*   5. *She had been calling for two days.*   6. *We have eaten.*   7. *We will have eaten by then* (para entonces).   8. *I was working on the computer all day yesterday.*   9. *He said he would have finished.*   10. *I thought it would be raining by now* (ya).

Ejercicio 6.22 Conteste las preguntas usando tiempos compuestos.

1. ¿Ha viajado usted alguna vez a otro país?   2. Antes de mudarse aquí, ¿había vivido usted en otro lugar?   3. Si en vez de venir a esta universidad usted hubiera podido ir a cualquier otra, ¿cuál habría preferido?   4. Indique una actividad en que ha participado aquí en que nunca antes se había imaginado participando.   5. ¿Cuáles son cinco cosas que quiere haber hecho antes de graduarse?

Ejercicio 6.23 Temas de ensayo y de práctica oral

a. Ensayo

Cuente el cuento de "Ricitos de Oro" *(Goldilocks)* en el pasado, usando el progresivo y el pluscuamperfecto cada vez que lo necesite.

> **Vocabulario: oso** *bear;* **cama** *bed;* **silla** *chair;* **la mamá osa** *mama bear;* **el papá oso** *papa bear;* **avena** *porridge;* **alguien** *somebody;* **sopa** *soup;* **el osito** *the little bear;* **estar acostado** *to be lying down [position];* **estar sentado** *to be*

sitting [position]; **dormirse** *to fall asleep;* **acostarse** *to lie down [change position from standing or sitting to lying down];* **sentarse** *to sit down [change position from standing to sitting];* **dormir** *to sleep;* **bosque** *woods*

b. Práctica oral

Hable con un(a) compañero(a) y cuéntele su versión de "Rizos de Oro" *(Goldilocks)*. Use el progresivo y el pluscuamperfecto cada vez que los necesite.

D WAYS OF EXPRESSING THE FUTURE

Chapter 6.D, page 199

(To practice the future forms, see exercises 5.21-22 and 5.24. We recommend that you do those exercises before these.)

Ejercicio 6.24   Traduzca de tres formas distintas. Para *you*, use el informal singular (tú).

1. *Tomorrow we will eat at a restaurant.*   **2.** *This evening we are going to the movies.*   **3.** *I will call you this afternoon.*   **4.** *What are you doing tonight?*

Ejercicio 6.25   Apunte las cosas que quiere que se cumplan antes de la actividad indicada, usando el futuro donde sea posible.

1. Antes de solicitar mi primer empleo profesional, (yo)…   **2.** Antes de que podamos votar por ese candidato, (él)…   **3.** Antes de que nuestros vecinos se quejen, (nosotros)…   **4.** Antes de que el mundo se destruya por nuestro descuido, (nosotros)…   **5.** Antes de morirme, (yo)…

Ejercicio 6.26   Temas de ensayo y de práctica oral

a. Ensayo

Usando el futuro cada vez que pueda, prepare una lista de diez promesas para mejorarse o para mejorar su vida; use verbos diferentes para cada promesa. (Por ejemplo: Me levantaré temprano. Haré mi cama cada mañana. No le gritaré a mi hermano aunque él me provoque.)

b. Práctica oral

En parejas de candidatos para la presidencia digan qué promesas harán para ganar el voto popular, alternando entre ustedes. Usen verbos diferentes para cada promesa y presten atención a las formas del futuro.

E CONDITIONAL

Chapter 6.E, pages 200–201

(To practice the conditional forms, see Exercises 5.25–5.27. We recommend that you do those exercises before these.)

Ejercicio 6.27 Cambie las oraciones siguientes para que sean más corteses.

1. ¿Puedes ayudarme con esto?   2. ¿Tienes tiempo para ayudarme?   3. No debes hacer eso.   4. Quiero que vengas.

Ejercicio 6.28 Cambie las oraciones al pasado.

1. Pienso que lo terminarán a tiempo.   2. Creo que llegarán pronto.   3. Dice que lo hará.   4. Sé que cumplirá con su promesa.

Ejercicio 6.29 Temas de ensayo y de práctica oral

a. Ensayo

Escriba un diálogo entre un mesero en un restaurante y un par de clientes difíciles, uno porque no quiere aumentar de peso, y el otro porque no tiene mucho dinero.

b. Práctica oral

Minidrama: El salón de clase es un restaurante, con clientes difíciles (el que está de dieta, el que no quiere gastar mucho, el que tiene alergias, el vegetariano, el que no come nada de color verde, etc.), y meseros que tratan de complacerlos, o que no tienen la libertad de cambiar los platos del menú. Antes de empezar, que cada cliente prepare algunas frases con el condicional para pedir sus platos especiales, y luego, dramaticen su escena, usando sus frases y prestando atención a sus formas verbales y expresiones de cortesía.

F PROBABILITY

Chapter 6.F, pages 201–203

(To practice the future and conditional forms, see Exercises 5.21–5.28. We recommend that you do those exercises before these.)

Ejercicio 6.30 Conteste las preguntas expresando conjetura y usando la información entre paréntesis.

1. ¿Por qué no puedo bajar de peso? (no controlar tu apetito)   **2.** ¿Por qué se veía verde ese hombre? (ser marciano) (estar enfermo) (algo asustarlo)   **3.** ¿Dónde está tu hermano? (estar en el sótano) (ir a la tienda)

Ejercicio 6.31   Temas de ensayo y de práctica oral

a. Ensayo

Usted es detective y debe escribir un informe de lo que cree que pasó basándose en los hechos *(facts)* que observa en un crimen: se encuentra el cadáver *(corpse)* de un hombre flotando boca abajo en la piscina *(swimming pool)* de la casa de su vecino; no hay ninguna evidencia de violencia física. El cadáver está casi completamente desnudo *(naked)*: solo tiene puesto un reloj *(watch)* que se paró a las tres y media. La autopsia revela que el hombre no murió ahogado *(drowned)*, sino envenenado *(poisoned)*. Escriba dos probables maneras en que pudo haber terminado así, usando un máximo de detalle descriptivo. Esto lo hace sin saber de seguro nada de nada *(without knowing anything at all for certain)*. (Por ejemplo: El hombre sería rico, y su esposa por alguna razón lo odiaría y querría deshacerse de él; lo habrá envenenado y luego, una vez que había muerto, ella habrá empujado su cadáver dentro de la piscina, con la ayuda de alguien.)

b. Práctica oral

En parejas y alternando su turno, háganse preguntas sobre lo que observan en la clase hoy. Contesten con formas de probabilidad, usando su imaginación. Por ejemplo: Estudiante 1: ¿Por qué se vistió de azul la profesora? Estudiante 2: Será su color favorito.

c. Tema de práctica oral

Piense en un evento misterioso reciente en las noticias, y dígale a un(a) compañero(a) lo que habrá pasado según usted, usando formas de probabilidad.

G SUBJUNCTIVE

(Nominal Clauses)

Chapter 6.G.2, pages 203–213

(To practice the subjunctive forms, see Exercises 5.29–5.38. We recommend that you do those exercises before these.)

Ejercicio 6.32   Conjugue cada verbo entre paréntesis en el presente del subjuntivo o del indicativo según lo requiera el contexto.

(continued)

1. Sus padres lo obligan a que (trabajar/él).   2. Creo que (tener/tú) razón.
3. Basta que (pagar/tú) la mitad.   4. Conviene que (salir/nosotros) temprano.
5. ¿Desea usted que le (servir/nosotros) en su habitación?   6. Mi padre se empeña en que yo no (ir) sola.   7. Es bueno que ellos (aprender) a nadar.   8. Es cierto que nosotros lo (ver).   9. Es evidente que tú (comer) demasiado temprano.
10. Es importante que yo la (llevar).   11. Es triste que ellos no (poder) salir de allí.   12. Es una lástima que tus vecinos no te (caer bien).   13. Eso no significa que tu novia no te (querer).   14. Veo que los pájaros no (poder) volar.
15. Insisto en que me (dejar/ustedes) pagar a mí.   16. Lamento que (ser) así.
17. Mi madre siempre me aconseja que (llevar/yo) más dinero del que necesito.
18. Nos encanta que nuestros amigos nos (sorprender) con sus visitas.   19. Te ruego que me (escuchar).   20. Ella siempre lo convence de que (quedarse) tarde.

Ejercicio 6.33 Conjugue cada verbo entre paréntesis en el presente del subjuntivo o del indicativo según lo requiera el contexto.

1. Piensan que les (deber/nosotros) dinero.   2. Más vale que ustedes (levantarse) temprano.   3. Le enoja que su hermano siempre (ganar).   4. ¿Necesitas que te (llevar/yo)?   5. El testigo niega que su hijo (ser) culpable.   6. No es que (llover) demasiado—al contrario.   7. No importa que no (querer/ellos); tienen que hacerlo.   8. Sé que me (querer/ella).   9. Los vecinos se quejan de que los niños (gritar) mucho.   10. Puede ser que ella (llegar) temprano.   11. Los adolescentes se avergüenzan de que sus padres los (controlar) en público.   12. Me opongo a que él lo (ver).   13. Estamos seguras de que mañana (ir) a llover.   14. Su hermana la persuade a que (hacer/ella) lo que ella quiere.   15. Mi madre me manda que le (llevar) sus cartas al correo.   16. Les advierto que (callarse/ustedes).
17. Me prohíben que (salir) tarde.   18. Tienen miedo que yo los (denunciar) a la policía.   19. Dice que no (saber/él) nada.   20. Tenemos que impedir que él (pagar) esta vez.

Ejercicio 6.34 Conjugue cada verbo entre paréntesis en el presente del subjuntivo o un tiempo *(tense)* del indicativo según lo requiera el contexto.

1. Ella cree que él no la (querer).   2. Ella no cree que él la (querer).   3. Su padre le dice que él (levantarse) temprano de niño. *[He used to get up early.]*   4. Su padre le dice que (levantarse) temprano. *[He tells her to get up early.]*   5. Te recomiendo que (dormir/tú) más.   6. ¿Te pide que (ir/tú) con él?   7. Espero que (poder/ellos) venir a la fiesta.   8. Me molesta que no me (hacer/ellos) caso.   9. Me alegro que (ser/tú) feliz.   10. No me gusta que me (gritar/ellos).   11. Parece que (estar/él) triste.   12. No parece que (estar/él) triste.   13. Parece increíble que ellos no lo (saber).   14. Me sorprende que no me (llamar/él).   15. Te sugiero que (tomar/tú) vitaminas.

Ejercicio 6.35 Traduzca. Para *you*, use el informal singular (tú).

1. *She lets me drive.*   **2.** *I hope I can do it.*   **3.** *I hope you can do it.*   **4.** *I feel it is going to rain.*   **5.** *I am sorry it is going to rain.*   **6.** *I am sorry I cannot do it.*

Ejercicio 6.36 Temas de ensayo y de práctica oral

a. Ensayo

Usando varias de las expresiones en la lista del capítulo 6.G.2.b ("Subjunctive after expressions of emotion"), describa en diez frases sus esperanzas, sus temores, lo que lamenta y lo que le emociona.

b. Práctica oral

Cuéntele a un(a) compañero(a) de sus esperanzas, temores, lo que lamenta y lo que le emociona, y luego pídale que haga lo mismo. Presten atención a sus formas verbales.

Ejercicio 6.37 Temas de ensayo y de práctica oral

a. Ensayo

Usando varias de las expresiones en la lista del capítulo 6.G.2.c ("Subjunctive after expressions of volition and influence"), describa en diez frases lo que sus padres le aconsejan, le prohíben, le recomiendan, etc.

b. Práctica oral

Hable con un(a) compañero(a) sobre lo que sus padres les aconsejan, les prohíben, les recomiendan, etc. Comparen sus experiencias prestando atención a sus formas verbales.

Ejercicio 6.38 Temas de ensayo y de práctica oral

a. Ensayo

Usando varias de las expresiones en la lista del capítulo 6.G.2.d ("Subjunctive after expressions of doubt and negation of reality"), describa en detalle una de sus dudas más importantes, como por ejemplo sobre el origen del mundo, la existencia de Dios, la vida en Marte *(Mars)*, el racismo, etc.

b. Práctica oral

Hable con un(a) compañero(a) sobre el momento en que usted empezó a dudar de un mito tradicional, como Santa Claus, los Reyes Magos, etc. Describa en detalle la transición entre estar seguro, dudar, y luego perder por completo la creencia. Comparen sus experiencias.

Ejercicio 6.39   Temas de ensayo y de práctica oral

a. Ensayo

Usando varias de las expresiones en la lista del capítulo 6.G.2.e ("Subjunctive after impersonal expressions with **ser**"), escriba diez consejos e ideas que usted le da a un(a) amigo(a) sobre un viaje a un país hispano.

b. Práctica oral

Usando varias de las expresiones en la lista del capítulo 6.G.2.e ("Subjunctive after impersonal expressions with **ser**"), dele consejos e ideas a un(a) amigo(a) sobre un viaje a un país hispano.

Ejercicio 6.40   Temas de ensayo y de práctica oral

a. Ensayo

Usando el mayor número posible de verbos de la lista de abajo para introducir cláusulas nominales, escriba un párrafo sobre el tema del amor en el mundo de hoy: piense en términos de establecer una pareja, la opción entre la soltería (no casarse) y el matrimonio (casarse), tener hijos o no y el divorcio. Si lo desea, puede hacer referencia a su vida personal para expresar su opinión. Preste atención al uso del subjuntivo, del infinitivo o del indicativo, dependiendo del contexto. Mire las páginas sobre las cláusulas nominales para ver ejemplos de usos de estos verbos.

> **querer, parecer, dudar, gustar, esperar, tener miedo de, alegrarse, enojar, molestar, sorprender, necesitar, preferir, oponerse a, dejar, obligar a, convencer, impedir, mandar, pedir, permitir, recomendar, sugerir, bastar, convenir, no creer, no ser, no significar, ser bueno (malo, raro, triste, importante, necesario, difícil, imposible, una lástima) que**

b. Práctica oral

1. Usando los verbos de arriba, y prestando atención a sus formas verbales, hable con un(a) compañero(a) sobre sus perspectivas del amor hoy en día: piensen en términos de establecer una pareja, la opción entre la soltería (no casarse) y el matrimonio (casarse), tener hijos o no y el divorcio.

2. Debate: El matrimonio de parejas interraciales, de religiones distintas, de edades muy diferentes o del mismo sexo. Prestando atención a sus formas verbales, opinen sobre estos temas controvertibles, sin perder de vista el requisito de tolerancia.

Subjunctive (Adjectival Clauses)

Chapter 6.G.3, pages 213–214

Ejercicio 6.41 Complete con el presente del subjuntivo o algún tiempo del indicativo de cada verbo entre paréntesis, según lo requiera el contexto.

1. Estamos esperando a la mujer que (calcular) nuestros impuestos. 2. Quiero encontrar a una mujer que (saber) hacerlo. 3. ¿Conoces a un hombre que (poder) hacerlo? 4. Yo conozco a un hombre que (poder) hacerlo. 5. No hay nadie que (poder) hacerlo como tú. 6. Hay alguien que (poder) hacerlo. 7. Haz lo que te (decir/yo) ayer. 8. Siempre hace lo que le (decir/ellos), sea lo que sea. 9. Digan lo que (decir/ellos), nunca te abandonaré.

Ejercicio 6.42 Temas de ensayo y de práctica oral

a. Ensayo

Haga una lista de diez deseos en su vida, usando cláusulas adjetivales. (Por ejemplo: Quiero conseguir un trabajo que me pague bien.)

b. Práctica oral

En parejas, comparen sus deseos y sueños en la vida, prestando atención a sus formas verbales.

Subjunctive (Adverbial Clauses)

Chapter 6.G.4, pages 215–218

Ejercicio 6.43 Conjugue cada verbo entre paréntesis en el presente del subjuntivo o un tiempo del indicativo según lo requiera el contexto.

1. Ellos llegaron después de que nosotros (salir). 2. Lo hago para que tú no (tener) que hacerlo. 3. Ven a visitarnos tan pronto como (poder/tú). 4. Mañana iremos al parque aunque (llover). 5. Quiero hablar con ella por teléfono antes de que (irse/ella). 6. Me lo dará, a no ser que (arrepentirse/él) primero. 7. Comerá después de que los niños (acostarse). 8. Caminó hasta que no (poder) más. 9. Caminará hasta que no (poder) más. 10. Tendrá el dinero, a menos que no le (pagar/ellos) hoy. 11. Lo haremos cuando (querer/tú). 12. Comí aunque no (tener) hambre. 13. Me gusta mirar por la ventana cuando (llover). 14. Los vemos a ellos sin que ellos nos (ver) a nosotros. 15. Lo haré con tal que no se lo (decir/tú) a los vecinos.

Ejercicio 6.44 Traduzca. Para *you*, use el informal singular (tú).

1. *She will not go unless we go.*   2. *I will do it as long as (or provided) you do not tell anyone.*   3. *We will leave as soon as you get dressed.*   4. *I will keep trying until it works.*   5. *I do not know anyone who can do that without your explaining how.*

Ejercicio 6.45   Temas de ensayo y de práctica oral

a. Ensayo

Usando el mayor número posible de conjunciones de la lista de abajo para introducir cláusulas adverbiales, escriba un diálogo entre dos compañeros de casa que están preparándose para una fiesta en su casa.

para que, a menos que, antes de que, con tal de que, sin que, en caso de que, cuando, en cuanto, aunque, a pesar de que, después de que, mientras, hasta que

b. Práctica oral

Usando el mayor número posible de conjunciones de la lista de arriba para introducir cláusulas adverbiales, planee con otros compañeros una fiesta en la clase.

Subjunctive (Sequence of Tenses)

Chapter 6.G.5, pages 219–228

Ejercicio 6.46   Combine cada dos oraciones, usando la que está entre paréntesis como cláusula principal. Haga las transformaciones necesarias.

1. Mañana llegarán nuestros amigos. (No creo que…)   2. Raúl vive en Suiza. (Parece increíble que…)   3. Los vecinos ya han visto esa película. (Me sorprende que…)   4. Ayer hacía calor. (Dudo que…)   5. Se levantó a las cinco. (Me sorprende que…)   6. Ya habrá terminado a esa hora. (Parece dudoso que…)   7. Mi abuelo ya había muerto cuando llegué. (Lamento que…)   8. Pronto estará lista la cena. (Mi padre dudaba que…)   9. Siempre hace frío en el monte. (Mi tía se quejaba de que…)   10. Tú bailabas el tango a los cinco años. (Era imposible que…)   11. Los perros se escaparon. (Temían que…)   12. Luisa nunca les ha dicho el secreto a sus hijos. (A Roberto le molestaba que…)   13. Habrán regresado para la medianoche. (Me sorprendería mucho que…)   14. Miguel ya había leído esa novela. (Yo tenía miedo que…)

Ejercicio 6.47 Transforme el verbo de cada cláusula subordinada (en negrilla) para concordar en el nuevo contexto con el verbo principal en el pasado (entre paréntesis).

1. No creo que **puedan** venir. (No creía que…)   **2.** Parece posible que **haga** calor hoy. (Parecía posible que… ese día.)   **3.** Lamento que no les **guste**. (Lamentaba que…)   **4.** ¿Conoces a alguien que **sea** de allí? (¿Conocías a alguien que…?)   **5.** Queremos encontrar una casa que **tenga** piscina. (Queríamos…)   **6.** Haremos lo que tú **quieras**. (Te dije que haríamos lo que…)   **7.** Te doy las llaves a fin de que tú **abras**. (Te di las llaves…)   **8.** Llama antes de que **sea** muy tarde. (Quería llamar antes de que…)

Ejercicio 6.48   Forme una frase usando la primera como subordinada.

1. Cantaban bien. (Me parecía increíble que…)   **2.** Ellos caminaron. (Dudo que…)   **3.** Yo había caminado. (Ellos no creyeron que…)   **4.** Perdí las llaves. (Ella se quejó de que yo…)   **5.** Por fin pudieron ver la película. (Me alegro de que…)   **6.** Los perros no habían ladrado en toda la noche. (A Pedro le sorprendió que…)

Ejercicio 6.49   Conjugue cada verbo entre paréntesis en la forma correcta.

1. Nosotros queríamos que ellos nos (llamar) primero.   **2.** A ella le gustaría que ustedes (ser) más directos.   **3.** El profesor dijo que no sabía si existía un texto que (explicar) más claramente ese punto.   **4.** ¿Había alguien que (poder) hacerlo?   **5.** Nos encantaría que las vacaciones (ser) más largas.   **6.** Me prometiste que me llamarías tan pronto (poder).   **7.** Les pedía que (callarse) a fin de que no (despertar) a los niños.   **8.** Me costaba trabajo creer que Marta (cortarse) el pelo la semana anterior.

Ejercicio 6.50   Temas de ensayo y de práctica oral

a. Ensayo

Deseos cambiados. Piense en su vida, y en los sueños y deseos que ha tenido desde la infancia. Algunos de sus deseos y sueños habrán cambiado a través de los años. Escriba un párrafo, describiendo cuatro o cinco de sus sueños y deseos en su infancia, cómo se lograron o no, y cómo cambiaron. Use al máximo las expresiones en la lista del capítulo 6.G.2.b ("Subjunctive after expressions of emotion").

b. Práctica oral

Hable con sus compañeros sobre sus deseos de infancia que han cambiado.

Ejercicio 6.51 Temas de ensayo y de práctica oral

a. Ensayo

Entreviste a alguien de una generación anterior a la suya, sobre la disciplina en la vida cuando era joven. Usando varias de las expresiones en la lista del capítulo 6.G.2.c ("Subjunctive after expressions of volition and influence"), escriba diez frases sobre lo que sus padres le aconsejaban, le prohibían, le recomendaban, etc., a este individuo.

b. Práctica oral

Usando el tema de ensayo de arriba, dé un informe oral sobre su entrevista.

Ejercicio 6.52 Temas de ensayo y de práctica oral

a. Ensayo

Entreviste a uno de sus padres, o a alguien de una generación anterior a la suya, sobre lo que pensaban de la guerra y de la política cuando tenían la edad que usted tiene ahora. Usando varias de las expresiones de la lista del capítulo 6.G.2.d ("Subjunctive after expressions of doubt and negation of reality"), escriba unas diez frases.

b. Práctica oral

Usando el tema de ensayo de arriba, dé un informe oral sobre su entrevista.

Ejercicio 6.53 Temas de ensayo y de práctica oral

a. Ensayo

Usando varias de las expresiones de la lista del capítulo 6.G.2.e ("Subjunctive after impersonal expressions with **ser**"), escriba diez consejos e ideas que usted le dio a un(a) amigo(a) antes de que este viajara a un país hispano. Por ejemplo: Le dije que era mejor que llevara ropa ligera, que era malo que no tratara de hablar español, etc.

b. Práctica oral

Hable con un(a) compañero(a) sobre una experiencia de su niñez en que sus padres o amigos le habían dado consejos que usted no siguió, y que luego descubrió que debió haberlos seguido. Prestando atención a las formas verbales, comparen sus experiencias.

Ejercicio 6.54 Temas de ensayo y de práctica oral

a. Ensayo

Entreviste a alguien que pertenezca a una generación anterior a la suya sobre el tema del amor cuando era adolescente, y sus sueños o sus ideales para el amor en su vida; averigüe si los padres de esta persona afectaron de alguna manera su punto de vista o su comportamiento. Usando el mayor número posible de verbos de la lista de abajo para introducir cláusulas nominales, escriba un párrafo sobre lo que pensaba esta persona. Preste atención al uso del subjuntivo, del infinitivo o del indicativo, dependiendo del contexto. Consulte las páginas sobre las cláusulas nominales para ver ejemplos de usos de estos verbos.

querer, parecer, dudar, gustar, esperar, tener miedo de, alegrarse, enojarse, molestar, sorprender, necesitar, preferir, oponerse a, dejar, obligar a, convencer, impedir, mandar, pedir, permitir, recomendar, sugerir, bastar, convenir, no creer, no ser, no significar, ser bueno (malo, raro, triste, importante, necesario, difícil, imposible, una lástima) que

b. Práctica oral

Use el tema de ensayo de arriba, y dé un informe oral sobre su entrevista.

Subjunctive (*If* [si] Clauses)

Chapter 6.G.6, pages 228–230

Ejercicio 6.55 Conjugue cada verbo entre paréntesis en la forma correcta.

1. Ella habría llegado a tiempo si no (haber) una tormenta. **2.** Si él tuviera dinero, (comprarse) todos los coches antiguos del mundo. **3.** Iría al supermercado si (ser) absolutamente necesario. **4.** Si hubiéramos estudiado más, no (tener) tantas dificultades en el examen de ayer. **5.** Si tuviera tiempo, te (ayudar/yo). **6.** Se abrazaron como si no (verse) en años. **7.** Lo trata como si (ser) adulto.

Ejercicio 6.56 Temas de ensayo y de práctica oral

a. Ensayo

Describa en un párrafo lo que pasaría si pudiera cambiar algún aspecto de su vida futura.

(continued)

b. Práctica oral

Hable con un(a) compañero(a) sobre algo que quisiera cambiar en su vida o en el mundo, imaginando lo que pasaría en el futuro si esto cambiara. Comparen sus sueños de cambio, prestando atención a las formas verbales.

Ejercicio 6.57 Temas de ensayo y de práctica oral

a. Ensayo

Describa en un párrafo cómo habría sido diferente su vida si algún elemento hubiera sido diferente desde el principio.

b. Práctica oral

Hable con un(a) compañero(a) sobre alguna característica de su familia o evento de su pasado que lo ha marcado hoy en día. Imagine cómo sería diferente su vida ahora si esa característica hubiera sido diferente, o si ese evento no hubiera ocurrido.

Subjunctive (Ojalá)

Chapter 6.G.7, pages 230–231

Ejercicio 6.58 Traduzca usando **Ojalá**. Para *you*, use el informal singular (tú).

1. *I wish she had not gone.*   2. *I wish you had listened to me.*   3. *I hope you eat today.*   4. *I wish he could see me now.*   5. *I hope they did not do it.*   6. *I hope we get there on time.*   7. *I hope they finished.*   8. *I hope she likes it.*   9. *I hope they bought it.*   10. *I wish you could hear me.*

Ejercicio 6.59 Haga una lista de deseos para usted usando **Ojalá**.

1. un deseo posible para el futuro   2. un deseo posible para el presente   3. un deseo posible para el pasado   4. un deseo contrario a la realidad presente   5. un deseo contrario a la realidad pasada

Subjunctive (Expressions of Leave-Taking)

Chapter 6.G.8, pages 231–234

Ejercicio 6.60 Traduzca estas expresiones usando las personas indicadas.

1. *Get well.* (tú)   2. *Have a good weekend.* (tú)   3. *Have a good day.* (ustedes)   4. *Have fun.* (usted)

Ejercicio 6.61 Despídase de las siguientes personas usando **irle bien a uno**.

1. de un amigo   2. de un profesor   3. de unos amigos (en Latinoamérica)
4. de unos amigos (en España)

Ejercicio 6.62 Despídase de las mismas personas usando **pasarlo bien**.

1. de un amigo   2. de un profesor   3. de unos amigos (en Latinoamérica)
4. de unos amigos (en España)

Ejercicio 6.63 Temas de escritura y de práctica oral

a. Escriba minidiálogos de despedida para cada situación.

1. despedida de un(a) amigo(a) en cualquier momento   2. despedida de un(a) profesor(a) un viernes antes de un fin de semana normal   3. despedida de una pareja de amigos antes de un viaje que va a hacer la pareja   4. despedida de varios amigos antes de una fiesta   5. despedida de un(a) amigo(a) enfermo(a)   6. despedida de unos amigos antes de una experiencia placentera

b. Usando los diálogos que preparó arriba, busque todas las oportunidades posibles cada día para practicarlos en contextos auténticos.

H   INFINITIVES AND PRESENT PARTICIPLES

Chapter 6.H, pages 234–239

(To practice the present participle forms, see Exercises 5.58–5.60. We recommend that you do those exercises before these.)

Ejercicio 6.64 Escoja la forma correcta entre paréntesis.

1. (Beber/Bebiendo) agua es muy saludable.   2. No les gusta (cantar/cantando).
3. Pensaban (viajar/viajando) al Caribe este invierno.   4. Se fueron sin (decir/diciendo) nada.   5. Eso es lo que te pasa por (hablar/hablando) tanto.   6. Estoy cansado de (rogar/rogando).   7. Al (salir/saliendo), no se les olvide llevarse el paraguas.   8. El anuncio decía: "No (fumar/fumando)".

Ejercicio 6.65 Traduzca las oraciones siguientes.

1. *That language is difficult to learn.*   2. *It is difficult to learn that language.*
3. *That recipe is easy to prepare.*   4. *It is easy to tell the truth.*   5. *It is possible to live longer than ninety years.*   6. *Some things are impossible to change.*

Ejercicio 6.66 Las frases siguientes tienen participios presentes en inglés. ¿En cuáles se usarían un participio presente en español también?

1. That is one of the world's **increasing** problems.   2. What an **interesting** subject!   3. She is one of the **leading** experts in that subject.   4. I need to buy some **writing** paper.   5. That psychologist says that all of the problems of adolescence are caused by **growing** pains.   6. They have **running** water.   7. Take a photo of the pitcher **containing** the blue liquid.   8. The court wanted a number of items **belonging** to her.   9. There he was, **standing** in the middle of the room.   10. The movie was **boring**.   11. That is an **amusing** game.   12. I found the dog **lying** on the bed.   13. She was **sitting** in front of me at the movies.   14. This exercise is **entertaining**.   15. Do you have any **drinking** water?

Ejercicio 6.67   Traduzca al español las frases del ejercicio anterior.

Ejercicio 6.68   Traduzca las oraciones siguientes.

1. *Look: they are **increasing** the weight.*   2. *They were **directing** the traffic to the side.*   3. *They left **running**.*   4. *The speaker was **boring** us all.*   5. *They were just **sitting** down (in the process of taking their seats) when the movie ended.*   6. *He was **entertaining** the guests.*

Ejercicio 6.69   Identifique la diferencia gramatical entre las palabras idénticas en cada par de frases; luego traduzca al español.

1a. *I am concerned about my **increasing** weight.*   **1b.** *They are **increasing** our taxes.*   **2a.** *That class is **boring**.*   **2b.** *Am I **boring** you?*   **3a.** *I was just **sitting** down (in the process) when the phone rang.*   **3b.** *I have serious news: are you **sitting** down?*

Ejercicio 6.70   Traduzca usando el infinitivo o el participio presente. Para *you*, use el informal singular (tú).

1. *They must have eaten.*   2. *She has to eat more.*   3. *They were planning on going to the beach.*   4. *I do not have anything to wear.*   5. *Put on your coat before leaving.*   6. *To see those effects, it is necessary to wear special glasses.*   7. *He was glad to see her.*   8. *Upon entering, they took off their shoes.*   9. *My brother had the veterinarian come.*   10. *Those seeds are hard to plant.*   11. *That book is easy to read.*   12. *It is easy to read that book.*   13. *Seeing is believing.*   14. *He forbids me to drive.*   15. *The children love playing online.*   16. *He left without saying a thing.*   17. *They were sorry after hanging up the phone.*   18. *They separated without really having gotten to know each other.*   19. *Do not stop me from moving.*   20. *My back hurts from having worked so much in the garden.*

Ejercicio 6.71 Temas de ensayo y de práctica oral

a. Ensayo

Imagine que es un médico muy concienzudo y debe indicarle a un paciente las actividades que son buenas o malas para la salud. Use una variedad de formatos: infinitivo como sujeto, como objeto directo, como objeto de preposición, con **hay que** o **tiene que**, con **nada que** y **poco que**, con **fácil de** y **difícil de** y con **al**.

b. Práctica oral

En parejas en que un estudiante hace de médico y otro de paciente, hablen de las actividades que son buenas o malas para la salud. El paciente le pregunta al doctor, y el doctor le da consejos al paciente.

Ejercicio 6.72 Temas de ensayo y de práctica oral

a. Ensayo

Escriba un párrafo sobre las acciones simultáneas de un individuo que está buscando como loco sus llaves perdidas *(lost keys)*. Haga lo posible por incorporar el equivalente correcto en español de las siguientes expresiones: *interesting, growing, existing, writing paper, containing, belonging, standing, sitting, lying down, boring, amusing, entertaining.*

b. Práctica oral

Compare con un(a) compañero(a) cómo acostumbra estudiar, o escribir trabajos para sus clases, o hablar por teléfono, etc. ¿Lo hace sentado, parado, acostado, caminando, comiendo, bebiendo, cantando, repitiendo en voz alta, etc.?

VERBS LIKE GUSTAR

Chapter 6.I, pages 239–244

Ejercicio 6.73 Traduzca usando la expresión **caer bien**. Para *you*, use el informal singular (tú).

1. *He likes you.* 2. *I like them.* 3. *She likes us.* 4. *They like her.* 5. *We like him.* 6. *You like them.*

Ejercicio 6.74 Traduzca las oraciones siguientes, usando los pronombres necesarios para enfatizar lo que está en negrilla. (Siga usando la expresión **caer bien**.)

1. *Nobody likes you.* ***She*** *likes me.*   2. *Yes, but* ***he*** *does not like you.*   3. ***You*** *like* ***her****, but* ***she*** *does not like* ***you****.*

Ejercicio 6.75 Conteste las siguientes preguntas con **a mí** o **yo**; luego traduzca la pregunta y la respuesta al inglés.

1. ¿A quién le interesa la magia?   2. ¿A quién le toca pagar la cuenta?   3. ¿A quién le gustó la cena?   4. ¿Quién comió más?

Ejercicio 6.76 Traduzca usando **caer bien, gustar, encantar** o **querer**.

1. *I love him.*   2. *I love your toys.*   3. *I like your house.*   4. *I like my neighbors.*

Ejercicio 6.77 Traduzca usando **faltar, hacer falta, quedar** o **sobrar**.

1. *They need food.*   2. *They have two days left.*   3. *We had time to spare (left over).*   4. *I miss you.*   5. *She needs twenty cents. (She is lacking twenty cents.)*

Ejercicio 6.78 Escoja la opción correcta entre paréntesis.

1. A mis vecinos (les/los/Ø) gustan las flores.   2. Tú ya no me (caigo/caes/cae) tan bien como antes.   3. Nos (encantamos/encanta/encantan) las cascadas del área.   4. Solo nos (faltamos/hacen falta/quedan) cinco días antes del final del semestre.   5. Después de la fiesta, ¿les (sobraron/sobró) mucha comida?

Ejercicio 6.79 Temas de ensayo y de práctica oral

a. Ensayo

Escriba un párrafo sobre sus gustos en general; indique lo que le gusta y lo que no le gusta, el tipo de gente que le cae bien, y quiénes le caen mal, a quién quiere, lo que le encanta, qué o quién le hace falta, lo que le importa, le interesa, le parece bien o mal o increíble.

b. Práctica oral

Usando el verbo **gustar**, y otros como **gustar** (**caer bien, caer mal, encantar, faltar, importar, interesar,** etc.) hable con un(a) compañero(a) sobre lo que constituye para ustedes el/la amigo(a) ideal.

J REFLEXIVE VERBS

Chapter 6.J, pages 245–252

(To practice the reflexive pronouns, see Exercises 3.20–3.22. We recommend that you do those exercises before these.)

Ejercicio 6.80 Traduzca usando verbos reflexivos. Para *you*, use el informal singular (tú).

1. We got bored at the party.   2. Did you remember the keys?   3. She got used to him very soon.   4. I am glad to see you.   5. He was ashamed of his lie.   6. I got off the bus at the third stop.   7. The other children always made fun of me.   8. You are going to have to confront that problem some day.   9. She realized that she had to say good-bye to me.   10. We must all make an effort to keep the environment clean.   11. How did he find out about that?   12. Do not trust anyone.   13. Notice their eyes when they dance.   14. Where are we going to meet him for lunch?   15. Why did your parents move?   16. What is his name?   17. Please do not leave now.   18. You must not interfere with those children.   19. They stayed with us for the summer.   20. He fought with his father.   21. You look like me.   22. Now he is going to start barking.   23. I feel sad today.   24. I sit here.   25. I felt sad yesterday.   26. I sat here yesterday.   27. I used to feel sad when I heard that song.   28. I used to sit here.   29. He kept my book.   30. Dry yourself well.

Ejercicio 6.81 Llene cada espacio en blanco con la preposición correcta, o con Ø si no se necesita preposición.

1. Me enamoré _____ ella hace mucho tiempo.   2. Se casó _____ él en junio.   3. Ella se reía _____ mí.   4. Se fijan _____ todo.   5. No te preocupes _____ mí.   6. Nos parecemos _____ nuestro padre.   7. Se interesa _____ las carreras de caballo.   8. No te deshagas _____ lo bueno.   9. Él se fiaba _____ todos.   10. Nos esforzábamos _____ hablar bajo.   11. Mi madre se empeñaba _____ que limpiara el cuarto todos los días.   12. Por fin se decidieron _____ salir.   13. Se atrevió _____ dirigirse _____ él después de unos minutos.   14. El vino se convirtió _____ vinagre.   15. Él se queja _____ todo.   16. ¿Te das cuenta _____ la hora que es?   17. Se curaron _____ los enfermos.   18. Me citaré _____ el dentista mañana.   19. Se arrepintieron _____ haber dicho eso.   20. ¡Aléjate _____ la calle!

Ejercicio 6.82   Temas de ensayo y de práctica oral

a. Ensayo

Usando al máximo los verbos reflexivos de las listas del capítulo 6.J, escriba el resumen de una telenovela *(soap opera)* imaginaria y melodramática.

b. Práctica oral

Competencia: En equipos de cuatro, comparen sus telenovelas, y preparen una todos juntos, usando un máximo de verbos reflexivos.

Que cada equipo le cuente a la clase su telenovela. El instructor escribe un punto en la pizarra cada vez que un verbo reflexivo está bien usado, con la preposición correcta. El equipo que tenga más verbos reflexivos usados correctamente gana la competencia.

K INDIRECT DISCOURSE

Chapter 6.K, pages 252–258

Ejercicio 6.83   Vuelva a escribir cada frase original usando la segunda como nuevo principio. Haga todos los cambios necesarios.

MODELO: Compró la casa. Dice que…

Dice que compró la casa.

1. Iremos al cine esta noche. Dice que…   **2.** Yo sé hacerlo. Ella supone que…
3. Yo hice tu trabajo. Te digo que…   **4.** Levántate. Te pido que…   **5.** Si pudiera ir ahora, lo haría. Dice que…   **6.** ¿Quieres que vayamos la semana entrante? Me preguntó esta mañana…   **7.** Si quieres comer, come. Me respondió que…
8. Llámame. Te ruego…   **9.** —¿Sabes qué hora es? —No. Siempre me pregunta… y yo siempre le contesto…

Ejercicio 6.84   Vuelva a escribir la frase original usando la segunda como nuevo principio. Haga todos los cambios necesarios.

MODELO: Compró la casa. Dice que…

Dice que compró la casa.

1. Iremos al cine esta noche. Ayer dijo que…   **2.** Yo sé hacerlo. Ella suponía que…   **3.** Yo hice tu trabajo. Le dije que…   **4.** Levántate. Me pidió que…

5. Si pudiera ir ahora, lo haría. Dijo que... **6.** ¿Quieres que vayamos la semana entrante? Me preguntó el mes pasado... **7.** Si quieres comer, come. Te estoy diciendo... **8.** Llámame. Me suplicó... **9.** —¿Sabes qué hora es? —No. Me preguntó... y yo le contesté...

Ejercicio 6.85 Vuelva a escribir la frase original usando la segunda como nuevo principio. Haga todos los cambios necesarios.

MODELO: Compró la casa. Dice que...

Dice que compró la casa.

1. Iremos al cine esta noche. Esta mañana dijo que... **2.** Yo sé hacerlo. Ella supuso que... **3.** Yo hice tu trabajo. Me dijo que... **4.** Levántate. Le pedí que... **5.** ¿Quieres que vayamos la semana entrante? Sé que me preguntará... **6.** Llámame. Insistió en que...

Ejercicio 6.86   Temas de ensayo y de práctica oral

a. Ensayo

Escriba uno de los diálogos siguientes usando lo más posible el discurso indirecto.

1. entre un testigo *(witness)* y un abogado *(lawyer)*, en que el abogado trata de demostrar que el testigo está mintiendo. (Por ejemplo: —Pero ayer usted dijo que...; —No, yo dije que...) Pueden ser personajes verdaderos o ficticios.

2. entre un padre y su hijo, en que el padre le recrimina al hijo algo que ha hecho en contra de las reglas que el padre le había dado y que el hijo dice que malentendió, o que contradicen otras cosas que dijo el padre.

3. entre dos compañeros de casa que tuvieron un malentendido *(misunderstood each other)* sobre quién iba a encargarse de qué *(who was going to take care of what)* en cuanto a las responsabilidades de la casa. Se acusan entre ellos de haber dicho que iban a hacer algo que luego no hicieron.

4. entre dos niños traviesos *(naughty)* que habían planeado alguna travesura *(naughty act, trick, practical joke)* y que fueron descubiertos por culpa de un error que cada uno de los niños cree que fue la culpa del otro.

b. Práctica oral

Prestando atención a las reglas del discurso indirecto, hable con un(a) compañero(a) sobre uno de los temas de ensayo de arriba.

Chapter 6 Review

Ejercicio 6.87 Conjugue cada verbo en el tiempo y modo más lógicos para el contexto. Lea todo el contexto antes de comenzar.

> **Vocabulario*: a caballo** *on horseback;* **aficionado** *fan;* **arena** *sand;* **asunto** *matter;* **banderilla** *colorfully decorated barbed stick used in bullfighting;* **bravo** *fierce;* **caballo** *horse;* **como si nada** *as if nothing were going on;* **corrida** *bullfight;* **criar** *to breed;* **daño (hacer)** *to injure;* **desequilibrio** *imbalance;* **desfilar** *to parade;* **estado de ánimo** *state of mind;* **estocada** *thrust of the sword;* **estoque** *sword of the bullfighter;* **grabado** *engraved;* **herir** *to injure;* **lanzar** *to toss;* **lidia** *bullfighting;* **lidia (toro de)** *bull bred for bullfighting;* **lidiar** *to fight (bulls);* **luchar** *to struggle;* **maltrato** *abuse;* **matador** *bullfighter of the highest rank, so named because he is to kill the bull;* **mezclar** *to mix;* **molestar** *to bother;* **oreja** *ear;* **pasodoble** *type of music;* **pena (dar)** *to be sorry;* **picador** *horseman that jabs the bull with a spear;* **plaza de toros** *bullring;* **por mi cuenta** *on my own;* **presenciar** *to witness;* **público** *audience;* **recuerdos** *memories;* **reverencia** *bow (bending at the waist);* **rito** *ritual;* **sangre** *blood;* **sangrienta** *bloody;* **temporada** *season;* **torero** *bullfighter;* **toro** *bull;* **traje de luces** *suit of lights, bullfighter's suit;* **valiente** *courageous;* **vencer** *to vanquish, beat;* **verónica** *cape pass*

Mi abuelo era un aficionado* de las corridas* de toros*: para él (**1.** ser) una necesidad cultural asistir a todas las corridas de toros durante la temporada*, no solo para él sino para toda la familia. Por eso cada domingo por la tarde (**2.** ir) todos juntos a la plaza de toros*, y (**3.** presenciar*) este espectáculo de música y de vida hispana. En esa época yo (**4.** ser) niña: hoy en día (**5.** recordar) muy poco de esas tardes; todas las corridas que (**6.** ver) se han (**7.** mezclar*) en una masa sin forma. Solo (**8.** quedar) grabados* en mi memoria los recuerdos* de los momentos que marcan el transcurso de la corrida: la música de pasodoble* que (**9.** tocar/ellos) al principio, la entrada de los toreros* y todos los ayudantes que (**10.** desfilar*) muy valientes* y elegantes en sus trajes de luces* y capas de colores vivos, el torero que (**11.** presentarse) con una reverencia* frente al presidente y que a veces le (**12.** lanzar*) su sombrero a alguien del público*, generalmente a una mujer; la entrada de cada toro que (**13.** salir) corriendo y (**14.** parecer) muy bravo, el público* que (**15.** gritar) "Olé" con cada pase de capa, el picador* a caballo*, las banderillas*, la llegada del matador* con su capa roja que (**16.** indicar) el final que se (**17.** acercar), y la estocada* final, que (**18.** dejar) al toro muerto o casi muerto. A veces le (**19.** cortar/ellos) una o ambas orejas* al toro para dárselas al torero, y este se (**20.** dar) la vuelta a la plaza con su premio, como héroe victorioso. Luego (**21.** limpiar/ellos) la arena* sangrienta* para que el próximo toro (**22.** entrar).

Solo hay una corrida que me (**23.** dejar) recuerdos más claros, y (**24.** ser) la vez que (**25.** venir) El Cordobés, que (**26.** ser) un torero español, de Córdoba, que (**27.** hacerse) famoso por su pelo largo y su personalidad; además, las mujeres (**28.** pensar) que (**29.** ser) muy guapo. Recuerdo que cuando él (**30.** ir) a empezar a lidiar*, (**31.** ir) al lugar de siempre frente al presidente, y cuando (**32.** quitarse) el sombrero, todo el público (**33.** gritar) y (**34.** reírse) por su pelo. En realidad no (**35.** tener) el pelo tan largo: hoy en día no (**36.** ser) nada sorprendente ver a alguien con el pelo así; pero en esa época (**37.** acabar) de hacerse famosos los Beatles por su pelo largo, y a cualquier hombre que (**38.** tener) pelo que le (**39.** tapar) las orejas se le (**40.** considerar) un rebelde o una anomalía.

La única otra imagen que tengo de ese día (**41.** ser) cuando El Cordobés, después de una verónica* que (**42.** dejar) al toro parado como hipnotizado, (**43.** pararse) de espaldas al toro y (**44.** sacar) de no sé dónde un enorme peine*, y (**45.** peinarse) tranquilamente, como si nada*. El público (**46.** morirse) de la risa.

En ningún momento pensé en la moralidad de lo que (**47.** pasar) en las corridas, y no (**48.** ser) sino hasta que (**49.** llegar) a ser adulta y que (**50.** mudarse) a los Estados Unidos que se me (**51.** ocurrir) que estos ritos* culturales (**52.** contener) elementos de injusticia. Debo confesar que en realidad no (**53.** ser) yo la que (**54.** pensar) en esto por mi cuenta*. (**55.** Ser) las preguntas de otros que me (**56.** hacer) ver el maltrato* hacia los toros. Yo no (**57.** saber) nada de lo que (**58.** pasar) antes de que el toro (**59.** entrar) a la plaza. Y nunca (**60.** pensar) en el toro. Para mí (**61.** tratarse) de un evento en que el torero (**62.** tener) que luchar* para que el toro no lo (**63.** matar) o (**64.** herir*). En realidad no me (**65.** gustar) que le (**66.** hacer/ellos) daño* al toro, y francamente me (**67.** molestar*) ver tanta sangre*, pero nunca (**68.** dejar) que eso (**69.** afectar) mi estado de ánimo*, o al menos la superficie. En mi familia, si yo (**70.** reaccionar) de alguna manera negativa en contra de las corridas, (**71.** haber) un escándalo. Para mi abuelo, una crítica (**72.** ser) una afrenta a la cultura.

Me da mucha pena* ahora que mi abuelo ya (**73.** morirse), porque si no, yo (**74.** poder) tener una conversación con él sobre el asunto*. Me (**75.** interesar) saber qué importancia le (**76.** dar) él al desequilibrio* de la batalla entre el hombre y el toro. Después de todo, es fácil (**77.** matar) a un toro si se considera todo el arsenal que se usa contra él. Yo (**78.** dudar) que un torero solo, con una capa y un estoque*, sin la ayuda de nadie, ni de banderillas ni de picadores, (**79.** poder) vencer* a un toro de lidia, sin que el toro lo (**80.** lastimar) mucho.

A pesar de todo, (**81.** tener/yo) que admitir que no (**82.** avergonzarse) de (**83.** asistir) a tantas corridas sin nunca (**84.** pensar) en el toro. Al contrario: si

(continued)

(**85.** tener/yo) la opción ahora de formar mi pasado, (**86.** preferir) haber tenido la experiencia, y no habérmela perdido. Las corridas de toros (**87.** representar) un aspecto importante de la cultura hispana, y (**88.** pensar/yo) que (**89.** ser) esencial que (**90.** reconocer/nosotros) este hecho y que (**91.** ser/nosotros) tolerantes de otros puntos de vista y sistemas de valores. Uno de los argumentos a favor de esta ceremonia (**92.** ser) que los toros de lidia se (**93.** criar*) con el único propósito de (**94.** participar) en las corridas. Pero (**95.** estar/yo) segura de que el debate (**96.** seguir) hasta que los críticos (**97.** lograr) que se (**98.** prohibir) las corridas y, cuando eso (**99.** ocurrir), (**100.** ser) el final de una gran tradición hispana.

Ejercicio 6.88   Temas de ensayo y de práctica oral

a. Ensayo

Prestando atención a la selección de tiempos y modos verbales, escriba un ensayo sobre uno de los temas siguientes. Narre su propia experiencia en el pasado con el tema, o sus observaciones de las experiencias de otros, y exprese su opinión, elaborando con cuidado los argumentos que se pueden hacer para cada lado del debate.

1. el uso de animales para experimentos en laboratorios
2. la legalización de la marihuana para propósitos medicinales
3. las ventajas y las desventajas de la estadidad (*statehood*) o independencia de Puerto Rico
4. la libertad de palabra (*freedom of speech*) para los grupos que odian (*hate*) a otros
5. los perros o los gatos: ¿cuáles son mejores como animales domésticos?
6. la eficiencia del sistema legal (escoja uno o dos casos específicos)
7. los deportes como espectáculo o diversión por un lado y como profesión por otro

b. Práctica oral

1. Pídale a un amigo hispano que le diga lo que piensa de uno de los temas del ejercicio 6.88a, o algún otro tema controvertible que le interese a usted. Escuche con cuidado para ver cómo usa las formas verbales para expresar su opinión. Mientras habla su amigo, si expresa una opinión que es diferente de lo que usted piensa, dígaselo, expresando su propia opinión (prestando atención a las formas verbales).
2. Conversación informal: En clase, hable con un(a) compañero(a) sobre uno de los temas presentados en el ejercicio 6.88a, o algún otro tema controvertible que le interese a usted.

3. Debate: Hagan un debate en clase sobre uno de los temas presentados en el ejercicio 6.88a, o algún otro tema controvertible que le interese a usted.

4. Encuesta: Fuera de clase, haga una encuesta *(poll)* informal entre estudiantes y profesores hispanos sobre uno de los temas presentados en el ejercicio 6.88a, o algún otro tema controvertible que le interese a usted. Preste atención a su uso de formas verbales. Tome apuntes para preparar un informe *(report)* para la clase.

Chapter 7
Ser, estar, haber, hacer, and tener

B SER VS. ESTAR

(With Equal Elements, Adjectives, Prepositions, and Adverbs)
Chapter 7.B.1–3, pages 262–269

Ejercicio 7.1   ¿**Es** o **está**? Si los dos son posibles, explique por qué.

Esa película _____…

1. mi favorita   2. la que quiero ver   3. la mejor   4. mía   5. de horror
6. aburrida   7. buena   8. dañada   9. interesante   10. de Argentina   11. lista para mostrarse   12. de Almodóvar   13. a las ocho esta noche   14. en la mesa
15. mostrándose ahora mismo

Ejercicio 7.2   ¿**Soy** o **estoy**? Si los dos son posibles, explique por qué.

1. _____ tu amiga.   2. No _____ lo que crees.   3. _____ de pie.   4. _____ donde quiero.   5. _____ alto y moreno.   6. _____ aburrido.   7. _____ bueno.   8. _____ bien.   9. _____ enfermo.   10. _____ emocionado.   11. _____ lista para salir.
12. _____ tuyo.   13. _____ harto de tanto trabajo.   14. _____ contento con la vida.   15. _____ llamando para pedir un favor.   16. _____ de Argentina.

Ejercicio 7.3   Traduzca de la manera más natural en español. Si hay más de una traducción posible, explique la diferencia, si la hay.

1. *I am done.*   2. *I am blind.*   3. *I am bored.*   4. *I am boring.*   5. *I am clever.*
6. *I am hot.*   7. *I am comfortable.*   8. *I am done.*   9. *I am excited.*   10. *I am fat.*
11. *I am fed up.*   12. *I am finished.*   13. *I am from Ithaca.*   14. *I am glad.*
15. *I am good (virtuous).*   16. *I am happy.*   17. *I am here.*   18. *I am dead (figuratively).*   19. *I am hungry.*   20. *I am at the university.*   21. *I am interested.*
22. *I am late.*   23. *I am standing.*   24. *I am okay.*   25. *I am quiet.*   26. *I am ready.*
27. *I am rich.*   28. *I am sad to hear that.*   29. *I am sick (ill).*   30. *I am sitting.*
31. *I am sorry.*   32. *I am mature.*   33. *I am short.*   34. *I am the one who gave you the flowers.*   35. *I am working.*   36. *I was born.*

Ejercicio 7.4 Traduzca de la manera más natural en español. Si hay más de una traducción posible, explique la diferencia, si la hay. Convendría repasar el uso del infinitivo y del subjuntivo.

1. *It is okay for you to be early.* **2.** *It was good to be there.* **3.** *"To be or not to be," that is the question.* **4.** *It is time to leave.* **5.** *We were comfortable because we were sitting.* **6.** *It was interesting to see that they were always late.* **7.** *It was clear that it wasn't working properly* (bien). **8.** *He was happy that I was done.* **9.** *I am sorry but I am not hungry.* **10.** *I am glad you agree with me.*

Ejercicio 7.5 ¿**Ser** o **estar**? Llene cada espacio en blanco con el verbo correcto.

1. Ese hombre _____ profesor. **2.** _____ importante llegar temprano. **3.** Martina _____ de vacaciones. **4.** _____ bien que estudien esta noche. **5.** Luisa _____ de Guadalajara. **6.** ¿Qué hora _____? **7.** _____ la una de la tarde. **8.** _____ las siete de la mañana. **9.** ¿ _____ claro lo que tienen que hacer? **10.** Los pisos en esa casa _____ de madera. **11.** Mis padres _____ de acuerdo con nosotros. **12.** Esta carta _____ para mi padre. **13.** ¿Para cuándo _____ la próxima composición? **14.** Este libro _____ de Mario. **15.** La ceremonia de la graduación siempre _____ en el gimnasio. **16.** Mis libros _____ en mi casillero. **17.** Su hermano _____ en Managua. **18.** Nosotros _____ en Sevilla. **19.** Tu mochila _____ en el escritorio. **20.** La conferencia _____ a las nueve de la mañana. **21.** Esa mujer _____ de gerente esta semana, hasta que regrese la gerente oficial. **22.** El vuelo _____ por salir. **23.** Ese puente _____ construido por un ingeniero famoso. **24.** Las ventanas _____ cerradas. ¿Quieres que las abra? **25.** Bertita _____ aprendiendo a caminar.

Ejercicio 7.6 ¿**Ser** o **estar**? Llene cada espacio en blanco con la forma correcta para el contexto.

1. Ese actor _____ muerto. **2.** Los cuellos de las jirafas _____ largos. **3.** El café de Colombia _____ bueno. **4.** Esa cantante _____ atlética. **5.** ¡Qué rico _____ el café esta mañana! **6.** Mi gatita _____ más flaca que hace un año. **7.** Mi coche _____ averiado. **8.** Su cuarto _____ desordenado hoy. ¿Qué pasaría? **9.** Su esposa _____ harta de tener que aguantar sus engaños. **10.** El presidente _____ contento con los resultados. **11.** —Hola, Quique. ¿_____ bien? —No, _____ (yo) enfermo, pero ya _____ mejor que hace una semana. **12.** Mi compañero de cuarto, que por lo general _____ muy platicador, ahora _____ callado. **13.** Mi hija _____ más lista que sus amiguitos. **14.** Ya _____ hora de irnos. ¿_____ listos? ¡Vámonos! **15.** Esa película _____ aburrida.

Ejercicio 7.7 ¿Ser o estar? En el diálogo que sigue, llene cada espacio en blanco con la forma correcta para el contexto.

SERGIO: Hola, Jacinto, tanto tiempo sin verte. ¿Cómo (**1**) ____?

JACINTO: Bien, pero agobiado de tanto trabajo. No sé ni qué día (**2**) ____ hoy. (**3**) ____ harto de no tener ni un minuto libre.

SERGIO: No (**4**) ____ tan negativo. Ven, sentémonos en ese banco a platicar un rato.

JACINTO: ¿Qué hora (**5**) ____? Tengo una clase de español a las 2.30.

SERGIO: (**6**) ____ temprano. Tenemos una hora para hablar. ¿Dónde (**7**) ____ la clase?

JACINTO: En Morrill Hall. El edificio (**8**) ____ cerca de aquí.

SERGIO: ¡Qué muchos libros llevas! ¿(**9**) ____ para la clase de español?

JACINTO: No, para la de biología.

SERGIO: Cuéntame de tus planes para los días de fiesta de la semana que viene. ¿Qué te gusta hacer cuando (**10**) ____ de vacaciones?

JACINTO: No quiero (**11**) ____ aquí. (**12**) ____ listo para irme al Caribe, a una isla que (**13**) ____ lejos de todo esto, donde la vida (**14**) ____ fácil, y no tenga que pensar que voy a (**15**) ____ estudiando en la biblioteca más tarde, donde pueda (**16**) ____ tirado al sol la mayor parte del tiempo, donde (**17**) ____ seguro…

SERGIO: Divagas, Jacinto… (**18**) ____ preocupado por ti. (**19**) ____ pálido y delgado, (**20**) ____ aquí sentado, (**21**) ____ hablando, pero no (**22**) ____ conmigo. ¿Qué te pasa?

JACINTO: Perdona, Sergio, (**23**) ____ que (**24**) ____ cansado. Llevo dos noches sin dormir. Tenía un trabajo escrito que (**25**) ____ para entregarse hoy, y no lo pude terminar. Sé que (**26**) ____ importante entregar todo a tiempo y sin embargo…

SERGIO: Tranquilo, hombre, (**27**) ____ en tu cuarto año de estudios y tienes que (**28**) ____ contento con tu futuro.

JACINTO: (**29**) ____ de acuerdo pero no (**30**) ____ que no (**31**) ____ contento. El problema (**32**) ____ que las clases este año (**33**) ____ muy difíciles y me he dado cuenta de que no (**34**) ____ muy listo.

SERGIO: ¿Cómo puedes decir eso? Uno no deja de (**35**) ____ listo así porque sí. Siempre has salido bien en todo. Eso no puede (**36**) ____. (**37**) ____ equivocado. Mira, creo que necesitas un cambio de rutina. ¿Qué te parece si vamos al concierto del sábado?

JACINTO: ¿De qué concierto hablas?

SERGIO: Ni te enteras. (38) _____ un concierto de un grupo venezolano que (39) _____ muy de moda. Sus conciertos no (40) _____ aburridos y (41) _____ seguro que lo pasarás bien. Te invito. Mira, aquí tengo dos entradas. Esta (42) _____ para ti.

JACINTO: Gracias, Sergio. (43) _____ un buen amigo. Ya (44) _____ hora de irme. ¿Qué tal si nos encontramos el sábado antes del concierto y cenamos juntos?

SERGIO: Eso me gustaría muchísimo. (45) _____ en mi cuarto hasta las cinco y podríamos ir a "Viva Taquería" como a las 6.

JACINTO: ¿A qué hora (46) _____ el concierto? A las 8, ¿no? Entonces podríamos cenar un poco más tarde.

SERGIO: No conviene porque el restaurante (47) _____ como a 10 minutos de aquí y no queremos llegar tarde al concierto.

JACINTO: (48) _____ bien. Hasta el sábado.

Ejercicio 7.8 Conteste las preguntas siguientes prestando atención a la elección de verbos. Elabore cada respuesta y dé como mínimo cinco elementos en su respuesta.

1. ¿Quién es usted?   2. ¿Cómo es usted? *(What are you like?)*   3. ¿Cómo está usted? *(How are you?)*   4. ¿Quién es su mejor amigo o amiga?   5. ¿Cómo es su mejor amigo o amiga?   6. ¿Por qué es esa persona su mejor amigo o amiga?   7. ¿Quién es Penélope Cruz?   8. ¿Cómo es Penélope Cruz?   9. ¿Quién era Che Guevara?   10. ¿Cómo era Che Guevara?

Ser vs. estar (With past participles: passive voice and resultant condition)

Chapter 7.B.4.b, pages 270–272

Ejercicio 7.9 ¿Activo, pasivo o **se** impersonal? Repase los usos del **se** impersonal (Chapter 3.B.4, pages 74–78), y luego traduzca las oraciones siguientes usando la estructura que sería **más natural** en español. Puede haber más de una posibilidad, dependiendo del contexto adicional que se visualice. Explique su razonamiento para cada traducción si da más de una.

1. *She was given the car.*   2. *The house was built by the owner.*   3. *Books are sold there.*   4. *Why wasn't I told?*   5. *She was not invited.*   6. *I was awakened by the light.*   7. *He was taken to the airport.*   8. *It is forbidden to smoke here.*   9. *The hunter was attacked by the lion, and was killed.*   10. *The man was not read his rights.*

Ejercicio 7.10 **Resultant Condition** En el diálogo que sigue, llene cada espacio en blanco con lo necesario para indicar condición resultante. Entre paréntesis se encuentra el equivalente en inglés para la expresión deseada.

La familia Escribano está casi lista para irse de vacaciones. Hay cuatro miembros en la familia: el padre, la madre y dos hijos, Rosa y Camilo. A cada uno le tocaba hacer varias tareas y ahora necesitan repasar para asegurarse que todo lo que se tenía que hacer se hizo.

MAMÁ: ¿Lo hicieron todo?
CAMILO Y ROSA: Sí, mamá, ya todo (**1**) _____. (*is done*)
MAMÁ: ¿Empacaron los trajes de baño?
CAMILO: Ya (**2**) _____. (*are packed*)
MAMÁ: ¿Y la ropa interior?
ROSA: Ya (**3**) _____. (*is packed*)
MAMÁ: ¿Pusieron la aspiradora en su lugar?
CAMILO: Ya (**4**) _____. (*is put away*)
ROSA: ¿Y tenemos que recoger el cuarto?
MAMÁ: No, ya (**5**) _____. (*is tidied up*)
PAPÁ: ¿Dónde están los pasajes?
MAMÁ: (**6**) _____ en mi cartera. (*stored*)
CAMILO: ¿Dónde está Fido?
ROSA: (**7**) _____ debajo de la cama. (*hiding*)
CAMILO: ¿Y la gatita?
PAPÁ: (**8**) _____ sobre la tele. (*sitting*)
MAMÁ: ¿Cerraste la puerta de atrás?
PAPÁ: Ya (**9**) _____. (*is closed*)
MAMÁ: ¿Abriste el baúl del coche?
PAPÁ: Ya (**10**) _____. (*is open*)
MAMÁ: ¿Estamos listos?
CAMILO Y ROSA: Sí, mamá, ya lo estamos. Vámonos ya.
Y se fueron.
(Nota: A los animalitos los venía a cuidar una tía que vivía cerca.)

Ejercicio 7.11 **Titulares** Imagine que trabaja en un periódico y necesita preparar los titulares para los artículos del día. Recuerde dar un máximo de información con un mínimo de palabras. Use la voz pasiva, el **se** impersonal o la voz activa.

MODELO: El poder ejecutivo de Agencias Radioemisoras de TeVé elabora un proyecto que aumentaría cuatro veces el tiempo actual de emisión en Jaén, que en la actualidad no supera la hora de emisión en los días de diario. Javier Pereda, gerente y portavoz del Consejo Asesor de Radio y Televisión en Jaén, indica que se transmitirían programas de diez de la mañana a dos de la tarde, y de seis a ocho y media de la tarde.
TITULARES POSIBLES:
SE VERÁ MÁS TELE QUE ANTES,
SE AUMENTARÁN EMISIONES DE TEVÉ,
etc.

Artículos:

1. A altas horas de la noche el Parque de Bombas de la barriada El Coto de Arecibo recibió una llamada para rescatar a un gatito de una rama de un árbol de flamboyán. Los bomberos de esta pequeña barriada lograron bajar al pobre animalito desamparado y se lo entregaron a su dueña, cuya emoción la mantuvo en silencio unos instantes.

2. El pasado 22 de diciembre se celebró la Lotería de Navidad, más conocida como EL PREMIO GORDO. El premio, que este año ascendió a 51 000 millones de pesetas, más de 307 millones de euros, ya fue entregado. La ganadora fue Josefina Rubio, ciudadana de este municipio.

3. Dos personas resultaron heridas a las 13.00 horas de ayer, sábado, en un accidente de tráfico que se produjo en la carretera de Sevilla a Huelva. Como consecuencia de la salida de la carretera de un autobús de turismo, resultaron heridos un joven de 15 años y un niño de 5. Fueron atendidos por la Unidad Medicalizada UME 91 en Cádiz. El primero de los heridos fue trasladado al Hospital San Ignacio y el segundo a la Clínica de Urgencias de Santa Lucía.

4. La línea 2 de Metro echa el cierre en agosto. Todas las estaciones, desde La Elipa hasta Cuatro Caminos, permanecerán cerradas desde el próximo sábado 7 de agosto hasta finales de agosto, aunque no se ha concretado la fecha, según han confirmado fuentes de la empresa.

    El motivo son las obras de mantenimiento de una de las líneas más antiguas de la red. Las obras consistirán, principalmente, en el cambio de la tensión de la

(continued)

catenaria (el dispositivo que abastece de electricidad a los trenes), la renovación de un tramo de vía entre las estaciones de Retiro y Cuatro Caminos y la mejora del revestimiento de las estaciones de Santo Domingo, Ópera, Sol, Sevilla, Banco de España y Retiro.

5. India quiere extender la tecnología a las zonas rurales más pobres y dar un salto cualitativo en educación. Para ello ha desarrollado una tableta táctil de 7 pulgadas que costará 35 dólares la unidad (unos 27 euros). La más barata del mundo.

   El ministro de Tecnología, Kapil Sibal, cree que este precio puede bajar incluso hasta los 10 dólares (7 euros) si el gobierno lo subvenciona.

   El dispositivo no tiene nada que envidiar al iPad teniendo en cuenta que el gadget de Apple cuesta como mínimo 479 euros.

6. A pesar del pasado incendio del 10 de octubre, el Museo Vidal «ha de continuar con sus actividades», afirma el consejero de Cultura Avelino Robles, que ayer visitó una vez más el Museo Vidal. El consejero afirma que antes de lo ocurrido estaba previsto que a fines de este mes se celebrara, con una inmensa exposición, el aniversario de los 40 años del museo. Robles asegura que se cumplirá con lo programado.

7. La Audiencia Municipal ha condenado a tres miembros de una misma familia, que viven en Córdoba, por dedicarse a vender heroína. Los condenados son una pareja de casados, de 50 y 46 años, y un primo del marido, de 37 años. La sentencia indica que deben cumplir una pena de cinco años de prisión, y deben pagar una multa de 200 000 pesetas.

8. El Servicio de Conservación de la Naturaleza de la Guardia Civil investiga un vertido de purín en un río del municipio coruñés, que ha causado la mortandad de peces.

   Según han informado a la prensa de las fuentes municipales y del instituto armado, se ha abierto una investigación después de que hace tres días pescadores que se encontraban en la zona alertaran al municipio de lo sucedido.

   Fuentes municipales han señalado que el vertido fue localizado en la parroquia de la Barranca, hace unos tres días por unos pescadores que se encontraron peces muertos.

9. Esta es una historia que solo se suele ver en las salas de cine. Un grupo de ladrones realizó un espectacular robo a un banco sueco llevándose más de cinco millones de dólares. Lo hicieron al estilo SWAT con helicópteros y cuerdas de por medio.

   Tal y como se puede ver en el vídeo grabado del local, los ladrones aterrizan directamente sobre el techo del banco. Este tiene una gran cristalera en forma de pirámide. Hicieron un agujero en el cristal. Eliminaron las alarmas. Bajaron. Se llevaron todo el dinero que pudieron y escaparon por donde vinieron.

Poco después diez de los que participaron en la operación fueron capturados por la policía y pronto se enfrentarán a un juicio a raíz del cual fue desvelado el vídeo de las cámaras de seguridad.

10. La universidad de Maracondo inicia el próximo lunes 15 el curso de verano 'Presente y futuro de la ingeniería ambiental'. Ernesto Parientes, del Departamento de Ingeniería Química y Tecnología del Medio Ambiente, será el director del curso, que durará toda la semana y que contará con la presencia de personalidades de diferentes universidades nacionales.

La mesa redonda del martes es una de las actividades más destacadas de todo el programa. A partir de las 13.00 horas, en el Aula 29 de la Facultad de Química, los participantes desarrollarán el tema "Agua y medio ambiente: problemas, prioridades y mitos".

11. La Fundación del Español Urgente, en una nota difundida hoy, recomienda que se prefiera "obispa" como femenino de "obispo" en lugar de "mujer obispo", como aparece en muchas informaciones relacionadas con la decisión de la Iglesia anglicana de abrir las puertas al obispado femenino.

La Fundéu BBVA, que cuenta con el asesoramiento de la Real Academia Española, ha observado que hay vacilación en la forma de referirse a las mujeres que reciben este cargo eclesiástico, y así se lee y escucha: "la mujer obispo" y en plural "las mujeres obispo" o "las mujeres obispos".

Esta institución recomienda que se prefiera "obispa" como femenino de "obispo", aunque esta forma carezca de tradición en el mundo católico.

12. Los atascos son ya habituales en las mañanas y las tardes de las carreteras de la provincia andaluza. El pasado año, los transeúntes tuvieron que soportar en sus vehículos más de 16 atascos diarios, según los datos aportados por las oficinias del Centro de Gestión de Tráfico.

En total, se contabilizaron 5966 retenciones en las carreteras sevillanas (para Tráfico, una retención debe tener como mínimo un kilómetro de longitud).

En comparación con el año pasado, las colas aumentaron en la provincia un 113%.

13. El cantante David Bisbal actuará este sábado, a partir de las 23.00 horas, en el Teatro Municipal de Sanlúcar de Barrameda, en un concierto organizado por el Ayuntamiento sanluqueño y que produce Producciones Guadalquivir.

En este concierto, el artista almeriense presentará la canciones más celebradas por el público como son 'Esclavo de sus besos', 'Sin mirar atrás', 'Mi princesa', la mundial 'Wavin' flag' o sus éxitos 'Silencio', 'Dígale' y 'Ave María'.

(continued)

Además, el cantante español —que cuenta con más de 350 000 seguidores en la red social Twitter— tiene en los conciertos de esta gira nuevas puestas en escena y una combinación de temas rápidos y baladas que pasan por un estilo moderno con ritmos de pop-rock y funky fusionados con elementos latinos de estilo internacional.

14. En opinión de la jerarquía eclesiástica, "respetando la pluralidad de opciones que se dan entre los cristianos y en nuestra sociedad, invitamos a todos a promover el diálogo y el entendimiento, para que se logre una convivencia pacífica, justa y duradera".

   "No nos corresponde a nosotros promover una solución política determinada a los problemas que plantea la manera de organizar la sociedad, pero deseamos, eso sí, colaborar para que los caminos que se vayan tomando reconozcan y respeten la dignidad y los derechos fundamentales de las personas y de los pueblos", afirman los obispos de la Conferencia Episcopal en la nota conclusiva de su reunión.

15. Veinticuatro horas de búsqueda terminaron felizmente. Los felices son los tres residentes de la zona Mairena del Aljarafe cuyo relato es, diríamos, inverosímil. Todo comenzó después del desayuno cuando estaban listos para salir de su casa e ir al trabajo. Según nos informa el Sr. Cadilla, padre de la familia, "como hacemos todas las mañanas, cerramos el piso, salimos a la calle y nos dirigimos al coche. En fin, que esta vez, ninguno de los tres tenía las llaves del coche. Buscamos pero no las encontramos en ningún lugar. Al día siguiente, las encontró el barrendero en el naranjo. Parece que nuestro gato las había subido al árbol, al menos no le puedo encontrar otra explicación, y hablar con el gato, bueno, ya sabe usted, solo maúllan".

C ESTAR VS. HABER

Chapter 7.C, page 273

Ejercicio 7.12   ¿**Están** o **hay**? Llene cada espacio en blanco.

1. _____ veinte estudiantes en esta clase.   2. Los estudiantes _____ sentados cerca de la ventana.   3. _____ muchas cosas que hacer.   4. Los libros _____ en la biblioteca.   5. _____ libros en la biblioteca.   6. No _____ suficientes fondos para cubrir su cheque.   7. ¿Dónde _____ taxis?   8. Ya no _____ tantos árboles como antes.   9. Los taxis _____ a dos cuadras de aquí.   10. Las leyes que _____ no bastan para controlar el crimen.

D. EXPRESSIONS WITH ESTAR AND TENER

Chapter 7.D, pages 274

Ejercicio 7.13   Llene cada espacio en blanco con la forma correcta de **estar** o **tener**.

1. Cuando entré en la tienda vi que el hombre _____ de pie frente a los iPods, y su novia _____ de rodillas buscando algo en un estante bajo. Se veía que los dos _____ prisa y parecía que _____ de muy mal humor porque no podían encontrar lo que necesitaban.   2. Yo _____ hambre y decidí ir a la panadería porque _____ ganas de comer un pan dulce.   3. Mi madre _____ a favor de la pena de muerte, pero mi padre dice que hay que _____ en cuenta que a veces se cometen errores y se condena a uno que no _____ la culpa por el crimen.
4. Ayer _____ ausente porque _____ tanto sueño que no me levanté cuando sonó el despertador. Ahora _____ vergüenza.   5. Nosotros _____ de visita ahora. _____ de vacaciones hasta septiembre, pero _____ de vuelta la semana entrante.
6. Tú _____ razón: me quejo mucho. Pero _____ (yo) de mal humor porque (yo) _____ frío, _____ sueño, _____ sed y _____ miedo de no pasar este examen.
7. Los obreros _____ de huelga porque sus salarios son muy bajos. Espero que (ellos) _____ éxito en conseguir lo que quieren.   8. Los vecinos _____ de viaje y no _____ de regreso hasta la semana entrante.

Ejercicio 7.14   Traduzca las oraciones siguientes usando las mejores estructuras en español.

1. *It seems they are in a hurry.*   2. *Roberto, hurry up!*   3. *I am sorry for being late.*
4. *I am glad.*   5. *I was standing and you were sitting.*   6. *Eva, sit down!*   7. *You are right and I am wrong.*   8. *I was sleepy, I fell asleep and I had a very strange dream.*

Ser, estar, tener, haber, and hacer (Review)

Chapter 7.A–D, pages 260–274

Ejercicio 7.15   Traduzca estas frases usando **ser**, **estar**, **tener**, **haber** o **hacer**.

1. *I have been on my knees too long.*   2. *Is it cold in winter here?*   3. *The children were thirsty.*   4. *I do not know why I am sad.*   5. *It is not that the party is boring, it is that the people are bored.*   6. *Is it raining?*   7. *How many rooms are there in that building?*   8. *Where are you from?*   9. *Is the conference in this building?*

Ejercicio 7.16 Complete con el presente de **ser, estar, haber** o **tener**.

1. El pan _____ cortado. ¿Tú comiste?   2. Las cuentas _____ pagadas por el banco.   3. Tú ya _____ visto esa película cuatro veces.   4. Ella lo _____ todo preparado para los invitados.

Ejercicio 7.17   Temas de ensayo y de práctica oral

a. Ensayo

Usando al máximo las expresiones con **estar** y **tener**, escriba un párrafo sobre un amigo.

b. Práctica oral

1. Juego de 20 preguntas: Un estudiante piensa en un objeto o una persona. Para adivinar de qué objeto o persona se trata, sus compañeros deben hacerle un máximo de veinte preguntas, usando correctamente los verbos **ser, estar, tener** y **haber**. El estudiante solo puede dar como respuesta "sí" o "no". Cuando alguien pueda adivinar cuál es el objeto o quién es la persona, debe alzar la mano. Solo se permiten tres adivinanzas sobre la identidad del objeto o la persona.

2. Hable con un(a) compañero(a) sobre su familia, prestando atención al uso correcto de los verbos **ser, estar, tener** y **haber**. Describan para cada miembro de la familia cómo es, dónde está ahora, cuántos años tiene, etc.

3. El mundo ideal: Entre todos, construyan la imagen del mundo ideal, describiendo cómo es, lo que hay y lo que no hay en ese mundo, lo que tienen o no tienen sus habitantes como derechos y posesiones, etc.

E TIME EXPRESSIONS

Chapter 7.E, pages 275–278

Ejercicio 7.18   Traduzca estas frases de dos formas si se puede, usando **hacer** y **llevar**.

1. *I have been here for an hour.*   2. *They had been working for twenty minutes when she came in.*   3. *We called him a week ago.*   4. *She had not cut her hair for many years.*   5. *My niece has been learning ballet for three years.*   6. *She came to visit us two months ago.*   7. *How long have we been waiting?*

Ejercicio 7.19 Escoja la opción correcta entre paréntesis.

1. ¿Cuánto tiempo (hace/haces/llevas) que no ves a tus padres?   **2.** Llevamos tres horas (que esperamos/esperar/esperando).   **3.** Lo vimos (hace/hacía/llevamos/lleva) una hora.   **4.** Ese chico (lleva/hace) dos meses sin cortarse el pelo.   **5.** Parece que hace años (que no llueve/sin llover/desde que llovió).

Ejercicio 7.20 Temas de ensayo y de práctica oral

a. Ensayo

Usando las expresiones **hace que** y **llevar,** haga una lista de los momentos más importantes de su vida pasada. (Hace diecinueve años que nací…)

b. Práctica oral

Use el tema de ensayo de arriba y platique con un(a) compañero(a), comparando los momentos más importantes de su vida pasada.

Chapter 7 Review

Ejercicio 7.21   Llene cada espacio en blanco con el verbo más lógico y en la forma correcta para el contexto.

Querida Luisa,
　　Te escribo desde Madrid donde Jorge y yo **(1)** _____ de visita por unos días. **(2)** _____ extraño porque **(3)** _____ más turistas que madrileños en la ciudad: todos **(4)** _____ de vacaciones en agosto. Pero **(5)** _____ bien, me mezclo con los demás turistas. En realidad, lo que yo **(6)** _____ ganas de hacer era de conocer Madrid porque dicen que **(7)** _____ una ciudad fascinante. Y los que dicen esto **(8)** _____ razón: esta ciudad **(9)** _____ un centro cultural impresionante. Siempre **(10)** _____ algo nuevo que hacer cada día.

　　(11) _____ (nosotros) muy contentos con el hotel, aunque **(12)** _____ mucho calor y parece que no **(13)** _____ aire acondicionado que pueda ser suficiente para dominar este calor. Casi siempre **(14)** _____ cansados por el calor y no podemos hacer tanto como quisiéramos cada día. Tenemos que **(15)** _____ cuidado y tomar la siesta cada día, como lo hacen los demás. Pero en fin, ya sabes cómo **(16)** _____ nosotros: nos quejamos de todo pero a fin de cuentas terminamos contentos.

　　¿Cómo **(17)** _____ ustedes? Espero que no **(18)** _____ lloviendo mucho allá. Creo que ayer **(19)** _____ el cumpleaños de Martita, ¿verdad? ¿Cuántos años **(20)** _____ ya? Salúdala de nuestra parte y dile que pronto **(21)** _____ de regreso con un regalito para ella.

　　Bueno, me despido por ahora: **(22)** _____ sueño y mañana **(23)** _____ un día de muchos planes.

　　　　　　　　　　Un fuerte abrazo para ti y para David,
　　　　　　　　　　　　　　　　　　Victoria

Ejercicio 7.22 Temas de ensayo y de práctica oral

a. Ensayo

Prestando atención a la selección del verbo correcto para indicar *to be*, escriba un párrafo sobre uno de los temas siguientes:

1. Describa a alguien a quien usted admira.
2. Escriba su autorretrato. Describa sus rasgos físicos y de personalidad, y los cambios por los que ha pasado.

b. Práctica oral

1. Adivina de qué personaje famoso hablo: Descríbales a sus compañeros un personaje famoso, hasta que adivinen de quién se trata. Preste atención al uso correcto de los verbos **ser, estar, tener** y **haber,** y de expresiones de tiempo.
2. Advina de qué compañero hablo: Descríbales a sus compañeros un(a) compañero(a) de la clase, hasta que adivinen de quién se trata. Preste atención al uso correcto de los verbos **ser, estar, tener** y **haber,** y de expresiones de tiempo.

Chapter 8
Lexical Variations

B TERMS AND EXPRESSIONS

1. Acabar

Chapter 8.B.1, pages 280–281

Ejercicio 8.1 Llene cada espacio en blanco con **acabé, acabé de, acababa, acababa de, acabo, acabo de** o **se me acabó**.

1. No tengo hambre ahora porque _____ comer.   **2.** Cuando yo era niña tenía una manía: siempre _____ ponerme los dos calcetines antes de ponerme los zapatos.   **3.** Estoy celebrando porque por fin _____ pintar el cuarto.   **4.** Tengo que ir a la tienda porque _____ la leche.   **5.** Anoche por fin _____ mi trabajo escrito para la clase de historia.   **6.** Cuando era joven, a la hora de comer siempre _____ primero y salía corriendo a jugar; ahora encuentro que como más despacio que los demás, y _____ último.

Ejercicio 8.2 Traduzca.

1. *I finished my work.*   **2.** *They finished repairing the bridge in October.*   **3.** *He will be finished with the construction by three in the afternoon.*   **4.** *I just got up.*   **5.** *The exam ended at ten.*   **6.** *When I got there, they had just eaten.*   **7.** *We finished the bread.*   **8.** *We ran out of bread.*

2. *Apply*

Chapter 8.B.2, pages 281–282

Ejercicio 8.3 Llene cada espacio en blanco con la expresión correcta: **aplicar, aplicación, solicitar** o **solicitud**.

1. Como no tenía suficiente dinero, tuve que _____ una beca.   **2.** Cuando el doctor me recetó este ungüento, me dijo que se debía _____ con cuidado.   **3.** Voy a _____ admisión a cuatro universidades.   **4.** El trabajo que iba a _____ para el verano ya no existe.   **5.** La _____ con la que estudia ese alumno es admirable.   **6.** Recibieron mi _____ para el préstamo, pero no han decidido todavía si me lo van a otorgar.

Ejercicio 8.4 Traduzca. Para *you*, use el informal singular (tú).

1. She applied for a scholarship. 2. The doctor applied pressure to the wound to stop the bleeding. 3. We will apply for a loan at the bank. 4. The job you applied for no longer exists. 5. I sent my application for the job yesterday. 6. Apply this ointment three times a day.

3. Ask

Chapter 8.B.3, page 282

Ejercicio 8.5 Llene cada espacio en blanco con la expresión correcta: **pedir, preguntar, hacer, pregunta, pedido** o **cuestión**. Si se trata de un verbo, conjúguelo en el pretérito. Es posible que se use una palabra más de una vez.

1. Luis me _____ si tenía tiempo. 2. Yo le _____ a María que me ayudara. 3. Les _____ un favor a mis amigos. 4. Roberto _____: —¿Cuándo nos vamos? 5. Los niños _____ mil preguntas antes de acostarse anoche.
6. No se trata de dinero: es una _____ de principios. 7. Necesito hacer otro _____ de papel de color: se nos está acabando. 8. Tengo una _____ para ti: ¿dónde conseguiste ese libro?

Ejercicio 8.6 Traduzca. Para *you*, use el informal singular (tú).

1. I want to ask you a favor. 2. I asked him a question. 3. She asked me to take her to town. 4. He asked me, "Are you really sixteen?" 5. We asked him if he had eaten. 6. They asked us why we had called. 7. Do not ask me so many questions. 8. I thought it was a question of ethics.

4. At

Chapter 8.B.4, page 283

Ejercicio 8.7 Llene cada espacio en blanco con **a** o **en**.

1. Los niños se quedaron _____ casa. 2. Ellos están _____ Nueva York.
3. La clase es _____ las diez, _____ el edificio de Morrill. 4. Me siento mejor _____ este momento. 5. No sé qué decir _____ veces. 6. Hay alguien _____ la puerta preguntando por ti. 7. Me parece que oí el timbre. Creo que hay alguien _____ la puerta. 8. Le gusta tener a su amiga _____ su lado.

Ejercicio 8.8 Traduzca.

1. *At this moment, I can't go.* 2. *My first class is at ten.* 3. *We are at the university.* 4. *They were not at home.* 5. *We are going to sit at the table.* 6. *In Buenos Aires I used to stay at my uncle's house at times.*

5. *Attend*

Chapter 8.B.5, page 284

Ejercicio 8.9 Llene cada espacio en blanco con la expresión correcta: **asistir, atender, asistencia** o **atento**. Si usa un verbo, conjúguelo en la forma correcta para el contexto.

1. La maestra, impaciente con la distracción de los alumnos, les dijo: "¡_____ (me)!" 2. El dependiente de la tienda se me acercó y me preguntó: "¿En qué puedo _____ la hoy, señora?" 3. Ayer yo no _____ a clase porque estaba enfermo. 4. La mesera nos _____ tan pronto entramos y nos trajo el menú. 5. Toda la familia _____ al funeral ayer. 6. La _____ a clase cuenta más que los exámenes. 7. Tu hermano siempre me abre la puerta: ¿por qué no puedes ser tan _____ como él? 8. Los servicios de _____ social son esenciales para mucha gente.

Ejercicio 8.10 Traduzca.

1. *We attended the lecture in the afternoon.* 2. *She did not attend class because she was ill.* 3. *May I assist you?* 4. *Tend to the guests, please.* 5. *Did you have a good audience?* 6. *Some politicians want to eliminate welfare.* 7. *Young people today are more polite with their elders than in the previous generation.*

6. *Because*

Chapter 8.B.6, page 285

Ejercicio 8.11 Llene cada espacio en blanco con la expresión correcta: **por, a causa de, porque** o **gracias a**. A veces se puede usar más de una: incluya todas las posibles.

1. Es _____ tus dudas que no ganamos la lotería. 2. Cerré las ventanas _____ el frío. 3. Me voy a poner un suéter _____ tengo frío. 4. No pude cerrar la puerta _____ la humedad: la madera está hinchada. 5. Sé que me curaré pronto _____ todo el apoyo y la ayuda de mis amigos. 6. Me dio dolor de cabeza _____ leer tanto. 7. _____ la tormenta no voy a poder ir al cine.

Ejercicio 8.12 Traduzca.

1. *I went home because of my brother's illness.* **2.** *They had to cancel the trial because of the news.* **3.** *They had to let him leave because of that.* **4.** *She lost her voice from screaming so much.* **5.** *They did not go out because it was snowing.* **6.** *It's because of your friendship that I managed to get where I am.*

7. *Become* or *Get*

Chapter 8.B.7, pages 285–287

Ejercicio 8.13 Llene cada espacio en blanco con la expresión correcta para significar *became*.

1. De joven _____ médico, y finalmente _____ millonario. **2.** Mi padre _____ muy contento cuando le dije que me había ganado la lotería. **3.** Esa noche, el conde _____ vampiro. **4.** Al ver el fantasma, la mujer _____ pálida. **5.** Tenía muchas ambiciones y finalmente _____ para todos un símbolo del éxito.

Ejercicio 8.14 Traduzca.

1. *I am glad it's Friday.* **2.** *The children became quiet.* **3.** *He calmed down after that.* **4.** *They got tired of walking.* **5.** *I got sick during the vacation.* **6.** *They got mad because I did not write.* **7.** *You get old fast in this job.* **8.** *The horse calmed down after the shot* (inyección). **9.** *I noticed she had become pale.* **10.** *She wanted to become a respected citizen.* **11.** *The flower had become a fruit.* **12.** *He became a doctor.*

Acabar, Apply, Ask, At, Attend, Because, Become (Review)

Chapter 8.B.1–7, pages 280–287

Ejercicio 8.15 Temas de ensayo y de práctica oral.

a. Ensayo

Prestando atención al uso correcto en español del léxico indicado, escriba un párrafo sobre uno de los temas que siguen. Refiérase a las páginas apropiadas del capítulo 8 para usar al máximo las expresiones que se deben practicar.

1. (si está en la universidad) Describa sus planes para venir a la universidad y el proceso por el que pasó para llegar aquí.

2. (si tiene planes de ir a la universidad) Describa sus planes para ir a la universidad y el proceso por el que está pasando para llegar allá.

3. Describa un trabajo que tenga o que haya tenido y el proceso por el que pasó para conseguirlo.

b. Práctica oral

Hable con un(a) compañero(a) sobre uno de los temas anteriores.

8. *But*

Chapter 8.B.8, pages 287–288

Ejercicio 8.16 Llene cada espacio en blanco con la expresión correcta para significar *but*.

1. Estudié el idioma, _____ no me atrevo a hablar.   **2.** No fueron a Honduras, _____ a Uruguay.   **3.** Ese hombre no es mi tío, _____ mi cuñado.   **4.** No lo compró, _____ se lo regaló su hermana.   **5.** No hablo el idioma, _____ voy a viajar al país.   **6.** Esta clase es interesante, _____ difícil.

9. *Come* and *Go*

Chapter 8.B.9, pages 288–289

Ejercicio 8.17 Llene cada espacio en blanco con la expresión correcta: **ven, voy, llegar, ir** o **vine**.

(La madre de Beto acaba de llegar del supermercado y, al entrar a la cocina, lo llama.)

—Beto, **(1)** _____ acá, necesito tu ayuda.
—Ya **(2)** _____, mami.

(Pasa un rato. La mamá sigue metiendo bolsas, pero Beto no aparece.)

—Apúrate, m'ijo, o **(3)** _____ a buscarte yo.

(Beto llega por fin.)

—¿Dónde estabas? ¿Por qué tardaste tanto en **(4)** _____?
—Pero mami, **(5)** _____ tan pronto como me llamaste.
—No, en lo que te esperaba, tuve tiempo de **(6)** _____ al coche dos veces.
—Lo siento, mami. No me di cuenta.

Ejercicio 8.18 Traduzca. Para *you*, use el informal singular (tú).

1. *When are your parents coming to see us?*   2. *I am going to the movies.*   3. *Can I come with you?*   4. *"Come here, Juanita!" "I'm coming!"*   5. *They are always late.*   6. *Do not be late.*   7. *I am sorry I am late.*   8. *When did you get here?*   9. *He went to the movies.*

10. Despedir

Chapter 8.B.10, page 289

Ejercicio 8.19 Llene cada espacio en blanco con la expresión correcta: **despidieron, nos despedimos, nos despidieron** o **los despedimos**.

1. Como no teníamos en ese trabajo la antigüedad que tenían los demás, _____.   2. Se formó una protesta cuando _____ a todos los empleados de esa empresa.   3. A los empleados que son menos productivos _____ cuando el mercado lo requiere.   4. Cuando fue hora de separarnos, mi novia y yo _____ con un abrazo.

Ejercicio 8.20 Traduzca.

1. *They fired me yesterday.*   2. *I said good-bye to my parents.*   3. *I fired him.*   4. *I said good-bye to her.*   5. *We said good-bye at the door.*

11. *Exit* and *Success*

Chapter 8.B.11, pages 289–290

Ejercicio 8.21 Llene cada espacio en blanco con la expresión correcta: **éxitos, salidas** o **sucesos**.

1. Para el periódico local, solo hay espacio para reportar los _____ de mayor importancia.   2. ¿Dónde están las _____ de emergencia?   3. Mis fracasos son mucho más frecuentes que mis _____.

Ejercicio 8.22 Traduzca.

1. *If we work hard, we shall be successful.*   2. *Our success depends upon our effort.*   3. *The exit is to the right.*   4. *My grandmother liked to talk about the terrible events of World War II.*

12. *Go* and *Leave*

Chapter 8.B.12, pages 290–292

Ejercicio 8.23 Llene cada espacio en blanco con la expresión correcta: **ir, irse, salir, dejar** o **dejar de**. Conjugue el verbo correctamente para el contexto.

Los turistas **(1)** _____ de su hotel temprano para **(2)** _____ al aeropuerto porque su vuelo iba a **(3)** _____ esa mañana: habían estado en Madrid dos semanas, y ya era hora de **(4)** _____. El viaje les había encantado: **(5)** _____ a muchos lugares turísticos, y todas las noches **(6)** _____ a restaurantes y bares. Tenían muchos recuerdos: uno de ellos se enfermó el tercer día, pero aun así no **(7)** _____ acompañar a los demás en todas sus aventuras. Otro **(8)** _____ sus tarjetas de crédito en casa en los Estados Unidos y tuvo que tomar dinero prestado de los demás. Y todos peleaban con doña Lupe, que quería comprarse objetos muy frágiles: por fin no la **(9)** _____ comprar más que uno o dos platos. El taxista los **(10)** _____ en el aeropuerto, y todos estaban tristes de que se terminara el viaje.

Ejercicio 8.24 Traduzca. Para *you*, use el informal singular (tú).

1. *We are going to school.*   2. *She left an hour ago.*   3. *The cat went outside.*   4. *They are going out tonight.*   5. *The nurse went out to lunch.*   6. *We were playing out in the park, and Luisito got mad and left.*   7. *At what time does your flight leave?*   8. *Could you leave me at the corner, please?*   9. *You will not let me do anything.*   10. *They stopped screaming.*

13. *Guide*

Chapter 8.B.13, page 292

Ejercicio 8.25 Llene cada espacio en blanco con **el** o **la**.

Al entrar al museo conocimos a Marcos, **(1)** _____ guía que nos habían asignado. Marcos nos dio **(2)** _____ guía de las diferentes exhibiciones del museo por si queríamos recorrer el lugar a solas. Había muchos estudiantes hoy en el museo y muchos llevaban **(3)** _____ guía en las manos.

Ejercicio 8.26 Traduzca. Para *you*, use el informal singular (tú).

1. *Our guide at the museum was an old man.*   2. *The tour guide was from Venezuela.*   3. *You will find the rules in the guide book.*

But, Come and Go, Despedir, Exit and Success, Go and Leave, Guide (Review)

Chapter 8.B.8–13, pages 287–292

Ejercicio 8.27 Temas de ensayo y de práctica oral

a. Ensayo

Prestando atención al uso correcto en español del léxico indicado, escriba un párrafo sobre uno de los temas que siguen. Refiérase a las páginas apropiadas del capítulo 8 para usar al máximo las expresiones que se deben practicar.

1. Describa las aventuras de unos turistas en un país hispano.
2. Describa una experiencia que usted haya tenido en un viaje.
3. Describa sus planes para su vida profesional.

b. Práctica oral

Hable con un(a) compañero(a) sobre uno de los temas anteriores.

14. Know

Chapter 8.B.14, pages 292–293

Ejercicio 8.28 Llene cada espacio en blanco con la expresión correcta para significar *know*. Conjugue el verbo correctamente para el contexto.

Yo **(1)** _____ que ellos **(2)** _____ la ciudad mejor que yo y que **(3)** _____ (ellos) exactamente dónde está la casa de su amigo. Hace muchos años que **(4)** _____ (ellos) a este amigo. Es un individuo que **(5)** _____ que lo andamos buscando, y **(6)** _____ esconderse bien. Me han dicho que **(7)** _____ disfrazarse. No **(8)** _____ (yo) qué vamos a hacer para **(9)** _____ dónde está.

Ejercicio 8.29 Traduzca. Para *you*, use el informal singular (tú).

1. *I know you.* 2. *He met his new wife in Guatemala.* 3. *He does not know the area.* 4. *He knows my phone number.* 5. *They know how to skate.* 6. *We knew it was cold.* 7. *They did not know what to say.* 8. *Do you know what time it is?* 9. *Do you know that hotel?* 10. *He did not know how to swim.*

15. *Learn*

Chapter 8.B.15, page 293

Ejercicio 8.30   Llene cada espacio en blanco con la expresión correcta: **aprender, enterarse de, averiguar** o **saber.** Conjugue el verbo correctamente para el contexto. Si existe más de una opción, explique la diferencia.

1. Me gustaría _____ a bailar la salsa.   2. Los jóvenes pensaban que nadie iba a _____ nada de lo que estaban haciendo.   3. Usando sus poderes de análisis, el detective _____ quiénes eran los ladrones.   4. Nunca _____ (yo) por qué no me habían invitado a su boda, pero verdaderamente no me importa.

Ejercicio 8.31   Traduzca. Para *you*, use el informal singular (tú).

1. *She learned to dance.* 2. *They found out about our secret.* 3. *When I found out that you were here, I came immediately.*

16. *Meet*

Chapter 8.B.16, page 294

Ejercicio 8.32   Llene cada espacio en blanco con la expresión correcta: **conocer, encontrar, encontrarse, encontrarse con, toparse con** o **tropezar con.** Conjugue el verbo correctamente para el contexto.

1. Ayer _____ al nuevo director del programa: me lo presentó el profesor López. 2. Voy a salir a almorzar con mi mejor amiga: vamos a _____ en el centro.   3. Me gustaría _____ a tus padres: si son como tú, han de ser muy interesantes.   4. No tengo ganas de _____ ningún conocido hoy.   5. Esta tarde voy a _____ mis amigos para repasar para el examen.   6. Ando buscando mis llaves y no las _____.

Ejercicio 8.33   Traduzca.

1. *Then they decided to meet in the afternoon to discuss the job.*   2. *Guess whom I met on my way to the library.*   3. *She met her in the office. (a first acquaintance)*

17. *Order*

Chapter 8.B.17, page 295

Ejercicio 8.34   Llene cada espacio en blanco con **el** o **la.**

1. Mi tía es una mujer obsesiva: para ella no hay nada más importante que _____ orden.   2. Los soldados dispararon cuando el general les dio _____ orden.

(continued)

3. ¿Cuál es _____ orden que siguieron para organizar estas fichas?   **4.** —Estoy a _____ orden del cliente —dijo el mesero.

Ejercicio 8.35   Traduzca.

1. Everything had to be placed in a specific order.   2. I did it because I received the order from above.   3. "Hello, my name is Rigoberta Menchú." "Hello, Elisabeth Burgos, at your service."

18. Pensar

Chapter 8.B.18, pages 295–296

Ejercicio 8.36   Llene cada espacio en blanco con **en, de** o **Ø** (nada).

1. Cuando pienso _____ mi niñez, no recuerdo nada que sea triste.   **2.** Este verano pienso _____ viajar a Europa.   **3.** Cada vez que veo a ese actor, pienso _____ mi padre.   **4.** ¿Qué pensarán _____ mí?

Ejercicio 8.37   Traduzca. Para *you*, use el informal singular (tú).

1. I cannot stop thinking of you.   2. What were you thinking of?   3. What do you think of me?   4. She refused to tell me what she thought of the workshop.   5. We are planning on visiting our family next week.

19. People vs. Machines

Chapter 8.B.19, pages 296–298

Ejercicio 8.38   Subraye la expresión correcta para cada contexto.

1. Mi reloj no (trabaja/funciona).   **2.** Jorge (apagó/salió) la luz.   **3.** El auto no (empieza/arranca).   **4.** Cuando primero compré este coche, (corría/andaba) muy bien.   **5.** Tuvimos que entregar el examen incompleto porque (corrimos fuera de/se nos acabó el) tiempo.

Ejercicio 8.39   Traduzca. Para *you*, use el informal singular (tú).

1. The children were running.   2. That motor stopped running.   3. They work from nine to five.   4. It does not work like that.   5. The batteries ran down.   6. I am going to start the car so it will get warm.   7. The lights went out after ten.   8. He works out every day.   9. We can work it out.   10. I ran out.   11. He ran into his cousin at the museum.   12. When did the movie start?   13. My watch ran down.   14. He ran down the stairs. **15.** *They ran into their friends at the bar.* **16.** *He ran into the wall.* **17.** *Turn out the lights.* **18.** *Everything turned out okay.*

20. *Play*

Chapter 8.B.20, pages 298–299

Ejercicio 8.40 Llene cada espacio en blanco con la expresión correcta: **jugar, tocar, obra, juego, jugada, partido** o **partida**. Si usa un verbo, conjúguelo correctamente para el contexto.

1. Fue una _____ de ajedrez especialmente interesante *(game)*. **2.** Con esa _____ *(game move)* ganaron el _____ *(game)* de baloncesto. **3.** Me encanta _____ *(play)* el piano y _____ *(play)* al tenis. **4.** Cuando fuimos a Montevideo asistimos a una _____ de teatro *(play)* y a un _____ *(game)* de fútbol. **5.** La canasta es un _____ *(game)* de cartas. **6.** Ella _____ *(play)* varios instrumentos musicales.

Ejercicio 8.41 Traduzca. Para *you*, use el informal singular (tú).

1. *They played tennis all afternoon.* **2.** *What are you playing?* **3.** *Do you play the guitar?* **4.** *Don't play with your sister's violin.* **5.** *She will be playing the violin tonight.*

Know, Learn, Meet, Order, **Pensar**, *People* vs. *Machines, Play* (Review)

Chapter 8.B.14–20, pages 292–299

Ejercicio 8.42 Temas de ensayo y de práctica oral

a. Ensayo

Prestando atención al uso correcto en español del léxico indicado, escriba un párrafo sobre uno de los temas que siguen. Refiérase a las páginas apropiadas del capítulo 8 para usar al máximo las expresiones que se deben practicar.

1. Describa una experiencia que haya tenido con problemas de automóvil.

2. Describa un día en que alguien nuevo entró en su vida.

3. Describa una aventura de un deportista o músico famoso con problemas mecánicos, eléctricos o electrónicos.

b. Práctica oral

En grupos, cuenten oralmente una de las experiencias enumeradas arriba, bajo "Temas de ensayo".

21. *Put*

Chapter 8.B.21, pages 299–300

Ejercicio 8.43 Llene cada espacio en blanco con la expresión correcta: **aguantar, apoyar, mantener, poner, ponerse** o **soportar**. Conjugue el verbo correctamente para el contexto.

Don José se levantó esa mañana y **(1)** _____ la ropa del día anterior porque no tenía nada limpio. Ya no lo **(2)** _____ más: su esposa no tenía tiempo de lavarle la ropa ahora que ella también trabajaba, y él no podía exigirle lo mismo que antes. El mundo moderno no era para él: no **(3)** _____ que los hombres y las mujeres se consideraran iguales. Él quería ser el único en **(4)** _____ a su familia y, por eso no **(5)** _____ a su esposa cuando esta le pidió permiso para conseguir empleo.

Ejercicio 8.44 Traduzca. Para *you*, use el informal singular (tú).

1. *She put her hand on my shoulder.* 2. *I put on my boots.* 3. *He put his hand in his jacket.* 4. *Help me set the table, please.* 5. *His face became green.* 6. *Do not put your finger in your sister's eye.* 7. *I can't stand your attitude.* 8. *My mother supports the family with two jobs.* 9. *My sister supports me, no matter what I want to do.* 10. *Why do you put up with such stupidity?*

22. *Realize*

Chapter 8.B.22, page 300

Ejercicio 8.45 Llene cada espacio en blanco con la expresión correcta: **darse cuenta de** o **realizar**.

1. Este es un ideal que nunca podré _____. 2. A veces es difícil _____ los sentimientos de los demás. 3. Si puedo _____ este proyecto de manera eficiente, estoy seguro que me darán el trabajo.

Ejercicio 8.46 Traduzca. Para *you*, use el informal singular (tú).

1. *I realize that I cannot fulfill your dreams in an instant.* 2. *If you carry out all your duties responsibly, you can stay.* 3. *She realized that he was unhappy.* 4. *He realized his dreams were impossible.*

23. *Serve*

Chapter 8.B.23, pages 300–301

Ejercicio 8.47 Llene cada espacio en blanco con **lo(s), la(s), le(s)** o **Ø** (nada).

(Dos meseras hablan en un restaurante.)

—Llegaron unos clientes nuevos a la mesa número 4. Te toca **(1)** servir_____.
—No, yo **(2)** _____ serví a los de la mesa 3 y 2.
—Sí, pero tienes tres mesas.
—Bueno, pues, si insistes.

(En la mesa)

—Buenas tardes, señores, ¿en qué puedo **(3)** servir_____?
—¿Podemos cenar a esta hora?
—Claro. La cena **(4)** _____ servimos a partir de las seis.
—¿Nos trae una botella de Marqués de Riscal, por favor?
—Bueno.

(Trae el vino.)

—Si le parece bien, abro ahora el vino y **(5)** _____ sirvo luego.
—No, no, **(6)** sírva_____ de inmediato.

Ejercicio 8.48 Traduzca.

1. *Do not serve me so much, please.* **2.** *How can I help you?* **3.** *Dinner is usually served at eight. Tonight we will serve it at nine thirty.*

24. *Spend*

Chapter 8.B.24, page 301

Ejercicio 8.49 Llene cada espacio en blanco con la expresión correcta: **desperdiciar, gastar** o **pasar.** Conjugue el verbo correctamente para el contexto.

1. Me encanta _____ *(spend)* tiempo con mi abuela en el campo. **2.** Me molesta _____ *(waste)* el agua. **3.** ¿Quieres _____ *(spend)* un rato conmigo? **4.** No quiero _____ *(spend)* mucho dinero esta vez. **5.** Solo _____ *(I only spent)* unos minutos en la cocina. **6.** No hay que _____ *(waste)* dinero: solo se debe _____ *(spend)* para lo que se necesita.

Ejercicio 8.50 Traduzca. Para *you*, use el informal singular (tú).

1. *You spend more money on your children than you do on yourself.*   2. *I spent three hours on this paper yesterday.*   3. *She spent some time abroad.*   4. *It is terrible to waste time and money.*

25. *Take*

Chapter 8.B.25, pages 301–303

Ejercicio 8.51 Llene cada espacio en blanco con la expresión más natural para el contexto. Use cada uno solo una vez: **apuntar, bajar, llevar, llevarse, quitarse, sacar, subir, tener, tomar, traer.**

1. Tenemos que _____ la basura hoy.   2. Voy a _____ tu número de teléfono en este papelito.   3. No quiero _____ esta caja al sótano porque tengo miedo que se moje.   4. Quisiera _____ un vaso de agua, por favor.   5. Los hombres deben _____ el sombrero al entrar a la iglesia.   6. ¿Podrían _____ a mi hermanita cuando se vayan?   7. Durante el desayuno, el niño le dijo a su mamá: "La maestra nos dijo que teníamos que _____ el libro a clase todos los días."   8. El mensajero tenía que _____ el paquete hasta el quinto piso.   9. En clase, la maestra le dijo a un niño al que se le había olvidado el libro: "¿No les dije que debían _____ su libro a clase todos los días?"   10. No sabemos cuándo va a _____ lugar ese evento.

Ejercicio 8.52 Traduzca. Para *you*, use el informal singular (tú).

1. *What would you like to drink?*   2. *He took his plate to the table.*   3. *She took the iPad and left.*   4. *"Can we take you?" "No, thanks, I will take the bus."*   5. *This is taking too long.*   6. *Here. This is yours.*   7. *We took the camera to the store.*   8. *They took away our towels.*   9. *Let me take (write) this down.*   10. *Do you want me to take your books down?*   11. *They took the food up to the room.*   12. *We have to take the garbage out.*   13. *Do not take off your socks.*   14. *The exam will take place here.*   15. *Can I bring a friend to your party?*   16. *Bring your own drink.*

26. *Time*

Chapter 8.B.26, pages 303–304

Ejercicio 8.53 Llene cada espacio en blanco con la expresión correcta: **tiempo, vez, hora** o **rato.**

1. ¿Qué _____ hace allá en invierno?   2. ¿Cuánto _____ nos queda?   3. Esta _____ no les voy a contar el final de la película.   4. Es _____ de cerrar la tienda.   5. Nos iremos dentro de un _____.   6. Es la primera _____ que oigo esa canción.

Ejercicio 8.54   Traduzca. Para *you*, use el informal singular (tú).

1. *Do you have time to talk to me?*   2. *What was the weather like?*   3. *How many times do I have to tell you?*   4. *That time it was different.*   5. *He would not tell me what time it was.*   6. *She will be here in a little while.*   7. *I knew it was time to get up.*   8. *We had a good time.*   9. *We had good weather.*

27. What

Chapter 8.B.27, pages 304–305

Ejercicio 8.55   Llene cada espacio en blanco con la expresión correcta: **qué, lo que, cuál** o **cómo**.

1. No le importaba _____ yo pensaba de la situación.   2. —¿_____ es? —Es el de piedra.   3. —¿_____ es? —Es un animal.   4. El niño, que no había oído lo que su padre le había dicho, preguntó: "¿_____?" Su padre rápidamente lo corrigió: "La gente bien educada no dice ¿_____? sino ¿_____?"

Ejercicio 8.56   Traduzca. Para *you*, use el informal singular (tú).

1. *What is cucurucho?*   2. *Which one is yours?*   3. *What cities did you visit?*   4. *Excuse me? (polite "What?")*   5. *What you do not know will not hurt you.*

Put, Realize, Serve, Spend, Take, Time, What (Review)

Chapter 8.B.21–27, pages 299–305

Ejercicio 8.57   Temas de ensayo y de práctica oral

a. Ensayo

Prestando atención al uso correcto en español del léxico indicado, escriba un párrafo sobre uno de los temas que siguen. Refiérase a las páginas apropiadas del capítulo 8 para usar al máximo las expresiones que se deben practicar.

1. Describa las aventuras de verano de un joven que trabaja de mesero en un restaurante.
2. Describa un día en su vida, usando las expresiones indicadas.
3. Describa una lección cultural que usted haya aprendido en su vida.

b. Práctica oral

En grupos, cuenten oralmente una de las experiencias enumeradas arriba, bajo "Temas de ensayo".

Chapter 9
Orthography

A GENERAL INFORMATION

Chapter 9.A, pages 314–318

Ejercicio 9.1   Deletree las palabras siguientes:

MODELO: **lago:** ele, a, ge, o

1. huevo   **2.** llano   **3.** riña   **4.** eficaz   **5.** yegua   **6.** aguja   **7.** bache   **8.** errores
9. balancearse   **10.** avestruz

B CONSONANTS: SPELLING ISSUES

Consonants (B, V)

Chapter 9.B.1, pages 319–320

Ejercicio 9.2   Escoja la opción correcta entre paréntesis.

1. ¡Qué (bello/vello) cuadro!   **2.** No sé si prefiero que mi primer hijo sea (barón/varón) o hembra.   **3.** No se te ocurra (rebelar/revelar) mi secreto.   **4.** ¿Cuándo (bienes/vienes) a visitarme?   **5.** Mi madre nunca (tubo/tuvo) la oportunidad de realizar sus sueños.   **6.** No te (vallas/vayas/bayas) todavía.   **7.** Quiero que (hierbas/hiervas) el agua para el té.

Ejercicio 9.3   En las frases siguientes las palabras entre corchetes ([ ]) están indicadas según su sonido. Escríbalas con su ortografía correcta, usando la lógica del contexto cuando tenga dudas. (Fíjese que las palabras entre corchetes están transcritas según un dialecto que usa seseo y yeísmo. Entre los corchetes el acento indica la vocal con énfasis, pero esto no significa que la palabra representada lleve acento escrito según las reglas de acentuación; por ejemplo, [káma] = cama.)

1. El [sábado] [bámos] adonde siempre [íba] mi familia para Año [nuébo].   **2.** En esta ciudad hay [bários] [bárrios] que son [béyos].   **3.** En [bes] de alejarse, le dio un [béso] en la [bóca] al [abogádo].   **4.** La [báse] de ese [báso] de cristal es de color diferente.   **5.** Todos tenemos [béyos] en los [brásos].   **6.** Se me [olbída] el nombre del [bisepresidénte]. **7.** ¿Cómo se dice [boy] en inglés? **8.** No [kábe] duda de que es un [jóben] [pribádo] de su [libertád]. **9.** Le [estúbe] [adbirtiéndo] que [andubiéra] con cuidado. **10.** Necesitas [kontribuír] sin [burlárte]. Pon a [erbír] el agua.

Ejercicio 9.4 Las palabras que siguen están indicadas entre corchetes ([ ]) por su sonido. Escríbalas con su ortografía correcta. (Fíjese que las palabras entre corchetes están transcritas según un dialecto que usa seseo. Entre los corchetes el acento indica la vocal con énfasis, pero esto no significa que la palabra representada lleve acento escrito según las reglas de acentuación; por ejemplo, [káma] = cama.)

1. [abía] **2.** [adbertír] **3.** [bebér] **4.** [benefísio] **5.** [bilaterál] **6.** [biolojía] **7.** [bisepresidénte] **8.** [bolbér] **9.** [boy] **10.** [budú] **11.** [debér] **12.** [ebadír] **13.** [esklábo] **14.** [eskribír] **15.** [estúbo] **16.** [íba] **17.** [irbió] **18.** [kabér] **19.** [kontribuír] **20.** [mobilidád] **21.** [posibilidád] **22.** [sabér] **23.** [serbír] **24.** [túbe]

Consonants (K, C, Qu, S)

Chapter 9.B.2, pages 321–324

Ejercicio 9.5 Complete cada espacio en blanco con la forma indicada del verbo.

1. Por lo general Rosa _____ (hacer/ella/presente indicativo) el postre, pero esta vez fue Marta la que lo _____ (hacer/ella/pretérito). **2.** Siempre me _____ (convencer/tú/presente indicativo) con ese razonamiento, pero yo nunca te _____ (convencer/yo/presente indicativo) a ti, aunque use exactamente la misma lógica. **3.** Aunque _____ (parecer/3.ª pers. sing/presente subjuntivo) que va a llover, no _____ (parecer/3.ª pers. sing./presente indicativo) que vaya a hacer viento. **4.** No _____ (merecer/yo/presente indicativo) tanta bondad de los que me rodean, sin embargo los que sí se lo _____ (merecer/ustedes/presente indicativo) son ustedes. **5.** Ojalá que no me _____ (torcer/yo/presente subjuntivo) el tobillo de nuevo, ayer me lo _____ (torcer/yo/pretérito) tan pronto me levanté.

Ejercicio 9.6 Complete las palabras incompletas con **-ción, -sión, -tión, -xión, -cion-, -sion-, -tion- o -xion.**

1. No me gusta la direc_____ que lleva esta asocia_____ en la cues_____ del cuidado de la pen_____ de los empleados. **2.** Las condi_____es de trabajo en esta empresa merecen nuestra aten_____. **3.** Las ac_____es que tomaron esos

(continued)

fotógrafos no me parecen muy profe_____ales.   **4.** Dicen que se puede controlar la diges_____ usando ejercicios de refle_____ semejantes a la medita_____.
5. Arrestaron a ese hombre por pose_____ de drogas: se dice que tiene cone_____es con la mafia.

Consonants (G, Gu, Gü, J)

Chapter 9.B.3, pages 324–328

Ejercicio 9.7   Subraye todas las **u** mudas (que no se pronuncian).

1. Aprendí a tocar la guitarra porque quería poder componer mis propias canciones.   **2.** Ese hombre es el que atestiguó en contra del acusado.
3. Averiguamos que ese queso era holandés y no uruguayo.   **4.** No paguemos nunca más los costos de la guerra.   **5.** ¿Qué producto químico usaron para preparar ese daguerrotipo?

Ejercicio 9.8   Subraye todas las **u** no mudas (que sí se pronuncian).

1. Aprendió a tocar la guitarra porque quería poder componer sus propias canciones.   **2.** Ese hombre es el que atestiguó en contra del acusado.
3. Averiguamos que ese queso era holandés y no uruguayo.   **4.** No paguemos nunca más los costos de la guerra.   **5.** Ayúdame a aguantar este cuadro de las cigüeñas, mientras cuelgo este otro aquí.

Ejercicio 9.9   Las palabras que siguen están indicadas entre corchetes ([ ]) por su sonido. Identifique las palabras de la lista que necesitan diéresis en la **u (ü)**, y escríbalas con su ortografía correcta al lado de su definición. (Fíjese que las palabras entre corchetes están transcritas según un dialecto que usa seseo y yeísmo. Entre los corchetes el acento indica la vocal con énfasis, pero esto no significa que la palabra representada lleve acento escrito según las reglas de acentuación; por ejemplo, [káma] = cama.)

[água]	[apasiguár]	[deguéyo]	[piraguísta]
[aguéro]	[atestiguár]	[deságue]	[regémos]
[agerrído]	[aberígue]	[distingímos]	[santiguár]
[albérge]	[bilíngue]	[linguístika]	[segí]
[amortiguár]	[siguéña]	[pinguíno]	[berguénsa]

1. La ciencia del lenguaje: _____   **2.** El que habla dos idiomas: _____   **3.** Se le dice también "pájaro bobo": _____   **4.** Acción de cortar el cuello: _____

5. Salida de aguas: _____ **6.** Tripulante de una nave parecida a la canoa: _____ **7.** Sentimiento de deshonra: _____ **8.** Presagio: _____ **9.** Sinónimo de "descubra", "se entere": _____ **10.** Ave zancuda que anida en las torres: _____

Ejercicio 9.10 Las palabras que siguen están indicadas entre corchetes ([ ]) por su sonido. Escríbalas con su ortografía correcta. (Fíjese que las palabras entre corchetes están transcritas según un dialecto que usa seseo. Entre los corchetes el acento indica la vocal con énfasis, pero esto no significa que la palabra representada lleve acento escrito según las reglas de acentuación; por ejemplo, [káma] = cama.)

1. [anjéliko] **2.** [apoplejía] **3.** [birjinál] **4.** [dijéramos] **5.** [finjámos]
6. [finjíamos] **7.** [fotojéniko] **8.** [garáje] **9.** [ijiéniko] **10.** [indíjena]
11. [jeólogo] **12.** [jésto] **13.** [kája] **14.** [kojeár] **15.** [konserjería] **16.** [májia]
17. [neuráljia] **18.** [ójo] **19.** [omojéneo] **20.** [pedagojía] **21.** [protéja]
22. [protejér] **23.** [tejído] **24.** [trajéra]

Consonants (H)

Chapter 9.B.4, pages 329–332

Ejercicio 9.11 Escoja la opción correcta para cada contexto.

1. Nunca he (echo/hecho) eso antes. **2.** Me dijo que iba (a ver/haber) una película nueva. **3.** Cuando voy a la playa, me hipnotizan las (holas/olas). **4.** Se le perdieron los lentes a mi abuela, y no los (halla/haya) en ningún lado. **5.** ¡(Has/Haz) tu tarea! **6.** (Asta/Hasta) mañana. **7.** Siempre le (hecho/echo) ajo al aderezo.

Ejercicio 9.12 Las palabras que siguen están indicadas entre corchetes ([ ]) por su sonido. Escríbalas con su ortografía correcta. (Fíjese que las palabras entre corchetes están transcritas según un dialecto que usa yeísmo. Entre los corchetes el acento indica la vocal con énfasis, pero esto no significa que la palabra representada lleve acento escrito según las reglas de acentuación; por ejemplo, [káma] = cama. En algunos casos hay más de una posibilidad: escriba todas las posibilidades.)

1. [an] **2.** [áya] **3.** [ayáste] **4.** [desidratádo] **5.** [ektárea] **6.** [elejír]
7. [eliotrópo] **8.** [ematóma] **9.** [emigrár] **10.** [emisfério] **11.** [emisión]
12. [emorrájia] **13.** [eptagonál] **14.** [ermáno] **15.** [ermíta] **16.** [érnia]
17. [etérno] **18.** [eterodókso] **19.** [inundár] **20.** [óiga] **21.** [ormíga]
22. [ostentár] **23.** [óye] **24.** [uébo] **25.** [uéso] **26.** [uésped] **27.** [uida]
28. [umbrál] **29.** [yamár]

Ejercicio 9.13 Las palabras que siguen están indicadas entre corchetes ([ ]) por su sonido. Escríbalas con su ortografía correcta. (Fíjese que las palabras entre corchetes están transcritas según un dialecto que usa seseo y yeísmo. Entre los corchetes el acento indica la vocal con énfasis, pero esto no significa que la palabra representada lleve acento escrito según las reglas de acentuación; por ejemplo, [káma] = cama.)

1. [ablandár] 2. [abláramos] 3. [andár] 4. [ayá] 5. [desisiéra] 6. [idroabión]
7. [inumáno] 8. [iperaktíbo] 9. [ipókrita] 10. [islám] 11. [istória]
12. [italiáno] 13. [ogár] 14. [olgánsa] 15. [olimpiáda] 16. [óya]
17. [omojéneo] 18. [ornaménto] 19. [ospitál] 20. [uéko] 21. [uélga]
22. [uérfano] 23. [uérta] 24. [uéya] 25. [umedád] 26. [yáto] 27. [yeléra]
28. [yélo] 29. [yéma] 30. [yérro]

Consonants (X)

Chapter 9.B.5, pages 333–335

Ejercicio 9.14 Ponga las palabras de la lista en tres grupos, una con la **x** pronunciada como /ks/, otra /s/ y otra /j/.

examen	excito	léxico	sexual
éxito	explorar	México	xenofobia
existe	experto	Oaxaca	xileno

1. /ks/ 2. /s/ 3. /j/

Consonants (Ll, Y, Í)

Chapter 9.B.6, pages 335–339

Ejercicio 9.15 Escoja la opción correcta para cada contexto.

1. Mi primo está muy (callado/cayado). 2. Caminé tanto por la playa que tengo (callos/cayos) en los pies. 3. En otoño las (ardías/ardillas) recogen nueces.

Ejercicio 9.16 Complete las palabras incompletas con **-ia, -ía** o **-illa**.

1. Esa librer___ tiene muchos libros sobre la histor___ de las cienc___s. 2. A mi famil___ le encanta cocinar cost___ a la parr___. 3. Esa secretar___ sabe más de geograf___ que de poes___. 4. Volvieron con alegr___ a la marav___ de la democrac___. 5. Por la lluv___ la pand___ entró a la cap___.

Consonants (R, Rr)

Chapter 9.B.7, pages 340–342

Ejercicio 9.17 Subraye las **r** que se pronuncian /rr/.

1. Nos sorprendió el calor en Roma. **2.** Fuimos a Israel para las vacaciones de verano. **3.** Viajaron alrededor del mundo en treinta días. **4.** Me da rabia que la gente sea deshonrada. **5.** El ratón de Roque no tiene rabo porque Ramón Ramírez se lo ha robado.

Consonants (Ph, Th, Ch; Double Consonants)

Chapter 9.B.8–9, pages 342–343

Ejercicio 9.18 Traduzca con el cognado en español de cada palabra indicada. Preste atención a la ortografía.

1. *photo, photographer, photography* **2.** *theater, theatrical* **3.** *character, characteristic* **4.** *occasion, occur, accident* **5.** *different, difference* **6.** *immediate, immortal, immigrant*

C VOWELS AND ACCENTS

(Syllabification: Consonants)

Chapter 9.C.1.a, pages 344–345

Ejercicio 9.19 Consonantes sencillas intervocálicas: Divida cada palabra en sílabas.

raza	meta	visa	callo	serrano
fecha	cerro	caballo	metiche	

Ejercicio 9.20 Dos consonantes intervocálicas: Divida cada palabra en sílabas.

campo	pantera	angelical	musgo	refresco
fantoche	mantilla	mercado	sincero	cencerro
vibra	hablan	autografiar	retrato	adrenalina
reflorecer	aglomerar	negro	aplastar	represión
declive				

Ejercicio 9.21 Tres o más consonantes intervocálicas: Divida cada palabra en sílabas.

anglosajón	empresario	constante	estrecho	espléndido
instituto	inspección	instrumento	embrollo	transmitir
resplandor	transcribir			

Accents (Syllabification: Vowels)

Chapter 9.C.1.b, pages 345–347

Ejercicio 9.22 Hiatos: Divida cada palabra en sílabas.

recaer	crear	creer	veo	sea
caos	boa	coactar	coexistir	gentío
frío	reí	vestía	etíope	ataúd
raíz	vía	mío	reúnan	continúa
rehúsa				

Ejercicio 9.23 Diptongos: Divida cada palabra en sílabas.

aviador	aire	bienestar	deleite	miope
oiga	resguardo	causa	fueron	endeudarse
fuimos	diurno	duodeno	Dios	hueso
cariátide	recién	comió	aguántate	acuérdense
cantáis	volvéis	óiganlos	enjáulalo	

Ejercicio 9.24 Triptongos y otras combinaciones: Divida cada palabra en sílabas.

veían	seáis	caíamos	esquiáis	vivíais
traían	caeríais	oíais	enviéis	creías
actuéis	adquirierais			

Ejercicio 9.25 La **h** intervocálica: Divida cada palabra en sílabas.

ahora	rehago	ahí	rehíce	prohíben
rehúsa	ahogar	desahogar	ahumado	cacahuate
alcahuete	cohete	rehúyen	sobrehumano	zaherir

Ejercicio 9.26 Repaso: Divida cada palabra en sílabas.

divida   las   siguientes   palabras   en
sílabas   luego   vea   cuando   necesitan
acentos   porque   rey   reina   voy
boina   bueno   bien

Accents (Stress)

Chapter 9.C.2, pages 347–354

Ejercicio 9.27 Indique para cada palabra si es **aguda, llana, esdrújula** o **sobresdrújula.**

1. camino   2. caminó   3. caminaba   4. caminábamos   5. caminad   6. compra
7. compró   8. compraba   9. comprábamos   10. cómpralo   11. cómpramelo
12. español   13. españoles   14. francés   15. trances   16. encéstalo

Ejercicio 9.28 Las siguientes palabras son agudas. Póngales acento a las que lo necesiten.

1. presto   2. enterrar   3. preparad   4. desperte   5. dividir   6. farol   7. piedad
8. pedi   9. peor   10. caiman   11. cocinar   12. imparcial   13. cajon
14. finlandes   15. trajin   16. temblor   17. cristal   18. riñon

Ejercicio 9.29 Las siguientes palabras son llanas. Póngales acento a las que lo necesiten.

1. lapiz   2. llamas   3. llaman   4. pluma   5. hablaron   6. españoles   7. dioses
8. dia   9. deme   10. españolita   11. peruano   12. consigo   13. traje
14. examen   15. caracter   16. lunes   17. labio   18. infertil

Ejercicio 9.30 Las siguientes palabras son esdrújulas y sobresdrújulas; la sílaba tónica (con énfasis) está en negrilla. ¿Necesitan acento?

1. **ma**talo   2. rega**la**melo   3. **ca**llense   4. es**tu**pido   5. **par**pado   6. ca**pi**tulo
7. **pro**jimo   8. **ba**jame   9. **a**nimo   10. **cas**cara   11. **de**cada   12. **e**xito
13. **pa**jaro   14. **as**pero   15. **hun**garo   16. **vin**culo   17. **ma**quina   18. **pil**dora

Ejercicio 9.31 Póngales acento a los adverbios que lo necesiten. (La sílaba con énfasis en la parte de cada adjetivo original está en negrilla.)

1. **ra**pidamente   2. **fa**cilmente   3. **len**tamente   4. di**fi**cilmente
5. pia**do**samente   6. bri**llan**temente   7. **fri**amente   8. despiada**da**mente
9. **se**camente   10. fe**liz**mente   11. **fi**jamente   12. **ca**lidamente
13. cien**ti**ficamente   14. misericor**dio**samente   15. **so**lamente
16. fi**nal**mente   17. **gra**vemente   18. pro**xi**mamente

Ejercicio 9.32 Las palabras siguientes son monosílabas; no hay nada subrayado porque el énfasis es único. Póngales acento si lo necesitan. (Las frases están traducidas por si se necesita.)

1. A el le va bien. *(It's going well for him.)*   2. Di que el rey te lo dio. *(Say that the king gave it to you.)*   3. Vio a Dios. *(She saw God.)*   4. El te no me da tos. *(Tea doesn't make me cough.)*   5. No se si se fue. *(I don't know if he left.)*   6. Tu no le des. *(Don't you give her any.)*   7. Tu voz se te va. *(Your voice is going.)*   8. Sin ti no se lo da. *(Without you she won't give it to her.)*   9. No le de la fe. *(Don't give him your faith.)*   10. Yo si se la di. *(I did give it to her.)*   11. A ti te doy lo que hay. *(I give you what there is.)*   12. No hay mas miel por mi. *(There is no more honey because of me.)*

Ejercicio 9.33 Ponga un acento donde se necesite; la sílaba tónica (con énfasis) de cada palabra de más de una sílaba está en negrilla. Si hay más de una opción, explique la diferencia.

1. Aun los **ri**cos nece**si**tan a**mor**.   2. Los **ni**ños a**un** no han co**mi**do.
3. Es**toy so**lo.   4. Me **sien**to **so**lo **cuan**do no es**tas**.   5. **Pa**same **e**sa **lla**ve, por fa**vor**.   6. No **quie**ro **es**ta **fru**ta, pre**fie**ro **e**sa.   7. Por **e**so no **qui**so ir con no**so**tros.   8. **Ten**go que recor**dar e**sa ma**ña**na.   9. ¡Que **bue**na **suer**te **tie**nes!   10. ¡**Co**mo **can**ta!   11. Es**ta**re **so**lo a**qui**.   12. No es**ta cla**ro por que te**ni**an **es**tos ta**tua**jes **pe**ro **e**sos no.

Ejercicio 9.34 Ponga un acento sobre los **que** que lo necesiten.

1. Prefiero **que** no llueva.   2. ¿**Que** dijiste?   3. No sé **que** dije.   4. Creo **que** dije **que** preferiría **que** no lloviera.   5. ¡**Que** locura!   6. Dime **que** crees.
7. El día **que** no llueva aquí, no sabremos **que** hacer.   8. Haremos lo **que** ustedes quieran.   9. La última vez **que** vinieron, nos costó mucho decidir **que** cuarto darles.   10. ¡**Que** duerman en el piso!

Ejercicio 9.35 Llene cada espacio en blanco con **porque** o **por qué**; traduzca las frases 4 y 5.

1. Te llamé ____ tengo noticias. **2.** ¿____ no me llamaste antes? **3.** No te puedo decir ____: ¡es un secreto! **4.** El asesino no pudo explicar ____ había matado al policía. **5.** El asesino no lo pudo explicar ____ había matado al policía. **6.** Yo creo que lo hizo ____ tenía miedo. **7.** ¿Tú matarías a alguien simplemente ____ tienes miedo? **8.** ¿ ____ no? **9.** ¡____ no se debe matar a nadie! **10.** No sé ____ se fue. **11.** Se fue ____ no le hacías caso.

Ejercicio 9.36 Póngale acento a **como** si lo necesita; traduzca las frases 4–7.

1. Como no tengo hambre, no **como**. **2.** ¿**Como** puedes decir eso? **3.** Necesitas pensar **como** yo para comprenderme. **4.** Muéstrame **como** comes con palillos. **5.** ¡**Como** comes! **6.** ¿**Como como**? **7. Como como como**. **8.** Ella se viste **como** yo. **9.** Es un libro **como** los demás. **10.** Si baila **como** canta, ha de ser una maravilla.

Ejercicio 9.37 Póngale acento a **cuanto** si lo necesita.

1. ¿**Cuanto** cuesta este cuarto? **2.** No sé **cuanto** cuesta. **3.** ¿**Cuantos** hermanos tienes? **4.** Me pregunto **cuantos** años tiene esa mujer. **5.** Nadie sabe **cuantas** veces se repetirá. **6.** Le di **cuanto** dinero tenía al ladrón. **7.** No sabe **cuanto** me arrepentí de darle mi dinero. **8.** La profesora le dará **cuanta** información tenga.

Ejercicio 9.38 Póngale acento a **donde** si lo necesita.

1. ¿**Donde** vives? **2.** Vivo **donde** viven mis padres. **3.** No sé **donde** vive mi amiga. **4.** Me dijo **donde** vivía, pero se me olvidó. **5.** Apunté su dirección en la libreta **donde** tengo todas las direcciones. **6.** No sé **donde** puse la libreta. **7.** ¿...No estará **donde** siempre la pones?

Ejercicio 9.39 Póngale acento a **cuando** si lo necesita; traduzca las frases 7 y 8.

1. Llegarán **cuando** estemos en la finca. **2.** ¿**Cuando** llegas? **3.** No me dijo **cuando** iban a llegar. **4. Cuando** lleguen, les serviremos cerveza. **5.** ¿Nos escondemos **cuando** los veamos llegar? **6. Cuando** me gradúe, iré al Caribe. **7.** ¿...**cuando** te gradúes? **8.** ¿**Cuando** te gradúas?

Ejercicio 9.40 Póngale acento a **quien** si lo necesita.

1. ¿Quien se llevó mi paraguas? 2. No sé quien se lo llevó. 3. El amigo con quien vino Marieta tenía paraguas. 4. ¿Te dijo quien era el chico con quien estaba? 5. No me dijo con quien había venido. 6. Dime con quien andas y te diré quien eres.

Accents (Review)

Ejercicio 9.41 Ponga un acento sobre cada vocal que lo necesite.

ARMANDO: ¿Esta Juan?

MIGUEL: Creo que fue al cine, y no se cuando va a regresar. ¿Para que lo quieres?

ARMANDO: Quiero pedirle prestado un libro para mi clase de español.

MIGUEL: ¿Sabes que libro es?

ARMANDO: Si. Es uno que tiene la portada negra.

MIGUEL: Yo se donde lo tiene, pero no estoy seguro si te lo podria prestar.

ARMANDO: A mi me dijo que no lo necesitaba este semestre.

MIGUEL: Si tu te lo llevas, y el lo necesita, yo voy a sentirme muy mal. ¿Por que no te tomas una taza de te, y esperas a que regrese Juan?

ARMANDO: Bueno. Mientras espero, prestame el libro para mirarlo, por favor.

MIGUEL: Voy a buscarlo. [...] ¿Es este, verdad?

ARMANDO: No, ese no. Es el otro, el de gramatica. Tiene casi la misma portada, pero un titulo diferente.

MIGUEL: A ver si lo encuentro; esperame. [...] Aqui lo tienes.

ARMANDO: Gracias.

Ejercicio 9.42 Ponga un acento sobre cada vocal que lo necesite; la sílaba con énfasis está en negrilla, a menos que sea monosílaba.

LUISA: Alo. ¿Con quien hablo?

EVA: Luisa, es Eva. ¿Estas ocupada?

LUISA: Estudiando desde esta mañana cuando te fuiste.

EVA: Mira, necesito un favor de ti. Anoche estaba trabajando en el esquema para la clase de ingles de esta tarde y se me quedo. ¿Recuerdas donde lo puse cuando termine?

LUISA: Ni idea. ¿Esta en tu escritorio?

EVA: No estoy segura de donde lo deje especificamente, pero se que esta en algun lugar por ahi.

LUISA: Dejame mirar. Ah, aqui esta.

EVA: ¡Que alivio! Llevamelo a la clase por favor.

LUISA: Que tal si nos encontramos en la cafeteria estudiantil para almorzar y te lo doy asi mas temprano.

EVA: Vale.

LUISA: ¿Como a las 11.30?

EVA: Claro, hasta entonces.

Ejercicio 9.43 Temas de ensayo y de práctica oral

a. Ensayo

Escriba un párrafo en el pasado sobre uno de los temas siguientes. Cada vez que escriba una palabra, piense en la pronunciación correcta de la palabra, y decida si necesita acento o no.

1. un momento inolvidable
2. una experiencia cómica
3. una lección cultural

b. Práctica oral

En parejas, estudien un párrafo escrito de los temas de ensayo de arriba. En español, analicen cada palabra juntos para determinar si la decisión de usar acento, o no, era correcta. ¿La palabra es aguda, llana, esdrújula o sobresdrújula? ¿Es monosílaba? ¿Necesita acento? ¿Por qué?

D LINKING BETWEEN WORDS: SYNALEPHA

Chapter 9.D, pages 354–356

Ejercicio 9.44 Lea en voz alta las siguientes transcripciones de frases, y luego escríbalas en español comprensible. Preste atención a la ortografía y a los acentos.

(continued)

Fíjese que los acentos escritos en la transcripción indican el lugar donde hay énfasis en la frase, y no necesariamente la sílaba donde hay acento escrito en las palabras. El dialecto usado aquí usa seseo.

1. [no-sé-ké-kié-res-de-sír]   2. [noái-ná-die]   3. [siém-pre-bié-nea-tiém-po]
4. [loí-so-sin-ke-rér]   5. [se-fué-sin-de-si-ra-diós]

Ejercicio 9.45 Lea en voz alta las siguientes transcripciones de frases, y luego escríbalas en español comprensible. Preste atención a la ortografía y a los acentos. Fíjese que los acentos escritos en la transcripción indican el lugar donde hay énfasis en la frase, y no necesariamente la sílaba donde hay acento escrito en las palabras. El dialecto usado aquí usa seseo.

1. [lo-man-dá-ro-na-la-kár-sel]   2. [a-bía-nué-be-le-fán-te-sen-fér-mos]
3. [noái-mál-ke-por-bié-no-bén-ga]   4. [ba-kam-biár-lo-po-rú-no-me-no-san-tí-guo]   5. [lo-ses-tu-dián-te-so-na-le-má-nes]

Ejercicio 9.46 Lea en voz alta las siguientes transcripciones de frases, y luego escríbalas en español comprensible. Preste atención a la ortografía y a los acentos. Fíjese que los acentos escritos en la transcripción indican el lugar donde hay énfasis en la frase, y no necesariamente la sílaba donde hay acento escrito en las palabras. El dialecto usado aquí usa seseo y yeísmo.

1. [bóya-la-fiés-taes-te-fín-de-se-má-na]   2. [tú-bo-ke-sa-lí-ra-la-no-che-sér]
3. [no-me-dí-jo-siu-bo-klá-se]   4. [ye-gó-suer-má-no-je-mé-lo]   5. [bióu-na-be-bo-lár-po-rel-sié-loa-sul]

E CAPITALIZATION

Chapter 9.E, pages 357–359

Ejercicio 9.47 Indique las palabras que requieren mayúscula en las siguientes oraciones.

1. el miércoles vamos a ver al señor del valle.   2. desde la revolución francesa hay separación de iglesia y estado.   3. los españoles celebran semana santa.   4. no sé cómo se dice eso en inglés.   5. me encantó leer *la casa de los espíritus* de isabel allende.

F NUMBERS

(Cardinal Numbers)
Chapter 9.F.1, pages 360–365

Ejercicio 9.48 Reescriba las frases, y transcriba las cifras en letras.

1. Murió el 23 de abril del 1616.   2. Hay más de 100 estudiantes en esa conferencia.   3. Cada 4 años se reúne toda la familia.   4. Siento que tengo 1000 problemas.   5. Ese país tiene más de 1 000 000 de habitantes.

Ejercicio 9.49 Conteste las siguientes preguntas usando cifras, y luego transcríbalas en letras.

MODELO: ¿En qué año viajaste a Tegucigalpa?
— En (el) 2003. (dos mil tres)

1. ¿Cuál es tu fecha de nacimiento?   2. ¿En qué año te graduaste del colegio?   3. ¿Cuántos libros has tenido que comprar este año?   4. ¿En qué año te vas a graduar de la universidad?

Ejercicio 9.50 Traduzca las oraciones siguientes, transcribiendo las cifras en letras.

MODELO: *In 2007, my brother studied in Argentina.*
En el (año) dos mil siete, mi hermano estudió en (la) Argentina.

1. *Since September 11th, 2001, the world has changed.* 2. *Almost 3,000 victims and the 19 hijackers* (secuestradores) *died.* 3. *The country was at war during my 1st 3 years in the Peace Corps* (el Cuerpo de Paz). 4. *That is a series that started on 08/10/2010.* 5. *My mother was born on July 21, 1971.*

Ejercicio 9.51 Traduzca el siguiente horario de trenes de Huelva a Sevilla al inglés, usando *A.M.* o *P.M.* para indicar si es de mañana o de tarde:

Salida	Llegada	Departure	Arrival
06.55	08.27		
14.25	15.57		
18.55	20.27		

(Ordinal Numbers)

Chapter 9.F.2, pages 366–368

Ejercicio 9.52 Complete los espacios en blanco traduciendo lo que está entre paréntesis en inglés. No use cifras en español, solo letras.

1. Este es el *(first)* _____ libro de lenguas que comprendo claramente.
2. Cuando estuvimos en Sevilla, vivíamos en el *(fifth floor)* _____ piso.
3. La mujer habló de la *(World War II)* _____. 4. Es difícil de creer que ya estamos en el siglo *(21st)* _____. 5. Hay muchas diferencias entre los reyes Juan Carlos I *(the 1st)* _____ y Alfonso XIII *(the 13th)* _____.

G PUNCTUATION

Chapter 9.G, pages 371–374

Ejercicio 9.53 Traduzca el texto siguiente, usando la puntuación correcta.

As we walked through the park we noticed reporters running toward a grey-haired man and yelling: "Please! Can we ask you some questions?" That weekend we saw a photo of the same grey-haired man in the paper. The article read: "It was Thursday morning when Mario Vargas Llosa heard the news that he had won the prize. At first, he couldn't believe it. 'It was a surprise,' said the Peruvian author, 'a perfect way to start the day.'"[3]

H DIALECTAL VARIATION, NORM, REGISTER

Chapter 9.H, pages 374–378

Ejercicio 9.54 Diario personal de variantes

1. Si es usted hablante nativo del español, prepare una lista de palabras o expresiones que usted usa y que ha observado que no se usan en clase, o que le han dicho que son informales, dialectales o agramaticales. Luego, entreviste a otros hablantes nativos del idioma sobre su uso de estas palabras o expresiones. Averigüe si tienen variantes, cuándo usan cuál, etc. Apunte sus observaciones en un diario personal.

---

[3] Gomez, Josie. 2010. Vargas Llosa Wins Nobel. *Manual Times*, 7 October.

2. Si no es usted hablante nativo del español, escuche el habla de hispanohablantes y haga una lista de palabras o expresiones que note que son diferentes de lo que se usa en su clase, o de lo que usted ha aprendido. Luego entreviste a dos o tres de los que usan estas palabras o expresiones, y averigüe si las consideran informales, dialectales o agramaticales, y en qué contexto las usan, y si usan variantes en otros contextos. Apunte sus observaciones en un diario personal.

VERB TABLES

A Lista de modelos de conjugación

B Modelos de conjugación (*Verb Tables*)

C Mini-índice de verbos

A. LISTA DE MODELOS DE CONJUGACIÓN

The table below lists the verb conjugation models of this section, with their corresponding numbers.

LISTA DE MODELOS DE CONJUGACIÓN				
1. actuar	16. conducir	31. haber	46. poner	61. teñir
2. adquirir	17. contar	32. hacer	47. prohibir	62. traer
3. andar	18. creer	33. ir	48. pudrir	63. valer
4. aprender	19. cruzar	34. jugar	49. querer	64. vencer
5. avergonzar	20. dar	35. llegar	50. regir	65. venir
6. averiguar	21. decir	36. lucir	51. reír	66. ver
7. buscar	22. dirigir	37. morir	52. reunir	67. vivir
8. caber	23. discernir	38. mover	53. rogar	68. volcar
9. caer	24. distinguir	39. negar	54. saber	69. volver
10. caminar	25. dormir	40. oír	55. salir	70. yacer
11. cerrar	26. enviar	41. oler	56. seguir	71. zambullir
12. cocer	27. errar	42. parecer	57. sentir	
13. coger	28. esparcir	43. pedir	58. ser	
14. comenzar	29. estar	44. perder	59. soler	
15. concluir	30. forzar	45. poder	60. tener	

Starting on the next page you will find the tables of conjugation models corresponding to the above list. Please note that in these tables, a bold letter or group of letters separated by an arrow indicates a spelling change.

After the tables, there is a mini-index of verbs with the numbers of the conjugation models they follow (the numbers are from the above table, and are also indicated in each conjugation table).

B. MODELOS DE CONJUGACIÓN

1. ACTUAR Verbo en -ar con cambio de u → ú
(to act) (Como **acentuar, continuar, evaluar, graduar, insinuar**)

Participio presente: actuando **Participio pasado:** actuado

Imperativo: actúa (no actúes), actúe Ud., actuemos, actuad (no actuéis), (no) actúen Uds.

INDICATIVO				CONDICIONAL	SUBJUNTIVO	
Presente	Imperfecto	Pretérito	Futuro	Presente	Presente	Imperfecto
actúo	actuaba	actué	actuaré	actuaría	actúe	actuara
actúas	actuabas	actuaste	actuarás	actuarías	actúes	actuaras
actúa	actuaba	actuó	actuará	actuaría	actúe	actuara
actuamos	actuábamos	actuamos	actuaremos	actuaríamos	actuemos	actuáramos
actuáis	actuabais	actuasteis	actuaréis	actuaríais	actuéis	actuarais
actúan	actuaban	actuaron	actuarán	actuarían	actúen	actuaran
Pres. Perfecto	**Pluscuamperf.**		**Futuro perfecto**	**Perfecto**	**Pres. perfecto**	**Pluscuamperf.**
he actuado	había actuado		habré actuado	habría actuado	haya actuado	hubiera actuado

2. ADQUIRIR Verbo en -ir con cambio de i → ie
(to acquire) (Como **coadquirir, inquirir**)

Participio presente: adquiriendo **Participio pasado:** adquirido

Imperativo: adquiere (no adquieras), adquiera Ud., adquiramos, adquirid (no adquiráis), (no) adquieran Uds.

INDICATIVO				CONDICIONAL	SUBJUNTIVO	
Presente	Imperfecto	Pretérito	Futuro	Presente	Presente	Imperfecto
adquiero	adquiría	adquirí	adquiriré	adquiriría	adquiera	adquiriera
adquieres	adquirías	adquiriste	adquirirás	adquirirías	adquieras	adquirieras
adquiere	adquiría	adquirió	adquirirá	adquiriría	adquiera	adquiriera
adquirimos	adquiríamos	adquirimos	adquiriremos	adquiriríamos	adquiramos	adquiriéramos
adquirís	adquiríais	adquiristeis	adquiriréis	adquiriríais	adquiráis	adquirierais
adquieren	adquirían	adquirieron	adquirirán	adquirirían	adquieran	adquirieran
Pres. Perfecto	**Pluscuamperf.**		**Futuro perfecto**	**Perfecto**	**Pres. perfecto**	**Pluscuamperf.**
he adquirido	había adquirido		habré adquirido	habría adquirido	haya adquirido	hubiera adquirido

3. ANDAR Verbo irregular
(to go, to walk)

Participio presente: andando **Participio pasado:** andado

Imperativo: anda (no andes), ande Ud., andemos, andad (no andéis), (no) anden Uds.

INDICATIVO				CONDICIONAL	SUBJUNTIVO	
Presente	Imperfecto	Pretérito	Futuro	Presente	Presente	Imperfecto
ando	andaba	anduve	andaré	andaría	ande	anduviera
andas	andabas	anduviste	andarás	andarías	andes	anduvieras
anda	andaba	anduvo	andará	andaría	ande	anduviera
andamos	andábamos	anduvimos	andaremos	andaríamos	andemos	anduviéramos
andáis	andabais	anduvisteis	andaréis	andaríais	andéis	anduvierais
andan	andaban	anduvieron	andarán	andarían	anden	anduvieran
Pres. Perfecto	**Pluscuamperf.**		**Futuro perfecto**	**Perfecto**	**Pres. perfecto**	**Pluscuamperf.**
he andado	había andado		habré andado	habría andado	haya andado	hubiera andado

4. APRENDER Verbo regular 2.ª conjugación
(to learn) (Como **depender, emprender, meter, prender, responder**)

Participio presente: aprendiendo **Participio pasado:** aprendido

Imperativo: aprende (no aprendas), aprenda Ud., aprendamos, aprended (no aprendáis), (no) aprendan Uds.

INDICATIVO				CONDICIONAL	SUBJUNTIVO	
Presente	Imperfecto	Pretérito	Futuro	Presente	Presente	Imperfecto
aprendo	aprendía	aprendí	aprenderé	aprendería	aprenda	aprendiera
aprendes	aprendías	aprendiste	aprenderás	aprenderías	aprendas	aprendieras
aprende	aprendía	aprendió	aprenderá	aprendería	aprenda	aprendiera
aprendemos	aprendíamos	aprendimos	aprenderemos	aprenderíamos	aprendamos	aprendiéramos
aprendéis	aprendíais	aprendisteis	aprenderéis	aprenderíais	aprendáis	aprendierais
aprenden	aprendían	aprendieron	aprenderán	aprenderían	aprendan	aprendieran
Pres. perfecto	Pluscuamperf.		Futuro perfecto	Perfecto	Pres. perfecto	Pluscuamperf.
he aprendido	había aprendido		habré aprendido	habría aprendido	haya aprendido	hubiera aprendido

5. AVERGONZAR Verbo en **-ar** con cambio de **u → ü** delante de **-e**; **z → c** delante de **-e**
(to shame) (Como **desvergonzarse**)

Participio presente: avergonzando **Participio pasado:** avergonzado

Imperativo: avergüenza (no avergüences), avergüence Ud., avergoncemos, avergonzad (no avergoncéis), (no) avergüencen Uds.

INDICATIVO				CONDICIONAL	SUBJUNTIVO	
Presente	Imperfecto	Pretérito	Futuro	Presente	Presente	Imperfecto
avergüenzo	avergonzaba	avergoncé	avergonzaré	avergonzaría	avergüence	avergonzara
avergüenzas	avergonzabas	avergonzaste	avergonzarás	avergonzarías	avergüences	avergonzaras
avergüenza	avergonzaba	avergonzó	avergonzará	avergonzaría	avergüence	avergonzara
avergonzamos	avergonzábamos	avergonzamos	avergonzaremos	avergonzaríamos	avergoncemos	avergonzáramos
avergonzáis	avergonzabais	avergonzasteis	avergonzaréis	avergonzaríais	avergoncéis	avergonzarais
avergüenzan	avergonzaban	avergonzaron	avergonzarán	avergonzarían	avergüencen	avergonzaran
Pres. perfecto	Pluscuamperf.		Futuro perfecto	Perfecto	Pres. Perfecto	Pluscuamperf.
he avergonzado	había avergonzado		habré avergonzado	habría avergonzado	haya avergonzado	hubiera avergonzado

6. AVERIGUAR Verbo en **-ar** con cambio de **u → ü** delante de **-e**
(to ascertain) (Como **aguar, amortiguar, apaciguar, atestiguar, santiguar**)

Participio presente: averiguando **Participio pasado:** averiguado

Imperativo: averigua (no averigües), averigüe Ud., averigüemos, averiguad (no averigüéis), (no) averigüen Uds.

INDICATIVO				CONDICIONAL	SUBJUNTIVO	
Presente	Imperfecto	Pretérito	Futuro	Presente	Presente	Imperfecto
averiguo	averiguaba	averigüé	averiguaré	averiguaría	averigüe	averiguara
averiguas	averiguabas	averiguaste	averiguarás	averiguarías	averigües	averiguaras
averigua	averiguaba	averiguó	averiguará	averiguaría	averigüe	averiguara
averiguamos	averiguábamos	averiguamos	averiguaremos	averiguaríamos	averigüemos	averiguáramos
averiguáis	averiguabais	averiguasteis	averiguaréis	averiguaríais	averigüéis	averiguarais
averiguan	averiguaban	averiguaron	averiguarán	averiguarían	averigüen	averiguaran
Pres. perfecto	Pluscuamperf.		Futuro perfecto	Perfecto	Pres. perfecto	Pluscuamperf.
he averiguado	había averiguado		habré averiguado	habría averiguado	haya averiguado	hubiera averiguado

7. BUSCAR — Verbo en -ar con cambio de c → qu delante de -e
(to look for) (Como **acercar, explicar, justificar, sacar, significar**)

Participio presente: buscando   **Participio pasado:** buscado

Imperativo: busca (no bus**ques**), bus**que** Ud., bus**que**mos, buscad (no bus**qué**is), (no) bus**quen** Uds.

INDICATIVO				CONDICIONAL	SUBJUNTIVO	
Presente	Imperfecto	Pretérito	Futuro	Presente	Presente	Imperfecto
busco	buscaba	bus**qué**	buscaré	buscaría	bus**que**	buscara
buscas	buscabas	buscaste	buscarás	buscarías	bus**ques**	buscaras
busca	buscaba	buscó	buscará	buscaría	bus**que**	buscara
buscamos	buscábamos	buscamos	buscaremos	buscaríamos	bus**quemos**	buscáramos
buscáis	buscabais	buscasteis	buscaréis	buscaríais	bus**quéis**	buscarais
buscan	buscaban	buscaron	buscarán	buscarían	bus**quen**	buscaran
Pres. perfecto	**Pluscuamperf.**		**Futuro perfecto**	**Perfecto**	**Pres. perfecto**	**Pluscuamperf.**
he buscado	había buscado		habré buscado	habría buscado	haya buscado	hubiera buscado

8. CABER — Verbo irregular
(to fit)

Participio presente: cabiendo   **Participio pasado:** cabido

Imperativo: cabe (no **quep**as), **quep**a Ud., **quep**amos, cabed (no **quep**áis), (no) **quep**an Uds.

INDICATIVO				CONDICIONAL	SUBJUNTIVO	
Presente	Imperfecto	Pretérito	Futuro	Presente	Presente	Imperfecto
quepo	cabía	**cup**e	cabré	cabría	**quep**a	**cup**iera
cabes	cabías	**cup**iste	cabrás	cabrías	**quep**as	**cup**ieras
cabe	cabía	**cup**o	cabrá	cabría	**quep**a	**cup**iera
cabemos	cabíamos	**cup**imos	cabremos	cabríamos	**quep**amos	**cup**iéramos
cabéis	cabíais	**cup**isteis	cabréis	cabríais	**quep**áis	**cup**ierais
caben	cabían	**cup**ieron	cabrán	cabrían	**quep**an	**cup**ieran
Pres. perfecto	**Pluscuamperf.**		**Futuro perfecto**	**Perfecto**	**Pres. perfecto**	**Pluscuamperf.**
he cabido	había cabido		habré cabido	habría cabido	haya cabido	hubiera cabido

9. CAER — Verbo irregular
(to fall) (Como **decaer, recaer**)

Participio presente: cayendo   **Participio pasado:** caído

Imperativo: cae (no **caig**as), **caig**a Ud., **caig**amos, caed (no **caig**áis), (no) **caig**an Uds.

INDICATIVO				CONDICIONAL	SUBJUNTIVO	
Presente	Imperfecto	Pretérito	Futuro	Presente	Presente	Imperfecto
ca**ig**o	caía	caí	caeré	caería	ca**ig**a	ca**y**era
caes	caías	caíste	caerás	caerías	ca**ig**as	ca**y**eras
cae	caía	ca**y**ó	caerá	caería	ca**ig**a	ca**y**era
caemos	caíamos	caímos	caeremos	caeríamos	ca**ig**amos	ca**y**éramos
caéis	caíais	caísteis	caeréis	caeríais	ca**ig**áis	ca**y**erais
caen	caían	ca**y**eron	caerán	caerían	ca**ig**an	ca**y**eran
Pres. perfecto	**Pluscuamperf.**		**Futuro perfecto**	**Perfecto**	**Pres. perfecto**	**Pluscuamperf.**
he caído	había caído		habré caído	habría caído	haya caído	hubiera caído

10. CAMINAR   Verbo regular 1.ª conjugación
(to walk)   (Como **acabar, comentar, enamorar, interesar, tardar**)

Participio presente: caminando   **Participio pasado:** caminado

Imperativo: camina (no camines), camine Ud., caminemos, caminad (no caminéis), (no) caminen Uds.

INDICATIVO				CONDICIONAL	SUBJUNTIVO	
Presente	Imperfecto	Pretérito	Futuro	Presente	Presente	Imperfecto
camino	caminaba	caminé	caminaré	caminaría	camine	caminara
caminas	caminabas	caminaste	caminarás	caminarías	camines	caminaras
camina	caminaba	caminó	caminará	caminaría	camine	caminara
caminamos	caminábamos	caminamos	caminaremos	caminaríamos	caminemos	camináramos
camináis	caminabais	caminasteis	caminaréis	caminaríais	caminéis	caminarais
caminan	caminaban	caminaron	caminarán	caminarían	caminen	caminaran
Pres. perfecto	**Pluscuamperf.**		**Futuro perfecto**	**Perfecto**	**Pres. perfecto**	**Pluscuamperf.**
he caminado	había caminado		habré caminado	habría caminado	haya caminado	hubiera caminado

11. CERRAR   Verbo en -ar con cambio de e → ie
(to close)   (Como **acertar, calentar, despertar, quebrar, sentar**)

Participio presente: cerrando   **Participio pasado:** cerrado

Imperativo: cierra (no cierres), cierre Ud., cerremos, cerrad (no cerréis), (no) cierren Uds.

INDICATIVO				CONDICIONAL	SUBJUNTIVO	
Presente	Imperfecto	Pretérito	Futuro	Presente	Presente	Imperfecto
cierro	cerraba	cerré	cerraré	cerraría	cierre	cerrara
cierras	cerrabas	cerraste	cerrarás	cerrarías	cierres	cerraras
cierra	cerraba	cerró	cerrará	cerraría	cierre	cerrara
cerramos	cerrábamos	cerramos	cerraremos	cerraríamos	cerremos	cerráramos
cerráis	cerrabais	cerrasteis	cerraréis	cerraríais	cerréis	cerrarais
cierran	cerraban	cerraron	cerrarán	cerrarían	cierren	cerraran
Pres. perfecto	**Pluscuamperf.**		**Futuro perfecto**	**Perfecto**	**Pres. perfecto**	**Pluscuamperf.**
he cerrado	había cerrado		habré cerrado	habría cerrado	haya cerrado	hubiera cerrado

12. COCER   Verbo en -er con cambio de o → ue; c → z delante de -a y -o
(to cook)   (Como **descocer, destorcer, retorcer, torcer**)

Participio presente: cociendo   **Participio pasado:** cocido

Imperativo: cuece (no cuezas), cueza Ud., cozamos, coced (no cozáis), (no) cuezan Uds.

INDICATIVO				CONDICIONAL	SUBJUNTIVO	
Presente	Imperfecto	Pretérito	Futuro	Presente	Presente	Imperfecto
cuezo	cocía	cocí	coceré	cocería	cueza	cociera
cueces	cocías	cociste	cocerás	cocerías	cuezas	cocieras
cuece	cocía	coció	cocerá	cocería	cueza	cociera
cocemos	cocíamos	cocimos	coceremos	coceríamos	cozamos	cociéramos
cocéis	cocíais	cocisteis	coceréis	coceríais	cozáis	cocierais
cuecen	cocían	cocieron	cocerán	cocerían	cuezan	cocieran
Pres. perfecto	**Pluscuamperf.**		**Futuro perfecto**	**Perfecto**	**Pres. perfecto**	**Pluscuamperf.**
he cocido	había cocido		habré cocido	habría cocido	haya cocido	hubiera cocido

13. COGER (to take hold of)
Verbo en -er con cambio de g → j delante de -a y -o
(Como acoger, encoger, escoger, proteger, recoger)

Participio presente: cogiendo	Participio pasado: cogido

Imperativo: coge (no cojas), coja Ud., cojamos, coged (no cojáis), (no) cojan Uds.

INDICATIVO				CONDICIONAL	SUBJUNTIVO	
Presente	Imperfecto	Pretérito	Futuro	Presente	Presente	Imperfecto
cojo	cogía	cogí	cogeré	cogería	coja	cogiera
coges	cogías	cogiste	cogerás	cogerías	cojas	cogieras
coge	cogía	cogió	cogerá	cogería	coja	cogiera
cogemos	cogíamos	cogimos	cogeremos	cogeríamos	cojamos	cogiéramos
cogéis	cogíais	cogisteis	cogeréis	cogeríais	cojáis	cogierais
cogen	cogían	cogieron	cogerán	cogerían	cojan	cogieran
Pres. perfecto	Pluscuamperf.		Futuro perfecto	Perfecto	Pres. perfecto	Pluscuamperf.
he cogido	había cogido		habré cogido	habría cogido	haya cogido	hubiera cogido

14. COMENZAR (to begin)
Verbo en -ar con cambio de e → ie; z → c delante de -e
(Como empezar, recomenzar, tropezar)

Participio presente: comenzando	Participio pasado: comenzado

Imperativo: comienza (no comiences), comience Ud., comencemos, comenzad (no comencéis), (no) comiencen Uds.

INDICATIVO				CONDICIONAL	SUBJUNTIVO	
Presente	Imperfecto	Pretérito	Futuro	Presente	Presente	Imperfecto
comienzo	comenzaba	comencé	comenzaré	comenzaría	comience	comenzara
comienzas	comenzabas	comenzaste	comenzarás	comenzarías	comiences	comenzaras
comienza	comenzaba	comenzó	comenzará	comenzaría	comience	comenzara
comenzamos	comenzábamos	comenzamos	comenzaremos	comenzaríamos	comencemos	comenzáramos
comenzáis	comenzabais	comenzasteis	comenzaréis	comenzaríais	comencéis	comenzarais
comienzan	comenzaban	comenzaron	comenzarán	comenzarían	comiencen	comenzaran
Pres. perfecto	Pluscuamperf.		Futuro perfecto	Perfecto	Pres. perfecto	Pluscuamperf.
he comenzado	había comenzado		habré comenzado	habría comenzado	haya comenzado	hubiera comenzado

15. CONCLUIR (to conclude)
Verbo en -ir con cambio de i → y
(Como atribuir, construir, distribuir, excluir)

Participio presente: concluyendo	Participio pasado: concluido

Imperativo: concluye (no concluyas), concluya Ud., concluyamos, concluid (no concluyáis), (no) concluyan Uds.

INDICATIVO				CONDICIONAL	SUBJUNTIVO	
Presente	Imperfecto	Pretérito	Futuro	Presente	Presente	Imperfecto
concluyo	concluía	concluí*	concluiré	concluiría	concluya	concluyera
concluyes	concluías	concluiste	concluirás	concluirías	concluyas	concluyeras
concluye	concluía	concluyó	concluirá	concluiría	concluya	concluyera
concluimos	concluíamos	concluimos	concluiremos	concluiríamos	concluyamos	concluyéramos
concluís*	concluíais	concluisteis	concluiréis	concluiríais	concluyáis	concluyerais
concluyen	concluían	concluyeron	concluirán	concluirían	concluyan	concluyeran
Pres. perfecto	Pluscuamperf.		Futuro perfecto	Perfecto	Pres. perfecto	Pluscuamperf.
he concluido	había concluido		habré concluido	habría concluido	haya concluido	hubiera concluido

*Fluir y huir se conjugan como concluir pero no llevan acento en las formas marcadas con asterisco (e.g. fluis, hui).

16. CONDUCIR (to conduct, to drive)
Verbo en -ir con cambio de c → zc delante de -a y -o; c → j
(Como **deducir, introducir, producir, reducir, traducir**)

Participio presente: conduciendo **Participio pasado:** conducido

Imperativo: conduce (no conduzcas), conduzca Ud., conduzcamos, conducid (no conduzcáis), (no) conduzcan Uds.

INDICATIVO				CONDICIONAL	SUBJUNTIVO	
Presente	Imperfecto	Pretérito	Futuro	Presente	Presente	Imperfecto
conduzco	conducía	conduje	conduciré	conduciría	conduzca	condujera
conduces	conducías	condujiste	conducirás	conducirías	conduzcas	condujeras
conduce	conducía	condujo	conducirá	conduciría	conduzca	condujera
conducimos	conducíamos	condujimos	conduciremos	conduciríamos	conduzcamos	condujéramos
conducís	conducíais	condujisteis	conduciréis	conduciríais	conduzcáis	condujerais
conducen	conducían	condujeron	conducirán	conducirían	conduzcan	condujeran
Pres. perfecto	**Pluscuamperf.**		**Futuro perfecto**	**Perfecto**	**Pres. perfecto**	**Pluscuamperf.**
he conducido	había conducido		habré conducido	habría conducido	haya conducido	hubiera conducido

17. CONTAR (to tell, to count)
Verbo en -ar con cambio de o → ue
(Como **acostar, costar, encontrar, mostrar, probar**)

Participio presente: contando **Participio pasado:** contado

Imperativo: **cuenta** (no **cuentes**), **cuente** Ud., contemos, contad (no contéis), (no) **cuenten** Uds.

INDICATIVO				CONDICIONAL	SUBJUNTIVO	
Presente	Imperfecto	Pretérito	Futuro	Presente	Presente	Imperfecto
cuento	contaba	conté	contaré	contaría	cuente	contara
cuentas	contabas	contaste	contarás	contarías	cuentes	contaras
cuenta	contaba	contó	contará	contaría	cuente	contara
contamos	contábamos	contamos	contaremos	contaríamos	contemos	contáramos
contáis	contabais	contasteis	contaréis	contaríais	contéis	contarais
cuentan	contaban	contaron	contarán	contarían	cuenten	contaran
Pres. perfecto	**Pluscuamperf.**		**Futuro perfecto**	**Perfecto**	**Pres. perfecto**	**Pluscuamperf.**
he contado	había contado		habré contado	habría contado	haya contado	hubiera contado

18. CREER (to believe)
Verbo irregular
(Como **descreer, leer, poseer, proveer*, releer**)

Participio presente: creyendo **Participio pasado:** creído

Imperativo: cree (no creas), crea Ud., creamos, creed (no creáis), (no) crean Uds.

INDICATIVO				CONDICIONAL	SUBJUNTIVO	
Presente	Imperfecto	Pretérito	Futuro	Presente	Presente	Imperfecto
creo	creía	creí	creeré	creería	crea	creyera
crees	creías	creíste	creerás	creerías	creas	creyeras
cree	creía	creyó	creerá	creería	crea	creyera
creemos	creíamos	creímos	creeremos	creeríamos	creamos	creyéramos
creéis	creíais	creísteis	creeréis	creeríais	creáis	creyerais
creen	creían	creyeron	creerán	creerían	crean	creyeran
Pres. perfecto	**Pluscuamperf.**		**Futuro perfecto**	**Perfecto**	**Pres. perfecto**	**Pluscuamperf.**
he creído	había creído		habré creído	habría creído	haya creído	hubiera creído

*__Proveer__ tiene dos formas de participio pasado: **proveído** y **provisto**.

19. CRUZAR Verbo en -ar con cambio de z → c delante de -e
(to cross) (Como **abrazar, bostezar, especializar, lanzar, reemplazar**)

Participio presente: cruzando					Participio pasado: cruzado	

Imperativo: cruza (no cruces), cruce Ud., crucemos, cruzad (no crucéis), (no) crucen Uds.

INDICATIVO				CONDICIONAL	SUBJUNTIVO	
Presente	Imperfecto	Pretérito	Futuro	Presente	Presente	Imperfecto
cruzo	cruzaba	crucé	cruzaré	cruzaría	cruce	cruzara
cruzas	cruzabas	cruzaste	cruzarás	cruzarías	cruces	cruzaras
cruza	cruzaba	cruzó	cruzará	cruzaría	cruce	cruzara
cruzamos	cruzábamos	cruzamos	cruzaremos	cruzaríamos	crucemos	cruzáramos
cruzáis	cruzabais	cruzasteis	cruzaréis	cruzaríais	crucéis	cruzarais
cruzan	cruzaban	cruzaron	cruzarán	cruzarían	crucen	cruzaran
Pres. perfecto	**Pluscuamperf.**		**Futuro perfecto**	**Perfecto**	**Pres. perfecto**	**Pluscuamperf.**
he cruzado	había cruzado		habré cruzado	habría cruzado	haya cruzado	hubiera cruzado

20. DAR Verbo irregular
(to give)

Participio presente: dando					Participio pasado: dado	

Imperativo: da (no des), dé Ud., demos, dad (no deis), (no) den Uds.

INDICATIVO				CONDICIONAL	SUBJUNTIVO	
Presente	Imperfecto	Pretérito	Futuro	Presente	Presente	Imperfecto
doy	daba	di	daré	daría	dé	diera
das	dabas	diste	darás	darías	des	dieras
da	daba	dio	dará	daría	dé	diera
damos	dábamos	dimos	daremos	daríamos	demos	diéramos
dais	dabais	disteis	daréis	daríais	deis	dierais
dan	daban	dieron	darán	darían	den	dieran
Pres. perfecto	**Pluscuamperf.**		**Futuro perfecto**	**Perfecto**	**Pres. perfecto**	**Pluscuamperf.**
he dado	había dado		habré dado	habría dado	haya dado	hubiera dado

21. DECIR Verbo irregular
(to say)

Participio presente: diciendo					Participio pasado: dicho	

Imperativo: di (no digas), diga Ud., digamos, decid (no digáis), (no) digan Uds.

INDICATIVO				CONDICIONAL	SUBJUNTIVO	
Presente	Imperfecto	Pretérito	Futuro	Presente	Presente	Imperfecto
digo	decía	dije	diré	diría	diga	dijera
dices	decías	dijiste	dirás	dirías	digas	dijeras
dice	decía	dijo	dirá	diría	diga	dijera
decimos	decíamos	dijimos	diremos	diríamos	digamos	dijéramos
decís	decíais	dijisteis	diréis	diríais	digáis	dijerais
dicen	decían	dijeron	dirán	dirían	digan	dijeran
Pres. perfecto	**Pluscuamperf.**		**Futuro perfecto**	**Perfecto**	**Pres. perfecto**	**Pluscuamperf.**
he dicho	había dicho		habré dicho	habría dicho	haya dicho	hubiera dicho

22. DIRIGIR — Verbo en -ir con cambio de **g → j** delante de -a y -o
(to direct) (Como **afligir, exigir, fingir, surgir, urgir**)

Participio presente: dirigiendo **Participio pasado:** dirigido

Imperativo: dirige (no dirijas), dirija Ud., dirijamos, dirigid (no dirijáis), (no) dirijan Uds.

INDICATIVO				CONDICIONAL	SUBJUNTIVO	
Presente	**Imperfecto**	**Pretérito**	**Futuro**	**Presente**	**Presente**	**Imperfecto**
dirijo	dirigía	dirigí	dirigiré	dirigiría	dirija	dirigiera
diriges	dirigías	dirigiste	dirigirás	dirigirías	dirijas	dirigieras
dirige	dirigía	dirigió	dirigirá	dirigiría	dirija	dirigiera
dirigimos	dirigíamos	dirigimos	dirigiremos	dirigiríamos	dirijamos	dirigiéramos
dirigís	dirigíais	dirigisteis	dirigiréis	dirigiríais	dirijáis	dirigierais
dirigen	dirigían	dirigieron	dirigirán	dirigirían	dirijan	dirigieran
Pres. perfecto	**Pluscuamperf.**		**Futuro perfecto**	**Perfecto**	**Pres. perfecto**	**Pluscuamperf.**
he dirigido	había dirigido		habré dirigido	habría dirigido	haya dirigido	hubiera dirigido

23. DISCERNIR — Verbo en -ir con cambio de **e → ie**
(to discern) (Como **cernir, concernir**)

Participio presente: discerniendo **Participio pasado:** discernido

Imperativo: discierne (no disciernas), discierna Ud., discernamos, discernid (no discernáis), (no) disciernan Uds.

INDICATIVO				CONDICIONAL	SUBJUNTIVO	
Presente	**Imperfecto**	**Pretérito**	**Futuro**	**Presente**	**Presente**	**Imperfecto**
discierno	discernía	discerní	discerniré	discerniría	discierna	discerniera
disciernes	discernías	discerniste	discernirás	discernirías	disciernas	discernieras
discierne	discernía	discernió	discernirá	discerniría	discierna	discerniera
discernimos	discerníamos	discernimos	discerniremos	discerniríamos	discernamos	discerniéramos
discernís	discerníais	discernisteis	discerniréis	discerniríais	discernáis	discernierais
disciernen	discernían	discernieron	discernirán	discernirían	disciernan	discernieran
Pres. perfecto	**Pluscuamperf.**		**Futuro perfecto**	**Perfecto**	**Pres. perfecto**	**Pluscuamperf.**
he discernido	había discernido		habré discernido	habría discernido	haya discernido	hubiera discernido

24. DISTINGUIR — Verbo en -ir con cambio de **gu → g** delante de -a y -o
(to distinguish) (Como **extinguir**)

Participio presente: distinguiendo **Participio pasado:** distinguido

Imperativo: distingue (no distingas), distinga Ud., distingamos, distinguid (no distingáis), (no) distingan Uds.

INDICATIVO				CONDICIONAL	SUBJUNTIVO	
Presente	**Imperfecto**	**Pretérito**	**Futuro**	**Presente**	**Presente**	**Imperfecto**
distingo	distinguía	distinguí	distinguiré	distinguiría	distinga	distinguiera
distingues	distinguías	distinguiste	distinguirás	distinguirías	distingas	distinguieras
distingue	distinguía	distinguió	distinguirá	distinguiría	distinga	distinguiera
distinguimos	distinguíamos	distinguimos	distinguiremos	distinguiríamos	distingamos	distinguiéramos
distinguís	distinguíais	distinguisteis	distinguiréis	distinguiríais	distingáis	distinguierais
distinguen	distinguían	distinguieron	distinguirán	distinguirían	distingan	distinguieran
Pres. perfecto	**Pluscuamperf.**		**Futuro perfecto**	**Perfecto**	**Pres. perfecto**	**Pluscuamperf.**
he distinguido	había distinguido		habré distinguido	habría distinguido	haya distinguido	hubiera distinguido

25. DORMIR Verbo en -ir con cambio de o → ue y o → u
(to sleep)

Participio presente: durmiendo **Participio pasado:** dormido

Imperativo: duerme (no duermas), duerma Ud., durmamos, dormid (no durmáis), (no) duerman Uds.

INDICATIVO				CONDICIONAL	SUBJUNTIVO	
Presente	Imperfecto	Pretérito	Futuro	Presente	Presente	Imperfecto
duermo	dormía	dormí	dormiré	dormiría	duerma	durmiera
duermes	dormías	dormiste	dormirás	dormirías	duermas	durmieras
duerme	dormía	durmió	dormirá	dormiría	duerma	durmiera
dormimos	dormíamos	dormimos	dormiremos	dormiríamos	durmamos	durmiéramos
dormís	dormíais	dormisteis	dormiréis	dormiríais	durmáis	durmierais
duermen	dormían	durmieron	dormirán	dormirían	duerman	durmieran
Pres. perfecto	**Pluscuamperf.**		**Futuro perfecto**	**Perfecto**	**Pres. perfecto**	**Pluscuamperf.**
he dormido	había dormido		habré dormido	habría dormido	haya dormido	hubiera dormido

26. ENVIAR Verbo en -ar con cambio de i → í
(to send) (Como **ampliar, confiar, enfriar, rociar, vaciar, variar**)

Participio presente: enviando **Participio pasado:** enviado

Imperativo: envía (no envíes), envíe Ud., enviemos, enviad (no enviéis*), (no) envíen Uds.

INDICATIVO				CONDICIONAL	SUBJUNTIVO	
Presente	Imperfecto	Pretérito	Futuro	Presente	Presente	Imperfecto
envío	enviaba	envié*	enviaré	enviaría	envíe	enviara
envías	enviabas	enviaste	enviarás	enviarías	envíes	enviaras
envía	enviaba	envió*	enviará	enviaría	envíe	enviara
enviamos	enviábamos	enviamos	enviaremos	enviaríamos	enviemos	enviáramos
enviáis*	enviabais	enviasteis	enviaréis	enviaríais	enviéis*	enviarais
envían	enviaban	enviaron	enviarán	enviarían	envíen	enviaran
Pres. perfecto	**Pluscuamperf.**		**Futuro perfecto**	**Perfecto**	**Pres. perfecto**	**Pluscuamperf.**
he enviado	había enviado		habré enviado	habría enviado	haya enviado	hubiera enviado

*****Criar, fiar, guiar, liar, piar,** y **triar** se conjugan como **enviar** pero no llevan acento en las formas marcadas con asterisco (e.g. **criais, fie, guio, lieis**).

27. ERRAR Verbo en -ar con cambio de e → ye*
(to wander, to err)

Participio presente: errando **Participio pasado:** errado

Imperativo: yerra (no yerres), yerre Ud., erremos, errad (no erréis), (no) yerren Uds.

INDICATIVO				CONDICIONAL	SUBJUNTIVO	
Presente	Imperfecto	Pretérito	Futuro	Presente	Presente	Imperfecto
yerro	erraba	erré	erraré	erraría	yerre	errara
yerras	errabas	erraste	errarás	errarías	yerres	erraras
yerra	erraba	erró	errará	erraría	yerre	errara
erramos	errábamos	erramos	erraremos	erraríamos	erremos	erráramos
erráis	errabais	errasteis	erraréis	erraríais	erréis	errarais
yerran	erraban	erraron	errarán	errarían	yerren	erraran
Pres. perfecto	**Pluscuamperf.**		**Futuro perfecto**	**Perfecto**	**Pres. perfecto**	**Pluscuamperf.**
he errado	había errado		habré errado	habría errado	haya errado	hubiera errado

*Existe también una conjugación regular de este verbo (e.g. **erro, erras, erra, erran; erre, erres, erre, erren**), de uso común en algunos países de América, y a veces en España para significar *to wander*. Las formas en ye- se consideran preferibles.

28. ESPARCIR — Verbo en -ir con cambio de c → z delante de -a y -o
(to scatter) (Como **fruncir, uncir, zurcir**)

Participio presente: esparciendo **Participio pasado:** esparcido

Imperativo: esparce (no esparzas), esparza Ud., esparzamos, esparcid (no esparzáis), (no) esparzan Uds.

INDICATIVO				CONDICIONAL	SUBJUNTIVO	
Presente	**Imperfecto**	**Pretérito**	**Futuro**	**Presente**	**Presente**	**Imperfecto**
esparzo	esparcía	esparcí	esparciré	esparciría	esparza	esparciera
esparces	esparcías	esparciste	esparcirás	esparcirías	esparzas	esparcieras
esparce	esparcía	esparció	esparcirá	esparciría	esparza	esparciera
esparcimos	esparcíamos	esparcimos	esparciremos	esparciríamos	esparzamos	esparciéramos
esparcís	esparcíais	esparcisteis	esparciréis	esparciríais	esparzáis	esparcierais
esparcen	esparcían	esparcieron	esparcirán	esparcirían	esparzan	esparcieran
Pres. perfecto	**Pluscuamperf.**		**Futuro perfecto**	**Perfecto**	**Pres. perfecto**	**Pluscuamperf.**
he esparcido	había esparcido		habré esparcido	habría esparcido	haya esparcido	hubiera esparcido

29. ESTAR — Verbo irregular
(to be)

Participio presente: estando **Participio pasado:** estado

Imperativo: está (no estés), esté Ud., estemos, estad (no estéis), (no) estén Uds.

INDICATIVO				CONDICIONAL	SUBJUNTIVO	
Presente	**Imperfecto**	**Pretérito**	**Futuro**	**Presente**	**Presente**	**Imperfecto**
estoy	estaba	estuve	estaré	estaría	esté	estuviera
estás	estabas	estuviste	estarás	estarías	estés	estuvieras
está	estaba	estuvo	estará	estaría	esté	estuviera
estamos	estábamos	estuvimos	estaremos	estaríamos	estemos	estuviéramos
estáis	estabais	estuvisteis	estaréis	estaríais	estéis	estuvierais
están	estaban	estuvieron	estarán	estarían	estén	estuvieran
Pres. perfecto	**Pluscuamperf.**		**Futuro perfecto**	**Perfecto**	**Pres. perfecto**	**Pluscuamperf.**
he estado	había estado		habré estado	habría estado	haya estado	hubiera estado

30. FORZAR — Verbo en -ar con cambio de o → ue; z → c delante de -e
(to force) (Como **almorzar, esforzar, reforzar**)

Participio presente: forzando **Participio pasado:** forzado

Imperativo: fuerza (no fuerces), fuerce Ud., forcemos, forzad (no forcéis), (no) fuercen Uds.

INDICATIVO				CONDICIONAL	SUBJUNTIVO	
Presente	**Imperfecto**	**Pretérito**	**Futuro**	**Presente**	**Presente**	**Imperfecto**
fuerzo	forzaba	forcé	forzaré	forzaría	fuerce	forzara
fuerzas	forzabas	forzaste	forzarás	forzarías	fuerces	forzaras
fuerza	forzaba	forzó	forzará	forzaría	fuerce	forzara
forzamos	forzábamos	forzamos	forzaremos	forzaríamos	forcemos	forzáramos
forzáis	forzabais	forzasteis	forzaréis	forzaríais	forcéis	forzarais
fuerzan	forzaban	forzaron	forzarán	forzarían	fuercen	forzaran
Pres. perfecto	**Pluscuamperf.**		**Futuro perfecto**	**Perfecto**	**Pres. perfecto**	**Pluscuamperf.**
he forzado	había forzado		habré forzado	habría forzado	haya forzado	hubiera forzado

31. HABER Verbo irregular
(to have)

Participio presente: habiendo	Participio pasado: habido

Imperativo: he (no hayas), haya Ud., hayamos, habed (no hayáis), (no) hayan Uds.

INDICATIVO				CONDICIONAL	SUBJUNTIVO	
Presente	Imperfecto	Pretérito	Futuro	Presente	Presente	Imperfecto
he	había	hube	habré	habría	haya	hubiera
has	habías	hubiste	habrás	habrías	hayas	hubieras
ha (hay*)	había*	hubo*	habrá*	habría*	haya*	hubiera*
hemos	habíamos	hubimos	habremos	habríamos	hayamos	hubiéramos
habéis	habíais	hubisteis	habréis	habríais	hayáis	hubierais
han	habían	hubieron	habrán	habrían	hayan	hubieran
Pres. perfecto	**Pluscuamperf.**		**Futuro perfecto**	**Perfecto**	**Pres. perfecto**	**Pluscuamperf.**
he habido	había habido		habré habido	habría habido	haya habido	hubiera habido

*Para la conjugación del uso impersonal, vea la 3.ª persona de cada tiempo excepto el presente del indicativo, que es **hay**.

32. HACER Verbo irregular
(to do) (Como **deshacer, rehacer, satisfacer**)

Participio presente: haciendo	Participio pasado: hecho

Imperativo: haz (no hagas), haga Ud., hagamos, haced (no hagáis), (no) hagan Uds.

INDICATIVO				CONDICIONAL	SUBJUNTIVO	
Presente	Imperfecto	Pretérito	Futuro	Presente	Presente	Imperfecto
hago	hacía	hice	haré	haría	haga	hiciera
haces	hacías	hiciste	harás	harías	hagas	hicieras
hace	hacía	hizo	hará	haría	haga	hiciera
hacemos	hacíamos	hicimos	haremos	haríamos	hagamos	hiciéramos
hacéis	hacíais	hicisteis	haréis	haríais	hagáis	hicierais
hacen	hacían	hicieron	harán	harían	hagan	hicieran
Pres. perfecto	**Pluscuamperf.**		**Futuro perfecto**	**Perfecto**	**Pres. perfecto**	**Pluscuamperf.**
he hecho	había hecho		habré hecho	habría hecho	haya hecho	hubiera hecho

33. IR Verbo irregular
(to go)

Participio presente: yendo	Participio pasado: ido

Imperativo: ve (no vayas), vaya Ud., vamos (no vayamos), id (no vayáis), (no) vayan Uds.

INDICATIVO				CONDICIONAL	SUBJUNTIVO	
Presente	Imperfecto	Pretérito	Futuro	Presente	Presente	Imperfecto
voy	iba	fui	iré	iría	vaya	fuera
vas	ibas	fuiste	irás	irías	vayas	fueras
va	iba	fue	irá	iría	vaya	fuera
vamos	íbamos	fuimos	iremos	iríamos	vayamos	fuéramos
vais	ibais	fuisteis	iréis	iríais	vayáis	fuerais
van	iban	fueron	irán	irían	vayan	fueran
Pres. perfecto	**Pluscuamperf.**		**Futuro perfecto**	**Perfecto**	**Pres. perfecto**	**Pluscuamperf.**
he ido	había ido		habré ido	habría ido	haya ido	hubiera ido

34. JUGAR Verbo en -ar con cambio de u → ue; g → gu delante de -e
(to play)

Participio presente: jugando				Participio pasado: jugado		
Imperativo: juega (no juegues), juegue Ud., juguemos, jugad (no juguéis), (no) jueguen Uds.						
INDICATIVO				**CONDICIONAL**	**SUBJUNTIVO**	
Presente	Imperfecto	Pretérito	Futuro	Presente	Presente	Imperfecto
juego	jugaba	jugué	jugaré	jugaría	juegue	jugara
juegas	jugabas	jugaste	jugarás	jugarías	juegues	jugaras
juega	jugaba	jugó	jugará	jugaría	juegue	jugara
jugamos	jugábamos	jugamos	jugaremos	jugaríamos	juguemos	jugáramos
jugáis	jugabais	jugasteis	jugaréis	jugaríais	juguéis	jugarais
juegan	jugaban	jugaron	jugarán	jugarían	jueguen	jugaran
Pres. perfecto	**Pluscuamperf.**		**Futuro perfecto**	**Perfecto**	**Pres. perfecto**	**Pluscuamperf.**
he jugado	había jugado		habré jugado	habría jugado	haya jugado	hubiera jugado

35. LLEGAR Verbo en -ar con cambio de g → gu delante de -e
(to arrive) (Como **abrigar, cargar, entregar, obligar, pagar**)

Participio presente: llegando				Participio pasado: llegado		
Imperativo: llega (no llegues), llegue Ud., lleguemos, llegad (no lleguéis), (no) lleguen Uds.						
INDICATIVO				**CONDICIONAL**	**SUBJUNTIVO**	
Presente	Imperfecto	Pretérito	Futuro	Presente	Presente	Imperfecto
llego	llegaba	llegué	llegaré	llegaría	llegue	llegara
llegas	llegabas	llegaste	llegarás	llegarías	llegues	llegaras
llega	llegaba	llegó	llegará	llegaría	llegue	llegara
llegamos	llegábamos	llegamos	llegaremos	llegaríamos	lleguemos	llegáramos
llegáis	llegabais	llegasteis	llegaréis	llegaríais	lleguéis	llegarais
llegan	llegaban	llegaron	llegarán	llegarían	lleguen	llegaran
Pres. perfecto	**Pluscuamperf.**		**Futuro perfecto**	**Perfecto**	**Pres. perfecto**	**Pluscuamperf.**
he llegado	había llegado		habré llegado	habría llegado	haya llegado	hubiera llegado

36. LUCIR Verbo en -ir con cambio de c → zc delante de -a y -o
(to shine) (Como **relucir, traslucir**)

Participio presente: luciendo				Participio pasado: lucido		
Imperativo: luce (no luzcas), luzca Ud., luzcamos, lucid (no luzcáis), (no) luzcan Uds.						
INDICATIVO				**CONDICIONAL**	**SUBJUNTIVO**	
Presente	Imperfecto	Pretérito	Futuro	Presente	Presente	Imperfecto
luzco	lucía	lucí	luciré	luciría	luzca	luciera
luces	lucías	luciste	lucirás	lucirías	luzcas	lucieras
luce	lucía	lució	lucirá	luciría	luzca	luciera
lucimos	lucíamos	lucimos	luciremos	luciríamos	luzcamos	luciéramos
lucís	lucíais	lucisteis	luciréis	luciríais	luzcáis	lucierais
lucen	lucían	lucieron	lucirán	lucirían	luzcan	lucieran
Pres. perfecto	**Pluscuamperf.**		**Futuro perfecto**	**Perfecto**	**Pres. perfecto**	**Pluscuamperf.**
he lucido	había lucido		habré lucido	habría lucido	haya lucido	hubiera lucido

37. MORIR Verbo en -ir con cambio de o → ue; participio pasado irregular
(to die)

Participio presente: muriendo **Participio pasado:** muerto

Imperativo: muere (no mueras), muera Ud., muramos, morid (no muráis), (no) mueran Uds.

INDICATIVO				CONDICIONAL	SUBJUNTIVO	
Presente	Imperfecto	Pretérito	Futuro	Presente	Presente	Imperfecto
muero	moría	morí	moriré	moriría	muera	muriera
mueres	morías	moriste	morirás	morirías	mueras	murieras
muere	moría	murió	morirá	moriría	muera	muriera
morimos	moríamos	morimos	moriremos	moriríamos	muramos	muriéramos
morís	moríais	moristeis	moriréis	moriríais	muráis	murierais
mueren	morían	murieron	morirán	morirían	mueran	murieran
Pres. perfecto	**Pluscuamperf.**		**Futuro perfecto**	**Perfecto**	**Pres. perfecto**	**Pluscuamperf.**
he muerto	había muerto		habré muerto	habría muerto	haya muerto	hubiera muerto

38. MOVER Verbo en -er con cambio de o → ue
(to move) (Como **doler, llover, morder, promover, remorder**)

Participio presente: moviendo **Participio pasado:** movido

Imperativo: mueve (no muevas), mueva Ud., movamos, moved (no mováis), (no) muevan Uds.

INDICATIVO				CONDICIONAL	SUBJUNTIVO	
Presente	Imperfecto	Pretérito	Futuro	Presente	Presente	Imperfecto
muevo	movía	moví	moveré	movería	mueva	moviera
mueves	movías	moviste	moverás	moverías	muevas	movieras
mueve	movía	movió	moverá	movería	mueva	moviera
movemos	movíamos	movimos	moveremos	moveríamos	movamos	moviéramos
movéis	movíais	movisteis	moveréis	moveríais	mováis	movierais
mueven	movían	movieron	moverán	moverían	muevan	movieran
Pres. perfecto	**Pluscuamperf.**		**Futuro perfecto**	**Perfecto**	**Pres. perfecto**	**Pluscuamperf.**
he movido	había movido		habré movido	habría movido	haya movido	hubiera movido

39. NEGAR Verbo en -ar con cambio de e → ie; g → gu delante de -e
(to deny) (Como **cegar, fregar, regar, renegar, restregar**)

Participio presente: negando **Participio pasado:** negado

Imperativo: niega (no niegues), niegue Ud., neguemos, negad (no neguéis), (no) nieguen Uds.

INDICATIVO				CONDICIONAL	SUBJUNTIVO	
Presente	Imperfecto	Pretérito	Futuro	Presente	Presente	Imperfecto
niego	negaba	negué	negaré	negaría	niegue	negara
niegas	negabas	negaste	negarás	negarías	niegues	negaras
niega	negaba	negó	negará	negaría	niegue	negara
negamos	negábamos	negamos	negaremos	negaríamos	neguemos	negáramos
negáis	negabais	negasteis	negaréis	negaríais	neguéis	negarais
niegan	negaban	negaron	negarán	negarían	nieguen	negaran
Pres. perfecto	**Pluscuamperf.**		**Futuro perfecto**	**Perfecto**	**Pres. perfecto**	**Pluscuamperf.**
he negado	había negado		habré negado	habría negado	haya negado	hubiera negado

40. OÍR   Verbo irregular
(to hear)

Participio presente: oyendo					Participio pasado: oído	
Imperativo: oye (no o**ig**as), o**ig**a Ud., o**ig**amos, oíd (no o**ig**áis), (no) o**ig**an Uds.						
INDICATIVO				**CONDICIONAL**	**SUBJUNTIVO**	
Presente	Imperfecto	Pretérito	Futuro	Presente	Presente	Imperfecto
o**ig**o	oía	oí	oiré	oiría	o**ig**a	oyera
oyes	oías	oíste	oirás	oirías	o**ig**as	oyeras
oye	oía	oyó	oirá	oiría	o**ig**a	oyera
oímos	oíamos	oímos	oiremos	oiríamos	o**ig**amos	oyéramos
oís	oíais	oísteis	oiréis	oiríais	o**ig**áis	oyerais
oyen	oían	oyeron	oirán	oirían	o**ig**an	oyeran
Pres. perfecto	**Pluscuamperf.**		**Futuro perfecto**	**Perfecto**	**Pres. perfecto**	**Pluscuamperf.**
he oído	había oído		habré oído	habría oído	haya oído	hubiera oído

41. OLER   Verbo en -er con cambio de o → hue
(to smell)

Participio presente: oliendo					Participio pasado: olido	
Imperativo: **hue**le (no **hue**las), **hue**la Ud., olamos, oled (no oláis), (no) **hue**lan Uds.						
INDICATIVO				**CONDICIONAL**	**SUBJUNTIVO**	
Presente	Imperfecto	Pretérito	Futuro	Presente	Presente	Imperfecto
huelo	olía	olí	oleré	olería	**hue**la	oliera
hueles	olías	oliste	olerás	olerías	**hue**las	olieras
huele	olía	olió	olerá	olería	**hue**la	oliera
olemos	olíamos	olimos	oleremos	oleríamos	olamos	oliéramos
oléis	olíais	olisteis	oleréis	oleríais	oláis	olierais
huelen	olían	olieron	olerán	olerían	**hue**lan	olieran
Pres. perfecto	**Pluscuamperf.**		**Futuro perfecto**	**Perfecto**	**Pres. perfecto**	**Pluscuamperf.**
he olido	había olido		habré olido	habría olido	haya olido	hubiera olido

42. PARECER   Verbo en -er con cambio de c → zc delante de -a y -o
(to seem)   (Como **agradecer, conocer, crecer, merecer, nacer**)

Participio presente: pareciendo					Participio pasado: parecido	
Imperativo: parece (no pare**zc**as), pare**zc**a Ud., pare**zc**amos, pareced (no pare**zc**áis), (no) pare**zc**an Uds.						
INDICATIVO				**CONDICIONAL**	**SUBJUNTIVO**	
Presente	Imperfecto	Pretérito	Futuro	Presente	Presente	Imperfecto
pare**zc**o	parecía	parecí	pareceré	parecería	pare**zc**a	pareciera
pareces	parecías	pareciste	parecerás	parecerías	pare**zc**as	parecieras
parece	parecía	pareció	parecerá	parecería	pare**zc**a	pareciera
parecemos	parecíamos	parecimos	pareceremos	pareceríamos	pare**zc**amos	pareciéramos
parecéis	parecíais	parecisteis	pareceréis	pareceríais	pare**zc**áis	parecierais
parecen	parecían	parecieron	parecerán	parecerían	pare**zc**an	parecieran
Pres. perfecto	**Pluscuamperf.**		**Futuro perfecto**	**Perfecto**	**Pres. perfecto**	**Pluscuamperf.**
he parecido	había parecido		habré parecido	habría parecido	haya parecido	hubiera parecido

43. PEDIR — Verbo en -ir con cambio de e → i
(to ask for) (Como **competir, despedir, medir, repetir, servir**)

| Participio presente: pidiendo | | | | | Participio pasado: pedido | | |

Imperativo: pide (no pidas), pida Ud., pidamos, pedid (no pidáis), (no) pidan Uds.

INDICATIVO				CONDICIONAL	SUBJUNTIVO	
Presente	Imperfecto	Pretérito	Futuro	Presente	Presente	Imperfecto
pido	pedía	pedí	pediré	pediría	pida	pidiera
pides	pedías	pediste	pedirás	pedirías	pidas	pidieras
pide	pedía	pidió	pedirá	pediría	pida	pidiera
pedimos	pedíamos	pedimos	pediremos	pediríamos	pidamos	pidiéramos
pedís	pedíais	pedisteis	pediréis	pediríais	pidáis	pidierais
piden	pedían	pidieron	pedirán	pedirían	pidan	pidieran
Pres. perfecto	**Pluscuamperf.**		**Futuro perfecto**	**Perfecto**	**Pres. perfecto**	**Pluscuamperf.**
he pedido	había pedido		habré pedido	habría pedido	haya pedido	hubiera pedido

44. PERDER — Verbo en -er con cambio de e → ie
(to lose) (Como **atender, defender, encender, entender, tender**)

| Participio presente: perdiendo | | | | | Participio pasado: perdido | | |

Imperativo: pierde (no pierdas), pierda Ud., perdamos, perded (no perdáis), (no) pierdan Uds.

INDICATIVO				CONDICIONAL	SUBJUNTIVO	
Presente	Imperfecto	Pretérito	Futuro	Presente	Presente	Imperfecto
pierdo	perdía	perdí	perderé	perdería	pierda	perdiera
pierdes	perdías	perdiste	perderás	perderías	pierdas	perdieras
pierde	perdía	perdió	perderá	perdería	pierda	perdiera
perdemos	perdíamos	perdimos	perderemos	perderíamos	perdamos	perdiéramos
perdéis	perdíais	perdisteis	perderéis	perderíais	perdáis	perdierais
pierden	perdían	perdieron	perderán	perderían	pierdan	perdieran
Pres. perfecto	**Pluscuamperf.**		**Futuro perfecto**	**Perfecto**	**Pres. perfecto**	**Pluscuamperf.**
he perdido	había perdido		habré perdido	habría perdido	haya perdido	hubiera perdido

45. PODER — Verbo irregular
(to be able)

| Participio presente: pudiendo | | | | | Participio pasado: podido | | |

Imperativo: puede (no puedas), pueda Ud., podamos, poded (no podáis), (no) puedan Uds.

INDICATIVO				CONDICIONAL	SUBJUNTIVO	
Presente	Imperfecto	Pretérito	Futuro	Presente	Presente	Imperfecto
puedo	podía	pude	podré	podría	pueda	pudiera
puedes	podías	pudiste	podrás	podrías	puedas	pudieras
puede	podía	pudo	podrá	podría	pueda	pudiera
podemos	podíamos	pudimos	podremos	podríamos	podamos	pudiéramos
podéis	podíais	pudisteis	podréis	podríais	podáis	pudierais
pueden	podían	pudieron	podrán	podrían	puedan	pudieran
Pres. perfecto	**Pluscuamperf.**		**Futuro perfecto**	**Perfecto**	**Pres. perfecto**	**Pluscuamperf.**
he podido	había podido		habré podido	habría podido	haya podido	hubiera podido

46. PONER Verbo irregular
(to put) (Como **componer, disponer, oponer, proponer, suponer**)

Participio presente: poniendo **Participio pasado:** puesto

Imperativo: pon (no pongas), ponga Ud., pongamos, poned (no pongáis), (no) pongan Uds.

INDICATIVO				CONDICIONAL	SUBJUNTIVO	
Presente	Imperfecto	Pretérito	Futuro	Presente	Presente	Imperfecto
pongo	ponía	puse	pondré	pondría	ponga	pusiera
pones	ponías	pusiste	pondrás	pondrías	pongas	pusieras
pone	ponía	puso	pondrá	pondría	ponga	pusiera
ponemos	poníamos	pusimos	pondremos	pondríamos	pongamos	pusiéramos
ponéis	poníais	pusisteis	pondréis	pondríais	pongáis	pusierais
ponen	ponían	pusieron	pondrán	pondrían	pongan	pusieran
Pres. perfecto	Pluscuamperf.		Futuro perfecto	Perfecto	Pres. perfecto	Pluscuamperf.
he puesto	había puesto		habré puesto	habría puesto	haya puesto	hubiera puesto

47. PROHIBIR Verbo en -ir con cambio de i → í
(to prohibit) (Como **cohibir**)

Participio presente: prohibiendo **Participio pasado:** prohibido

Imperativo: prohíbe (no prohíbas), prohíba Ud., prohibamos, prohibid (no prohibáis), (no) prohíban Uds.

INDICATIVO				CONDICIONAL	SUBJUNTIVO	
Presente	Imperfecto	Pretérito	Futuro	Presente	Presente	Imperfecto
prohíbo	prohibía	prohibí	prohibiré	prohibiría	prohíba	prohibiera
prohíbes	prohibías	prohibiste	prohibirás	prohibirías	prohíbas	prohibieras
prohíbe	prohibía	prohibió	prohibirá	prohibiría	prohíba	prohibiera
prohibimos	prohibíamos	prohibimos	prohibiremos	prohibiríamos	prohibamos	prohibiéramos
prohibís	prohibíais	prohibisteis	prohibiréis	prohibiríais	prohibáis	prohibierais
prohíben	prohibían	prohibieron	prohibirán	prohibirían	prohíban	prohibieran
Pres. perfecto	Pluscuamperf.		Futuro perfecto	Perfecto	Pres. perfecto	Pluscuamperf.
he prohibido	había prohibido		habré prohibido	habría prohibido	haya prohibido	hubiera prohibido

48. PUDRIR* Verbo irregular
o **PODRIR** *(to rot)*

Participio presente: pudriendo **Participio pasado:** podrido

Imperativo: pudre (no pudras), pudra Ud., pudramos, pudrid (no pudráis), (no) pudran Uds.

INDICATIVO				CONDICIONAL	SUBJUNTIVO	
Presente	Imperfecto	Pretérito	Futuro	Presente	Presente	Imperfecto
pudro	pudría	pudrí; podrí*	pudriré; podriré*	pudriría	pudra	pudriera
pudres	pudrías	pudriste	pudrirás	pudrirías	pudras	pudrieras
pudre	pudría	pudrió	pudrirá	pudriría	pudra	pudriera
pudrimos	pudríamos	pudrimos	pudriremos	pudriríamos	pudramos	pudriéramos
pudrís	pudríais	pudristeis	pudriréis	pudriríais	pudráis	pudrierais
pudren	pudrían	pudrieron	pudrirán	pudrirían	pudran	pudrieran
Pres. perfecto	Pluscuamperf.		Futuro perfecto	Perfecto	Pres. perfecto	Pluscuamperf.
he podrido	había podrido		habré podrido	habría podrido	haya podrido	hubiera podrido

*Donde hay dos opciones, las formas con **-u-** predominan en la norma culta.

49. QUERER Verbo irregular
(to want) (Como **bienquerer**)

Participio presente: queriendo **Participio pasado:** querido

Imperativo: quiere (no quieras), quiera Ud., queramos, quered (no queráis), (no) quieran Uds.

INDICATIVO				CONDICIONAL	SUBJUNTIVO	
Presente	Imperfecto	Pretérito	Futuro	Presente	Presente	Imperfecto
quiero	quería	quise	querré	querría	quiera	quisiera
quieres	querías	quisiste	querrás	querrías	quieras	quisieras
quiere	quería	quiso	querrá	querría	quiera	quisiera
queremos	queríamos	quisimos	querremos	querríamos	queramos	quisiéramos
queréis	queríais	quisisteis	querréis	querríais	queráis	quisierais
quieren	querían	quisieron	querrán	querrían	quieran	quisieran
Pres. perfecto	**Pluscuamperf.**		**Futuro perfecto**	**Perfecto**	**Pres. perfecto**	**Pluscuamperf.**
he querido	había querido		habré querido	habría querido	haya querido	hubiera querido

50. REGIR Verbo en -ir con cambio de e → i; g → j delante de -a y -o
(to rule) (Como **colegir, corregir, elegir, reelegir**)

Participio presente: rigiendo **Participio pasado:** regido

Imperativo: rige (no rijas), rija Ud., rijamos, regid (no rijáis), (no) rijan Uds.

INDICATIVO				CONDICIONAL	SUBJUNTIVO	
Presente	Imperfecto	Pretérito	Futuro	Presente	Presente	Imperfecto
rijo	regía	regí	regiré	regiría	rija	rigiera
riges	regías	registe	regirás	regirías	rijas	rigieras
rige	regía	rigió	regirá	regiría	rija	rigiera
regimos	regíamos	regimos	regiremos	regiríamos	rijamos	rigiéramos
regís	regíais	registeis	regiréis	regiríais	rijáis	rigierais
rigen	regían	rigieron	regirán	regirían	rijan	rigieran
Pres. perfecto	**Pluscuamperf.**		**Futuro perfecto**	**Perfecto**	**Pres. perfecto**	**Pluscuamperf.**
he regido	había regido		habré regido	habría regido	haya regido	hubiera regido

51. REÍR Verbo irregular
(to laugh) (Como **freír**)

Participio presente: riendo **Participio pasado:** reído

Imperativo: ríe (no rías), ría Ud., riamos, reíd (no riais*), (no) rían Uds.

INDICATIVO				CONDICIONAL	SUBJUNTIVO	
Presente	Imperfecto	Pretérito	Futuro	Presente	Presente	Imperfecto
río	reía	reí	reiré	reiría	ría	riera
ríes	reías	reíste	reirás	reirías	rías	rieras
ríe	reía	rio*	reirá	reiría	ría	riera
reímos	reíamos	reímos	reiremos	reiríamos	riamos	riéramos
reís	reíais	reísteis	reiréis	reiríais	riais*	rierais
ríen	reían	rieron	reirán	reirían	rían	rieran
Pres. perfecto	**Pluscuamperf.**		**Futuro perfecto**	**Perfecto**	**Pres. perfecto**	**Pluscuamperf.**
he reído	había reído		habré reído	habría reído	haya reído	hubiera reído

*Refreír, sofreír y sonreír se conjugan como reír pero llevan acento en las formas marcadas con asterisco (e.g. sofrió, sonriáis).

52. REUNIR Verbo en -ir con cambio de u → ú
(to assemble)

Participio presente: reuniendo				Participio pasado: reunido		
Imperativo: reúne (no reúnas), reúna Ud., reunamos, reunid (no reunáis), (no) reúnan Uds.						
INDICATIVO				**CONDICIONAL**	**SUBJUNTIVO**	
Presente	Imperfecto	Pretérito	Futuro	Presente	Presente	Imperfecto
reúno	reunía	reuní	reuniré	reuniría	reúna	reuniera
reúnes	reunías	reuniste	reunirás	reunirías	reúnas	reunieras
reúne	reunía	reunió	reunirá	reuniría	reúna	reuniera
reunimos	reuníamos	reunimos	reuniremos	reuniríamos	reunamos	reuniéramos
reunís	reuníais	reunisteis	reuniréis	reuniríais	reunáis	reunierais
reúnen	reunían	reunieron	reunirán	reunirían	reúnan	reunieran
Pres. perfecto	**Pluscuamperf.**		**Futuro perfecto**	**Perfecto**	**Pres. perfecto**	**Pluscuamperf.**
he reunido	había reunido		habré reunido	habría reunido	haya reunido	hubiera reunido

53. ROGAR Verbo en -ar con cambio de o → ue; g → gu delante de -e
(to beg) (Como **colgar, descolgar**)

Participio presente: rogando				Participio pasado: rogado		
Imperativo: ruega (no ruegues), ruegue Ud., roguemos, rogad (no roguéis), (no) rueguen Uds.						
INDICATIVO				**CONDICIONAL**	**SUBJUNTIVO**	
Presente	Imperfecto	Pretérito	Futuro	Presente	Presente	Imperfecto
ruego	rogaba	rogué	rogaré	rogaría	ruegue	rogara
ruegas	rogabas	rogaste	rogarás	rogarías	ruegues	rogaras
ruega	rogaba	rogó	rogará	rogaría	ruegue	rogara
rogamos	rogábamos	rogamos	rogaremos	rogaríamos	roguemos	rogáramos
rogáis	rogabais	rogasteis	rogaréis	rogaríais	roguéis	rogarais
ruegan	rogaban	rogaron	rogarán	rogarían	rueguen	rogaran
Pres. perfecto	**Pluscuamperf.**		**Futuro perfecto**	**Perfecto**	**Pres. perfecto**	**Pluscuamperf.**
he rogado	había rogado		habré rogado	habría rogado	haya rogado	hubiera rogado

54. SABER Verbo irregular
(to know)

Participio presente: sabiendo				Participio pasado: sabido		
Imperativo: sabe (no sepas), sepa Ud., sepamos, sabed (no sepáis), (no) sepan Uds.						
INDICATIVO				**CONDICIONAL**	**SUBJUNTIVO**	
Presente	Imperfecto	Pretérito	Futuro	Presente	Presente	Imperfecto
sé	sabía	supe	sabré	sabría	sepa	supiera
sabes	sabías	supiste	sabrás	sabrías	sepas	supieras
sabe	sabía	supo	sabrá	sabría	sepa	supiera
sabemos	sabíamos	supimos	sabremos	sabríamos	sepamos	supiéramos
sabéis	sabíais	supisteis	sabréis	sabríais	sepáis	supierais
saben	sabían	supieron	sabrán	sabrían	sepan	supieran
Pres. perfecto	**Pluscuamperf.**		**Futuro perfecto**	**Perfecto**	**Pres. perfecto**	**Pluscuamperf.**
he sabido	había sabido		habré sabido	habría sabido	haya sabido	hubiera sabido

55. SALIR — Verbo irregular
(to go out) (Como **sobresalir**)

Participio presente: saliendo					Participio pasado: salido	

Imperativo: sal (no salgas), salga Ud., salgamos, salid (no salgáis), (no) salgan Uds.

INDICATIVO				CONDICIONAL	SUBJUNTIVO	
Presente	Imperfecto	Pretérito	Futuro	Presente	Presente	Imperfecto
salgo	salía	salí	saldré	saldría	salga	saliera
sales	salías	saliste	saldrás	saldrías	salgas	salieras
sale	salía	salió	saldrá	saldría	salga	saliera
salimos	salíamos	salimos	saldremos	saldríamos	salgamos	saliéramos
salís	salíais	salisteis	saldréis	saldríais	salgáis	salierais
salen	salían	salieron	saldrán	saldrían	salgan	salieran
Pres. perfecto	Pluscuamperf.		Futuro perfecto	Perfecto	Pres. perfecto	Pluscuamperf.
he salido	había salido		habré salido	habría salido	haya salido	hubiera salido

56. SEGUIR — Verbo en -ir con cambio de gu → g delante de -a y -o; e → i
(to follow, to continue) (Como **conseguir, perseguir, proseguir**)

Participio presente: siguiendo					Participio pasado: seguido	

Imperativo: sigue (no sigas), siga Ud., sigamos, seguid (no sigáis), (no) sigan Uds.

INDICATIVO				CONDICIONAL	SUBJUNTIVO	
Presente	Imperfecto	Pretérito	Futuro	Presente	Presente	Imperfecto
sigo	seguía	seguí	seguiré	seguiría	siga	siguiera
sigues	seguías	seguiste	seguirás	seguirías	sigas	siguieras
sigue	seguía	siguió	seguirá	seguiría	siga	siguiera
seguimos	seguíamos	seguimos	seguiremos	seguiríamos	sigamos	siguiéramos
seguís	seguíais	seguisteis	seguiréis	seguiríais	sigáis	siguierais
siguen	seguían	siguieron	seguirán	seguirían	sigan	siguieran
Pres. perfecto	Pluscuamperf.		Futuro perfecto	Perfecto	Pres. perfecto	Pluscuamperf.
he seguido	había seguido		habré seguido	habría seguido	haya seguido	hubiera seguido

57. SENTIR — Verbo en -ir con cambio de e → ie; e → i
(to feel) (Como **arrepentirse, divertir, mentir, preferir, sugerir**)

Participio presente: sintiendo					Participio pasado: sentido	

Imperativo: siente (no sientas), sienta Ud., sintamos, sentid (no sintáis), (no) sientan Uds.

INDICATIVO				CONDICIONAL	SUBJUNTIVO	
Presente	Imperfecto	Pretérito	Futuro	Presente	Presente	Imperfecto
siento	sentía	sentí	sentiré	sentiría	sienta	sintiera
sientes	sentías	sentiste	sentirás	sentirías	sientas	sintieras
siente	sentía	sintió	sentirá	sentiría	sienta	sintiera
sentimos	sentíamos	sentimos	sentiremos	sentiríamos	sintamos	sintiéramos
sentís	sentíais	sentisteis	sentiréis	sentiríais	sintáis	sintierais
sienten	sentían	sintieron	sentirán	sentirían	sientan	sintieran
Pres. perfecto	Pluscuamperf.		Futuro perfecto	Perfecto	Pres. perfecto	Pluscuamperf.
he sentido	había sentido		habré sentido	habría sentido	haya sentido	hubiera sentido

58. SER   Verbo irregular
(to be)

Participio presente: siendo					Participio pasado: sido	
Imperativo: sé (no seas), sea Ud., seamos, sed (no seáis), (no) sean Uds.						

INDICATIVO				CONDICIONAL	SUBJUNTIVO	
Presente	Imperfecto	Pretérito	Futuro	Presente	Presente	Imperfecto
soy	era	fui	seré	sería	sea	fuera
eres	eras	fuiste	serás	serías	seas	fueras
es	era	fue	será	sería	sea	fuera
somos	éramos	fuimos	seremos	seríamos	seamos	fuéramos
sois	erais	fuisteis	seréis	seríais	seáis	fuerais
son	eran	fueron	serán	serían	sean	fueran
Pres. perfecto	Pluscuamperf.		Futuro perfecto	Perfecto	Pres. perfecto	Pluscuamperf.
he sido	había sido		habré sido	habría sido	haya sido	hubiera sido

59. SOLER   Verbo irregular defectivo*
(to accustom, to do habitually)

Participio presente: soliendo					Participio pasado: solido	
Imperativo:						

INDICATIVO				CONDICIONAL	SUBJUNTIVO	
Presente	Imperfecto	Pretérito	Futuro	Presente	Presente	Imperfecto
suelo	solía				suela	soliera
sueles	solías				suelas	solieras
suele	solía				suela	soliera
solemos	solíamos				solamos	soliéramos
soléis	solíais				soláis	solierais
suelen	solían				suelan	solieran
Pres. perfecto	Pluscuamperf.		Futuro perfecto	Perfecto	Pres. perfecto	Pluscuamperf.
he solido	había solido				haya solido	hubiera solido

*Un verbo defectivo es uno que no se usa en todos los modos, tiempos o personas.

60. TENER   Verbo irregular
(to have)   (Como atenerse, contener, detener, mantener, obtener, retener, sostener)

Participio presente: teniendo					Participio pasado: tenido	
Imperativo: ten (no tengas), tenga Ud., tengamos, tened (no tengáis), (no) tengan Uds.						

INDICATIVO				CONDICIONAL	SUBJUNTIVO	
Presente	Imperfecto	Pretérito	Futuro	Presente	Presente	Imperfecto
tengo	tenía	tuve	tendré	tendría	tenga	tuviera
tienes	tenías	tuviste	tendrás	tendrías	tengas	tuvieras
tiene	tenía	tuvo	tendrá	tendría	tenga	tuviera
tenemos	teníamos	tuvimos	tendremos	tendríamos	tengamos	tuviéramos
tenéis	teníais	tuvisteis	tendréis	tendríais	tengáis	tuvierais
tienen	tenían	tuvieron	tendrán	tendrían	tengan	tuvieran
Pres. perfecto	Pluscuamperf.		Futuro perfecto	Perfecto	Pres. perfecto	Pluscuamperf.
he tenido	había tenido		habré tenido	habría tenido	haya tenido	hubiera tenido

61. TEÑIR Verbo en -ir con cambio de e → i; pierde la -i- átona de la terminación
(to dye) (Como **ceñir, desteñir, estreñir, reñir**)

Participio presente: tiñendo				Participio pasado: teñido		
Imperativo: tiñe (no tiñas), tiña Ud., tiñamos, teñid (no tiñáis), (no) tiñan Uds.						
INDICATIVO				**CONDICIONAL**	**SUBJUNTIVO**	
Presente	Imperfecto	Pretérito	Futuro	Presente	Presente	Imperfecto
tiño	teñía	teñí	teñiré	teñiría	tiña	tiñera
tiñes	teñías	teñiste	teñirás	teñirías	tiñas	tiñeras
tiñe	teñía	tiñó	teñirá	teñiría	tiña	tiñera
teñimos	teñíamos	teñimos	teñiremos	teñiríamos	tiñamos	tiñéramos
teñís	teñíais	teñisteis	teñiréis	teñiríais	tiñáis	tiñerais
tiñen	teñían	tiñeron	teñirán	teñirían	tiñan	tiñeran
Pres. perfecto	**Pluscuamperf.**		**Futuro perfecto**	**Perfecto**	**Pres. perfecto**	**Pluscuamperf.**
he teñido	había teñido		habré teñido	habría teñido	haya teñido	hubiera teñido

62. TRAER Verbo irregular
(to bring) (Como **atraer, contraer, detraer, distraer, extraer**)

Participio presente: trayendo				Participio pasado: traído		
Imperativo: trae (no traigas), traiga Ud., traigamos, traed (no traigáis), (no) traigan Uds.						
INDICATIVO				**CONDICIONAL**	**SUBJUNTIVO**	
Presente	Imperfecto	Pretérito	Futuro	Presente	Presente	Imperfecto
traigo	traía	traje	traeré	traería	traiga	trajera
traes	traías	trajiste	traerás	traerías	traigas	trajeras
trae	traía	trajo	traerá	traería	traiga	trajera
traemos	traíamos	trajimos	traeremos	traeríamos	traigamos	trajéramos
traéis	traíais	trajisteis	traeréis	traeríais	traigáis	trajerais
traen	traían	trajeron	traerán	traerían	traigan	trajeran
Pres. perfecto	**Pluscuamperf.**		**Futuro perfecto**	**Perfecto**	**Pres. perfecto**	**Pluscuamperf.**
he traído	había traído		habré traído	habría traído	haya traído	hubiera traído

63. VALER Verbo irregular
(to be worth) (Como **equivaler, prevaler**)

Participio presente: valiendo				Participio pasado: valido		
Imperativo: vale (no valgas), valga Ud., valgamos, valed (no valgáis), (no) valgan Uds.						
INDICATIVO				**CONDICIONAL**	**SUBJUNTIVO**	
Presente	Imperfecto	Pretérito	Futuro	Presente	Presente	Imperfecto
valgo	valía	valí	valdré	valdría	valga	valiera
vales	valías	valiste	valdrás	valdrías	valgas	valieras
vale	valía	valió	valdrá	valdría	valga	valiera
valemos	valíamos	valimos	valdremos	valdríamos	valgamos	valiéramos
valéis	valíais	valisteis	valdréis	valdríais	valgáis	valierais
valen	valían	valieron	valdrán	valdrían	valgan	valieran
Pres. perfecto	**Pluscuamperf.**		**Futuro perfecto**	**Perfecto**	**Pres. perfecto**	**Pluscuamperf.**
he valido	había valido		habré valido	habría valido	haya valido	hubiera valido

64. VENCER — Verbo en -er con cambio de c → z delante de -a y -o
(to conquer) (Como **coercer, convencer, ejercer, mecer**)

Participio presente: venciendo **Participio pasado:** vencido

Imperativo: vence (no venzas), venza Ud., venzamos, venced (no venzáis), (no) venzan Uds.

INDICATIVO				CONDICIONAL	SUBJUNTIVO	
Presente	Imperfecto	Pretérito	Futuro	Presente	Presente	Imperfecto
venzo	vencía	vencí	venceré	vencería	venza	venciera
vences	vencías	venciste	vencerás	vencerías	venzas	vencieras
vence	vencía	venció	vencerá	vencería	venza	venciera
vencemos	vencíamos	vencimos	venceremos	venceríamos	venzamos	venciéramos
vencéis	vencíais	vencisteis	venceréis	venceríais	venzáis	vencierais
vencen	vencían	vencieron	vencerán	vencerían	venzan	vencieran
Pres. perfecto	**Pluscuamperf.**		**Futuro perfecto**	**Perfecto**	**Pres. perfecto**	**Pluscuamperf.**
he vencido	había vencido		habré vencido	habría vencido	haya vencido	hubiera vencido

65. VENIR — Verbo irregular
(to come) (Como **convenir, intervenir, prevenir, provenir, reconvenir**)

Participio presente: viniendo **Participio pasado:** venido

Imperativo: ven (no vengas), venga Ud., vengamos, venid (no vengáis), (no) vengan Uds.

INDICATIVO				CONDICIONAL	SUBJUNTIVO	
Presente	Imperfecto	Pretérito	Futuro	Presente	Presente	Imperfecto
vengo	venía	vine	vendré	vendría	venga	viniera
vienes	venías	viniste	vendrás	vendrías	vengas	vinieras
viene	venía	vino	vendrá	vendría	venga	viniera
venimos	veníamos	vinimos	vendremos	vendríamos	vengamos	viniéramos
venís	veníais	vinisteis	vendréis	vendríais	vengáis	vinierais
vienen	venían	vinieron	vendrán	vendrían	vengan	vinieran
Pres. perfecto	**Pluscuamperf.**		**Futuro perfecto**	**Perfecto**	**Pres. perfecto**	**Pluscuamperf.**
he venido	había venido		habré venido	habría venido	haya venido	hubiera venido

66. VER — Verbo irregular
(to see)

Participio presente: viendo **Participio pasado:** visto

Imperativo: ve* (no veas), vea Ud., veamos, ved (no veáis), (no) vean Uds.

INDICATIVO				CONDICIONAL	SUBJUNTIVO	
Presente	Imperfecto	Pretérito	Futuro	Presente	Presente	Imperfecto
veo	veía	vi	veré	vería	vea	viera
ves	veías	viste	verás	verías	veas	vieras
ve*	veía	vio	verá	vería	vea	viera
vemos	veíamos	vimos	veremos	veríamos	veamos	viéramos
veis	veíais	visteis	veréis	veríais	veáis	vierais
ven	veían	vieron	verán	verían	vean	vieran
Pres. perfecto	**Pluscuamperf.**		**Futuro perfecto**	**Perfecto**	**Pres. perfecto**	**Pluscuamperf.**
he visto	había visto		habré visto	habría visto	haya visto	hubiera visto

*****Entrever** y **prever** se conjugan como **ver** pero tienen acento en las formas marcadas con asterisco (e.g. **entrevé, prevé**).

67. VIVIR — Verbo regular 3.ª conjugación
(to live) (Como **compartir, decidir, emitir, permitir, resumir**)

Participio presente: viviendo					Participio pasado: vivido	

Imperativo: vive (no vivas), viva Ud., vivamos, vivid (no viváis), (no) vivan Uds.

INDICATIVO				CONDICIONAL	SUBJUNTIVO	
Presente	Imperfecto	Pretérito	Futuro	Presente	Presente	Imperfecto
vivo	vivía	viví	viviré	viviría	viva	viviera
vives	vivías	viviste	vivirás	vivirías	vivas	vivieras
vive	vivía	vivió	vivirá	viviría	viva	viviera
vivimos	vivíamos	vivimos	viviremos	viviríamos	vivamos	viviéramos
vivís	vivíais	vivisteis	viviréis	viviríais	viváis	vivierais
viven	vivían	vivieron	vivirán	vivirían	vivan	vivieran
Pres. Perfecto	**Pluscuamperf.**		**Futuro perfecto**	**Perfecto**	**Pres. perfecto**	**Pluscuamperf.**
he vivido	había vivido		habré vivido	habría vivido	haya vivido	hubiera vivido

68. VOLCAR — Verbo en -ar con cambio de o → ue; c → qu delante de -e
(to tip over) (Como **revolcar, trocar**)

Participio presente: volcando					Participio pasado: volcado	

Imperativo: vuelca (no vuelques), vuelque Ud., volquemos, volcad (no volquéis), (no) vuelquen Uds.

INDICATIVO				CONDICIONAL	SUBJUNTIVO	
Presente	Imperfecto	Pretérito	Futuro	Presente	Presente	Imperfecto
vuelco	volcaba	volqué	volcaré	volcaría	vuelque	volcara
vuelcas	volcabas	volcaste	volcarás	volcarías	vuelques	volcaras
vuelca	volcaba	volcó	volcará	volcaría	vuelque	volcara
volcamos	volcábamos	volcamos	volcaremos	volcaríamos	volquemos	volcáramos
volcáis	volcabais	volcasteis	volcaréis	volcaríais	volquéis	volcarais
vuelcan	volcaban	volcaron	volcarán	volcarían	vuelquen	volcaran
Pres. perfecto	**Pluscuamperf.**		**Futuro perfecto**	**Perfecto**	**Pres. perfecto**	**Pluscuamperf.**
he volcado	había volcado		habré volcado	habría volcado	haya volcado	hubiera volcado

69. VOLVER — Verbo en -er con cambio de o → ue; participio pasado irregular
(to return) (Como **devolver, disolver, envolver, resolver, revolver**)

Participio presente: volviendo					Participio pasado: vuelto	

Imperativo: vuelve (no vuelvas), vuelva Ud., volvamos, volved (no volváis), (no) vuelvan Uds.

INDICATIVO				CONDICIONAL	SUBJUNTIVO	
Presente	Imperfecto	Pretérito	Futuro	Presente	Presente	Imperfecto
vuelvo	volvía	volví	volveré	volvería	vuelva	volviera
vuelves	volvías	volviste	volverás	volverías	vuelvas	volvieras
vuelve	volvía	volvió	volverá	volvería	vuelva	volviera
volvemos	volvíamos	volvimos	volveremos	volveríamos	volvamos	volviéramos
volvéis	volvíais	volvisteis	volveréis	volveríais	volváis	volvierais
vuelven	volvían	volvieron	volverán	volverían	vuelvan	volvieran
Pres. perfecto	**Pluscuamperf.**		**Futuro perfecto**	**Perfecto**	**Pres. perfecto**	**Pluscuamperf.**
he vuelto	había vuelto		habré vuelto	habría vuelto	haya vuelto	hubiera vuelto

70. YACER* Verbo irregular
(to lie [usually dead])

Participio presente: yaciendo **Participio pasado:** yacido

Imperativo: yace o yaz (no yazcas), yazca Ud., yazcamos, yaced (no yazcáis), (no) yazcan Uds.

INDICATIVO				CONDICIONAL	SUBJUNTIVO	
Presente	Imperfecto	Pretérito	Futuro	Presente	Presente	Imperfecto
yazco	yacía	yací	yaceré	yacería	yazca	yaciera
yaces	yacías	yaciste	yacerás	yacerías	yazcas	yacieras
yace	yacía	yació	yacerá	yacería	yazca	yaciera
yacemos	yacíamos	yacimos	yaceremos	yaceríamos	yazcamos	yaciéramos
yacéis	yacíais	yacisteis	yaceréis	yaceríais	yazcáis	yacierais
yacen	yacían	yacieron	yacerán	yacerían	yazcan	yacieran
Pres. perfecto	**Pluscuamperf.**		**Futuro perfecto**	**Perfecto**	**Pres. perfecto**	**Pluscuamperf.**
he yacido	había yacido		habré yacido	habría yacido	haya yacido	hubiera yacido

*Existen otras formas de este verbo, menos usuales, en las que en vez de -zc- se usa -zg- o -g-.

71. ZAMBULLIR Verbo irregular
(to submerge)

Participio presente: zambullendo **Participio pasado:** zambullido

Imperativo: zambulle (no zambullas), zambulla Ud., zambullamos, zambullid (no zambulláis), (no) zambullan Uds.

INDICATIVO				CONDICIONAL	SUBJUNTIVO	
Presente	Imperfecto	Pretérito	Futuro	Presente	Presente	Imperfecto
zambullo	zambullía	zambullí	zambulliré	zambulliría	zambulla	zambullera
zambulles	zambullías	zambulliste	zambullirás	zambullirías	zambullas	zambulleras
zambulle	zambullía	zambulló	zambullirá	zambulliría	zambulla	zambullera
zambullimos	zambullíamos	zambullimos	zambulliremos	zambulliríamos	zambullamos	zambulléramos
zambullís	zambullíais	zambullisteis	zambulliréis	zambulliríais	zambulláis	zambullerais
zambullen	zambullían	zambulleron	zambullirán	zambullirían	zambullan	zambulleran
Pres. perfecto	**Pluscuamperf.**		**Futuro perfecto**	**Perfecto**	**Pres. perfecto**	**Pluscuamperf.**
he zambullido	había zambullido		habré zambullido	habría zambullido	haya zambullido	hubiera zambullido

C MINI-ÍNDICE DE VERBOS

*(El número de la derecha de cada verbo es el que corresponde al verbo modelo de conjugación. Vea la "Lista de modelos de conjugación" para la referencia. Note: Los verbos con -se al final son reflexivos. Es necesario usarlos con los pronombres reflexivos: "yo **me** abstengo", por ejemplo.)*

abandonar 10	ablandecer 42	aborrecer 42	abrumar 10	acaecer 42
abanicar 7	abnegar 39	abortar 10	absolver 69	acallar 10
abaratar 10	abobar 10	abotonar 10	absorber 4	acalorar 10
abarcar 7	abocar 7	abrasar 10	abstenerse 60	acampar 10
abarrotar 10	abochornar 10	abrazar 19	abstraer 62	acaparar 10
abastecer 42	abofetear 10	abreviar 10	abultar 10	acaramelar 10
abatir 67	abogar 35	abrigar 35	abundar 10	acariciar 10
abdicar 7	abombar 10	abrillantar 10	aburguesarse 10	acarrear 10
aberrar 10	abominar 10	abrir 67	aburrir 67	acceder 4
abjurar 10	abonar 10	abrochar 10	abusar 10	accidentar 10
ablandar 10	abordar 10	abrogar 35	acabar 10	acechar 10

aceitar 10	adentrar 10	agolpar 10	almacenar 10	angostar 10
acelerar 10	aderezar 19	agonizar 19	almidonar 10	angustiar 10
acentuar 1	adeudar 10	agraciar 10	almorzar 30	anhelar 10
acepillar 10	adherir 57	agradar 10	alocar 7	anidar 10
aceptar 10	adicionar 10	agradecer 42	alojar 10	anihilar 10
acequiar 10	adiestrar 10	agrandar 10	alquilar 10	animalizar 19
acercar 7	adivinar 10	agravar 10	alterar 10	animar 10
acertar 11	adjetivar 10	agregar 35	altercar 7	aniñarse 10
achacar 7	adjudicar 7	agriar 10	alternar 10	aniquilar 10
achaparrarse 10	adjuntar 10	agrietar 10	alucinar 10	anivelar 10
achatar 10	administrar 10	agringarse 35	aludir 67	anochecer 42
achicar 7	admirar 10	agrumar 10	alumbrar 10	anonadar 10
achicharrar 10	admitir 67	agrupar 10	alzar 19	anotar 10
achocar 7	adobar 10	aguantar 10	amadrinar 10	anquilosar 10
acinturar 10	adoctrinar 10	aguar 6	amaestrar 10	ansiar 26
aclamar 10	adoptar 10	aguardar 10	amalgamar 10	anteceder 4
aclarar 10	adorar 10	agudizar 19	amamantar 10	antedatar 10
aclimatar 10	adormecer 42	aguijonear 10	amanecer 42	anteponer 46
acobardar 10	adornar 10	agujerear 10	amanerarse 10	anticipar 10
acobijar 10	adosar 10	aguzar 19	amansar 10	antojarse 10
acodar 10	adquirir 2	aherrumbrar 10	amar 10	antorchar 10
acoger 13	adscribir 67	ahogar 35	amargar 35	anular 10
acojinar 10	adular 10	ahorcar 7	amarillear 10	anunciar 10
acolchonar 10	adulterar 10	ahorrar 10	amarillecer 42	añadir 67
acomedirse 43	adverbializar 19	ahuecar 7	amarrar 10	añejar 10
acometer 4	advertir 57	ahuyentar 10	amasar 10	añorar 10
acomodar 10	afanar 10	airear 10	ambicionar 10	apabilar 10
acompañar 10	afectar 10	ajetrear 10	ambientar 10	apacentar 11
acompasar 10	afeitar 10	ajorar 17	ambular 10	apachurrar 10
acomplejar 10	afeminar 10	ajustar 10	amedrentar 10	apaciguar 6
aconchabarse 10	aferrar 11	alabar 10	amelcochar 10	apadrinar 10
acondicionar 10	afianzar 19	alagar 35	amenazar 19	apagar 35
acongojar 10	aficionar 10	alargar 35	amenizar 19	apalear 10
aconsejar 10	afilar 10	albergar 35	amenorar 10	aparcar 7
acontecer 42	afiliar 10	alborotar 10	americanizar 19	aparear 10
acordar 17	afinar 10	alcahuetear 10	ametrallar 10	aparecer 42
acorralar 10	afincar 7	alcanzar 19	aminorar 10	aparentar 10
acorrer 4	afirmar 10	alegar 35	amodorrarse 10	apartar 10
acortar 10	afligir 22	alegorizar 19	amolar 17	apasionar 10
acosar 10	aflojar 10	alegrar 10	amoldar 10	apear 10
acostar 17	aflorar 10	alejar 10	amonestar 10	apedrear 10
acostumbrar 10	afluir 15	alentar 11	amontonar 10	apegar 35
acrecentar 11	afrancesar 10	alertar 10	amortiguar 6	apellidar 10
acreditar 10	afrentar 10	alfabetizar 19	amortizar 19	apestar 10
acribillar 10	africanizar 19	alfombrar 10	amparar 10	apetecer 42
activar 10	afrontar 10	alforzar 19	ampliar 26	apiadar 10
actualizar 19	agachar 10	aligerar 10	amplificar 7	apilar 10
actuar 1	agarrar 10	alijar 10	ampollar 10	apiñar 10
acuchillar 10	agasajar 10	alimentar 10	amputar 10	aplacar 7
acuclillarse 10	agazapar 10	alinear 10	analizar 19	aplanar 10
acudir 67	agermanarse 10	alisar 10	anclar 10	aplastar 10
acurrucarse 7	agilizar 19	alistar 10	andar 3	aplaudir 67
acusar 10	agitanar 10	alivianar 10	anegar 35	aplazar 19
adaptar 10	agitar 10	aliviar 10	anestesiar 10	aplicar 7
adelantar 10	aglomerar 10	allanar 10	anexar 10	apocar 7
adelgazar 19	agobiar 10	allegar 35	anexionar 10	apocopar 10

Verb Tables **A-27**

apodar 10	arrestar 10	atesorar 10	bastar 10	calificar 7
apoderar 10	arriar 26	atestar 10	batallar 10	caligrafiar 26
apolillar 10	arribar 10	atestiguar 6	batir 67	callar 10
aporrear 10	arriesgar 35	atinar 10	bautizar 19	calmar 10
aportar 10	arrimar 10	atolondrar 10	beatificar 7	calumniar 10
apostar 17	arrinconar 10	atomizar 19	beber 4	calzar 19
apostrofar 10	arrojar 10	atontar 10	beneficiar 10	cambiar 10
apoyar 10	arropar 10	atorar 10	berrear 10	caminar 10
apreciar 10	arrugar 35	atormentar 10	besar 10	camuflar 10
aprehender 4	arruinar 10	atornillar 10	bienquerer 49	canalizar 19
apremiar 10	arrullar 10	atraer 62	bifurcarse 7	cancelar 10
aprender 4	articular 10	atragantarse 10	blanquear 10	canjear 10
aprestar 10	asaltar 10	atrancar 7	blanquecer 42	canonizar 19
apresurar 10	asar 10	atrapar 10	blindar 10	cansar 10
apretar 11	ascender 44	atrasar 10	bloquear 10	cantar 10
apretujar 10	asear 10	atravesar 11	bofetear 10	capacitar 10
aprisionar 10	asechar 10	atribuir 15	boicotear 10	capar 10
aprobar 17	asediar 10	atrofiar 10	bombardear 10	capitalizar 19
aprontar 10	asegurar 10	atronar 17	bordear 10	capitular 10
apropiar 10	asemejar 10	atropellar 10	borrar 10	captar 10
aprovechar 10	asentar 11	aturdir 67	borronear 10	capturar 10
aprovisionar 10	asentir 57	augurar 10	bosquejar 10	caracolear 10
aproximar 10	aserrar 11	aumentar 10	bostezar 19	caracterizar 19
apuntar 10	asesinar 10	auscultar 10	botar 10	caramelizar 19
apuntillar 10	asesorar 10	ausentar 10	boxear 10	carbonizar 19
apuñalar 10	asestar 10	auspiciar 10	bramar 10	carcomer 4
apurar 10	asfaltar 10	autenticar 7	bregar 35	cardar 10
arar 10	asfixiar 10	autentificar 7	brillar 10	carecer 42
arbitrar 10	asignar 10	autografiar 26	brincar 7	cargar 35
arbolecer 42	asimilar 10	automatizar 19	brindar 10	caricaturizar 19
archivar 10	asistir 67	autorizar 19	bromear 10	casar 10
arder 4	asociar 10	avanzar 19	broncear 10	castigar 35
argentinizar 19	asolear 10	aventajar 10	brotar 10	castrar 10
argüir 15	asomar 10	aventar 11	brutalizar 19	catalogar 35
argumentar 10	asombrar 10	aventurar 10	bucear 10	catapultar 10
aridecer 42	aspirar 10	avergonzar 5	burocratizar 19	catar 10
aristocratizar 19	asquear 10	averiguar 6	buscar 7	causar 10
armar 10	astillar 10	avisar 10		cauterizar 19
armonizar 19	asumir 67	avivar 10	cabalgar 35	cautivar 10
aromatizar 19	asustar 10	ayudar 10	cabecear 10	cavar 10
arquear 10	atacar 7	ayunar 10	caber 8	cazar 19
arraigar 35	atajar 10	azorar 10	cablegrafiar 26	cazcalear 10
arrancar 7	atapuzar 19	azotar 10	cabrear 10	cebar 10
arrasar 10	atar 10	azucarar 10	cacarear 10	cecear 10
arrastrar 10	atarantar 10	azuzar 19	cachetear 10	ceder 4
arrear 10	atardecer 42		caducar 7	cegar 39
arrebatar 10	atarear 10	babear 10	caer 9	cejar 10
arreglar 10	atascar 7	babosear 10	cagar 35	celar 10
arrellanarse 10	atemorizar 19	bailar 10	calar 10	celebrar 10
arremangar 35	atender 44	bajar 10	calcar 7	cementar 10
arremedar 10	atenerse 60	balancear 10	calcificar 7	cenar 10
arremeter 4	atentar 10	balbucear 10	calcinar 10	censurar 10
arremolinar 10	atenuar 1	barnizar 19	calcografiar 26	centralizar 19
arrempujar 10	aterrar 11	barrenar 10	calcular 10	centrar 10
arrendar 11	aterrizar 19	barrer 4	calentar 11	ceñir 61
arrepentirse 57	aterrorizar 19	basar 10	calibrar 10	cepillar 10

cercar 7	codiciar 10	computar 10	consentir 57	corroborar 10
cerciorar 10	codificar 7	computarizar 19	conservar 10	cortar 10
cernir 23	coercer 64	comulgar 35	considerar 10	cortejar 10
cerrar 11	coexistir 67	comunicar 7	consignar 10	cosechar 10
certificar 7	coger 13	concatenar 10	consistir 67	coser 4
cesar 10	cohabitar 10	concebir 43	consolar 17	costar 17
chantajear 10	cohibir 47	conceder 4	consolidar 10	costear 10
chapotear 10	coincidir 67	concentrar 10	consonantizar 19	cotizar 19
charlar 10	cojear 10	conceptuar 1	conspirar 10	cotorrear 10
chequear 10	colaborar 10	concernir 23	constar 10	crear 10
checar 7	colar 10	concertar 11	constatar 10	crecer 42
chicanear 10	coleccionar 10	concienciar 10	consternar 10	creer 18
chiflar 10	colegir 50	concientizar 19	constipar 10	crepitar 10
chillar 10	colgar 53	conciliar 10	constitucionalizar 19	criar 26
chinear 10	colindar 10	concluir 15	constituir 15	criminalizar 19
chingar 35	colmar 10	concordar 17	construir 15	cristalizar 19
chirriar 26	colocar 7	concretar 10	consultar 10	criticar 7
chismear 10	colonizar 19	concurrir 67	consumar 10	croar 10
chismorrear 10	colorear 10	concursar 10	consumir 67	cronometrar 10
chismotear 10	columpiar 10	condecorar 10	contactar 10	crucificar 7
chispear 10	comadrear 10	condenar 10	contagiar 10	crujir 67
chistar 10	combatir 67	condensar 10	contaminar 10	cruzar 19
chocar 7	combinar 10	condescender 44	contar 17	cuadrar 10
chocarrear 10	comentar 10	condicionar 10	contemplar 10	cuajar 10
chorrear 10	comenzar 14	condimentar 10	contender 44	cualificar 7
chotear 10	comer 4	condolecerse 42	contener 60	cuantificar 7
chupar 10	comercializar 19	condonar 10	contentar 10	cubrir 67
chutar 10	cometer 4	conducir 16	contestar 10	cucar 7
cicatrizar 19	comisionar 10	conectar 10	continuar 1	cucharear 10
cimentar 11	compactar 10	conferir 57	contonearse 10	cuchichear 10
circular 10	compadecer 42	confesar 11	contorsionarse 10	cuestionar 10
circundar 10	compadrear 10	confiar 26	contraer 62	cuidar 10
circunferir 57	compaginar 10	configurar 10	contraponer 46	culminar 10
circunscribir 67	comparar 10	confinar 10	contrariar 26	culpar 10
circunvenir 65	comparecer 42	confirmar 10	contrarrestar 10	cultivar 10
circunvolar 17	compartir 67	confiscar 7	contrastar 10	cumplir 67
citar 10	compasar 10	conformar 10	contratar 10	curar 10
civilizar 19	compeler 4	confortar 10	contribuir 15	curiosear 10
clamar 10	compendiar 10	confrontar 10	controlar 10	cursar 10
clamorear 10	compendizar 19	confundir 67	controvertir 57	curtir 67
clarear 10	compenetrarse 10	congelar 10	convalecer 42	curvear 10
clarecer 42	compensar 10	congestionar 10	convencer 64	
clarificar 7	competir 43	conglomerar 10	convenir 65	dactilografiar 26
clasificar 7	compilar 10	congregar 35	conversar 10	danzar 19
claudicar 7	complementar 10	conjeturar 10	convertir 57	dañar 10
clausurar 10	completar 10	conjugar 35	convidar 10	dar 20
clavar 10	complicar 7	conllevar 10	convivir 67	deambular 10
clavetear 10	complotar 10	conmemorar 10	convocar 7	debatir 67
climatizar 19	componer 46	conmocionar 10	cooperar 10	deber 4
coadquirir 2	comportarse 10	conmover 38	coordinar 10	debilitar 10
coagular 10	comprar 10	conmutar 10	copiar 10	decaer 9
cobijar 10	comprender 4	connotar 10	coquetear 10	decampar 10
cobrar 10	comprimir 67	conocer 42	corregir 50	decantar 10
cocer 12	comprobar 17	conquistar 10	correr 4	decapitar 10
cocinar 10	comprometer 4	consagrar 10	corresponder 4	decepcionar 10
codear 10	computadorizar 19	conseguir 56	corretear 10	decidir 67

Verb Tables **A-29**

decir 21	deprimir 67	descalificar 7	desempeñar 10	deshojar 10
declamar 10	depurar 10	descansar 10	desemperezar 19	deshonrar 10
declarar 10	derivar 10	descargar 35	desempolvar 10	deshuesar 10
declinar 10	derogar 35	descarrillar 10	desencadenar 10	deshumanizar 19
decolorar 10	derramar 10	descartar 10	desencajar 10	designar 10
decorar 10	derrengar 39	descender 44	desencarcelar 10	desigualar 10
decrecer 42	derretir 43	descentralizar 19	desencerrar 11	desilusionar 10
decretar 10	derribar 10	descentrar 10	desenchufar 10	desinfectar 10
decuplar 10	derrocar 7	descifrar 10	desenfadar 10	desinflar 10
dedicar 7	derrochar 10	desclasificar 7	desenfilar 10	desintegrar 10
deducir 16	derrotar 10	descoagular 10	desenfocar 7	desintoxicar 7
defender 44	derrumbar 10	descobijar 10	desenfrenar 10	desistir 67
deferir 57	desabotonar 10	descocar 7	desenfundar 10	desmaquillar 10
definir 67	desabrigar 35	descocer 12	desenfurecer 42	desmarañar 10
deforestar 10	desabrochar 10	descolgar 53	desenganchar 10	desmayar 10
deformar 10	desacomodar 10	descompaginar 10	desengañar 10	desmejorar 10
defraudar 10	desacordar 17	descomponer 46	desenlazar 19	desmentir 57
degenerar 10	desacreditar 10	desconcertar 11	desenlodar 10	desmenuzar 19
deglutir 67	desactivar 10	desconchinflar 10	desenmarañar 10	desmitificar 7
degollar 17	desaferrar 11	desconectar 10	desenmascarar 10	desmontar 10
degradar 10	desafiar 26	desconfiar 26	desenmohecer 42	desmoralizar 19
degustar 10	desafilar 10	descongelar 10	desenredar 10	desmoronar 10
deificar 7	desafinar 10	descongestionar ... 10	desenrollar 10	desnivelar 10
dejar 10	desagradar 10	desconocer 42	desenroscar 7	desnudar 10
delatar 10	desagradecer 42	descontaminar 10	desensamblar 10	desobedecer 42
delegar 35	desaguar 6	descontar 17	desensartar 10	desocupar 10
deleitar 10	desahogar 35	descontinuar 1	desensillar 10	desodorizar 19
deletrear 10	desajustar 10	descoser 4	desenterrar 11	desorbitar 10
deliberar 10	desalentar 11	descotar 10	desentonar 10	desordenar 10
delimitar 10	desalojar 10	descoyuntar 10	desentrenar 10	desorganizar 19
delinear 10	desamarrar 10	descrecer 42	desentumecer 42	desorientar 10
delirar 10	desamontonar 10	descreer 18	desentumir 67	despabilar 10
deludir 67	desamparar 10	describir 67	desenvainar 10	despachar 10
demandar 10	desanimar 10	descruzar 19	desenvolver 69	desparramar 10
demarcar 7	desaparecer 42	descuartizar 19	desequilibrar 10	despedazar 19
democratizar 19	desapegar 35	descubrir 67	desertar 10	despedir 43
demorar 10	desapreciar 10	descuidar 10	desesperar 10	despegar 35
demostrar 17	desapretar 11	desdentar 11	desestabilizar 19	despeinar 10
denegar 39	desaprobar 17	desdeñar 10	desestancar 7	despejar 10
denigrar 10	desapropiar 10	desdibujar 10	desfallecer 42	despellejar 10
denominar 10	desarmar 10	desdoblar 10	desfavorecer 42	desperdiciar 10
denotar 10	desarmonizar 19	desdorar 10	desfigurar 10	despertar 11
densificar 7	desarreglar 10	desear 10	desfilar 10	despilfarrar 10
dentar 11	desarrollar 10	desecar 7	desfondar 10	despintar 10
denunciar 10	desarropar 10	desechar 10	desgajar 10	despiojar 10
deparar 10	desarrugar 35	desembalar 10	desgarrar 10	despistar 10
departir 67	desatar 10	desembarazar 19	desgastar 10	desplegar 39
depender 4	desatinar 10	desembarcar 7	desgraciar 10	desplomar 10
depilar 10	desatornillar 10	desembarrar 10	desgreñar 10	despoblar 17
deplorar 10	desayunar 10	desembocar 7	deshacer 32	despojar 10
deponer 46	desbarajustar 10	desemejar 10	deshebrar 10	despreciar 10
deportar 10	desbaratar 10	desempacar 7	deshelar 11	desprender 4
depositar 10	desbordar 10	desempañar 10	desheredar 10	despreocuparse 10
depravar 10	desboronar 10	desempaquetar 10	deshidratar 10	desprestigiar 10
deprecar 7	desbridar 10	desemparejar 10	deshilachar 10	desquiciar 10
depreciar 10	descalcar 7	desempatar 10	deshinchar 10	desquitar 10

destacar 7	dilucidar 10	domar 10	embolsar...............10	encender...............44
destapar...............10	diluir 15	domesticar.............7	emborrachar.........10	encerar 10
desteñir 61	diminuir 15	dominar.................10	emboscar 7	encerrar 11
desterrar................11	dimitir 67	donar 10	embotellar.............10	encestar 10
destetar.................10	dinamitar..............10	dopar 10	embriagar 35	enchilar 10
destilar..................10	diplomar................10	dorar 10	embrollar...............10	enchinar 10
destinar.................10	diptongar...............35	dormir 25	embromar 10	enchuecar................7
destituir.................15	diputar 10	dormitar 10	embrujar.................10	enchufar 10
destorcer 12	dirigir 22	dosificar...................7	embrutecer 42	encoger 13
destornillar............10	discernir 23	dotar 10	emburujar...............10	encomendar 11
destrabar...............10	disciplinar..............10	dramatizar.............19	embustir 67	encontrar 17
destrenzar..............19	discordar 17	duchar 10	emerger 13	encorvar 10
destripar................10	discriminar 10	dudar 10	emigrar 10	encuadernar 10
destrizar.................19	disculpar 10	dulcificar 7	emitir......................67	encuerar 10
destrozar................19	discurrir 67	duplicar 7	emocionar 10	enderezar...............19
destruir..................15	discursar 10	durar 10	empacar...................7	endeudarse 10
desunir 67	discutir 67		empachar................10	endiablar 10
desvalijar 10	disecar 7	echar 10	empadronar...........10	endomingarse.......35
desvalorar..............10	diseminar 10	eclipsar 10	empalagar 35	endosar 10
desvalorizar 19	disentir 57	economizar............19	empalidecer 42	endulzar 19
desvanecer.............42	diseñar 10	edificar 7	empañar 10	endurecer 42
desvariar................26	disertar 10	editar 10	empapar 10	enfadar 10
desvelar..................10	disfrazar 19	educar 7	empapelar 10	enfangar 35
desvencijar.............10	disfrutar 10	efectuar 1	empaquetar 10	enfatizar 19
desvergonzarse........5	disgustar 10	egresar 10	emparedar 10	enfermar 10
desvestir 43	disimular 10	ejecutar 10	emparejar 10	enfilar 10
desviar 26	disipar 10	ejemplarizar 19	empedrar 11	enflacar 7
desvivirse...............67	dislocar 7	ejemplificar 7	empelotarse............10	enfocar 7
desyerbar...............10	disminuir 15	ejercer 64	empeñar 10	enfrentar 10
detallar 10	disolver...................69	ejercitar 10	empeorar 10	enfriar....................26
detectar 10	disparar 10	elaborar 10	empequeñecer 42	enfurecer 42
detener 60	dispensar 10	electrificar 7	empezar..................14	enganchar 10
deteriorar 10	dispersar 10	electrocutar 10	empilar 10	engañar 10
determinar 10	disponer 46	electrolizar 19	empinar 10	engendrar 10
detestar 10	disputar 10	elegir 50	emplear 10	engordar 10
detractar.................10	distanciar 10	elevar 10	empobrecer 42	engrasar 10
detraer 62	distar 10	elidir 67	empolvar 10	enharinar 10
devaluar...................1	distinguir 24	eliminar 10	emprender 4	enjabonar 10
devastar 10	distorsionar 10	elogiar 10	empujar 10	enjaular..................10
devengar................35	distraer 62	elucidar 10	emular 10	enjuagar.................35
devolver.................69	distribuir 15	eludir 67	emulsionar 10	enlatar 10
devorar 10	disuadir 67	emanar 10	enamorar 10	enlazar 19
diagnosticar.............7	divagar 35	emancipar 10	encabezar 19	enlodar 10
dialogar 35	divergir 22	emascular 10	encadenar 10	enloquecer.............42
dibujar 10	diversificar 7	embabucar 7	encajar 10	enlutar 10
dictar 10	divertir 57	embadurnar 10	encaminar 10	enmarcar 7
difamar 10	dividir 67	embalar 10	encandilar 10	enmascarar 10
diferenciar.............10	divisar 10	embanderar 10	encantar 10	enmendar 11
diferir 57	divorciar 10	embarazar 19	encapricharse 10	enmudecer 42
dificultar................10	divulgar 35	embarcar 7	encaramar 10	enmugrar 10
difundir..................67	doblar 10	embargar 35	encarar 10	ennegrecer 42
digerir....................57	doblegar 35	embarrar.................10	encarcelar 10	enojar 10
dignarse.................10	doctrinar 10	embellecer..............42	encargar 35	enorgullecer..........42
dignificar.................7	documentar 10	embestir 43	encariñar 10	enredar 10
dilapidar 10	dogmatizar 19	embobar 10	encarnar 10	enriquecer 42
dilatar....................10	doler 38	embocar 7	encebollar...............10	enrojecer 42

enrollar 10	erradicar 7	estornudar 10	expresar 10	fosilizarse 19
enroscar 7	errar 27	estrangular 10	exprimir 67	fotocopiar 10
ensamblar 10	eructar 10	estratificar 7	expulsar 10	fotografiar 26
ensanchar 10	escalar 10	estrellar 10	expurgar 35	fracasar 10
ensangrentar 11	escalofriar 26	estremecer 42	extasiarse 26	fracturar 10
ensayar 10	escandalizar 19	estrenar 10	extender 44	fragmentar 10
enseñar 10	escapar 10	estreñir 61	extenuar 1	fraternizar 19
ensillar 10	escarbar 10	estribar 10	exteriorizar 19	frecuentar 10
ensimismarse 10	escasear 10	estropear 10	exterminar 10	fregar 39
ensordecer 42	escavar 10	estructurar 10	extinguir 24	freír 51
ensuciar 10	escenificar 7	estrujar 10	extirpar 10	frenar 10
entablar 10	esclavizar 19	estudiar 10	extraer 62	frotar 10
entender 44	escoger 13	eternizar 19	extrañar 10	fruncir 28
enterar 10	esconder 4	etiquetar 10	extrapolar 10	frustrar 10
enternecer 42	escribir 67	evacuar 10	extraviar 26	fugarse 35
enterrar 11	escuchar 10	evadir 67		fumar 10
entibiar 10	escudriñar 10	evaluar 1	fabricar 7	fumigar 35
entiesar 10	esculcar 7	evaporar 10	facilitar 10	funcionar 10
entiznar 10	esculpir 67	evitar 10	facturar 10	fundar 10
entonar 10	escupir 67	evocar 7	fallar 10	fundir 67
entornar 10	escurrir 67	evolucionar 10	fallecer 42	fusilar 10
entorpecer 42	esforzar 30	exacerbar 10	falsificar 7	fusionar 10
entrar 10	esfumar 10	exagerar 10	faltar 10	
entreabrir 67	esmaltar 10	exaltar 10	familiarizar 19	galantear 10
entrecerrar 11	esmerar 10	examinar 10	fascinar 10	galardonar 10
entregar 35	espantar 10	exasperar 10	fastidiar 10	galopear 10
entrenar 10	esparcir 28	excarcelar 10	favorecer 42	ganar 10
entretejer 4	esparramar 10	excavar 10	fechar 10	garabatear 10
entretener 60	espatarrarse 10	exceder 4	felicitar 10	garantizar 19
entrever 66	especializar 19	excepcionar 10	fermentar 10	gargarizar 19
entrevistar 10	especificar 7	exceptuar 1	festejar 10	gastar 10
entristecer 42	especular 10	excitar 10	fiar 26	gatear 10
entrometer 4	esperar 10	exclamar 10	fichar 10	gemir 43
entumecer 42	espesar 10	excluir 15	figurar 10	generalizar 19
entumirse 67	espiar 26	excomulgar 35	fijar 10	generar 10
entusiasmar 10	espolvorear 10	excretar 10	filar 10	germinar 10
enumerar 10	espulgar 35	exculpar 10	filmar 10	gestar 10
enunciar 10	esquiar 26	excusar 10	filtrar 10	gesticular 10
envasar 10	esquivar 10	exentar 10	finalizar 19	gestionar 10
envejecer 42	estabilizar 19	exhalar 10	financiar 10	girar 10
envenenar 10	establecer 42	exhibir 67	fincar 7	glorificar 7
enverdecer 42	estacionar 10	exigir 22	fingir 22	gobernar 11
enviar 26	estafar 10	exiliar 10	firmar 10	golpear 10
envidiar 10	estallar 10	eximir 67	fiscalizar 19	gotear 10
envigorizar 19	estancar 7	existir 67	florear 10	gozar 19
enviudar 10	estandardizar 19	exonerar 10	florecer 42	grabar 10
envolver 69	estandarizar 19	exorcizar 19	flotar 10	graduar 1
enyesar 10	estar 29	expandir 67	fluctuar 1	granizar 19
equilibrar 10	estereotipar 10	expatriarse 26	fluir 15	gratificar 7
equipar 10	esterilizar 19	expectorar 10	fomentar 10	gravitar 10
equiparar 10	estigmatizar 19	experimentar 10	forjar 10	gritar 10
equivaler 63	estimar 10	expiar 26	formalizar 19	guardar 10
equivocar 7	estimular 10	explicar 7	formar 10	guarnecer 42
erigir 22	estipular 10	explorar 10	formular 10	guerrear 10
erizar 19	estirar 10	explotar 10	forrar 10	guerrillear 10
erosionar 10	estorbar 10	exponer 46	forzar 30	guiar 26

guindar 10	idiotizar 19	infringir 22	intimar 10	lamer 4
guiñar 10	idolatrar 10	infundir 67	intimidar 10	laminar 10
guisar 10	ignorar 10	ingerir 57	intoxicar 7	lancear 10
gustar 10	igualar 10	ingresar 10	intricar 7	languidecer 42
	iluminar 10	inhalar 10	intrigar 35	lanzar 19
haber 31	ilustrar 10	inhibir 67	intrincar 7	laquear 10
habilitar 10	imaginar 10	iniciar 10	introducir 16	largar 35
habitar 10	imitar 10	injuriar 10	intuir 15	lastimar 10
habituar 1	impacientar 10	inmigrar 10	inundar 10	lateralizar 19
hablar 10	impedir 43	inmiscuir 15	invadir 67	latinizar 19
hacer 32	impersonalizar 19	inmovilizar 19	invalidar 10	latir 67
hachear 10	implantar 10	inmunizar 19	inventar 10	laudar 10
halagar 35	implicar 7	inmutar 10	inventariar 26	lavar 10
halar 10	implorar 10	innovar 10	invernar 11	leer 18
hallar 10	imponer 46	inocular 10	invertir 57	legalizar 19
harmonizar 19	imposibilitar 10	inquietar 10	investigar 35	legar 35
hechizar 19	impresionar 10	inquirir 2	invitar 10	legislar 10
heder 44	imprimir 67	inscribir 67	invocar 7	legitimar 10
helar 11	improvisar 10	insensibilizar 19	involucrar 10	lesionar 10
heredar 10	impulsar 10	insinuar 1	inyectar 10	levantar 10
herir 57	imputar 10	insistir 67	ionizar 19	liar 26
herrar 11	inaugurar 10	inspeccionar 10	ir 33	liberalizar 19
hervir 57	incapacitar 10	inspirar 10	irradiar 10	liberar 10
hilar 10	incendiar 10	instalar 10	irrigar 35	libertar 10
hilvanar 10	incitar 10	instar 10	irritar 10	librar 10
hincar 7	inclinar 10	instaurar 10	irrumpir 67	licenciar 10
hinchar 10	incluir 15	instigar 35	italianizar 19	licuar 1
hipnotizar 19	incomodar 10	instilar 10	iterar 10	lidiar 10
hipotecar 7	incorporar 10	institucionalizar ... 19	izar 19	ligar 35
hispanizar 19	incrementar 10	instituir 15		lijar 10
hojear 10	incriminar 10	instruir 15	jactarse 10	limar 10
homenajear 10	incrustar 10	insubordinar 10	jadear 10	limitar 10
homogeneizar 19	inculcar 7	insultar 10	jalar 10	limosnear. 10
homologar 35	incumbir 67	integrar 10	jalear 10	limpiar 10
honrar 10	incurrir 67	intelectualizar 19	jaspear 10	lindar 10
hormiguear 10	indagar 35	intentar 10	jerarquizar 19	liquidar 10
hornear 10	indemnizar 19	intercalar 10	jorobar 10	lisiar 10
horrificar 7	independizar 19	intercambiar 10	jubilar 10	lisonjear 10
horripilar 10	indicar 7	interceder 4	jugar 34	litigar 35
horrorizar 19	indignar 10	interceptar 10	juguetear 10	lividecer 42
hospedar 10	indisciplinarse 10	interesar 10	juntar 10	llamar 10
hospitalizar 19	indisponer 46	interferir 57	jurar 10	llegar 35
hostigar 35	individualizar 19	interiorizar 19	justiciar 10	llenar 10
huir 15	inducir 16	intermediar 10	justificar 7	llevar 10
humanizar 19	indultar 10	internacionalizar .. 19	juzgar 35	llorar 10
humectar 10	industrializar 19	internar 10		lloriquear 10
humedecer 42	infectar 10	interpelar 10	kilometrar 10	llover 38
humillar 10	inferir 57	interpolar 10		lloviznar 10
hundir 67	infestar 10	interponer 46	labrar 10	loar 10
hurgar 35	infiltrar 10	interpretar 10	lacerar 10	localizar 19
hurgonear 10	inflamar 10	interrogar 35	lactar 10	lograr 10
husmear 10	inflar 10	interrumpir 67	ladear 10	lubricar 7
	infligir 22	intersecarse 7	ladrar 10	lubrificar 7
idealizar 19	influir 15	intervenir 65	lagrimear 10	luchar 10
identificar 7	informar 10		lamentar 10	lucir 36

Verb Tables **A-33**

lucrar 10	mecer 64	molestar 10	ñangotarse 10	originar 10
lucubrar 10	mediar 10	molificar 7		orillar 10
lustrar 10	medicamentar 10	mondar 10	obedecer 42	orinar 10
	medir 43	monologar 35	objetar 10	ornamentar 10
macanear 10	meditar 10	monopolizar 19	objetivar 10	ornar 10
macerar 10	mejorar 10	montar 10	obligar 35	ornear 10
machacar 7	melancolizar 19	moralizar 19	obliterar 10	orquestar 10
machetear 10	melcochar 10	morar 10	obrar 10	ortografiar 26
machucar 7	mellar 10	morder 38	obscurecer 42	osar 10
macizar 19	memorar 10	mordisquear 10	obsequiar 10	oscilar 10
madrugar 35	memorizar 19	morir 37	observar 10	oscurecer 42
madurar 10	mencionar 10	mortificar 7	obsesionar 10	osificar 7
magnetizar 19	mendigar 35	mostrar 17	obstaculizar 19	ostentar 10
magnificar 7	menear 10	motivar 10	obstar 10	otorgar 35
magullar 10	menguar 6	motorizar 19	obstinarse 10	ovalar 10
majar 10	menospreciar 10	mover 38	obstruir 15	oxidar 10
malcriar 26	menstruar 1	movilizar 19	obtemperar 10	oxigenar 10
malentender 44	mensualizar 19	mudar 10	obtener 60	
malgastar 10	mentar 11	mugir 22	obturar 10	pacer 42
maliciar 10	mentir 57	multar 10	obviar 10	pacificar 7
mallugar 35	mercantilizar 19	multicopiar 10	ocasionar 10	pactar 10
malograr 10	mercerizar 19	multiplicar 7	occidentalizar 19	padecer 42
maltratar 10	merecer 42	municipalizar 19	ocluir 15	paganizar 19
mamar 10	merendar 11	murmurar 10	ocultar 10	pagar 35
manar 10	mermar 10	musitar 10	ocupar 10	paginar 10
manchar 10	merodear 10	mutilar 10	ocurrir 67	palear 10
mandar 10	mestizar 19		odiar 10	palidecer 42
manejar 10	metaforizar 19	nacer 42	ofender 4	palmear 10
manifestar 11	metalizar 19	nacionalizar 19	oficializar 19	palpar 10
maniobrar 10	metamorfosear ... 10	nadar 10	oficiar 10	palpitar 10
manipular 10	meter 4	narrar 10	ofrecer 42	parafrasear 10
manosear 10	metodizar 19	nasalizar 19	ofuscar 7	paralelar 10
mantener 60	mexicanizar 19	naturalizar 19	oír 40	paralizar 19
manufacturar 10	mezclar 10	naufragar 35	ojear 10	parapetar 10
maquinar 10	militar 10	nausear 10	oler 41	parar 10
maravillar 10	militarizar 19	navegar 35	olfatear 10	parcelar 10
marcar 7	mimar 10	necesitar 10	olvidar 10	parchear 10
marchar 10	mimeografiar 26	negar 39	omitir 67	parcializar 19
marchitar 10	minar 10	negociar 10	ondear 10	parear 10
marear 10	mineralizar 19	neutralizar 19	ondular 10	parecer 42
marginar 10	miniaturizar 19	nevar 11	opacar 7	parir 67
martillear 10	minimizar 19	neviscar 7	opalizar 19	parodiar 10
martirizar 19	mirar 10	nidificar 7	operar 10	parpadear 10
mascar 7	mistificar 7	nivelar 10	opinar 10	parquear 10
masculinizar 19	mitigar 35	noctambular 10	oponer 46	parrafear 10
mascullar 10	mitotear 10	nombrar 10	oprimir 67	parrandear 10
masticar 7	mochar 10	nominar 10	optar 10	partear 10
matar 10	modelar 10	noquear 10	optimar 10	participar 10
materializar 19	moderar 10	normalizar 19	optimizar 19	particularizar 19
matizar 19	modernizar 19	normar 10	orar 10	partir 67
matraquear 10	modificar 7	notar 10	ordenar 10	pasar 10
matricular 10	mofar 10	notificar 7	ordeñar 10	pasear 10
maximizar 19	mojar 10	nublar 10	organizar 19	pasmar 10
mecanizar 19	moldear 10	numerar 10	orientalizar 19	pastar 10
mecanografiar .. 26	moler 38	nutrir 67	orientar 10	pasteurizar 19

pastorear 10	persistir 67	posar 10	prevaricar 7	publicar 7
patalear 10	personalizar 19	poseer 18	prevenir 65	pudrir 48
patear 10	personificar 7	posesionar 10	prever 66	pujar 10
patentar 10	persuadir 67	posibilitar 10	privar 10	pulsar 10
patentizar 19	pervertir 57	posponer 46	privilegiar 10	pulular 10
patinar 10	pesar 10	postergar 35	probar 17	pulverizar 19
patrocinar 10	pescar 7	postrar 10	proceder 4	puntualizar 19
patrullar 10	pespuntar 10	postular 10	procesar 10	puntuar 1
pausar 10	pespuntear 10	potenciar 10	proclamar 10	punzar 19
pautar 10	pestañear 10	practicar 7	procrastinar 10	purgar 35
pavonear 10	petardear 10	precaver 4	procrear 10	purificar 7
payasear 10	petrificar 7	preceder 4	procurar 10	
pealar 10	piafar 10	preciar 10	prodigar 35	quebrajar 10
pecar 7	pialar 10	precipitar 10	producir 16	quebrantar 10
pedalear 10	piar 26	precisar 10	profanar 10	quebrar 11
pedir 43	picanear 10	preconcebir 43	proferir 57	quedar 10
pedorrear 10	picar 7	preconizar 19	profesar 10	quejar 10
pegar 35	picardear 10	predefinir 67	profesionalizar 19	quejumbrar 10
peinar 10	picotear 10	predeterminar 10	profetizar 19	quemar 10
pelar 10	pigmentar 10	predicar 7	profundar 10	querer 49
pelear 10	pincelar 10	predisponer 46	profundizar 19	quimerizar 19
peligrar 10	pinchar 10	predominar 10	programar 10	quintuplicar 7
pellizcar 7	pintar 10	preestablecer 42	progresar 10	quitar 10
pelotear 10	piropear 10	preexistir 67	prohibir 47	
penalizar 19	pisar 10	prefabricar 7	proletarizar 19	rabiar 10
penar 10	pisotear 10	preferir 57	proliferar 10	raciocinar 10
pender 4	pitar 10	prefigurar 10	prologar 35	racionalizar 19
penetrar 10	pizcar 7	prefijar 10	prolongar 35	racionar 10
penitenciar 10	plagar 35	pregonar 10	promediar 10	radicalizar 19
pensar 11	plagiar 10	preguntar 10	prometer 4	radicar 7
pensionar 10	planchar 10	premeditar 10	promover 38	radiodifundir 67
percatar 10	planear 10	premiar 10	promulgar 35	radiografiar 26
perchonar 10	planificar 7	prender 4	pronosticar 7	radiotelegrafiar 26
percibir 67	plantar 10	prensar 10	pronunciar 10	rajar 10
percudir 67	plantear 10	preñar 10	propagar 35	rallar 10
percutir 67	plantificar 7	preocupar 10	propasar 10	ramificar 7
perder 44	plasmar 10	preparar 10	propiciar 10	ranciar 10
perdonar 10	plastificar 7	preponer 46	proponer 46	rapar 10
perdurar 10	platicar 7	presagiar 10	proporcionar 10	raptar 10
perecer 42	plisar 10	prescindir 67	propulsar 10	rarificar 7
peregrinar 10	pluralizar 19	prescribir 67	prorrogar 35	rasar 10
perfeccionar 10	poblar 17	presenciar 10	prorrumpir 67	rascar 7
perfilar 10	podar 10	presentar 10	proscribir 67	rasgar 35
perforar 10	poder 45	presentir 57	proseguir 56	rasguear 10
perfumar 10	podrir 48	preservar 10	prosificar 7	rasguñar 10
perjudicar 7	poetizar 19	presidiar 10	prosperar 10	raspar 10
permanecer 42	polarizar 19	presidir 67	prosternarse 10	rastrear 10
permitir 67	polemizar 19	presionar 10	prostituir 15	rastrillar 10
permutar 10	politizar 19	prestar 10	protagonizar 19	rasurar 10
pernoctar 10	ponderar 10	presumir 67	proteger 13	ratificar 7
perorar 10	poner 46	presuponer 46	protestar 10	rayar 10
perpetrar 10	pontificar 7	presupuestar 10	proveer 18	razonar 10
perpetuar 1	popularizar 19	pretender 4	provenir 65	reabrir 67
perseguir 56	pordiosear 10	pretextar 10	provocar 7	reabsorber 4
perseverar 10	porfiar 26	prevalecer 42	proyectar 10	reaccionar 10
persignar 10	portar 10	prevaler 63		

reactivar 10	reconsiderar 10	refunfuñar 10	remitir 67	reseñar 10
readmitir 67	reconstituir 15	refutar 10	remojar 10	reservar 10
reafirmar 10	reconstruir 15	regalar 10	remolcar 7	resfriar 26
reagrupar 10	reconvenir 65	regañar 10	remontar 10	resguardar 10
reajustar 10	recopilar 10	regar 39	remorder 38	residir 67
realizar 19	recordar 17	regatear 10	remover 38	resignar 10
realzar 19	recorrer 4	regenerar 10	remplazar 19	resistir 67
reanimar 10	recoser 4	regentar 10	rempujar 10	resollar 17
reanudar 10	recostar 17	regimentar 11	remunerar 10	resolver 69
reaparecer 42	recrear 10	regionalizar 19	renacer 42	resonar 17
reapretar 11	recriminar 10	regir 50	rendir 43	resoplar 10
reasegurar 10	rectificar 7	registrar 10	renegar 39	resorber 4
reasumir 67	recubrir 67	reglamentar 10	renovar 17	respaldar 10
reavivar 10	recuperar 10	regocijar 10	renquear 10	respetar 10
rebajar 10	recurrir 67	regresar 10	rentabilizar 19	respingar 35
rebanar 10	recusar 10	regular 10	rentar 10	respirar 10
rebasar 10	redactar 10	regularizar 19	renunciar 10	resplandecer 42
rebautizar 19	redimir 67	regurgitar 10	reñir 61	responder 4
rebelarse 10	redituar 1	rehabilitar 10	reordenar 10	responsabilizar 19
rebosar 10	redoblar 10	rehacer 32	reorganizar 19	resquebrajar 10
rebotar 10	redoblegar 35	rehogar 35	repagar 35	restablecer 42
rebozar 19	redolar 10	rehuir 15	reparar 10	restar 10
rebuscar 7	redondear 10	rehumedecer 42	repasar 10	restaurar 10
rebuznar 10	reducir 16	reimprimir 67	repatriar 26	restituir 15
recaer 9	redundar 10	reinar 10	repeinar 10	restregar 39
recalcitrar 10	reduplicar 7	reincidir 67	repensar 11	restringir 22
recalentar 11	reedificar 7	reincorporar 10	repercutir 67	resucitar 10
recapacitar 10	reeditar 10	reingresar 10	repetir 43	resultar 10
recapitular 10	reeducar 7	reinscribir 67	repicar 7	resumir 67
recargar 35	reelegir 50	reinstalar 10	replegar 39	resurgir 22
recatar 10	reembarcar 7	reintegrar 10	repletar 10	retar 10
recaudar 10	reembolsar 10	reír 51	replicar 7	retardar 10
recavar 10	reemplazar 19	reiterar 10	repoblar 17	retener 60
recetar 10	reemprender 4	reivindicar 7	repodar 10	retirar 10
rechazar 19	reengendrar 10	rejonear 10	reponer 46	retocar 7
rechinar 10	reensayar 10	rejuntar 10	reportar 10	retoñar 10
recibir 67	reestructurar 10	rejuvenecer 42	reposar 10	retorcer 12
reciclar 10	reexaminar 10	relacionar 10	reprender 4	retozar 19
reciprocar 7	reexpedir 43	relajar 10	representar 10	retraer 62
recitar 10	refaccionar 10	relamer 4	reprimir 67	retransmitir 67
reclamar 10	referir 57	relampaguear 10	reprobar 17	retrasar 10
reclinar 10	refilar 10	relatar 10	reprochar 10	retratar 10
reclutar 10	refinar 10	releer 18	reproducir 16	retribuir 15
recobrar 10	refirmar 10	relegar 35	reptar 10	retroceder 4
recodar 10	reflejar 10	relinchar 10	repudiar 10	retumbar 10
recoger 13	reflexionar 10	relingar 35	repugnar 10	reunificar 7
recolectar 10	reflorecer 42	rellenar 10	repulsar 10	reunir 52
recomendar 11	reforestar 10	relucir 36	requebrar 11	revalidar 10
recomenzar 14	reformar 10	remachar 10	requerir 57	revalorizar 19
recompensar 10	reforzar 30	remar 10	resaltar 10	revaluar 1
recomponer 46	refregar 39	rematar 10	resbalar 10	revelar 10
reconcentrar 10	refreír 51	rembolsar 10	rescatar 10	revenir 65
reconciliar 10	refrenar 10	remedar 10	rescindir 67	reventar 11
reconfirmar 10	refrescar 7	remediar 10	rescribir 67	reverberar 10
reconocer 42	refrigerar 10	rememorar 10	resecar 7	reverdecer 42
reconquistar 10	refugiar 10	remendar 11	resentirse 57	reverenciar 10

revestir 43	saltear 10	sincopar 10	soslayar 10	tachar 10
revindicar 7	saludar 10	sincronizar 19	sospechar 10	taconear............. 10
revisar................ 10	salvar 10	sindicar................ 7	sostener 60	tajar 10
revistar 10	sanar 10	singularizar.......... 19	suavizar 19	taladrar 10
revitalizar 19	sancionar 10	sintetizar 19	subdividir 67	talar 10
revivificar 7	sancochar 10	sintonizar 19	subentender 44	tallar 10
revivir 67	sangrar................ 10	sisear 10	subestimar 10	tambalear 10
revocar 7	santificar.............. 7	sistematizar 19	subir 67	tamizar 19
revolcar 68	santiguar.............. 6	situar 1	sublevar 10	tantear 10
revolotear 10	saquear 10	sobar 10	sublimar 10	tapar 10
revolucionar 10	satirizar 19	sobornar 10	subordinar 10	tapizar 19
revolver 69	satisfacer 32	sobrar 10	subrayar 10	tararear 10
rezar 19	saturar 10	sobrealimentar 10	subrogar 35	tardar................. 10
rezongar 35	sazonar 10	sobrealzar 19	subscribir 67	tarifar................. 10
rezumar 10	secar 7	sobrecargar 35	subsistir 67	tartamudear......... 10
ridiculizar 19	secuestrar 10	sobrecoger........... 13	substanciar 10	tatuar 1
rifar 10	seducir 16	sobrepasar 10	substantivar 10	tejer 4
rilar 10	segar 39	sobreponer 46	substituir 15	telefonear 10
rimar 10	segmentar 10	sobresalir 55	substraer 62	telegrafiar........... 26
rivalizar 19	segregar 35	sobresaltar 10	subtitular 10	televisar 10
rizar 19	seguetear 10	sobrestimar 10	subvencionar 10	temblar 11
robar 10	seguir 56	sobrevenir 65	subyugar 35	temer 4
robustecer 42	segundar 10	sobrevivir 67	suceder 4	templar 10
rociar 26	seleccionar.......... 10	sobrevolar............ 17	sucumbir 67	tender 44
rodar 17	sellar 10	socializar 19	sudar 10	tener 60
rodear 10	sembrar 11	socorrer 4	sufrir 67	tentar 11
rogar 53	sementar 11	sofisticar 7	sugerir 57	teñir 61
romper 4	sensibilizar 19	sofocar 7	sugestionar 10	teorizar 19
roncar 7	sentar 11	sofreír 51	suicidarse............. 10	terminar 10
rondar 10	sentenciar 10	soldar 17	sujetar 10	testificar 7
ronquear............. 10	sentir 57	solear 10	sumar 10	tintinear 10
ronronear 10	señalar 10	solemnizar 19	sumergir 22	tipificar 7
rotar 10	señalizar 19	soler 59	suministrar 10	tiranizar 19
rotular 10	separar 10	solicitar 10	superar 10	tirar 10
roturar 10	septuplicar 7	solidarizar 19	superponer 46	tiritar 10
rozar 19	sepultar 10	solidificar 7	supervisar 10	tironear 10
ruborizar 19	ser 58	sollozar 19	supervivir 67	tirotear 10
rubricar 7	serenar 10	soltar 17	suplantar 10	titubear 10
rugir 22	sermonear 10	solucionar 10	suplicar 7	titular 10
rusticar 7	serpentear........... 10	sombrear 10	suplir 67	tiznar 10
	serrar 11	someter 4	suponer 46	tocar 7
saber 54	serruchar 10	sonar 17	suprimir 67	tolerar 10
saborear 10	serviciar 10	sondar 10	supurar 10	tomar 10
sabotear 10	servir 43	sondear 10	surcar 7	tonsurar 10
sacar 7	sesear 10	sonetizar 19	surgir 22	topar 10
saciar 10	sesgar 35	sonorizar 19	suscitar 10	torcer 12
sacrificar 7	sestear 10	sonreír 51	suscribir 67	torear 10
sacudir 67	significar 7	sonrojar 10	suspender 4	tormentar 10
salar 10	silabear 10	sonsacar 7	suspirar 10	tornar 10
salariar 10	silbar 10	soñar 17	sustanciar 10	tornear................ 10
saldar 10	silenciar 10	sopesar 10	sustantivar 10	torpedear 10
salir 55	silogizar 19	sopetear 10	sustentar 10	torear 4
salivar 10	simbolizar 19	soplar 10	sustituir 15	tostar 17
salpicar 7	simpatizar 19	sorber 4	sustraer 62	totalizar 19
salpimentar 11	simplificar 7	sorprender............. 4	susurrar 10	trabajar 10
saltar 10	simular 10	sosegar 39	suturar 10	trabar 10

traducir 16	trastear 10	unir 67	ver 66	voltear 10
traer 62	trastornar 10	universalizar 19	veranear 10	volver 69
traficar 7	tratar 10	untar 10	verdecer 42	vomitar 10
tragar 35	traumatizar 19	urbanizar 19	verificar 7	vosear 10
traicionar 10	trazar 19	urgir 22	versificar 7	votar 10
trajinar 10	trenzar 19	usar 10	verter 44	vulcanizar 19
tramar 10	trepar 10	usurpar 10	vestir 43	vulgarizar 19
tramitar 10	trepidar 10	utilizar 19	vetar 10	
trancar 7	triar 26		viajar 10	xerocopiar 10
tranquilizar 19	trillar 10	vaciar 26	vibrar 10	
transcender 44	trinar 10	vacilar 10	viciar 10	yacer 70
transcribir 67	trincar 7	vacunar 10	victimar 10	yuxtaponer 46
transcurrir 67	trinchar 10	vagabundear 10	vigilar 10	
transferir 57	triplicar 7	vagar 35	vigorizar 19	zabordar 10
transformar 10	triturar 10	vaguear 10	vincular 10	zafar 10
transitar 10	triunfar 10	valer 63	vindicar 7	zaherir. 57
translucirse 36	trocar 68	validar 10	violar 10	zahoriar 10
transmitir 67	trompetear 10	valorar 10	violentar 10	zalear 10
transparentarse ... 10	tronar 17	valorizar 19	virar 10	zambullir 71
transpirar 10	tropezar 14	valuar 1	virilizar 19	zampar 10
transplantar 10	trotar 10	vanagloriarse 10	visar 10	zanjar 10
traquetear 10	tumbar 10	vaporizar 19	visitar 10	zorrear 10
trascender 44	turbar 10	variar 26	vislumbrar 10	zangolotear 10
trascribir 67	tutear 10	vaticinar 10	visualizar 19	zapatear 10
trascurrir 67		vedar 10	vitalizar 19	zarandear 10
trasladar 10	ubicar 7	vegetar 10	vivaquear 10	zarpar 10
traslucir 36	ufanarse 10	velar 10	vivificar 7	zigzaguear 10
traslumbrar 10	ulcerar 10	vencer 64	vivir 67	zonificar 7
trasmitir 67	ultrajar 10	vendar 10	vocalizar 19	zozobrar 10
trasnochar 10	ulular 10	vender 4	vocear 10	zumbar 10
traspasar 10	uncir 28	vendimiar 10	vociferar 10	zurcir 28
traspirar 10	undular 10	venerar 10	volar 17	zurrar 10
trasplantar 10	unificar 7	vengar 35	volatilizar 19	
trasponer 46	uniformar 10	venir 65	volatizar 19	
trasquilar 10	uniformizar 19	ventilar 10	volcar 68	

INDEX

NOTE: Page numbers followed by "t" indicate the presence of tables. Cited Spanish terms are in bold font, cited English terms are in italics.

A

a, letter of the alphabet, 314
a
  a caballo, 104, 119, 235; **a casa**, 17, 112, 198, 223, 283; **a causa de**, 104, 118, 285; **a clase**, 32, 106, 225, 283; **a eso de**, 104, 118, 120, 364; **a fin de (que)**, 216–217, 217; **a fin de cuentas**, 145, 311, 314; **a fondo**, 104, 118, 119; **a fuerza de**, 104, 118, 120; **a gusto**, 132; **a la casa**, 137, 373; **a la vez**, 14, 104, 118, 119, 304; **a lo mejor**, 105, 118, 119, 141; **a los x años**, 31, 103, 363; **a mano**, 105; **a medias**, 132; **a menudo**, 84, 105, 113, 119, 132; **a mi lado**, 283; **a misa**, 32; **a no ser que**, 216; **a ojo**, 105; **a personal**, 26–27, 50, 51, 77, 91, 103t, 105; a personal in examples, 7, 22, 26–27, 43, 55, 57, 60, 62, 69, 71, 77, 91, 103t, 105, 179, 182, 186, 190, 208, 212, 214, 225, 242, 255, 292, 294; **a pesar de**, 12, 105, 118, 120, 143, 216, 218; **a pie**, 105, 119; **a por**, 100; **a su vez**, 142; **a tiempo**, 105, 116, 119, 210, 212, 225, 274, 282, 304; **a veces**, 105, 119, 283, 304, 356; **a ver**, pronunciation, 330; 103t; expressions with, 94, 104–106, 283; following verbs, 252
-a, 23, 36
a.m., 364
abajo, 133–135, 137, 190
  ¡Abajo...!, 135
abarrotería, 308
abogado / a, 95, 287
abrazar, 55
abrir, 57, 126, 167, 168, 169, 170, 171, 174, 187, 197, 216, 270
abroad, 22
aburrido / a, 79, 239, 264
aburrir(se), 193, 215, 245, 248, 250
abuse vs. **abusar**, 306
acá / allá, 114, 133–134, 289
acabar (de), 87, 109, 179, 186, 266, 280–281, 331
acabarse, 64, 216, 281, 296–297
acaso, 129–130, 141
accents, 65, 315, 347–354
  adjectives into adverbs, 121; adverbs ending in **-mente**, 121, 348; **aguda, palabra**, 347; **aquel** vs. **aquél**, 351; **aun** vs. **aún**, 124, 350; on capital letters, 359; change with plurals, 25, 37; **como** vs. **cómo**, 351–353; **cuando** vs. **cuándo**, 352–353; **cuanto** vs. **cuánto**, 352–353; demonstratives, 351, 359; **de** vs. **dé**, 164, 349; diphthong, 346; direct vs. indirect discourse, 352; **donde** vs. **dónde**, 96, 351–352, 353–354; **el** vs. **él**, 349; errors by association, 323; **esdrújula, palabra**, 347; **ese** vs. **ése**, 351; **eso** vs. **esto** vs. **aquello**, 351; **este** vs. **éste**, 351; exclamatives, 351; hiatus, 345; homonyms, 349; on imperatives, 168; interrogatives, 96–97, 351–353; **llana, palabra**, 347; **mas** vs. **más**, 350; **mi** vs. **mí**, 349; monosyllables, 349–350; with homonyms, 349t; multiple vowels, 345t; plural of vowel names, 314; **porque** vs. **por qué**, 352, 353; and pronouns after infinitives, 65; **que** vs. **qué**, 232, 352–353; **quien** vs. **quién**, 354; rules for written, 348–354; **se** vs. **sé**, 349; **si** vs. **sí**, 349; **sobresdrújula, palabra**, 347; **solo** vs. **sólo**, 350; stressed syllables, 65, 345–346; stressed vowel in pronunciation, 345; syllabification, 344–347; **te** vs. **té**, 349; triphthong, 346; **tu** vs. **tú**, 349; weak and strong vowels, 345–346
accommodate vs. **acomodar**, 306
acentuar, 152
acercarse, 14, 103, 171, 248, 250, 252
acomodar, 306
acompañar, 4, 27, 182, 208, 232, 234
aconsejar, 208, 235
acordarse de, 109, 119, 120, 246, 249, 250, 252
acostarse, 17
acostumbrarse a, 105, 118, 120, 249, 250, 252
active vs. passive voice, 75–76, 270–272
  English-Spanish contrast, 76t; formation, 270t
actor, 23, 24
actriz, 24
actual vs. **actual**, 306
actually vs. **actualmente**, 306
actualmente, 142, 306
actuar, 152
actuar (conjugation), A-3
acuerdo, 307
adelantarse, 248, 250
adelante, 133, 136, 137
adelgazar, 237
además, 143, 144
adentro, 22, 133, 135, 137
adiós, 41, 232
adiosito, 377
adjectival clauses, 6–9, 92, 213–214

adjectives
  + **-mente**, 348; in adverb formation, 121–122, 348; as adverbs, 122; agreement, 36–38; capitalization, 357–359; in comparisons, 43–47; **cuyo**, 96; demonstrative, 34–36; descriptive, 36–38, 38–42; **estar** + adj., 260, 262–268, 274t; exclamative, 85–88, 351; function, 2, 4; *how* + adjective, 84–85; indefinite, 89–91, 99t; interrogative, 351–353; **llegar a ser** + adj., 287; with **lo**, 21; **lo** as replacement, 60; nominalized, 20–22, 28; as noun companion, 22; **parecer** + adj., 204; past participles as --, 175, 238, 270; **ponerse** +adj., 287, 299; position, 38–42
  possessive, 27, 35–36
    long, 35t; short, 35t
  pronunciation, 320; **¡qué!** + adj., 87; **ser** + adj., 211–213, 261, 262–268; Table of adjectives with multiple meanings, 41
admitir, 303
adonde / adónde, 133–134, 192
adquirir (conjugation), A-3
adverbial clauses, 7–8, 8, 9, 12, 29, 215–218, 269
adverbs, 121–149
  adverbial phrases, 6, 32, 89–90, 132t; in comparisons, 43–47; of confirmation, doubt, or negation, 129t; definition, 121; ending in **-mente**, 121–122, 348; exclamative, 351; function, 2, 4; *how* + verb, 83–84; indefinite, 89–90, 89t; interrogative, 351–353; of manner, 126–127, 126t; of place, 133–136, 133t, 269; of quantity, 128–129, 128t; **¡qué!** + adv., 87; and related prepositions, 136–137t; of time, 124–126, 124t, 269; and word order, 122
advertisement vs. **advertencia**, 306
aéreo, 264
afasia, 342
aforismo, 342
afrenta, 318
afrodisíaco, 342
afuera, 54, 133, 135, 137, 265
agarrar, 308
age, 363
agradecer, 102, 119, 120, 151, 306
agreement, subject–verb, 13–18
agrio, 21
aguacate, 266
agua, el, feminine, 28, 41
aguantar, 300
aguda, palabra --, 347
águila, el, feminine, 28
ahí, 133
ahogar, 307

ahora, 32, 55, 82, 124, 126, 127, 130, 134, 199, 256, 265, 300
    (pronunciation), 329
ahorita, 377
ahorrar, 6, 299
ajedrez, 298, 328
al + infinitive, 103, 236
albedrío, 42
alcalde, 309
alcance, 101, 137
alcanzar, 157, 164, 165
al día siguiente, 252, 256
alegrarse de, 109, 118, 120, 205, 206, 245, 249, 250, 252, 267, 285
alegre, 121, 267
alegría, 338, 372
alemán, 37
alfabeto, 314, 314t, 315
al final, 104, 132, 140
alfombra, 307
algo, 3, 55, 88, 118, 122, 128, 207, 223, 235, 236, 248–251, 282, 299, 301, 375
alguien, 3, 75, 88, 103, 118, 214
    (with personal a), 27, 223, 225, 248, 310, 332
algún, 4, 38, 88, 89, 141
alguna parte, 132
alguna vez, 90, 132
algún día, 38, 89–90, 141
algunos / as, 14, 88, 90
allá, 133–134, 277
al lado, 22, 93, 269
allí (ahí), 77, 133–134, 224, 268
alma, agreement, 17, 28, 375
al menos, 104
al mismo tiempo, 14, 304
¿aló?, 130
alphabet, 314t, 315, 378
al principio, 104, 140
alquilar, 45
al rato, 304
alrededor, 137
    (pronunciation), 318, 340; (telling time), 364
altamente, 123
alternativo, 6
alterno, 74
alteza, agreement, 17
alto, 28, 41, 47, 84, 121, 123, 261, 262
alto el fuego, 212
alubia, 376
alzar, 116
amable, 308
ama, el, feminine, 28
amanecer, 15, 24, 106, 184, 291
ambientalista, 273
ambiguo, 308
ambos, 16, 38
amenaza, 288
amontonarse, 14
amor
    agreement, 17; in examples, 15, 25, 29, 144; plural, 25; pronunciation, 341
amorcito, 377
anciano, 27
Andalucía, 322, 375
andaluz, 37
andar, 57, 155, 296
    (as auxiliary), 179, 320, A-3
ángel, masculine, 25

anglicism, 30
anillo, 52
anoche, 27, 108, 124, 126, 181, 188, 189, 204, 223, 229, 235, 256, 299, 305
anochecer, 15
another, 33, 38, 53, 126, 138, 142, 193
answer, 13
anteayer, 124, 126, 377
antelación (con), 209
antemano (de), 238
anterior, 144, 256
antes, 77, 124, 126, 180, 223, 230
    antes de, 193, 216–217, 221–222, 236, 319; antes de que, 215–217, 224; antes que, 91
anticipar, 46
antiguo / a, 41
antipático, 263, 287
antojarse, 124
anuncio, 306
any, anything, anyone, 91t
año(s), 14, 31, 103, 106, 136, 180, 182, 198, 203, 260, 264, 274, 278, 301, 361, 363
Año Nuevo, 359
apagar, 296, 298
    apagarse, 73, 192, 296–297
aparecer(se), 109, 151
apartamento, 376
apenar, 267
apenas, 91, 128, 216, 218
apenas si, 128
apenitas, 377
aplicado, 33
aplicar vs. solicitar, 281–282
apology vs. apología, 306
apóstrofe, 342
apoyar, 300, 311
application vs. aplicación, 306
apply, 281–282, 306
appreciate vs. apreciar, 306
aprender, 31, 105, 235, 293, A-4
apresurarse a, 105
apuntar, 302
apunte, 65
apurarse, 131
aquel, aquella, aquellos, aquellas
    accentuation rules, 379; demonstrative adjective, 34; demonstrative pronoun, 78; in examples, 14, 34, 79, 350
aquello, 79
aquí, 133–134
    in examples, 14, 27, 36, 38, 45, 88, 89, 115, 116, 134, 137, 143, 199, 205, 209, 214, 262, 268, 276
aquí / allí, 133–134
árbol, 96
archivar, 295
archivo, 96
    ardilla, 335
ardilla, 260
arena vs. arena, 306
Argentina, 56
arma, 20, 208
arrancar, 296
arrebatar, 308
arreglar, 341
arrepentirse de, 110, 119, 120, 247, 249, 250, 252
arriba, 133–135, 269
¡Arriba...!, 135

arrive, 13
arroba, 371
arroz, masculine, 23
arrugarse, 73
articles
    definite
        agreement with nouns, 28
        capitalization, 357–359
        and nominalization, 20–22, 28
        with dates, 362; with days of the week, 142; for English possessive, 31, 64, 69, 71–74, 109, 116, 194, 216, 229, 246, 299, 300; with infinitives, 235, 326; with languages, 30, 122
        omission of, 32
            examples, 13, 14, 15, 17, 21, 28, 102, 107, 111, 122, 135, 193, 195, 241, 254, 262, 264, 266, 281, 290, 293, 296, 298, 357, 358, 361–362
        omission with **cien** and **mil**, 361; with ordinal numbers, 366t, 367, 370; with parts of body, 31; with percentages, 371; with possessives, 79–80; with subjects, 235, 262; with superlatives, 46; table, 28; with titles, 30, 290; with **todo(s)**, 14, 62, 69, 74; with years, 361–362
    function, 2, 4, 28–32; with **gustar**-type verbs, 243
    indefinite
        agreement with nouns, 32; omission of, 33; table, 32; usage, 33; used as the number one, 34
        with names of languages, 30; with reflexive verbs, 31; vs. possessives, 31
arveja, 376
asco, 307
asfalto, 342
así, 29, 36, 87, 106, 126–127, 226, 243, 262, 286
así que, 59, 215
asir, 308
asistencia, 284
asistir (a), 106, 284, 306
ask, 59, 102, 118, 140, 208, 209, 282
Asociación de Academias de la Lengua Española, 314; website, 378
aspiration of s, 322
assist vs. asistir, 306
assume vs. asumir, 306
asunto, 56, 236
ataúd, masculine, 23
atender, 284
atento, 284
at, expressions for, 283
atrás, 13, 133, 137
atrasarse, 248, 250
atravesar corriendo, 297
atreverse a, 59, 106, 118, 120, 200, 247, 248, 250
attend, 284; vs. atender, 306
attribute, agreement, 15
atún, 311
audience, 29
aula, el, feminine, 28
aumentar, 29
aumento, 295

aunque, 4, 216, 218
aun vs. aún, 124, 350
    aun cuando, 218
ausencia, 30
autobús, 102, 302, 376
auxiliary, 65, 158, 160, 161, 166, 167, 173, 179, 191–198, 237, 255, 261
    acabar de, deber, ir a, poder, querer, 186–188; **andar, ir, seguir,** 179; **deber, haber de, ir a, tener que, poder, venir,** 198; modal auxiliary, 184, 186–188, 331, 332
avance, 39
ave, el, feminine, 28
avergonzado / a, 118, 308
avergonzar, A-4
avergonzarse de, 110, 118, 120, 205, 226, 245, 248, 250, 252
averiguar, 223, 293, 325, 328, A-4
avisar, 77, 109
aviso, 309
ay, 330
ayer, 9, 20, 22, 27, 52, 58, 65, 66, 92, 93, 106, 110, 124, 126, 144, 181, 182, 223, 256, 262, 290, 292, 304, 328
ayudar, 6, 7, 11, 30, 106, 107, 111, 118, 120, 187, 194, 200, 203, 236, 303, 306
azafate, 376
azúcar, 281, 350
azul, 20, 22, 28, 36, 95, 108, 243, 288, 318, 352

B

b, letter of the alphabet, 314
b, v
    homophones, 319t; spelling, 320t
bachelor vs. **bachiller,** 306
backslash, 371
baile, 307
bajamente, 123
bajar, 297, 302
bajar corriendo, 297
bajo, 123, 135, 137, 267, 301
    guion bajo, 371; **planta baja,** 367; **ve baja,** 319–320
balneario, 311
ban, 74
bandeja, 376
baraja, 216, 242, 298, 325
barba, 18
barco, 207
barra, 371
barrio, 26, 108
Basque, 375
bastante, 122, 128, 204
bastar, 209, 243, 314
basura, 110, 237, 332
be, letter of the alphabet, 314
bean, 376
bebé, 27, 69, 186
beca, 281
because, 8, 29, 60, 66, 104, 115, 118, 143, 144, 195, 200, 215, 236, 263, 285, 352, 353
become, 95, 112, 118, 195, 245, 248–259, 285–287, 299
belga, 37
bendecido, 175
bendito, 175

bestial, 87
biblioteca, 309
bien, 4, 22, 46, 51, 58, 70, 87, 93, 95, 106, 114, 121, 122, 126–127, 141, 144, 232, 264, 268, 302, 317, 320, 351
    caer bien / mal, 22, 51, 61, 63, 95, 106, 241–242; **irle bien / mal a uno,** 232–234; **llevarse bien / mal,** 67, 248; **por tu bien,** 141; **salir bien / mal,** 298; **sentarle bien / mal a uno,** 243; **sentirse bien / mal,** 265
bigote, 108
billion, 360
billón, with **un,** 360
bizcocho, 320
blanquito, 370
bodega, 308
Bolivia, 87
bombero, 192, 224
both, 16
bother, 15
botones, 302
brackets, 319
-bs- to -s-, 320
buen, 37, 42, 108, 114, 232–233, 260, 269, 274, 303, 304
buenaventura, 42
¿bueno?, 130
bueno (adv.), 129, 130
bueno(s) / a(s), 20, 21, 29, 37, 41, 42, 44, 86, 109, 119, 211, 232, 264–265, 268
Buenos Aires, 90
buenos días, 42
bufanda, 36
burlar, 320
burlarse de, 110, 118, 249
bus, 376
buscar, 118
    conjugation, 157, A-5; in examples, 26, 53, 77, 102, 103, 179, 224
but, 287–288
buzo, 376

C

c, letter of the alphabet, 314
c, k, qu, s, 321
caber, 155, 159, 161, 163, 166, 320, A-5
cada, 342
    cada vez más / menos, 141
caer, 137, 153, 157, 240, 246, 336, A-5
    caer bien / mal, 22, 51, 52, 61, 63, 95, 106, 241–242, 243; **caerse,** 73, 116, 145, 241, 246, 250, 294; **caérsele a uno,** 64, 68, 73, 190; **dejar caer,** 73
cake, 376
cal, 317
calcetines, 73
call, 11
callado, 55, 265
    vs. **cayado,** 335
callar, 335
callarse, 170, 172, 208, 209, 248, 285
callo vs. **cayo,** 335
calmarse, 286
calor, 86, 128, 138, 260, 265, 267, 274, 293, 300
caminar, 191
    conjugation, A-6; pronunciation, 318

camión, 376
camp, refugee, 14; vs. **campo,** 307
    campamento, 307
campo, 14, 307
Canadá, 358
Canarias, 322, 375
cansado, 17, 139, 197, 236
cansancio, 86, 266
cansarse, 237, 286
cántaro, 109, 304
capital, feminine, 23
capitalization, 357–359
capital letters, accentuation, 359
carácter, 342, 348
cárcel, feminine, 23
card vs. **carta,** 307
cardinal numbers, 360–365, 360t
career vs. **carrera,** 307
Caribbean, 84, 87, 88, 375
cariño, agreement, 17
carne, 16
carpet vs. **carpeta,** 307
carrera, 307
carretera, 224
carta, 307
cartel, 14
casa, 17
    a casa, 17, 112, 198, 223, 283; with **a, de, en,** omit article, 32; **de casa,** 291; **en casa,** 32, 73, 202, 283
casado, 126
casarse (con), 107, 112, 118, 249
casi, 128–129, 364
casi nunca, 141
casi siempre, 141
casita, 377
caso, 106
    en caso de (que), 216–217 223–224; **en todo caso,** 145; **hacer caso,** 212, 309
castigar, 76
catalán, 292
Catalan, 375
Catalonia, 314
Cataluña, 322, 375
catedral, feminine, 23
cazador, 26
ce, letter of the alphabet, 314
ceceo, 322
ceder, 63
célula, 36
celular, 22
Cenicienta, 190
centavo, 33
centímetro, 364
cerca, 66, 133, 134, 137, 377
cero, 317, 342, 360, 362, 364
    de cero, 365; **un cero a la izquierda,** 365
cerrar
    conjugation, 148, A-6; in examples, 21, 73, 93, 108, 168, 169, 170, 171, 172
-ces, 25
cesar (sin), 15
césped, (masculine), 23, 195, 260
ceta, letter of the alphabet, 314
chapa, 376
chaqueta, 376
character vs. **carácter,** 307
charola, 376

Index **I-3**

chaucha, 376
ch, che
  English words with ch, ph, th, 342–343; history as letter of the alphabet, 314
chequera, 100
chévere, 87
chícharo, 376
  chico / a, ve chica, 314
Chile, 90, 93, 223, 225
chiste, 111
chocar, 74, 297
  chocarle a uno, 198
choke vs. **chocar**, 307
chompa, 376
CIA, 359
ciego, 265
cien, 33, 294
científico, 25
ciento, 18, 360, 361
  por ciento, 18, 371
cierto, 15, 33, 41, 204, 211, 213
  por cierto, 132–133
ciervo, 14
cincuentón (-tona), 363
cinta, 105, 317, 322
-ción, 23, 323–324
claro, 6, 123, 213, 268
clase, with a, de, en, omit article, 32
clauses
  adjectival (relative), 3, 7, 13, 93, 96, 98, 188, 213–214, 262; adverbial, 7, 8, 9, 215–218, 269; in comparisons, 45t; dependent (subordinate), 3, 6–12; examples, 8t; independent, 6–7, 8; main, 6, 7; main (principal), 8–12; nominal (noun), 6–9, 203–205; si, 229; types, 8t
cláusula, 6–7
cliente, 309
clima, masculine, 23, 116
cobrar, 140
cocer, A-6
coche, 6, 31, 33, 41, 317
coger, 150, A-7
cognado, 315
cognate, 272
  false cognates and false friends, 306–311t
colectivo, 376
collar vs. **collar**, 307
collective nouns, 14
college vs. **colegio**, 307
Colombia, 108
colon, 371
colored vs. **colorado**, 307
come and *go*, 289–290
come close, 14
comenzar, 149, A-7
comenzar a, 106
comer, 148, 154, 155, 159, 161, 162, 165
comida, 14, 45, 100, 112, 216, 217, 240, 242, 266, 301, 305
comillas, 371
comma
  with decimals, 360; punctuation, 371
communication, verbs of, 52, 208, 253, 256
como, 7, 46, 57, 66, 67, 74, 88, 126–127, 142, 143, 144, 215–216, 218, 230, 352–353; como consecuencia, 142; como resultado, 142; como si, 230; vs. cómo, 351–353

cómo, 76, 81, 83–84, 85, 87, 126–127, 298, 300, 305, 351–353, 372
comparisons, 43–47
  of inequality; adverbs, adjectives, nouns, 43t; clause; noun compared, 45t; clause; verb, adjective or adverb compared, 45t
compasión, 311
compasivo, 311
complacer, 306
complejo, 96
componer, 153
compound tenses
  perfect, 191–193; progressive, 194–196, 194t; table, 191
comprar, 31
compra y venta, 15
comprender, 31
comprensivo, 311
compromise vs. **compromiso**, 307
computadora, 376
común, 42
con, 4, 6, 21, 28, 30, 55, 56, 66, 67, 73, 76, 78, 83, 84, 93, 94, 97, 100, 101, 105, 107–120, 122, 140, 142, 144, 169, 195, 198, 208, 209, 212, 237, 238, 257, 267, 274, 281, 286, 294, 298, 314, 352, 354, 372, 373
  con antelación, 209; con facilidad, 30; conmigo, 67, 101, 107, 116, 206, 255, 257, 286, 298; con respecto a, 107, 140; consigo, 67, 70; con tal (de) que, 107, 216, 217; contigo, 67, 108, 206, 240, 255, 269; following reflexive verbs, 120, 252; and indefinite article, 34; table, 107
concesión, 307
concluir, 157, A-7
concluir (present indicative conjugation), 152
condición, feminine, 23
conditional
  formation
    perfect, 161t; present, 160–161, 160t; future of the past, 201; irregular stems, 161t; for probability, 193, 202; probability in the past, 201; usage, 185, 200–201
conducir, 151, A-8
conductor vs. **conductor**, 307
conference vs. **conferencia**, 307
conferencia, 29, 114, 221, 222, 269, 307
confianza, 236
confiar, 152
confront, 248
confundir, 315
conjunctions, 138t
  of coordination, 6, 9, 10–11, 138–139, 379; followed by indicative, 215; followed by subjunctive, 215–218; function, 2, 3, 4; subordinate, 6; of subordination, 8, 139–140, 215–218; table of conjunctions: always subjunctive; occasionally subjunctive, 216; table of conjunctions and the subjunctive (examples), 217–218; usage, 137
conmigo, 67, 101, 107, 116, 206, 255, 257, 286, 298
conocer, 163, 185–186, 292, 292–293
  in examples, 27
conocido, 30, 39
conocimiento, 29

conseguir, 65, 106, 149, 151, 310
consejero / a, 51
consentir en, 112
conservador, 310
consigo, 67, 70
consiguiente (por —), 142
consistir en, 112
consonante, 315
consonants
  role in syllable, 344–345; spelling issues, 318–343
constipated vs. **constipado**, 307
construir, 152
consulta, 307
consultar, 198, 307
contar, 149, A-8
contender, 307
contento, 11, 264, 267, 274
contest vs. **contestar**, 307
contestar, 13, 307
contigo, 67, 108, 112, 206, 240, 255, 269
continuar, 152
contra, 211
  en contra de, 13, 108, 274
contrario a, 96
contrato, 41
contribuir, 152
convencer (conjugation), 151
convenir (en), 17, 112, 118
conversions, 364
convertirse en, 112, 120, 287
convidado, 62
copy vs. **copia**, 307
corazón, agreement, 17
corchetes, 371
corregir, 150, 271
correo, 211
  correo electrónico, 77
correr, 84, 122, 296
correr del tiempo, 28
correspondence, punctuation, 372
correspondencia, pronunciation, 337
cortar, 107, 195
cortés, 188, 308
cortesía, 338
corto / a, 268
  ve corta, 314
cosa, 36, 104, 138, 298
  cosas así, 127, 243; cualquier cosa, 91; tal cosa, 33
costar, 149
costilla, 339
costumbre, feminine, 23
cotidiano, 142
Counting Back
  from the past: hacer, 277t; from the past: llevar, 277t; from the present: hacer, 276t; from the present: llevar, 276t
courtesy, expressions of, 200
creciente, 238
crecimiento, 238
creer, 33, 36, 45, 60, 107, 134, 157, 180, 181, 192, 196, 204, 210, 220, 237, 241, 273, 288, A-8
  creerlo vs. creerle, 62
crew, 96
criar(se), 92, 152, 380
crisis, plural, 25
crucigrama, masculine, 23

cruzar, A-9
cu, letter of the alphabet, 314
cuadrado, 364
cuadro, 51
cual
cual (el / la / lo), cuales (los / las), 92–97, 100; cual (tal —), 350; cuál, 20, 80, 81–82, 83, 110, 127, 282, 304, 362; cuál vs. qué, 304
cualquier, cualquiera, 88, 91, 103
cuán, 84
cuando, 6, 12, 31, 64, 91, 102, 124, 126, 141, 142, 180, 183, 185, 186, 192, 195, 197, 215–216, 218, 223, 226, 239, 245, 269, 280, 291, 295, 299
  aun cuando, 218; de vez en cuando, 109, 119, 304; para cuando, 197
cuándo, 64, 85, 258, 269, 282, 293, 352–354, 363
cuándo vs. cuando, 352–354
cuanto, 122, 128–129, 352–353
  en cuanto (a), 112, 118, 140, 216, 218
cuánto, 54, 81, 84, 85, 87–88, 128, 302, 352–354, 363
cuanto vs. cuánto, 128, 352
cuarto, 43
Cuba, 268
cubetera, 376
cubierto, 174
cubrir, 40
cuello, 307
cuenta (darse cuenta de), 110, 119, 120, 140, 246, 249–252, 286, 300, 310
  cuentas, a fin de cuentas, 145; en resumidas cuentas, 144
cuenta (n.), 62, 178, 303
  tener en cuenta, 274
cuento, 144
cuerda, 297, 310
cuerdo, 311
cuero, 194
cuesta, 317
cuestión, 282, 306, 310
cuidado, 274
cuidar, 196
culpa, 274, 308
culpable, 204, 210
cult vs. **culto**, 307
cumpleaños, 126
cumplir (años), 180, 363
cumplir (con), 6, 223
cup vs. **copa**, 307
cura, el vs. la, 24
cuyo, 3, 6, 92, 93, 96

D

d, letter of the alphabet, 314
-d, 23, 170, 171
Dalí, 39
dama, 368
damas, 299, 328
dance vs. **danza**, 307
dar, 8, 9, 43, 45, 51, 61, 62, 68, 77, 103, 108, 115, 153, 223, 255, 281, 297, 317, 336, 349, A-9
  dar con, 297; darle a alguien (=pegarle), 62; darse cuenta de, 110, 119, 246, 249, 286, 300, 310; dar un paso, 136

dash, 371
date, 362
dato, 142
days of the week
  with article, 32; with *by*, 254; and capitalization, 359; gender, 24; with *on*, 32
de
  de acuerdo, 108, 269, 274; de antemano, 238; de aquí en adelante, 136; de buena / mala gana, 109; de buen / mal humor, 108; de color, 307; de esta manera, 109; and definite articles, 28, 31; de hecho, 142; de huelga, 108, 274; de lo anterior, 144; de lo que, 45–46; del que, de la que, de los que, de las que, 45; de luto, 108; de más en más, 141; de menos en menos, 141; de modo que, 109; de noche, 116; de nuevo, 109; de pie, 109, 261; de regreso, 108; de repente, 106, 109, 119, 181, 291, 292; de rodillas, 108; de todos modos, 145; de vacaciones, 108; de veras, 109; de vez en cuando, 109; de viaje, 108; de visita, 27; de vuelta, 108; expressions with, 109; following reflexive verbs, 252; to indicate origin, possession, 268; with infinitives, 236; with numerical comparisons, 43; table, 108; usage, 108; verbs with, 109–111; vs. dé, 164, 349
de, letter of the alphabet, 314
debajo, 100, 133–135, 137, 269
debajo de, 100
debate, 307
deber, 21, 112, 186, 320
  as modal auxiliary, 112, 198, 200, 235, 237, 331
debido a que, 143
década, 362
deception vs. **decepción**, 307
decimals, 362
decir, 8, 9, 11, 12, 16, 153, 156, 159, 161, 166, 168, 169, 170, 174, A-9
decisión, feminine, 23
declaración, 41
deer, 13
defecto, 308
defender, 149
definite articles, 28t
dejar, 65, 70, 116, 120, 134, 144, 197, 208, 209, 235, 237, 269, 285, 292, 319
  dejar caer, 73; dejar de, 110, 292, 310
delante, 133, 136, 137
  delante de, 100, 137; por delante de, 101
deleite, 307
deletrear, deletreo, 314
deliberación, 307
delight vs. **delito**, 307
demand vs. **demandar**, 307
demás, 22, 70, 140
demasiado, 92, 128, 129
de modo que, 109, 119
demonstrative adjectives, 34–36, 34t, 43, 351
demonstrative pronouns, 78–79, 78t (neutral); 79t, 351
de ningún modo, 89, 90
dentista, 31

dentro, 133, 135, 137
dentro de, 100
departamento, 376
depender de, 110, 118, 289
de pie, 109, 261
deportar, 285
deportivo, 229
depress, 21
depressed, 331
deprimido, 331
deprimir, 21
derecha, 62
derecho (adv.), 123
derechos humanos, 6
desamparado, 307
desarrollo, 74
desastre, 86, 116
descansar, 311
descargarse, 297
desconocido, 190, 284
desde, 4, 143, 145, 183
  desde hace, 198; desde que, 215
desdecir, 153
deshonra, 307
desigual, 308
desnudo, 309
despacho, 269, 309
despedir, 246, 332
despedir vs. despedirse, 246, 289
despedirse (de), 110, 119, 216, 236, 246, 250
desperdiciar, 301, 370
despertar(se), 69, 75, 184, 246, 250, 282
después, 59, 124, 126, 190
  después de, 33, 187, 216, 218, 237; después de que, 216, 218; después de todo, 145
despuesito, 377
destitute vs. **destituido**, 307
destruir, 152
detalladamente, 122
detenerse a, 106
de todos modos, 145
detrás, 133, 136, 137
  detrás de, 101, 137
devolver, 52, 149, 174
Diccionario panhispánico de dudas, website, 378
dicho, 12, 174, 186, 212, 221, 222, 224, 237, 331, 351
diente, 31
diéresis, 325
diferente, 41, 136, 308
¿diga?, 130
diminutives, 377
dinero, 6, 38, 43, 85, 102, 106, 107, 204, 267, 282, 287, 299, 301, 309
diphthong, 57, 346
Direct Object Pronouns, 57
director, 307
dirigir, 327, A-10
  dirigir la palabra, 372
  dirigirse, 103, 250, 373
discernir, A-10
disculpa, 306
disculpar, 209, 372
disculparse, 122
discussion vs. **discusión**, 307
disgrace vs. **desgracia**, 308
disgust vs. **disgusto**, 308

dismiss, 289
disparate vs. **disparate**, 308
distinct vs. **distinto**, 308
distinguir, 15, A-10
distinto, 123, 308
distribuir, 152, 336
divertido, 7, 8, 213, 239
divertirse, 56, 132, 232, 233, 245, 248, 250, 304
doble uve, letter of the alphabet, 315, 378
doctor(a), and definite article, 30, 287
dólar, 33, 115
dolerle a uno, 67, 76, 243
dolor, 115, 238, 309
domingo, 195, 358; masculine, 24; capitalization, 358–359; with article, 32; **los domingos**, 358; **Santo Domingo**, 37
don, and definite article, 30
donde, 92, 96, 133, 134, 262, 269, 352, 353, 365; vs. **adonde**, 133–134
dónde, 58, 81, 83, 88, 89, 96, 133–134, 137, 201, 258, 278, 290, 293, 301, 352, 353, 372; **de dónde**, 83, 88
doña, and definite article, 30
dormir(se), conjugation, 149, 156, 162, 166, 173, A-11; in examples, 57, 108, 126, 137, 179, 245, 246, 268, 276
  mal dormir, 42
dos, 12, 14, 33, 103, 104, 106, 115, 180, 181, 183, 194, 213, 216, 242, 244, 276, 278, 301, 360–365, 367, 369–371
  los/las dos (both), 183, 304, 351
dos puntos, 371
dot com, 371
double consonants, 343
drama, masculine, 23
dream, 17, 38, 274, 300
droga, 15
dulce, 21
duda, 33, 342
Diccionario de dudas, 357, 378
dudar, 129, 197, 209–210, 221–228, 253, 254, 327, pronunciation 342
duro, 62, 123, 341, 342

E

e, letter of the alphabet, 314
e, conjunction, 138, 143
E, 357
-e, 36
-es, 25, 38
echar, 330, 332
  echar de menos, 332; **echar la culpa**, 332
Ecuador, 87
education vs. **educación**, 308
efe, letter of the alphabet, 314
effective vs. **efectivo**, 308
eficaz, 308
either/or, 16
ejemplar, 77, 307
ejemplo, 33
  por ejemplo, 141
ejercer, 151
ejote, 376
el, 3, 20, 349
  accent, 349; **Alfonso el Sabio**, 357; article in Spanish omitted in English, 15, 17, 28, 102, 107, 111, 122, 135, 193, 195, 234, 241, 254, 262, 265, 281, 290, 293, 296, 298; capitalization, 358–359; with dates, 362; **el 2015**, 362; **el Cinco de Mayo**, 359; **el cual**, 92–94, 97; **el de**, 80; **el lunes / martes / etc.**, 111, 254; **el Mal**, 357; **el mío / tuyo / etc.**, 3, 20, 35, 46, 79–80, 82; **El País**, 358; **el que**, 3, 6, 13, 20, 92–95, 188; **El Salvador**, 358; **el uno al otro**, 70; for English possessive, 31, 69, 73, 74, 109, 116, 194, 216, 229, 246, 299, 300, 323; with feminine nouns, 28; with infinitives, 331; with languages, 122; with ordinal numbers, 366–368; with parts of body, 31; with percentages, 371; with subjects, 235, 262; with superlatives, 46; with titles, 30, 290; **todo el**, 195, 246, 269; with years, 362
ele, letter of the alphabet, 314
elefante, 342
elegir, 150
elle, 314
ellipsis, 371
embarrassed vs. **embarazada**, 308
eme, letter of the alphabet, 314
eminencia, agreement, 17
emoción, 308
emocionado, 261, 267, 308
empate, 109
empeñarse en, 112
empezar (a), 106, 149
empleado / a, 41, 77, 223, 289, 300
empobrecerse, 286
empresa, 289, 308
en
  for at, 283; **en alguna parte**, 89, 132; **en cambio**, 112; **en casa**, 32, 73, 202, 283; **en caso (de) (que)**, 216–217, 223–224; **en conclusión**, 144; **en contra de**, 13; **en cuanto (a)**, 112, 140; **en esa época**, 304; **en ese / este momento**, 283, 304; **en fin**, 132; **en frente de**, 112, 137; **en gran parte**, 141; **en lo tocante a**, 140; **en primer lugar**, 141; **en punto**, 364; **en realidad**, 142, 306; **en resumen**, 132, 144; **en resumidas cuentas**, 144; **en seguida**, 112, 118; **en segundo lugar**, 141; **en todo caso**, 145; **en vez de**, 112, 304; expressions with, 112; followed by name of language, 30; following reflexive verbs, 252; table, 111; usage, 111; verbs with, 112–113
enamorado, 110, 118, 245
enamorarse de, 110, 118, 245, 248, 268
encantarle a uno, 21, 51, 52, 108, 204, 206, 224, 235, 241, 243
encararse (con), 248
encender, 149
encima, 133–135, 137
encima de, 101
encontrar, 21, 62, 66, 75, 89, 102, 149, 190, 205, 222, 294, 331
encontrarse (con), 107, 112, 120, 186, 239, 244, 249, 290, 294, 298, 358
end of line word division, 373–374
ene, letter of the alphabet, 314
énfasis, 315
enfermarse, 286

enfermo, 30
enfrente, 133, 136, 137
enfrente de, 101, 137
enfurecerse, 286
engaño, 307
engordar, 237
enloquecerse, 286
enojarse con, 107, 286
enough, 128, 129, 131, 204, 209, 243, 273, 287
enredo, 318
enriquecerse, 286
enseñanza, 113, 308
enseñar, 31
  enseñar a, 106
ensuciarse, 73
entender, 31, 149
enterarse (de), 110, 293
entonces, 54, 124, 126, 142, 193, 256
entrar en, 113
entre, 14, 66, 304
entristecerse, 286
enviar, 51, 152, A-11
eñe, letter of the alphabet, 314
epithet, agreement, 17
equipaje, 74, 302
equis, letter of the alphabet, 314
equivocal vs. **equivocado**, 308
ere, letter of the alphabet, 314
errar, A-11
erre, 314
escaleras, 14, 297
  escaleras abajo, 190
escoger, 150, 298, 327
escribir, 34
escrito, 174
escrupuloso, 308
escurrir, 297
esdrújula, palabra --, 347
ese, 314
  accentuation rules, 351; demonstrative pronoun, 78–79; **ese, esa, esos, esas**, demonstrative adjective, 34; in examples, 20, 21, 27, 46, 100
esforzarse por, 117
esfuerzo, 187, 237
esmerarse, 289
eso, 3, 21, 62, 74, 76, 79, 83, 91, 96, 97, 101, 104, 105, 186, 200, 204, 210, 235, 236, 257, 262, 286
  a eso de, 104, 118, 120, 364; **eso, esto, aquello**, accentuation rules, 351; **eso sí que no**, 131; **por eso**, 116, 142, 285
espantarse, 14
español, 9, 13
  (language) masculine, 23, 30, 37, 235
esparcir, A-12
especializarse en, 113
esperar, 46, 55
  (no preposition), 102, 120, 197, 205, 304, 319, 362
espléndido, 335
esplendor, 335
espliego, 335
esquina, 102, 108, 273
estadio, 306
Estados Unidos, 358
estadounidense, 306

esta mañana, 17, 29, 34
estar, 153, 155, A-12
   with adjectives, 262–268; **caliente**, 16; **cansado**, 17; **claro**, 6; **contento**, 11; **enamorado de**, 110; **enfermo**, 30; expressions with, 268, 274t; to indicate place, 268–269; **limpio**, 35; with past participle (resultant condition), 261, 270; with prepositions, 261; in progressive tenses, 179, 191, 194–197, 194t, 261, 269; **prohibido**, 15; vs. **haber**, 273; in weather descriptions, 260
estar vs. ser. *see* ser vs. estar
este (*east*), 357
este, esta, estos, estas
   accentuation rules, 351; demonstrative adjective, 351; demonstrative pronoun, 78–79; in examples, 21, 29, 43, 100, 260
estreñido, 307
estudiante, 31
eterno, 29
evitar, 22, 116, 320
ex-, 335
examen, plural, 25
excavar, 335
excelencia, agreement, 17
excéntrico, 335
excepcional, 310
excepto, 66, 288
excited vs. **excitado / a**, 308
excitement vs. **excitación**, 308
exclamación, signo de, 371
exclamar, 333, 335
exclamatives, 85–88, 85t, 351
exculpar, 335
exigir, 150, 208, 307
exiliado, 14
existe, 318
exit and *success*, 289–290
exit vs. **éxito**, 308
éxito, 289, 308
explicación, 122
explicar, 30, 64, 238, 292
explosión, 14, 86
explotar, 333, 335
expresión, 309, 335
expressions
   with estar, 274t; leave-taking, 232–234t; with prepositions, 118–120; probability, 202t; with tener, 274t
exprimir, 335
extra-, 335
extracurricular, 335
extramuros, 335
extranjero, 22, 114
extrañar, 62
extraño, 211, 223, 225
extraterrestre, 335
extravagante, 39

F

f, letter of the alphabet, 314
fabric vs. **fábrica**, 308
fábrica, 42, 308
facilidad, 30
facultad, 308
faculty vs. **facultad**, 308
false cognates, 306–311
faltar, 30

faltarle a uno, 61, 194, 240, 241, 242
fantasma, 23, 342
farmacia, 108, 337, 342
fastidious vs. **fastidioso / a**, 308
fault vs. **falta**, 308
favor, 317
felicitar, 126, 285
feliz, 15, 267
fenómeno, 342
fidelidad, 42
fijarse en, 113, 119, 246
fijo (idea fija), 42
Filadelfia, 342
fin, 308
   a fin de (que), 216–217; a fin de cuentas, 145, 311; al fin, 297; en fin, 132; fin de semana, 232, 298; por fin, 116, 132–133
final, 36
fingir, 150, 310
fire (verb), 289
firm vs. **firma**, 308
flamenco, 375
florero, 311
folleto, 295
a fondo, 104, 118, 119
fondo, 140
fonética, 342
football vs. **fútbol**, 308
foreign, 22
foreigner, 22
formación, 308
formal vs. informal, 16
forzar, A-12
foto, feminine, 23, 45, 317, 342
fotogénico, 326
fotografía, 338
fractions, 369t
francés, 25, 37
frase, 6, 309
freído vs. frito, 175
frente a, 66, 101, 136, 245
freshman, 368
frijol, 376
frío, 9, 29
frito vs. freído, 175
fritura, 122
frontera, 208, 295
fuego, 73, 192
   alto el fuego, 212
fuente, 74
fuera, 133, 135, 137, 206
fuera de, 101, 137
función, 300
funcionar, 268, 296
funcionario, 41
fundamental, 311
fútbol, 298, 308
future, 159t
   ir a + infinitive for, 199; irregular stems, 159t; for present conditional, 201; present for, 199; ways of expressing, 199
future perfect, 160t, 192, 290–292
future progressive, 195, 201

G

g, letter of the alphabet, 314
g, gu, gü, j, 324–326

g o j (spelling), 326t
gala, 317
Galician, 375
gana, 109, 119
ganar, 21, 28, 62, 106, 125, 140, 145, 206, 231, 235
ganas, 274
gang vs. **ganga**, 308
gastar, 87, 301
gaveta, 137, 269
ge, letter of the alphabet, 314
general (por lo), 116, 118, 140
genial, 265
gente
   collective noun, 14; in examples, 15, 29, 30; *people*, 309
   pronunciation, 317
gerente, 287, 290, 291
gerund, 173–174, 237
gesto, 139, 326
get, 65, 83, 100, 106, 112, 115, 197, 205, 245, 246, 285–287, 289, 293; *get ahead*, 248, 250; *get along*, 67, 248; *get angry*, 118, 222, 286; *get better*, 287; *get bored*, 245, 248, 250; *get dirty*, 72; *get divorced*, 248; *get down*, 246, 248, 250; *get fat*, 237; *get hurt*, 141; *get in touch*, 140, 144; *get involved*, 108; *get lost*, 249; *get married*, 118, 141, 249, 250; *get near*, 248, 250; *get off*, 248, 250; *get old*, 286; *get on (to)*, 249; *get out*, 187; *get rich*, 286; *get rid of*, 249, 250; *get sick*, 249, 286; *get tired*, 286; *get together*, 186; *get up*, 15, 69, 78, 125, 170, 172, 249, 297; *get used to*, 113, 249, 250; *get well*, 232–233, 249, 250; *get wet*, 246, 249; *get worse*, 249
Ginebra, 317
girasol, 264
gitano / a, 325
globo, 317
glossaries
   chapter, 9, 315t; sentence structure, 8
goal vs. **gol**, 308
go and *leave*, 290–292
goleador, 295
good-bye (to say), 289
go out (people vs. machines), 296
gotear, 297
grab vs. **grabar**, 308
grabar, 308
gracias, 38, 88, 302
   gracias a, 285
gracious vs. **gracioso**, 308
grade vs. **grado**, 308
graduar, 152
gran, 14
gran vs. grande, 37, 41
grande, 309
granizar, 15
granizo, 260
grocery vs. **grosería**, 308
grosero, 310
guagua, 376
guante, 61
guapo, 17
guardar, 299
Guatemala, 261
guay, 87
guerra, 46, 111, 141, 192, 193, 318, 325, 358, 367

Primera Guerra Mundial, 358, 367;
Segunda Guerra Mundial, 111, 367
guía, el vs. la, 24, 292
guiar, 152
guide, 292
guillemets, 371
guion, 371
guisante, 376
gustar, 8, 15, 16, 20, 28, 29, 35, 38, 46, 51, 52, 55, 61, 67, 83, 87, 90, 95, 98, 105, 106, 111, 116, 180, 204, 206, 224, 235, 239–240, 243, 298, 305, 324
gustar-type verbs
    articles with, 243; followed by subjunctive, 206; formation, 235, 239–240; meaning changes, 241–242; with subject and direct object only, 51
gusto, 324
    a gusto, 132

H

h, letter of the alphabet, 314
h
    homophones, 330t; pronunciation, 329; spelling, 329t; syllabification, 347; in word division, 374
haber, 330–331
    conjugation, 153, 155, 159, A-13; **de** + infinitive, 198; impersonal use of, 273; as modal auxiliary, 198; negative, omit indefinite article, 33; pronunciation, 330; usage, impersonal, 14
habichuela, 376
habilidad, 41
habitable, 309
habitante, 18
habit, negative of, 185
hablar, 30, 148, 154, 155, 159, 161, 162, 165
hacer, 153, 159
    conjugation, A-13; **ejercicio,** 297; in examples, + inf, 7
    in examples, 9
        in time expressions, 14
    hacer daño, 141, 243; **hacer falta,** 63, 240–241; **hacer frío,** 7; **hacer ruido,** 22; **hacer una pregunta,** 282; table: counting back from the past: **hacer,** 277; table: counting back from the present: **hacer,** 276; in weather descriptions, 260
    hacer caso (no), 309
hacerle falta a uno, 63, 240–241, 242
hacerse, 287
hacha, el, feminine, 28
hache, letter of the alphabet, 314
hacia, 364
halla, haya, 331
hallazgo, 285
hambre, el, feminine, 28
    in examples, 32, 86, 126, 131, 143, 260, 267, 274
happy, 15, 205, 264, 267, 274, 285
harina, 29
harto, 264
has, haz, 331–332
hasta, 32, 55, 59, 132, 183, 216, 218
    hasta el + day, 32; **hasta luego,** 232; **hasta que,** 216, 218, 297
hay, 14, 21, 260, 273, 330
    hay que, 236

he allí / aquí, 268
hecho (n.), 332
hecho (v.), 10, 174, 223, 225, 256, 267, 330
    de hecho, 142; **hecho a mano,** 105
hecho, echo, pronunciation, 332
herida (n.), 281
herido (n.), 88
herido / a (adj.), 350
heritage learners, 318, 354, 374
hermoso, 39
hiato, 345
hielo, 262
hierbabuena, 42
hijo, 30
hispano, 329
hispanoamericano, 374
hombre, 24
home, 17, 112, 198, 223, 283
homophones
    with b / v, 319t; with h, 330t
hondo, 123
honest vs. **honesto,** 308
honrado, 17, 308
hora, 31, 73, 104, 115, 116, 184, 197, 235, 243, 245, 246, 275, 276–278, 291, 300, 303, 317, 364, 370
    hora de, 204, 301, 303; **media hora,** 370; pronunciation, 317; ¿Qué hora es?, 262, 282, 303
hot, 16
how
    in examples, 21, 54, 76, 84, 85, 86, 87, 127, 132, 284, 298, 300, 302, 351; in exclamations, 86–88, 263, 264, 351; *how?* + adjective or adverb, 84t; *how to,* 105, 293; in questions, 83–84, 126
however, 112, 116, 118, 143, 144
hoy, 17, 32, 124, 126
hoy en día, 142
huelga, 104, 181
    de huelga, 108, 274
huésped, 23, 289, 290, 303
huevo, 76, 85, 216, 329
huir, 152
huracán, 22
hurt, 67, 141, 243
hyphen, 371

I

i, letter of the alphabet, 314
i griega, 314
-ía, 337t
-ía, 160, 338t
identificar, 106, 314
idiom vs. **idioma,** 309
idioma, masculine, 23, 112, 182
-iendo, 173–174
ignore vs. **ignorar,** 309
igual, 123
-illa, 339t
imperative
    direct commands, 167–172; indirect commands, 172; **tú** irregular forms, 168t; **usted(es)** forms, 169–170t
imperfect
    indicative, formation, 185–188; indirect discourse with, 184–185; irregular stems, 166t; and present parallelism, 184t; subjunctive, formation,

165–166; vs. preterite, 179–188, 179t, 181t
impersonal
    expressions, 209, 211–213; reflexive, 78; verbs, agreement, 14
implicación, 300
implicar, 74
importar, 138, 209, 243
importar(le a uno), 243, 298
impreso, 175
imprimido, 175
impuesto, 226
incluir, 152
incomodo, 128
increíble, 21, 204, 243
indefinite article, omission, 33
indefinites, 88–91
    tables
        indefinite adjectives, 89; indefinite adverbials, 89; indefinite articles, 32; indefinite pronouns, 88
indicative
    adverbial clauses, 215; after impersonal expressions with **ser,** 211
    formation
        imperfect, 154; perfect tenses, 158t, 160; pluperfect, 158t; present, 148–154, 155–157; preterite, 155–157; simple future, 159
    usage
        equivalence with English present, present progressive, 179; past tenses, 179–183; present with **probablemente,** 202–203; projected actions / indirect discourse, 184–185; for *would,* 185
indicio, 74
indígena, 21
indirect discourse, 252–258
    compared to direct discourse, 252t; connectives with, 257t; definition, 252; demonstratives and, 257; with imperfect, 184–185; no verb-tense changes, 254–255; person changes, 255; time changes, 255–256; verbs of communication in, 257; verb-tense changes, 253–254, 255t; word order, 258
indirect object pronouns, 60t
infinidad, 13
infinitives
    after expressions of emotion, 205; after expressions of volition, 207; after expressions of volition and influence, 207; after que, 236; in commands, advertising, questions, signs, 237; **deber** +, 186; as direct object, 235–236; following object pronoun and verb, 232–234, 235; formation, 173; as nouns, 20, 24, 235; with passive meaning, 237; perfect, 237; as subject, 17, 235; verbs of influence followed by, 209
infinitves, as subjects, 235
influir en, 113
informe, 54
ingeniosidad, 308
ingenuity vs. **ingenuidad,** 308
inglés, 31, 37
ingrediente, 318
inhabitable vs. **inhabitable,** 309

inscribir, 310
insistir en, 113
interés, 90, 238
interesado, 140
interesar, 9
interesarle a uno, 243, 267
interesarse por / en, 117, 118, 243, 248
interrogación, signo de, 371
interrogatives, 81–85, 81t
   direct vs. indirect discourse, 351–353; qué vs. cuál, 81–82; translation of "how?", 83–84; vs. noninterrogatives, 352t
intransitive, 123, 291
intransitive vs. transitive, 52–53
introduce vs. **introducir**, 309
introducir, 151, 309
invernadero, 222
invitado, 33
invitar a, 106, 208
ir a
   a + infinitive, 106, 184, 187, 198, 199; conjugation, A-13; **ir,** + present participle, 198; **irle bien / mal a uno,** 232–234; **irse (de),** 110, 291; as modal auxiliary, 186, 198, 199, 331; signifying come, 290; signifying toward, 291
iraní, 37
iraquí, 37
irse (de), 8, 21
ir y venir, 15
israelí, 37, 318
-ista, 36
-ivo, 320
-ívoro, 320
Ixtapa, 335
ixtle, 335

J

j, letter of the alphabet, 314
j, g, gu, gü, pronunciation, 324
jabón, 21, 311
jamás, 89, 91, 124, 325
   nunca jamás, 124
Japón, 244
japonés / -esa, 94
Jerez, 348
jersey, 376
jinete, 317
jota, letter of the alphabet, 314
judía, 376
juego, 298
   capitalization, 359
jueves
   with article, 32; masculine, 24
jugada, 298
jugar, 50, 150, 298, A-14
junior, 368
junto(s) / a(s), 12, 15, 55, 59, 186, 187
just, 281

K

k, letter of the alphabet, 314
k, c, qu, s, 321
k sound, 321
ka, letter of the alphabet, 314
karaoke, 317
karate, 321

kilo, 33, 321, 365, 370
kilómetro, 364, 365
know, 292–293
Kremlin, 340
kurdo, 76, 321

L

l, letter of the alphabet, 314
-l, 23
la (see el) -l
   a la vez, 118; la mayor parte, 14; la mitad, 14; la una a la otra, 70
labor vs. **labor,** 309
lado, al --, 22
ladrillo, 268
ladrón, 224
lamentar, 11
languages, and definite article, 30–31
lápiz
   masculine, 23; plural, 25
large vs. **largo,** 309
largo, 46
lástima, 212
lastimar, 243
Latin America, dialect, 16, 56, 58, 80, 87, 115, 189, 316, 322, 375, 377
lavarse, 31
lavo, 317
learn, 293
leave, 8, 21, 32, 85, 111, 115, 120, 204, 208, 211, 216, 218, 223, 225, 246, 249, 290–292, 303
leave-taking, expressions of, 232–234t
lecture vs. **lectura,** 309
leer, 7, 9, 31, 157
le, ind. obj., 8
leísmo, 58, 322
leísta, 58
lejos, 133, 137
león, 26
let, 73, 116, 120, 144, 172, 197, 208, 235, 292
letter vs. **letra,** 309
letters
   alphabet, 314t; Sound Representation of, 317–318t
levantar, 31
levantarse, 53
ley, plural, 25
libanés, 37
libertad, feminine, 23
library vs. **librería,** 309
libre, 42
like that / this, 29, 87, 106, 126–127, 243, 262, 286
like, to (verb), 29
limosnero, 265
limpio, 35, 123
linking between words, 354–356
listo, 46, 60, 265
litro, 41
ll
   history as letter of the alphabet, 314; the sound, 376
llamar, 11, 12, 22
llana, palabra --, 347
llave (key), 61, 69, 80, 102, 258, 299, 302, 317, 349
llaves (brackets), 371

llegar, 11, 12, 14, 22, 28, 30, 50, 52, 157, 289, A-14
llegar a ser, 287
lleno, 40
llevar, 22, 302
   Table: counting back from the past: **llevar,** 277; Table: counting back from the present: **llevar,** 276
llevarse, 302
llevarse bien / mal, 67, 248
llorar, 27
llover, 15, 109, 116, 149, 178, 194, 195, 204, 210, 220, 221, 229, 230, 243, 260
   llover a cántaros, 109
lloviznar, 15
lo, 17, 21, 22, 60, 80
   a lo mejor, 105, 141; lo cual, 95; lo de, 238; lo demás, 140; lo mismo, 195; lo que, 15, 92, 93, 95, 96, 214, 305; nominalization with, 21; por lo general, 116, 140; por lo menos, 116; por lo que se refiere a, 140; por lo tanto, 142
loco, 262
   Juana la Loca, 357
locura, 15
lograr, 106, 135, 203, 235
lo mismo, 195
long possessives, 35
look (n.), 36
look (v.), 17, 53, 60, 109, 134, 137, 330, 351
   look at / for, 26, 53, 65, 87, 102, 103, 118, 179, 190, 220, 224, 245, 263, 297; *look like,* 244, 249
los, (see el)
   los de al lado, 22; los demás, 22, 70; los vs. os, 58t
love (n.), 15, 17, 25, 29, 144
love (v.)
   fall in love, 110, 118, 245, 248, 268 *someone,* 57, 126, 210, 242; *something,* 21, 51, 108, 206, 235, 241, 243
lucha, 142
lucir, A-14
luego, 1, 124, 126
lugar, 36, 41
lujo, 309
lunes, 111
   with article, 32; capitalization, 359; masculine, 24; **para el lunes,** 254; plural, 25
luxury vs. **lujuria,** 309
luz, feminine, 23, 73, 96, 296, 298
   luz del día, 96

M

m, letter of the alphabet, 314
Madrid, 291
   (pronunciation), 341
madrugada, 364
maduro, 222, 266
maíz, masculine, 23
majestad, agreement, 17
mal, 37, 42, 87, 126, 260
   caer mal, 22, 51, 52, 61, 67, 95, 106, 241–242; de mal humor, 108; el Mal, 357; mal dormir, 42; mal vs. malo, 37
maldecido, 175
maldecir, 153

maldito, 175
maleducado, 310
malhumor, 42
malo, 21, 37, 44, 211
malparto, 42
maltratar, 306
mandar, 61, 64, 115, 209, 237
   manera, de esa / esta manera, 220
manera, de esa / esta manera, 109
manifestante, 14, 319
manifestar, 14
mano, 31, 34, 35, 69, 73, 265, 365
   alzar o levantar la mano, 31; a mano, 105; ¡Arriba las manos!, 135; equipaje de mano, 74; hecho a mano, 105
mano de obra, 309
mano, feminine, 23
mantener, 300, 311
manzana, 39, 41, 61, 89, 222, 264
mañana, 17, 29, 124, 126, 364
mapa, masculine, 23
marcado, 308
marchar, 246
marcharse, 246, 249, 290
mark vs. **marca**, 309
marroquí, 37
martes
   with article, 32; capitalization, 359; hásta el martes, 32; martes trece, 365; masculine, 24
más, 55, 73, 79, 80, 83, 86, 104, 135, 143, 144, 198, 212, 229, 300, 350
   cada vez más, 141; de más en más, 141; más de, 43–45, 273, 363; más del que / de la que / de lo que, 45–46; más grande, 47, 79; más pequeño, 47; más que, 44, 80, 91, 286; más tarde, 223; más vale, 107, 209, 365; nada más, 80; por más que, 116, 185
mas vs. más, 350
mass vs. **masa**, 309
matar, 26, 317
materia, 138, 309
material vs. **material**, 309
matiz, masculine, 23
matter, 282
máximo, 295
mayor, 14, 44, 47, 363, 373
mayor parte, 14
   los mayores, 21
mayor vs. **mayor**, 309
me, 61, 67
mecer, 151
medianoche, 364
médico, 34, 106, 294
medio / a, 33, 41, 128, 262, 363, 369, 370
   a medias, 132; media hora, 370; medios, 209
mediodía, 364
Mediterráneo, 20
meet, 294
mejor, 17, 20, 44, 88, 91, 144, 211, 265, 299, 377
   a lo mejor, 105, 141; lo mejor, 21, 117, 327
mejora, 362
mejorarse, 217, 233, 249, 287
menor, 44, 47, 363
menos, 66, 67, 106, 128, 288, 363
   al menos, 104, 118; a menos que, 216–217, 223, 225; cada vez menos, 141; de menos en menos, 141; echar de menos, 332; menos de / que, 43, 91; por lo menos, 116, 118
mensaje, 51
-mente, 121–122, 348
mentir, 13, 149
mentira, 15, 33, 74, 221, 222, 224
menudo (a —), 84, 105, 113, 119, 132
merecer, 151
merienda, 61
mes, 183
mesa, 311
mesero, 272, 302, 303
meta, 308
meter, 299
meterse con, 108
metro, 364
mexicanismo, 335
mexicano, 33, 335
México, 38, 84, 87, 95, 130, 142, 183, 264, 318, 335, 376
mezquita, 31, 273
mi, 35, 349
mí, 66, 349
mi vs. mí
   with homonyms, 349t; monosyllables, 349–350
miedo, 200, 205, 274
miel, feminine, 23
mientras, 124, 126, 190, 216, 218, 275, 373
miércoles, masculine, 24
   capitalization, 359; with ser, 32
mil, 33, 273, 360, 361–362, 364, 365
   de mil maravillas, 365
milla, 104, 182, 339, 365
millón, with un and de, 361
mínimo, 74
minusvalía, 212
minusválido, 304
mío, mía, míos, mías, 35
   el mío, 20; los míos, 28; vida mía, 17
mirada, 36, 341
mirar, 53, 58, 65, 87, 109, 134, 137, 218, 220, 237, 245, 330, 351
misa, with a, de, en, omit article, 32, 309
mismo, a mí / ti / sí mismo / a, 71
mitad, 14, 43, 369, 370
mochila, 80, 101, 111
modal auxiliaries, 198
   in conditional, 200; courtesy, expressions of with conditional, 200; in past, 186–188
modelo, 24
modismo, 308
modo, de algún modo, 89, 90
molest vs. **molestar**, 309
molestar, 15, 96, 110
   molestarle a uno, 206, 220
money vs. **moneda**, 309
montar a caballo, 235
monte, 40
moral, 23, 123
moreno, 21
morir, 149, 186, 202, A-15
mostrar, 149
moto, feminine, 23
motor, 136
move, 142, 145, 195, 246, 250, 251
move away from, 250
mover, 149, A-15

much, 38, 112
   as much, 46, 128–129, 352–353; *however much*, 116, 118; *how much*, 81, 85, 87, 128, 185, 351, 352–353; *so much*, 38, 87, 115, 126, 128–129, 236, 265, 285; *too much*, 128–129
muchacho, 317
muchas gracias, 38
muchedumbre, 13
mucho, 8, 9, 15, 20, 55, 62, 112, 113, 122–123, 128–129, 204, 242, 267, 268, 301, 304
mucho(s) / a(s), 38, 45, 55, 76, 96, 122–123, 181, 187, 200, 242, 277, 284, 301
muda (u), 325
mudarse, 142, 145, 195, 246, 249, 251
mudo, 265
Muerte, 26, 269, 357
muerto, 174, 266
mujer, 24, 27
multitud, 13
mundial, 111, 358
Museo del Prado, 39, 40
must, 195, 197, 198, 200, 202, 236, 237, 331, 373
musulmán, 37, 107, 273
muy, 4, 9, 17, 29, 30, 33, 60, 70, 85, 114, 121, 122, 128, 129, 132, 137, 142, 203, 205, 242, 263, 265, 266, 284, 303

N

n, letter of the alphabet, 314
N, 357
nacer, 268
nada, 3, 55, 56, 70, 80, 90, 90–91, 128–129, 137, 185, 208, 224, 237, 292, 302, 328
   nada más, 80; nada que, 236
nadar, 198
nadie, 27, 57, 90, 90–91, 100, 103, 116, 141, 145, 198, 208, 214, 223, 224, 226, 286, 377
nariz, 39
NE, 357
necesitar, 12, 33, 38
negar, 149, 210, A-15
negarse a, 106
negatives, 88–91
negrito, 377
neither/nor, 16
nevar, 15, 46
ni, 16, 365
   ni... ni, 16, 21, 138; ni un, 33
nieve, 40, 54
ninguno, 90
   agreement, 18; in examples, 18
niño / a, 51, 317
nivel, 121
no, 11, 129, 130
   no estar para bromas, 114; no... hasta, 132; no... ninguno, 18; no obstante, 143; no ser para tanto, 114
NO, 357
noche, 46, 104, 116, 130, 197, 201, 256, 269, 276, 290, 303, 305, 317, 364, 368
   de la noche, 364; de noche, 116, 130; día y noche, 104; esta noche, 201, 269, 290, 303, 305; la noche anterior, 256; Noche de Reyes, 368; toda la noche, 197

nominal clauses, 203–213
nominalization of words and phrases, 20–22
noreste, 357
norm, linguistic, 377
noroeste, 357
norte, 357
nota, 308
note reference, 373
notice vs. **noticia**, 309
noticia, 21, 30, 50, 110, 286
notificar, 77
noun companions, 22
nouns
    and article agreement, 28; collective, 14; definition, 20; and equivalents, 20–22; function, 2, 3; gender, 23–35; nominalization of words and phrases, 20–22; number, 25; with prepositions, 100
novio / a, 107, 241
nublado, 15, 260
nude vs. **nudo**, 309
nuestro / a, nuestros / as, 35
    el nuestro, 46
Nueva Revista, 358
nuevo, 41, 287
    Año Nuevo, 359; **de nuevo**, 109, 118
Nuevo México, 335
number of nouns (singular, plural), 25
numbers
    cardinal, 360–365, 360t; fractions, 369t, 370–371; ordinal, 366–368, 366t
number vs. **nombre**, 309
número, 309
    as collective noun, 14; in examples, 13; singular vs. plural, 25
nunca, 27, 33, 44, 90–91, 124, 126, 373
ñ, 314, 317

O

o, letter of the alphabet, 314
o, conjunction, 10, 11
o…o, agreement, 16
o vs. **u**, 138
O, 357
-o, 23, 36, 155, 158, 160, 161, 164, 166, 167, 366
Oaxaca, 334
obedecer, 151
objetivo, 308
obra, 299
obrero, 42
obscuro vs. **oscuro**, 320
obstante (no), 143
obtener, 310
ocurrir, 224, 362
ocurrirse, 73
odiar, 68, 206
oeste, 357
office vs. **oficio**, 309
ofrecer, 151
oír
    conjugation, 154, 157, A-16; in examples, 50, 65, 217, 235, 331
ojalá, 77, 203, 230–231
ojo, 21
oler, 150, A-16
olvidar, 28, 73
    olvidarse (de), 110, 118, 246; **olvidársele a uno**, 64, 68, 73

ombligo, 39
ómnibus, 376
on, with days of the week, 32
one, in nominalization, 21, 22
oponerse (a), 207, 249
oración, 7, 311
ordenador, 376
orden, el vs. **la**, 295
ordinal numbers, 366–368, 366t
ortografía, 2010 rules, 378–380
os, 57, 58, 60, 63, 69, 171, 233–234
os vs. **los**, 58t
oscuro, 46, 320
oso, 317
otro, 33, 38, 54, 70, 80, 126, 134, 135, 138, 142, 193, 238
ought, 186

P

p, letter of the alphabet, 314
p.m., 364
padre, 87
padres, 51, 309
pagar, 62, 107, 113, 157, 172, 178, 200, 207, 209, 211, 226, 292, 303
pain vs. **pena**, 309
País Vasco, 322, 375
pakistaní, 37
pálido, 263, 287
pan, 318
pandilla, 108, 308, 339
panorama, masculine, 23
pantalones, 73
papa, 376
papa, el vs. **la**, 24
papel, 238
paper vs. **papel**, 309
para, 22, 32, 114t
    para con, 101; **para que**, 12, 215–217; **para resumir**, 144; **para siempre**, 114
paracaídas, 200
paraguas, 70, 72, 116, 229, 268
Paraguay, 56
parar, 187, 297
    sin parar, 197
pararse, 373
parecer, 204
    conjugation, 151, 163, A-16; in examples, 15, 60, 140, 187, 204, 235, 244, 323
parecerse, 244, 249
pared, 211
pareja, 13
paréntesis, 371
parentheses, 371
parents, 51
parents vs. **parientes**, 309
parientes, 309
párrafo, 367
parte, 66, 367, 370–371
    en alguna parte, 89, 132; **en gran parte**, 141; **en ninguna parte**, 89; with fractions, 369; **la mayor parte de**, 14; **por otra parte**, 116, 119; **por su parte**, 142
participle
    with **estar**, 270
    formation
        irregular past participles, 174t; past, 174–175; present (gerund), 173–174

past for expressing postures, 239; in perfect tenses, 192; present as adverb, 237; present as gerund, 237; present in idiomatic expressions, 239; present in weather descriptions, 260; in progressive tenses, 179, 191, 194–197, 194t, 196t; with **ser**, 270
particular, 308
partida, 291, 299
partido, 109, 299
partir, 291
pasar, 301
    pasarlo / la bien, 232–233; **pasar un buen fin de semana**, 232–233
paso, 310
passive voice, 75–76, 270–272
    English-Spanish contrast, 76t; formation, 270t
pastel, 376
past perfect (pluperfect) indicative, 158t, 192
past progressive, 195
patata, 376
patinar, 105
patrocinador, 236, 310
patrón, 140
patron vs. **patrón**, 309
pausadamente, 122
paz, 106, 203
pe, letter of the alphabet, 314
pea, 376
pedido, 282
pedir, 61, 102, 118, 140, 149, 156, 208, 209, 215, 257, 282, A-17
    + thing, 102
pegajoso, 94
pegar, 62, 123
película, 45, 50
peligro, 77, 116, 286
pelo, 317
peluquería, 192
pena, 212, 267, 310
Peninsular Spanish, 375–377
pensar, 149
    + **de**, 110, 295; + **en**, 113, 295; + infinitive, 102, 295; subjunctive with, 204
people, 22, 30
people vs. machines, 296–298
people vs. **pueblo**, 309
peor, 44
    el peor, 94
pequeño, 39, 47
percentages, 371
    agreement of verb, 18
perder, 97, 148, 286, 331, A-17
    perderse, 72, 249
pérdida, 21
perdido / a, 294, 350
perdonar, 30
perfect progressive tenses, 196t
perfect tenses, 192–193, 192t
periferia, 342
period, 371
periódico, 96
permanecer, 151
permitir, 208, 235, 282, 331
pero, 10, 11, 138, 143, 144, 287, 318
perro, 318
perseguir, 65
persona, 25, 238, 300
personaje, 96, 140, 307

personal **a**, 26–27, 50–51, 77, 103t
persuadir, 208
peruano, 261
pesadilla, 339
pésame, 311
pesar, 33, 80, 364
    a pesar de, 12, 105, 118, 120, 143, 216, 218
peso, 44, 61, 294, 361, 370
pez, 23, 322
ph, English words with **ch**, **ph**, **th**, 342
phrase, 7
phrase vs. *frase*, 309
pianista, 24
piano, 206, 298
picante, 180
Pichichi, 235
pico (y —), 363
pie
    a pie, 105, 119; **de pie**, 109
    pie (measurement), 364, 365
piel, feminine, 23
Pirineos, masculine, 23
piso, 376
pistola, 224
placa, 376
place, 268–269
placer, 307
planchado, 261
planeta, masculine, 23
planta baja, 367
platillo, 76
play, 298–299
pluma, 34
pluperfect indicative, 158t, 189–190
pluperfect subjunctive, 167t, 193, 198
pobre, 41, 42, 143
poco, 12, 38, 60, 122, 128, 129, 142, 236
    poco a poco, 179, 198, 286; **por poco**, 116, 118, 132–133
poder, 7, 11, 12, 24, 33, 45, 66, 74, 91, 96, 104, 130, 144, 149, 155, 159, 187, 198, 199, 204, 210, 211, 218, 237, 256, 284, 285, 295, 300, 323, 330, 331, 373, A-17
    puede ser, 210
poder (n.), 24, 63
podrir, A-18
poema, 23, 235
poeta, masculine, 23
point of view, 190, 255
policía, 24, 197, 338
policy vs. *policía*, 310
política, 310
politician vs. **política**, 310
político, 310
poner, 101, 134, 135, 137, 153, 155, 159, 163, 168, 169, 170, 171, 299, A-18
    poner en marcha, 296; **poner la mesa**, 280, 299; **ponerse**, 73, 109, 168, 172, 248, 249, 287, 299, 305, 348; **ponerse a**, 106, 118, 248
póquer, 298
por
    a por, 100; expressions with, 116; following reflexive verbs, 252; with infinitives, 285; with nouns, 285; **por ciento**, 18, 371; **por cierto**, 132–133; **por consiguiente**, 142; **por delante de**, 101; **por desgracia**, 141; **por ejemplo**, 141; **por encima de**, 101; **por esa razón**, 142; **por ese motivo**, 142; **por eso**, 116, 118,

120, 142, 285; **por favor**, 34; **por fin**, 116, 132, 133; **por lo general**, 116, 140; **por lo menos**, 116, 118; **por lo que se refiere a**, 140; **por lo tanto**, 142; **por más que**, 116, 185; **por otra parte**, 116; **por otro lado**, 142; **por poco**, 116, 132, 133; **por qué**, 30, 59, 74, 81, 85, 96, 144, 193, 195, 197, 237, 265, 352–353; **por suerte**, 141; **por su parte**, 142; **por supuesto**, 116; **por tu bien**, 141; with pronouns, 285; **tomar por**, 117; usage, 115t
porcentaje, 371
poroto, 376
porque, 7, 9, 29, 60, 104, 115, 143, 144, 195, 215, 263, 284, 285, 352–353
por qué, 30, 59, 74, 81, 85, 96, 144, 193, 196, 197, 237, 265, 352, 353
por qué / cómo / cuánto, 352t
position of descriptive adjectives, 38–42
possessives
    adjectives, 35–36; long, 35t; pronouns, 79–80; short, 35t; vs. articles, 31
postre, 67, 295
potato, 376
precavido, 365
precepto, 375
precio, 140, 283, 370
preferir, 81, 96, 105, 137, 149, 207, 223, 327
prefix, 320, 335
pregnant, 308
pregunta, 118, 282, 310
preguntar, 59, 93, 257, 282
preguntar (por), 117, 118
preguntarse, 258, 282
premiar, 77
premiere, 368
prendido, 175
preocuparse (por), 30, 117, 119, 138, 245, 250, 372
preparar, 55, 76, 194, 198, 209, 216, 217, 238, 241, 295
prepositions
    with **billón** and **millón**, 361; capitalization in surnames, 357; in combinations, 100; expressions with, 118–120t; following reflexive verbs, 252; function, 4, 22, 100; with infinitives, 100; with nouns, 100; object of, 31; and related adverbs, 137–138t; with relative pronouns, 94; as sentence component, 3; with **sonar**, 315; usage, 103
present
    conditional, 160t; and imperfect parallelism, 184t
    indicative
        formation, 148–154; usage, 178–179, 202–203
    subjunctive
        formation, 162–165; usage, 203–213
presentación, 122
presentar, 122, 309
present participle, 237–239
present perfect, 5
    indicative, 158, 192, 196, 253;
    subjunctive, 166, 193, 196, 219, 221, 225, 227, 228, 253
present perfect vs. preterite, 189, 331
present vs. **presente**, 310
preservative vs. **preservativo**, 310
presidente, 121

preso (adjective), 175
preso, (noun), 6
prestar atención, 208
presumido, 46
pretend vs. **pretender**, 310
preterite
    irregular stems with **i**, 155t; irregular stems with **u**, 155t; vs. imperfect, 179–188, 179t, 181t; vs. present perfect, 189, 331
prevail, 143
prevent, 208, 235
primaria, 145
primavera, 207
primer
    de primer año, 367; **el primer piso**, 367; **en primer lugar**, 141; in examples, 38; ordinal number, 367; **primer plano**, 368; **primer** vs. **primero**, 367
primera, 366t
    por primera vez, 368; **primera dama**, 368; **primera infancia**, 368; **primera plana**, 368
Primera Guerra Mundial, 358
primerizo, 368
primero, 13, 21, 59, 134, 198, 207, 368–370
    in dates, 367; **el primero en**, 111; **primeros auxilios**, 367
primo / a, 22, 55, 260, 294
    primo hermano, 368
primogénito, 326, 367
principal, 373
príncipe, 190
principio (al —), 104, 140
prisoner, 6, 175, 208
probabilidad, 36
probability, 201–203, 202t
probable, 212
probablemente, 202–203, 373
probar, 149
problema, masculine, 23
    in examples, 41, 46, 73, 83, 86, 142, 238, 268, 297, 331, 349, 361, 373; with **¡Qué!**, omit indefinite article, 33
procure vs. **procurar**, 310
producir, 87, 151, 156
producto, 286
profesión, 307
profesional, 324
profesor / a, and definite article, 30, 31, 39, 114, 122, 241, 269, 349
profesor / a, and indefinite article, 38
profesorado, 308
programa, masculine, 23, 112
progressive tenses, 179, 199
    perfect progressive, 196t; present progressive, 194t
prohibición, 74
prohibido, 15, 237
prohibir, 208, 235, 329, A-18
projected actions, 184–185
prometer, 256
pronouns
    definition, 20
    demonstrative, 78–79, 78t (neutral), 79t, 351
    direct object, 27, 57t; function, 2, 3; with **gustar**-type verbs, 61; indefinite, 88; indirect object, 60–62, 60t; interrogative, 351–353
    personal, 50–67

combining object, 63t; direct object, 50, 57–58; indirect object, 51, 60–62, 60t, 63; object of preposition, 66t, 68; and personal a, 27; position of object pronouns, 65t; reciprocal, 70t; reflexive, 68t; reflexive prepositional, 70t; repetitive object, 62–63; stressed and unstressed object, 58–59; stressed object, 70; subject, 50, 53–55, 53t, 55–55; **usted** and **ustedes**, 53; **voseo, vosotros** and **vos**, 53–54
possessives
   adjectives, 35–36
     long, 35t; short, 35t
   pronouns, 79–80, 79t
     vs. articles, 31
reciprocal, 70t
relative pronouns, 92–98, 92t
   options, 93t
se, 68t; subject, 53–55; usage, 178
pronto, 112, 126, 184, 194, 209, 221–222, 285, 287, 340
   tan pronto como, 6, 7, 215, 216, 218
pronunciation, 314–315, 342, 375–376
pronunciation and spelling
   b / v, 319–320; **c / qu / f / t**, 342; **g / gu / gü / j**, 324–330; **h**, 329–332; **k / c / qu / s**, 321–324; **ll / y / í**, 335–339; **r / rr**, 340–341; **x**, 333–335
proper nouns, 3, 27, 39, 40, 357
proteger, 150
protest, 14
protester, 14, 319
prueba, 32, 237
pruebas, 197
publicar, 193
público, 29, 89, 264, 284, 371
pudrir, A-18
pueblo, 13, 116, 309
puerta, 73, 197, 283
puerto, 376
Puerto Rico, 87, 283, 376
puertorriqueño, 94
pues, 131
puesto (adj.), 174, 194
puesto (n.), 281
puesto que, 143
pulgada, 364, 365
pulóver, 376
punctuation, 371–374, 371t
punto, 371
   dos puntos, 371; **en punto**, 371; **punto com**, 371; **puntos suspensivos**, 371; **punto y coma**, 371
puro, 41
put (on, in, etc.), 299
   in examples, 101, 134, 135, 137, 373; *put arms around*, 55; *put away*, 280, 299; *put in*, 299, 373; *put on (clothes)*, 69, 73, 109, 168–172, 216, 249; *put up with*, 300

Q

q, letter of the alphabet, 314
quantitative adjectives, position, + noun, 304
quantitative adjectives, position, 38
   as conjunction, 139–140, 232; **el que**, 13, 95; in examples, 7–8, 13; as exclamative, 17, 33, 87; infinitives after, 235; as interrogative, 81, 84, 352; **qué, + es**, 305; **que**, after **a / de / en / con**, 94; as relative pronoun, 92–98, 213–214; vs. **qué**, 352–353
que, as conjunction, 139–140
quechua, 122, 321
quedar, 84, 109
   quedarle a uno, 43, 60, 104, 115, 142, 240–241, 242; **quedarse**, 55, 73, 120, 209, 283; **quedarse con**, 108, 120, 249
queja, 300
quejarse (de), 107, 110, 118, 223, 247
quemadura, 375
quemar, 72
   quemarse, 72, 92, 224
queque, 376
querer, 6, 53, 55, 59, 74, 87, 97, 111, 126, 144, 149, 155, 159, 161, 166, 185, 186, 187, 200, 207, 214, 223, 242, 253, 257, 282, 298, 305, 325, 350, A-19
querido, 372
queso, 318
question, 282
question vs. **cuestión**, 310
question mark, 371
questions, 84, 371
qué, vs. **cuál**, 81–82, 304
quien, 92, 95
   with personal **a**, 27
quién, 88
   with personal **a**, 26
quien vs. **quién**, 352t
quiet vs. **quieto**, 310
quince, 180, 360, 363
quincuagésimo, 366t
quingentésimo, 366t
quinientos, 360, 370
quinto, 367, 369, 370
   Carlos V, 367; **el siglo quinto**, 367
quiquiriquí, 7, 321
quitar, 61, 224, 310
   quitarse, 31, 73, 250, 303
quit vs. **quitar**, 310
quizá(s), 129, 141, 203
qu / k / c / s, 321–324
quórum, 379
quotation marks, 371

R

r, letter of the alphabet, 314
r, soft d, 341–342
-r, 23, 170, 171, 340–341
   r, rr, pronunciation, 340–341; spelling, 341t
rabia, 340
race vs. **raza**, 310
radicar, 139
radio, feminine, 23, 238
rama, 96
ranchero, 30
rápidamente, 4, 7, 46, 215
rápido, 55, 78, 84, 87, 100, 109, 123, 303, 318
rare vs. **raro**, 310
raro, 41, 73, 123, 211

rastro, 142
rate vs. **rato**, 310
rato, 310
raya, 371
Real Academia Española, 314
   website, 378
realizar, 300
realize, 110, 119, 140, 246, 249–252, 286, 300, 310
realize vs. **realizar**, 310
real vs. **real**, 310
rebelarse, 249, 319
recado, 61
receipt vs. **receta**, 310
rechazar, 74, 212
recibo, 310
recién casados, 126
reciprocal pronouns, 70t
recomendar, 10
reconocer, 151
Reconquista, 358
record vs. **recordar**, 310
recordar, 149, 310
recuerdo (n.), 207
red vs. **red**, 310
reflexión, 324
reflexionar, 324
reflexive pronouns, 69–71
   reciprocal, 70t; reflexive (stressed), 71t; reflexive (unstressed), 69t; reflexive prepositional, 70t
reflexive verbs, 245–247t
   after expressions of emotion, 205; with characteristic prepositions, 252t; compared to non-reflexive, 245; to indicate change of state, 245–246; obligatory, 247; and reflexive pronouns, 246; Spanish with English equivalent, 248–251
refugee, 14
refugiado, 14, 21
regalar, 35, 52, 61, 64, 95, 139, 213, 215, 288
regalo, 45, 61, 310
regañar, 27
regar, 89
regio, 326
regir, A-19
register, linguistic, 377
register vs. **registrar a alguien**, 310
registrar, 310
regla, 71, 223
regresar, 12, 192, 202, 208, 209, 350
regreso (de), 108, 274
rehén, 43
rehilar, 347
rehundir, 347
reina, 24, 357
reír, 7, 112, 156, 213, A-19
reírse de, 111, 120, 249
reja, 301
relampaguear, 15
relative pronouns, 92–98
   options, 93t; Table, 92
relative vs. **relativo**, 310
reloj, 109, 296, 297
relucir, 144
remoto, 36
Renacimiento, 358
rent vs. **renta**, 310

reparación, 224
repasar, 30
repente (de), 106, 109, 119, 181, 291, 292
reportero, 214, 373
requisito, 284
rescatar, 22
residencia, 27
resignarse a, 106
resolución, 235
resolver, 104, 297, 330
resorte, 310
resort vs. **resorte**, 310
respaldar, 235
respecto (con — a), 107, 119, 140
respetar, 21, 22, 207
respirar, 123
responsable, 16
respuesta, 14, 33, 55, 93, 109, 198
rest vs. **restar**, 310
restaurante, 283, 294, 296
restroom, 372
resuelto, 174
resultado, 267, 332
   como resultado, 142
resultant condition, 260–261, 270
resumen (en), 132, 144
resumidas cuentas (en), 144
resumir, 54, 144
return, 12, 52, 124, 192, 202, 208, 347, 350
reunión, 284
reunir (conjugation), 152, A-20
revelar, 319
Revolución, 358
rey, 24
   Noche de Reyes, 368; **Rey**, 357
rezar, 269, 357
rico, 28, 87, 185, 266
   riquísimo, 79
ritmo, 310
robar, 62, 74, 331, 365
rogar, 209, 235, A-20
rojizo, 326
rojo, 22, 36, 47, 127, 310
romper, 71, 174
romperse, 71, 72, 94
rope vs. **ropa**, 310
roto, 174
rubio, 28
rubí, plural, 25
rude, 200, 310
rude vs. **rudo**, 310
ruido, 22, 206, 217
rumbo, 350
run (across, down, into, out), 297
run (people vs. machines), 296, 297
Rusia, 204
ruso, 31

S

s, pronunciation, 317
s, letter of the alphabet, 314
s sound, 322
s, k, c, qu, spelling, 321
S, 357
-s, 25
   -bs- to -s-, 320; capitalization, 359; plural, 25; sé vs. se, 349

sábado
   with article, 32; **los sábados**, 142; masculine, 24
saber, 11, 14, 18, 20, 60, 85, 97, 99, 104, 105, 107, 109, 112, 125, 144, 155, 185–186, 192, 193, 195, 197, 205, 229, 235, 258, 293, 300, 320, A-20
   conjugation, 154
saberse, 246
sacar, 31, 45, 303
saco, 376
sal, 23, 244, 269
salary vs. **salario**, 310
salida, 62, 290, 291, 308
salir, 7, 12, 33, 50, 290–291
   bien, mal, etc., 298
salir (conjugation), 153, A-21
salir, vs. **irse**, 291
salón, 31
salsa, 16
saltar, 14, 200
salud, 20, 235, 264
saludar, 188, 230, 236
salvo que, 216–217
san, and definite article, 30
sane vs. **sano**, 310
   pronunciation, 318
San Juan de la Cruz, 37
San Nicolás, 37
Santo Domingo, 37
santo, santa, and definite article, 30
   san vs. santo, 37
Santo Tomás, 37
school vs. **escuela**, 311
se, 68–78
   impersonal
      for actions with no specific subject, 68, 69, 71–78; with inanimate objects, 76; with persons, 76–77; reflexive construction with **uno**, 78
   irresponsible or accidental, 68, 69, 71–74; reciprocals, 70; reflexive, 68, 69–70; se, 69t; se vs. sé, 349t; transformation of le(s), 68, 69
secar, 33, 280
   secarse, 246
seco, 229
secta, 307
sed, 116, 260, 274
seguir
   conjugation, A-21; as modal auxiliary, 179
según, 66, 126, 140
Segunda Guerra Mundial, 367
segundo
   ordinal number, 366t–368; part of a minute, 371; position, 38
seguridad, 286
seguro (adj.), 129
seguro (n.), 106, 223
semana, 185, 186, 232, 256, 291, 298, 363
Semana Santa, 42
semejante, 33
semicolon, 371
senado, 74
senior, 368
sensato, 311
sense vs. **sentir**, 311
sensible vs. **sensible**, 311
sentarle bien / mal a uno, 243

sentarse, 100, 101, 137
sentences, 2–4
   components of, 2–4t, 5; English / Spanish terminology, 7t; impersonal, 74–76; multiple-function words in, 122–123; structure, 6–12
sentence vs. **sentencia**, 311
sentir, 144, 148, 156, 173, 205, A-21
   sentirlo, 87, 267, 291; sentirse, 87, 248; sentirse bien / mal, 87, 265; subjunctive with, 205
señal, feminine, 23, 309
señor, 30, 290, 357
señora, 30, 357
señoría, 17
señorita, 30, 357, 372
sequence of tenses
   aspect relativity, 225–226; chronological relativity, 219–224; tense relativity from indicative to subjunctive, 226–228
sequía, 74
ser, 154, 156, A-22
   with adjectives, 262–268; conjugation, 154; with **de** to indicate origin, possession, 268; with equal elements, 262
   in examples
      + adj., 13, 17, 20; **eres tú el que**, 13; **es cierto**, 15; **fui yo la que**, 13
   with expressions of time, 262, 269; in imperfect, 188; impersonal expressions with, 267–268; long possessives and, 36; and omission of definite article, 32; in passive voice, 270–272; with past participle, 261; with possessive pronouns, 80; with prepositions, 269; **qué** vs. **cuál** with, 81–82; subject–verb agreement, 13
ser vs. **estar**, 262–266
serio, 287, 288
serrucho, 107
serve, 300–301
servir, 21, 45, 83, 91, 114, 272, 284, 300–301, 320
seseo, 317, 318, 322, 330t, 331, 356, 375
short possessives, 36
should, 21, 112, 178, 186, 198, 200
si, 56, 73, 128, 178, 185, 194, 197, 200, 223, 224, 228–230, 229t, 243, 254, 257, 282, 286, 289, 293, 330, 332
   como si, 230
sí (affirmative), 27, 59, 60, 76, 112, 116, 129, 131, 144, 256, 257, 300, 302
   ahora sí, 131, 256, 300; **eso sí que no**, 131
sí (pronoun), 59, 66, 67, 70, 71
   en sí, 349
si clause, 229t
si vs. sí, 349
siempre, 20, 35, 89, 126
siglo, 367
significar, 210
signo, 371
siguiente, 195, 252, 254, 256
sílaba, 315
silencioso, 310
silent u, 318, 321, 324, 325, 328
simpático, 241, 263
simple, 41
sin, omit indefinite article, 33
sinalefa, 354–356

since, 143, 145, 215
sin cesar, 14
sin embargo, 143, 288
sino, 138, 139, 143, 288
    sino que, 11, 139, 288
sin que, 216–217, 223–224
síntoma, masculine, 23
-sión, 23, 323–324
sistema, masculine, 23
slash, 371
soap vs. **sopa**, 311
sobrar, 240–241, 242
sobre (n.), 168
sobre (prep.), 214, 281, 299, 370
sobresdrújula, palabra --, 347
sobrino, 43
sofocar, 307
soga, 310
soldado, 20
soler, A-22
solicitar vs. **aplicar**, 281–282, 306
solicitud, 77, 282, 306
solo, 43, 96, 128, 129, 180, 207, 303
    no solo, sino también, 139; rules of accentuation, 350
soltado, 175
soltar, 6
soltero, 33, 306
sombra, 96
sombrero, 28, 36
sonar, 315
sonido, 315
soñar, 16, 38
    soñar con, 108
sophomore, 368
soportar, 300
sorprender, 20
sorpresa, 22
sospecha, 301
Sound Representation of Letters, 317–318t
Spain
    dialect, 16, 56, 58, 80, 87, 100, 189, 316, 322, 376; in examples, 44, 74, 125, 138, 178, 181, 183, 238, 275, 291, 331
speech, 29
spend, 301
Sr., 357
Sra., 357
Srta., 357
start (people vs. machines), 296
su, sus, 35
subgerente, 281
subir, 302
subirse, 235
subject
    pronouns, 53–55, 53t; subject–verb agreement, 13–18; unaccompanied, 29
subject vs. **sujeto**, 311
subjunctive, 203–213
    adjectival clauses, 213–214; with adverbial clauses, 215–218; after **como si**, 230; after expressions of doubt, 204, 209–210; after expressions of emotion, 205–206; after expressions of emotion, desire, 204; after expressions of volition and influence, 204, 206–209; after impersonal expressions, 209; after impersonal expressions with **ser**, 211–213; after negations of reality, 209–210; after **ojalá**, 230–231

chronological relativity
    chart, 220t; examples, 221t
with expressions of leave-taking, 232–234
formation
    imperfect, 165–166; imperfect irregular stems, 166t; perfect tenses, 166t, 167; pluperfect, 167t; present, 162–165; present irregular stems, 163t
with independent clauses, 203; sequence of tenses, 219–228; **si** clauses, 228–230; with subordinate clauses, 203; tense relativity
    past set, 228 [Chart]; past set examples, 227t; present set, 227 [Chart]; present set examples, 226t
subordinate clauses
    adjectival, 6–9, 92, 213–214; adverbial, 7, 215–218, 269; with indicative, 204; nominal (noun), 7, 203–205; relative, 7, 8, 13, 93, 97–98, 188, 262; with subjunctive, 203
succeed vs. **suceder**, 311
success vs. **suceso**, 311
suceso, 290, 311
Sudamérica, 102, 300, 305
suegra, 27
sueldo, 311
suelto, 175
suerte, 42, 375
    por suerte, 141
suéter, 108, 376
suficiente, 267, 273, 287
sufrir, 135, 221, 373
sugerir, 209
Suiza, 76
superlatives, 46–47
suplicar, 257
suponer, 306
support, 300
support vs. **soportar**, 311
supuesto (por), 116
sur, 357
sureste, 357
suroeste, 357
suspirar, 55
sustancia, 320
sustantivo, 3
sustitución, 320
sustraer, 320
suyo, suya, suyos, suyas, 36
    vs. **de + él, ella**, etc., 36
syllabification, 344–347
sympathetic vs. **simpático**, 311
sympathy vs. **simpatía**, 311

T

t, letter of the alphabet, 314
Tables and Charts
    a (preposition), 103
    active vs. passive voice, 270
    adjectives with multiple meanings, 41
    adverbial phrases, 132
    adverbs, and related prepositions, 137; of confirmation, doubt or negation, 129; of manner, 126; of place, 133; of quantity, 128; of time, 124

any, anything, anyone, 91
b / v (spelling), 320; homophones, 319–320
cardinal numbers, 360–365
chapter 9 glossary, 315
clause examples, 8; clause types, 8
comparison, adverbs, adjectives, nouns, 43; clause, noun compared, 45; clause, verb, adjective or adverb compared, 45; numerical expression, 43
compound tenses, 191
con, 107
conditional, 160; conditional perfect, 161; irregular stems, 161
conjunctions, 138; always subjunctive / occasionally subjunctive, 216; examples re: the subjunctive, 217–218
counting back from the past, **hacer** 277; **llevar**, 277; from the present **hacer**, 276; **llevar**, 276
de, 108
definite articles, 28
demonstrative adjectives, 34
demonstrative pronouns, 78
El alfabeto, 314
en, 111
English /Spanish Terminology, 7
exclamatives, 85
expressions of leave-taking, 232–234
expressions of probability, 202
expressions with **estar**, 274
expressions with prepositions, 118–120
expressions with **tener**, 274
false cognates and false friends, 306–311
fractions, 368
future perfect, 160
future tense, 159; (irregular stems), 159
g o j(spelling), 326
h (spelling), 329
homophones **b / v**, 319–320; **h**, 330
How? + adjective or adverb, 84
imperative **tú**, 168; **usted(es)**, 169–170
imperfect, vs. preterite (examples), 181; imperfect/present parallelism, 184; imperfect subjunctive; (irregular stems), 166
indefinite articles, 32
indefinites, adjectives, 89; adverbials, 89; pronouns, 88
indirect discourse, 252; verb changes, 255; other changes, 257
interrogatives, 81; interrogatives vs. noninterrogatives, 352
irregular past participles, 174
monosyllables with homonyms, 349
multiple vowels, 345
neutral demonstrative pronouns, 79
order of object pronouns when combined, 63
ordinal numbers, 366
os, vs. **los**, 58
para, 114
passive, Spanish vs. English rules, 76; passive formation, Spanish vs. English, 271
perfect progressive tenses, 196
perfect tenses, 192

personal **a**, 103
pluperfect indicative, 158
pluperfect subjunctive, 167
por, 115
por qué, cómo, cuánto, 352
position of object pronouns, 65
possessives, adjectives, long/short, 35; possessive pronouns, 79
possessive pronouns, 79
prepositional object pronouns, 66
prepositions and related adverbs, 137
present conditional, 160
present perfect indicative, 158
present perfect subjunctive, 166
present subjunctive (irregular stems), 163
preterite (irregular stems with **i**), 155
preterite (irregular stems with **u**), 155
preterite/imperfect (Principles), 179
present progressive, 194
perfect progressive, 196
pronouns
    demonstrative, 78–79; direct object, 58; indefinite, 88; indirect object, 60;
    order when combined, 63; **os** vs. **los**, 58; position of object pronouns, 65;
    possessive, 79; prepositional object, 66; reflexive pronouns, reciprocal, 70; reflexive (stressed), 71; reflexive (unstressed), 69; reflexive prepositional, 70; relative pronouns, 92; **se** (overview of uses of), 69; **seseo**, 322; subject, 53
punctuation, 371
r / rr (spelling), 341
reciprocal pronouns, 70
reflexive pronouns
    reciprocal, 70; reflexive (stressed), 71; reflexive (unstressed), 69; reflexive prepositional, 70
reflexive verbs, 248–252
relative pronoun options, 93; relative pronouns, 92
se (overview of uses of), 69
sentence components, chart, 2; functions, 3–4
seseo, 322
si clause, 229
sound representation of letters, 317
subject pronouns, 53
subjunctive
    chronological relativity (chart), 220; chronological relativity (examples), 221; tense relativity (past set, chart), 228; tense relativity (past set, examples), 227; tense relativity (present set, chart), 227; tense relativity (present set, examples), 226
time expressions with **hacer** and **llevar**, counting back from the past, 277; from the present, 276
transitions, 140–145
tú imperative, 168
u / ü (spelling), 325
usted(es) imperatives, (affirmative forms), 169; (negative forms), 170
verb formation, 148–175

verb structure, 5
vocabulary, dialectal variation, 376
word categorization by stress, 347
words ending in **-ia**, 337; **-ía**, 338; **-illa**, 339
x (spelling), 335
table vs. **tabla**, 311
take, 301–303
tal, 33
    tal cual, 350; **tal vez**, 129, 141, 203
también, 89, 131, 143
tampoco, 89–90, 129, 131
tan, 7, 46
tan pronto como, 6, 7, 215, 216, 218
tanto, 38, 46, 128, 129
tapete, 307
tardar (en), 113, 116, 120, 197
tarde (adv.), 11, 124, 125, 128, 131, 203, 205, 208, 209, 223, 267, 274, 289
tarde (n.), 140, 181, 183, 195, 199, 284, 291, 364
tarde o temprano, 125
tarea, 32
tarjeta, 307
tarta, 376
tasa, 310
taza, 307
te, letter of the alphabet, 314
técnica, 139
tela, 308
telegrama, masculine, 23
tema, masculine, 23, 311
temprano, 68, 78, 124, 125, 128, 202, 211, 215, 235, 285, 289
    tarde o temprano, 125
tenedor, 302
tener, 153, 155, A-22
    años, 31; **éxito**, 289, 311; expressions with, 274t; **hambre**, 32; **la impresión**, 311; **lugar**, 303; negative, omit indefinite article, 33; **que** + infinitive, 21, 188, 198; **que ver con**, 236; **tiempo**, 12; usage with personal **a**, 26–27
tenses
    perfect progressive, 196–198; simple progressive, 194–195
tense vs. **tenso**, 311
teñir, A-23
tercer
    ordinal number, 366–368; position, 38
terminar de, 111
terremoto, 212
terrorista, 36, 282
texano, 335
Texas, 334, 335
th, English words with **ch, ph, th**, 343
tiempo, 37, 60, 144, 235, 260, 277, 296, 302, 303–304
    al mismo --, 14, 304; **a tiempo**, 105, 116, 119, 210, 212, 225, 274, 282, 304; **correr del --**, 28; with **tener**, 12, 141; **verbal**, 311; **tienda**, 100, 114, 115, 126, 239, 288, 294
time, 269, 303–304
    adverbs of, 124–126; ago, 277–278; to count backward, 275, 276–277t; to count forward, 275; duration, 276–277; expressions of, 262; telling time, 363
tío, 25
tirante, 194

titles of address, 17, 30
toalla, 302
to be, Spanish equivalents for, 260–275
tocadiscos, plural, 25
tocante (en lo -- a), 140
tocar, 82, 157, 206, 244, 298
tocarle a uno, 243
todavía, 124, 125
todavía no, 124, 125
todo, 28, 56, 63, 70, 89–100, 107, 109, 136, 143, 145, 181, 195, 217, 229, 244, 246, 269, 298
todos, 14, 22, 47, 62, 67, 69, 74, 142, 145, 193, 196, 236, 288, 297
todos los días, 69, 196
tomar, 10, 302
tomar por, 117
tonight, 201, 269, 290, 303, 305
tono, 41
too, 89, 92, 128–129, 131, 203, 205
toparse (con), 294
torcer, 151
tormenta, 104, 181, 212, 270, 285
tormento, 311
torment vs. **tormenta**, 311
toro, 24
torta, 39, 376
tortilla, 376
trabajar, 18, 296
trabajo, 309
trabajo escrito, 309
traducir, 151, 311
traer, 153, 156, 303, A-23
trama, feminine, 23
tramp vs. **trampa**, 311
tranquilizarse, 287
tranquilo, 29
transitions, 140–145
    words used for, 140–145t
transitive, 70, 102, 123, 292
    vs. intransitive, 52–53
translate vs. **trasladar**, 311
tranvía, masculine, 23
tratar, 116, 144
tratar(se) de, 111
tray, 376
tregua, 21
tribunal, 358
Tribunal Supremo, 358
trillion, 360
triphthongs, 346
tripulación, 96
triste, 41
tronar, 15
tropezar (con), 294, 297
tu, tus, 35
tú (accent), 349t
    imperative irregular forms, 168t
tuna vs. **tuna**, 311
turn out, 298
tuyo, el --, 20
tuyo, tuya, tuyos, tuyas, 35

U

u, letter of the alphabet, 314
u muda, 324
u (silent), 318, 321, 324, 325, 328

u / ü (spelling), 325t
ultimate vs. **último**, 311
ultimately vs. **últimamente**, 311
último, 21
-umbre, 23
umlaut, 324–325
una, becomes **un** in front of feminine noun starting with stressed **a-** or **ha-**, 32
unaccompanied subject, 29
único, 41
universidad, 307
uno, 78, 367
unos a otros / unas a otras, 70–71
unos, unas, 22
un, una, 32–34, 318
uña, 72
Uruguay, 56, 376
usted, agreement, 17
vs. **tú**, 16
usted(es) imperatives (Affirmative forms), 169t; (negative forms), 170t
ustedes, vs. **vosotros**, 16, 169–171
uve, letter of the alphabet, 314

V

v, letter of the alphabet, 314
v / b, spelling, 320
vaca, 24
vacaciones, 12
vagabundo, 311
vainita, 376
valentía, 307
valer, 153, A-23
valor, 307, 318
varios, 38
vase vs. **vaso**, 311
vaso, 40
vecindario, 13
velo, 22
velocidad, 310
vencer, 143, 323, A-24
venir, 11, 153, 155, 199, 290, A-24
ventana, 21
ver
 conjugation, 154, A-24; in examples, 27
verano, 15
verbs, 51
 with **a**, 140–145; agreement with subject, 13–18; of communication, indicative following, 208; of communication, subjunctive following, 208; conjugation with **voseo, vosotros**, 56; **cuál**, 84–85; with **de**, 109–111; of emotion, 205–206; with **en**, 112–113
 formation
  compound tenses, 191–198;
   conditional, 160–161;
   imperative, 168–172
  indicative
   future, 159–160; future perfect, 160; imperfect, 154; pluperfect, 158; present, 140–145; present perfect, 158; preterite, 155–157
  irregular past participles, 174t; participles, 173–175
 subjunctive
  imperfect, 165–166; perfect tenses, 166, 167; present, 162–165
 function, 2, 4; **gustar**-type, 51, 239–243; of influence, 207–209; intransitive, 52–53; list of conjugated, A-2; **mini-índice de verbos**, A-26–A-38; modal auxiliaries, 186–188; with **por**, 116; progressive tenses, 194–197; reflexive, 248–252t; with reflexive and nonreflexive uses, 245, 246; and reflexive, articles vs. possessives, 31; sequence of tenses, 219–228; structure, 5t; subject–verb agreement, 13–18; transitive, 52–53
 usage
  compound tenses, 191–198;
   conditional, 200–201
  indicative
   imperfect, 184; present indicative, 178–179; preterite vs. imperfect, 179–183, 185–188
  subjunctive, 203–213
 used without prepositions, 102; of volition, 206–207
verdad, 17, 42, 64, 96, 110, 198, 209, 210, 211, 218, 272, 293, 328, 351
¿verdad?, 55
verdadero, 306, 310
vez, 182, 185, 281, 303, 365, 367, 368
 a la vez, 14, 104, 304; **alguna vez**, 89–90, 132; **a su vez**, 142; **a veces**, 105, 283, 356; **cada vez más / menos**, 141; **de vez en cuando**, 109, 304; **en vez de**, 112, 304; **tal vez**, 129, 141, 203; **una vez**, 89
vicepresidente, 320
víctima, 25
vida, agreement, 17
viejo, 36, 41
 with article, 41; capitalization, 359
viernes, masculine, 33
vínculo, 282
violate vs. **violar**, 311
virrey, 320
visita, 27
vivir, 148, 154, 155, 159, 161, 162, 165, A-25
vizconde, 320
vocabulary, dialects, 376t
vocal, 315
voice, active vs. passive, 75–76, 270–272
 English-Spanish contrast, 76t; formation, 270t
volcar, A-25
volver
 conjugation, 149, A-25; in examples, 38, 52, 124, 128
volver a, 106, 120, 372
volverse, 246, 262
vos, voseo, 56
vosotros, 170–171, 322
 vs. **ustedes**, 16; and **vos**, 56
vowel, 344–347
voz, 33, 41, 55
vuelo, 74, 110, 185, 225, 291
vuelto, 174
vuestro, vuestra, vuestros, vuestras, 35

W

w, letter of the alphabet, 314
Wagner, 318
what, 21, 304–305
word categorization by stress, 347t
word division, end of line, 373–374
word order
 with adjectival clauses, 214; with adjectives, 38–39; with adverbs, 122; with the direct object, 77; with **gustar**-type verbs, 240; with indirect discourse, 258; interrogative, 85, 258; with pronouns, 66, 78; punctuation, 230; with the subject, 26, 30
words ending in
 -ia, 337t; **-ía**, 338t; **-illa**, 339t
work (people vs. machines), 296
work out, 297
would, 5, 10, 11, 12, 15, 21, 46, 55, 74, 91, 99, 105, 109, 114, 116, 140, 142, 144, 185, 187, 195, 197, 200, 201, 206, 217, 220, 222, 223, 224, 228, 229, 238, 243, 252, 253, 254, 256
 different translations, 185

X

x, letter of the alphabet, 314
 pronunciation, 333; spelling, 335t
xenofobia, 318, 333
xerografía, 335
xilófono, 335
xóchil, 335
Xochimilco, 335

Y

-y, 25
y, letter of the alphabet, 314
y, the sound, 336
y, pronunciation, 335–336
 y, conjunction, 10, 27, 143; **y pico**, 364; **y** vs. **e**, 138
ya, 28, 50, 60, 73, 124, 125, 128, 129, 131, 189, 192, 193, 198, 221, 222, 224, 225, 254, 261, 265, 266, 267, 290, 291, 301, 318
ya no, 124, 125, 268, 300
ya que, 143
yacer, A-26
ye, letter of the alphabet, 314
yeísmo, 376
yo, 13

Z

z, letter of the alphabet, 314
-z, 23, 25
zambullir, A-26
zapato, 194, 243, 318
zigzag, 317
zorro, 322
zero, 342, 360
zeta, 378